Daily Readings
from all four Gospels

For morning and evening

J. C. Ryle

Compiled by Robert Sheehan

EVANGELICAL PRESS

EVANGELICAL PRESS
Grange Close, Faverdale North Industrial Estate, Darlington,
DL3 0PH, England

First published in 2 volumes:
  vol. 1 (Matthew, Mark, Luke) published 1982
  vol. 2 (John) published 1985

This combined edition first published 1998

ISBN 0 85234 420 1

British Library Cataloguing in Publication Data available

Printed and bound in Great Britain by Creative Print & Design,
Ebbw Vale, Wales.

Introduction

J. C. Ryle produced his *Expository Thoughts* on each of the four Gospels. When the Gospels repeat a particular incident in the life of our Lord, Ryle either repeated the teaching he had given in his previous commentaries, or developed those lines of thought peculiar to the individual Gospel writer. In forming J. C. Ryle's commentaries into daily readings there has inevitably been a considerable amount of editing, but it has been my aim to bring a large proportion of the treasure from Ryle's abundant store.

In order to gather together the comments on the first three Gospels into some sort of order without constant repetition the material is presented according to the chronological framework set out in Loraine Boettner's *A Harmony of the Gospels* (Presbyterian and Reformed, 1976). Where several of the Gospels mention the same incident the longest record is chosen as the reading for the day and the parallel passages are listed in brackets, or the Gospel on which Ryle bases his main comments is chosen, the alternative passages again being in brackets.

On each day there are two things which are not extracted from Bishop Ryle's writings. They are the additional reading, which has been chosen because it emphasizes one of the themes in Ryle's exposition, and the closing meditation, which seeks to focus attention on one particular point for further thought.

My thanks to the staff of Evangelical Press, who have coped with a cut-and-paste manuscript, and to my wife, who always gives encouragement. They, I and Ryle will, to use his words, 'be more than repaid' if the result of this volume is 'to exalt the Lord Jesus Christ and make him beautiful and glorious in the eyes of men and to promote the increase of repentance, faith and holiness upon earth'.

Robert Sheehan

Publishers' note: For suggestions on how to use these readings, see last page.

Suggested further reading: Hebrews 12:4-13

What high testimony is borne in this passage to the character of Zacharias and Elisabeth! It matters little whether we interpret this 'righteousness' as that which is imputed to all believers for their justification, or that which is wrought inwardly in believers by the operation of the Holy Spirit for their sanctification. The two sorts of righteousness are never disjoined. There are none justified who are not sanctified, and there are none sanctified who are not justified. Suffice it for us to know that Zacharias and Elisabeth had grace when grace was very rare, and kept all the burdensome observances of the ceremonial law with devout conscientiousness when few Israelites cared for them except in name and form.

The main thing that concerns us all is the example which this holy pair hold up to Christians. Let us all strive to serve God faithfully and live fully up to our light, even as they did.

It was a heavy trial that God was pleased to lay on Zacharias and Elisabeth (v. 7). The full force of these words can hardly be understood by a modern Christian. To an ancient Jew they would convey the idea of a very weighty affliction. To be childless was one of the bitterest of sorrows (1 Sam. 1:10).

The grace of God exempts no one from trouble. Let us remember this, if we serve Christ, and let us count trial no strange thing. Let us believe that a hand of perfect wisdom is measuring out all our portion, and that when God chastises us, it is to make us 'partakers of his holiness' (Heb. 12:10). If afflictions drive us nearer to Christ, the Bible and prayer, they are positive blessings. We may not think so now. But we shall think so when we wake up in another world.

For meditation: *God works out our circumstances, for our good if we love him (Rom. 8:28). He knows what might have been if our circumstances were other than they are (Ps. 81:13-15; Matt. 11:21-23). Can we not trust his wisdom to have worked out the best circumstances for us in every situation?*

Suggested further reading: Colossians 1:15-18

The Gospel of St John, which begins with these verses, is in many respects very unlike the other three Gospels. But it is enough to remember that Matthew, Mark, Luke and John wrote under the direct inspiration of God. In the general plan of their respective Gospels and in the particular details, in everything that they record and in everything that they do not record, they were all four equally and entirely guided by the Holy Ghost.

About the matters which St John was specially inspired to relate in his Gospel one general remark will suffice. The things which are peculiar to his Gospel are among the most precious possessions of the church of Christ. No one of the four Gospel writers has given us such full statements about the divinity of Christ, about justification by faith, about the offices of Christ, about the work of the Holy Ghost and about the privileges of believers as we read in the pages of St John.

The five verses now before us contain a statement of matchless sublimity concerning the divine nature of our Lord Jesus Christ. He it is, beyond all question, whom St John means when he speaks of 'the Word'. No doubt there are heights and depths in that statement which are far beyond man's understanding. And yet there are plain lessons in it which every Christian would do well to treasure up in his mind.

Our Lord Jesus Christ is eternal. St John tells us that 'In the beginning was the Word.' He did not begin to exist when the heavens and the earth were made. Much less did he begin to exist when the gospel was brought into the world. He had glory with the Father 'before the world was' (John 17:5). He was existing when matter was first created and before time began. He was 'before all things' (Col. 1:17). He was from all eternity.

For meditation: *Our Lord is the great unifying theme of all Scripture because he is not a word to us among many, but **the** Word.*

Suggested further reading: Psalm 111

God announced the coming birth of John the Baptist by an angel (v. 11). The ministry of angels is undoubtedly a deep subject. At no time do we read of so many appearances of angels as about the time of our Lord's incarnation and entrance into the world. The meaning of this circumstance is sufficiently clear. It was meant to teach the church that Messiah was no angel, but the Lord of angels, as well as of men.

One thing about angels we must never forget. They take a deep interest in the work of Christ and the salvation that Christ has provided. They sang high praise when the Son of God came down to make peace by his own blood between God and man. They rejoice when sinners repent. They delight to minister to those who shall be heirs of salvation. Let us strive to be like them, while we are on earth — to be of their mind, and to share their joys.

The appearance of an angel produced a marked effect on the mind of Zacharias (v. 12). The experience of this righteous man tallies exactly with that of other saints who saw visions of things belonging to another world (Exod. 3:6; Dan. 10:7-9; Matt. 28:8; Rev. 1: 17). They trembled and were afraid.

How are we to account for this fear? It arises from our inward sense of weakness, guilt and corruption. The vision of an inhabitant of heaven reminds us forcibly of our own imperfection and of our natural unfitness to stand before God. If angels are so great and terrible, what must the Lord of angels be?

Let us bless God that we have a mighty Mediator between God and man, the man Christ Jesus. Believing on him, we may draw near to God with boldness and look forward to the Day of Judgement without fear. But let us tremble when we think of the terror of the wicked at the last day.

For meditation: *Our modern world is a testimony to the wisdom and knowledge of men who have thrown off the fear of God* (Rom. 3:18). *But where God is not feared there is no true wisdom and knowledge* (Ps. 111:10; Prov. 1:7).

Suggested further reading: Hebrews 1:1-14

Our Lord Jesus Christ is a person distinct from God the Father and yet one with him. St John tells us that 'The Word was with God.' The Father and the Word, though two persons, are joined by an ineffable union. Where God the Father was from all eternity, there also was the Word, even God the Son — their glory equal, their majesty co-eternal and yet their Godhead one. This is a great mystery! Happy is he who can receive it as a little child without attempting to explain it.

The Lord Jesus Christ is very God. St John tells us that 'The Word was God.' He is not merely a created angel, or a being inferior to God the Father and invested by him with power to redeem sinners. He is nothing less than perfect God — equal to the Father as touching his Godhead, God of the substance of the Father, begotten before the worlds.

The Lord Jesus Christ is the Creator of all things. St John tells us that 'By him were all things made, and without him was not anything made that was made.' So far from being a creature of God, as some heretics have falsely asserted, he is the being who made the worlds and all that they contain. 'He commanded and they were created' (Ps. 148:5).

The Lord Jesus Christ is the source of all spiritual life and light. St John tells us that 'In him was life; and the life was the light of men.' He is the eternal fountain, from which alone the sons of men have ever derived life. The vast majority of mankind in every age have refused to know him, have forgotten the Fall and their own need of a Saviour. The light has been constantly shining 'in darkness'. The most have 'not comprehended the light'. But if any men and women out of the countless millions of mankind have ever had spiritual life and light, they have owed all to Christ.

For meditation: *Our Lord has life in himself and is light. All life, whether physical or spiritual, and all light, all goodness and truth, have him as their source.*

Suggested further reading: Psalm 40:1-10

Prayers are not necessarily rejected because the answer is long delayed. Zacharias, no doubt, had often prayed for the blessing of children and, to all appearance, had prayed in vain. At his advanced time of life he had probably long ceased to mention the subject before God, and had given up all hope of being a father. Yet the very first words of the angel show plainly that the bygone prayers of Zacharias had not been forgotten (v. 13).

We shall do well to remember this fact whenever we kneel to pray. We must beware of hastily concluding that our supplications are useless, and especially in the matter of intercessory prayer on behalf of others. It is not for us to prescribe either the time or the way in which our requests are to be answered.

Verse 14 teaches us that no children cause such true joy as those who have the grace of God. It is a thousand times better for them than beauty, riches, honours, rank and high connections. Till they have grace we never know what they might do. They may bring down our grey hairs with sorrow to the grave.

Children are never too young to receive the grace of God (v. 15). There is no greater mistake than to suppose that infants, by reason of their tender age, are incapable of being operated upon by the Holy Spirit. Let us beware of limiting God's power and compassion. With him nothing is impossible.

True greatness may receive little honour in this life (v. 15). The measure of greatness which is common among men is utterly false and deceptive. Princes and potentates, conquerors and leaders of armies, statesmen and philosophers, artists and authors — these the world calls 'great'. Such greatness is not recognized among the angels of God. Those who do great things for God they reckon great. Those who do little for God they reckon little.

For meditation: *Are we seeking the praise and esteem of God, or of men?* (John 5:44: Rom. 2:29; 1 Cor. 4:2-5).

Suggested further reading: Philippians 2:5-11

These wonderful verses appear to contain much in them, without controversy, which is above our reason, but there is nothing contrary to it. There is much that we cannot explain and must be content humbly to believe. Let us, however, never forget that there are plain practical consequences flowing from the passage which we can never grasp too firmly, or know too well.

Would we know, for one thing, the exceeding sinfulness of sin? Let us often read these first five verses of St John's Gospel. Let us mark what kind of being the Redeemer of mankind must needs be, in order to provide eternal redemption for sinners. If no one less than the eternal God, the Creator and Preserver of all things, could take away the sin of the world, sin must be a far more abominable thing in the sight of God than most men suppose. The right measure of sin's sinfulness is the dignity of him who came into the world to save sinners. If Christ is so great, then sin must indeed be sinful!

Would we know, for another thing, the strength of a true Christian's foundation for hope? Let us often read these first five verses of St John's Gospel. Let us mark that the Saviour in whom the believer is bid to trust is nothing less than the eternal God, one able to save to the uttermost all that come to the Father by him. He that was 'with God' and 'was God' is also 'Emmanuel, God with us'. Let us thank God that our help is laid on one that is mighty (Ps. 89:19). In ourselves we are great sinners. But in Jesus Christ we have a great Saviour. He is a strong foundation-stone, able to bear the weight of a world's sin. He that believeth on him shall not be confounded (1 Peter 2:6).

For meditation: *Only a man could die as a substitute for men, but only God could die as a substitute for millions of men. Therefore Christ, as God and man, is the very Saviour we need.*

Suggested further reading: Hebrews 3:7-13

What a striking example we have here of the power of unbelief in a good man! Righteous and holy as Zacharias was, the announcement of the angel appears to him incredible (v. 18).

A well-instructed Jew, like Zacharias, ought not to have raised this question. No doubt he was well acquainted with the Old Testament. He ought to have remembered the wonderful births recorded there (Gen. 18:11-14; 21:1-3; Judg. 13:2-3; 1 Sam. 1:5,20) and that what God has done once he can do again. With him nothing is impossible. But he forgot all this. He thought of nothing but the arguments of mere human reason and sense. And it often happens in religious matters that, where reason begins, faith ends.

How exceeding sinful the sin of unbelief is in the sight of God! (v. 20). The doubts and questionings of Zacharias brought down upon him a heavy chastisement peculiarly suited to the offence. The tongue that was not ready to speak the language of believing praise was struck dumb. For nine long months at least, Zacharias was condemned to silence, and was daily reminded that by unbelief he had offended God.

Few sins appear to be so peculiarly provoking to God as the sin of unbelief. It is a practical denial of God's almighty power to doubt whether he can do a thing when he undertakes to do it. It is giving the lie to God to doubt whether he means to do a thing when he has plainly promised that it shall be done.

Let us watch and pray daily against this soul-ruining sin. Concessions to it rob believers of their inward peace, weaken their hands in the day of battle, bring clouds over their hopes. Unbelief is the true cause of a thousand spiritual diseases. In all that respects the pardon of our sins and the acceptance of our souls, the duties and trials of our daily lives, let it be a settled maxim in our religion, to trust every word of God implicitly, and to beware of unbelief.

For meditation: *Do you profit so little from God's Word read and preached because you receive so little of it with faith?* (Heb. 4:2).

Suggested further reading: Acts 20:17-24

St John, after beginning his Gospel with a statement of our Lord's nature as God, proceeds to speak of his forerunner, John the Baptist. The contrast between the language used about the Saviour and that used about his forerunner ought not to be overlooked. Of Christ we are told that he was the eternal God, the Creator of all things, the source of life and light. Of John the Baptist we are told simply that 'There was a man sent from God, whose name was John.'

We see in these verses the true nature of a Christian minister's office. We have it in the description of John the Baptist. He 'came for a witness, to bear witness of the Light, that all men through him might believe'. Christian ministers are not priests, nor mediators between God and man. They are not agents into whose hands men may commit their souls and carry on their religion by deputy. They are witnesses. They are intended to bear testimony to God's truth and specially to the great truth that Christ is the only Saviour and light of the world. This was St Peter's ministry on the Day of Pentecost: 'With many other words did he *testify*' (Acts 2:40). This was the whole tenor of St Paul's ministry: '*Testifying* both to the Jews and also to the Greeks, repentance toward God, and faith toward our Lord Jesus Christ' (Acts 20:21). Unless a Christian minister bears a full testimony to Christ, he is not faithful to his office. So long as he does testify of Christ, he has done his part and will receive his reward, although his hearers may not believe his testimony. Until a minister's hearers believe on that Christ of whom they are told, they receive no benefit from the ministry. They may be pleased and interested, but they are not profited until they believe. The great end of a minister's testimony is 'that through him, men may believe'.

For meditation: *Your minister may have many faults — and is probably more aware of them than you are — but, if he preaches Christ, value him.*

Suggested further reading: Matthew 12:46-50

We have in these verses the announcement of the most marvellous event that ever happened in this world, the incarnation and birth of our Lord Jesus Christ.

The first advent of Messiah was to be an advent of humiliation. That humiliation was to begin even from the time of his conception and birth. Let us beware of despising poverty in others or ourselves. The condition of life which Jesus voluntarily chose ought always to be regarded with holy reverence. The common tendency of the day to bow down before rich men, and make an idol of money, ought to be carefully resisted and discouraged. The example of our Lord is a sufficient answer to a thousand grovelling maxims about wealth which pass current among men (2 Cor. 8:9).

What a high privilege the Virgin Mary had! She is addressed in remarkable language (vv. 28,30). The Roman Catholic Church pays an honour to her hardly inferior to that which it pays to her blessed Son. She is formally declared to be 'conceived without sin'. She is held up as an object of worship, and prayed to as a mediator between God and man, no less powerful than Christ himself. For all this, be it remembered, there is not the slightest warrant in Scripture. But while we say this, we must in fairness admit that no woman was ever so highly honoured as the mother of our Lord. By the child-bearing of one woman, life and immortality were brought to light when Christ was born.

One thing in connection with this subject should never be forgotten by Christians. There is a relationship to Christ within reach of us all, a relationship far nearer than that of flesh and blood, a relationship which belongs to all who repent and believe (Mark 3:35; Luke 11:28).

What a glorious account is given of our Lord Jesus Christ! (vv. 32-33). Of his greatness we know something already. He has brought in a great salvation. He has shown himself a prophet greater than Moses. He is a great High Priest. And he shall be greater still when he is owned as a King.

For meditation: *Our Lord's true brothers share a family likeness* (Rom. 8:29).

Suggested further reading: John 3:16-21

We see in these verses one principal position which our Lord Jesus Christ occupies towards mankind. We have it in the words: He 'was the true light, which lighteth every man that cometh into the world'.

Christ is to the souls of men what the sun is to the world. He is the centre and source of all spiritual light, warmth, life, health, growth, beauty and fertility. Like the sun, he shines for the common benefit of all mankind — for high and for low, for rich and for poor, for Jew and for Greek. Like the sun, he is free to all. All may look at him and drink health out of his light. If millions of mankind were mad enough to dwell in caves underground, or to bandage their eyes, their darkness would be their own fault and not the fault of the sun. So, likewise, if millions of men and women love spiritual 'darkness rather than light', the blame must be laid on their blind hearts and not on Christ. We see in these verses the desperate wickedness of man's natural heart. We have it in the words: Christ 'was in the world, and the world was made by him, and the world knew him not. He came unto his own, and his own received him not.' He came to the very people whom he had brought out from Egypt and purchased for his own. He came to the Jews, whom he had separated from other nations and to whom he had revealed himself by the prophets. He came to those very Jews who had read of him in the Old Testament Scriptures, seen him under types and figures in their temple services and professed to be waiting for his coming. And yet, when he came, those very Jews received him not. They even rejected him, despised him and slew him. Well may the natural heart be called 'desperately wicked'!

For meditation: *No statement during our Lord's earthly ministry is more tragic than his rebuke to unbelieving Jews* (Matt. 23:37).

Suggested further reading: Matthew 26:36-42

The angel Gabriel speaks of the mystery of Christ's incarnation in a reverent and discreet manner (v. 35). We shall do well to follow this example in all our reflections on this deep subject, regarding it with holy reverence and abstaining from speculations. Scripture reveals the truth (John 1:14; Heb. 10:5; 2:14; Gal. 4:4) and there we must stop, not prying beyond this point. In a religion that comes down from heaven there must needs be mysteries.

The angel Gabriel lays down a mighty principle to silence all objections about the incarnation (v. 37). A hearty reception of this great principle is of immense importance to our own inward peace. Among many antidotes to a doubting, questioning state of mind, few will be found more useful than that before us now — a thorough conviction of the almighty power of God. Faith never rests so calmly and peacefully as when it lays its head on the pillow of God's omnipotence.

The Virgin Mary gives meek and ready acquiescence to God's revealed will concerning her (v. 38). There is far more of admirable grace in this answer than at first appears. A moment's reflection will show us that it was no light matter to become the mother of our Lord in this unheard of and mysterious way. It brought with it, no doubt, at a distant period great honour; but it brought with it for the present no small danger to Mary's reputation, and no small trial to Mary's faith. But she asks no further questions. She raises no further objections. She accepts the honour laid upon her with all its attendant perils and inconveniences.

Let us seek in our daily practical Christianity to exercise the same blessed spirit of faith. Let us be willing to go anywhere, and do anything, and be anything, whatever be the present inconvenience, so long as God's will is clear and the path of duty is plain.

For meditation: *It is an easy thing within the context of a highly emotional, pressurized meeting to promise to go anywhere, at any time, at any cost. It is entirely another thing to put the vow into practice in the real world.*

Suggested further reading: Galatians 3:26 - 4:7

We see in these verses the vast privileges of all who receive Christ and believe on him. We are told that 'As many as received him, to them gave he power to become the sons of God, even to them that believe on his name.'

Christ will never be without some servants. If the vast majority of the Jews did not receive him as the Messiah, there were, at any rate, a few who did. To them he gave the privilege of being God's children. He adopted them as members of his Father's family. He reckoned them his own brethren and sisters, bone of his bone and flesh of his flesh. He conferred on them a dignity which was ample recompense for the cross which they had to carry for his sake. He made them sons and daughters of the Lord Almighty.

Privileges like these, be it remembered, are the possession of all, in every age, who receive Christ by faith and follow him as their Saviour. They are 'children of God by faith in Christ Jesus' (Gal. 3:26). They are born again by a new and heavenly birth and adopted into the family of the King of kings. Few in number, and despised by the world as they are, they are cared for with infinite love by a Father in heaven who, for his Son's sake, is well pleased with them. In time he provides them with everything that is for their good. In eternity he will give them a crown of glory that fadeth not away. These are great things! But faith in Christ gives men an ample title to them. Good masters care for their servants and Christ cares for his.

Are we ourselves sons of God? Have we been born again? Have we the marks which always accompany the new birth — sense of sin, faith in Jesus, love of others, righteous living, separation from the world? Let us never be content till we can give a satisfactory answer to these questions.

For meditation: *The idea of his being a child of God filled John with praise, anticipation and longings to be holy* (1 John 3:1-3). *What does it do for you?*

Suggested further reading: Hebrews 11:1-6

Observe the benefit of fellowship and communion between believers. We read of a visit paid by the Virgin Mary to her cousin Elisabeth. We are told in a striking manner how the hearts of both these holy women were cheered, and their minds lifted up, by this interview.

We should always regard communion with other believers as an eminent means of grace. It is a refreshing break in our journey along the narrow way to exchange experience with our fellow-travellers. There are many who fear the Lord and think upon his name and yet forget to speak often one to another (Mal. 3:16). First let us seek the face of God. Then let us seek the face of God's friends.

What clear spiritual knowledge appears in the language of Elisabeth! She calls Mary 'the mother of my Lord' (v. 43). The words 'my Lord' at the time they were spoken implied far more than we are apt to suppose. They were nothing less than a distinct declaration that the child who was to be born was the long-promised Messiah (Ps. 110:1), the Christ of God. Let us beware of using these words lightly. With holy reverence let them fall from our lips. There are two texts connected with the expression which should often come to our minds (1 Cor. 12:3; Phil. 2:11).

What high praise Elisabeth bestows upon the grace of faith! (v. 45). We need not wonder that this holy woman should thus commend faith. She was well acquainted with the Old Testament. She knew the great things faith had done. What is the whole history of God's saints in every age, but a record of men and women who obtained a good report by faith?

Do we know anything of this precious faith? Do we know anything of the faith of God's elect? (Titus 1:1). Let us never rest till we know it by experience. Better a thousand times be rich in faith than rich in gold. Gold will be worthless in the unseen world to which we are all travelling. Faith will be owned in that world before God the Father and the holy angels.

For meditation: *Nothing will be able to make up for lack of faith on the great and terrible Day of Judgement.*

Suggested further reading: Hebrews 2:14-18

The main truth which this verse teaches is the reality of our Lord Jesus Christ's incarnation or being made man. St John tells us that 'The Word was made flesh, and dwelt among us.'

The plain meaning of these words is that our divine Saviour really took human nature upon him, in order to save sinners. He really became a man like ourselves in all things, sin only excepted. Like ourselves, he was born of a woman, though born in a miraculous manner. Like ourselves, he grew from infancy to boyhood and from boyhood to man's estate, both in wisdom and in stature (Luke 2:52). Like ourselves, he hungered, thirsted, ate, drank, slept, was wearied, felt pain, wept, rejoiced, marvelled, was moved to anger and compassion. Having become flesh and taken a body, he prayed, read the Scriptures, suffered, being tempted, and submitted his human will to the will of God the Father. And finally, in the same body, he really suffered and shed his blood, really died, was really buried, really rose again and really ascended up into heaven. And yet all this time he was God as well as man!

This constant undivided union of two perfect natures in Christ's person is exactly that which gives infinite value to his mediation and qualifies him to be the very Mediator that sinners need. Our Mediator is one who can sympathize with us, because he is very man. And yet at the same time he is one who can deal with the Father for us on equal terms, because he is very God. It is the same union which gives infinite value to his righteousness, when imputed to believers. It is the righteousness of one who was God as well as man. It is the same union which gives infinite value to the atoning blood which he shed for sinners on the cross. It is the blood of one who was God as well as man.

For meditation: *God the Son shares with us a common experience of living in a fallen world. His understanding of us is not therefore theoretical but personally experienced.*

Suggested further reading: James 1:19-25

What full acquaintance with Scripture this hymn exhibits! We are reminded as we read it of many phrases in the book of Psalms. Above all, we are reminded of the song of Hannah, in the book of Samuel (1 Sam. 2:2-10). It is evident that the memory of the blessed Virgin was stored with Scripture. She was familiar, whether by hearing or by reading, with the Old Testament. And so, when out of the abundance of her heart her mouth spoke, she gave vent to her feelings in scriptural language. Moved by the Holy Spirit to break forth in praise, she chooses language which the Holy Spirit had already consecrated and used.

Let us strive, every year we live, to become more deeply acquainted with Scripture. Let us study it, search into it, meditate on it, until it dwells in us richly (Col. 3:16). In particular, let us labour to make ourselves familiar with those parts of the Bible which, like the book of Psalms, describe the experience of the saints of old. We shall find it most helpful to us in all our approaches to God. It will supply us with the best and most suitable language both for the expression of our wants and thanksgivings. Such knowledge of the Bible can doubtless never be attained without regular daily study. But the time spent on such study is never mis-spent. It will bear fruit after many days.

Although Mary was chosen of God to the high honour of being Messiah's mother, she speaks of her low estate (v. 47) and her need of a Saviour (v. 47). In her deep humility she does not regard herself as sinless. On the contrary, she uses the language of one who has been taught by the grace of God to feel her own sins and, so far from being able to save others, requires a Saviour for her own soul.

Let us copy this holy humility of our Lord's mother, while we steadfastly refuse to regard her as a mediator or pray to her. Like her, let us be lowly in our own eyes, and think little of ourselves. Humility is the highest grace that can adorn the Christian character. It is the grace that is in the reach of every converted person.

For meditation: *Humility is needed before the Word and world.*

Suggested further reading: Ephesians 1:3-14

Did the Word become flesh? Then he is one who can be touched with the feeling of his people's infirmities, because he has suffered himself, being tempted. He is almighty, because he is God, and yet he can feel with us, because he is man.

Did the Word become flesh? Then he can supply us with a perfect pattern and example for our daily life. Had he walked among us as an angel or a spirit, we would never have copied him. But having dwelt among us as a man, we know that the true standard of holiness is to 'walk even as he walked' (1 John 2:6). He is a perfect pattern, because he is God. But he is also a pattern exactly suited to our wants, because he is man.

It is Christ alone who supplies all the spiritual wants of all believers. It is written that 'Of his fulness have we all received, and grace for grace.'

There is an infinite fulness in Jesus Christ. As St Paul says, 'It pleased the Father that in him should all fulness dwell.' 'In him are hid all the treasures of wisdom and knowledge' (Col. 1:19; 2:3). There is laid up in him, as in a treasury, a boundless supply of all that any sinner can need, either in time or in eternity. The Spirit of life is his special gift to the church and conveys from him, as from a great root, sap and vigour to all the believing branches. He is rich in mercy, grace, wisdom, righteousness, sanctification and redemption. Out of Christ's fulness, all believers in every age of the world have been supplied. They did not clearly understand the fountain from which their supplies flowed in Old Testament times. The Old Testament saints only saw Christ afar off and not face to face. But from Abel downwards, all saved souls have received all they have had from Jesus Christ alone. Every saint in glory will at last acknowledge that he is Christ's debtor for all he is. Jesus will prove to have been all in all.

For meditation: *Every blessing that God gives may be summarized by one word — Christ. With him all things are freely given to us* (Rom. 8:32).

Suggested further reading: Philippians 4:4-9

There is a lively thankfulness in Mary's hymn. Verses 46-49 are full of what God has done for her. We can scarcely enter into the full extent of feelings which a holy Jewess would experience on finding herself in Mary's position. But we should try to recollect them as we read Mary's repeated expressions of praise.

We, too, shall do well to walk in Mary's steps and cultivate a thankful spirit. It has ever been a mark of God's most distinguished saints in every age; David in the Old Testament and Paul in the New are remarkable for their praise. We seldom read much of their writings without finding them blessing and praising God. Let us rise from our beds every morning with a deep conviction that we are debtors, and that every day we have more mercies than we deserve. Let us look around us every week, as we travel through the world, and see whether we have not much to thank God for. Well would it be if our prayers and supplications were more mingled with thanksgiving (1 Sam. 7:12; Phil. 4:6).

It is evident that the Virgin Mary possessed an experimental acquaintance with God's former dealings with his people. Verses 50-55 trace the handiwork of Israel's covenant God in Old Testament history. The true Christian should always give close attention to Bible history. Such study throws light on God's mode of dealing with his people. He is of one mind. What he does for them and to them in time past, he is likely to do in times to come. Such study will teach us what to expect, check unwarrantable expectations and encourage us when cast down. Such knowledge will make men patient and hopeful.

The Virgin Mary had a clear grasp of Bible promises (vv. 54-55). Let us learn to lay firm hold on Bible promises. We walk by faith, and this faith leans on promises. But on those promises we may lean confidently. They will bear all the weight we can lay on them. We shall find one day that God keeps his word, and that what he has spoken he will always in due time perform.

For meditation: *'Be still before the Lord and wait patiently for him; do not fret when men succeed in their ways, when they carry out their wicked schemes... But the meek will inherit the land and enjoy great peace'* (Ps. 37:7-11).

Suggested further reading: 2 Corinthians 3:6-11

Moses was employed by God 'as a servant', to convey to Israel the moral and ceremonial law (Heb. 3:5). As a servant, he was faithful to him who appointed him, but he was only a servant. The moral law, which he brought down from Mount Sinai, was holy and just and good. But it could not justify. It had no healing power. It could wound, but it could not bind up. It 'worked wrath' (Rom. 4:15). It pronounced a curse against any imperfect obedience. The ceremonial law, which he was commanded to impose on Israel, was full of deep meaning and typical instruction. Its ordinances and ceremonies made it an excellent schoolmaster to guide men towards Christ (Gal. 3:24). But the ceremonial law was only a schoolmaster. It could not make him that kept it perfect, as pertaining to the conscience (Heb. 9:9). It laid a grievous yoke on men's hearts, which they were not able to bear. It was a ministration of death and condemnation (2 Cor. 3:7-9). The light which men got from Moses and the law was at best only starlight compared to noonday.

Christ, on the other hand, came into the world 'as a Son', with the keys of God's treasury of grace and truth entirely in his hands (Heb. 3:6). Grace came by him when he made fully known God's gracious plan of salvation by faith in his own blood and opened the fountain of mercy to all the world. Truth came by him when he fulfilled in his own person the types of the Old Testament and revealed himself as the true sacrifice, the true mercy-seat and the true Priest. No doubt there was much of 'grace and truth' under the law of Moses. But the whole of God's grace and the whole truth about redemption were never known until Jesus came into the world and died for sinners.

For meditation: *The requirements of the law are very demanding* (Gal. 3:10), *but salvation is a gift of grace* (Acts 15:10-11).

Suggested further reading: 1 Corinthians 12:18-26

We have a striking example of the kindness we owe to one another in the conduct of Elisabeth's neighbours and cousins (v. 58). Sympathy in one another's joys and sorrows costs little, and yet is a grace of the most mighty power. Like the oil on the wheels of some great machine, it may seem a trifling and unimportant thing, yet in reality it has an immense influence on the comfort and well-working of the whole machine of society. To the heart that is warmed by good news or chilled by affliction, sympathy is often more precious than gold (Rom. 12:15). Our Lord was ready to go to a marriage and weep at a grave (John 2:1-11; 11:1-46). Let us be ready to do likewise.

How beneficial affliction was to Zacharias! He resists the wishes of his relatives and clings to the name commanded by the angel Gabriel (vv. 62-63). He now believes every word which Gabriel had spoken to him, and every word of his message shall be obeyed.

Let us take heed that affliction does us good as it did to Zacharias. We cannot escape trouble in a sin-laden world. Man is born to trouble (Job 5:7). But in the time of trouble let us make it our prayer that we may learn wisdom by the rod, and not harden our hearts against God. The sorrow that humbles us and drives us nearer to God is a blessing and gain. No case is more hopeless than that of a man who, in time of affliction, turns his back upon God (2 Chr. 28:22).

The Lord's hand was with John the Baptist (v. 66). This is the blessing that we should desire for all young children. It is the best portion, the happiest portion, the only portion that can never be lost, and will endure beyond the grave. It is good to have over them the 'hand' of teachers and instructors, but it is better still to have the 'hand' of the Lord. We may be thankful if they obtain the patronage of the great and the rich, but we ought to far more care for their obtaining of the favour of God. If we would have the hand of the Lord with our children we must diligently seek him for it.

For meditation: *God uses affliction to shape character* (Rom. 5:3-4).

Suggested further reading: John 14:8-11

It is Christ alone who has revealed God the Father to man. It is written that 'No man hath seen God at any time; the only begotten Son, which is in the bosom of the Father, he hath declared him.'

The eye of mortal man has never beheld God the Father. No man could bear the sight. Even to Moses it was said, 'Thou canst not see my face: for there shall no man see me, and live' (Exod. 33:20). Yet all that mortal man is capable of knowing about God the Father is fully revealed to us by God the Son. He, who was in the bosom of the Father from all eternity, has been pleased to take our nature upon him and to exhibit to us, in the form of a man, all that our minds can comprehend of the Father's perfections. In Christ's words and deeds and life and death we learn as much concerning God the Father as our feeble minds can at present bear. His perfect wisdom, his almighty power, his unspeakable love to sinners, his incomparable holiness, his hatred of sin could never be represented to our eyes more clearly than we see them in Christ's life and death. In truth, 'God was manifest in the flesh,' when the Word took on him a body (1 Tim. 3:16). He was 'the brightness of the Father's glory, and the express image of his person' (Heb. 1:3). He says himself, 'I and my Father are one' (John 10:30). 'He that hath seen me hath seen the Father' (John 14:9). 'In him dwelleth all the fulness of the Godhead bodily' (Col. 2:9). These are deep and mysterious things. But they are true.

And now, after reading this passage, can we ever give too much honour to Christ? Can we ever think too highly of him? Christ is the meeting-point between the Trinity and the sinner's soul.

For meditation: *Our understanding of the character of God need not be vague and indistinct, because our Lord has lived as God with us and made him known.*

Suggested further reading: Numbers 23:18-24

What deep thankfulness marked the Jewish believer's heart at the prospect of Messiah's appearing! Praise is the first word that falls from Zacharias' mouth as soon as his dumbness is removed and his speech restored.

At this period of the world we can hardly understand the depth of this good man's feelings. We must imagine ourselves in his position, seeing the fulfilment of the oldest promise in the Old Testament, the promise of a Saviour, and beholding the accomplishment of this promise brought near to our own door. Then perhaps we may have some idea of the feelings of Zacharias when he cried out (v. 68).

Zacharias stresses God's fulfilment of his promises (vv. 68-75). He speaks of these things in the manner of the prophets as a thing already accomplished, because sure to take place.

It is clear that the souls of Old Testament believers fed much on God's promises. They were obliged to walk by faith far more than we are. They knew nothing of the great facts which we know about Christ's life and death and resurrection. They looked forward to redemption as a thing hoped for, but not yet seen — and their only warrant for hope was God's covenanted Word. Their faith may well put us to shame.

Let us learn to rest on promises and embrace them as Zacharias did. Let us not doubt that every word of God about his people concerning future things shall be as surely fulfilled as every word about them has been fulfilled concerning things past. Their safety is secured by promise. The world, the flesh, the devil shall never prevail against any believer. Their acquittal is secured by promise, as is their final glory. Let us be persuaded of these promises. Let us embrace them and not let them go. They will never fail us. God's Word is never broken. He is not a man that he should lie. We have a seal on every promise that Zacharias never saw. We have the seal of Christ's blood to assure us that what God has promised God will perform.

For meditation: *'For no matter how many promises God has made, they are "Yes" in Christ. And so through him the "Amen" is spoken by us to the glory of God'* (2 Cor. 1:20).

Suggested further reading: Luke 22:24-27

John the Baptist was an eminent saint of God. There are few names which stand higher than his in the Bible calendar of great and good men. The Lord Jesus himself declared that 'Among them that are born of women there hath not risen a greater than John the Baptist' (Matt. 11:11). The Lord Jesus himself declared that he was 'a burning and a shining light' (John 5:35). Yet here in this passage we see this eminent saint lowly, self-abased and full of humility. He puts away from himself the honour which the Jews from Jerusalem were ready to pay him. He declines all flattering titles. He speaks of himself as nothing more than the 'voice of one crying in the wilderness' and as one who 'baptized with water'. He proclaims loudly that there is one standing among the Jews far greater than himself, one whose shoe-latchet he is not worthy to unloose. He claims honour not for himself, but for Christ. To exalt Christ was his mission and to that mission he steadfastly adhered.

If we profess to have any real Christianity, let us strive to be of John the Baptist's spirit. Let us study humility. This is the grace with which all must begin who would be saved. We have no true religion about us until we cast away our high thoughts and feel ourselves sinners. This is the grace which all saints may follow after and which none have any excuse for neglecting. All God's children have not gifts, or money, or time to work, or a wide sphere of usefulness, but all may be humble. This is the grace, above all, which will appear most beautiful in our latter end. Never shall we feel the need of humility so deeply as when we lie on our deathbeds and stand before the judgement-seat of Christ. Our whole lives will then appear a long catalogue of imperfections, ourselves nothing and Christ all.

For meditation: *All that we become and all that we accomplish is due to the grace of God at work in us* (1 Cor. 15:10). *Self-congratulation is, therefore, always wrong.*

Suggested further reading: Ephesians 2:1-10

What clear views of Christ's kingdom Zacharias possessed! He speaks as if he had a view of a temporal deliverer from Gentile power and a temporal kingdom (v. 74). But he does not stop there. He declares how his people are to serve him in that kingdom (vv. 74-75). This kingdom he proclaimed as drawing nigh. Prophets had long foretold that it would one day be set up. In the birth of his son John the Baptist, and the near approach of Christ, Zacharias saw this kingdom close at hand.

The foundation of this kingdom of Messiah was laid by the preaching of the gospel. From that time the Lord Jesus has been continually gathering out subjects from an evil world. The full completion of the kingdom is an event yet to come. The saints of the Most High shall one day have entire dominion. But whether in its incomplete or complete state, the subjects of the kingdom are always of one character. They serve God without fear in holiness and righteousness (vv. 74-75). Let us give diligence to belong to this kingdom.

What clear views of doctrine Zacharias enjoyed! He ends the hymn of praise by addressing his infant son John the Baptist. He foretells that he shall go before the face of Messiah (v. 76) and give knowledge of the salvation that he is about to bring in (v. 77), a salvation that is all of grace and mercy (v. 78), of which the leading privileges are forgiveness of sins (v. 77), light (vv. 78-79) and peace (v. 79).

What do we know of these glorious privileges? Do we know anything of pardon? Have we turned from darkness to light? Have we tasted peace with God? These, after all, are the realities of Christianity. These are the things without which church membership and sacraments save no one's soul. Let us never rest till we are experientially acquainted with them. Mercy and grace have provided them. Mercy and grace will give them to all who call on Christ's name. Let us never rest till the Spirit witnesses with our spirit that we are walking in the way of peace.

For meditation: *'Make every effort to live in peace with all men and to be holy; without holiness no one will see the Lord'* (Heb. 2:14).

Suggested further reading: 1 Corinthians 1:18-25

We have in these verses a mournful example of the blindness of unconverted men. That example is supplied by the state of the Jews who came to question John the Baptist.

These Jews professed to be waiting for the appearance of Messiah. Like all the Pharisees, they prided themselves on being children of Abraham and possessors of the covenants. They rested in the law and made their boast of God. They professed to know God's will and to believe God's promises. They were confident that they themselves were guides of the blind and lights of them that sat in darkness (Rom. 2:17-19). And yet at this very moment their souls were utterly in the dark. 'There was standing among them,' as John the Baptist told them, 'one whom they knew not.' Christ himself, the promised Messiah, was in the midst of them, and yet they neither knew him, nor saw him, nor received him, nor acknowledged him, nor believed him. And worse than this, the vast majority of them never would know him! The words of John the Baptist are a prophetic description of a state of things which lasted during the whole of our Lord's earthly ministry. Christ 'stood among the Jews' and yet the Jews knew him not and the greater part of them died in their sins.

It is a solemn thought that John the Baptist's words in this place apply strictly to thousands in the present day. Christ is still standing among many who neither see, nor know, nor believe. Christ is passing by in many a parish and many a congregation and the vast majority have neither an eye to see him, nor an ear to hear him. The spirit of slumber seems poured out upon them. Money and pleasure and the world they know, but they know not Christ. The kingdom of God is close to them, but they sleep. Salvation is within their reach, but they sleep.

For meditation: *It is not enough to be near to Christ, to listen to him and to admire his words and works. We must believe in him* (Luke 13:24-27).

Suggested further reading: 1 Peter 1:22 - 2:3

Let no one think that these verses are useless. Nothing is useless in creation. The least mosses and the smallest insects serve some good end. Nothing is useless in the Bible. Every word of it is inspired. The chapters and verses which seem at first sight unprofitable are all given for some good purpose.

We learn from this list of names that God always keeps his word. He had promised that in Abraham's seed all the nations of the earth should be blessed. He had promised to raise up a Saviour of the family of David (Gen. 12:3; Isa. 11:1). These sixteen verses prove that Jesus was the son of David and the son of Abraham, and that God's promise was fulfilled. Thoughtless and ungodly people should be afraid. Whatever they may think, God will keep his word. If they repent not, they shall surely perish. True Christians should take comfort. Their Father in heaven will be true to all his engagements. He has said that he will save all believers in Christ. If he has said it, he will certainly do it.

What a frail and dying creature man is! How little we know of many of those whose names are recorded. They all had their joys and sorrows, their hopes and fears, their cares and troubles, their schemes and plans, like any of ourselves. But they have all passed away from earth, and gone to their place. And so it will be with us. We, too, are passing away and will soon be gone.

Forever let us bless God that in a dying world we are able to turn to a living Saviour (Rev. 1:18; John 11:25). Let our main care be to be one with Christ, and Christ with us. Joined to the Lord Jesus by faith, we shall rise to live for evermore. The second death shall have no power over us (John 14:19).

For meditation: *The stark contrast in this passage is between man who passes away like the grass, being here today and gone tomorrow, and the Word of God which lives and abides for ever. This contrast is prominent in Scripture and worthy of study (Isa. 40:6-8; 1 Peter 1:22 - 2:3).*

Suggested further reading: 1 Peter 1:18-21

Let us notice in this passage the peculiar name which John the Baptist gives to Christ. He calls him 'the Lamb of God'.

This name did not merely mean, as some have supposed, that Christ was meek and gentle as a lamb. This would be truth, no doubt, but only a very small portion of the truth. There are greater things here than this! It meant that Christ was the great sacrifice for sin, who was come to make atonement for transgression by his own death upon the cross. He was the true Lamb which Abraham told Isaac at Moriah God would provide (Gen. 22:8). He was the true Lamb to which every morning and evening sacrifice in the temple had daily pointed. He was the Lamb of which Isaiah had prophesied that he would be 'brought to the slaughter' (Isa. 53:7). He was the true Lamb of which the Passover lamb in Egypt had been a vivid type. In short, he was the great propitiation for sin which God had covenanted from all eternity to send into the world. He was God's Lamb.

Let us take heed that, in all our thoughts of Christ, we first think of him as John the Baptist here represents him. Let us serve him faithfully as our Master. Let us obey him loyally as our King. Let us study his teaching as our Prophet. Let us walk diligently after him as our Example. Let us look anxiously for him as our coming Redeemer of body as well as soul. But above all, let us prize him as our sacrifice and rest our whole weight on his death as an atonement for sin. Let his blood be more precious in our eyes every year we live. Whatever else we glory in about Christ, let us glory above all things in his cross. This is the cornerstone, this is the citadel, this is the rule of true Christian theology. We know nothing rightly about Christ until we see him with John the Baptist's eyes and can rejoice in him as 'the Lamb that was slain'.

For meditation: *Only where God saw the blood of the lamb did the destroyer pass over in Egypt* (Exod. 12:23). *Christ our Passover Lamb is sacrificed* (1 Cor. 5:7), *so destruction will pass us by.*

Suggested further reading: Hebrews 2:10-18

This list of names teaches us the sinfulness and corruption of human nature. Observe how many godly parents in this catalogue had wicked and ungodly sons. The names of Rehoboam, Joram, Amon and Jechoniah should teach us humbling lessons. They all had pious fathers, but they were all wicked men. Grace does not run in families. It needs something more than good examples and good advice to make us children of God. They that are born again are not born of blood, nor of the will of the flesh, nor of the will of man, but of God (John 1:13). Praying parents should pray night and day that their children may be born of the Spirit.

How great is the mercy and grace of our Lord Jesus Christ! Think how defiled and unclean our nature is; and then think what a condescension it was in him to be born of a woman and made in the likeness of men. Some of the names we read in this catalogue remind us of shameful and sad histories. Some of the names are of persons never mentioned elsewhere in the Bible. But at the end of all comes the name of the Lord Jesus Christ. Though he is the eternal God, he humbled himself to become man in order to provide salvation for sinners (2 Cor. 8:9).

We should always read this catalogue with thankful feelings. We see here that no one who partakes of human nature can be beyond the reach of Christ's sympathy and compassion. Our sins may have been as black and great as any of those whom St Matthew names. But they cannot shut us out of heaven if we repent and believe the gospel. If Jesus was not ashamed to be born of a woman whose pedigree contained such names as those we have read today, we need not think that he will be ashamed to call us brethren and to give us eternal life.

Note: Part of the genealogy as recorded by Matthew differs from part of that recorded by Luke. How can this difference be reconciled? The most probable explanation of the difficulty is to regard Luke's genealogy as the genealogy of Mary and not of Joseph.

For meditation: *God becoming man is worse than man becoming a slug.*

Suggested further reading: 1 Peter 2:21-25

Let us notice in this passage the peculiar work which John the Baptist describes Christ as doing. He says that 'He taketh away the sin of the world.'

Christ is a Saviour. He did not come on earth to be a conqueror, or a philosopher, or a mere teacher of morality. He came to save sinners. He came to do that which man could never do for himself — to do that which money and learning can never obtain, to do that which is essential to man's real happiness — he came to 'take away sin'.

Christ is a complete Saviour. He 'taketh away sin'. He did not merely make vague proclamations of pardon, mercy and forgiveness. He 'took' our sins upon himself and carried them away. He allowed them to be laid upon himself and 'bore them in his own body on the tree' (1 Peter 2:24). The sins of everyone that believes on Jesus are made as though they had never sinned at all. The Lamb of God has taken them clean away.

Christ is an almighty Saviour and a Saviour for all mankind. He 'taketh away the sin of the world'. He did not die for the Jews only, but for the Gentile as well as the Jew. The payment that he made on the cross was more than enough to make satisfaction for the debts of all. The blood that he shed was precious enough to wash away the sins of all. His atonement on the cross was sufficient for all mankind, though efficient only to them that believe. The sin that he took up and bore on the cross was the sin of the whole world.

Last, but not least, Christ is a perpetual and unwearied Saviour. He 'taketh away' sin. He is daily taking it away from everyone that believes on him — daily purging, daily cleansing, daily washing the souls of his people, daily granting and applying fresh supplies of mercy.

For meditation: *My sin — oh, the bliss of this glorious thought! —*
My sin, not in part, but the whole,
Is nailed to the cross, and I bear it no more!
Praise the Lord! Praise the Lord! O my soul!
　　　　　　　　　　　　　　(H. G. Spafford).

Suggested further reading: Philippians 2:5-11

The name 'Jesus' means Saviour (v. 21). The special office of our Lord is to save his people from their sins. He saves them from the guilt of sin by washing them in his atoning blood. He saves them from the dominion of sin by putting in their hearts the sanctifying Spirit. He saves them from the presence of sin when he takes them out of this world to rest with him. He will save them from all the consequences of sin when he shall give them a glorious body at the last day. They are saved from sin for evermore. He who cleaves to sin is not yet saved.

Jesus is very encouraging to heavy-laden sinners. He who is King of kings and Lord of lords might lawfully have taken some more high-sounding title. But he does not do so. The rulers of this world have often called themselves Great, Conqueror, Bold, Magnificent, and the like. The Son of God is content to call himself Saviour. The souls which desire salvation may draw nigh to the Father with boldness and have access with confidence through Christ (John 3:17).

Jesus is a name which is peculiarly sweet and precious to believers. It has often done them good when the favour of kings and princes would have been heard of with unconcern. It has given them what money cannot buy, even inward peace. It has eased their weary consciences and given rest to their heavy hearts. Happy is that person who trusts not merely in vague notions of God's mercy and goodness, but in Jesus.

The conduct of Joseph described in these verses is a beautiful example of godly wisdom and tender consideration for others. He saw 'the appearance of evil' in his espoused wife. But he did nothing rashly. He waited patiently to have the line of duty made clear.

The patience of Joseph was rewarded. He received a direct message from God upon the subject of his anxiety and was at once relieved from all his fears. How good it is to wait upon God! Who ever cast his cares upon God in hearty prayer and found him fail? (Prov. 3:6).

For meditation: *The name Jesus is not given to us to make him an object of glib familiarity, but to fill us with awe at his saving condescension.*

Suggested further reading: Acts 15:6-11

Let us notice in this passage the peculiar office which John the Baptist attributes to Christ. He speaks of him as him 'which baptizeth with the Holy Ghost'.

The baptism here spoken of is not the baptism of water. It does not consist either of dipping or sprinkling. It does not belong exclusively either to infants or to grown-up people. It is not a baptism which any man can give, Episcopalian or Presbyterian, Independent or Methodist, layman or minister. It is a baptism which the great Head of the church keeps exclusively in his own hands. It consists of the implanting of grace into the inward man. It is the same thing with the new birth. It is a baptism, not of the body, but of the heart. It is a baptism which the penitent thief received, though neither dipped nor sprinkled by the hand of man. It is a baptism which Ananias and Sapphira did not receive, though admitted into church communion by apostolic men.

Let it be a settled principle in our religion that the baptism of which John the Baptist speaks here is the baptism which is absolutely necessary to salvation. The baptism of water is a most blessed and profitable ordinance and cannot be neglected without great sin. But the baptism of the Holy Ghost is of far greater importance. The man who dies with his heart not baptized by Christ can never be saved.

Let us ask ourselves, as we leave this passage, whether we are baptized with the Holy Ghost and whether we have any real interest in the Lamb of God. Thousands, unhappily, are wasting their time in controversy about water baptism and neglecting the baptism of the heart. Thousands more are content with a head-knowledge of the Lamb of God, or have never sought him by faith that their own sins may be actually taken away. Let us take heed that we ourselves have new hearts and believe to the saving of our souls.

For meditation: *The Pharisees were very concerned to have clean bodies. Our Lord was concerned with clean hearts* (Matt. 15:1,2,10,11,16-20). *Are you more concerned with your body or your soul?*

Suggested further reading: John 1:1-5, 14-18

The name Emmanuel (v. 23) is given to our Lord from his nature as God manifest in the flesh. Let us take care that we have clear views of our Lord's nature and person. We should settle it firmly in our minds that our Saviour is perfect man as well as perfect God, and perfect God as well as perfect man. If we once lose sight of this great foundational truth we may run into fearful heresies. The name Emmanuel takes in the whole mystery. Jesus is 'God with us'. He had a nature like our own in all things, sin only excepted. But though Jesus was 'with us' in human flesh and blood, he was at the same time very God.

We shall often find, as we read in the Gospels, that our Saviour could be weary, hungry and thirsty, could weep, groan and feel pain, like one of ourselves. In all this we see the man Christ Jesus. We see the nature he took on him when he was born of the Virgin Mary.

But we shall also find in the same Gospels that our Saviour knew men's hearts and thoughts, that he had power over devils, that he could work the mightiest miracles with a word, that he was ministered to by angels, that he allowed a disciple to call him 'my God', and that he said, 'I and the Father are one' (John 10:30) and 'Before Abraham was, I am' (John 8:58). In all this we see the eternal God. We see him 'who is over all, God blessed for ever' (Rom. 9:5).

Would you have a strong foundation for your faith and hope? Then keep in constant view your Saviour's divinity. He in whose blood you are taught to trust is the almighty God. All power is his in heaven and on earth. None can pluck you out of his hand. If you are a true believer in Jesus let not your heart be troubled or afraid.

Would you have sweet comfort in suffering and trial? Then keep in constant view your Saviour's humanity. He knows the heart of a man. He can be touched with the feeling of your infirmities, temptations, hunger, tears and pain. Trust him at all times with your sorrows. He will not despise you. He can sympathize with his people.

For meditation: *Christ is between God and men, as God and man.*

Suggested further reading: 1 Corinthians 2:1-5

We see, for one thing, in these verses, what good is done by continually testifying of Christ. This simple story is a pattern of the way in which good has been done to souls in every age of the Christian church. By such testimony as that before us, and by none else, men and women are converted and saved. It is by exalting Christ, not the church, Christ, not the sacraments, Christ, not the ministry — it is by this means that hearts are moved and sinners are turned to God. To the world such testimony may seem weakness and foolishness. Yet, like the ram's horns before whose blast the walls of Jericho fell down, this testimony is mighty to the pulling down of strongholds. The story of the crucified Lamb of God has proved in every age the power of God unto salvation. Those who have done most for Christ's cause in every part of the world have been men like John the Baptist. They have not cried, 'Behold me!' or 'Behold the church!' or 'Behold the ordinances!' but 'Behold the Lamb!' If souls are to be saved, men must be pointed directly to Christ.

One thing, however, must never be forgotten. There must be patient continuance in preaching and teaching the truth, if we want good to be done. Christ must be set forth again and again as the 'Lamb of God which taketh away the sin of the world'. The story of grace must be told repeatedly, line upon line and precept upon precept. It is the constant dropping which wears away the stone. The promise shall never be broken that 'God's word shall not return unto him void' (Isa. 55:11). But it is nowhere said that it shall do good the very first time that it is preached. It was not the first proclamation of John the Baptist, but the second, which made Andrew and his companion follow Jesus.

For meditation: *Persistence in the work of evangelism, and in all service to God, has a promise of ultimate blessing connected to it* (Gal. 6:9).

Suggested further reading: Psalm 31:9-20

The sceptre was practically departing from Judah (Gen. 49:10). The Jews were coming under the dominion and taxation of a foreign power. Strangers were beginning to rule over them. They had no longer a really independent government of their own. The 'due time' had come for the promised Messiah to appear. Augustus taxes the world and at once Christ is born.

It was a time peculiarly suited for the introduction of Christ's gospel. The whole civilized world was at length governed by one master (Dan. 2:40). There was nothing to prevent a preacher of a new faith going from city to city and from country to country. The princes and priests of the heathen world had been weighed in the balances and found wanting. Egypt, Assyria, Babylon, Persia, Greece and Rome had all successively proved that 'the world by wisdom knew not God' (1 Cor. 1:21). Notwithstanding their mighty conquerors, poets, historians, architects and philosophers, the kingdoms of the world were full of dark idolatry. It was indeed 'due time' for God to interpose from heaven and send down an almighty Saviour. It was 'due time' for Christ to be born (Rom. 5:6).

Let us ever rest our souls on the thought that our times are in God's hands (Ps. 31:15). He knows the best season for sending help to his church and new light to the world. Let us beware of giving way to over-anxiety about the course of events around us, as if we knew better than the King of kings what time relief should come. 'Cease, Philip, to try to govern the world,' was a frequent saying of Luther to an anxious friend. It was a saying full of wisdom.

The prophet Micah had foretold that the Christ would be born at Bethlehem. God overruled the time when Augustus decreed the taxing and directed the enforcement of the decree in such a way that Mary must needs be at Bethlehem for the birth. Little did the haughty Roman emperor imagine he was an instrument in the hands of the God of Israel, carrying out the purposes of the King of kings.

For meditation: *God rules* (Ps. 115:3) *in all things* (Eph. 1:11).

Suggested further reading: Mark 5:18-20

No sooner does Andrew become a disciple than he tells his brother Simon what a discovery he has made. Like one who has unexpectedly heard good tidings, he hastens to impart it to the one nearest and dearest to him. And to Andrew's outspoken testimony, under God, the great apostle Peter owed the first beginning of light in his soul.

The fact before us is most striking and instructive. Out of the three first members of the Christian church, one at least was brought to Jesus by the private, quiet word of a relative. He seems to have heard no public preaching. He saw no mighty miracle wrought. He was not convinced by any powerful reasoning. He only heard his brother telling him that he had found a Saviour himself and at once the work began in his soul. The simple testimony of a warm-hearted brother was the first link in the chain by which Peter was drawn out of the world and joined to Christ. The first blow in that mighty work by which Peter was made a pillar of the church was struck by Andrew's words: 'We have found the Christ.'

Well would it be for the church of Christ, if all believers were more like Andrew! Well would it be for souls, if all men and women who have been converted themselves would speak to their friends and relatives on spiritual subjects and tell them what they have found! How much good might be done! How many might be led to Jesus who now live and die in unbelief! The work of testifying to the gospel of the grace of God ought not to be left to ministers alone. All who have received mercy ought to find a tongue and to declare what God has done for their souls. Thousands, humanly speaking, would listen to a word from a friend who will not listen to a sermon. Every believer ought to be a home missionary, a missionary to his family, children, servants, neighbours and friends.

For meditation: *Has every member of your family heard the gospel at least once from you? If you do not evangelize them, who will?*

Suggested further reading: 1 Corinthians 1:26-31

The birth of a king's son is generally made an occasion of public revelling and rejoicing. The announcement of the birth of the Prince of peace was made privately, at midnight, and without anything of worldly pomp and ostentation.

The tidings that Christ was born first came to shepherds (vv. 8-9) — to shepherds, not to priests and rulers; to shepherds, not to scribes and Pharisees. To shepherds an angel appeared with the proclamation of a Saviour (v. 11).

The saying of James should come into our minds (James 2:5). The lack of money debars no one from spiritual privileges. The things of God's kingdom are often hid from the great and noble, and revealed to the poor. The busy labour of the hands need not prevent a man from being favoured with special communion with God. Moses was keeping sheep, Gideon was threshing wheat, Elisha was ploughing, when they were each honoured by direct calls and revelations from God. Let us resist the suggestion of Satan that religion is not for the working man. The weak of the world are often called before the mighty. The last are often first and the first last.

We need not wonder at the remarkable language used by the angel in announcing Christ's birth to the shepherds (v. 10). The spiritual darkness which had covered the earth for four thousand years was about to be rolled away. The way to pardon and peace with God was about to be thrown open to all mankind. The head of Satan was about to be bruised. Liberty was about to be proclaimed to the captives, the recovering of sight to the blind. The mighty truth was about to be proclaimed that God could be just, and yet, for Christ's sake, justify the ungodly. Salvation was no longer to be seen through types and figures, but openly and face to face. The knowledge of God was no longer to be confined to the Jews, but to be offered to the whole Gentile world. If this was not 'good news', then there were never tidings that deserved that name.

For meditation: *Neither intellect nor social standing count, only faith.*

Suggested further reading: Acts 8:26-35

Let us observe, as we read these verses, how various are the paths by which souls are led into the narrow way of life.

We are told of a man named Philip being added to the little company of Christ's disciples. He does not appear to have been moved, like Andrew and his companions, by the testimony of John the Baptist. He was not drawn, like Peter, by the outspoken declaration of a brother. He seems to have been called directly by Christ himself and the agency of man seems not to have been used in his calling. Yet in faith and life he became one with those who were disciples before him. Though led by different paths, they all entered the same road, embraced the same truths, served the same Master and at length reached the same home.

The fact before us is a deeply important one. It throws light on the history of all God's people in every age and of every tongue. There are diversities of operations in the saving of souls. All true Christians are led by one Spirit, washed in one blood, serve one Lord, lean on one Saviour, believe one truth and walk by one general rule. But all are not converted in one and the same manner. All do not pass through the same experience. In conversion, the Holy Ghost acts as a sovereign.

We must beware of making the experience of other believers the measure of our own. We must beware of denying another's grace, because he has not been led by the same way as ourselves. Has a man got the real grace of God? This is the only question that concerns us. Is he a penitent man? Is he a believer? Does he live a holy life? Provided these inquiries can be answered satisfactorily, we may well be content. It matters nothing by what path a man has been led, if he has only been led at last into the right way.

For meditation: *In accepting fellow believers it is not race, social standing, gender, etc. that matters, but their acceptance by our Lord* (Gal. 3:28; Rom. 15:7).

Suggested further reading: Revelation 5:6-14

Angels first praised God when Christ was born (v. 13). Angels, not men — angels who had never sinned and needed no Saviour, angels who had not fallen, and required neither Redeemer nor atoning blood.

This fact is full of deep spiritual lessons. It shows us what good servants the angels are. All that their heavenly Master does pleases and interests them. It shows us what clear knowledge they have. They know what misery sin has brought into creation. They know the blessedness of heaven and the privilege of an open door into it. Above all, it shows us the deep love and compassion with which the angels view poor lost man. They rejoice in the glorious prospect of many souls being saved and many brands plucked from the burning.

Let us strive to be more like-minded with the angels. Our spiritual ignorance and deadness appear most painfully in our inability to enter into the joy which we see them here expressing. Surely if we hope to dwell with them in heaven, we ought to share something of their feelings while we are here upon earth. Let us seek a more deep sense of the sinfulness and misery of sin, and then we shall have a more deep sense of thankfulness for redemption.

The hymn of praise (v. 14) declares that the highest degree of glory to God is come by the appearing of his Son. He, by his life and death, will glorify God's attributes, his justice, holiness, mercy and wisdom, as they were never glorified before.

The song declares the coming to earth of the peace of God which passes all understanding, the perfect peace between a holy God and sinful man, which Christ was to purchase with his own blood, the peace which is freely offered to all mankind, which, once admitted to the heart, makes men live at peace one with another, and which will overspread the earth.

The song declares that the time is come when God's kindness and goodwill towards guilty man is to be fully made known. His mercy is fully revealed by the appearing and atonement of Jesus Christ.

For meditation: *If sinless angels praise God for the Saviour, should not we?*

Suggested further reading: 2 Timothy 2:23-26

Let us observe in these verses the good advice which Philip gave to Nathanael. The mind of Nathanael was full of doubts about the Saviour of whom Philip told him. 'Can there any good thing', he said, 'come out of Nazareth?' And what did Philip reply? He said, 'Come and see.'

Wiser counsel than this it would be impossible to conceive! If Philip had reproved Nathanael's unbelief, he might have driven him back for many a day and given offence. If he had reasoned with him, he might have failed to convince him, or might have confirmed him in his doubts. But by inviting him to prove the matter for himself, he showed his entire confidence in the truth of his own assertion and his willingness to have it tested and proved. And the result shows the wisdom of Philip's words. Nathanael owed his early acquaintance with Christ to that frank invitation: 'Come and see.'

If we call ourselves true Christians, let us never be afraid to deal with people about their souls as Philip dealt with Nathanael. Let us invite them boldly to make proof of our religion. Let us tell them confidently that they cannot know its real value until they have tried it. Let us assure them that vital Christianity courts every possible inquiry. It has no secrets. It has nothing to conceal. Its faith and practice are spoken against, just because they are not known. Its enemies speak evil of things with which they are not acquainted. They understand neither what they say nor whereof they affirm. Philip's mode of dealing, we may be sure, is one principal way to do good. Few are ever moved by reasoning and argument. Still fewer are frightened into repentance. The man who does most good to souls is often the simple believer who says to his friends, 'I have found a Saviour; come and see him.'

For meditation: *It sometimes gives us great satisfaction to win an argument with an unbeliever. We should, however, be more concerned to win the person.*

Suggested further reading: 1 Corinthians 9:19-23

Our Lord rendered obedience as an infant to the Jewish law by being circumcised on the eighth day (v. 21). Our Lord's circumcision was a public testimony to Israel that, according to the flesh, he was a Jew, made of a Jewish woman and made under the law (Gal. 4:4). Without it he could never have fulfilled the law's requirements. Without it he could never have been recognized as the son of David and the seed of Abraham. Let us remember that circumcision was absolutely necessary before our Lord could be heard as a teacher in Israel. Without it he could have no place in any lawful Jewish assembly and no right to any Jewish ordinance. Without it he would have been regarded by all Jews as nothing better than an uncircumcised Gentile and an apostate from the faith of the fathers.

Let our Lord's submission to an ordinance that he did not need for himself be a lesson to us in our daily life. Let us endure much rather than increase the offence of the gospel or hinder in any way the cause of God. Paul walked very closely in the footsteps of his Master and his words deserve pondering (1 Cor. 9:19-22).

Our Lord was called 'Jesus' by God's special command (v. 21). The Son of God could have chosen the King, the Lawgiver, the Prophet, the Priest, the Judge of fallen man as his proper title. But he bypassed them all. He selects a name which speaks of mercy, grace, help and deliverance for a lost world. It is as a Deliverer and Redeemer that he desires principally to be known. Let us ask ourselves what our own hearts know of the Son of God. Is he our Jesus, our Saviour? Do we know him as our Deliverer from the guilt and power of sin, and our Redeemer from Satan's bondage?

The offering given was that of a poor man and woman (v. 24; Lev. 12:6,8). Poverty was our Lord's portion from the days of his earliest infancy. Let the poor believer remember that his mighty Mediator in heaven is accustomed to poverty and is the true poor man's Friend.

For meditation: *What inconveniences will we face for the salvation of men?*

Suggested further reading: Luke 24:25-27,44-48

How much of Christ there is in the Old Testament Scriptures! We read that when Philip described Christ to Nathanael, he said, 'We have found him of whom Moses in the law and the prophets did write.'

Christ is the sum and substance of the Old Testament. To him the earliest promises pointed in the days of Adam and Enoch and Noah and Abraham and Isaac and Jacob. To him every sacrifice pointed in the ceremonial worship appointed at Mount Sinai. Of him every high priest was a type and every part of the tabernacle was a shadow and every judge and deliverer of Israel was a figure. He was the Prophet like unto Moses, whom the Lord God promised to send, and the King of the house of David, who came to be David's Lord as well as Son. He was the Son of the virgin and the Lamb foretold by Isaiah, the righteous Branch mentioned by Jeremiah, the true Shepherd foreseen by Ezekiel, the Messenger of the covenant promised by Malachi and the Messiah who, according to Daniel, was to be cut off, though not for himself. The further we read in the volume of the Old Testament, the clearer do we find the testimony about Christ. The light which the inspired writers enjoyed in ancient days was, at best, but dim, compared to that of the gospel. But the coming person they all saw afar off, and on whom they all fixed their eyes, was one and the same. The Spirit, which was in them, testified of Christ (1 Peter 1:11).

Do we stumble at this saying? Do we find it hard to see Christ in the Old Testament, because we do not see his name? Let us pray for a more humble, childlike and teachable spirit. May we never rest till we can subscribe to our Lord's words about the Old Testament Scriptures: 'They are they which testify of me' (John 5:39).

For meditation: *In the earliest days of the church the Christians only had the Old Testament to prove that Jesus is the Christ. How would you have managed?*

Suggested further reading: Philippians 1:19-26

Simeon reminds us that God has a believing people even in the worst of places and in the darkest times. Religion was at a very low ebb when Christ was born. The faith of Abraham was spoiled by the doctrines of the Pharisees and Sadducees. Yet in the midst of Jerusalem is a man of the character of Simeon (v. 25).

It is a cheering thought that God never leaves himself without a witness. Small as his believing church may sometimes be, the gates of hell shall never completely prevail against it. The true church may be driven into the wilderness and be a scattered flock, but it never dies. There was a Lot in Sodom (Gen. 19; 2 Peter 2:7), an Obadiah in Ahab's house (1 Kings 18:3-4), a Daniel in Babylon (Dan. 6:4), and in the last days of the Jewish church, when its iniquity was almost full, there were godly people like Simeon, even in Jerusalem.

Christians in every age should remember this and take comfort. It is a truth which they are apt to forget and in consequence to give way to despondency. Elijah's complaint that he alone was left was answered by God's keeping of seven thousand faithful in Israel (1 Kings 19:14,18).

In Simeon we see how completely a believer can be delivered from the fear of death (v. 29). He speaks like one for whom the grave has lost its terrors, and the world its charms. He desires to be released from the miseries of this pilgrim state and to be allowed to go home (2 Cor. 5:8). He speaks as one who knows where he is going when he departs this life and cares not how soon he goes. The change with him will be a change for the better and he desires that change may come.

What is it that can enable a mortal man to use such language as this? What can deliver us from that fear of death to which so many are in bondage? What can take the sting of death away? Nothing but strong faith can do it. Faith laying hold on an unseen Saviour, faith resting on the promises of an unseen God, faith, and only faith, can enable a man to look death in the face and say, 'I depart in peace.'

For meditation: *Are Hebrews 2:14-15 a living reality in your life?*

Suggested further reading: 1 Samuel 3:2-10

Let us observe, lastly, in these verses the high character which Jesus gives of Nathanael. He calls him 'an Israelite indeed, in whom is no guile'.

Nathanael, there can be no doubt, was a true child of God and a child of God in difficult times. He was one of a very little flock. Like Simeon and Anna and other pious Jews, he was living by faith and waiting prayerfully for the promised Redeemer when our Lord's ministry began. He had that which grace alone can give — an honest heart, a heart without guile. His knowledge was probably small. His spiritual eyesight was dim. But he was one who had lived carefully up to his light. He had diligently used such knowledge as he possessed. His eye had been single, though his vision had not been strong. His spiritual judgement had been honest, though it had not been powerful. What he saw in Scripture, he had held firmly, in spite of Pharisees and Sadducees and all the fashionable religion of the day. He was an honest Old Testament believer who had stood alone. And here was the secret of our Lord's peculiar commendation! He declared Nathanael to be a true son of Abraham, a Jew inwardly, possessing circumcision in the spirit as well as in the letter, an Israelite in heart, as well as a son of Jacob in the flesh.

Let us pray that we may be of the same spirit as Nathanael. An honest, unprejudiced mind, a childlike willingness to follow the truth, wherever the truth may lead us, a simple, hearty desire to be guided, taught and led by the Spirit, a thorough determination to use every spark of light which we have, are a possession of priceless value. A man of this spirit may live in the midst of much darkness and be surrounded by every possible disadvantage to his soul. But the Lord Jesus will take care that such a man does not miss the way to heaven. 'The meek will he guide in judgement: and the meek will he teach his way' (Ps. 25:9).

For meditation: *How teachable are you? Or are you self-opinionated and puffed up with your own knowledge?*

Suggested further reading: Ephesians 2:11-22

What clear views of Christ's work and office some Jewish believers attained even before the gospel was preached! Well would it have been for the letter-learned scribes and Pharisees of Simeon's time if they had sat at his feet and listened to his word concerning Jew and Gentile (v. 32).

Christ was indeed light to the Gentiles. Without him they were sunk in gross darkness and superstition. They knew not the way of life. They worshipped the work of their own hands. Their wisest philosophers were utterly ignorant in spiritual things (Rom. 1:22). The gospel of Christ was like sunrise to Greece and Rome and the whole heathen world. The light which it let in on men's minds on the subject of religion was as great as the change from night to day.

Christ was indeed the glory of Israel. The descent from Abraham, the covenants, the promises, the law of Moses, the divinely ordered temple service — all these were mighty privileges. But all were nothing compared to the mighty fact that out of Israel was born the Saviour of the world. This was to be the highest honour of the Jewish nation, that the mother of Christ was a Jewish woman, and that the blood of one made of the seed of David according to the flesh was to make atonement for the sin of mankind (Rom. 1:3).

The words of old Simeon, let us remember, will yet receive a fuller accomplishment. The light which he saw by faith, as he held the child Jesus in his arms, shall yet shine so brightly that all the nations of the Gentile world shall see it. The glory of that Jesus whom Israel crucified shall one day be revealed so clearly to the scattered Jews that they shall look on him whom they pierced and repent and be converted. The day shall come when the veil shall be taken away from the heart of Israel and all shall glory in the Lord (Isa. 45:25). If Christ be the light and glory of our souls that day cannot come too soon.

For meditation: *The Scriptures do not promise the salvation of everyone but do promise the salvation of an innumerable host from every nation.*

Suggested further reading: Ephesians 5:22-33

How honourable in the sight of Christ is the estate of matrimony! To be present at a 'marriage' was almost the first public act of our Lord's earthly ministry.

Marriage is not a sacrament, as the church of Rome asserts. It is simply a state of life ordained by God for man's benefit. But it is a state which ought never to be spoken of with levity, or regarded with disrespect. The Prayer Book service has well described it as 'an honourable estate, instituted of God in the time of man's innocency, and signifying unto us the mystical union that is betwixt Christ and his church'. Society is never in a healthy condition and true religion never flourishes in that land where the marriage tie is lightly esteemed. They who lightly esteem it have not the mind of Christ. He who 'beautified and adorned the estate of matrimony by his presence and first miracle that he wrought in Cana of Galilee' is one who is always of one mind. 'Marriage', says the Holy Ghost by St Paul, 'is honourable in all' (Heb. 13:4).

One thing, however, ought not to be forgotten. Marriage is a step which so seriously affects the temporal happiness and spiritual welfare of two immortal souls that it ought never to be taken in hand 'unadvisedly, lightly, wantonly and without due consideration'. To be truly happy, it should be undertaken 'reverently, discreetly, soberly and in the fear of God'. Christ's blessing and presence are essential to a happy wedding. The marriage at which there is no place for Christ and his disciples is not one that can justly be expected to prosper.

We learn from these verses that there are times when it is lawful to be merry and rejoice. Our Lord himself sanctioned a wedding feast by his own presence. He did not refuse to be a guest at 'a marriage in Cana of Galilee'.

For meditation: *In days of soaring divorce rates and rampant immorality, faithfulness and purity among Christians should be guarded.*

Suggested further reading: 1 Corinthians 1:18-25

Every word of old Simeon on the results which would follow when Jesus Christ and his gospel came into the world deserves private meditation. The whole forms a prophecy which is daily being fulfilled.

Christ was to be 'a sign spoken against' (v. 34). He was to be a mark for all the fiery darts of the wicked one. He was to be despised and rejected by men. He and his people were to be a city set on a hill assailed on every side and hated by all sorts of enemies. And so it proved. Men who agreed in nothing else have agreed in hating Christ. From the very first thousands have been persecutors and unbelievers.

Christ was to be the occasion of the fall of many in Israel (v. 34). He was to be a stone of stumbling and a rock of offence to many proud and self-righteous Jews, who would reject him and perish in their sins. And so it was proved. To multitudes among them Christ crucified was a stumbling-block and his gospel a savour of death (1 Cor. 1:23; 2 Cor. 2:16).

Christ was to be the occasion of the rising of many in Israel (v. 34). He was to prove the Saviour of many who at one time rejected, blasphemed and reviled him, but afterwards repented and believed. And so it proved. When the thousands who crucified him repented, and Saul who persecuted him was converted, there was nothing less than a rising again of the dead.

Christ was to be the occasion of the thoughts of many hearts being revealed (v. 35). His gospel was to bring to light the real characters of many people. The enmity to God of some, the inward weariness and hunger of others would be discovered by the preaching of the cross. It would show what men really were. And so it proved.

What do we think of Christ? This is the question that ought to occupy our minds. What thoughts does he call forth in our hearts? This is the enquiry which ought to receive our attention. Are we for him or against him? Do we love him or neglect him? Do we stumble at his doctrine, or do we find it life from the dead?

For meditation: *'For the word of God is living and active... Everything is uncovered and laid bare before the eyes of him to whom we must give account'* (Heb. 4:12-13).

Suggested further reading: Matthew 11:16-19

'A feast', it is written, 'is made for laughter, and wine maketh merry' (Eccles. 10:19). Our Lord, in the passage before us, countenances both the feast and the use of wine.

True religion was never meant to make men melancholy. On the contrary, it was intended to increase real joy and happiness among men. The servant of Christ unquestionably ought to have nothing to do with races, balls, theatres and suchlike amusements, which tend to frivolity and dissipation, if not to sin. But he has no right to hand over innocent recreations and family gatherings to the devil and the world. The Christian who withdraws entirely from the society of his fellow men and walks the earth with a face as melancholy as if he was always attending a funeral does injury to the cause of the gospel. A cheerful, kindly spirit is a great recommendation to a believer. It is a positive misfortune to Christianity when a Christian cannot smile. A merry heart and a readiness to take part in all innocent mirth are gifts of inestimable value. They go far to soften prejudices, to take up stumbling-blocks out of the way and to make way for Christ and the gospel.

The subject, no doubt, is a difficult and delicate one. On no point of Christian practice is it so hard to hit the mean between that which is lawful and that which is unlawful, between that which is right and that which is wrong. It is very hard indeed to be both merry and wise.

One golden rule on the subject may be laid down, the use of which will save us much trouble. Let us take care that we always go to feasts in the spirit of our divine Master and that we never go where he would not have gone. Let us endeavour to bring the salt of grace into every company and to drop the word in season in every ear we address.

For meditation: *A life lived in reverent fear* (1 Peter 1:17) *and set on pleasing Christ and gaining his approval* (2 Cor. 5:9-10) *will avoid much sin.*

Suggested further reading: 1 Corinthians 9:24 - 10:6

The facts recorded about Anna are few and simple but full of instruction. Anna was a woman of irreproachable character. After a married life of only seven years' duration she had spent eighty-four years as a lone widow (vv. 36-37). The trials, desolations and temptation of such a condition were probably very great. But Anna, by grace, overcame them all. She answered the description given by Paul (1 Tim. 5:5).

Anna was a woman who loved God's house (v. 37). She regarded it as the place where God especially dwelt. 'Nearer to God, nearer to God,' was the desire of her heart, and she felt never so near as within the walls that contained the ark, the altar and the holy of holies. She could enter into David's words (Ps. 84:2).

Anna was a woman of great self-denial (v. 37). She was continually crucifying the flesh and keeping it in subjection by voluntary fastings. Being fully persuaded in her own mind that the practice was helpful to her soul, she spared no pains to keep it up.

Anna was a woman of much prayer (v. 37). She was continually communing with God, as her best Friend, about the things that concerned her own peace. She was never weary of pleading with him on behalf of others and, above all, for the fulfilment of his promises of Messiah.

Anna was a woman who held communion with other saints (v. 38). As soon as she had seen Jesus she spoke of him to others in Jerusalem who enjoyed the same hope. With her they walked by faith and not by sight. They lived in faith that the coming Redeemer would bring in holiness and righteousness.

Anna received a rich reward for all her diligence in God's service before she left the world. She was allowed to see him who had been so long promised and for whose coming she had so often prayed. Her faith was at last changed to sight and her hope to certainty.

For meditation: *Anna is an example to us by which we will do well to measure our own lives. She was consistent, holy, prayerful and self-denying. Are we?*

Suggested further reading: Psalm 27:1-6

We learn from these verses the almighty power of our Lord Jesus Christ. We are told of a miracle which he wrought at the marriage feast when the wine failed. By a mere act of will he changed water into wine and so supplied the need of all the guests.

The manner in which the miracle was worked deserves especial notice. We are not told of any outward visible action which preceded or accompanied it. It is not said that he touched the waterpots containing the water that was made wine. It is not said that he commanded the water to change its qualities, or that he prayed to his Father in heaven. He simply willed the change and it took place. We read of no prophet or apostle in the Bible who ever worked a miracle after this fashion. He who could do such a mighty work, in such a manner, was nothing less than very God.

It is a comfortable thought that the same almighty power of will which our Lord here displayed is still exercised on behalf of his believing people. They have no need of his bodily presence to maintain their cause. They have no reason to be cast down because they cannot see him with their eyes interceding for them, or touch him with their hands, that they may cling to him for safety. If he 'wills' their salvation and the daily supply of all their spiritual need, they are as safe and well provided for as if they saw him standing by them. Christ's *will* is as mighty and effectual as Christ's *deed*. The will of him who could say to the Father, 'I will that they whom thou hast given me be with me where I am' (John 17:24) is a will that has all power in heaven and earth and must prevail.

Happy are those who, like the disciples, believe on him by whom this miracle was wrought!

For meditation: *Whatever has been determined by God must happen. It is unable to be stopped and is above any legitimate criticism* (Dan. 4:35).

Suggested further reading: Matthew 11:20-30

These verses teach us that there may be true servants of God in places where we should not expect to find them. The Lord Jesus has many 'hidden ones' like these wise men. Their history on earth may be as little known as that of Melchizedek and Jethro and Job. But their names are in the book of life and they will be found with Christ at the day of his appearing. It is well to remember this. We must not look around the earth concluding all is barren. The grace of God is not tied to places and families. The Holy Spirit can lead souls to Christ without the help of many outward means.

It is not always those who have most religious privileges that give Christ most honour. We might have thought that the scribes and Pharisees would have been the first to hasten to Bethlehem on the slightest rumour that the Saviour was born. But it was not so. A few unknown strangers from a distant land were the first, except the shepherds, to rejoice at his birth (John 1:11). What a mournful picture this is of human nature! How often those people who live nearest to the means of grace are those who reject them most. There is too much truth in the old proverb: 'The nearer the church, the further from God.' Familiarity with sacred things has an awful tendency to make men despise them.

There may be knowledge of Scripture in the head, while there is no grace in the heart. King Herod sent to enquire of the priests and elders where Christ was to be born (v. 4). They quickly gave him the answer and showed an acquaintance with the letter of Scripture. But they never went to Bethlehem to seek for the coming Saviour. They would not believe in him when he ministered amongst them. Their heads were better than their hearts. Let us all beware of resting satisfied with head knowledge. It is an excellent thing when rightly used. But a man may have much of it, yet perish everlastingly. What is the state of our hearts? A little grace is better than many gifts. Gifts alone save no one. But grace leads on to glory.

For meditation: *What are you doing with all the spiritual privileges you have?*

Suggested further reading: Ezekiel 33:30-33

How much Christ disapproves all irreverent behaviour in the house of God! We are told that he drove out of the temple those whom he found selling oxen and sheep and doves within its walls, that he poured out the changers' money and overthrew their tables and that he said to them that sold doves, 'Take these things hence; make not my Father's house an house of merchandise.' On no occasion in our Lord's earthly ministry do we find him acting so energetically and exhibiting such righteous indignation as on the occasion now before us. Nothing seems to have called from him such a marked display of holy wrath as the gross irreverence which the priests permitted in the temple, notwithstanding all their boasted zeal for God's law.

The passage is one that ought to raise deep searchings of heart in many quarters. Are there none who profess and call themselves Christians, behaving every Sunday just as badly as these Jews? Are there none who secretly bring into the house of God their money, their lands, their houses, their cattle and a whole train of worldly affairs? Are there none who bring their bodies only into the place of worship and allow their hearts to wander into the ends of the earth? Are there none who are 'almost in all evil, in the midst of the congregation'? (Prov. 5:14). Multitudes, it may be feared, could not give a satisfactory answer. Christian churches and chapels, no doubt, are very unlike the Jewish temple. They are not built after a divine pattern. They have no altars or holy places. Their furniture has no typical meaning. But they are places where God's Word is read and where Christ is specially present. The man who professes to worship in them should surely behave with reverence and respect. The man who brings his worldly matters with him when he professes to worship is doing that which is evidently most offensive to Christ.

For meditation: *Our Lord detests that worship which is only outward and insincere* (Matt. 15:7-8).

Suggested further reading: Hebrews 11:32-38

What spiritual diligence these wise men showed! What troubles it must have cost them to travel from their homes to the house where Jesus was born! How many weary miles they must have journeyed! The fatigues of an eastern traveller are far greater than we in England can at all understand. The time that such a journey would occupy must necessarily have been very great. The dangers to be encountered were neither few nor small. But none of these things moved them. They had set their hearts on seeing him that was born King of the Jews, and they never rested till they saw him. They prove to us the truth of that old saying: 'Where there is a will, there is a way.'

It would be well for all professing Christians if they were more ready to follow the wise men's example. Where is our self-denial? What pains do we take about our souls? What diligence do we show about following Christ? What does our religion cost us? These serious questions deserve serious consideration.

Theirs is a striking example of faith. They believed in Christ when they had never seen him. They believed in him when the scribes and Pharisees were unbelieving. They believed in him when they saw a little infant on Mary's knee and worshipped him as a King. This was the crowning point of their faith. They saw no miracles. They heard no teaching to convince them. They beheld no signs of divinity and greatness to overawe them. They saw nothing but a newborn infant, helpless and weak, and needing a mother's care like any one of ourselves. And yet when they saw that infant they believed they saw the divine Saviour of the world (v. 11).

This is the kind of faith God delights to honour. Wherever the Bible is read, the conduct of these wise men is known and told as a memorial to them. Have we not a thousandfold more evidence than the wise men had to make us believe that Jesus is the Christ? Beyond doubt we have. Yet where is our faith?

For meditation: *Then Jesus told him, 'Because you have seen me, you have believed; blessed are those who have not seen and yet have believed' (John 20:29). ' "... if someone from the dead goes to them, they will repent." [Abraham] said to him, "If they do not listen to Moses and the Prophets, they will not be convinced even if someone rises from the dead"' (Luke 16:30-31).*

Suggested further reading: Daniel 9:1-14

Men may remember words of religious truth long after they are spoken and may one day see a meaning in them which at first they did not see. We are told that our Lord said to the Jews, 'Destroy this temple and in three days I will raise it up.' St John informs us distinctly that 'He spake of the temple of his body,' that he referred to his own resurrection. Yet the meaning of the sentence was not understood by our Lord's disciples at the time that it was spoken. It was not till 'he was risen from the dead', three years after the events here described, that the full significance of the sentence flashed on their hearts. For three years it was a dark and useless saying to them. For three years it lay sleeping in their minds, like a seed in a tomb, and bore no fruit. But at the end of that time the darkness passed away. They saw the application of their Master's words and as they saw it were confirmed in their faith. 'They remembered that he had said this,' and as they remembered 'they believed'.

It is a comfortable and cheering thought that the same kind of thing that happened to the disciples is often going on at the present day. The sermons that are preached to apparently heedless ears in churches are not all lost and thrown away. The instruction that is given in schools and pastoral visits is not all wasted and forgotten. The texts that are taught by parents to children are not all taught in vain. There is often a resurrection of sermons and texts and instruction after an interval of many years. The good seed sometimes springs up after he that sowed it has been long dead and gone. Let preachers go on preaching and teachers go on teaching and parents go on training up children in the way they should go. Let them sow the good seed of Bible truth in faith and patience. Their labour is not in vain in the Lord.

For meditation: *In a day when everything has to be instant and readily disposable, patience in sowing God's Word is needed* (Eccles. 11:1).

Suggested further reading: Psalm 146

The rulers of this world are seldom friendly to the cause of God. The Lord Jesus comes down from heaven to save sinners and at once Herod the king seeks to destroy him (v. 13).

Greatness and riches are a perilous possession for the soul. They know not what they seek who seek to have them. They lead men into many temptations. They are likely to fill the heart with pride and to chain the affections down to things below (1 Cor. 1:26-29; Matt. 19:23-24).

Do you envy the rich and the great? Does your heart long for their place, rank and substance? Beware of giving way to the feeling. The very wealth which you admire may be gradually sinking its possessor down into hell. A little more money might be your ruin. Like Herod you might run into every excess of wickedness and cruelty (Luke 12:15).

Do you think that Christ's cause depends on the power and patronage of princes? You are mistaken. They have seldom done much for the advancement of true religion. They are far more frequently the enemies of the truth. Learn the truth of Psalm 146:3. Those who are like Herod are many. Those who are like Josiah and Edward VI of England are few.

Death removes the kings of this world like other men. The rulers of millions have no power to retain life when the hour of their departure comes. The murderer of helpless infants must die himself. Joseph and Mary return to their own land in safety when Herod is dead (vv. 19-20).

True Christians should never be greatly moved by the persecution of man. Their enemies may be strong and they may be weak; but still they ought not to be afraid. What has become of the Pharaohs, Neros, Diocletians, Bloody Marys who at one time persecuted the people of God? They did their utmost to cast the truth down to the ground. But the truth rose again from the earth and still lives; and they are dead and mouldering in the grave. Death is a mighty leveller, and can take any mountain out of the way of Christ's church.

For meditation: *Many Christians put more weight on political programmes and economic packages than on the power of the gospel in the nation. Do you?*

Suggested further reading: Jeremiah 17:5-10

How perfect is our Lord Jesus Christ's knowledge of the human heart! We are told that when our Lord was at Jerusalem the first time he 'did not commit himself' to those who professed belief in him. He knew that they were not to be depended on. They were astonished at the miracles which they saw him work. They were even intellectually convinced that he was the Messiah whom they had long expected. But they were not 'disciples indeed' (John 8:31). They were not converted and true believers. Their hearts were not right in the sight of God, though their feelings were excited. Their inward man was not renewed, whatever they might profess with their lips. Our Lord knew that nearly all of them were stony-ground hearers (Luke 8:13). As soon as tribulation or persecution arose because of the Word, their so-called faith would probably wither away and come to an end. All this our Lord saw clearly, if others around him did not. Andrew and Peter and John and Philip and Nathanael perhaps wondered that their Master did not receive these seeming believers with open arms. But they could only judge things by the outward appearance. Their Master could read hearts. 'He knew what was in man.'

The truth now before us is one which ought to make hypocrites and false professors tremble. They may deceive men, but they cannot deceive Christ. They may wear a cloak of religion and appear, like whited sepulchres, beautiful in the eyes of men. But the eyes of Christ see their inward rottenness and the judgement of Christ will surely overtake them except they repent. Christ is already reading their hearts and, as he reads, he is displeased. They are known in heaven, if they are not known on earth, and they will be known at length to their shame before assembled worlds if they die unchanged. It is written: 'I know thy works, that thou hast a name that thou livest, and art dead' (Rev. 3:1).

For meditation: *There is no limit to God's knowledge of us. He sees the motives of the heart* (Heb. 4:12-13).

Suggested further reading: Philippians 2:1-8

Our Lord Jesus was 'a man of sorrows' even from his infancy. Trouble awaits him as soon as he enters the world. His life is in danger from Herod's hatred. His mother and Joseph are obliged to take him away by night, and flee into Egypt. It was only a type and figure of all his experience upon earth. The waves of humiliation began to beat over him even when he was a sucking child.

The Lord Jesus is just the Saviour that the suffering and sorrowful need. He knows well what we mean when we tell him in prayer of our troubles. He can sympathize with us when we cry to him under cruel persecution. Let us keep nothing back from him. Let us make him our bosom friend. Let us pour out our hearts before him. He has had great experience of affliction.

A lesson of humility is taught us by the dwelling-place of the Son of God when he was on earth (v. 23). Nazareth was a small town in Galilee. It was an obscure, retired place, not so much as once mentioned in the Old Testament. Hebron, Shiloh, Gibeon and Bethel were far more important places, but the Lord Jesus passed by them all and chose Nazareth. This was humility.

In Nazareth the Lord Jesus lived thirty years. We know little of the manner in which those thirty years were spent. We only know that almost five-sixths of the time the Saviour of the world was on earth was passed among the poor of this world and in complete retirement. Truly this was humility.

Let us learn from our Saviour's example. We are far too ready to seek great things in this world. To have a place, and a title, and a position in society is not nearly as important as people think. It is a great sin to be covetous, worldly, proud and carnal-minded. But it is no sin to be poor. It matters not so much where we live as what we are in the sight of God. Pride is the oldest and commonest of sins. Humility is the rarest and most beautiful of graces.

For meditation: *Before he was highly exalted our Lord was humbled greatly.*

Suggested further reading: Matthew 12:15-21

There can be little doubt that Nicodemus acted as he did on this occasion from fear of man. He was afraid of what man would think, or say, or do, if his visit to Jesus was known. He came 'by night', because he had not faith and courage enough to come by day. And yet there was a time afterwards when this very Nicodemus took our Lord's part in open day in the council of the Jews. 'Doth our law judge any man,' he said, 'before it hear him and know what he doeth?' (John 7:51). Nor was this all. There came a time when this very Nicodemus was one of the only two men who did honour to our Lord's dead body. He helped Joseph of Arimathea to bury Jesus, when even the apostles had forsaken their Master and fled. His last things were more than his first. Though he began ill, he ended well.

The history of Nicodemus is meant to teach us that we should never 'despise the day of small things' in religion (Zech. 4: 10). We must not set down a man as having no grace, because his first steps towards God are timid and wavering and the first movements of his soul are uncertain, hesitating and stamped with much imperfection. We must remember our Lord's reception of Nicodemus. He did not 'break the bruised reed, or quench the smoking flax' which he saw before him (Matt. 12:20). Like him, let us take inquirers by the hand and deal with them gently and lovingly. In everything there must be a beginning. It is not those who make the most flaming profession of religion at first who endure the longest and prove the most steadfast. Judas Iscariot was an apostle when Nicodemus was just groping his way slowly into full light. Yet afterwards, when Nicodemus was boldly helping to bury his crucified Saviour, Judas Iscariot had betrayed him and hanged himself! This is a fact which ought not to be forgotten.

For meditation: *Even Paul dismissed the usefulness of Mark after he had deserted him in Pamphylia* (Acts 15:37-38) *but later recognized his value* (Col. 4:10). *Hasty judgements are best avoided.*

Suggested further reading: Ephesians 5:22-33

There is a lesson in this passage for all married people in the conduct of Joseph and Mary. We are told that they regularly honoured God's appointed ordinances and that they honoured them together (v. 41). The distance from Nazareth to Jerusalem was great. The journey, to poor people without any means of conveyance, was troublesome and fatiguing. To leave house and home for ten days or a fortnight was no slight expense. But God had given Israel a command and Joseph and Mary strictly obeyed it. God had appointed an ordinance for their spiritual good and they regularly kept it. And all that they did concerning the Passover they did together. When they went up to the feast they always went side by side.

So ought it to be with all Christian husbands and wives. They ought to help one another in spiritual things and to encourage one another in the service of God. Marriage, unquestionably, is not a sacrament, as the Roman church vainly asserts. But marriage is a state of life which has the greatest effect on the souls of those who enter it. It helps them upwards or downwards. It leads them nearer to heaven or nearer to hell. We all depend much on the company we keep. Our characters are insensibly moulded by those with whom we pass our time. To none does this apply so much as to married people. Husbands and wives are continually doing good or harm to one another's souls.

Let all who are married, or think of being married, ponder these things well. Let them take example from the conduct of Mary and Joseph, and resolve to do likewise. Let them pray together, and read the Bible together, go to the house of God together and talk to one another about spiritual matters. Above all, let them beware of throwing obstacles and discouragements in one another's way about the means of grace. Blessed are those who say to their partners as Leah and Rachel did to Jacob in Genesis 31:16.

For meditation: *Whether married or not, all Christians need the company of others. Scripture lays great emphasis on doing good to those with whom we fellowship* (Heb. 10:24-25; Col. 3:16).

Suggested further reading: Ephesians 2:1-10

What a mighty change our Lord declares to be needful to salvation, and what a remarkable expression he uses in describing it! He speaks of a new birth. He says to Nicodemus, 'Except a man be born again, he cannot see the kingdom of God.' He announces the same truth in other words, in order to make it more plain to his hearer's mind: 'Except a man be born of water and of the Spirit, he cannot enter into the kingdom of God.' By this expression he meant Nicodemus to understand that no one could become his disciple, unless his inward man was as thoroughly cleansed and renewed by the Spirit as the outward man is cleansed by water. To possess the privileges of Judaism a man only needed to be born of the seed of Abraham after the flesh. To possess the privileges of Christ's kingdom a man must be born again of the Holy Ghost.

The change which our Lord here declares needful to salvation is evidently no slight or superficial one. It is not merely reformation, or amendment, or moral change, or outward alteration of life. It is a thorough change of heart, will and character. It is a resurrection. It is a new creation. It is a passing from death to life. It is the implanting in our dead hearts of a new principle from above. It is the calling into existence of a new creature, with a new nature, new habits of life, new tastes, new desires, new appetites, new judgements, new opinions, new hopes and new fears. All this, and nothing less than this, is implied when our Lord declares that we all need a 'new birth'.

Would we know what the marks of the new birth are? The man born of God 'believes that Jesus is the Christ', 'doth not commit sin', 'doeth righteousness', 'loves the brethren', 'overcomes the world', 'keepeth himself from the wicked one'. This is the man born of the Spirit!

For meditation: *It is no use dealing with sin's symptoms without dealing with its root — the sinful heart of man.*

Suggested further reading: Matthew 10:34-42

All young persons should note the conduct of the Lord Jesus Christ when he was left by himself in Jerusalem at the age of twelve. For four days he was out of the sight of Mary and Joseph. For three days they sorrowfully looked for him, not knowing what had befallen him. Who can imagine the anxiety of such a mother at losing such a child? And where did they find him at last? Not idling his time away, or getting into mischief. Not in vain and unprofitable company. They found him in the temple of God, sitting in the midst of the Jewish teachers, hearing what they had to say and asking questions about things he wished them to explain to him (v. 46).

So ought it to be with the younger members of Christian families. They ought to be steady and trustworthy behind the backs of their parents, as well as before their faces. They ought to seek the company of the wise and prudent, and to use every opportunity of getting spiritual knowledge before the cares of life come upon them and while their memories are fresh and strong.

Let boys and girls remember that if they are old enough to do wrong they are also old enough to do right, and that if able to read story-books and to talk, they are also able to read their Bibles and pray. Let them remember that they are accountable to God even while they are yet young.

All Christians have an example in the answer our Lord gave to his mother's question (vv. 48-49). A mild reproof was evidently implied in that reply. It reminded his mother he was no common person, and had come into the world to do no common work. It was a solemn reminder that, as God, he had a Father in heaven and that this heavenly Father's work demanded first priority.

Are we about our Father's business? Let this be the mark at which we aim in our daily lives, and the test by which we try our habits and conversation. Let it quicken us when we begin to be slothful, and check us when we are inclined to go back into the world.

For meditation: *The purpose of life is to bring honour to God. Do we?*

Suggested further reading: Ezekiel 37:1-10

This change of heart is rendered absolutely necessary to salvation by the corrupt condition in which we are all without exception born. 'That which is born of the flesh is flesh.' Our nature is thoroughly fallen. The carnal mind is enmity against God (Rom. 8:7). We come into the world without faith, or love, or fear towards God. We have no natural inclination to serve him or obey him and no natural pleasure in doing his will. Left to himself, no child of Adam would ever turn to God. The truest description of the change which we all need in order to make us real Christians is the expression 'new birth'.

This mighty change, it must never be forgotten, we cannot give to ourselves. The very name which our Lord gives to it is a convincing proof of this. He calls it a birth. No man is the author of his own existence and no man can quicken his own soul. We might as well expect a dead man to give himself life as expect a natural man to make himself spiritual. A power from above must be put in exercise, even that same power which created the world (2 Cor. 4:6). Man can do many things, but he cannot give life either to himself or to others. To give life is the peculiar prerogative of God. Well may our Lord declare that we need to be 'born again'!

This mighty change, we must above all remember, is a thing without which we cannot go to heaven and could not enjoy heaven if we went there. Our Lord's words on this point are distinct and express: 'Except a man be born again, he can neither see nor enter the kingdom of God.' Heaven may be reached without money, or rank, or learning. But it is clear as daylight, if words have any meaning, that nobody can enter heaven without a 'new birth'.

For meditation: *Thank God that he intervenes in the lives of men to save them from their state of spiritual stupor and death.*

Suggested further reading: 1 Corinthians 9:16-18

How wicked were the times when Christ's gospel was brought into the world! Verses 1-2 tell us the names of some who were rulers and governors in the earth when the ministry of John the Baptist began. It is a melancholy list and full of instruction. There is hardly a name in it that is not infamous for wickedness. Tiberius, Pontius Pilate, Herod, his brother, Annas and Caiaphas were men of whom we know little or nothing but evil. When such were the rulers, what must the people have been? Such was the state of things when Christ's forerunner was commissioned to begin preaching.

Let us never despair about the cause of God's truth, however black and unfavourable its prospects might appear. At the very time when things seem hopeless God may be preparing a mighty deliverance. Let us beware of slacking our hands from any work of God because of the wickedness of the times or the number and power of our adversaries (Eccles. 11:4). Let us work on, and believe that help will come from heaven when it is most wanted.

John the Baptist received a special call from God to begin preaching and baptizing (v. 2). A message from heaven was sent to his heart and, under the impulse of that message, he undertook his marvellous work.

This account throws great light on the office of all ministers of the gospel. It is an office which no man has the right to take up unless he has an inward call from God as well as an outward call from man. Visions and revelations, of course, we have no right to expect. Fanatical claims to special gifts of the Spirit must always be checked and discouraged. But an inward call a man must have before he puts his hand to the work of the ministry.

Let it be a part of our daily prayers that our churches may have no ministers except those who are really called of God. An unconverted minister is an injury and burden to a church.

For meditation: *How faithful are you in praying for those whom God has called to minister his Word? How faithful are you in obeying that Word?*

Suggested further reading: 1 John 2:28 - 3:10

We should notice in these verses the instructive comparison which our Lord uses in explaining the new birth. He saw Nicodemus perplexed and astonished by the things he had just heard. He graciously helped his wondering mind by an illustration drawn from the wind. A more beautiful and fitting illustration of the work of the Spirit it is impossible to conceive.

There is much about the wind that is mysterious and inexplicable. 'Thou canst not tell', says our Lord, 'whence it cometh and whither it goeth.' We cannot handle it with our hands, or see it with our eyes. When the wind blows, we cannot point out the exact spot where its breath first began to be felt and the exact distance to which its influence shall extend. But we do not on that account deny its presence. It is just the same with the operations of the Spirit in the new birth of man. They may be mysterious, sovereign and incomprehensible to us in many ways. But it is foolish to stumble at them because there is much about them that we cannot explain.

But whatever mystery there may be about the wind, its presence may always be known by its sound and effects. 'Thou hearest the sound thereof,' says our Lord. When our ears hear it whistling in the windows and our eyes see the clouds driving before it, we do not hesitate to say, 'There is wind.' It is just the same with the operations of the Holy Spirit in the new birth of man. Marvellous and incomprehensible as his work may be, it is work that can always be seen and known. The new birth is a thing that 'cannot be hid'. There will always be visible 'fruits of the Spirit' in everyone that is born of the Spirit.

Have we been born again? A day will come when those who are not born again will wish that they had never been born at all.

For meditation: *When there is no evidence of physical life a person is pronounced dead and is buried. A fruitless Christian is a spiritual corpse* (John 15:5-6).

Suggested further reading: Luke 13:1-5

There is a close connection between true repentance and forgiveness (v. 3). The plain meaning of this expression in verse 3 is that John preached the necessity of being baptized in token of repentance, and that he told his hearers that except they repented of sin they would not be forgiven.

We must carefully bear in mind that no repentance can make atonement for sin. The blood of Christ, and nothing else, can wash away sin from man's soul. No quantity of repentance can ever justify us in the sight of God. We are accounted righteous before God only for the sake of our Lord Jesus Christ, by faith, and not for our own works or deservings. It is of the utmost importance to understand this clearly. The trouble that men bring upon their souls by misunderstanding this subject is more than can be expressed.

But while we say all this, we must carefully remember that without repentance no soul was ever yet saved. We must know our sins, mourn over them, forsake them, abhor them, or else we shall never enter the kingdom of heaven. There is nothing meritorious in this. It forms no part whatever of the price of our redemption. Our salvation is all of grace, from first to last. But the great fact still remains that saved souls are always penitent souls, and that saving faith in Christ and true repentance towards God are never found asunder. This is a mighty truth and one that ought never to be forgotten.

Do we ourselves repent? This, after all, is the question that most concerns us. Have we been convinced of sin by the Holy Spirit? Have we fled to Jesus for deliverance from the wrath to come? Do we know anything of a broken and contrite heart and a thorough hatred of sin? Can we say, 'I repent,' as well as 'I believe'? If not, let us not delude ourselves with the idea that our sins are yet forgiven. It is written that 'Except ye repent, ye shall all likewise perish' (Luke 13:3).

For meditation: *We can feel sorry for our sins without turning from them. This is remorse, but it is not repentance. Repentance forsakes sin.*

Suggested further reading: 1 Corinthians 2:6-15

What gross spiritual ignorance there may be in the mind of a great and learned man! We see a 'master of Israel' unacquainted with the first elements of saving religion. Nicodemus is told about the new birth and at once exclaims, 'How can these things be?' When such was the darkness of a Jewish teacher, what must have been the state of the Jewish people? It was indeed due time for Christ to appear! The pastors of Israel had ceased to feed the people with knowledge. The blind were leading the blind and both were falling into the ditch (Matt. 15:14).

Ignorance like that of Nicodemus is unhappily far too common in the church of Christ. We must never be surprised if we find it in quarters where we might reasonably expect knowledge. Learning and rank and high ecclesiastical office are no proof that a minister is taught by the Spirit. The successors of Nicodemus in every age are far more numerous than the successors of St Peter. On no point is religious ignorance so common as on the work of the Holy Ghost. That old stumbling-block, at which Nicodemus stumbled, is as much an offence to thousands in the present day as it was in the days of Christ. The natural man receiveth not the things of the Spirit of God' (1 Cor. 2:14). Happy is he who has been taught to prove all things by Scripture and to call no man master upon earth! (1 Thess. 5:21; Matt. 23:9).

These verses show us the original source from which man's salvation springs. That source is the love of God the Father. Our Lord says to Nicodemus, 'God so loved the world that he gave his only begotten Son, that whosoever believeth in him should not perish, but have everlasting life.'

This wonderful verse has been justly called by Luther 'the Bible in miniature'. No part of it, perhaps, is so deeply important as the first five words: 'God so loved the world.'

For meditation: *Our salvation does not depend on the level of education we have, but on God giving us spiritual sight.*

Suggested further reading: Mark 9:42-50

John's ministry had an immense effect on the Jews (v. 7; Matt. 3:5). Our Lord also bore testimony to John in a remarkable way (Matt. 11:11). What then was the character of John's ministry?

John addressed the multitudes that came to his ministry with holy boldness (v. 7). He saw the rottenness and hypocrisy of the profession that the crowd around him made, and used language descriptive of their case. His head was not turned by popularity. He cared not who was offended by his words. The spiritual disease of those before him was desperate and of long standing, and he knew that desperate diseases need strong remedies.

Well would it be for the church of Christ if it possessed more plain-speaking ministers like John the Baptist in these latter days. Personality and uncharitable language are no doubt always to be deprecated, but there is no charity in flattering unconverted people by abstaining from any mention of their vices or in applying smooth epithets to their damnable sins.

How plainly John speaks about hell and danger! (vv. 7,9). The subject of hell is always offensive to human nature. The minister who dwells much upon it will be regarded as coarse, violent, unfeeling and narrow-minded. Men love to hear 'smooth things' and be told of peace and not of danger (Isa. 30:10). But the subject is one that ought not to be kept back if we desire to do good to souls.

Let us never be ashamed to avow our firm belief that there is a 'wrath to come' for the impenitent and that it is possible for a man to be lost as well as to be saved. To be silent on this subject only encourages men to persevere in wickedness and fosters in their minds the devil's old delusion that they will not die (Gen. 3:4). Never will a man flee till he sees there is a real cause to be afraid. The religion in which there is no mention of hell is not the religion of John the Baptist, nor of our Lord Jesus and his apostles.

For meditation: *Sinners need do nothing more to go to hell. Damnation is easy.*

Suggested further reading: Numbers 21:4-9

By being 'lifted up', our Lord meant nothing less than his own death upon the cross. That death, he would have us know, was appointed by God to be 'the life of the world' (John 6:51). It was ordained from all eternity to be the great propitiation and satisfaction for man's sin. It was the payment, by an almighty Substitute and Representative, of man's enormous debt to God. When Christ died upon the cross, our many sins were laid upon him. He was made 'sin' for us (2 Cor. 5:21). He was made 'a curse' for us (Gal. 3:13). By his death he purchased pardon and complete redemption for sinners.

The brazen serpent, lifted up in the camp of Israel, brought health and cure within the reach of all who were bitten by serpents. Christ crucified, in like manner, brought eternal life within reach of lost mankind. Christ has been lifted up on the cross and man looking to him by faith may be saved.

The truth before us is the very foundation-stone of the Christian religion. Christ's death is the Christian's life. Christ's cross is the Christian's title to heaven. Christ 'lifted up' and put to shame on Calvary is the ladder by which Christians 'enter into the holiest' and are at length landed in glory. It is true that we are sinners, but Christ has suffered for us. It is true that we deserve death, but Christ has died for us. It is true that we are great debtors, but Christ has paid our debts with his own blood. This is the real gospel! This is the good news! On this let us lean while we live. To this let us cling when we die. Christ has been 'lifted up' on the cross and has thrown open the gates of heaven to all believers.

For meditation: *The serpent on the pole gave life but suffered nothing. Bronze does not feel pain. Our Saviour gave a better life, but at terrible personal cost.*

Suggested further reading: James 2:14-26

What a blow John strikes at the common notion that connection with godly people can save our souls! (v. 8). The strong hold that this notion has obtained on the heart of man in every part of the world is an affecting proof of the fallen and corrupt state of humanity. Thousands have lived and died in the blind delusion that because they were allied to holy people by ties of blood or church membership they might themselves hope to be saved.

Let it be a settled thing with us that saving religion is a personal thing. It is a business between each man's own soul and Christ. It will save no one to have had godly men's blood in his veins if he does not possess godly men's faith and works.

John exposes the uselessness of a repentance not accompanied by fruits in the life (vv. 8-9). It can never be pressed on our minds too strongly that religious talking and profession are utterly worthless without religious doing and practice. It is vain to say with our lips that we repent, if we do not at the same time repent in our lives. To say that we are sorry for our sins is mere hypocrisy unless we show that we are really sorry for them by giving them up. Doing is the very life of repentance. Tell us not merely what a man says in religion. Tell us rather what he does.

John bade each man who made a profession of repentance to begin by breaking off from those sins which especially beset him (vv. 10-14). Let us see here the right way to prove our own hearts. It must not content us to cry out against sins to which, by natural temperament, we are not inclined, while we deal gently with other sins of a different character. Let us find out our own peculiar corruptions. Let us know our own besetting sins. Against them let us wage unceasing war.

For meditation: *It is a trick of Satan to cause us to paint the sins of others in the darkest colours and to dismiss our own sins as little faults, failings and weaknesses. But our sins have crucified Christ and merit hell also. It is of our sins that we must repent, not the sins of others.*

Suggested further reading: Psalm 145:8-17

The love here spoken of is not that special love with which the Father regards his own elect, but that mighty pity and compassion with which he regards the whole race of mankind. Its object is not merely the little flock which he has given to Christ from all eternity, but the whole 'world' of sinners, without any exception. There is a deep sense in which God loves that world. All whom he has created he regards with pity and compassion. Their sins he cannot love, but he loves their souls. 'His tender mercies are over all his works' (Ps. 145:9).

Let us take heed that our views of the love of God are scriptural and well-defined. We must maintain firmly that God hates wickedness and that the end of all who persist in wickedness will be destruction. It is not true that God's love is 'lower than hell'. It is not true that God so loved the world that all mankind will be finally saved, but that he so loved the world that he gave his Son to be the Saviour of all who believe. His love is offered to all men freely, fully, honestly and unreservedly, but it is only through the one channel of Christ's redemption. He that rejects Christ cuts himself off from God's love and will perish everlastingly. On the other hand, we must beware of narrow and contracted opinions. We must not hesitate to tell any sinner that God loves him. It is not true that God cares for none but his own elect, or that Christ is not offered to any but those who are ordained to eternal life. There is a 'kindness and love' in God towards all mankind. It was in consequence of that love that Christ came into the world and died upon the cross. Let us not be wise above that which is written, or more systematic in our statements than Scripture itself. God has no pleasure in the death of the wicked. God is not willing that any should perish. God would have all men to be saved. God loves the world (John 6:33; Titus 3:4; 1 John 4:10; 2 Peter 3:9; 1 Tim. 2:4; Ezek. 33:11).

For meditation: *God's love to us requires more than a smile in response!*

Suggested further reading: Acts 10:44-48; 15:7-11

One effect of a faithful ministry is to set men thinking (v. 15). The cause of true religion has gained a great step when people begin to think. Thoughtlessness about spiritual things is one great feature of unconverted man. It cannot be said, in many cases, that they either like or dislike the gospel. They do not give it a place in their thoughts.

Let us always thank God when we see a spirit of reflection on religious subjects coming over the mind of an unconverted man. Consideration is the high road to conversion. Thinking, no doubt, is not faith and repentance. But it is always a hopeful symptom.

A faithful minister will always exalt Christ (vv. 15-16). A true man of God will never allow anything to be credited to him, or his office, which belongs to the divine Master. He will follow Paul's adage (2 Cor. 4:5). To commend Christ dying and rising again for the ungodly, to make known Christ's love and power to save sinners, this will be the main object of his ministry. He will be content that his own name is forgotten so long as Christ crucified is exalted. A minister who is really doing us good will make us think more of Jesus every year we live.

There is an essential difference between the Lord Jesus and even the best and holiest of his ministers. An ordained man can administer the outward ordinances of Christianity with a prayerful hope that God will graciously bless the means which he himself has appointed. He can preach the gospel faithfully to their ears, but he cannot make them receive it into their consciences. He can apply baptismal water but he cannot cleanse their inward nature. Christ alone can do this by the power of the Holy Spirit (v. 16). It is his peculiar office to do it, and it is an office which he has deputed to no child of man.

There must not only be the work of Christ for us, but the work of the Holy Spirit in us. There must not only be a title to heaven by the blood of Christ, but a preparedness for heaven wrought in us by the Spirit of Christ. This is the baptism of the Spirit.

For meditation: *Baptism in water washes the body, baptism in the Spirit washes the heart* (Acts 15:8-9).

Suggested further reading: Romans 4:1-8

These verses show us the way in which the benefits of Christ's death are made our own. That way is simply to put faith and trust in Christ. Faith is the same thing as believing. Three times our Lord repeats this glorious truth to Nicodemus. Twice he proclaims that 'Whosoever believeth shall not perish.' Once he says, 'He that believeth on the Son of God is not condemned.'

Faith in the Lord Jesus is the very key of salvation. He that has it has life and he that has it not has not life. Nothing whatever *beside* this faith is necessary to our complete justification; but nothing whatever *except* this faith will give us an interest in Christ. We may fast and mourn for sin and do many things that are right and use religious ordinances and give all our goods to feed the poor and yet remain unpardoned and lose our souls. But if we will only come to Christ as guilty sinners and believe on him, our sins shall at once be forgiven and our iniquities shall be entirely put away. Without faith there is no salvation, but through faith in Jesus the vilest sinner may be saved.

If we would have a peaceful conscience in our religion, let us see that our views of saving faith are distinct and clear. Let us beware of supposing that justifying faith is anything more than a sinner's simple trust in a Saviour, the grasp of a drowning man on the hand held out for his relief. Let us beware of mingling anything else with faith in the matter of justification. Here we must always remember faith stands entirely alone. A justified man, no doubt, will always be a holy man. True believing will always be accompanied by godly living. But that which gives a man an interest in Christ is not his living, but his faith.

For meditation: *Salvation is through Christ alone, by God's grace alone, received by faith alone.*

Suggested further reading: 2 Thessalonians 1:6-10

There will be an awful separation at the last day. The unerring judgement of the King of kings shall at length divide the wheat from the chaff (v. 17), and divide them for evermore.

This again is a teaching that is deeply important. We need to be straitly warned that it is no light matter whether we repent or not. There is a hell as well as a heaven, an everlasting punishment for the wicked as well as everlasting life for the godly. We are fearfully apt to forget this. We talk of the love and the mercy of God and we do not remember sufficiently his justness and holiness. Let us be very careful on this point. It is no real kindness to keep back the terrors of the Lord. It is good for us all to be taught that it is possible to be lost for ever, and that all unconverted people are hanging over the brink of the pit.

John the Baptist spoke also about the safety of true believers. This again is a teaching that human nature greatly requires. The best of believers need much encouragement. They are yet in the body. They live in a wicked world. They are often tempted by the devil. They ought to be reminded that Jesus will never leave them nor forsake them. He will guide them safely through this life and at length to eternal glory. They shall be hid in the day of wrath, as safe as Noah in the ark.

We need to remember that the reward of God's servants is often not in this world. John was imprisoned by Herod and ultimately beheaded. All true servants of Christ must be content to wait for their wages. Their best things are yet to come. They must count it no strange thing if they meet with hard treatment from men. The world that persecuted Christ will never hesitate to persecute Christians (1 John 3:13).

But let us take comfort in the thought that the great Master has laid up in heaven for his people such things as pass man's understanding. When all who have suffered for the truth are at last gathered together they will find it true that heaven makes amends for all.

For meditation: *'Therefore we do not lose heart. Though outwardly we are wasting away, yet inwardly we are being renewed day by day... For what is seen is temporary, but what is unseen is eternal'* (2 Cor. 4:16-18).

Suggested further reading: Ezekiel 33:1-11

These verses show us the true cause of the loss of man's soul. Our Lord says to Nicodemus, 'This is the condemnation, that light is come into the world, and men loved darkness rather than light, because their deeds were evil.'

The words before us form a suitable conclusion to the glorious tidings which we have just been considering. They completely clear God of injustice in the condemnation of sinners. They show in simple and unmistakable terms that, although man's salvation is entirely of God, his ruin, if he is lost, will be entirely from himself. He will reap the fruit of his own sowing.

'God sent not his Son into the world to condemn the world, but that the world through him might be saved.' There is no unwillingness on God's part to receive any sinner, however great his sins. God has sent 'light' into the world and if man will not come to the light the fault is entirely on man's side. His blood will be on his own head if he makes shipwreck of his soul. The blame will be at his own door if he misses heaven. His eternal misery will be the result of his own choice. His destruction will be the work of his own hand. God loved him and was willing to save him, but he loved darkness and therefore darkness must be his everlasting portion. He would not come to Christ and therefore he could not have life (John 5:40).

The truths we have been considering are peculiarly weighty and solemn. Do we live as if we believed them? Salvation by Christ's death is close to us today. Have we embraced it by faith and made it our own? Let us never rest till we know Christ as our own Saviour. Let us look to him without delay for pardon and peace, if we have never looked before. Let us go on believing on him, if we have already believed. 'Whosoever' is his own gracious word — '*whosoever* believeth on him, shall not perish, but have eternal life.'

For meditation: *Every mouth is stopped before God. The unbeliever's condemnation is above criticism because entirely just.*

Suggested further reading: Acts 16:30-34

What high honour the Lord Jesus has put on baptism! When the Jewish priests took up their office at the age of thirty they were washed with water. When our great High Priest begins the great work he came into the world to accomplish, he is publicly baptized.

An ordinance which the Son of God was pleased to use and afterwards to appoint for the use of his church ought always to be held in peculiar reverence by his people. Baptism cannot be a thing of slight importance if Christ himself was baptized.

However, errors of every sort and description abound on the subject of baptism. Some make an idol of it and exalt it above the place the Bible assigned to it. We must not expect the water to act as a charm. We must not suppose that all baptized persons, as a matter of course, receive the grace of God in the moment that they are baptized, regardless of whether they come in faith and prayer or in utter carelessness.

Others degrade and dishonour baptism and seem almost to forget that it was ordained by Christ himself. It is dishonoured when it is thrust out of sight and never publicly noticed in the congregation. A sacrament ordained by Christ himself ought not to be treated in this way. The admission of every new member into the ranks of a visible church is an event which ought to excite a lively interest in a Christian assembly. It is an event that ought to call forth the fervent prayers of all praying people.

Baptism was graciously intended by our Lord to be a help to his church and a means of grace and, when rightly and worthily used, we may confidently look upon it for a blessing. But let us never forget that the grace of God is not tied to any sacrament, and that we might be outwardly baptized with water without being inwardly baptized by the Holy Spirit.

For meditation: *Because baptism is an issue that divides Christians there is a temptation to ignore it. Faithfulness to the Great Commission will not allow such a procedure* (Matt. 28:18-20). *Are you baptized?*

Suggested further reading: 1 Corinthians 1:10-17

We have in these verses a humbling example of the petty jealousies and party spirit which may exist among professors of religion. We are told that the disciples of John the Baptist were offended, because the ministry of Jesus began to attract more attention than that of their master. 'They came unto John, and said unto him, Rabbi, he that was with thee beyond Jordan, to whom thou barest witness, behold the same baptizeth, and all men come to him.'

The spirit exhibited in this complaint is unhappily too common in the churches of Christ. The succession of these complainers has never failed. There are never wanting religious professors who care far more for the increase of their own party than for the increase of true Christianity and who cannot rejoice in the spread of religion if it spreads anywhere except within their own pale. There is a generation which can see no good doing except in the ranks of its own congregations and which seems ready to shut men out of heaven if they will not enter therein under its banner.

The true Christian must watch and pray against the spirit here manifested by John's disciples. It is very insidious, very contagious and very injurious to the cause of religion. Nothing so defiles Christianity and gives the enemies of truth such occasion to blaspheme as jealousy and party spirit among Christians. Wherever there is real grace, we should be ready and willing to acknowledge it, even though it may be outside our own pale. We should strive to say with the apostle, 'If Christ be preached, I rejoice, yea, and will rejoice' (Phil. 1:18). If good is done, we ought to be thankful, though it even may not be done in what we think the best way. If souls are saved, we ought to be glad, whatever be the means that God may think fit to employ.

For meditation: *We must be careful to distinguish between the enemies of the gospel, whom we are to avoid* (2 John 10-11), *and brethren, whom we are to receive* (3 John 5-8).

Suggested further readings: Matthew 28:18-20; 2 Corinthians 13:14; Revelation 1:4-5

The presence of all three persons of the blessed Trinity is evident. God the Son, manifest in the flesh, is baptized (v. 16). God the Spirit descends like a dove and lights upon him (v. 16). God the Father speaks from heaven with a voice (v. 17). In a word, we have the manifested presence of Father, Son and Holy Spirit. Surely we may regard this as a public announcement that the work of Christ was the result of the eternal counsels of all the Three. It was the whole Trinity which at the beginning of creation said, 'Let us make man' (Gen. 1:26). It was the whole Trinity again which at the beginning of the gospel seemed to say, 'Let us save man.'

All three persons in the Godhead are equally concerned in the deliverance of our souls from hell. The thought should cheer us when disquieted and cast down. The thought should hearten and encourage us when weary of the conflict with the world, the flesh and the devil. The enemies of our souls are mighty, but the Friends of our souls are mightier still. The whole power of the triune Jehovah is engaged upon our side (Eccles. 4:12).

We are told of a voice from heaven (v. 17). We read of no voice from heaven before this except at the giving of the law at Sinai. God marks the introduction of both law and gospel with the peculiar honour of his own voice speaking.

His words are a divine declaration that our Lord Jesus Christ is the promised Redeemer, whom God from the beginning undertook to send into the world, and that with his incarnation, sacrifice and substitution for man God the Father is satisfied and well pleased. In him he regards the claim of his holy law as fully discharged. Through him he is willing to receive poor, sinful men to mercy and remember their sins no more.

Let all true Christians rest their souls on these words and draw from them daily consolation. If we believe in Jesus God regards us as members of his own dear Son with whom he is well pleased.

For meditation: *Are we obeying Matthew 17:5: 'While he was still speaking ... a voice from the cloud said, "This is my Son ... listen to him" '?*

Suggested further reading: Philippians 2:5-8

We have in these verses a splendid pattern of true and godly humility. We see in John the Baptist a very different spirit from that displayed by his disciples. He begins by laying down the great principle that acceptance with man is a special gift of God and that we must therefore not presume to find fault when others have more acceptance than ourselves. 'A man can receive nothing except it be given him from heaven.' He goes on to remind his followers of his repeated declaration that one greater than himself was coming: 'I said, I am not the Christ.' He tells them that his office, compared to that of Christ, is that of the bridegroom's friend, compared to the bridegroom. And, finally, he solemnly affirms that Christ must and will become greater and greater and that he himself must become less and less important until, like a star eclipsed by the rising sun, he has completely disappeared.

A frame of mind like this is the highest degree of grace to which mortal man can attain. The greatest saint in the sight of God is the man who is most thoroughly 'clothed with humility' (1 Peter 5:5). Would we know the prime secret of being men of the stamp of Abraham and Moses and Job and David and Daniel and St Paul and John the Baptist? They were all eminently humble men. Living at different ages and enjoying very different degrees of light, in this matter at least they were all agreed. In themselves they saw nothing but sin and weakness. To God they gave all the praise of what they were. Let us walk in their steps. Let us covet earnestly the best gifts, but above all let us covet humility. The way to true honour is to be humble. No man ever was so praised by Christ as the very man who says here, 'I must decrease,' the humble John the Baptist.

For meditation: *Self-effacement is a rare quality in a day of personality cults in Christendom.*

Suggested further reading: Hebrews 4:14 - 5:5

The first event recorded in our Lord's history after his baptism is his temptation by the devil. From a season of honour and glory he passed immediately to a season of suffering and conflict. The Father testified to his sonship (Matt. 3:17); Satan sneered 'if' (vv. 3,6). The portion of Christ will often prove the portion of the Christian. From great privilege to great trial there will often be but a step.

It would be well for believers if they remembered this. They are too apt to forget it. They often find evil thoughts arising within their minds which they can truly say they hate. Doubts, questions and sinful imaginings are suggested to them, against which their whole inward man revolts. But let not these things rob them of their comforts. Let them remember there is a devil and not be surprised to find him near them. To be tempted is in itself no sin. It is the yielding to the temptation, and giving it a place in our hearts, that we must fear.

What a sympathizing Saviour our Lord is! (Heb. 2:18). Believers should never forget that they have a mighty Friend in heaven who feels for them in all their temptations and can enter into all their spiritual anxieties. Are they ever tempted to distrust God's care and goodness? So was Jesus (v. 3). Are they ever tempted to presume on God's mercy and run into danger without warrant? So was Jesus (v. 6). Are they ever tempted to commit some one great private sin for the sake of some great seeming advantage? So was Jesus (v. 9). Are they ever tempted to listen to some misapplication of Scripture as an excuse for doing wrong? So was Jesus (v. 6). He is just the Saviour that a tempted people require. Let them flee to him for help and spread before him all their troubles. They will find his ear ever ready to hear and his heart ever ready to feel. He can understand their sorrows. The Lord Jesus is not an austere man. He knows what we mean when we complain of temptation and is both able and willing to give us help.

For meditation: *God understands our experience by his perfect knowledge and his Son's experience.*

Suggested further reading: 1 John 5:9-13

John the Baptist teaches his disciples once more the true greatness of the person whose growing popularity offended them. Once more, and perhaps for the last time, he proclaims him as one worthy of all honour and praise. He uses one striking expression after another to convey a correct idea of the majesty of Christ. He speaks of him as 'the bridegroom' of the church, as 'him that cometh from above', as 'him whom God hath sent', as 'him to whom the Spirit is given without measure', as him 'whom the Father loves' and into 'whose hands all things are given', to believe in whom is life everlasting and to reject whom is eternal ruin. Each of these phrases is full of deep meaning and would supply matter for a long sermon. All show the depth and height of John's spiritual attainments. More honourable things are nowhere written concerning Jesus than these verses recorded as spoken by John the Baptist.

John the Baptist declares, 'He that believeth on the Son hath everlasting life.' He is not intended to look forward with a sick heart to a far distant privilege. He 'hath' everlasting life as soon as he believes. Pardon, peace and a complete title to heaven are an immediate possession. They become a believer's own from the very moment he puts faith in Christ. They will not be more completely his own if he lives to the age of Methuselah.

The truth before us is one of the most glorious privileges of the gospel. There are no works to be done, no conditions to be fulfilled, no price to be paid, no wearing years of probation to be passed before a sinner can be accepted with God. Let him only believe on Christ and he is at once forgiven. Salvation is close to the chief of sinners. Let him only repent and believe and this day it is his own. By Christ all that believe are at once justified from all things.

For meditation: *As our Lord is the one in whom we receive every spiritual blessing* (Eph. 1:3), *to have Christ is to be unspeakably rich.*

Suggested further reading: Genesis 3:1-6

That old serpent who tempted Adam to sin in paradise was not afraid to assault the second Adam, the Son of God. Whether he understood that Jesus was 'God manifest in the flesh' might be doubted. But that he saw in Jesus one who had come into the world to overthrow his kingdom is plain and clear. He had seen what had happened at our Lord's baptism. He had heard the marvellous words from heaven. He felt that the great Friend of man was come and that his own dominion was in peril. The Redeemer had come. The prison door was about to be thrown open. The lawful captives were about to be set free. All this, we need not doubt, Satan saw, and resolved to fight for his own. The prince of this world would not give way to the Prince of peace without a mighty struggle. He had overcome the first Adam in the garden; why should he not overcome the second Adam in the wilderness? He had spoiled man once of Paradise; why should he not spoil him of the kingdom of God?

Let it never surprise us if we are tempted of the devil. Let us rather expect it as a matter of course if we are living members of Christ. The Master's lot will be the lot of his disciples. That mighty spirit who did not fear to attack Jesus himself is still going about as a roaring lion seeking whom he may devour. That murderer and liar who vexed Job and overthrew David and Peter still lives and is not yet bound (Job 1:12; 2:6; 1 Chr. 21:1; Luke 22:31-32). If he cannot rob us of heaven, he will at any rate make our journey thither painful. If he cannot destroy our souls, he will at least bruise our heels (Gen. 3:15). Let us beware of despising him, or thinking lightly of his power. Let us rather put on the whole armour of God and cry to the strong for strength (James 4:7). Let us all watch and pray daily against his devices. There is no enemy worse than an enemy who is never seen and never dies, who is near to us wherever we live, and goes with us wherever we go.

For meditation: *The devil is considered in the modern world as a symbol of sensual enjoyment or a mythical figure from a past age. Let none of us encourage a false picture of the destroyer of men's souls.*

Suggested further reading: 1 Corinthians 1:13-17

We read that 'Jesus himself baptized not, but his disciples.' To baptize is not the principal work for which Christian ministers are ordained. Frequently we read of our Lord preaching and praying. Once we read of his administering the Lord's Supper. But we have not a single instance recorded of his ever baptizing anyone. And here we are distinctly told that it was a subordinate work, which he left to others. Jesus 'himself baptized not, but his disciples'.

The lesson is one of peculiar importance in the present day. Baptism, as a sacrament ordained by Christ himself, is an honourable ordinance and ought never to be lightly esteemed in the churches. It cannot be neglected or despised without great sin. When rightly used, with faith and prayer, it is calculated to convey the highest blessings. But baptism was never meant to be exalted to the position which many nowadays assign to it in religion. It does not act as a charm. It does not necessarily convey the grace of the Holy Ghost. The benefit of it depends greatly on the manner in which it is used. The doctrine taught and the language employed about it in some quarters are utterly inconsistent with the fact announced in the text. If baptism was all that some say it is, we should never have been told that 'Jesus himself baptized not'.

Let it be a settled principle in our minds that the first and chief business of the church of Christ is to preach the gospel. The words of St Paul ought to be constantly remembered: 'Christ sent me not to baptize, but to preach the gospel' (1 Cor. 1:17). When the gospel of Christ is faithfully and fully preached we need not fear that the sacraments will be undervalued. Baptism and the Lord's Supper will always be most truly reverenced in those churches where the truth as it is in Jesus is most fully taught and known.

For meditation: *The dying thief had nothing but faith in Christ, but paradise was gained* (Luke 23:42-43). *Christ saves, not water.*

Suggested further reading: Deuteronomy 6:4-9

How subtle our great enemy the devil is! Each assault on our Lord showed the hand of a master in the art of temptation. Each assault was the work of one long acquainted with every weak point in human nature.

Satan's first device was to persuade our Lord to distrust his Father's providential care. He comes to him when weak and exhausted with forty days' hunger, and suggests to him to work a miracle to gratify his physical appetite. Why should he wait any longer? Why should the Son of God sit still and starve? Why not create bread? (v. 3). Satan uses the weapon of unbelief.

Satan's second device was to persuade the Lord to an act of presumption. He takes him to the pinnacle of the temple and suggests that he cast himself down to give public proof that God had sent him. In so doing he might expect to be kept from harm. Was there not a text of Scripture which especially applied to the Son of God in such a position? (v. 6). Satan uses the weapon of presumption.

Satan's last device was to persuade the Lord to grasp at worldly power by unlawful means. He asks for a small concession and gives a large promise. Why not by a little momentary act obtain an enormous gain? (vv. 8-9). Satan uses the weapon of worldliness.

In resisting each suggestion of rebellion against God the chief weapon used was the Bible. Three times the offers are refused because 'It is written' (vv. 4,7,10).

We ought to be diligent Bible-readers because the Word of God is the sword of the Spirit. We shall never fight a good fight if we do not use it as our principal weapon. It may well be feared that there is not enough Bible-reading amongst us. It is not enough to have the book. We must actually read it and pray over it ourselves. It will do us no good if it only lies still in our houses. Knowledge of the Bible can only be got by hard, regular, daily, attentive wakeful reading.

For meditation: *Memorized Scripture is a stronghold against sin in the hands of the Spirit of God* (Ps. 119:11).

Suggested further reading: Hebrews 2:14-18

Jesus was 'wearied with his journey'. We learn from this, as well as many other expressions in the Gospels, that our Lord had a body exactly like our own.

The truth before us is full of comfort for all who are true Christians. He to whom sinners are bid to come for pardon and peace is one who is man as well as God. He had a real human nature when he was upon earth. He took a real human nature with him when he ascended up into heaven. We have at the right hand of God a High Priest who can be touched with the feeling of our infirmities, because he has suffered himself, being tempted. When we cry to him in the hour of bodily pain and weakness, he knows well what we mean. When our prayers and praises are feeble through bodily weariness, he can understand our condition. He knows our frame. He has learned by experience what it is to be a man. To say that the Virgin Mary, or anyone else, can feel more sympathy for us than Christ is ignorance no less than blasphemy. The man Christ Jesus can enter fully into everything that belongs to man's condition. The poor, the sick and the suffering have in heaven one who is not only an almighty Saviour, but a most feeling Friend.

Power and sympathy are marvellously combined in him who died for us on the cross. Because he is God, we may repose the weight of our souls upon him with unhesitating confidence. He is mighty to save. Because he is man, we may speak to him with freedom about the many trials to which flesh is heir. He knows the heart of a man. Here is rest for the weary! Here is good news! Our Redeemer is man as well as God and God as well as man. He that believeth on him has everything that a child of Adam can possibly require, either for safety or for peace.

For meditation: *The perfect Mediator relates to God as God and to man as man.*

Suggested further reading: Isaiah 61:1-7

What a striking account our Lord gave the congregation at Nazareth of his own office and ministry! When our Lord read Isaiah 61:1-2 he told the listening crowd that he himself was the Messiah of whom these words were written, and that in him and his gospel the marvellous figures of the passage were about to be fulfilled.

Our Lord desired to impress on his Jewish hearers the true character of the Messiah. He well knew they were looking for a mere temporal king who would deliver them from Roman dominion. He would have them understand that Messiah's kingdom was to be a spiritual kingdom over hearts. His victories were not to be over worldly enemies, but over sin. His redemption was not to be from the power of Rome, but from the power of the devil and the world.

Let us take care that we know for ourselves in what light we ought chiefly to regard Christ. It is right and good to reverence him as very God, as Head over all things, the mighty Prophet, the Judge of all, the King of kings. But we must not rest here if we hope to be saved. We must know Jesus as the Friend of the poor in spirit, the Physician of the diseased heart, the Deliverer of the soul in bondage.

How instructive these verses are in showing us how religious teaching is often heard! His hearers were impressed (v. 22). They could not find any flaw in the exposition of Scripture that they had heard. They could not deny the beauty of the well-chosen language to which they had listened. Except a temporary feeling of admiration their hearts were unmoved and unaffected.

There are thousands who listen regularly to preaching, admire it, do not dispute its truth and who find an intellectual pleasure in hearing a good and powerful sermon. But their religion never goes beyond that point. Their sermon-hearing does not prevent them living a life of thoughtlessness, worldliness and sin.

For meditation: *What sort of a hearer are you? What change to your life did the last sermon you heard make?*

Suggested further reading: 1 Corinthians 9:19-23

The Samaritan woman shows us how our Lord dealt with an ignorant, carnal-minded woman, whose moral character was more than ordinarily bad.

We should mark the mingled tact and condescension of Christ in dealing with a careless sinner.

Our Lord was sitting by Jacob's well when a woman of Samaria came thither to draw water. At once he says to her, 'Give me to drink.' He does not wait for her to speak to him. He does not begin by reproving her sins, though he doubtless knew them. He opens communication by asking a favour. He approaches the woman's mind by the subject of 'water', which was naturally uppermost in her thoughts. Simple as this request may seem, it opened a door to spiritual conversation. It threw a bridge across the gulf which lay between her and him. It led to the conversion of her soul.

Our Lord's conduct in this place should be carefully remembered by all who want to do good to the thoughtless and spiritually ignorant. It is vain to expect that such persons will voluntarily come to us and begin to seek knowledge. We must begin with them and go down to them in the spirit of courteous and friendly aggression. It is vain to expect that such persons will be prepared for our instruction and will at once see and acknowledge the wisdom of all we are doing. We must go to work wisely. We must study the best avenues to their hearts and the most likely way of arresting their attention. There is a handle to every mind and our chief aim must be to get hold of it. Above all, we must be kind in manner and beware of showing that we feel conscious of our own superiority. If we let ignorant people fancy that we think we are doing them a great favour in talking to them about religion, there is little hope of doing good to their souls.

For meditation: *How willing are you to think carefully before you speak to others about the Lord or are you too lazy to bother whether they understand or not?*

Suggested further reading: Isaiah 46:8-13

How apt men are to despise the highest privileges when they are familiar with them! The men of Nazareth could find no fault in our Lord's sermon. They could point to no inconsistency in his past life. But because the preacher had lived with them for thirty years, and his face, appearance and voice were familiar to them, they would not receive his doctrine (v. 22), just as our Lord expected (v. 24).

We shall do well to remember this lesson in the matter of ordinances and means of grace. We are always in danger of undervaluing them when we have them in abundance. We are apt to think lightly of the privilege of an open Bible, a preached gospel, and the liberty of meeting together for public worship. We grow up in the midst of these things and are apt to have them without trouble. The consequence is that we often hold them very cheap. We soon lose reverence for the name of Christ, the Bible and other sacred things.

How bitterly human nature dislikes the doctrine of the sovereignty of God! Our Lord reminded the men of Nazareth that God was under no obligation to work miracles among them. He could bypass Israel and work elsewhere (vv. 24-27).

Such doctrine as this was intolerable to the men of Nazareth. It wounded their pride and self-conceit. It taught them that God was no man's debtor, and that if they themselves were passed over in the distribution of his mercies, they had no right to find fault. They could not bear it. They thrust the Lord out of the city and, had it not been for an exercise of miraculous power on his part, they would doubtless have put him to a violent death (vv. 28-30).

The sovereignty of God is clearly taught in the Bible (Rom. 9:10-18). Upon no other principle can we explain why some are converted and some not, some nations enlightened by Christianity and others buried in heathenism. All is ordered by the sovereign hand of God. Let us pray for humility in respect of this deep thing.

For meditation: *We do not understand God's plans, but we can know our duties.*

Suggested further reading: Matthew 6:25-33

We should mark Christ's readiness to give mercies to careless sinners. He tells the Samaritan woman that if she had asked, 'he would have given her living water'.

The infinite willingness of Christ to receive sinners is a golden truth, which ought to be treasured up in our hearts and diligently impressed on others. The Lord Jesus is far more ready to hear than we are to pray and far more ready to give favours than we are to ask them. All day long he stretches out his hands to the disobedient and gainsaying. He has thoughts of pity and compassion towards the vilest of sinners, even when they have no thoughts of him. He stands waiting to bestow mercy and grace on the worst and most unworthy, if they will only cry to him. He will never draw back from that well-known promise: 'Ask and ye shall receive: seek and ye shall find.' The lost will discover at the last day that they had not because they asked not.

We should mark the priceless excellence of Christ's gifts when compared with the things of this world. Our Lord tells the Samaritan woman, 'He that drinketh of this water shall thirst again, but he that drinketh of the water that I shall give him shall never thirst.'

The truth of the principle here laid down may be seen on every side by all who are not blinded by prejudice or love of the world. Thousands of men have every temporal good thing that heart could wish and are yet weary and dissatisfied. Riches and rank and place and power and learning and amusements are utterly unable to fill the soul. He that only drinks of these waters is sure to thirst again.

There is no heart satisfaction in this world until we believe on Christ. Jesus alone can fill up the empty places of our inward man. Jesus alone can give solid, lasting, enduring happiness. The peace that he imparts is a fountain which, once set flowing within the soul, flows on to all eternity.

For meditation: *Which is more important to you: time or eternity?*

Suggested further reading: Romans 2:1-11

There is no office so honourable as that of the preacher. There is no work so important to the souls of men. It is an office which the Son of God was not ashamed to take up. It is an office to which he appointed twelve apostles. It is an office to which St Paul in his old age especially directs Timothy's attention. He charges him with almost his last breath to 'preach the word' (2 Tim. 4:2). It is the means which God has been pleased to use above any other for the conversion and edification of souls. The brightest days of the church have been those when preaching has been honoured. The darkest days of the church have been those when preaching has been lightly esteemed. Let us honour the sacraments and public prayers of the church, and reverently use them. But let us beware that we do not place them above preaching.

The first doctrine that our Lord proclaimed to the world was repentance (v. 17). The necessity of repentance is one of the great foundations which lie at the very bottom of Christianity (Heb. 6:1). It needs to be pressed on all mankind without exception. High or low, rich or poor, all have sinned and are guilty before God; and all must repent and be converted if they are to be saved. And true repentance is no light matter. It is a thorough change of heart about sin, a change showing itself in godly sorrow and humiliation (2 Cor. 7:10), in heartfelt confession before the throne of grace, in a complete breaking off from sinful habits, and an abiding hatred of sin. Such repentance is the inseparable companion of saving faith in Christ. Let us prize the doctrine highly. It is of the highest importance. No Christian teaching can be sound which does not constantly bring forward repentance towards God and faith towards the Lord Jesus Christ (Acts 20:21).

For meditation: *True repentance involves a change of mind, a change of affections, a change of desires, a change of direction, a change of life and a change of destination. It is no mere decision or clean-up of a life but a radical transformation of a whole person so that a hell-bound sinner becomes a heaven-bound saint.*

Suggested further reading: Matthew 15:1-8

We should mark the absolute necessity of conviction of sin before a soul can be converted to God. The Samaritan woman seems to have been comparatively unmoved until our Lord exposed her breach of the seventh commandment. Those heart-searching words, 'Go, call thy husband,' appear to have pierced her conscience like an arrow. From that moment, however ignorant, she speaks like an earnest, sincere enquirer after truth. And the reason is evident. She felt that her spiritual disease was discovered. For the first time in her life she saw herself.

To bring thoughtless people to this state of mind should be the principal aim of all teachers and ministers of the gospel. They should carefully copy their Master's example in this place. Till men and women are brought to feel their sinfulness and need, no real good is ever done to their souls. Till a sinner sees himself as God sees him, he will continue careless, trifling and unmoved.

Never does a soul value the gospel medicine until it feels its disease. Never does a man see any beauty in Christ as a Saviour until he discovers that he is himself a lost and ruined sinner. Ignorance of sin is invariably attended by neglect of Christ.

We should mark the uselessness of any religion which only consists of formality. The Samaritan woman, when awakened to spiritual concern, started questions about the comparative merits of the Samaritan and Jewish modes of worshipping God. Our Lord tells her that true and acceptable worship depends not on the place in which it is offered, but on the state of the worshipper's heart. The heart is the principal thing in all our approaches to God. 'The Lord looketh on the heart' (1 Sam. 16:7). The feeblest gathering of three or four poor believers in a cottage to read the Bible and pray is a more acceptable sight to him who searches the heart than the fullest congregation which is ever gathered in St Peter's at Rome.

For meditation: *Have our consciences been convicted and cleansed and our hearts been given to the Lord?*

Suggested further reading: Matthew 8:18-22

Our Lord had an unwearied readiness for every good work. Our Lord preaches to a crowd, not in any consecrated building or place set apart for public worship, but in the open air — not in a pulpit constructed for the preacher's use, but in a fisherman's boat (vv. 1-3). Souls were waiting to be fed. Personal inconvenience was not allowed a place in his consideration. God's work must not stand still.

Servants of Christ should learn a lesson from the Master. We are not to wait until every little obstacle or difficulty is removed before we put our hand to the plough or go forth to sow the seed of the Word. Let us work with the tools that we have. While we are lingering and delaying, souls are perishing. It is the slothful heart that is always looking at the hedge of thorns and the lion in the way (Prov. 15:19; 22:13). Where we are, and as we are, in season or out of season, by one means or another, by tongue or pen, by speaking or writing, let us strive to be ever working for God. Let us never stand still.

What encouragement our Lord gives to unquestioning obedience! Our Lord's command to Simon (v. 4) receives a reply which exhibits in a striking manner the mind of a good servant (v. 5). And what was the reward of this ready compliance with the Lord's command? Verse 6 tells us.

A practical lesson for all Christians is contained under these simple circumstances. We are meant to learn the lesson of ready, unhesitating obedience to every command of Christ. The path of duty may sometimes be hard and disagreeable. The wisdom of the course we follow may not be apparent to the world. But none of these things must move us. We are to go straight forward when Jesus says, 'Go'; and do a thing decidedly, boldly and unflinchingly, when Jesus says, 'Do it.' We are to walk by faith and not by sight, and believe that what we see not now to be reasonable and right we shall see hereafter. So acting we shall never find in the long run that we are losers. Sooner or later we shall reap a great reward.

For meditation: *Disobedience can always make reasons out of excuses, but God knows the motive of the heart* (1 Cor. 4:5).

Suggested further reading: Luke 7:36-50

We should mark Christ's gracious willingness to reveal himself to the chief of sinners. He concludes his conversation with the Samaritan woman by telling her openly and unreservedly that he is the Saviour of the world. 'I that speak to thee', he says, 'am the Messiah.' Nowhere in all the Gospels do we find our Lord making such a full avowal of his nature and office as he does in this place. And this avowal, be it remembered, was made not to learned scribes, or moral Pharisees, but to one who up to that day had been an ignorant, thoughtless and immoral person!

Dealings with sinners such as these form one of the grand peculiarities of the gospel. Whatever a man's past life may have been, there is hope and a remedy for him in Christ. If he is only willing to hear Christ's voice and follow him, Christ is willing to receive him at once as a friend and to bestow on him the fullest measure of mercy and grace. The Samaritan woman, the penitent thief, the Philippian jailor, the publican Zacchaeus are all patterns of Christ's readiness to show mercy and to confer full and immediate pardons. It is his glory that, like a great physician, he will undertake to cure those who are apparently incurable and that none are too bad for him to love and heal. Let these things sink down into our hearts. Whatever else we doubt, let us never doubt that Christ's love to sinners passeth knowledge and that Christ is as willing to receive as he is almighty to save.

What are we ourselves? This is the question, after all, which demands our attention. We may have been up to this day careless, thoughtless, sinful as the woman whose story we have been reading. But yet there is hope. He who talked with the Samaritan woman at the well is yet living at God's right hand and never changes. Let us only ask and he will 'give us living water'.

For meditation: *The gospel is for the chief of sinners. Do we 'write off' the openly wicked, or do we call them to the Saviour of sinners?*

Suggested further reading: Isaiah 6:1-8

A sense of God's presence abases man and makes him feel his sin-fulness. This is strikingly illustrated by Peter's words when the miraculous draught of fishes convinced him that one greater than man was in the boat (v. 8).

In measuring these words of Peter, we must, of course, remember the time at which they were spoken. He was, at best, a babe in grace, weak in faith, experience and knowledge. At a later period of his life he would, doubtless, have said, 'Abide with me,' and not 'Depart'. But still, after every deduction of this kind, the words of Peter exactly express the first feelings of man when he is brought into anything like close contact with God. The sight of divine greatness and holiness makes him feel strongly his own littleness and sinfulness. Like Adam after the Fall, his first thought is to hide himself. Like Israel, he fears to die in God's presence (Exod. 20:19).

Let us strive to know more and more, every year we live, our need of a mediator between ourselves and God. Let us seek more and more to realize that without a mediator our thoughts of God can never be comfortable, and the more clearly we see God, the more uncomfortable we feel. Above all, let us be thankful that we have in Jesus the very Mediator our souls require. Out of Christ, God is a consuming fire. In Christ, he is a reconciled Father.

Jesus holds out a mighty promise to Peter (v. 10). The promise was intended for all faithful ministers of the gospel who walk in the apostle's steps. It was spoken for their encouragement and consolation, to support them under that sense of weakness and unprofitableness by which they are sometimes almost overwhelmed. They are often tempted to give up in despair and to leave off preaching. But here stands the promise (v. 10).

Let us pray that all ministers may preach the same gospel Peter preached and live the same holy life he lived. Only such ministers will ever prove successful fishermen.

For meditation: *If congregations prayed more for their ministers, God might well be pleased to give them more blessing in their labours.*

Suggested further reading: Luke 15:1-7

How marvellous in the eyes of man are Christ's dealings with souls! We are told that the disciples 'marvelled that he talked with the woman'. That their Master should take the trouble to talk to a woman at all, and to a Samaritan woman, and to a strange woman at a well, when he was wearied with his journey — all this was wonderful to the eleven disciples.

The feeling displayed by the disciples on this occasion does not stand alone in the Bible. When our Lord allowed publicans and sinners to draw near to him and be in his company, the Pharisees marvelled. They exclaimed, 'This man receiveth sinners and eateth with them' (Luke 15:2). When Saul came back from Damascus, a converted man and a new creature, the Christians at Jerusalem were astonished. 'They believed not that he was a disciple' (Acts 9:26). When Peter was delivered from Herod's prison by an angel and brought to the door of the house where disciples were praying for his deliverance, they were so taken by surprise that they could not believe it was Peter. 'When they saw him they were astonished' (Acts 12:16).

If there was more real faith on the earth, there would be less surprise felt at the conversion of souls. If Christians believed more, they would expect more, and if they understood Christ better, they would be less startled and astonished when he calls and saves the chief of sinners. We should consider nothing impossible and regard no sinner as beyond the reach of the grace of God. The astonishment expressed at conversions is a proof of the weak faith and ignorance of these latter days. The thing that ought to fill us with surprise is the obstinate unbelief of the ungodly and their determined perseverance in the way to ruin. This was the mind of Christ. It is written that he thanked the Father for conversions. But he marvelled at unbelief (Matt. 11:25; Mark 6:6).

For meditation: *Have we the Father's heart for the returning prodigal (Luke 15:20-24), or a cold, repulsive look of disapproval?*

Suggested further reading: Matthew 9:10-13

The men whom the Lord Jesus chose to be his disciples were of the poorest and humblest rank in life. They were all fishermen. The religion of our Lord Jesus was not intended for the rich and learned only, but for the world. Poverty and ignorance of books excluded thousands from the notice of the boastful philosophers of the heathen world. They exclude no one from the highest place in the service of Christ. Intellect and money are worth nothing without grace.

The religion of Christ must have been from heaven or it never could have prospered and overspread the earth as it has done. A religion that did not flatter the rich, the great and the learned, which offered no licence to the carnal inclinations of the heart, whose first teachers were poor fishermen, without rank, wealth or power — such a religion could never have turned the world upside down, if it were not of God.

The miracles by which the Lord confirmed his mission were miracles of mercy and kindness. Our Lord went about doing good (Acts 10:38). These miracles are meant to teach us our Lord's power. He could heal sick people with a touch, and cast out devils with a word. He is able to save to the uttermost all those who come unto God by him (Heb. 7:25). He is almighty.

These miracles are meant to be types and emblems of our Lord as a spiritual Physician. He, before whom no bodily disease proved incurable, is mighty to cure every ailment of our souls. There is no broken heart that he cannot heal. There is no wound of conscience that he cannot cure. Fallen, crushed, bruised, plague-stricken as we all are by sin, Jesus by his blood and Spirit can make us whole. Only let us go to him.

These miracles, not least, are intended to show us Christ's heart. He is a most compassionate Saviour. He rejected no one who came to him. He refused no one, however loathsome and diseased. He had an ear to hear all, a hand to help all and a heart to feel for all. There is no kindness like his. His compassions fail not.

For meditation: *'Christ Jesus came into the world to save sinners... I was shown mercy so that in me Christ Jesus might display his unlimited patience as an example for those who would believe on him and receive eternal life'* (1 Tim. 1:15-16).

Suggested further reading: Matthew 13:44-46

How absorbing is the influence of grace when it first comes into a believer's heart! We are told that after our Lord had told the woman he was the Messiah, 'She left her waterpot and went her way into the city, and saith to the men, Come, see a man which told me all things that ever I did.' She had left her home for the express purpose of drawing water. She had carried a large vessel to the well, intending to bring it back filled. But she found at the well a new heart and new objects of interest. She became a new creature. Old things passed away. All things became new. At once everything else was forgotten for the time. She could think of nothing but the truths she had heard and the Saviour she had found. In the fulness of her heart she 'left her waterpot' and hastened away to express her feelings to others.

Conduct like that here described is doubtless uncommon in the present day. Rarely do we see a person so entirely taken up with spiritual matters that attention to this world's affairs is made a secondary matter or postponed. And why is it so? Simply because true conversions to God are uncommon. Few really feel their sins and flee to Christ by faith. Few really pass from death to life and become new creatures. Yet these few are the real Christians of the world. These are the people whose religion, like the Samaritan woman's, tells on others. Happy are they who know something by experience of this woman's feelings and can say with Paul, 'I count all things but loss for the excellency of the knowledge of Christ' (Phil. 3:8). Happy are they who have given up everything for Christ's sake, or at any rate have altered the relative importance of all things in their minds! 'If thine eye be single, thy whole body shall be full of light' (Matt. 6:22).

For meditation: *Is your relationship with Christ a polite interest or a healthy obsession?*

Suggested further reading: Matthew 19:16-22

We are especially told that the unclean spirits knew our Lord (v. 24). They knew Christ when scribes and Pharisees were ignorant of him and would not acknowledge him. And yet their knowledge was not unto salvation. This knowledge was a knowledge unaccompanied by faith, hope or charity. Those who possessed it were miserable fallen beings, full of bitter hatred against both God and man.

The mere belief of the facts and doctrines of Christianity will never save our souls. Such belief is no better than the belief of devils. They all believe and know that Jesus is the Christ. They believe that he will one day judge the world and cast them down into endless torment. It is a solemn and sorrowful thought that on these points some professing Christians have even less faith than the devil. There are some who doubt the reality of hell and the eternity of punishment. Such doubts as these find no place except in the hearts of self-willed men and women. There is no infidelity among devils (James 2:19).

Let us beware of an unsanctified knowledge of Christianity. It is a dangerous possession, but a fearfully common one in these latter days. We may know the Bible intellectually and have no doubt about the truth of its contents. We may have our memories well stored with its leading texts, and be able to talk glibly about its leading doctrines. And all this time the Bible may have no influence over our hearts, wills and consciences. We may, in reality, be nothing better than devils.

Let us take heed that our faith is a faith of the heart, as well as the head. We may go on all our lives saying, 'I know that and I know that' and sink at last into hell with the words upon our lips. Let us see that our knowledge bears fruit in our lives.

It is one thing to say, 'Christ is a Saviour.' It is quite another to say, 'Christ is my Saviour and my Lord.' The devil can say the first. The true Christian alone can say the second.

For meditation: *Without faith we are worse than devils; with a mere head faith we are equal to devils; with life-changing faith we are unlike devils.*

Suggested further reading: Acts 9:15-22

How zealous a truly converted person is to do good to others! We are told that the Samaritan woman 'went into the city, and said to the men, Come, see a man which told me all things that ever I did: is not this the Christ?' In the day of her conversion she became a missionary. She felt so deeply the amazing benefit she had received from Christ that she could not hold her peace about him. Just as Andrew told his brother Peter about Jesus, and Philip told Nathanael that he had found Messiah, and Saul when converted straightaway preached Christ, so, in the same way, the Samaritan woman said, 'Come and see Christ.' She used no abstruse arguments. She attempted no deep reasoning about our Lord's claim to be the Messiah. She only said, 'Come and see.' Out of the abundance of her heart her mouth spoke.

That which the Samaritan woman here did, all true Christians ought to do likewise. The church needs it. The state of the world demands it. Common sense points out that it is right. Everyone who has received the grace of God and tasted that Christ is gracious ought to find words to testify of Christ to others. Where is our faith, if we believe that souls around us are perishing and that Christ alone can save them and yet hold our peace? Where is our charity if we can see others going down to hell and yet say nothing to them about Christ and salvation? We may well doubt our own love to Christ if our hearts are never moved to speak of him. We may well doubt the safety of our own souls if we feel no concern about the souls of others.

Do we ever talk to others about God and Christ and eternity and the soul and heaven and hell? If not, what is the value of our faith? Where is the reality of our Christianity?

For meditation: *Are you more talkative about the weather, your family and your hobbies than about your Saviour?*

Suggested further reading: Hebrews 10:11-14

In time of trouble we should resort first to Jesus, as the friends of Simon's wife's mother did (v. 30). There is no remedy like this. Means are to be used diligently without question in time of need. Doctors are to be sent for in sickness. Lawyers are to be consulted when property or character needs defence. The help of friends is to be sought. But still, the first thing to be done is to cry to the Lord Jesus for help. No one is so compassionate and so willing to relieve. Scripture gives many examples of this (Gen. 32:11; 2 Kings 19:19; John 11:3; Ps. 55:22; 1 Peter 5:7; Phil. 4:6).

The almighty power of the Lord Jesus Christ is seen in that sicknesses and devils alike yield to his command. He rebukes unclean spirits and they come forth from the unhappy people whom they possessed (vv. 25,26,34). He rebukes a fever, lays his hands on sick people and at once their diseases depart and the sick are healed (vv. 31,34).

Such miracles occur so frequently in the Gospels that we are apt to read them with a thoughtless eye, and forget the mighty lesson that each one is meant to convey. They are all intended to fasten our minds on the great truth that Christ is the appointed Healer of every evil that sin has brought into this world. Christ is the true antidote and remedy for all the soul-ruining mischief which Satan has wrought on mankind.

The Lord Jesus makes a complete and perfect cure when he heals. Not only did the fever leave Simon's mother-in-law, but she served them (v. 31). That weakness and prostration of strength that as a general rule fever leaves behind was entirely removed in her case. The fevered woman was not only made well in a moment, but in the same moment made strong and able to work. What an emblem of Christ's dealings with sin-sick souls! The sin-sick soul is not merely cured and then left to itself. It is also supplied with a new heart and a right spirit, and enabled to live so as to please God.

For meditation: *'Cast all your anxiety on him because he cares for you'* (1 Peter 5:7).

Suggested further reading: Acts 20:17-35

We have in these verses an instructive pattern of zeal for the good of others. We read that our Lord Jesus Christ declares, 'My meat is to do the will of him that sent me, and to finish his work.' To do good was not merely duty and pleasure to him. He counted it as his food, meat and drink. Job, one of the holiest Old Testament saints, could say that he esteemed God's Word 'more than his necessary food' (Job 23:12). The great Head of the New Testament church went even further. He could say the same of God's work.

Do we do any work for God? Do we try, however feebly, to set forward his cause on earth, to check that which is evil, to promote that which is good? If we do, let us never be ashamed of doing it with all our heart and soul and mind and strength. Whatsoever our hand finds to do for the souls of others, let us do it with our might (Eccles. 9:10). The world may mock and sneer and call us enthusiasts. The world can admire zeal in any service but that of God and can praise enthusiasm on any subject but that of religion. Let us work on unmoved. Whatever men may say and think, we are walking in the steps of our Lord Jesus Christ.

Let us, beside this, take comfort in the thought that Jesus Christ never changes. He that sat by the well of Samaria and found it 'meat and drink' to do good to an ignorant soul is always in one mind. High in heaven at God's right hand, he still delights to save sinners and still approves zeal and labour in the cause of God. The work of the missionary and the evangelist may be despised and ridiculed in many quarters. But while man is mocking, Christ is well pleased. Thanks be to God, Jesus is the same yesterday and today and for ever.

For meditation: *What are you doing in the service of the Lord, for the good of others and the glory of God?*

Suggested further reading: 1 Timothy 2:1-8

We have here an example of our Lord Jesus Christ's habits about private prayer (v. 35). This was no isolated incident (Luke 3:21; 9:29; 6:12; Matt. 14:23; Mark 14:32). In short, our Lord always prayed and did not faint. Sinless as he was, he was an example of diligent communion with his Father. His Godhead did not render him independent of the use of means as a man. His very perfection was a perfection kept up through the exercise of prayer. His nature was kept sinless in the regular use of the means of grace, and not in the neglect of them.

There is an example here that all who desire to grow in grace and walk closely with God would do well to follow. We must make time for private meditation and for being alone with God. It must not content us to pray regularly and read the Scriptures, to hear the gospel regularly and receive the Lord's Supper. All this is well, but something more is needed. We should set apart special seasons for solitary self-examination and meditation on the things of God. The hurrying, bustling times imperil our souls. The more we have to do, the more we ought to imitate our Master in prayer and private communion with God.

What shall we say to those who never pray at all? There are many such church people who rise up in the morning without prayer and lay down at night without prayer, never speaking one word to God. Are such people Christians at all? A praying Master like Jesus can have no prayerless servants. To be prayerless is to be Christless, Godless and on the road to destruction.

What shall we say to those who pray, but give little time to their prayers? We are obliged to say that they show at present very little of the mind of Christ. Asking little, they must expect to have little. Seeking little, they cannot be surprised if they possess little. It will always be found that when prayers are few, grace, strength, peace and hope are small.

For meditation: *The spiritually careless are inevitably prayerless. Spiritual stature is measured by prayerfulness before God.*

Suggested further reading: Psalm 126

Work for the souls of men is undoubtedly attended by great discouragements. The heart of natural man is very hard and unbelieving. The blindness of most men to their own lost condition and peril of ruin is something past description. 'The carnal mind is enmity against God' (Rom. 8:7). No one can have any just idea of the desperate hardness of men and women until he has tried to do good. No one can have any conception of the small number of those who repent and believe until he has personally endeavoured to 'save some' (1 Cor. 9:22). To suppose that everybody who is told about Christ and entreated to believe will become a true Christian is mere childish ignorance. 'Few there be that find the narrow way!' The labourer for Christ will find the majority of those among whom he labours unbelieving and impenitent, in spite of all that he can do. 'The many' will not turn to Christ. These are discouraging facts. But they are facts, and facts that ought to be known.

The true antidote against despondency in God's work is an abiding recollection of such promises as that before us. There are 'wages' laid up for faithful reapers. They shall receive a reward at the last day, far exceeding anything they have done for Christ — a reward proportioned not to their success, but to the quantity of their work. They are gathering 'fruit' which shall endure when this world has passed away — fruit in some souls saved, if many will not believe, and fruit in evidences of their own faithfulness, to be brought out before assembled worlds. Do our hands ever hang down and our knees wax faint? Do we feel disposed to say, 'My labour is in vain and my words without profit'? Let us lean back at such seasons on this glorious promise. There are 'wages' yet to be paid. One single soul saved shall outlive and outweigh all the kingdoms of the world.

For meditation: *Christ has promised to bring all his chosen sheep into the flock. He cannot fail. Therefore evangelism cannot be in vain* (John 10:16).

Suggested further reading: 2 Timothy 3:14 - 4:5

Our Lord made a remarkable statement as to the purpose for which he came into the world (v. 38). The meaning of these words is plain and unmistakable. Our Lord declares that he came on earth to be a preacher and a teacher. He came to fulfil the prophetical office, to be the 'Prophet greater than Moses' who had been so long foretold (Deut. 18:15). He left the glory which he had from all eternity to do the work of an evangelist. He came down to earth to show to man the way of peace, to proclaim deliverance to the captives and recovering of sight to the blind. One principal part of his work on earth was to go up and down and publish glad tidings, to offer healing to the broken-hearted, light to them that sat in darkness and pardon to the chief of sinners.

What infinite honour the Lord puts on the office of preacher! It is an office which the eternal Son of God himself undertook. He might have spent his earthly ministry in instituting and keeping up ceremonies, like Aaron. He might have ruled and reigned as a king, like David. Until the time when he died as a sacrifice for sins, his daily, and almost hourly, work was to preach.

Let us never be moved by those who cry down the preacher's office. Let us give to every part of the public worship its proper place, but let us beware of placing any part of it above preaching. By preaching the church of Christ was first gathered together and founded, and by preaching it has ever been maintained in health and prosperity. By preaching sinners are awakened and enquirers are led on and saints are built up.

Those who sneer at and ridicule preaching ridicule the work which turned the world upside down, the very work which Christ himself undertook. The King of kings and Lord of lords was a preacher for three long years.

For meditation: *Paul shunned all attempts in his day to make the gospel attractive by gimmicks and cleverness (1 Cor. 2:1). He gloried in a plain setting forth of the truth (2 Cor. 4:2). New Testament communication is always verbal: drama, dance and mime are nowhere to be found.*

Suggested further reading: Matthew 10:1-4

We have in these verses a most teaching instance of the variety of ways by which men are led to believe Christ. We read that 'Many of the Samaritans believed on Christ for the saying of the woman.' But this is not all. We read again, 'Many more believed because of Christ's own word.' In short, some were converted through the means of the woman's testimony and some were converted by hearing Christ himself.

The words of St Paul should never be forgotten: 'There are diversities of operations, but it is the same God which worketh all in all' (1 Cor. 12:6). The way in which the Spirit leads all God's people is always one and the same. But the paths by which they are severally brought into that road are often widely different. There are some in whom the work of conversion is sudden and instantaneous. There are others in whom it goes on slowly, quietly and by imperceptible degrees. Some have their hearts gently opened, like Lydia. Others are aroused by violent alarm, like the jailor at Philippi. All are finally brought to repentance towards God, faith towards our Lord Jesus Christ and holiness of conversation. But all do not begin with the same experience. The weapon which carries conviction to one believer's soul is not the one which first pierces another. The arrows of the Holy Ghost are all drawn from the same quiver. But he uses sometimes one and sometimes another, according to his own sovereign will.

Are we converted ourselves? This is the one point to which our attention ought to be directed. Our experience may not tally with that of other believers. But that is not the question. Do we feel sin, hate it and flee from it? Do we love Christ and rest solely on him for salvation? Are we bringing forth fruits of the Spirit in righteousness and true holiness? If these things are so, we may thank God and take courage.

For meditation: *The twelve disciples were of diverse backgrounds. The church consists of a variety of people bound together by the one thing that matters: a common faith in Christ* (Gal. 3:26-28).

Suggested further reading: Numbers 5:1-4

Leprosy is a complaint of which we know little in our climate. In Bible lands it is far more common. It is a radical disease of the whole man, attacking not merely the skin but the blood, the flesh, the bones until the unhappy patient begins to rot. Amongst the Jews the leper was reckoned unclean and was cut off from the congregation of Israel and the ordinances of religion. He was obliged to dwell in a separate house. None might touch him or minister to him. What remarkable wretchedness belonged to the leprous person!

There is something like leprosy in us. There is a foul sin disease, which is ingrained into our very natures and cleaves to our bones and marrows with deadly force. That disease is the plague of sin. Like leprosy it is a deep-seated disease, infecting every part of our natures: our heart, will, conscience, understanding, memory and affections. Like leprosy it makes us loathsome and abominable, unfit for the company of God and the glory of heaven. But far worse than leprosy, it is a disease from which no mortal is exempt (Isa. 64:6).

Our Lord is able and willing to heal those in need (vv. 41-42). Our Lord responded to the leper's request (vv. 40-41) and made him well. At once the cure was effected (vv. 41-42). That very instant the deadly plague departed from the poor sufferer and he was healed. It was but a word, and a touch, and there stood before the Lord not a leper, but a sound and healthy man.

Who can conceive the greatness of the change in the feelings of this leper when he found himself healed? The morning sun rose upon him, a miserable being more dead than alive, a mass of sores and corruption. The evening sun saw him full of hope and joy, free from pain and fit for society.

So with spiritual leprosy. No heart disease is so deep-seated but he is able to cure it. No plague of soul is so virulent but our Great Physician can heal it.

For meditation: *Christ is willing to save. Sinners are not willing to come to him for salvation* (Matt. 23:37; John 5:40).

Suggested further reading: Romans 8:18-25

The rich have afflictions as well as the poor. We read of a nobleman in deep anxiety because his son was sick. We need not doubt that every means of restoration was used that money could procure. But money is not almighty. The sickness increased and the nobleman's son lay at the point of death.

The lesson is one which needs to be constantly impressed on the minds of men. There is no more common or more mischievous error than to suppose that the rich have no cares. The rich are as liable to sickness as the poor and have a hundred anxieties beside, of which the poor know nothing at all.

Let the servant of Christ beware of desiring riches. They are certain cares and uncertain comforts. Let him pray for the rich and not envy them. How hardly shall a rich men enter the kingdom of God! Above all, let him learn to be content with such things as he has. He only is truly rich who has treasure in heaven.

Sickness and death come to the young as well as to the old. We read of a son sick unto death and a father in trouble about him. We see the natural order of things inverted. The elder is obliged to minister to the younger, and not the younger to the elder. The child draws nigh to the grave before the parent, and not the parent before the child.

He that is wise will never reckon confidently on long life. We never know what a day may bring forth. The strongest and fairest are often cut down and hurried away in a few hours, while the old and feeble linger on for many years. The only true wisdom is to be always prepared to meet God, to put nothing off which concerns eternity and to live like men ready to depart at any moment. So living, it matters little whether we die young or old. Joined to the Lord Jesus, we are safe in any event.

For meditation: *Freedom from sickness and death are future blessings for the Christian* (Rev. 21:3-4). *While we stay in this world we are subject to the effects of the Fall.*

Suggested further reading: Luke 24:25-27,44-49

Our Lord Jesus paid respect to the ceremonial law (v. 44), even though he knew well that the ceremonies of the Mosaic law were only shadows and figures of the good things to come, and had in themselves no inherent power (Heb. 10:1). He knew well that the last days of the Levitical institutions were close at hand and that they were soon to be laid aside for ever. But so long as they were not abrogated he would have them respected. They were pictures and emblems of the gospel and not to be lightly esteemed.

Christians should remember this lesson, not despising the ceremonial law because its work is done. Let us beware of neglecting those parts of the Bible which contain it under the idea that the believer in the gospel has nothing to do with them. It is true that we have nothing to do with altars, sacrifices or priests. But we must never forget that the ceremonial law is full of instruction. It contains the same gospel in bud that we now see in full flower.

There is a time to be quiet about the work of Christ as well as a time to speak (v. 44). In the warmth of his zeal the cured man disobeyed the Lord's command and brought consequences on our Lord he had wanted to avoid (v. 45).

There is a lesson in all this of deep importance, however difficult it might be to use it rightly. There are times when our Lord would have us work for him quietly and silently rather than attract public attention by noisy zeal.

Unquestionably the majority of Christians are far more inclined to be silent about their glorious Master than to confess him before men and do not need the bridle so much as the spur. But there are good men who have more zeal than discretion and even help the enemy of truth by unseasonable acts and words.

For meditation: *Christian wives are encouraged to win their husbands by their lives rather than their words* (1 Peter 3:1). *Unless people see that we are different our words will count for nothing* (James 2:18).

Suggested further reading: Hebrews 12:4-13

What benefits affliction can confer on the soul! We read that anxiety about a son led the nobleman to Christ, in order to obtain help in time of need. Once brought into Christ's company, he learned a lesson of priceless value. In the end, 'He believed, and his whole house.' All this, be it remembered, hinged upon the son's sickness. If the nobleman's son had never been ill, his father might have lived and died in his sins.

Affliction is one of God's medicines. By it he often teaches lessons which would be learned in no other way. By it he often draws souls away from sin and the world, which would otherwise have perished everlastingly.

Let us beware of murmuring in the time of trouble. Let us settle it firmly in our minds that there is a meaning, a needs-be and a message from God in every sorrow that falls upon us. There are no lessons so useful as those learned in the school of affliction.

Christ's word is as good as Christ's presence. We read that Jesus did not come down to Capernaum to see the sick young man, but only spoke the word: 'Thy son liveth.' Almighty power went with that little sentence. That very hour the patient began to amend. Christ only spoke and the cure was done. Christ only commanded and the deadly disease stood fast.

The fact before us is singularly full of comfort. It gives enormous value to every promise of mercy, grace and peace which ever fell from Christ's lips. He that by faith has laid hold on some word of Christ has got his feet upon a rock. What Christ has said, he is able to do, and what he has undertaken, he will never fail to make good. The sinner who has really reposed his soul on the word of the Lord Jesus is safe to all eternity. He could not be safer if he saw the book of life and his own name written in it.

For meditation: *It is better to be sick and have Christ than to be well and on a road to hell.*

Suggested further reading: Philippians 2:7-11

Some persons enjoy great spiritual privileges yet make no use of them. No city in Palestine appears to have enjoyed so much of our Lord's presence as did Capernaum. It was the place where he dwelt after he left Nazareth (Matt. 4:13). It was the place where many of his miracles were worked and many of his sermons delivered. But nothing that Jesus said or did seems to have had any effect on the hearts of the inhabitants. They crowded to hear him (v. 2). They were amazed and astonished at his mighty works (v. 12), but they were not converted. For this they drew heavy condemnation from our Lord (Matt. 11:23-24).

We are apt to suppose that it needs nothing but the powerful preaching of the gospel to convert men's souls, and that if that gospel is brought into a place everybody must believe. We forget the amazing power of unbelief and the depth of man's enmity towards God. The Capernaites heard the most faultless preaching and saw it confirmed by the most surprising miracles, and yet remained dead in trespasses and sins. Nothing seems to harden men's hearts so much as to hear the gospel regularly, and yet deliberately prefer the service of sin and the world.

However, what pains men will take about an object when they are in earnest! The friends of the sick man overcome all obstacles to bring him to Jesus (v. 4). By pains, labour and perseverance the friends gained for him a complete cure. In any activity there are no gains without pains.

Pains and diligence are just as essential to the well-being and prosperity of our souls as of our bodies. In all our endeavours to draw near to God, in all our approaches to Christ, there ought to be the same determined earnestness shown by the sick man's friends. We must allow no difficulties to check us and no obstacle to keep us back from anything which is really for our spiritual good. Men who are not in spiritual earnest about salvation have no time for Bible-reading, prayer and hearing the gospel. They have time for money, business, pleasure and politics!

For meditation: *Modern Christians work shorter hours than ever, but always have less time for God than their forefathers. Why?*

Suggested further reading: Genesis 3:13-19

We read of a man who had been ill for no less than thirty-eight years! For eight-and-thirty weary summers and winters he had endured pain and infirmity. He had seen others healed at the waters of Bethesda and going to their homes rejoicing. But for him there had been no healing.

When we read of cases of sickness like this, we should remember how deeply we ought to hate sin! Sin was the original root and cause and fountain of every disease in the world. God did not create man to be full of aches and pains and infirmities. These things are the fruits of the Fall. There would have been no sickness if there had been no sin.

No greater proof can be shown of man's inbred unbelief than his carelessness about sin. 'Fools', says the wise man, 'make a mock at sin' (Prov. 14:9). Thousands delight in things which are positively evil and run greedily after that which is downright poison. They love that which God abhors and dislike that which God loves. They are like the madman who loves his enemies and hates his friends. Their eyes are blinded. Surely if men would only look at hospitals and infirmaries and think what havoc sin has made on this earth, they would never take pleasure in sin as they do.

Well may we be told to pray for the coming of God's kingdom! Well may we be told to long for the second advent of Jesus Christ! Then, and not till then, shall there be no more curse on the earth, no more suffering, no more sorrow and no more sin. Tears shall be wiped from the faces of all who love Christ's appearing, when their Master returns. Weakness and infirmity shall all pass away. Hope deferred shall no longer make hearts sick. There will be no chronic invalids and incurable cases, when Christ has renewed this earth.

For meditation: *Christ promises his people a glorious body like his own* (Phil. 3:20-21), *a body transformed by his power.*

Suggested further reading: Psalm 139:1-6

How great a blessing affliction may prove to a man's soul! The man who had been carried from his house that morning weak, dependent and bowed down in body and soul returned to his own house rejoicing in body and soul. Who can doubt that this man to the end of his days would thank God for his palsy? It was the beginning of eternal life to his soul.

Let us beware of murmuring under affliction. Every cross is meant to call us nearer to God. Bereavements have proved mercies. Losses have proved real gains. Sicknesses have led many to the great Physician of souls, sent them to the Bible, shut out the world, shown them their foolishness and taught them to pray. Thousands echo David's words (Ps. 119:71).

Our Lord Jesus has perfect knowledge of men's thoughts (v. 8). It should be a daily and habitual reflection with us that we can keep nothing secret from Christ. To him belong the solemn expressions of the 139th Psalm, which Christians should often study (Heb. 4:13; Ps. 139:4).

How many searchings of the heart this mighty truth should awaken within us! Christ ever sees us! Christ always knows us! Christ daily reads and observes our acts, words and thoughts! The recollection of this should alarm the wicked and drive them from their sins. Their wickedness is not hid and will one day be fearfully exposed if they do not repent. It should frighten hypocrites out of their hypocrisy. They can deceive men, but not Christ. It should comfort all sincere believers. They should remember that a loving Master is looking at them and fairly and justly measuring them in his eye (John 21:17).

The Lord Jesus possesses the priestly power to forgive sins (vv. 5,10). He laid claim to be the true High Priest who has the power of absolving sinners. No angel in heaven, no man upon earth, no church in council, no minister of any denomination can take away the sinner's conscience-load of guilt and give him peace with God. They may declare with authority whose sins God is willing to forgive, but they cannot absolve by their own authority. This is the peculiar prerogative of God, which he has put into the hands of his Son, Jesus Christ.

For meditation: *The Christ who knows us completely can forgive us entirely.*

Suggested further reading: Psalm 119:65-71

How great are the mercy and compassion of Christ! He 'saw' the poor sufferer lying in the crowd. Neglected, overlooked and forgotten in the great multitude, he was observed by the all-seeing eye of Christ. 'He knew' full well, by his divine knowledge, how long he had been 'in that case' and pitied him. He spoke to him unexpectedly, with words of gracious sympathy. He healed him by miraculous power, at once and without tedious delay, and sent him home rejoicing.

This is just one among many examples of our Lord Jesus Christ's kindness and compassion. He is full of undeserved, unexpected, abounding love towards man. 'He delighteth in mercy' (Micah 7:18). He is far more ready to save than man is to be saved, far more willing to do good than man is to receive it.

We are taught the lesson that recovery from sickness ought to impress upon us. That lesson is contained in the solemn words which our Saviour addressed to the man he had cured: 'Sin no more, lest a worse thing come unto thee.'

Every sickness and sorrow is the voice of God speaking to us. Each has its peculiar message. Happy are they who have an eye to see God's hand and an ear to hear his voice in all that happens to them. Nothing in this world happens by chance.

And as it is with sickness, so it is with recovery. Renewed health should send us back to our post in the world with a deeper hatred of sin, a more thorough watchfulness over our own ways and a more constant purpose of mind to live to God. Far too often the excitement and novelty of returning health tempt us to forget the vows and intentions of the sick-room. There are spiritual dangers attending a recovery! Well would it be for us all after illness to grave these words on our hearts: 'Let me sin no more, lest a worse thing come unto me.'

For meditation: *Are we making the most of God's kindnesses towards us or building up wrath?* (Rom. 2:5).

Suggested further reading: Romans 14:1-12

What excessive importance hypocrites attach to small things! The hypocritical Pharisees find fault with the disciples plucking corn on the sabbath (vv. 1-2). This exaggerated zeal of the Pharisees for the sabbath did not extend to other commandments. These men who pretended such strictness on one little point were more than lax and indifferent about other points of infinitely greater importance. While they stretched the commandment about the sabbath beyond its true meaning, they openly trampled on the tenth commandment and were notorious for covetousness (Luke 16:14). Our Lord well illustrated the hypocrite in Matthew 23:24.

It is a bad symptom of any man's state of soul when he begins to put the second things in religion in the first place, and the first in the second, or the things ordained by man above the things ordained by God. There is something sadly wrong when it is more important to us whether others are of our denomination and ceremonies rather than whether they repent of sin, believe on Christ and live holy lives. These are the chief points to which our attention ought to be directed. We are not to be accusers of the disciples.

How graciously our Lord pleaded the cause of his disciples and defended them against their accusers! We are told that he answered the cavils of the Pharisees with arguments by which they were silenced, if not convinced. He did not leave his disciples to fight their battle alone. He came to their rescue and spoke for them.

We have in this fact a cheering illustration of the work that Jesus is ever doing on behalf of his people. There is an accuser of the brethren, even Satan, the prince of this world (Rev. 12:10). How many grounds of accusation we give him by reason of our sins! How many charges he may justly lay against us before God! But let us thank God that believers have an Advocate with the Father, Jesus Christ the righteous, who is ever maintaining the cause of his people in heaven, and continually making intercession for them. Let us take comfort in this cheering thought.

For meditation: *Men and devils criticize; Christ sympathizes and intercedes.*

Suggested further reading: Mark 3:1-6

These verses begin one of the most deep and solemn passages in the four Gospels. They show us the Lord Jesus asserting his own divine nature, his unity with God the Father and the high dignity of his office. Nowhere does our Lord dwell so fully on these subjects as in the chapter before us. And nowhere, we must confess, do we find out so thoroughly the weakness of man's understanding! There is much, we must all feel, that is far beyond our comprehension in our Lord's account of himself. Such knowledge, in short, is too wonderful for us. 'It is high: we cannot attain unto it' (Ps. 139:6). How often men say that they want clear explanations of such doctrines as the Trinity! Yet here we have our Lord handling the subject of his own person and, behold, we cannot follow him! We seem only to touch his meaning with the tip of our fingers.

There are some works which it is lawful to do on the sabbath day. The Jews, as on many other occasions, found fault because Jesus healed a man who had been ill for thirty-eight years on the sabbath. They charged our Lord with a breach of the fourth commandment.

Our Lord's reply to the Jews is very remarkable. 'My Father', he says, 'worketh hitherto, and I also work.' It is as though he said, 'Though my Father rested on the seventh day from his work of creation, he has never rested for a moment from his providential government of the world and from his merciful work of supplying the daily wants of all his creatures. Were he to rest from such work, the whole frame of nature would stand still. And I also work works of mercy on the sabbath day. I do not break the fourth commandment when I heal the sick, any more than my Father breaks it when he causes the sun to rise and the grass to grow on the sabbath.'

For meditation: *Those who are too busy to spend time worshipping God must not be surprised to find God absent from them.*

Suggested further reading: Matthew 23:15-24

Our Lord freed the sabbath from incorrect interpretations and puri-fied it from man-made traditions. He stripped off the miserable tra-ditions with which the Pharisees had encrusted the day, and by which they had made it a burden rather than a blessing.

Our Lord allows all works of real necessity and mercy to be done on the sabbath day. This is a principle which is abundantly established in the Scripture we are now considering. We find our Lord justifying his disciples for plucking ears of corn on a sabbath. It was an act permitted in Scripture (Deut. 23:25). They were hungry and in need of food and therefore not to blame (Matt. 12:1). We find him maintaining the lawfulness of healing a sick man on the sabbath day. The man was suffering from disease and pain. In such a case it was no breach of God's commandment to afford relief. We ought never to rest from doing good.

The arguments by which our Lord supports the lawfulness of any work of necessity and mercy on the sabbath are striking and unanswerable. He reminds the Pharisees, who charged him and his disciples with breaking the law, of the actions of David (vv. 3-4), of priests in the temple (Matt. 12:5) and of their own care for animals (Matt. 12:11). Above all, he lays down the great principle that no ordinance of God is to be pressed so far as to make us neglect the plain duties of charity (v. 9; Matt. 12:7). The first table of the law is not to be interpreted so as to make us break the second. The fourth commandment is not to be so explained as to make us unkind and unmerciful to our neighbour.

Our Lord again shows his perfect knowledge of men's thoughts (v. 8). It belongs only to God to read hearts. He who could discern the secret intents and imaginations of others must have been more than man. No doubt he was man like ourselves, sin only excepted. But there are other texts in Scripture which prove our Lord was God as well as man. Our Lord's perfect knowledge should always exercise a humbling influence upon our souls. Jesus Christ is hourly reading our hearts.

For meditation: *Zeal for truth must be matched with love for others.*

Suggested further reading: John 14:8-11

The errors of Christians on the sabbath in these latter days are of a very different kind from those of the Jews. There is little danger of men keeping the sabbath too strictly. The thing to be feared is the disposition to keep it loosely and partially, or not to keep it at all. The tendency of the age is not to exaggerate the fourth commandment, but to cut it out of the Decalogue and throw it aside altogether. Against this tendency it becomes us all to be on our guard.

We learn from these verses the dignity and greatness of our Lord Jesus Christ. The Jews, we are told, sought to kill Jesus because he said 'that God was his Father, making himself equal with God'. Our Lord, in reply, on this special occasion enters very fully into the question of his own divine nature. In reading his words, we must all feel that we are reading mysterious things and treading on very holy ground. But we must feel a deep conviction, however little we may understand, that the things he says could never have been said by one who was only man. The speaker is nothing less than 'God manifest in the flesh' (1 Tim. 3:16).

He asserts his own unity with God the Father. No other reasonable meaning can be put on the expressions: 'The Son can do nothing of himself, but what he seeth the Father do: for what things soever he doeth, these also doeth the Son likewise... The Father loveth the Son, and showeth him all things that himself doeth.' Such language, however deep and high, appears to mean that in operation and knowledge and heart and will the Father and the Son are one — two persons, but one God. Truths such as these are, of course, beyond man's power to explain particularly. Enough for us to believe and rest upon them.

For meditation: *Christ must be given equal honour with his Father, or neither can be honoured* (John 5:23).

Suggested further reading: John 7:1-9

The desperate wickedness of the human heart is exemplified in the Pharisees, who, silenced and defeated by our Lord's arguments, plunged deeper and deeper into sin (v. 14). What evil had our Lord done that he should be so treated? None, none at all. No charge could be brought against his life: he was holy, harmless, undefiled and separate from sinners. His days were spent in doing good. No charge could be brought against his teaching: he had proved it to be agreeable to Scripture and reason, and no reply had been made to his proofs. But it mattered little how perfectly he lived or taught. He was hated.

This is human nature appearing in its true colours. The unconverted heart hates God and will show its hatred whenever it dares and has a favourable opportunity. It will persecute God's witnesses. It will dislike all who have anything of God's mind and are renewed after his image. Why were so many of the prophets killed? Why were the names of the apostles cast out as evil by the Jews? Why were the martyrs slain? Why were so many Reformers burned? Not for any sins they had committed. They all suffered because they were godly men. And human nature, unconverted, hates godly men because it hates God.

It must never surprise true Christians if they meet with the same treatment that the Lord Jesus met with (1 John 3:13). It is not the utmost consistency, or the closest walk with God, that will exempt them from the enmity of the natural man. They need not torture their consciences by fancying that if they were only more faultless and consistent everybody would surely love them. It is all a mistake. They should remember that there was never but one perfect Man on earth, and that he was not loved but hated. It is not the sins of the believer that the world dislikes but his goodness. It is not the remains of the old nature that call forth the world's enmity, but the exhibition of the new. Let us remember these things and be patient. The world hated Christ and the world will hate Christians.

For meditation: *Light let in under a lifted stone sends creatures scurrying back to the dark. So it is with sinners in the presence of holiness* (John 3:19-20).

Suggested further reading: Colossians 1:15-18

Life is the highest and greatest gift that can be bestowed. It is precisely that thing that man, with all his cleverness, can neither give to the work of his hands, nor restore when taken away. But life, we are told, is in the hands of the Lord Jesus, to bestow and give at his discretion. Dead bodies and dead souls are both alike under his dominion. He has the keys of death and hell. In him is life. He is the life (John 1:4; Rev. 1:18).

He asserts his own authority to judge the world. 'The Father', we are told, 'has committed all judgement unto the Son.' All power and authority over the world is committed to Christ's hands. He is the King and the Judge of mankind. Before him every knee shall bow and every tongue shall confess that he is Lord. He that was once despised and rejected of man, condemned and crucified as a malefactor, shall one day hold a great assize and judge all the world. 'God shall judge the secrets of man by Jesus Christ' (Rom. 2:16).

Is it possible to make too much of Christ in our religion? If we have ever thought so, let us cast aside the thought for ever. Both in his own nature as God, and in his office as commissioned Mediator, he is worthy of all honour. He that is one with the Father, the Giver of life, the King of kings, the coming Judge, can never be too much exalted. 'He that honoureth not the Son, honoureth not the Father that sent him.'

If we desire salvation, let us lean our whole weight on this mighty Saviour. So leaning, we never need be afraid. Christ is the rock of ages and he that builds on him shall never be confounded — neither in sickness, nor in death, nor in the judgement day. The hand that was nailed to the cross is almighty. The Saviour of sinners is 'mighty to save' (Isa. 63:1).

For meditation: *As the Father intends his Son to have supremacy in all things we should not be slow to fulfil his will.*

Suggested further reading: Mark 9:14-24

Great encouragement can be drawn from the description of our Saviour's character (v. 20). What are we to understand by the bruised reed and the smoking flax? The language of the prophet no doubt is figurative. The simplest explanation seems to be that the Holy Spirit is here describing persons whose grace is at present weak, whose repentance is feeble and whose faith is small. Towards such persons the Lord Jesus Christ will be tender and compassionate. Weak as the bruised reed is, it shall not be broken. Small as the spark of fire may be within the smoking flax, it shall not be quenched. It is a standing truth in the kingdom of grace that weak grace, weak faith and weak repentance are all precious in our Lord's sight.

The doctrine here laid down is full of comfort and consolation. There are thousands in every church of Christ to whom it ought to speak peace and hope. There are some who are ready to despair of their salvation because their strength seems so small. They are full of fears and despondency, because their knowledge, faith, hope, love appear so dwarfish and diminutive. Let them drink comfort out of this text. Let them know that weak faith gives a man as real and true an interest in Christ as strong faith, though it may not give him the same joy. There is fire in a spark as truly as in a burning flame.

Does Satan make light of the beginning of repentance towards God and faith towards our Lord Jesus Christ? No. Indeed, he does not! He has great wrath because his time is short. Do the angels of God think lightly of the first signs of penitence and feeling after God in Christ? No, indeed! There is joy among them when they behold the sight. Does the Lord Jesus regard no faith and repentance with interest unless they are strong and mighty? No, indeed. As soon as that bruised reed Saul of Tarsus begins to cry to him he sends Ananias to him saying that he prays (Acts 9:11). We err greatly if we do not encourage the very first movements of a soul towards Christ. A spark is better than utter darkness, and little faith better than no faith at all.

For meditation: *The Scriptures never ask how much faith saves.*

Suggested further reading: Matthew 7:24-27

The salvation of our souls depends on hearing Christ. It is the man, we are told, who 'hears Christ's word' and believes that God the Father sent him to save sinners who 'has everlasting life'. Such 'hearing', of course, is something more than mere listening. It is hearing as a humble scholar, hearing as an obedient disciple, hearing with faith and love, hearing with a heart ready to do Christ's will — this is the hearing that saves. It is the very hearing of which God spoke in the famous prediction of a 'prophet like unto Moses': 'Unto him shall ye hearken... Whosoever will not hearken unto my words which he shall speak in my name, I will require it of him' (Deut. 18:15-19).

To 'hear' Christ in this way, we must never forget, is just as needful now as it was nineteen hundred years ago. It is not enough to hear sermons and run after preachers, though some people seem to think this makes up the whole of religion. We must go much further than this: we must 'hear Christ'. To submit our hearts to Christ's teaching, to sit humbly at his feet by faith and learn of him, to enter his school as penitents and become his believing scholars, to hear his voice and follow him — this is the way to heaven. Till we know something experimentally of these things, there is no life in us.

How rich and full are the privileges of the true hearer and believer! Such a man enjoys a present salvation. Even now, at this present time, he 'hath everlasting life'. Such a man is completely justified and forgiven. There remains no more condemnation for him. His sins are put away. 'He shall not come into condemnation.' Such a man is in an entirely new position before God. He is like one who has moved from one side of a gulf to another: 'He is passed from death unto life.'

For meditation: *We can have assurance of salvation now — in the same way as Paul* (2 Tim. 1:12).

Suggested further reading: Psalm 51

Would we know what kind of people Christians ought to be? Would we know the character at which Christians ought to aim? Would we know the outward walk and inward habit of mind which are fitting for a follower of Jesus? Then let us often study the Sermon on the Mount (Matt. 5-7). Let us ponder each sentence and prove ourselves by it.

The Lord Jesus calls those blessed who are poor in spirit (v. 3). He means the humble, lowly-minded and self-abased. He means those who are deeply convinced of their own sinfulness in the sight of God, those who are not wise in their own eyes and holy in their own sight. They do not fancy they need nothing. They regard themselves as wretched, miserable, poor, blind and naked. Blessed are all such! Humility is the very first letter in the alphabet of Christianity. We must begin low if we would build high.

The Lord Jesus calls those blessed who mourn (v. 4). He means those who sorrow for sin, and grieve daily over their shortcomings. These are they who trouble themselves more about sin than anything on earth. The remembrance of it is grievous to them. The burden of it is intolerable. Blessed are all such. 'The sacrifices of God are a broken and contrite spirit' (Ps. 51:17). One day they shall weep no more. They shall be comforted.

The Lord calls those blessed who are meek (v. 5). He means those who are of a patient and contented spirit. They are willing to put up with little honour here below. They can bear injuries without resentment. They are not ready to take offence. Like Lazarus in the parable, they are content to wait for their good things (Luke 16:25). They are never losers in the long run. One day they shall reign (Rev. 5:10).

The Lord Jesus calls those blessed who hunger and thirst for righteousness (v. 6). He means those who desire above all things to be entirely conformed to the mind of God. They long not so much to be rich, or wealthy, or learned, but holy. Blessed are all such! They shall have enough one day (Ps. 17:15).

For meditation: *How ravenous for all that pleases God are you?* (2 Cor. 5:9).

Suggested further reading: 1 Corinthians 15:51-58

Our Lord tells us that 'The hour is coming, and now is, when the dead shall hear the voice of the Son of God: and they that hear shall live.' It seems most unlikely that these words were meant to be confined to the rising of men's bodies and were fulfilled by such miracles as that of raising Lazarus from the grave. It appears far more probable that what our Lord had in view was the quickening of souls, the resurrection of conversion (Eph. 2:1; Col. 2:13). Whenever any men or women among ourselves awaken to a sense of their souls' value and become alive to God, the words are made good before our eyes. It is Christ who has spoken to their hearts by his Spirit. It is the dead hearing Christ's voice and living.

Our Lord tells us that 'The hour is coming when all that are in the grave shall hear his voice, and shall come forth; they that have done good to the resurrection of life, and they that have done evil to the resurrection of damnation.'

The passage is one of those that ought to sink down very deeply into our hearts and never be forgotten. All is not over when men die. Whether they like it or not, they will have to come forth from their graves at the last day and to stand at Christ's bar. None can escape his summons. When his voice calls them before him, all must obey. When men rise again, they will not all rise in the same condition. There will be two classes, two parties, two bodies. Not all will go to heaven. Not all will be saved. Some will rise again to inherit eternal life, but some will rise again only to be condemned. These are terrible things! But the words of Christ are plain and unmistakable. Thus it is written and thus it must be.

For meditation: *Your resurrection is a certainty — but where will you spend eternity afterwards?*

Suggested further reading: Colossians 3:12-17

The Lord Jesus calls those blessed who are merciful (v. 7). He means those who are full of compassion towards others. They pity all who are suffering either from sin or sorrow, and are tenderly desirous to make their sufferings less. They are full of good works and endeavours to do good. Blessed are all such! Both in this life and that to come they shall reap a rich reward.

The Lord Jesus calls those blessed who are pure in heart (v. 8). He means those who do not aim merely at outward correctness, but at inward holiness. They are not satisfied with a mere external show of religion. They strive to keep a heart and a conscience void of offence, and to serve God with the spirit and the inner man. Blessed are all such. The heart is the man (1 Sam. 16:7). He that is most spiritual-minded will have most communion with God.

The Lord Jesus calls those blessed who are peacemakers. He means those who use their influence to promote peace and charity on earth, in private and public, at home and abroad. He means those who strive to make all men love one another by teaching the principles of the gospel (Rom. 13:10). They are doing the very work which the Son of God began when he came to earth the first time and which he will finish when he comes to earth the second time.

Lastly, the Lord Jesus calls those blessed who are persecuted for righteousness' sake. He means those who are laughed at, mocked, despised and ill-used because they endeavour to live as true Christians. Blessed are all such! They drink of the same cup that their Master drank. They are now confessing him before men and he will confess them before his Father and the angels at the last day (Matt. 10:32-33).

Such are the eight great foundation-stones which our Lord lays down. Eight great testing truths are placed before us. They are opposed to the principles of the world and despised by it, but they are the standard for which all true believers should aim.

For meditation: *It would not be possible for the world to ignore people who lived like this, but the modern world does largely ignore the church.*

Suggested further reading: Hebrews 6:7-12

In these verses we see the proof of our Lord Jesus Christ being the promised Messiah set forth before the Jews in one view. Four different witnesses are brought forward. Four kinds of evidence are offered. His Father in heaven, his forerunner, John the Baptist, the miraculous works he had done, the Scriptures, which the Jews professed to honour — each and all are named by our Lord as testifying that he was the Christ, the Son of God. Hard must those hearts have been which could hear such testimony and yet remain unmoved! But it only proves the truth of the old saying that unbelief does not arise so much from want of evidence as from want of will to believe.

What honour Christ puts on his faithful servants! See how he speaks of John the Baptist: 'He bare witness of the truth ... he was a burning and a shining light.' John had probably passed away from his earthly labours when these words were spoken. He had been persecuted, imprisoned and put to death by Herod, none interfering, none trying to prevent his murder. But this murdered disciple was not forgotten by his divine Master. If no one else remembered him, Jesus did. He had honoured Christ and Christ honoured him.

There things ought not to be overlooked. They are written to teach us that Christ cares for all his believing people and never forgets them. Forgotten and despised by the world, perhaps, they are never forgotten by their Saviour. He knows where they dwell and what their trials are. A book of remembrance is written for them. Their 'tears are all in his bottle' (Ps. 56:8). Their names are graven on the palms of his hands. He notices all they do for him in this evil world, though they think it not worth notice, and he will confess it one day publicly before his Father and the holy angels. He that bore witness to John the Baptist never changes. Let believers remember this. In their worst estate they may boldly say with David, 'I am poor and needy; yet the Lord thinketh upon me' (Ps. 40:17).

For meditation: *'He will not forget'* (Heb. 6: 10). *He will 'never forsake' his own people* (Heb. 13:5).

Suggested further reading: Titus 2:11 - 3:8

The Lord Jesus reveals the character that the true Christian must support and maintain in the world. It is of great importance that we have clear views on this subject.

True Christians are to be like salt in the world (v. 13). Now salt has a peculiar taste of its own utterly unlike anything else. When mingled with other substances it preserves them from corruption. It imparts a portion of its taste to everything it is mixed with. It is useful so long as it preserves its savour, but no longer. Are we true Christians? Then take note of our place and its duties!

True Christians are to be like light in the world (v. 14). It is the property of light to be utterly distinct from darkness. The least spark in a dark room can be seen at once. Of all things created light is the most useful. It fertilizes. It guides. It cheers. It was the first thing called into being. Without it the world would be a gloomy blank. Are we true Christians? Then take note of our position and its responsibilities!

Surely, if words mean anything, we are to learn from these two figures that there must be something marked, distinct and peculiar about our character if we are true Christians. It will never do to idle through life, thinking and living like others, if we mean to be owned by Christ as his people. Have we grace? Then it must be seen. Have we the Spirit? Then there must be fruit. Have we any saving religion? Then there must be a difference of habits, tastes and turn of mind between us and those who think only of the world. It is perfectly clear that true Christianity is something more than being baptized and going to church. Salt and light evidently imply peculiarity both of heart and life, of faith and practice. We must dare to be singular and unlike the world if we mean to be saved.

For meditation: *The emphasis in the church at present is to get alongside the world and build bridges between it and the church. The Scriptures have an emphasis on separateness and distinctiveness. The church is to be different, not similar.*

Suggested further reading: John 14:8-14

Let us observe for another thing the honour Christ puts upon miracles, as an evidence of his being the Messiah. He says, 'The works which the Father hath given me to finish, the same works that I do, bear witness of me that the Father hath sent me.'

The miracles of the Lord receive far less attention in the present day as proofs of his divine mission than they ought to do. Too many regard them with a silent incredulity as things which, not having seen, they cannot be expected to care for. Not a few openly avow that they do not believe in the possibility of such things as miracles and would fain strike them out of the Bible as weak stories, which, like burdensome lumber, should be cast overboard to lighten the ship.

But, after all, there is no getting over the fact that in the days when our Lord was upon earth, his miracles produced an immense effect on the minds of men. They aroused attention to him that worked them. They excited inquiry, if they did not convert. They were so many, so public and so incapable of being explained away that our Lord's enemies could only say that they were done by satanic agency. That they were done they could not deny. 'This man', they said, 'doeth many miracles' (John 11:47). The facts which wise men pretend to deny now no one pretended to deny nineteen hundred years ago.

Let the enemies of the Bible take our Lord's last and greatest miracle, his own resurrection from the dead, and disprove it if they can. When they have done that, it will be time to consider what they say about miracles in general. They have never answered the evidence of it yet and they never will. Let the friends of the Bible not be moved by objections against miracles until that one miracle has been fairly disposed of.

For meditation: *The only sort of person who has problems with the miracles of the Bible is the person who does not know the God of the Bible.*

Suggested further reading: Hebrews 10:1-18

The relation between our Lord's teaching and that of the Old Testament is cleared up by our Lord in one striking sentence (v. 17). These are remarkable words. They were deeply important when spoken, as satisfying the natural anxiety of the Jews on this point. They will be deeply important as long as the world stands, as a testimony that the religion of the Old and New Testament is one harmonious whole.

The Lord Jesus came to fulfil the predictions of the prophets who had long foretold that a Saviour would one day appear. He came to fulfil the ceremonial law by becoming the great sacrifice for sin to which all the Mosaic offerings had ever pointed. He came to fulfil the moral law, by yielding to it a perfect obedience which we could never have yielded, and by paying the penalty for our breach of it with his atoning blood which we could never have paid. In all these ways he exalted the law of God and made its importance more evident than it had been before (Isa. 42:21).

Let us beware of despising the Old Testament under any pretence whatever. Let us never listen to those who bid us throw it aside as obsolete, antiquated and useless. The religion of the Old Testament is the germ of Christianity. The Old Testament is the gospel in bud. The New Testament is the gospel in full bloom. The saints in the Old Testament saw many things in a glass darkly. But they all looked by faith to the same Saviour and were led by the same Spirit as ourselves. Much infidelity begins with an ignorant contempt of the Old Testament.

Let us beware of supposing that the gospel has lowered the standard of personal holiness and that the Christian is not expected to be as strict and particular in this matter as the Jew. So far from this being the case, the sanctification of the New Testament saint ought to exceed that of him who had nothing but the Old Testament for his guide. The more light we have, the more we ought to love God.

For meditation: *Initially the early church proved Christianity from the Old Testament not the New! It speaks of Christ* (John 5:39; Luke 24:27,44).

Suggested further reading: Isaiah 53

Let us observe in these verses the honour that Christ puts upon the Scriptures. He refers to them in concluding his list of evidences as the great witnesses to him. 'Search the Scriptures,' he says, 'they are they which testify of me.'

The 'Scriptures' of which our Lord speaks are, of course, the Old Testament. And his words show the important truth which too many are apt to overlook — that every part of our Bibles is meant to teach us about Christ. Christ is not merely in the Gospels and epistles. Christ is to be found directly and indirectly in the Law, the Psalms and the Prophets. In the promises to Adam, Abraham, Moses and David, in the types and emblems of the ceremonial law, in the predictions of Isaiah and the other prophets, Jesus, the Messiah, is everywhere to be found in the Old Testament.

How is it that men see these things so little? The answer is plain. They do not 'search the Scriptures'. They do not dig into that wondrous mine of wisdom and knowledge and seek to become acquainted with its contents. Simple, regular reading of our Bibles is the grand secret of establishment in the faith. Ignorance of the Scriptures is the root of all error.

What a plain duty it is to read the Scriptures! Men have no right to expect spiritual light if they neglect the great treasury of all light. If even of the Old Testament our Lord said, 'Search ... it testifies of me,' how much more is it a duty to search the whole Bible!

And now what will men believe, if they do not believe the divine mission of Christ? Great indeed is the obstinacy of infidelity. A cloud of witnesses testify that Jesus was the Son of God. To talk of wanting evidence is childish folly. The plain truth is that the chief seat of unbelief is the heart. Many do not wish to believe and therefore remain unbelievers.

For meditation: *The Scriptures make us wise unto salvation — they teach about Christ — but only faith in Christ saves* (2 Tim. 3:15).

Suggested further reading: Matthew 23:25-28

A right understanding of the doctrines contained in these verses lies at the very root of Christianity. Here the Lord Jesus explains verse 17 more fully. He teaches us that the gospel magnifies the law and exalts its authority. He shows us that the law, as expounded by him, was a far more spiritual and heart-searching rule than most of the Jews supposed. He proves this by selecting three of the ten commandments as examples of what he means.

He expounds the sixth commandment (v. 21; Exod. 20:13). Many thought that they kept this part of God's law so long as they did not commit actual murder. The Lord Jesus shows that it condemns all angry and passionate language. Let us mark this well. We may be perfectly innocent of taking life away and yet be guilty of breaking the sixth commandment.

He expounds the seventh commandment (v. 27; Exod. 20:14). Many supposed that they kept this part of God's law if they did not actually commit adultery. The Lord Jesus teaches that we may break it in our thoughts, hearts and imaginations, even when our outward conduct is moral and correct. The God with whom we have to do looks far beyond actions. With him even a glance of the eye may be a sin.

He expounds the third commandment (v. 33; Exod. 20:7). Many fancied that they kept this part of God's law so long as they did not swear falsely and performed their oaths. The Lord forbids all vain and light swearing altogether. All swearing by created things is a great sin.

Let us learn from this the exceeding holiness of God. He is a pure and most perfect Being who sees faults and imperfections where man's eyes often see none. He reads our inward motives. He notes our words and thoughts as well as our actions (Ps. 51:6). Oh, that men would consider this part of God's character more than they do! There would be no room for pride, self-righteousness and carelessness if they saw God as he is.

For meditation: *That God holds back his judgement does not mean he does not see nor care* (Ps. 50:21).

Suggested further reading: 2 Peter 3:8-14

The Lord Jesus says to the unbelieving Jews, 'Ye will not come to me that ye might have life.'

It is want of will to come to Christ for salvation that will be found, at last, to have shut the many out of heaven. It is not men's sins. All manner of sin may be forgiven. It is not any decree of God. We are not told in the Bible of any whom God has only created to be destroyed. It is not any limit in Christ's work of redemption. He has paid a price sufficient for all mankind. It is something far more than this. It is man's own innate unwillingness to come to Christ, repent and believe. Either from pride, or laziness, or love of sin, or love of the world, the many have no mind, or wish, or heart, or desire to seek life in Christ. 'God has given to us eternal life, and this life is in his Son' (1 John 5:11). But men stand still and will not stir hand or foot to get life. And this is the whole reason why many of the lost are not saved.

This is a painful and solemn truth, but one that we can never know too well. It contains a first principle in Christian theology. Thousands, in every age, are constantly labouring to shift the blame of their condition from off themselves. They talk of their inability to change. They tell you complacently that they cannot help being what they are! They know that they are wrong, but they cannot be different! It will not do. Such talk will not stand the test of the Word of Christ before us. The unconverted are what they are because they have no will to be better. 'Light is come into the world, and men love darkness rather than light' (John 3:19). The words of the Lord Jesus will silence many: 'I would have gathered you, and ye would not be gathered' (Matt. 23:37).

For meditation: *Condemnation comes to those who have not believed the truth but have delighted in wickedness* (2 Thess. 2:12). *Is that a description of you?*

Suggested further reading: Matthew 19:16-22

How exceedingly ignorant man is in spiritual things! There are ten thousands of professing Christians who know no more of the requirements of God's law than the most ignorant Jews. They know the letter of the ten commandments, but fancy that they have kept them all from their youth (Matt. 19:20). They never dream that it is possible to break the commandments if they do not break them by outward deed or act. And so they live on satisfied with themselves and their little bit of religion. Happy indeed are they who really understand God's law!

This passage teaches us our great need of the Lord Jesus' atoning blood to save us. What man or woman can ever stand before such a God as this and plead 'not guilty'? Who is there who has not broken the commandments thousands of times? 'There is none righteous, not one' (Rom. 3:10). Without a mighty Mediator we should everyone be condemned in the Judgement. Ignorance of the real meaning of the law is one plain reason why so many do not value the gospel as they ought and content themselves with a little formal Christianity. They do not see the strictness and holiness of God's commands. If they did they would never rest until they were safe in Christ.

How important it is to avoid all occasions of sin! If we really desire to be holy we must take heed to our tongues. We must be ready to make up quarrels and disagreements lest they gradually lead on to greater evils. We must labour to crucify our flesh and mortify our members, to make any sacrifice and endure any bodily inconvenience rather than sin. We must keep our lips as with a bridle, and exercise an hourly strictness over our words. Let men call us precise and too particular if they will. We need not be moved. We are merely doing as our Lord Jesus Christ bids us, and we have no need to be ashamed in doing that.

For meditation: *No one has ever yet been condemned by God for being too holy. The world condemned the 'too holy' Christ and will condemn his 'too holy' followers, but no such condemnation can come from the mouth of God without condemning himself, for he is holy* (1 Peter 1:16).

Suggested further reading: John 12:37-43

We are all by nature dead in trespasses and sins. Spiritual life is laid up for sinners in Christ alone. To receive benefit from Christ men must come to him by faith. The real reason why men do not come to Christ, and consequently die in their sins, is their want of will to come.

Let us mark in this passage one principal cause of unbelief. The Lord Jesus says to the Jews, 'How can ye believe which receive honour one of another, and seek not the honour that cometh of God only?' He meant by that saying that they were not honest in their religion. With all their apparent desire to hear and learn, they cared more in reality for pleasing man than God. In this state of mind they were never likely to believe.

A deep principle is contained in this saying of our Lord's and one that deserves special attention. True faith does not depend merely on the state of man's head and understanding, but on the state of his heart. His mind may be convinced. His conscience may be pricked. But so long as there is anything the man is secretly loving more than God, there will be no true faith. The man himself may be puzzled and wonder why he does not believe. He does not see that he is like a child sitting on the lid of his box and wishing to open it, but not considering that his own weight keeps it shut. Let a man make sure that he honestly and really desires first the praise of God. It is the want of an honest heart which makes many stick fast in their religion all their days and die at length without peace. Those who complain that they hear and approve and assent, but make no progress and cannot get any hold on Christ, should ask themselves this simple question: 'Am I honest? Am I sincere? Do I really desire first the praise of God?'

For meditation: *Which is more important to you — the praise of your friends or the approval of God?*

Suggested further reading: 1 Peter 2:21-25

In our feeling and acting towards our fellow man our Lord forbids everything like an unforgiving and revengeful spirit. A readiness to resent injuries, a quickness in taking offence, a quarrelsome and contentious disposition, a keenness in asserting our rights — all, all are contrary to the mind of Christ. The world may see no harm in these habits of mind but they do not become the character of a Christian.

The Lord Jesus enjoins on us a spirit of universal love and charity. We ought to put away all malice. We ought to return good for evil and blessing for cursing. We ought to love even our enemies not in word only but in deed. We are to deny ourselves and take trouble in order to be kind and courteous. We are to put up with much and bear much rather than hurt one another and give offence. Our thought must never be 'How do others behave to me?' but 'What would Christ have me to do?'

A standard of conduct like this may seem extravagantly high. But we must never content ourselves with aiming at one lower. Our Lord tells us that if we do not aim at the spirit and temper here recommended we are not yet children of God (vv. 44-45). Our Father in heaven is kind to all. He sends rain on good and evil alike. He causes his sun to shine on all without distinction. A son should be like his father. But where is our likeness to our Father in heaven if we cannot show mercy and kindness to everybody? Where is the evidence that we are new creatures if we lack love? It is altogether lacking and we must be born again (John 3:7).

If we do not aim at the spirit and temper here recommended we are manifestly yet of this world. Even those who have no religion can love those who love them (vv. 46-47). They can do good and show kindness when their affection or interest move them. But a Christian ought to be influenced by higher principles than these. Do we flinch from the test? Do we find it impossible to do good to our enemies? If that is the case we must be sure we have not yet been converted.

For meditation: *The claim that we love the unseen God is empty if we do not love men we can see* (1 John 4:20).

Suggested further reading: 2 Timothy 3:12 - 4:4

That there really was such a person as Moses, that he really was the author of the writings commonly ascribed to him — on both these points our Lord's testimony is distinct: 'He wrote of me.' Can we suppose for a moment that our Lord was only accommodating himself to the prejudices and traditions of his hearers and that he spoke of Moses as a writer though he knew in his heart that Moses never wrote at all? Such an idea is profane. It would make out our Lord to have been dishonest. Can we suppose for a moment that our Lord was ignorant about Moses and did not know the wonderful discoveries which learned men, falsely so called, have made in the twentieth century? Such an idea is ridiculous blasphemy. To imagine the Lord Jesus speaking ignorantly in such a chapter as the one before us is to strike at the root of all Christianity. There is but one conclusion about the matter. There was such a person as Moses. The writings commonly ascribed to him were written by him. The facts recorded in them are worthy of all credit. Our Lord's testimony is an unanswerable argument. The sceptical writers against Moses and the Pentateuch have greatly erred.

Let us beware of handling the Old Testament irreverently and allowing our minds to doubt the truth of any part of it because of alleged difficulties. The simple fact that writers of the New Testament continually refer to the Old Testament and speak even of the most miraculous events recorded in it as undoubtedly true should silence our doubts. Is it at all likely, probable or credible, that men of the twentieth century are better informed about Moses than Jesus and his apostles? God forbid that we should think so! Then let us stand fast and not doubt that every word in the Old Testament, as well as in the New, was given by inspiration of God.

For meditation: *Anti-biblical theologians and theology still dominate the academic world and professing church, but they have never saved one soul by their lies.*

Suggested further reading: John 13:31-35

There is much in all this which calls loudly for solemn reflection. There are few passages of Scripture so calculated to raise in our minds humbling thoughts. We have a lovely picture of the Christian as he ought to be. We cannot look at it without painful feelings. We must all allow that it differs widely from the Christian as he is. Let us carry away from it two general lessons.

In the first place, if the spirit of these ten verses were more continually remembered by true believers they would recommend Christianity to the world far more than they do. We must not allow ourselves to imagine that the least words in this passage are trifling or of small moment. They are not so. It is attention to the spirit of this passage which makes our religion beautiful. It is the neglect of the things which it contains which makes our religion deformed. Unfailing courtesy, kindness, tenderness and consideration for others are some of the greatest ornaments to the character of the child of God. The world can understand these things if it cannot understand doctrine. There is no religion in rudeness, roughness, bluntness and incivility. The perfection of practical Christianity consists in attending to the little duties of holiness as well as to the great.

In the second place, if the spirit of these ten verses had more dominion and power in the world how much happier the world would be! Who does not know what quarrellings, strifes, selfishness and unkindness cause half the miseries by which mankind is visited? Who can fail to see that nothing would so much tend to increase happiness as the spread of Christian love, as here recommended by our Lord? Those who fancy that true religion has any tendency to make men unhappy are greatly mistaken. It is the absence of it that does that, and not the presence. True religion makes men happy because it promotes peace, love, kindness and goodness.

For meditation: *There is a dangerous tendency to point men away from the example of our own lives when they want a proof of Christianity. Our lives, however, are supposed to be living testimonies to our faith* (John 13:35).

Suggested further reading: Romans 4:18-25

These verses describe one of our Lord's most remarkable miracles. Of all the great works that he did, none was done so publicly as this and before so many witnesses. Of all the miracles related in the Gospels, this is the only one which all the four Gospel writers alike record. This fact alone (like the four times repeated account of the crucifixion and resurrection) is enough to show that it is a miracle demanding special attention.

We have, for one thing, in this miracle a lesson about Christ's almighty power. We see our Lord feeding five thousand men with 'five barley loaves and two small fishes'. We see clear proof that a miraculous event took place in the 'twelve baskets of fragments' that remained after all had eaten. Creative power was manifestly exercised. Food was called into existence that did not exist before. In healing the sick and raising the dead something was amended or restored that had already existed. In feeding five thousand men with five loaves something must have been created which before had no existence.

Such a history as this ought to be specially instructive and encouraging to all who endeavour to do good to souls. It shows us the Lord Jesus 'able to save to the uttermost'. He is one who has all power over dead hearts. Not only can he mend that which is broken, build up that which is ruined, heal that which is sick, strengthen that which is weak; he can do even greater things than these. He can call into being that which was not before and call it out of nothing. We must never despair of anyone being saved. So long as there is life there is hope. Reason and sense may say that some poor sinner is too hardened, or too old to be converted. Faith will reply, 'Our Master can create as well as renew. With a Saviour who, by his Spirit, can create a new heart, nothing is impossible.'

For meditation: *'Is anything too hard for the Lord?'* (Gen. 18:14).

Suggested further reading: John 5:41-44

Our Lord takes it for granted that all who call themselves his disciples will give to the needy (v. 2). He assumes they will consider it a solemn duty to relieve the needs of others. In speaking of the manner in which this is done he condemns the selfish stinginess of those who never give a penny to do good to the bodies and souls of men. A giving Saviour should have giving disciples.

Our Lord takes it for granted that all who call themselves disciples will pray (v. 5). This teaches plainly that prayerless people are not Christians. It is not enough to join in the prayers of Sunday's congregation, or of the family during the week. There must be private prayer also.

In giving our Lord desires that we should abhor and avoid ostentation. We are not to give as if we wanted everyone to know how liberal and charitable we are (v. 2), and as if we desired the praise of our fellow men. We are to shun everything like display. We are to give quietly, making as little noise as possible about our acts of charity (v. 3).

In praying we are to seek to be alone with God (v. 6). We should endeavour to find some place where no mortal eye sees us and where we can pour out our hearts with the feeling that no one is looking at us but God. This can be difficult but 'necessity is the mother of invention'!

Whether giving or praying, the great thing to be kept in mind is that we have to do with a heart-searching and all-knowing God (vv. 4,6,8). Everything like formality, affectation or mere bodily service is abominable and worthless in God's sight. He takes no account of the quantity of money we give or the quantity of words that we use. The one thing at which his all-seeing eye looks is the nature of our motives and the state of our hearts (vv. 4,6).

Here lies a rock on which many are continually making shipwreck. They flatter themselves that all must be right with their souls if they fulfil a certain number of religious duties. They forget that God does not regard the quantity but the quality of our service.

For meditation: *In your worship and service is the vertical or the horizontal relationship most prominent?*

Suggested further reading: 2 Kings 4:1-7

We see the Lord Jesus supplying the hunger of a huge multitude of five thousand men. The provision seemed, at first sight, utterly inadequate for the occasion. To satisfy so many craving mouths with such scanty fare, in such a wilderness, seemed impossible. But the event showed that there was enough and to spare. There was not one who could complain that he was not filled.

There can be no doubt that this was meant to teach the adequacy of Christ's gospel to supply the necessities of the whole world. Weak and feeble and foolish as it may seem to man, the simple story of the cross is enough for all the children of Adam in every part of the globe. The tidings of Christ's death for sinners and the atonement made by that death is able to meet the hearts and satisfy the consciences of all nations and peoples and kindreds and tongues. Carried by faithful messengers, it feeds and supplies all ranks and classes. 'The preaching of the cross is to them that perish foolishness, but to us who are saved it is the power of God' (1 Cor. 1:18). Five barley loaves and two small fishes seemed scanty provision for a hungry crowd. But blessed by Christ and distributed by his disciples, they were more than sufficient.

Let us never doubt for a moment that the preaching of Christ crucified — the old story of his blood and righteousness and substitution — is enough for all the spiritual necessities of all mankind. It is not worn out. It is not obsolete. It has not lost its power. We want nothing new, nothing more broad and kind, nothing more intellectual, nothing more efficacious. We want nothing but the true bread of life which Christ bestows, distributed faithfully among starving souls. Let men sneer or ridicule as they will. Nothing else can do good in this sinful world. No other teaching can fill hungry consciences and give them peace.

For meditation: *The provision of God is always adequate for the need that arises.*

Suggested further reading: Malachi 1:6-14

The first sentence of this prayer declares to whom we are to pray (v. 9). We are not to cry to saints and angels, but to the everlasting Father, the Father of spirits, the Lord of heaven and earth. We call him Father in the lowest sense as our Creator, as Paul told the Athenians, 'In him we live and move and have our being — we are also his offspring' (Acts 17:28). We call him Father in the highest sense as the Father of our Lord Jesus Christ, who reconciles us to himself through the death of his Son (Col. 1:21-22). We profess that which the Old Testament saints saw dimly, if at all; we profess to be his children by faith in Christ and to have the Spirit of adoption, by which we cry, 'Abba, Father' (Rom. 8:15). This, we must never forget, is the sonship that we must desire, if we would be saved. Without faith in Christ's blood and union with him, it is vain to talk of trusting in the fatherhood of God.

The second sentence is a petition respecting God's name (v. 9). By the 'name' of God we mean all the attributes under which he is revealed to us: his power, wisdom, holiness, justice, mercy and truth. By asking that they be hallowed we mean that they may be known and glorified. The glory of God is the first thing that God's children should desire. It is the object of one of our Lord's own prayers (John 12:28). It is the purpose for which the world was created. It is the end for which the saints are called and converted. It is the chief thing we should seek (1 Peter 4:11).

The third sentence is a petition concerning God's kingdom (v. 10) — the kingdom of grace which God sets up and maintains in the hearts of his people by the Word and the Spirit, and the kingdom that Jesus shall establish at his coming in glory. That time is a time above all things to be desired and therefore has a foremost place in the Lord's Prayer.

For meditation: *So often our prayers are little more than a string of petitions. Our Lord began his pattern prayer by concern not for his own needs, nor even the needs of others, but with concern that God might be honoured and glorified. True prayer is concerned for the person and work of God.*

Suggested further reading: Luke 22:24-27

We are told that, after feeding the multitude, he 'perceived that they would come and take him by force to make him a king'. At once he departed and left them. He wanted no such honours as these. He had come, 'not to be ministered unto, but to minister and to give his life a ransom for many' (Matt. 20:28).

We see the same spirit and frame of mind all through our Lord's earthly ministry. From his cradle to his grave he was 'clothed with humility' (1 Peter 5:5). He was born of a poor woman and spent the first thirty years of his life in a carpenter's house at Nazareth. He was followed by poor companions, many of them no better than fishermen. He was poor in his manner of living: 'The foxes had holes, and the birds of the air their nests: but the Son of man had not where to lay his head' (Matt. 8:20). When he went on the Sea of Galilee, it was in a borrowed boat. When he rode into Jerusalem, it was on a borrowed ass. When he was buried, it was in a borrowed tomb. 'Though he was rich, yet for our sakes he became poor' (2 Cor. 8:9).

The example is one which ought to be far more remembered than it is. How common are pride and ambition and high-mindedness! How rare are humility and lowly-mindedness! How few ever refuse greatness when offered to them! How many are continually seeking great things for themselves and forgetting the injunction: 'Seek them not!' (Jer. 45:5).

Our Lord, after washing the disciples' feet, said, 'I have given you an example that ye should do as I have done' (John 13:15). There is little, it may be feared, of that feet-washing spirit among Christians.

'Tell me', it has been said, 'how much humility a man has, and I will tell you how much religion he has.'

For meditation: *We are to be ambitious to please Christ, not to promote self* (2 Cor. 5:9).

Suggested further reading: Matthew 18:21-35

The fourth sentence is a petition concerning God's will (v. 10). We here pray that God's laws may be obeyed by men as perfectly, readily and unceasingly as they are by the angels in heaven. We ask that those who obey not his laws might be taught to obey them and that those who do obey them may obey them better. Our truest happiness is perfect submission to God's will and it is the highest love to pray that all mankind may know, obey and submit to it.

The fifth sentence is a petition regarding our own daily needs (v. 11). We are here taught to acknowledge our entire dependence on God for our daily necessities. We, as weak, poor, needy creatures, beseech our Maker to take care of us.

The sixth petition respects our sins (v.12). We confess that we are sinners and in daily need of pardon and forgiveness. This deserves especially to be remembered. It condemns all self-righteousness and self-justifying. We are instructed here to keep up a continual habit of confession at the throne of grace and a continual habit of seeking mercy and remission.

The seventh petition is a profession respecting our feelings towards others (v. 12). This is the only profession in the whole prayer, and the only part on which our Lord comments and dwells, when he has concluded the prayer. The plain object of it is to remind us that we must not expect our prayers for forgiveness to be heard if we pray with malice and spite in our hearts towards others. To pray in such a frame of mind is mere formality and hypocrisy. It is as much as saying, 'Do not forgive me at all.' Our prayer is nothing without love. We must not expect to be forgiven if we cannot forgive.

For meditation: *The Scriptures do not permit us to divorce our relationships with our fellow men from our relationship with God. The law contained commandments concerning our duties to both. The teaching of the Old Testament applies to both* (Matt. 22:37-40). *The gospel has implications for both* (1 John 4:20). *Recipients of grace from God must be gracious to men.*

Suggested further reading: Job 23:1-10

We should notice in these verses the trials through which Christ's disciples had to pass. We are told that they were sent over the lake by themselves, while their Master tarried behind. And then we see them alone in a dark night, tossed about by a great wind on stormy waters and, worst of all, Christ not with them. It was a strange transition. From witnessing a mighty miracle and helping it instrumentally, amidst an admiring crowd, to solitude, darkness, winds, waves, storm, anxiety and danger, the change was very great! But Christ knew it and Christ appointed it and it was working for their good.

Trial, we must distinctly understand, is part of the diet which all true Christians must expect. It is one of the means by which their grace is proved and by which they find out what there is in themselves. Winter as well as summer, cold as well as heat, clouds as well as sunshine are all necessary to bring the fruit of the Spirit to ripeness and maturity. We do not naturally like this. We would rather cross the lake with calm weather and favourable winds, with Christ always by our side and the sun shining down on our faces. But it may not be. It is not in this way that God's children are made 'partakers of his holiness' (Heb. 12:10).

The Lord Jesus came to his disciples as they were rowing on the stormy lake, 'walking on' the waters. He walked on them as easily as we walk on dry land. They bore him as firmly as the pavement of the temple, or the hills around Nazareth. That which is contrary to all natural reason was perfectly possible to Christ.

It was just as easy for him to walk on the sea as to form the sea at the beginning, just as easy to suspend the common laws of nature, as they are called, as to impose those laws at the first.

For meditation: *He who created and sustains this world can keep his people secure through its trials and snares.*

Suggested further reading: 1 Corinthians 10:1-13

The eighth petition concerns our weakness (v. 13). It teaches us that we are liable at all times to be led astray and fall. It instructs us to confess our infirmity and beseech God to hold us up and not allow us to run into sin. We ask him who orders all things in heaven and on earth to restrain us from going into that which would injure our souls, and never to allow us to be tempted above that which we are able to bear (1 Cor. 10:13).

The ninth petition is a request concerning our dangers (v. 13). We are here taught to ask God to deliver us from the evil that is in the world, the evil that is within our hearts and, not least, from that evil one, the devil. We confess that, as long as we are in the body, we are constantly seeing, hearing and feeling the presence of evil. It is about us, within us and around us on every side. And we entreat him who alone can preserve us to be continually delivering us from its power (John 17:15).

The last sentence is an ascription of praise (v. 13). We declare in these words our belief that the kingdoms of this world are the rightful property of the Father, that to him alone belongs all power, and that he alone deserves to receive all glory. We conclude by offering to him the profession of our hearts that we give him all honour and praise and rejoice that he is King of kings and Lord of lords.

Let us examine ourselves and see whether we really have the desire to have the things which we are taught to ask for in the Lord's prayer. Thousands repeat the form without considering what they say. They care nothing for the glory or kingdom or will of God. They have no sense of dependence, sinfulness, weakness or danger. They have no love to their enemies. But they pray the Lord's Prayer! These things ought not to be so. May we resolve that, by God's help, our hearts shall go together with our lips!

For meditation:
I often say my prayers, but do I ever pray?
And do the wishes of my heart go with the words I say?
                                        (John Burton).

Suggested further reading: Revelation 2:18-29

What knowledge of man's heart our Lord Jesus Christ possesses! We see him exposing the false motives of those who followed him for the sake of the loaves and fishes. They had followed him across the Lake of Galilee. They seemed at first sight ready to believe in him and do him honour. But he knew the inward springs of their conduct and was not deceived. 'Ye seek me,' he said, 'not because ye saw the miracles, but because ye did eat of the loaves and were filled.'

The Lord Jesus, we should never forget, is still the same. He never changes. He reads the secret motives of all who profess and call themselves Christians. He knows exactly why they do all they do in their religion.

Let us be real, true and sincere in our religion, whatever else we are. The sinfulness of hypocrisy is very great, but its folly is greater still. It is not hard to deceive ministers, relatives and friends. A little decent outward profession will often go a long way. But it is imposs-ible to deceive Christ. 'His eyes are as a flame of fire' (Rev. 1:14). He sees us through and through. Happy are those who can say, 'Thou, Lord, who knowest all things, knowest that we love thee' (John 21:17).

Our Lord told the crowds who followed him so diligently for the loaves and fishes 'not to labour for the meat that perisheth'.

What our Lord did mean to rebuke was that excessive attention to labour for the body, while the soul is neglected, which prevails everywhere in the world. What he reproved was the common habit of labouring only for the things of time and letting alone the things of eternity, of minding only the life that now is and disregarding the life to come. Against this habit he delivers a solemn warning. Happy are those who learn the respective value of soul and body and give the first and best place in their thoughts to salvation.

For meditation: *No one will be more pathetic and tragic on the Day of Judgement than the unmasked hypocrite who looked good but lacked life.*

Suggested further reading: Matthew 9:14-17

Fasting, or occasional abstinence from food, in order to bring the body into subjection to the spirit, is a practice frequently mentioned in the Bible and generally in connection with prayer. David fasted when his child was sick (2 Sam. 12:16-17). Daniel fasted when he sought special light from God (Dan. 9:3). Paul and Barnabas fasted when they appointed elders (Acts 14:23). Esther fasted before going in to the king (Esth. 4:16).

It is a subject about which we find no direct command in the New Testament. It seems to be left to one's discretion whether one will fast or not. There is a great wisdom in this — especially in relation to the very poor and sick. It is a matter in which everyone should be persuaded in his own mind, and not hasty to condemn others who do not agree with him.

Those who fast should do it quietly, secretly and without ostentation. They are not to fast to man but to God (v. 18). Their fasting is to be accompanied by cheerfulness (v. 17). Men should not see Christianity making us sad, but happy. Our religion does not consist in gloomy, melancholy looks. Are we dissatisfied with Christ's wages and Christ's service? Surely not! Then let us not look as if it were so!

Worldliness is one of the greatest of dangers that besieges men's souls. It is no wonder that we find our Lord speaking strongly about it. It is an insidious, specious, plausible enemy. It seems so harmless to seek our happiness in this world as long as we keep clear of open sins! Yet here is a rock on which many shipwreck to all eternity. Laying up treasure on earth causes them to forget treasure in heaven. May we all remember this! Where are our hearts? What do we love best? Are our chiefest affections on things on earth or things in heaven? Life or death depends on the answer that we give to these questions! If our treasure is earthly our heart will be earthly also (v. 21). Let us watch and pray against an earthly spirit. Open transgression of God's law slays its thousands, but worldliness its tens of thousands.

For meditation: *We need to be citizens of heaven in temporary residence on earth. Our roots are not to be here but there* (Col. 3:1-4).

Suggested further reading: Luke 13:22-27

Christ tells us to 'labour for the meat that endureth to everlasting life'. He would have us take pains to find food and satisfaction for our souls. That food is provided in rich abundance in him. But he that would have it must diligently seek it.

How are we to labour? There is but one answer. We must labour in the use of all appointed means. We must read our Bibles like men digging for hidden treasure. We must wrestle earnestly in prayer like men contending with a deadly enemy for life. We must take our whole heart to the house of God and worship and hear like those who listen to the reading of a will. We must fight daily against sin, the world and the devil like those who fight for liberty and must conquer or be slaves. These are the ways we must walk in if we would find Christ and be found of him. This is 'labouring'. This is the secret of getting on about our souls.

Labour like this no doubt is very uncommon. In carrying it on we shall have little encouragement from man and shall often be told that we are 'extreme' and go too far. Strange and absurd as it is, the natural man is always fancying that we may take too much thought about religion and refusing to see that we are far more likely to take too much thought about the world. But whatever man may say, the soul will never get spiritual food without labour. We must 'strive', we must 'run', we must 'fight', we must throw our whole heart into our soul's affairs. It is 'the violent' who take the kingdom (Matt. 11:12).

Never let us rest till we have eaten of the meat which Christ alone can give. They that are content with any other spiritual food will sooner or later 'lie down in sorrow' (Isa. 50:11).

For meditation: *Half-heartedness does not find God, but earnest seeking is always rewarded* (Heb. 11:6).

Suggested further reading: Luke 12:13-21

Singleness of purpose is one great secret of spiritual prosperity. If our eyes do not see distinctly, we cannot walk without stumbling or falling. If we attempt to work for two masters, we can be sure to give satisfaction to neither. It is just the same with respect to our souls. We cannot serve Christ and the world at the same time. It is vain to attempt it. The thing cannot be done. The ark and Dagon will never stand together (1 Sam. 5:1-5). God must be King over our hearts. His law, his will, his precepts must receive our first attention. Then, and not till then, everything in our inward man will fall into its right place. Unless our hearts are so ordered everything will be confusion (v. 23).

This lack of singleness of purpose is at the root of so many failures in religion. Those in our churches who are uncomfortable, ill at ease and dissatisfied with themselves, hardly knowing why, have the reason revealed here (v. 24). They are trying to keep in with both sides. They are endeavouring to please God and please man, to serve Christ and serve the world at the same time. Let us not commit this mistake. Let us be decided, thoroughgoing, uncompromised followers of Christ. Let us do one thing (Phil. 3:13).

But maybe we will push away these warnings about serving this world by the argument that we cannot help being anxious about the things of this life. As we have families and bodies to provide for, how can we get through life if we think first of our souls? The Lord Jesus saw such thoughts and furnished an answer.

He forbids us to keep an anxious spirit about the things of this world. Four times over he tells us to take no anxious thought (vv. 25,28,31,34). There is to be no anxiety about life, food, clothing or the morrow. Be not overcareful. Be not over-anxious. Prudent provision for the future is right. Wearing, corroding, self-tormenting anxiety is wrong.

For meditation: *So many try to have a foot on earth and a foot in heaven. But heaven and earth are like two boats separating from each other. We cannot stay in both and we can end up losing both.*

Suggested further reading: Ephesians 2:1-10

If any two things are put in strong contrast in the New Testament, they are faith and works. Not working, but believing, not of works, but through faith, are words familiar to all careful Bible-readers. Yet here the great Head of the church declares that believing on him is the highest and greatest of all 'works'! It is 'the work of God'.

Doubtless our Lord did not mean that there is anything meritorious in believing. Man's faith, at the very best, is feeble and defective. Regarded as a 'work', it cannot stand the severity of God's judgement, deserve pardon or purchase heaven. But our Lord did mean that faith in himself, as the only Saviour, is the first act of the soul which God requires at a sinner's hands. Till a man believes on Jesus and rests on Jesus as a lost sinner, he is nothing. Our Lord did mean that faith in himself is that act of the soul which specially pleases God. When the Father sees a sinner casting aside his own righteousness and simply trusting in his dear Son, he is well pleased. Without such faith it is impossible to please God. Our Lord did mean that faith in himself is the root of all saving religion. There is no life in a man till he believes. Above all, our Lord did mean that faith in himself is the hardest of all spiritual acts to the natural man. Did the Jews want something to do in religion? Let them know that the greatest thing they had to do was to cast aside their pride, confess their guilt and need and humbly believe.

Let all who know anything of true faith thank God and rejoice. Blessed are they that believe! It is an attainment which many of the wise of this world have never yet reached. We may feel ourselves poor, weak sinners. But do we believe? We may fail and come short in many things. But do we believe?

For meditation: *Receiving a free gift involves activity but it does not imply merit in the recipient.*

Suggested further reading: Deuteronomy 8:1-5

Our Lord reminds us of the providential care that God continually takes of everything that he has created. Has he given us life? Then he will surely not let us lack anything for its maintenance. Has he given us a body? Then he will surely not let us die for lack of clothing. He that calls us into being will doubtless find food to feed us.

He points out the uselessness of over-anxiety (v. 27). Our life is entirely in God's hands. All the anxiety in the world will not make us continue a minute beyond the time which God has appointed. We shall not die till our work is done.

He sends us to the birds of the air for our instruction (v. 26). They make no provision for the future. They lay up no stores for times to come. They literally live from day to day on what they can pick up by using the instinct that God has put in them. They ought to teach us that no man doing his duty in the work to which God has called him shall ever come to poverty.

He bids us observe the flowers of the field (vv. 28-30). Year after year they are decked in gayest colours without the slightest labour or exertion on their part. God, by his almighty power, clothes them every season. The same God is the Father of all believers. Why should they doubt that they can be clothed by him as well as the flowers? He who takes thought for perishable flowers will surely not neglect bodies in which are immortal souls.

He suggests to us that over-anxiety about the things of this world is most unworthy of a Christian. One great feature of heathenism (v. 32) is anxiously living for the present. The unbeliever knows nothing of a Father in heaven. But let the Christian who has clearer light and knowledge give proof of it by his faith and contentment. We are not to be anxious as if we had no God and no Christ.

For meditation: *Serenity of spirit in a world when men's hearts fail them for fear is a great witness to the gospel. If men can face death with this serenity (Dan. 3:16-18) can we not face the lesser problems of life?*

Suggested further reading: Mark 6:1-6

When our Lord bade his hearers 'labour for the meat which endureth to eternal life', they immediately began to think of works to be done and a goodness of their own to be established. 'What shall we do that we might work the works of God?' Doing, doing, doing was their only idea of the way to heaven. Again, when our Lord spoke of himself as one sent of God and the need of believing on him at once, they turn round with the question: 'What sign showest thou? What dost thou work?' Fresh from the mighty miracle of the loaves and fishes, one might have thought they had had a sign sufficient to convince them. Taught by our Lord Jesus Christ himself, one might have expected a greater readiness to believe. But, alas! there are no limits to man's dullness, prejudice and unbelief in spiritual matters. It is a striking fact that the only thing which our Lord is said to have 'marvelled' at during his earthly ministry was man's 'unbelief' (Mark 6:6).

We shall do well to remember this, if we ever try to do good to others in the matter of religion. We must not be cast down because our words are not believed and our efforts seem thrown away. We must not complain of it as a strange thing and suppose that the people we have to deal with are peculiarly stubborn and hard. We must recollect that this is the very cup of which our Lord had to drink and like him we must patiently work on. If even he, so perfect and so plain a teacher, was not believed, what right have we to wonder if men do not believe us? Happy are the ministers and missionaries and teachers who keep these things in mind! It will save them much bitter disappointment. In working for God, it is of first importance to understand what we must expect in man. Few things are so little realized as the extent of human unbelief.

For meditation: *Let us not be amazed at unbelief, but let us not be discouraged by it either. All the chosen sheep shall hear the voice of Christ* (John 10:16,27).

Suggested further reading: Psalm 37:23-29

Our Lord offers us a gracious promise as a remedy against an anxious spirit. He assures us that if we seek first and foremost to have a place in the kingdom of grace and glory, then everything that we really need in this world will be given to us. It shall be added over and above our heavenly inheritance as all things are worked together for our good and nothing good is withheld (v. 33; Rom. 8:28; Ps. 84:11).

He seals up his instruction on this subject by laying down one of the wisest maxims (v. 34). We are not to carry cares before they come. We are to attend to today's business and leave tomorrow's anxieties till tomorrow dawns. We may die before tomorrow. We know not what may happen on the morrow. This only we may be assured of, that if tomorrow brings a cross he who sends it can and will send the grace to bear it.

In all this passage there is a treasury of golden lessons. Let us seek to use them in our daily life. Let us not only read them but turn them to practical account. Let us watch and pray against an anxious and overcareful spirit. It deeply concerns our happiness. Half our miseries are caused by fancying things that we think are coming upon us. Half the things that we expect to come upon us never come at all! Where is our faith? Where is our confidence in our Saviour's words? We may well feel ashamed of ourselves as we read these verses and then look into our hearts. But this we may be sure of, that David's words are true: 'I have been young, and now am old, yet have I not seen the righteous forsaken, nor his seed begging bread' (Ps. 37:25).

The man who seeks first God's kingdom shall never lack anything that is for his good. He may not have so much health as some. He may not have so much wealth as some. He may not have a richly spread table or royal dainties. But he shall always have enough (Isa. 33:16).

For meditation: *While God does not promise to give us everything we want, he does bind himself to give us everything that is for our good (Matt. 7:11). If he gave us everything we wanted, even though it might not be for our good, it would be more an act of judgement than of love (Rom. 1:28).*

Suggested further reading: Acts 4:8-12

Our Lord would have us know that he himself is the appointed food of man's soul. The soul of every man is naturally starving and famishing through sin. Christ is given by God the Father to be the satisfier, the reliever and the physician of man's spiritual need. In him and his mediatorial office, in him and his atoning death, in him and his priesthood, in him and his grace, love and power — in him alone will empty souls find their wants supplied. In him there is life. He is 'the bread of life'.

With what divine and perfect wisdom this name is chosen! Bread is necessary food. We can manage tolerably well without many things on our table, but not without bread. So is it with Christ. We must have Christ, or die in our own sins. Bread is food that suits all. Some cannot eat meat and some cannot eat vegetables. But all like bread. It is food both for the queen and for the pauper. So is it with Christ. He is just the Saviour that meets the wants of every class. Bread is food that we need daily. Other kinds of food we take, perhaps, only occasionally. But we want bread every morning and evening in our lives. So is it with Christ. There is no day in our lives but we need his blood, his righteousness, his intercession and his grace. Well may he be called 'the bread of life'!

Do we know anything of spiritual hunger? Do we feel anything of craving and emptiness in conscience, heart and affections? Let us distinctly understand that Christ alone can relieve and supply us and that it is his office to relieve. We must come to him by faith. We must believe on him and commit our souls into his hands. So coming, he pledges his royal word we shall find lasting satisfaction for both time and eternity. It is written: 'He that cometh unto me shall never hunger, and he that believeth on me shall never thirst.'

For meditation: *Our Lord is not a spiritual delicacy to decorate the plate of a gourmet but necessary food for the spiritually starving.*

Suggested further reading: Matthew 10:11-15

It is possible to so press, abuse and misapply these words that they yield poison, not medicine. Our Lord does not mean that it is wrong under any circumstances to pass an unfavourable judgement on the conduct and opinions of others. We are exhorted to pass judgement (1 Thess. 5:21; 1 John 4:1), and so to condemn sin and error.

What our Lord means to condemn is a censorious and fault-finding spirit. A readiness to blame others for trifling offences, or matters of indifference, a habit of passing rash and hasty judgements, a disposition to magnify the errors and infirmities of our neighbour, and make the worst of them — this is what our Lord condemns. Christian love teaches us to be slow to find fault and to think the best of others (1 Cor. 13:7).

Our Lord emphasizes the importance of exercising discretion as to the person with whom we speak on the subject of religion. Everything is beautiful in its place and season. Our zeal is to be tempered by a prudent consideration of times, places and persons. Solomon gives us a warning (Prov. 9:8). It is not everyone to whom it is wise to open our mouths on spiritual subjects. There are many who from violent tempers or openly profligate habits are utterly incapable of valuing the things of the gospel. They will even fly into a passion and run into greater excesses of sin if you try to do good to their souls. To name the name of Christ to such people is to disobey verse 6. It rouses all their corruption and makes them angry. They are like the Jews at Corinth (Acts 18:6) and Nabal (1 Sam. 25:17).

This is a lesson which it is peculiarly difficult to use in a proper way. Great wisdom is needed because we are likely to err on the side of overcaution rather than of overzeal, to be silent rather than to speak too much. But what of ourselves? Do we not too often check our friends from giving us good advice by our moroseness and irritability of temper? Have we never turned against our kind advisers and silenced them by violence, passion, pride and impatient contempt of counsel?

For meditation: *When the truth makes us angry, and nothing more, it is barren in its effect* (James 1:19-21).

Suggested further reading: Romans 8:28-39

What does 'coming' mean? It means that movement of the soul which takes place when a man, feeling his sins and finding out that he cannot save himself, hears of Christ, applies to Christ, trusts in Christ, lays hold on Christ and leans all his weight on Christ for salvation. When this happens a man is said, in Scripture language, to 'come' to Christ.

What did our Lord mean by saying, 'I will in no wise cast him out'? He meant that he will not refuse to save anyone who comes to him, no matter what he may have been. His past sins may have been very great. His present weakness and infirmity may be very great. But does he come to Christ by faith? Then Christ will receive him graciously, pardon him freely, place him in the number of his dear children and give him everlasting life.

We are taught in verse 40 that Christ has brought into the world a salvation open and free to everyone. Our Lord draws a picture of it from the story of the brazen serpent, by which bitten Israelites in the wilderness were healed. Everyone that chose to 'look' at the brazen serpent might live. Just in the same way, everyone who desires eternal life may 'look' at Christ by faith and have it freely. There is no barrier, no limit, no restriction. The terms of the gospel are wide and simple. Everyone may 'look and live'.

We are taught in verse 39 that Christ will never allow any soul that is committed to him to be lost and cast away. He will keep it safe, from grace to glory, in spite of the world, the flesh and the devil. Not one bone of his mystical body shall ever be broken. Not one lamb of his flock shall ever be left behind in the wilderness. He will raise to glory, in the last day, the whole flock entrusted to his charge and not one shall be found missing.

For meditation: *With such a clear invitation to come to Christ and such great promises made to those who come, the foolishness and sinfulness of not coming are surely clear.*

Suggested further reading: Luke 11:5-13

In the second of our two readings our Lord stresses perseverance in prayer by means of an illustration. We are reminded what man can obtain from man in times of difficulty. Selfish and indolent as we are, we are capable of being roused to exertion by continual asking. The man who would not give three loaves at midnight for friendship's sake at length gave them to save himself from further trouble. The meaning is clear. If this is the case between man and man, how much more may we expect to obtain mercies from God in prayer?

We need to remember that it is far more easy to begin a habit of prayer than to keep it up. Myriads of professing Christians are taught to pray when they are young and then gradually leave off the practice as they grow up. Thousands take up the habit of praying for a while, after some special mercy or special affliction, and then little by little become cold about it, and at last lay it aside. The secret thought comes stealing over men's minds: 'It is no use to pray.' They see no visible benefit from it. They persuade themselves that they can get on just as well without prayer. Laziness and unbelief prevail over their hearts and at last they altogether 'restrain prayer before God' (Job 15:4).

Let us resist this feeling whenever we feel it rising within us. Let us resolve by God's grace that, however feeble and poor our prayers may seem to us, we will pray on. It is not for nothing that the Bible tells us to persist in prayer (Luke 18:1; Eph. 6:18; 1 Thess. 5:17). These expressions all look one way. They are meant to remind us of a danger and quicken us to a duty. The time and way in which our prayers shall be answered are matters we must leave entirely to God. But that every petition we offer in faith shall surely be answered we need not doubt. Let us lay our matters before God again and again, day after day, week after week, month after month, year after year. The answer may be long in coming, as it was in the case of Hannah and Zacharias (1 Sam. 1:27; Luke 1:13). But though it tarry let us pray on and wait for it.

For meditation: *Our prayers go into God's 'in-tray'. His wisdom determines the right time for their removal to the 'out-tray'. Shall we not trust his wisdom rather than ours?*

Suggested further reading: Romans 8:1-11

Christ's lowly condition, when he was upon earth, is a stumbling-block to the natural man. We read that 'The Jews murmured, because Jesus said, I am the bread that came down from heaven. And they said, Is not this Jesus, the son of Joseph, whose father and mother we know? How is it then that he saith, I came down from heaven?' Had our Lord come as a conquering king, with wealth and honours to bestow on his followers and mighty armies in his train, they would have been willing enough to receive him. But a poor and lowly and suffering Messiah was an offence to them. Their pride refused to believe that such a one was sent from God.

There is nothing that need surprise us in this. It is human nature showing itself in its true colours. We see the same thing in the days of the apostles. Christ crucified was 'to the Jews a stumbling-block, and to the Greeks foolishness' (1 Cor. 1:23). The cross was an offence to many wherever the gospel was preached.

The salvation of a believer is a present thing. Our Lord Jesus Christ says, 'Verily, verily, I say unto you, he that believeth on me hath everlasting life.' How many seem to think that forgiveness and acceptance with God are things which we cannot attain in this life, that they are things which are to be earned by a long course of repentance and faith and holiness — things which we may receive at the bar of God at last, but must never pretend to touch while we are in this world! It is a complete mistake to think so. The very moment a sinner believes on Christ he is justified and accepted. There is no condemnation for him. He has peace with God and that immediately and without delay. His name is in the book of life, however little he may be aware of it. He has a title to heaven, which death and hell and Satan cannot overthrow. Happy are they that know this truth! It is an essential part of the good news of the gospel.

For meditation: *True joy in the Lord can only exist where certainty rather than doubt reigns.*

Suggested further reading: Psalm 84:8-12

Our Lord employs three different words to express the idea of prayer — ask, seek, knock. He holds out the fullest, broadest promise to those who pray (v. 8). He illustrates God's readiness to hear our prayers by an argument drawn from the practice of parents on earth. Evil and selfish as they are by nature, they do not neglect the needs of their children according to the flesh. Much more will a God of love and mercy attend to the cries of those who are his children by grace.

Let us take special note of these words of our Lord about prayer. The poorest and most unlearned man can tell you that if we seek not we shall not find. But what is the good of knowing it if we do not use it? Knowledge not improved and well employed will only increase our condemnation at the last day.

Do we know anything of this asking, seeking and knocking? Why should we not? There is nothing so simple and plain as praying if a man really has a will to pray. There is nothing, unhappily, which men are so slow to do. They will use many forms of religion, attend many ordinances, do many things that are right before they will do this. And yet without it no soul can be saved!

God promises to give all good gifts (v. 11), especially the Holy Spirit (Luke 11:13). The Holy Spirit is beyond doubt the greatest gift which God can bestow on man. Having this gift we have all things: life, light, hope and heaven. Having this gift we have God the Father's boundless love, God the Son's atoning blood and full communion with all three persons of the blessed Trinity. And yet this mighty gift is held out by our Lord Jesus Christ as a gift to be obtained by prayer!

There are few Bible passages which so completely strip the unconverted man of his common excuses as this passage. He says that he is 'weak and helpless'. But does he ask to be made strong? He says he is 'wicked and corrupt'. But does he seek to be made better? He says he 'can do nothing of himself'. But does he pray for the grace of the Holy Spirit? So often we are what we are because we do not ask to be changed.

For meditation: *'What causes fights and quarrels among you? ... You want something but don't get it... When you ask, you do not receive, because you ask with wrong motives, that you may spend what you get on your pleasures'* (James 4:1-3).

Suggested further reading: Isaiah 65:1-7

We find our Lord saying, 'No man can come unto me, except the Father which hath sent me draw him.' Until the Father draws the heart of man by his grace, man will not believe.

The solemn truth contained in these words is one that needs careful weighing. It is vain to deny that without the grace of God no one ever can become a true Christian. We are spiritually dead and have no power to give ourselves life. We need a new principle put in us from above. Facts prove it. Preachers see it.

But after all, of what does this inability of man consist? In what part of our inward nature does this impotence reside? Here is a point on which many mistakes arise. For ever let us remember that the *will* of man is the part of him which is in fault. His inability is not physical, but moral. It would not be true to say that a man has a real wish and desire to come to Christ, but no power to come. It would be far more true to say that a man has no power to come because he has no desire or wish. It is not true that he would come if he could. It is true that he could come if he would. The corrupt will, the secret disinclination, the want of heart are the real causes of unbelief. It is here the mischief lies. The power that we want is a new will. It is precisely at this point that we need the 'drawing' of the Father.

These things, no doubt, are deep and mysterious. By truths like these God proves the faith and patience of his people. Can they believe him? Can they wait for a fuller explanation at the last day? What they see not now, they shall see hereafter. One thing at any rate is abundantly clear and that is man's responsibility for his own soul. His inability to come to Christ does not make an end of his accountableness. Both things are equally true. If lost at last, it will prove to have been his own fault. His blood will be on his own head.

For meditation: *Are you 'a man who remains stiff-necked after many rebukes, who will suddenly be destroyed'* (Prov. 29:1), *or are you willing to submit to the will of the Lord?* (Acts 22:10).

Suggested further reading: 1 Kings 18:16-24

In all doubtful matters between man and man we have a general principle for our guidance (v. 12). We are not to deal with others as others deal with us. This would be pure heathenism and mere selfishness. Real Christianity deals with others as it would like to be dealt with.

This is the golden rule indeed! It does not merely forbid all petty malice and revenge, all cheating and overreaching. It does much more. It settles a hundred difficult points which arise between men, not by laying down endless rules, but by one mighty principle. It gives a balance and measure by which duty is defined. What would we like others to do to us? Let us do it to them. What would we never want others to do to us? Let us not do it to them. A rule for honest use which decides many problems!

We are also given a caution about the way of the many in religion. It is not enough to think and do as others, to follow the fashion and swim with the stream. The way that leads to life is narrow and few travel on it. The way that leads to everlasting destruction is broad and full of travellers. These are fearful truths which ought to raise great searchings of heart in the minds of all who hear them. Which of the two roads are we on?

We may well tremble and be afraid if our religion is that of the multitude. To go and worship and hope like the rest is to pronounce our own condemnation. This is the broad way whose end is destruction. It is not saving religion.

We have no reason to be discouraged and downcast if the religion we profess is not popular and few agree with us. We must remember our Lord's words (v. 13). Repentance, faith in Christ and holiness of life have never been fashionable. The true flock of Christ has always been small. It must not move us to find that we are reckoned singular, peculiar, bigoted and narrow-minded. This is the 'narrow way'. Surely it is better to enter into life eternal with the few than to go to destruction with a great company.

For meditation: *Human religions can easily gain adherents because all that is required is obedience to rules. Christianity requires a change of heart. This is a work of God and far more radical than rule-keeping.*

Suggested further reading: Luke 23:39-43

The 'eating and drinking' of which Christ speaks do not mean any literal eating and drinking. Above all, the words were not spoken with any reference to the sacrament of the Lord's Supper.

For one thing, a literal 'eating and drinking' of Christ's body and blood would have been an idea utterly revolting to all Jews and flatly contradictory to an often-repeated precept of their law.

For another thing, to take a literal view of 'eating and drinking' is to interpose a bodily act between the soul of man and salvation. This is a thing for which there is no precedent in Scripture. The only things without which we cannot be saved are repentance and faith.

Last, but not least, to take a literal view of 'eating and drinking' would involve most blasphemous and profane consequences. It would shut out of heaven the penitent thief. He died long after these words were spoken, without any literal eating and drinking. Will any dare to say he had 'no life' in him? It would admit to heaven thousands of ignorant, godless communicants in the present day. They literally eat and drink, no doubt! But they have no eternal life and will not be raised to glory at the last day. Let these reasons be carefully pondered.

The plain truth is, there is a morbid anxiety in fallen man to put a carnal sense on scriptural expressions, wherever he possibly can. He struggles hard to make religion a matter of forms and ceremonies, of doing and performing, of sacraments and ordinances, of sense and sight. He secretly dislikes that system of Christianity which makes the state of heart the principal thing and labours to keep sacraments and ordinances in the second place. Happy is that Christian who remembers these things and stands on his guard!

For meditation: *Many of the Jews expected acceptance with God because of their outward ordinances — yet they perished* (1 Cor. 10:1-5).

Suggested further reading: 2 Timothy 4:1-5

The Lord Jesus gives us a general warning against false teachers in the church. If we would keep clear of the 'broad way' (v. 13) we must beware of false prophets. They will arise. They began in the days of the apostles. Even then the seeds of error were sown. They have appeared continually since. We must be prepared for them and be on our guard.

This is a warning that is much needed. There are thousands who seem to believe anything in religion if they hear it from an ordained minister. They forget that ministers may err as others. They are not infallible. Their teaching must be weighed in the balance of Holy Scripture. They are to be followed and believed as long as their doctrine agrees with the Bible, and not a minute longer. We are to try them by their fruits (v. 20). Sound doctrine and holy living are the marks of true prophets. Let us remember this. Our minister's mistakes will not excuse our own.

What is the best safeguard against false teaching? Beyond all doubt the regular study of God's Word with prayer for the teaching of the Holy Spirit. The Bible was given to be a lamp to our feet and a light to our path (Ps. 119:105). The man who reads it aright will never be allowed greatly to err. It is neglect of the Bible which makes so many a prey to the first false teacher whom they hear. They would fain have us believe that they are not learned and do not pretend to have decided opinions. The plain truth is that they are lazy and idle about reading the Bible and do not like the trouble of thinking for themselves. Nothing supplies false prophets with followers so much as spiritual sloth under a cloak of humility.

The world, the flesh and the devil are not the only dangers the Christian faces. There remains another yet, and that is the false prophet, the wolf in sheep's clothing. Happy is he who prays over his Bible and knows the difference between truth and error in religion. There is a difference, and we are meant to know it and use our knowledge.

For meditation: *Are you like the Bereans* (Acts 17:11) *or an easy prey for error?*

Suggested further reading: Hebrews 9:11-14

Few passages of Scripture have been so painfully wrested and perverted as that which we have now read. The Jews are not the only
people who have striven about its meaning. A sense has been put
upon it which it was never intended to bear. Fallen man, in interpreting the Bible, has an unhappy aptitude for turning meat into poison.
The things that were written for his benefit, he often makes an occasion for falling.

Let us consider carefully what these verses do mean. The expressions they contain are, no doubt, very remarkable. Let us try to
get some clear notion of their meaning.

The 'flesh and blood of the Son of man' mean that sacrifice of
his own body, which Christ offered up on the cross, when he died
for sinners. The atonement made by his death, the satisfaction made
by his sufferings as our Substitute, the redemption effected by his
enduring the penalty of our sins in his own body on the tree — this
seems to be the true idea that we should set before our minds.

The 'eating and drinking', without which there is no life in us,
means that reception of Christ's sacrifice which takes place when a
man believes on Christ crucified for salvation. It is an inward and
spiritual act of the heart and has nothing to do with the body. Whenever a man, feeling his own guilt and sinfulness, lays hold on Christ
and trusts in the atonement made for him by Christ's death, at once
he 'eats the flesh of the Son of man, and drinks his blood'. His soul
feeds on Christ's sacrifice by faith just as his body would feed on
bread. Believing, he is said to 'eat'. Believing, he is said to 'drink'.
And the special thing that he eats and drinks and gets benefit from is
the atonement made for his sins by Christ's death for him on Calvary.

For meditation: *Food left on a plate is of no benefit to the body.
When Christ is not received by faith he is of no benefit to the soul.*

Suggested further reading: John 6:60-71

Here is heart-piercing application. Our Lord turns from false prophets to false professors. How useless a mere outward profession of Christianity is! Not all that profess themselves and call themselves Christians shall be saved.

Let us take notice of this. It requires far more than most people seem to think necessary to save a soul. We may be baptized in the name of Christ and boast confidently of our ecclesiastical privileges. We may possess head knowledge and be quite satisfied with our own state. We may even be preachers and teachers of others and do many wonderful works in connection with our church. But all this time are we practically doing the will of our Father in heaven? Do we truly repent, truly believe and live holy and humble lives? If not, in spite of all our privileges and profession we shall miss heaven at last and be ever cast away. We shall hear those awful words: 'I never knew you: depart from me.'

The Day of Judgement will reveal strange things. The hopes of many who were thought great Christians while they lived will be utterly confounded. The rottenness of their religion will be exposed and put to shame before the whole world. It will then be proved that being saved means more than making a profession. We must practise our Christianity as well as profess it. Let us often think of that great day. Let us often judge ourselves, that we be not judged and condemned by our Lord. Whatever else we are, let us aim at being real, true and sincere.

For meditation: *It is vital in these days that we realize that gifts do not indicate conversion. A man may have gifts and be damned. Balaam was a prophet of God* (Num. 22:18-19), *but was killed by the Israelites as an evil man* (Num. 31:8,16) *and is always condemned in subsequent Scriptures* (2 Peter 2:15; Jude 11; Rev. 2:14). *Judas was an apostle* (Matt. 10:4), *with gifts of healing and 'exorcism'* (Matt. 10:1), *yet a traitor* (Matt. 10:4) *and a devil* (John 6:70-71). *As gifts cannot save they are no basis for fellowship and no sure guide to the possession of saving grace.*

Suggested further reading: Exodus 12:1-13

The practical lessons which may be gathered from the whole passage are weighty and important. The point being once settled that 'the flesh and blood' in these verses mean Christ's atonement and the 'eating and drinking' mean faith, we may find in these verses great principles of truth which lie at the very root of Christianity.

We may learn that faith in Christ's atonement is a thing of absolute necessity to salvation. Just as there was no safety for the Israelite in Egypt who did not eat the Passover lamb, in the night when the first-born were slain, so there is no life for the sinner who does not eat the flesh of Christ and drink his blood.

We may learn that faith in Christ's atonement unites us by the closest possible bonds to our Saviour and entitles us to the highest privileges. Our souls shall find full satisfaction for all their wants: 'His flesh is meat indeed, and his blood is drink indeed.' All things are secured to us that we can need for time and eternity: 'Whoso eateth my flesh and drinketh my blood hath eternal life, and I will raise him up at the last day.'

Last, but not least, we may learn that faith in Christ's atonement is a personal act, a daily act and an act that can be felt. No one can eat and drink for us and no one, in like manner, can believe for us. We need food every day, and not once a week or once a month, and, in like manner, we need to employ faith every day. We feel benefit when we have eaten and drunk, we feel strengthened, nourished and refreshed and, in like manner, if we believe truly, we shall feel the better for it, by sensible hope and peace in our inward man.

For meditation: *It is because Christ died at Calvary that salvation is freely offered to us in the gospel. It is by faith that salvation is freely received by us to our eternal benefit.*

Suggested further reading: James 1:19-25

Here is a striking picture of two classes of hearers: those who hear and do nothing, and those who hear and do as well as hear. They, their histories and their ends are placed before us.

We have the man who hears Christian teaching and practises what he hears. He does not content himself with listening to exhortations to repent, believe in Christ and live a holy life. He actually repents, believes, ceases to do evil, learns to do well, abhors that which is sinful and cleaves to that which is good. He hears and does (James 1:22).

What is the result? In the time of trial his religion does not fail him. The floods of sickness, sorrow, poverty, disappointments, bereavements beat upon him in vain. His faith does not give way. His comforts do not utterly forsake him. His religion may have cost him trouble in times past and have been obtained with labour and tears, earnest seeking and wrestling in prayer. But his labour has not been thrown away. He now reaps a rich reward. The religion that can stand trial is true religion.

We have the man who hears Christian teaching but never gets beyond hearing. He satisfies himself with listening and approving but goes no further. He flatters himself, perhaps, that all is right with his soul because he has feelings, conviction and desires of a spiritual kind. In these he rests. He never really breaks off from sin, and casts aside the spirit of the world. He never really lays hold of Christ. He never really takes up the cross. He is a hearer of the truth but nothing more.

What is the result? This man's religion breaks down entirely under the first flood of tribulation. It fails him completely like a sun-dried stream when his need is greatest. It leaves its possessor high and dry like a wreck on a sandbank, a scandal to the church, a byword to the infidel and a misery to himself. Most true it is that what costs little is worth little! A religion that consists in nothing but hearing sermons is a useless thing.

For meditation: *We remember very little of what we hear and read as it is. If we then go on to apply very little of what is remembered, what spiritual benefit can possibly accrue?*

Suggested further reading: 1 Corinthians 1:18-25

The true antidote to wrong views of baptism and the Lord's Supper is a right understanding of the third and sixth chapters of St John's Gospel and the whole of St John's First Epistle. While he altogether omits to describe the institution of the Lord's Supper, and says little or nothing about baptism in the Gospel, he dwells at the same time most strongly on these two mighty truths, which he foresaw were in danger of being forgotten — viz. the new birth and faith in the atonement. Surely it is possible to honour baptism and the Lord's Supper without thrusting them in everywhere in our interpretation of Scripture.

We are told that 'many' who had followed our Lord for a season were offended when he spoke of 'eating his flesh and drinking his blood'. They murmured and said, 'This is an hard saying; who can hear it?' Murmurs and complaints of this kind are very common. It must never surprise us to hear them. They have been, they are, they will be as long as the world stands. To some Christ's sayings appear hard to understand. To others, as in the present case, they appear hard to believe and harder still to obey. It is just one of the many ways in which the natural corruption of man shows itself. So long as the heart is naturally proud, worldly, unbelieving and fond of self-indulgence, if not of sin, so long there will never be wanting people who will say of Christian doctrines and precepts, 'These are hard sayings; who can hear them?'

Humility is the frame of mind which we should labour and pray for, if we would not be offended. If we find any of Christ's sayings hard to understand, we should humbly remember our present ignorance and believe that we shall know more by and by. If we find any of his sayings difficult to obey, we should humbly recollect that he will never require of us impossibilities and that, what he bids us do, he will give us grace to perform.

For meditation: *Salvation by works is always popular because it exalts the efforts of men. Salvation through the blood of Christ is repugnant to many because it exalts the efforts of another in the light of the inadequacy of self.*

Suggested further reading: Matthew 8:5-13

These verses describe the miraculous cure of a sick man. A centurion in the Roman army applies to our Lord on behalf of his servant and obtains what he requests. A greater miracle of healing than this is nowhere recorded in the Gospels. Without even seeing the sufferer, without touch of hand or look of eye, our Lord restores health to a dying man by a single word. He speaks and the sick man is cured. He commands and the disease departs. We read of no prophet or apostle who wrought miracles in this manner. We see here the finger of God.

The kindness of the centurion appears in three ways. He cares for his servant tenderly when sick and takes pains to have him restored to health (v. 3). He does not despise the Jewish people as many other Gentiles did. The elders of the Jews bear a strong testimony to this (v. 5). He liberally supported the Jewish place of worship at Capernaum, not loving Israel in words and tongue only, but in deed (v. 5).

Let us learn a lesson from this centurion's example. Let us, like him, show kindness to everyone with whom we have to do. Let us strive to have an eye ready to see, and a hand ready to help, and a heart ready to feel, and a will ready to do good to all. Let us be ready to weep with them that weep and rejoice with them that rejoice (Rom. 12:15). This is the way to recommend our religion and make it beautiful before men. Kindness is a grace that all can understand. This is one way to be like our blessed Saviour. If there is one feature in his character more notable than another it is his unwearied kindness and love. There is one way to be happy in the world and see good days. Kindness always brings its own reward. The kind person will seldom be without friends.

For meditation: *Kindness to all is a characteristic of God* (Luke 6:32-36). *Christians are exhorted to show similar kindnesses, doing good to those who are fellow believers in Christ especially, but also to men in general* (Gal. 6:10). *Even our enemies are to be the recipients of our kindness* (Luke 6:35) *and such action in the face of evil has its effect in overcoming evil and turning hostility into friendship* (Rom. 12:20-21).

Suggested further reading: Ezekiel 37:1-10

Our Lord says, 'It is the Spirit that quickeneth.' By this he means that it is the Holy Ghost who is the special author of spiritual life in man's soul. By his agency it is first imparted and afterwards sustained and kept up. If the Jews thought he meant that men could have spiritual life by bodily eating or drinking, they were greatly mistaken.

Our Lord says, 'The flesh profiteth nothing.' By this he means that neither his flesh nor any other flesh, literally eaten, can do good to the soul. Spiritual benefit is not to be had through the mouth, but through the heart. The soul is not a material thing and cannot therefore be nourished by material food.

Our Lord says, 'The words that I speak unto you, they are spirit and they are life.' By this he signifies that his words and teachings, applied to the heart by the Holy Ghost, are the true means of producing spiritual influence and conveying spiritual life. By words thoughts are begotten and aroused. By words mind and conscience are stirred. And Christ's words especially are spirit-stirring and life-giving.

The principle contained in this verse, however faintly we may grasp its full meaning, deserves peculiar attention in these times. There is a tendency in many minds to attach an excessive importance to the outward and visible or 'doing' part of religion. They seem to think that the sum and substance of Christianity consists in baptism and the supper of the Lord, in public ceremonies and forms, in appeals to the eye and ear and bodily excitement. Surely they forget that it is 'the Spirit that quickeneth' and that the 'flesh profiteth nothing'. It is not so much by noisy public demonstrations as by the still quiet work of the Holy Ghost on hearts that God's cause prospers. It is Christ's words entering into consciences which 'are spirit and life'.

For meditation: *Truth and life come by God's Word and God's Spirit. Never separate the two.*

Suggested further reading: Acts 10:1-8

The humility of the centurion appears in his remarkable message when the Lord was not far from his house (vv. 6-7). Such expressions are in striking contrast to the attitude of the Jews (vv. 4-5).

Humility like this is one of the strongest evidences of the indwelling of the Spirit of God. We know nothing of it by nature, for we are all born proud. The principle that the Holy Spirit works in the soul of man is to make him convinced of his sin, to show him his vileness and corruption, to put him in his right place, to make him lowly and self-abased. Few of our Lord's sayings are so often repeated as that which closes the parable of the Pharisee and the publican (Luke 18:14). To have great gifts and do great works for God is not given to all believers. But all believers ought to strive to be clothed with humility.

We have a beautiful example of faith in the request that he made to our Lord (v. 7). He thinks it needless for our Lord to come to the place where his servant lay dying. He regards our Lord as one possessing authority over diseases as complete as his own authority over his soldiers, or a Roman emperor's authority over himself. He believes that a word of command from Jesus is sufficient to send sickness away. He asks to see no sign or wonder. He declares his confidence that Jesus is an almighty Master and King, and that diseases, like obedient servants, will at once depart at his orders.

Faith like this was indeed rare when our Lord was on the earth. The Pharisees and the people wanted miracles and signs. Our Lord responds to his faith (v. 9) and rebukes the Jews. The faith of a Roman soldier proved stronger than that of the Jews.

Let us not forget to walk in the steps of this blessed spirit of faith which the centurion here exhibited. Our eyes do not yet behold things spiritual, but we have the word of Christ's promises. Let us rest on it and fear nothing. Let us not doubt that every word that Christ has spoken shall be made good. The word of Christ is a sure foundation.

For meditation: *We love to undermine faith by telling ourselves that we must be 'practical' as well as religious.*

Suggested further reading: Psalm 139:1-6

Christ has a perfect knowledge of the hearts of men. We read that 'He knew from the beginning who they were that believed not, and who should betray him.'

Sentences like this are found so frequently in the Gospels that we are apt to underrate their importance. Yet there are few truths which we shall find it so good for our souls to remember as that which is contained in the sentence before us. The Saviour with whom we have to do is one who knows all things!

What light this throws on the marvellous patience of the Lord Jesus in the days of his earthly ministry! He knew the sorrow and humiliation before him and the manner of his death. He knew the unbelief and treachery of some who professed to be his familiar friends, allowing one whom he knew to be about to betray him to be one of his apostles. It was doubtless meant to teach us that false profession must be expected everywhere and must not surprise us. How much we ought to tolerate and put up with, if our Lord tolerated Judas near him! But 'for the joy that was set before him' he endured it all (Heb. 12:2).

What light this throws on the folly of hypocrisy and false profession in religion! Let those who are guilty of it recollect that they cannot deceive Christ. He sees them, knows them and will expose them at the last day, except they repent. Whatever we are as Christians and however weak, let us be real, true and sincere.

Finally, what light this throws on the daily pilgrimage of all true Christians! Let them take comfort in the thought that their Master knows them. However much unknown and misunderstood by the world, their Master knows their hearts and will comfort them at the last day. Happy is he who, in spite of many infirmities, can say with Peter, 'Lord, thou knowest all things; thou knowest that I love thee' (John 21:17).

For meditation: *Nothing goes unnoticed. The smallest good shall receive its reward* (Matt. 10:42).

Suggested further reading: 1 Corinthians 15:50-58

What sorrow sin has brought into the world! Here we have the death of the only son of a widowed mother. All this misery is the result of sin. God made all things very good (Gen. 1:31) but sin entered the world and death through sin (Rom. 5:12). This world is full of sickness, pain, infirmity, poverty, labour and trouble. Universally the history of families is full of lamentation, weeping, mourning and woe. It can all be traced to sin. How much we ought to hate sin! Instead of loving it, cleaving to it, dallying with it, excusing it, playing with it, we ought to hate it with a deadly hatred, waging a ceaseless warfare against it, abhorring it (Rom. 12:9).

How deep is the compassion of our Lord's heart! He did not wait to be applied to for help but addressed the weeping mother (v. 13). A few seconds later the meaning of his words became plain. The widow's son was restored to her alive. Her darkness was turned into light and her sorrow into joy.

Our Lord has not changed (Heb. 13:8). His heart is still as compassionate. His sympathy with sufferers is still as strong. There is no friend or comforter who can be compared to Christ. In all our days of darkness, which must needs be many, let us turn first to Christ for comfort. He will never fail us, never disappoint us, never refuse to take interest in our sorrows. He lives to heal the brokenhearted and to be a Friend that sticks closer than a brother.

What almighty power our Lord has to bring the dead corpse back to life! He speaks to a dead corpse and at once it becomes a living person. In a moment, in the twinkling of an eye, the heart, the lungs, the brain, the senses again resume their work and discharge their duties (vv. 14-15).

This is a pledge of the solemn resurrection. This same Jesus that raised one man shall one day raise all (John 5:28-29). When the trumpet sounds and Christ commands, there can be no refusal or escape. All must appear before him in their bodies to be judged.

For meditation: *Pause and ask the question: 'Am I ready to meet God?'*

Suggested further reading: Matthew 13:18-23

What an old sin backsliding is! We read that when our Lord had explained what he meant by 'eating and drinking his flesh and blood', 'from that time many went back and walked no more with him'.

The true grace of God no doubt is an everlasting possession. From this men never fall away entirely when they have once received it. 'The foundation of God standeth sure' (2 Tim. 2:19). 'My sheep shall never perish' (John 10:28). But there is counterfeit grace and unreal religion in the church, wherever there is true, and from counterfeit grace thousands may and do fall away. Like the stony-ground hearers in the parable of the sower, many 'have no root in themselves, and so in time of temptation fall away'. All is not gold that glitters. All blossoms do not come to fruit. All are not Israel which are called Israel. Men may have feelings, desires, convictions, resolutions, hopes, joys, sorrows in religion and yet never have the grace of God. They may run well for a season and bid fair to reach heaven and yet break down entirely after a time, go back to the world and end like Demas, Judas Iscariot and Lot's wife.

It must never surprise us to see and hear of such cases in our own days. If it happened in our Lord's time and under our Lord's teaching, much more may we expect it to happen now. Above all, it must never shake our faith and discourage us in our course. On the contrary, we must make up our minds that there will be backsliders in the church as long as the world stands. The sneering infidel who defends his unbelief by pointing at them must find some better argument than their example. He forgets that there will always be counterfeit coin where there is true money.

For meditation: *Machines that are never serviced prove inefficient and break down. Christians that neglect their relationship with God decline and grow cold.*

Suggested further reading: 1 Corinthians 1:18-25

When John was a prisoner of Herod (Matt. 11:2) and his active life was drawing to a close, he still sends men to Christ. John exhibited great forethought about his disciples before he left the world. He sent them to Jesus with a question (v. 19), doubtless calculating that they would receive such an answer as would make an indelible impression on their minds. He sends them to Jesus that they might see what sort of teacher he is and become acquainted with him for their benefit after John has gone. Should not all ministers, parents and friends have similar concern for the spiritual welfare of those they will leave behind? While we are here let us often instruct them in the things of the gospel so that we might die peacefully, knowing that we have told others to go to Jesus and follow him.

In response our Lord makes no formal declaration of his Messiahship. He simply supplies the messengers with facts to report as he does miracles and sends them away (vv. 21-22). Christ will have them know him by his fruits (Matt. 7:20), by his works and teaching. This is the right way to test churches and ministers. We examine the works they do for God and the fruits they bring forth.

Our Lord gave a solemn warning to John's disciples (v. 23). He knew what danger they were in. He knew they were disposed to question his claim to be the Messiah because of his lowly appearance. They saw no signs of a king about him: no riches, no royal apparel, no guards, no courtiers and no crown. They only saw a poor man attended by fishermen and publicans and their pride rebelled against the idea that this was the Messiah. Our Lord read their hearts and cautioned them.

The warning is just as needful now. So long as the world stands, Christ and his gospel will be a stumbling-block to many. To hear that we are all lost and guilty sinners and cannot save ourselves, that we must give up our own righteousness and trust in one who was crucified between two thieves, to hear that we must be saved by free grace, in the same way as publicans and harlots, offends our pride, but it is so!

For meditation: *Whether jewel-bedecked or lice-ridden, there is only one Saviour and one way of salvation for all.*

Suggested further reading: Matthew 16:13-20

Our Lord had said to the twelve, when many went back, 'Will ye also go away?' At once Peter replied, with characteristic zeal and fervour, 'Lord, to whom shall we go? Thou hast the words of eternal life. And we believe and are sure that thou art that Christ, the Son of the living God.'

The confession contained in these words is a very remarkable one. Living in a professedly Christian land and surrounded by Christian privileges, we can hardly form an adequate idea of its real value. For a humble Jew to say of one whom scribes and Pharisees and Sadducees agreed in rejecting, 'Thou hast the words of eternal life; thou art the Christ,' was an act of mighty faith. No wonder that our Lord said in another place, 'Blessed art thou, Simon Bar-jona: for flesh and blood hath not revealed it unto thee, but my Father which is in heaven' (Matt. 16:17).

But the question with which Peter begins is just as remarkable as his confession. 'To whom shall we go?' said the noble-hearted apostle. 'Whom shall we follow? To what teacher shall we take ourselves? Where shall we find any guide to heaven to compare with thee? What shall we gain by forsaking thee?'

The question is one which every true Christian may boldly ask when urged and tempted to give up his religion and go back to the world. It is easy for those who hate religion to pick holes in our conduct, to make objections to our doctrines, to find fault with our practices. It may be hard sometimes to give them any answer. But after all, 'To whom shall we go,' if we give up our religion? Where shall we find such peace and hope and solid comfort as in serving Christ, however poorly we serve him? Can we better ourselves by turning our back on Christ and going back to our old ways? We cannot. Then let us hold on our way and persevere.

For meditation: *Our Lord is not a way, a truth and a life amongst many others, but **the** way, **the** truth, **the** life* (John 14:6).

Suggested further reading: 1 Peter 1:10-12

Jesus takes care of the characters of his faithful servants. He defended the reputation of John the Baptist as soon as his messengers were departed, lest the people should think lightly of John because of his imprisonment or his questions. He pleads the cause of his absent friend, warmly rejecting the idea that John was a wavering and unstable character (v. 24), a hanger-on at the court of kings (v. 25). He exalts him as a prophet who himself was the subject of a prophecy (vv. 26-27).

There is comfort here for all believers who are suspected, slandered and falsely accused. The accuser of the brethren is ever active. He knows that slanders are easily produced, received and propagated, and only with great difficulty silenced. But the Christian has a heavenly Advocate who knows his sorrows, will not desert him and who will one day plead his cause before the whole world.

Believers under the new covenant have vastly superior privileges to those under the old. Jesus commends John's grace and gifts but contrasts his privileges with those of later believers (v. 28). The weakest believer understands things, with the teaching of Paul this side of Calvary, that John the Baptist could never have explained. Truths which were seen through a glass darkly are now as plain as noonday. The child who knows the story of the cross possesses a key to religious knowledge which patriarchs and prophets never enjoyed. Let us learn to be thankful for our privileges.

Every man possesses a power to ruin himself in hell. Like the Pharisees we may reject God's offer of salvation (v. 30). By continued impenitence and unbelief, by persevering in the love and practice of sin, by pride, self-will, laziness and determined love of the world, we may bring upon ourselves everlasting destruction. If this takes place we shall have no one to blame but ourselves. God has no pleasure in our deaths (Ezek. 18:32). Christ is willing to gather men (Matt. 23:37) but they will not come.

For meditation: *The greater our privileges, the greater our responsibilities* (Luke 12:47-48).

Suggested further reading: Matthew 19:16-22

What little benefit some men get from religious privileges! We read that our Lord said, 'Have not I chosen you twelve, and one of you is a devil?' And it goes on, 'He spake of Judas Iscariot, the son of Simon.'

If ever there was a man who had great privileges and opportunities, that man was Judas Iscariot. A chosen disciple, a constant companion of Christ, a witness of his miracles, a hearer of his sermons, a commissioned preacher of his kingdom, a fellow and friend of Peter, James and John — it would be impossible to imagine a more favourable position for a man's soul. Yet if anyone ever fell hopelessly into hell and made shipwreck at last for eternity, that man was Judas Iscariot. The character of that man must have been black indeed, of whom our Lord could say he is 'a devil'.

Let us settle it firmly in our minds that the possession of religious privileges alone is not enough to save our souls. It is neither place, nor light, nor company, nor opportunities, but grace that man needs to make him a Christian. With grace we may serve God in the most difficult position — like Daniel in Babylon, Obadiah in Ahab's court and the saints in Nero's household. Without grace we may live in the full sunshine of Christ's countenance and yet, like Judas, be miserably cast away. Then let us never rest till we have grace reigning in our souls. Grace is to be had for the asking. There is one sitting at the right hand of God who has said, 'Ask, and it shall be given you' (Matt. 7:7). The Lord Jesus is more willing to give grace than man is to seek it. If men have it not, it is because they do not ask it.

For meditation: *Those who are so near to Christ yet so far from him will have an eternity of irreversible regret.*

Suggested further reading: Luke 15:14-24

The hearts of unconverted men are often desperately perverse as well as wicked. Children at play were not more wayward, perverse and hard to please than the Jews of our Lord's day. Nothing would satisfy them. They were always finding fault. Whatever ministry God employed amongst them, they took exception to it. Whatever messenger God sent amongst them, they were not pleased. John the Baptist, living a retired, ascetic, self-denying life, was accused of being indwelt by a devil (v. 33). Our Lord, with his normal social habits of eating and drinking, was accused of being a gluttonous drunkard (v. 34). It was evident that the Jews intended to receive no message from God at all. Their pretended objections were only a cloak to cover over their hatred of God's truth. What they really disliked was, not so much God's ministers, as God himself!

The world has not changed! Is it not a fact that many who strive to serve Christ faithfully and walk closely with God find their neighbours and relations always dissatisfied with their conduct? No matter how holy and consistent their lives may be, they are always thought to be wrong. If they withdraw entirely from the world, the cry is raised that they are too exclusive, narrow-minded, sour-spirited and righteous overmuch. If they go into society and endeavour to take an interest in their neighbours' pursuits, the remark is soon made that they are no better than other people and have no more real religion than those that make no profession at all. Whatever God's servants do, they are blamed.

The plain truth is that the natural heart of man hates God. The carnal mind dislikes God's law, God's gospel and God's people. It will always find some excuse for disbelieving and disobeying. The doctrine of repentance is too strict for it! The doctrine of faith is too easy! John the Baptist is too other-worldly. Our Lord is too worldly. And so the heart of man excuses itself for sitting in its sins. We must make up our minds that we cannot please everybody. We must be content to walk in Christ's steps and let the world say what it likes.

For meditation: *It is easy to justify disobedience by calling the excuses we have reasons.*

Suggested further reading: 1 Kings 22:1-8

The chapter we now begin is divided from the preceding one by a wide interval of time. The many miracles which our Lord wrought while he 'walked in Galilee' are passed over by St John in comparative silence. The events which he was specially inspired to record are those which took place in or near Jerusalem.

We are told that even our Lord's 'brethren did not believe in him'. Holy and harmless and blameless as he was in life, some of his nearest relatives according to the flesh did not receive him as the Messiah. It was bad enough that his own people, 'the Jews sought to kill him'. But it was even worse that 'his brethren did not believe'.

Verse 7 reveals one of those secret principles which influence men in their treatment of religion. They help to explain that deadly enmity with which many during our Lord's earthly ministry regarded him and his gospel. It was not so much the high doctrines which he preached as the high standard of practice which he proclaimed which gave offence. It was not even his claim to be the Messiah which men disliked so much as his witness against the wickedness of their lives. In short, they could have tolerated his opinions if he would only have spared their sins.

The principle, we may be sure, is one of universal application. It is at work now just as much as it was nineteen hundred years ago. The real cause of many people's dislike to the gospel is the holiness of living which it demands. Teach abstract doctrines only and few will find any fault. Denounce the fashionable sins of the day and call on men to repent and walk consistently with God and thousands at once will be offended. The true reason why many profess to be infidels and abuse Christianity is the witness that Christianity bears against their own bad lives. Like Ahab, they hate it, 'because it does not prophesy good concerning them, but evil' (1 Kings 22:8).

For meditation: *Does a lack of opposition suggest a lack of godliness?* (2 Tim. 3:12).

Suggested further reading: Proverbs 8:1-11

The wisdom of God's ways is always recognized and acknowledged by those who are wise-hearted (v. 35). Though the vast majority of the Jews were hardened and unreasonable, there were some who were not. Those few were the children of wisdom. Those few by their lives and obedience declared their full conviction that God's ways of dealing with the Jews were wise and right, and that John the Baptist and the Lord Jesus were both worthy of all honour.

The saying of our Lord about the generation among whom he lived describes a state of things that will always be found in the church of Christ. In spite of the cavils, sneers, objections and unkind remarks with which the gospel is received by the majority of mankind, there will always be some in every country who will assent to it and obey it with delight. A 'little flock' will never be lacking who hears the voice of the Shepherd gladly and counts all his ways right. The children of this world may mock at the gospel and pour contempt on the lives of believers. They may count their practice madness and see no wisdom and beauty in their ways. But God will take care to see that he has a people in every age. There will always be some who will assert the perfect excellence of the doctrine and requirements of the gospel and who will justify the wisdom of him who sent it. And these, however much the world may despise them, are they whom Jesus calls wise. They are 'wise unto salvation through faith in Christ Jesus' (2 Tim. 3:15).

Do we deserve to be called children of wisdom? Have we been taught by the Spirit to know the Lord Jesus Christ? Have the eyes of our understanding been opened? Have we the wisdom that comes from above? If we are truly wise let us not be ashamed to confess our Master before men. Let us declare boldly that we approve the whole of his gospel, all its doctrines and its requirements.

For meditation: *Paul said that his ability to speak of the things of God was rooted in his belief of their truth (2 Cor. 4:13-14). In an age when Christians have an increasing tendency to be silent, could it be that the root of the problem is a lack of conviction about the gospel and its doctrines?*

Suggested further reading: 2 Timothy 4:9-18

That great scriptural doctrine, man's need of preventing and converting grace, stands out here, as if written with a sunbeam. It becomes all who question that doctrine to look at this passage and consider. Let them observe that seeing Christ's miracles, hearing Christ's teaching, living in Christ's own company were not enough to make men believers. The mere possession of spiritual privileges never yet made anyone a Christian. All is useless without the effectual and applying work of God the Holy Ghost. No wonder that our Lord said in another place, 'No man can come to me, except the Father which hath sent me draw him' (John 6:44).

The true servants of Christ in every age will do well to remember this. They are often surprised and troubled to find that in religion they stand alone. They are apt to fancy that it must be their own fault that all around them are not converted like themselves. They are ready to blame themselves because their families remain worldly and unbelieving. But let them look at the verse before us. In our Lord Jesus Christ there was no fault either in temper, word, or deed. Yet even Christ's own 'brethren did not believe in him'.

Our blessed Master has truly learned by experience how to sympathize with all his people who stand alone. This is a thought 'full of sweet, pleasant and unspeakable comfort'. He knows the heart of every isolated believer and can be touched with the feeling of his trials. He has drunk this bitter cup. He has passed through this fire. Let all who are fainting and cast down, because brothers and sisters despise their religion, turn to Christ for comfort and pour out their hearts before him. He 'has suffered himself being tempted' in this way and he can help as well as feel (Heb. 2:18).

For meditation: *Never has anyone known desertion as our Lord knew it* (Matt. 27:46). *He is uniquely suited to sympathize with the lonely.*

Suggested further reading: Amos 2:1 - 3:2

There is an exceeding wickedness in wilful impenitence. Our Lord declares that it shall be more tolerable for Tyre, Sidon and Sodom in the Day of Judgement than for those towns where people had heard his sermons and seen his miracles but not repented.

There is something very solemn in this saying. Let us look at it well. Let us think for a moment what dark, immoral, profligate places Tyre and Sidon must have been. Let us call to mind the unspeakable wickedness of Sodom. Let us remember that the cities named by our Lord, Chorazin, Bethsaida and Capernaum, were probably no worse than other Jewish towns and at all events were far better than Tyre, Sidon and Sodom. And then let us observe that the people of Chorazin, Bethsaida and Capernaum are to be in lowest hell, because they heard the gospel and yet did not repent, because they had the greatest religious advantages and yet did not use them. How awful this sounds!

Surely these words ought to make the ears of everyone tingle who hears the gospel regularly and yet remains unconverted. How great is the guilt of such a man before God! How great the danger in which he daily stands! Moral and decent and respectable as his life may be, he is actually more guilty than an idolatrous Tyrian or Sidonian, or a miserable inhabitant of Sodom. They had no spiritual light; he has and neglects it. They heard no gospel; he hears but does not obey it. Their hearts might have been softened if they had enjoyed his privileges. Tyre and Sidon would have repented. Sodom would have remained to this day. His heart under the full blaze of the gospel remains hard and unmoved. There is but one painful conclusion to be drawn. His guilt will be found greater than theirs at the last day.

May we often think about Chorazin, Bethsaida and Capernaum! Let us settle it in our minds that it will never do to be content with merely hearing and liking the gospel. We must go further than this. We must actually repent and be converted.

For meditation: *Every hearing of the gospel robs men of their excuses and makes them culpable before God.*

Suggested further reading: Matthew 10:34-39

We are told that 'There was much murmuring among the people concerning him: for some said, He is a good man: others said, Nay; but he deceiveth the people.' The words which old Simeon had spoken thirty years before were here accomplished in a striking manner. He had said to our Lord's mother, 'This child is set for the fall and rising again of many in Israel: and for a sign which shall be spoken against ... that the thoughts of many hearts may be revealed' (Luke 2:34-35). In the diversities of opinion about our Lord which arose among the Jews, we see the good old man's saying fulfilled.

In the face of such a passage as this, the endless differences and divisions about religion, which we see on all sides in the present day, ought never to surprise us. The open hatred of some towards Christ, the carping, fault-finding, prejudiced spirit of others, the bold confession of the few faithful ones, the timid, man-fearing temper of the many faithless ones, the unceasing war of words and strife of tongues with which the churches of Christ are so sadly familiar are only modern symptoms of an old disease. Such is the corruption of human nature that Christ is the cause of division among men wherever he is preached. So long as the world stands, some when they hear of him will love and some will hate; some will believe and some will believe not. That deep, prophetical saying of his will be continually verified: 'Think not that I come to send peace on earth; I came not to send peace, but a sword' (Matt. 10:34).

What think we of Christ ourselves? This is the one question with which we have to do. Let us never be ashamed to be of that little number who believe on him, hear his voice, follow him and confess him before men. While others waste their time in vain jangling and unprofitable controversy, let us take up the cross and give all diligence to make our calling and election sure.

For meditation: *Many divisions are unnecessary in this world and ought to be avoided, but divisions over Christ are essential and eternal.*

Suggested further reading: Matthew 18:1-5

Let us learn the excellence of a childlike and teachable frame of mind (v. 25). It is not for us to attempt to explain why some receive and believe the gospel while others do not. The sovereignty of God in this matter is a great mystery: we cannot fathom it. But one thing, at all events, stands out in the Scriptures as a great practical truth to be had in everlasting remembrance. Those from whom the gospel is hidden are generally wise and prudent in their own eyes. Those to whom the gospel is revealed are generally humble, simple-minded and willing to learn. The words of the Virgin Mary are continually being fulfilled (Luke 1:53).

Let us watch against pride in every shape — pride of intellect, pride of wealth, pride in our own goodness, pride in our own deserts. Nothing is so likely to keep a man out of heaven and prevent him seeing Christ as pride. So long as we think we are something we shall never be saved. Let us pray for and cultivate humility. Let us seek to know ourselves aright and to find out our place in the sight of a holy God. The beginning of the way to heaven is to feel that we are on the way to hell and to be willing to be taught of the Spirit.

Our Lord Jesus Christ has a greatness and a majesty (v. 27). The psalmist's words are fitting as we contemplate these words (Ps. 139:6). We see something of the perfect union that exists between the First and Second Persons of the Trinity. We see something of the immeasurable superiority of the Lord Jesus to all who are nothing more than men. But still we must confess that there are heights and depths in this verse which are beyond our feeble comprehension.

Let us draw from these words the great practical truth that all power and authority in everything that concerns our soul's interests is placed in our Lord Jesus Christ's hands. He bears the keys: to him we must go for admission into heaven. He is the door: through him we must enter. He is the Shepherd: we must hear his voice and follow him. If we have Christ we have all things (v. 27; 1 Cor. 3:22).

For meditation: *Man contributes nothing to his salvation but his sin. Where then is his ground for boasting and pride?*

Suggested further reading: Acts 18:24-28

The difficulty of finding out 'what is truth' in religion is a common subject of complaint among men. They point to the many differences which prevail among Christians on matters of doctrine and profess to be unable to decide who is right. In thousands of cases this professed inability to find out truth becomes an excuse for living without any religion at all.

The saying of our Lord before us is one that demands the serious attention of persons in this state of mind. It supplies an argument whose edge and point they will find it hard to evade. It teaches that one secret of getting the key of knowledge is to practise honestly what we know, and that if we conscientiously use the light that we now have, we shall soon find more light coming down into our minds. In short, there is a sense in which it is true that by doing we shall come to knowing.

There is a mine of truth in this principle. Well would it be for men if they would act upon it. Instead of saying, as some do, 'I must first know everything clearly, and then I will act,' we should say, 'I will diligently use such knowledge as I possess and believe that in the using fresh knowledge will be given to me.' How many mysteries this simple plan would solve! How many hard things would soon become plain if men would honestly live up to their light and 'follow on to know the Lord'! (Hosea 6:3).

It should never be forgotten that God deals with us as moral beings and not as beasts or stones. He loves to encourage us to self-exertion and diligent use of such means as we have in our hands. The plain things in religion are undeniably very many. Let a man honestly attend to them and he shall be taught the deep things of God. Let him humbly use what little knowledge he has got and God will soon give him more.

For meditation: *Because Apollos told others what he knew, he learned more of what he needed to know. When we use the little we have, we gain more.*

Suggested further reading: Isaiah 55:1-7

The invitations of Christ's gospel have a breadth and a fulness. The last three verses of the chapter are precious. They meet the trembling sinner who asks, 'Will Christ reveal his Father's love to such a one as me?' with the most gracious encouragement.

Our Lord does not invite those who feel themselves righteous and worthy. He addresses the weary and heavy-laden. It is a wide description. It comprises multitudes in this weary world. All who feel a load on their heart, of which they would get free, a load of sin or a load of sorrow, a load of anxiety or a load of remorse — all, whosoever they may be, and whatsoever their past lives, all such are invited to come to Christ.

What a gracious offer Jesus makes! He gives soul rest. Unrest is one great characteristic of the world. Hurry, vexation, failure, disappointment stare us in the face on every side. But there is hope. There is an ark of refuge for the weary. There is rest in Christ, rest of conscience, rest of heart, rest built on pardon of sin, rest flowing from peace with God.

Jesus makes a simple request to the labouring and weary-laden ones. He interposes no hard conditions. He speaks nothing of works to be done first and deservingness of his gifts to be established. He only asks us to come with all our sins, just as we are, and to submit ourselves like children to his teaching.

Jesus gives an encouraging account of himself. He is meek and lowly of heart. Mary and Martha at Bethany (John 11:17-45), Peter after his fall (John 21:15-19), Thomas after his cold unbelief (John 20:24-29) — all tasted the meekness and gentleness of Christ.

Jesus gives an encouraging account of his service. No doubt there is a cross to be carried if we follow Christ. No doubt there are trials to be endured and battles to be fought. But the comforts of the gospel far outweigh the cross. Compared to the service of the world and sin, compared to the yoke of Jewish ceremonies and the bondage of human superstition, his yoke is no more a burden than feathers are to a bird (1 John 5:3).

For meditation: *An invitation unreceived is of no value* (Matt. 23:37-39).

Suggested further reading: 2 Corinthians 4:1-6

A self-exalting spirit in ministers of religion is entirely opposed to the mind of Christ. Our Lord says, 'He that speaketh of himself seeketh his own glory; but he that seeketh his glory that sent him, the same is true, and no unrighteousness is in him.'

The wisdom and truth of this sentence will be evident at once to any reflecting mind. The minister truly called of God will be deeply sensible of his Master's majesty and his own infirmity and will see in himself nothing but unworthiness. He, on the other hand, who knows that he is not 'inwardly moved by the Holy Ghost' will try to cover over his defects by magnifying himself and his office. The very desire to exalt ourselves is a bad symptom. It is a sure sign of something wrong within.

Does anyone ask illustrations of the truth before us? He will find them, on the one side, in the scribes and Pharisees of our Lord's times. If one thing more than another distinguished these unhappy men, it was their desire to get praise for themselves. He will find them, on the other side, in the character of the apostle St Paul. The keynote that runs through all his epistles is personal humility and zeal for Christ's glory: 'I am less than the least of all saints' (Eph. 3:8). 'I am not meet to be called an apostle' (1 Cor. 15:9). 'I am chief of sinners' (1 Tim. 1:15). 'We preach not ourselves but Christ Jesus the Lord, and ourselves your servants for Jesus' sake' (2 Cor. 4:5).

Does anyone ask for a test by which he may discern the real man of God from the false shepherd in the present day? Let him remember our Lord's weighty words and notice carefully what is the main object that a minister loves to exalt. Not he who is ever crying, 'Behold the church! Behold the sacraments! Behold the ministry!' but he who says, 'Behold the Lamb!' is the pastor after God's own heart.

For meditation: *Many modern ministers and evangelists parade self rather than exalting Christ. So do many non-ministers!*

Suggested further reading: John 21:15-18

Men may show some outward respect to Christ and yet remain un-converted. The Pharisee before us is a case in point. He showed our Lord more respect than many did (v. 36) but all this time was pro-foundly ignorant of the nature of Christ's gospel. His proud heart secretly revolted at the sight of a poor contrite sinner being allowed to wash the Lord's feet. Even the hospitality he showed seems to be cold and niggardly (vv. 44-46). In all the Pharisee did there was one great defect. There was outward civility but no heart love.

It is quite possible to have a decent form of religion and yet to know nothing of the gospel of Christ, to treat Christianity with re-spect and yet to be utterly blind about its cardinal doctrines, to be-have with great correctness and propriety at church and yet to hate justification by faith and salvation by grace. Do we really feel affec-tion towards the Lord Jesus? Have we cordially embraced his whole gospel? Are we willing to enter heaven side by side with the chief of sinners and owe all our hopes to free grace? If not, the Lord may have something to tell us (v. 40).

Grateful love is the secret of doing much for Christ. The penitent woman showed far more honour to the Lord than the Pharisee. She proved her reverence and respect by her acts (vv. 37-38,44-46). She loved our Lord and thought nothing too much to do for him.

More doing for Christ is the universal demand of all the churches; more good works, more self-denial, more practical obedience to Christ's commands. But what will produce these things? Nothing, nothing but love. The fear of punishment, the desire for reward, the sense of duty are all useful arguments to persuade men to holiness. But they are all weak and powerless until a man loves Christ. Once let a man get hold of that mighty principle, and you will see his whole life changed.

However much the world may sneer at feelings in religion, and however false unhealthy religious feelings may sometimes be, the great truth still remains that feeling is the secret of doing. The hands hang down when the heart is not engaged for Christ.

For meditation: *When love for Christ is lost we are to remember, repent and do* (Rev. 2:5).

Suggested further reading: Matthew 7:21-23

We learn in this passage the danger of forming a hasty judgement. The Jews at Jerusalem were ready to condemn our Lord as a sinner against the law of Moses, because he had done a miracle of healing on the sabbath day. They forgot in their blind enmity that the fourth commandment was not meant to prevent works of necessity or works of mercy. And hence they drew down on themselves the rebuke: 'Judge not according to the appearance, but judge righteous judgement.'

The practical value of the lesson before us is very great. We shall do well to remember it as we travel through life and to correct our estimate of people and things by the light which it supplies.

We are often too ready to be deceived by an appearance of good. We are in danger of rating some men as very good Christians because of a little outward profession of religion and a decent Sunday formality — because, in short, they talk the language of Canaan and wear the garb of pilgrims. We forget that all is not good that appears good, even as all is not gold that glitters, and that daily practice, choice, tastes, habits, conduct, private character are the true evidence of what a man is. In a word, we forget our Lord's saying: 'Judge not according to the appearance.'

We are too ready, on the other hand, to be deceived by the appearance of evil. We must remember that the best of men are but men at their very best and that the most eminent saints may be overtaken by temptation and yet be saints at heart after all. We must not hastily suppose that all is evil where there is an occasional appearance of evil. The holiest man may fall sadly for a time and yet the grace within him may finally get a victory. Is a man's general character godly? Then let us suspend our judgement when he falls and hope on. Let us 'judge righteous judgement'.

For meditation: *The failing saint is to be treated differently to the brazenly rebellious* (Gal. 6:1; 1:8).

Suggested further reading: 1 Timothy 1:12-17

The sense of having our sins forgiven is the mainspring and life-blood of love to Christ. This, beyond doubt, was the lesson which our Lord wished Simon the Pharisee to learn when he told him the story of the two debtors. Both owed different sums of money. Neither could pay. Both were forgiven freely. And then came the searching question as to which would love him most? Here was the true explanation, the Lord told Simon, of the deep love which the penitent woman before him had displayed. Her many tears, her deep affection, her public reverence, her action in anointing his feet were all traceable to one cause. She had been forgiven much, so she loved much. Her love was the effect of her forgiveness, not the cause; the consequence of her forgiveness, not the condition; the result of her forgiveness, not the reason; the fruit of her forgiveness, not the root. Would the Pharisee know why this woman showed so much love? It was because she felt much forgiven. Would he know why he himself had shown his guest so little love? It was because he felt no obligation. He had no consciousness of having obtained forgiveness, no sense of debt to Christ.

The mighty principle laid down by our Lord in this passage is one of the great cornerstones of the whole gospel. The only way to make men holy is to teach and preach free and full forgiveness through Jesus Christ. The secret of being holy ourselves is to know and feel that Christ has pardoned our sins. We shall do nothing until we are reconciled to God. We must work from life, and not for life. Our best works before we are justified are little better than splendid sins. The heart which has experienced the pardoning love of Christ is the heart which loves Christ and strives to glorify him.

There is an encouragement, in our Lord's amazing mercy and compassion to this woman, to anyone, however bad he may be, to come to him for pardon and forgiveness. Never, never need anyone despair of salvation if he will only come to Christ.

For meditation: *If our love for Christ is a reflection of how much we appreciate what he has done for us, how much are we thankful?*

Suggested further reading: James 2:14-20

We are told that some of our Lord's hearers knew clearly where Christ was to be born. They referred to Scripture, like men familiar with its contents. And yet the eyes of their understanding were not enlightened. Their own Messiah stood before them and they neither received, nor believed, nor obeyed him.

A certain degree of religious knowledge, beyond doubt, is of vast importance. Ignorance is certainly not the mother of true devotion and helps nobody towards heaven. An 'unknown God' can never be the object of a reasonable worship. Happy indeed would it be for Christians if they all knew the Scriptures as well as the Jews seem to have done when our Lord was on earth!

But while we value religious knowledge, we must take care that we do not overvalue it. We must not think it enough to know the facts and doctrines of our faith, unless our hearts and lives are thoroughly influenced by what we know. The very devils know the creed intellectually and 'believe and tremble', but remain devils still (James 2:19). It is quite possible to be familiar with the letter of Scripture and to be able to quote texts appropriately and reason about the theory of Christianity and yet to remain dead in trespasses and sins. Like many of the generation to which our Lord preached, we may know the Bible well and yet remain faithless and unconverted.

Heart-knowledge, we must always remember, is the one thing needful. It is something which schools and universities cannot confer. It is the gift of God. To find out the plague of our own hearts and hate sin, to become familiar with the throne of grace and the fountain of Christ's blood, to sit daily at the feet of Jesus and humbly learn of him — this is the highest degree of knowledge to which mortal man can attain. Let anyone thank God who knows anything of these things.

For meditation: *What is more awful than to be always learning but never coming to a knowledge of the truth?* (2 Tim. 3:7).

Suggested further reading: Matthew 25:31-46

Our Lord showed unwearied diligence in doing good (v. 1) regardless of the reception that he found. Man's unbelief did not move our Lord or hinder his working. He was always about his Father's work. His short ministry comprised much work. Here is the Christian's example. Let us labour to do good in our day and generation (1 John 2:6), redeeming the time. Few have an idea what can be done in twelve hours if men will stick to their business and avoid idleness and frivolity. Time is short. In the world to come there will be no ignorant to instruct, no mourners to comfort, no spiritual darkness to enlighten, no distress to relieve, no sorrow to make less. Souls are perishing and time is flying!

The power of the grace of God and the constraining influence of the love of Christ are seen in these women. We can well imagine the difficulties these holy women had to face in becoming Christ's disciples: the contempt and scorn of the Pharisees towards all who became Christ's disciples, the hard words and actions against any Jewish woman who thought seriously on religion. But, grateful for the mercies received from the Lord and renewed by the Holy Spirit, they were able to endure much, to cleave to Jesus and not give way. It was not women who betrayed, forsook and denied our Lord. They wailed and lamented at his crucifixion. They stood at his cross. They were first to his tomb. Let all women take note. Busy mothers, wives of ungodly husbands, daughters of worldly parents should follow Christ, serve him and glorify him.

The Lord grants his faithful followers work to do (v. 3). As a man like ourselves in all things, except sin, our Lord lived the life of faith in his Father's providence. He allowed his followers to minister to him to prove their love and regard for him. True love will count it a pleasure to give anything to the object loved. False love will often talk and profess much, but do and give nothing at all. Our lives are continually showing whether we love Christ or whether we love the world. When we serve Christ's people we serve Christ.

For meditation: *We cannot all be great preachers like Paul, but we can and should serve Christ according to the abilities given us* (Rom. 12:4-5).

Suggested further reading: Luke 1:1-4

We see in these verses the obstinate blindness of the unbelieving Jews. We find them defending their denial of our Lord's Messiahship by saying, 'We know this man whence he is: but when Christ cometh no man knoweth whence he is.' And yet in both these assertions they were wrong!

They were wrong in saying that they 'knew whence our Lord came'. They meant no doubt to say that he was born at Nazareth and belonged to Nazareth and was therefore a Galilean. Yet the fact was that our Lord was born at Bethlehem. It is incredible to suppose that the Jews could not have found this out, if they had honestly searched and inquired. It is notorious that pedigrees, genealogies and family histories were most carefully kept by the Jewish nation. Their ignorance was without excuse.

They were wrong again in saying that no man was to know whence Christ came. There was a well-known prophecy, with which their whole nation was familiar, that Christ was to come out of the town of Bethlehem (Micah 5:2; Matt. 2:6; John 7:42). It is absurd to suppose that they had forgotten this prophecy. But apparently they found it inconvenient to remember it on this occasion.

Men's memories are often sadly dependent on their wills. They shut their eyes against the plainest facts and doctrines of Christianity. They pretend to say that they do not understand and cannot therefore believe the things that we press on their attention as needful to salvation. But, alas, in nineteen cases out of twenty it is a wilful ignorance! They do not believe what they do not like to believe. They will neither read, nor listen, nor search, nor think, nor enquire honestly after truth. Can anyone wonder if such persons are ignorant? Faithful and true is that old proverb: 'There are none so blind as those who will not see.'

For meditation: *Luke searched out the facts to give Theophilus certainty. The unbelieving Jews guessed and were wrong. Are you studious or lazy in the things of God?*

Suggested further reading: Mark 3:20-30

There is nothing too blasphemous for hardened and prejudiced men to say against religion. Our Lord casts out a devil and at once the Pharisees declare he does it by the prince of devils (v. 24).

This was an absurd charge. Our Lord shows that it was unreasonable to suppose that the devil would help to pull down his own kingdom (vv. 25-26). But there is nothing too absurd and unreasonable to say when men are thoroughly set against religion. The Pharisees are not the only people who have lost their logic, good sense and temper when they have attacked the gospel of Christ.

Strange as this charge may sound, it is one that has often been made against the servants of Christ. Their enemies have been obliged to confess that they are doing a work and producing an effect on the world. The results of Christian labour stare them in the face. As they cannot deny them, they attribute them to the devil.

We must never be surprised to hear of dreadful charges being made against the best of men without cause. It is an old device (Matt. 10:25). When the Christian's arguments cannot be answered and the Christian's work cannot be denied, the last resource of the wicked is to blacken the Christian's character. Let us bear this patiently. False charges will not keep us out of heaven.

How evil religious divisions are! Our Lord shows the folly of the charge that he casts out devils by Beelzebub, because division results in a fall. He teaches Christians here a lesson that they have been mournfully slow to learn. Religious divisions of some kind there must always be. Division and separation from those who adhere to false and unscriptural doctrine is a duty, and not a sin. But divisions on matters not needful to salvation, forms, ceremonies and ecclesiastical arrangements on which Scripture is silent, are to be deplored. They bring scandal on religion and weakness to the church.

For meditation: *When our fellow Christians are abused we should be very careful in our judgements. We are not to give encouragement to those whose occupation is the destruction of the characters of others.*

Suggested further reading: Matthew 25:1-13

We see in these verses the miserable end to which unbelievers may one day come. We find our Lord saying to his enemies, 'Ye shall seek me, and shall not find me; and where I am, thither ye cannot come.'

We can hardly doubt that these words were meant to have a prophetical sense. Whether our Lord had in view individual cases of unbelief among his hearers, or whether he looked forward to the national remorse which many would feel too late in the final siege of Jerusalem, are points which we cannot perhaps decide. But that many Jews did remember Christ's sayings long after he had ascended into heaven and did in a way seek him and wish for him when it was too late, we may be very sure.

It is far too much forgotten that there is such a thing as finding out truth too late. There may be convictions of sin, discoveries of our own folly, desires after peace, anxieties about heaven, fears of hell — but all too late. The teaching of Scripture on this point is clear and express. It is written in Proverbs: 'Then shall they call upon me, but I will not answer; they shall seek me early, but they shall not find me' (Prov. 1:28). It is written of the foolish virgins in the parable that when they found the door shut they knocked in vain, saying, 'Lord, Lord, open to us' (Matt. 25:11). Awful as it may seem, it is possible, by continually resisting light and warnings, to sin away our own souls. It sounds terrible, but it is true.

Let us take heed to ourselves lest we sin after the example of the unbelieving Jews and never seek the Lord Jesus as a Saviour till it is too late. The door of mercy is still open. The throne of grace is still waiting for us. Let us give diligence to make sure our interest in Christ, while it is called today. Better never have been born than hear the Son of God say at last, 'Where I am, thither ye cannot come.'

For meditation: *When we are tempted to put off what God requires us to do today, let us remember the wise saying: 'Tomorrow never comes.'*

Suggested further reading: Luke 11:14-23

Neutrality in religion is impossible (v. 30). There are many persons who endeavour to steer a middle course in religion. They are not as bad as many sinners, but they are not saints. They feel the truth of Christ's gospel when it is brought before them, but are afraid to confess what they feel. Because they have these feelings they flatter themselves that they are not as bad as others. And yet they shrink from the standard of faith and practice which the Lord Jesus sets up. They are not boldly on Christ's side and yet they are not openly against him. Our Lord warns all such that they are in a dangerous position. There are only two parties in religious matters, two camps, two sides. Are we with Christ and working in his cause? If not, we are against him. Are we doing good in the world? If not, we are doing harm. There can be no peace until we are thoroughgoing and decided in our Christianity.

How exceedingly sinful are sins against knowledge! This is the practical conclusion that seems to flow naturally from our Lord's words about the blasphemy against the Holy Spirit. Difficult as these words are, they seem fairly to prove that there are degrees in sin. The brighter the light, the greater the guilt of him who rejects it. The clearer a man's knowledge of the nature of the gospel, the greater his sin if he wilfully refuses to repent and believe.

The doctrine taught here is in other Scriptures, too (Heb. 6:4-8; 10:26-27). The unconverted children of godly parents, the unconverted members of evangelical congregations are the hardest people on earth to impress. They seem past feeling. The same fire which melts the wax hardens the clay. In a Pharaoh, a Saul, an Ahab and a Judas Iscariot there was a combination of clear knowledge and deliberate rejection of Christ. There was light in the head and hatred of truth in the heart.

May God give us a will to use our knowledge, whether it be little or great! May we beware of neglecting our opportunities! Let us live up to the light we have and walk in the truth we know.

For meditation: *Men ever seek to create a third group within humanity but Scripture only ever recognizes two. In which are you?*

Suggested further reading: Isaiah 55:1-7

We have in these verses a case supposed. The Lord Jesus says, 'If any man thirst.' These words no doubt were meant to have a spiritual meaning. The thirst before us is of a purely spiritual kind. It means anxiety of soul, conviction of sin, desire of pardon, longing after peace of conscience. When a man feels his sins and wants forgiveness, is deeply sensible of his soul's need and earnestly desires help and relief, then he is in that state of mind which our Lord had in view when he said, 'If any man thirst.' The Jews who heard Peter preach on the Day of Pentecost and were 'pricked in their hearts', the Philippian jailer who cried to Paul and Silas, 'What must I do to be saved?' are both examples of what the expression means. In both cases there was a 'thirst'.

Such thirst as this, unhappily, is known by few. All ought to feel it and all would feel it if they were wise. Sinful, mortal, dying creatures as we all are, with souls that will one day be judged and spend eternity in heaven or hell, there lives not the man or woman on earth who ought not to 'thirst' after salvation. And yet the many thirst after everything almost except salvation. Money, pleasure, honour, rank, self-indulgence — these are the things which they desire. There is no clearer proof of the fall of man and the utter corruption of human nature than the careless indifference of most people about their souls.

Happy are those who know something by experience of spiritual 'thirst'. The beginning of all true Christianity is to discover that we are guilty, empty, needy sinners. Till we know that we are lost, we are not in the way to be saved. The very first step towards heaven is to be thoroughly convinced that we deserve hell.

'Blessed indeed are they which do hunger and thirst after righteousness, for they shall be filled' (Matt. 5:6).

For meditation: *With such a clear invitation to come and drink, shall we stay thirsty and die?*

Suggested further reading: James 3:1-12

It is immensely important to be careful about our daily words. There are few of our Lord's statements that are so heart-searching as this (vv. 36-37). There is nothing to which men pay less attention than their words. They go through their daily work speaking and talking without thought or reflection and seem to fancy that if they do what is right it matters but little what they say.

But is it so? We dare not say so in the face of this Scripture. Our words are the evidence of the state of our hearts, as surely as the taste of water is the evidence of the state of the spring. The lips only utter what the mind conceives (v. 34). Our words will form one subject of enquiry at the Day of Judgement. We shall have to give an account of our sayings as well as our doings. Truly these are solemn considerations. This passage ought to convince us of our guilt before God (Rom. 3:20) and our need of a righteousness better than our own (Phil. 3:9).

Let us be humble as we read this passage in recollection of times past. How many idle, foolish, vain, frivolous, sinful and unprofitable things we have all said! How many words we have used which have flown far and wide and sown mischief in the hearts of others that will never die! How often we must repent of what we have said! Even when a man has died his evil words may live on in the memories of others. A word spoken is physically transient but morally permanent.

Let us be watchful as we read this passage about words when we look forward to our days yet to come. Let us resolve by God's grace to be more careful over our tongues and more particular about our use of them. Let us pray that our speech may always be with grace (Col. 4:6). Let us watch our words every day so that we do not sin with our tongues. Let us cry to the Strong for strength and ask him to put a watch over our mouths and to keep the door of our lips (Ps. 39:1; 141:3). Well might James call the man who controls his tongue a perfect man! (James 3:2).

For meditation: *A few well-chosen words are sufficient to destroy a man in the eyes of others, whatever his innocence might be. Satan is the father of lies. Let us not be his children.*

Suggested further reading: Ephesians 2:1-10

We have in these verses a remedy proposed. The Lord Jesus says, 'If any man thirst, let him come unto me and drink.' He declares that he is the true fountain of life, the supplier of all spiritual necessities, the reliever of all spiritual wants. He invites all who feel the burden of sin heavy to apply to him and proclaims himself their helper.

Those words, 'Let him come unto me,' are few and very simple. But they settle a mighty question which all the wisdom of Greek and Roman philosophers could never settle: they show how man can have peace with God. They show that peace is to be had in Christ by trusting in him as our Mediator and Substitute — in one word, by believing. To 'come' to Christ is to believe on him and to 'believe' on him is to come. The remedy may seem a very simple one, too simple to be true. But there is no other remedy than this and all the wisdom of the world can never find a flaw in it, or devise one better.

To use this grand prescription of Christ is the secret of all saving Christianity. The saints of God in every age have been men and women who drank of this fountain by faith and were relieved. They felt their guilt and emptiness and thirsted for deliverance. They heard of a full supply of pardon, mercy and grace in Christ crucified for all penitent believers. They believed the good news and rested upon it. They cast aside all confidence in their own goodness and worthiness and came to Christ by faith as sinners. So coming they found relief. So coming daily they lived. So coming they died. Really to feel the sinfulness of sin and to thirst and really to come to Christ and believe are the two steps which lead to heaven. But they are mighty steps. Thousands are too proud and careless to take them. Few, alas, think, and still fewer believe!

For meditation:
None but Jesus, none but Jesus
Can do helpless sinners good

(Joseph Hart).

Suggested further reading: Matthew 16:1-4

In their desperate unbelief the Jews of our Lord's day still professed to be waiting for a sign (v. 38). They pretended to want more evidence before they believed. Our Lord declares that the Queen of Sheba and the men of Nineveh would put the Jews to shame at the last day. The Queen of Sheba had such faith that she travelled a great distance to hear the wisdom of Solomon (v. 42). Yet Solomon, with all his wisdom, was an erring and imperfect king. The Ninevites had such faith that they believed the message Jonah brought from God and repented (v. 41). Yet even Jonah was a weak and unstable prophet. The Jews of our Lord's time had far higher light and infinitely clearer teachings than either Solomon or Jonah could supply. They had amongst them the Prophet greater than Moses. Yet the Jews neither repented nor believed.

Let it never surprise us to see unbelief abounding. Rather than marvelling that some men disbelieve, we should marvel that any believe at all! Why should we wonder to see that old disease which began with Adam and Eve infecting all their children? Why should we expect to see more faith in men and women today than in our Lord's time? The enormous amount of unbelief and hardness on every side may well grieve and pain us. But it ought not to surprise us.

Let us thank God if we have received the gift of faith. It is a great thing to believe all the Bible. Have we faith, however weak and small? Let us praise God for the privilege. Who are we that God should have made us to differ? Let us watch against unbelief. Let us guard our faith with a godly jealousy.

Our Lord testifies to the truth of a resurrection and life to come (vv. 41-42). This reminds us that our world is not all, and that the life which man lives in the body on earth is not the only life of which we ought to think. The kings, queens and vast multitudes that have lived shall yet be raised. Graves receive their tenants until the earth casts out her dead (Isa. 26:19). Some may tremble at the thought. Christians should rejoice.

For meditation: *God is not in the business of giving personal proof and miracles to the hearts of the unbelieving. We must trust his Word or perish.*

Suggested further reading: John 4:10-14

We have in these verses a promise held out. The Lord Jesus says, 'He that believeth on me, out of his belly shall flow rivers of living water.' These words, of course, were meant to have a figurative sense. They have a double application. They teach, for one thing, that all who come to Christ by faith shall find in him abundant satisfaction. They teach, for another thing, that believers shall not only have enough for the wants of their own souls, but shall also become fountains of blessings to others.

The fulfilment of the first part of the promise could be testified by thousands of living Christians in the present day. They would say, if their evidence could be collected, that when they came to Christ by faith, they found in him more than they expected. They have tasted peace and hope and comfort since they first believed, which, with all their doubts and fears, they would not exchange for anything in this world. They have found grace according to their need and strength according to their days. In themselves and their own hearts they have often been disappointed, but they have never been disappointed in Christ.

The fulfilment of the other half of the promise will never be fully known until the Judgement Day. That day alone shall reveal the amount of good that every believer is made the instrument of doing to others, from the very day of his conversion. Some do good while they live, by their tongues, like the apostles and first preachers of the gospel. Some do good when they are dying, like Stephen and the penitent thief and our own martyred Reformers at the stake. Some do good long after they are dead by their writings, like Baxter and Bunyan and M'Cheyne. But in one way or another, probably, almost all believers will be found to have been fountains of blessings. They know it not now, but they will find at last that it is true.

For meditation: *What is promised here is not a special blessing for the spiritual élite, but a fulness of blessing for every believer.*

Suggested further reading: 1 Peter 5:6-11

Next to his friends and allies a soldier ought to be acquainted with his enemies. We ought not to be ignorant of Satan. Our Lord draws a picture of his power.

Christ speaks of Satan as a 'strong man'. The strength of Satan has been only too well proved by his victories over the souls of men. He who tempted Adam and Eve to rebel against God and brought sin into the world, he who has led captive the vast majority of mankind and robbed them of heaven — that evil one is indeed a mighty foe. He who is called the prince of this world is not to be despised (John 14:30). He is very strong.

Christ speaks of Satan as a 'strong, armed man'. Satan is well supplied with defensive armour. He is not to be overcome with slight assaults and feeble exertions. He that would overcome him must put forth all his strength. Satan is also well supplied with offensive weapons. He is never at a loss for a means to injure the soul of man. He has snares of every kind, rank and description. He knows exactly how every rank, class, age, nation and people can be assailed with most advantage. The devil is well armed.

Christ speaks of man's heart as being Satan's 'palace'. The natural heart is the favourite abode of the evil one and all its faculties and power are his servants to do his will. He sits upon the throne which God ought to occupy and governs the inward man. He works in the disobedient (Eph. 2:2).

Christ speaks of Satan's possessions as safe. A man dead in sin is at ease about spiritual things and does not fear the future. He has no anxiety about hell. He has a devil-given thoughtlessness and insensibility about his soul. Let us no more jest about the devil than about the executioner at the gallows.

Thank God, Christ is stronger than Satan. Jesus overcame him on the cross, plucks his captives from his hands and breaks the chains with which he binds them. Are you delivered? (v. 22).

For meditation: *Disbelief in the devil is a trick of the devil.*

Suggested further reading: Daniel 3:8-18

We see, for another thing, in these verses the overruling hand of God over all his enemies. We find that the unbelieving Jews 'sought to take' our Lord, 'but no man laid hands on him, because his hour was not yet come'. They had the will to hurt him, but by an invisible restraint from above, they had not the power.

There is a mine of deep truth in the words before us which deserves close attention. They show us plainly that all our Lord's sufferings were undergone voluntarily and of his own free will. He did not go to the cross because he could not help it. He did not die because he could not prevent his death. Neither Jew nor Gentile, Pharisee nor Sadducee, Annas nor Caiaphas, Herod nor Pontius Pilate, could have injured our Lord, except power had been given them from above. All that they did was done under control and by permission. The crucifixion was part of the eternal counsels of the Trinity. The passion of our Lord could not begin until the very hour which God had appointed. This is a great mystery. But it is a truth.

The servants of Christ in every age should treasure up the doctrine before us and remember it in time of need. It is full of sweet, pleasant and unspeakable comfort to godly persons. Let such never forget that they live in a world where God overrules all times and events and where nothing can happen but by God's permission. The very hairs of their heads are all numbered. Sorrow and sickness and poverty and persecution can never touch them unless God sees fit. They may boldly say to every cross, 'Thou couldst have no power against me, except it were given thee from above.' Then let them work on confidently. They are immortal till their work is done. Let them suffer patiently, if needs be that they suffer. Their 'times are in God's hand' (Ps. 31:15). That hand guides and governs all things here below and makes no mistakes.

For meditation: *The joy of the martyr in death is a joy in the Lord who reigns over all and in all.*

Suggested further reading: 2 Peter 2:17-22

How dangerous it is to be content with any change in religion that is short of thorough conversion to God! This is a truth that our Lord teaches by an awful picture of one from whom a devil has been cast forth but into whose heart the Holy Spirit has not entered. He describes the evil spirit after his expulsion as seeking rest and finding none. He describes him planning a return to the heart which he once inhabited and carrying his plan into execution. He describes him finding the heart empty of any good but ready for his reception. He describes him as again entering in with seven devils worse than himself to create an even worse state than before!

These words, which we faintly comprehend, no doubt illustrate the state of things that existed in the Jewish nation at that time. But the main lesson concerns the danger of our own individual souls. We must never be satisfied with religious reformation without heart conversion.

There is no safety except in thorough Christianity. To lay aside open sin is nothing unless grace reigns in our hearts. To cease to do evil is a small matter if we do not also learn to do well. The house must not only be swept and whitewashed. A new tenant must also be introduced. The outward life must not only be garnished with the outward trappings of religion. The power of vital religion must be experienced in the inward man. The devil must not only be cast out. The Holy Spirit must take his place. We must not only be moralized. We must be spiritualized. We must not only be reformed but born again.

Many professing Christians are deceiving themselves. They are no longer daring sinners and so they dream that they are Christians. They do not see that they have changed one devil for another. They are now governed by a decent, Pharisaic devil instead of an audacious, riotous unclean spirit. But the tenant within is the devil still! From such an end may we pray to be delivered. Let us not be fair without and worthless within.

For meditation: *Even a moral, religious Pharisee like Nicodemus needed the rebirth* (John 3:1-8). *There are no exceptions.*

Suggested further reading: Jeremiah 1:4-10

How eminent must have been our Lord's gifts as a public teacher of religion! We are told that even the officers of the chief priests, who were sent to take him, were struck and amazed.

Of the *manner* of our Lord's public speaking, we can of necessity form little idea. It was probably something very unlike what the Jewish officers were accustomed to hear. There is much in what is said in another place: 'He taught them as one having authority, and not as the scribes' (Matt. 7:29).

Of the *matter* of our Lord's public speaking, we may form some conception from the discourses which are recorded in the four Gospels. The leading features of these discourses are plain and unmistakable. The world has never seen anything like them, since the gift of speech was given to man. They often contain deep truths, which we have no line to fathom. But they often contain simple things, which even a child can understand. They are bold and outspoken in denouncing national and ecclesiastical sins and yet they are wise and discreet in never giving needless offence. They are faithful and direct in their warnings and yet loving and tender in their invitations. For a combination of power and simplicity, of courage and prudence, of faithfulness and tenderness, we may well say, 'Never man spake like this man!'

It would be well for the church of Christ if ministers and teachers of religion would strive more to speak after their Lord's pattern. Let them remember that fine bombastic language and a sensational, theatrical style of address are utterly unlike their Master. Let them realize that an eloquent simplicity is the highest attainment of public speaking. Of this their Master left them a glorious example. Surely they need never be ashamed of walking in his steps.

For meditation: *One difference between a man who preaches as a hobby and a preacher sent by God is that only the latter speaks with authority.*

Suggested further reading: Hebrews 2:10-18

How great are the privileges of those who hear and keep God's Word! They are regarded by Christ with as much honour as if they were his nearest relatives. It is more blessed to be a believer in the Lord Jesus than it would have been to have been one of the family in which he was born after the flesh. It was a greater blessing to the Virgin Mary to have Christ dwelling in her heart by faith than to have been the mother of Christ and have nursed him at her bosom.

We are apt to fancy that to have seen Christ, heard Christ, lived near Christ and have been a relative of Christ would have had some mighty effect upon our souls. We are all naturally inclined to attach a great importance to a religion of sight, sense, touch, eye and ear. We love a sensuous, tangible, material Christianity far better than one of faith. We need reminding that seeing is not always believing. Thousands saw Christ continually while he was on this earth and clung to their sins. Even his brethren at one time disbelieved (John 7:5). A mere fleshly knowledge of Christ saves no one (2 Cor. 5:16).

Faith brings to us far more privileges with respect to Christ than we would ever have by pressing Christ's hand, hearing his voice, or being numbered among his earthly relatives. To hear Christ's voice, to follow him and cleave to him is our highest privilege.

There is a solemn warning for all who mock true religion and persecute Christians. They are persecuting the near relations of the King of kings (Acts 9:4). They will find at the last day what it is to have mocked those whom the Judge calls his brother, sister and mother.

There is rich encouragement here for all believers. They are far more precious in their Lord's eyes than they are in their own. Their faith may be feeble, their repentance weak, their strength small. But whosoever believes is a relation of Christ (Matt. 12:50). Jesus will richly provide for his relations for eternity.

For meditation: *The poorest, most despised, most lonely Christian on earth is a joint-heir with Christ of all that is his for ever* (Rom. 8:16-17).

Suggested further reading: Mark 8:22-26

How slowly and gradually the work of grace goes on in some hearts! We are told that Nicodemus stood up in the council of our Lord's enemies and mildly pleaded that he deserved fair dealing.

This very Nicodemus, we must remember, is the man who eighteen months before had come to our Lord by night as an ignorant enquirer. He evidently knew little then and dared not come to Christ in open day. But now, after eighteen months, he has got on so far that he dares to say something on our Lord's side. It was but little that he said, no doubt, but it was better than nothing at all. And a day was yet to come when he would go further still. He was to help Joseph of Arimathaea in doing honour to our Lord's dead body when even his chosen apostles had forsaken him and fled.

The case of Nicodemus is full of useful instruction. It teaches us that there are diversities in the operation of the Holy Spirit. All are undoubtedly led to the same Saviour, but all are not led precisely in the same way. It teaches us that the work of the Spirit does not always go forward with the same speed in the hearts of men. In some cases it may go forward very slowly indeed and yet may be real and true.

We shall do well to remember these things in forming our opinion of other Christians. We are often ready to condemn some as graceless, because their experience does not exactly tally with our own, or to set them down as not in the narrow way at all, because they cannot run as fast as ourselves. We must beware of hasty judgements. It is not always the fastest runner that wins the race. It is not always those who begin suddenly in religion and profess themselves rejoicing Christians who continue steadfast to the end. Slow work is sometimes the surest and most enduring. Nicodemus stood firm when Judas Iscariot fell away.

For meditation: *In the hard grind of pioneer missionary work William Carey's claim was 'I can plod'. To 'plod' and arrive is better than to run and fall asleep.*

Suggested further reading: 1 Samuel 16:1-13

Our Lord was ready when needful to go into the company of the unconverted. Our Lord is our pattern as well as our propitiation. Nothing must induce the Christian to be a partaker of the world's sins and frivolous amusements, but he must not be uncourteous, entirely withdrawing himself from the society of the unconverted and becoming a hermit or ascetic.

In such company we need to follow the Lord's example of always being engaged in the work of his Father. Let us remember his boldness in speaking of the things of God, his faithfulness in rebuking sin. He spared not even the sins of those who entertained him when his attention was publicly called to them. Let us go into company in the same state of mind, or stay at home.

Foolishness accompanies hypocrisy in religion. Our Lord's failure to wash was seen as something unholy, a sign of moral impurity (v. 38). Our Lord points out the absurdity of attaching such importance to the cleansing of the body when the cleansing of the heart is overlooked (v. 39). He reminds his host that God looks at the inward part of us, the hidden man of the heart, far more than the outward skin.

For ever let us bear in mind that the state of our souls is the principal thing that demands our attention if we would know what we are in religion. Bodily washings, fastings, gestures, postures and self-imposed mortifications of the flesh are all utterly useless if the heart is wrong. External devoutness of conduct, a grave face, a bowed head, a solemn countenance, a loud amen are all abominable in God's sight so long as our hearts are not washed from their wickedness and renewed by the Holy Spirit. The idea that men can be devout before they are converted is a grand delusion of the devil against which we need to be on our guard. Two Scriptures make weighty statements on this subject (Prov. 4:23; 1 Sam. 16:7).

For meditation: *Hypocrisy is easy. It is godliness that is difficult. Attending all the right meetings, expressing the correct sentiments, doing the expected things — these have a show of religiosity, but it is the state of the heart that really matters.*

Suggested further reading: Matthew 7:1-5

To suppose, as some have thought, that the narrative before us palliates the sin of adultery and exhibits our Lord as making light of the seventh commandment is surely a great mistake. There is nothing in the passage to justify such an assertion. There is not a sentence in it to warrant our saying anything of the kind. Of all whose words are recorded in the Bible there is none who has spoken so strongly about the breach of the seventh commandment as our divine Master. It is he who has taught that it may be broken by a look or a thought, as well as by an open act (Matt. 5:28). It is he who has spoken more strongly than any about the sanctity of the marriage relation (Matt. 19:5). In all that is recorded here, we see nothing inconsistent with the rest of his teaching. He simply refused to usurp the office of the judge and to pronounce condemnation on a guilty woman for the gratification of his deadly enemies.

He refused to be a 'judge' and lawgiver among them and specially in a case which their own law had already decided. He gave them at first no answer at all. But 'when they continued asking', our Lord silenced them with a withering and heart-searching reply. 'He that is without sin among you,' he said, 'let him first cast a stone at her.' He did not say that the woman had not sinned, or that her sin was a trifling and venial one. But he reminded her accusers that they at any rate were not the persons to bring a charge against her. Their own motives and lives were far from pure. They themselves did not come into the case with clean hands. What they really desired was not to vindicate the purity of God's law and punish a sinner, but to wreak their malice on himself.

For meditation: *We are to condemn sin in order to lead others to repentance, not so that we feel 'smug' and self-righteous.*

Suggested further reading: Jude 12-23

Hypocrites often exhibit gross inconsistency in religion (Matt. 23:23). The Pharisees carried certain things to great extremes and yet neglected the plainest duties to God and their neighbours. They were scrupulous to an extreme about small matters in the ceremonial law and yet were utterly regardless of the simplest principles of justice to man and love to God. In secondary matters they were zealots and enthusiasts and in great primary matters no better than the heathen.

Thousands today also make a great deal of ado about daily services, keeping Lent, frequent communion, turning east in churches, gorgeous ceremonial, but nothing more. They know little or nothing of the great spiritual duties of humility, love, meekness, spiritual-mindedness, Bible reading, private devotion and separation from the world. They plunge into every gaiety with greediness. They exhibit nothing of the mind of Christ in their daily lives. We need scriptural proportion in our religion and to beware of putting secondary things so to the fore as to lose sight of the first things entirely.

The hypocrite in religion is characterized by hollowness and falseness. Our Lord's picture of the Pharisees (v. 44) shows these boasting teachers of the Jews were full of corruption and uncleanness to an extent of which their deluded hearers had no conception.

The picture here drawn is painful and disgusting. Yet the accuracy and truthfulness of it have often been proved by the conduct of hypocrites in every age of the church. What shall we say of the lives of the monks and nuns which were exposed at the time of the Reformation? Thousands of so-called holy men and women were found to be sunk in every kind of wickedness. How often the leaders of heresies prove to be men sunk in corruption! Hypocrisy and unclean living have often been found side by side. Let us watch and pray against hypocrisy. Let us be real, thorough, genuine and sincere.

For meditation: *We should always beware of those who are zealous for some new interpretation or make much of some obscure reference of Scripture. Obsession with the new and the weird are not marks of genuine piety.*

Suggested further reading: 2 Samuel 12:1-15

We learn, for one thing, the power of conscience. We read of the woman's accusers that, when they heard our Lord's appeal, 'being convicted by their own conscience, they went out one by one, beginning at the eldest, even unto the last'. Wicked and hardened as they were, they had something within which made them cowards. Fallen as human nature is, God has taken care to leave within every man a witness that will be heard.

Conscience is a most important part of our inward man and plays a most prominent part in our spiritual history. It cannot save us. It never yet led anyone to Christ. It is blind and liable to be misled. It is lame and powerless and cannot guide us to heaven. Yet conscience is not to be despised.

Happy is he who never stifles his conscience, but strives to keep it tender! Still happier is he who prays to have it enlightened by the Holy Ghost and sprinkled with Christ's blood.

We learn, for another thing, the nature of true repentance. When our Lord had said to the sinful woman, 'Neither do I condemn thee,' he dismissed her with the solemn words: 'Go and sin no more.' He did not merely say, 'Go home and repent.' He pointed out the chief thing which her case required — the necessity of immediately breaking off from her sin.

Let us never forget this lesson. It is the very essence of genuine repentance, as the church catechism well teaches, to 'forsake sin'. That repentance which consists in nothing more than feeling, talking, professing, wishing, meaning, hoping and resolving is worthless in God's sight. Action is the very life of 'repentance unto salvation not to be repented of'. Till a man ceases to do evil and turns from his sins, he does not really repent.

For meditation: *Only the blood of Christ can cleanse the conscience; only it is adequate to deal with the guilt of sin.*

Suggested further reading: Romans 2:17-24

Without fear or favour our Lord rebuked the sins of the Jewish expounders of the law. That false love that calls it 'unkind' to say anyone is in error finds no encouragement in the language used by our Lord. He would not agree with everything a man said, but told him the truth.

He shows us that there is a great sin in professing to teach others what we do not practise ourselves (v. 46). They required others to observe wearisome ceremonies in religion that they themselves neglected. They had the impudence to lay yokes on the consciences of other men and yet to grant exemptions from these yokes for themselves. They had one set of measures and weights for their hearers and one set for themselves.

There is a word of special power to all teachers of young people, to all mothers and fathers, to all ministers of religion. Let all these beware of telling others to aim at a standard which they do not aim at themselves. Such conduct is gross inconsistency.

Perfection is, no doubt, unattainable in this world. If nobody is to lay down rules, or teach, or preach, until he is faultless himself, the whole fabric of society will be thrown into confusion. But we have a right to expect some agreement between a man's words and a man's actions, between his teaching and his doing, his preaching and his practice. Let us follow Paul's example (Phil. 4:9).

It is much easier to admire dead saints than living ones (v. 47). They professed to honour the memory of the prophets while they lived in the very same ways that the prophets had condemned. Thousands of wicked men in every age have tried to deceive themselves and others by loud professions of admiration for the saints of the past, hoping to be thought of as like them. The real question, however, is how we respond to God's people now. Do we love them and cleave to them? Or do we view them with displeasure as fanatics and over-righteous?

For meditation: *The fact that Paul was an apostle did not mean that he had special grace for living his life that other Christians do not have. Paul's level of holiness is attainable by all Christians. We do not have his gifts, but we may have his graces.*

Suggested further reading: Isaiah 8:19 - 9:2

Let us notice, for one thing, in these verses, what the Lord Jesus says of himself. He proclaims, 'I am the light of the world.'

These words imply that the world needs light and is naturally in a dark condition. It is so in a moral and spiritual point of view and it has been so for nearly 6,000 years. In ancient Egypt, Greece and Rome, in modern England, France and Germany, the same report is true. The vast majority of men neither see nor understand the value of their souls, the true nature of God, nor the reality of a world to come! Notwithstanding all the discoveries of art and science, 'Darkness still covers the earth, and gross darkness the people' (Isa. 60:2).

For this state of things, the Lord Jesus Christ declares himself to be the only remedy. He has risen, like the sun, to diffuse light and life and peace and salvation in the midst of a dark world. He invites all who want spiritual help and guidance to turn to him and take him for their leader. What the sun is to the whole solar system — the centre of light and heat and life and fertility — that he has come into the world to be to sinners.

Let this saying sink down into our hearts. It is weighty and full of meaning. False lights on every side invite man's attention in the present day. Reason, philosophy, earnestness, liberalism, conscience and the voice of the church are all, in their various ways, crying loudly that they have got 'the light' to show us. Their advocates know not what they say. Wretched are those who believe their high professions! He only is the true light who came into the world to save sinners, who died as our Substitute on the cross and sits at God's right hand to be our Friend. 'In his light we shall see light' (Ps. 36:9).

For meditation: *Christ is our sunrise, who sheds light on our way and dispels our gloom* (Luke 1:78-79).

Suggested further reading: Luke 18:1-8

A reckoning day for persecutors shall surely come (vv. 50-51). There is something solemn in this statement. The number of those who have been put to death for the faith of Christ in every age of the world is exceedingly great. Thousands of men and women have laid down their lives rather than deny the Saviour and have shed their blood for the truth. At the time they died they seemed to have no helper. Like Zacharias, James, Stephen, John the Baptist, Ignatius, Huss, Hooper and Latimer, they died without resistance. They were soon buried and forgotten on earth and their enemies seemed to triumph utterly. But their deaths were not forgotten in heaven. Their blood was had in remembrance before God. The persecutions of Herod, Nero, Diocletian, Bloody Mary and Charles IX are not forgotten. There will be a great assize one day when the psalmist's words shall be seen to be true (Ps. 116:15).

Let us often look ahead to the Judgement Day. There are many things going on in the world that try our faith. The frequent triumphing of the wicked is perplexing. The frequent depression of the godly is a problem that appears hard to solve. But it shall all be made clear one day. All shall be unravelled and put in its right place. Every drop of righteous blood that has been spilt shall be required.

How wicked it is to keep others back from religious knowledge! (v. 52). The sin denounced here is awfully common. It is the sin of the Roman priest who forbids his people to read the Bible. It is the sin of the unconverted Protestant minister who warns his people against extreme views and sneers at the idea of conversion. It is the sin of the marriage partner or parents who hold back their loved ones from getting involved or becoming serious in religion. All these bring down our Lord's denunciation on themselves by hindering others from entering heaven.

Let us watch ourselves that we never hinder any from reading the Bible, hearing the gospel or private prayer. Let us rather cheer them, encourage them, help them and thank God if they are better than ourselves.

For meditation: *'In fact, everyone who wants to live a godly life in Christ Jesus will be persecuted'* (2 Tim. 3:12).

Suggested further reading: 1 John 1:5 - 2:2

Let us notice in these verses what the Lord Jesus says of those that follow him. He promises, 'He that followeth me shall not walk in darkness, but shall have the light of life.'

To follow Christ is to commit ourselves wholly and entirely to him as our only Leader and Saviour and to submit ourselves to him in every matter, both of doctrine and practice. 'Following' is only another word for 'believing'. It is the same act of soul, only seen from a different point of view. As Israel followed the pillar of cloud and fire in all their journeyings — moving whenever it moved, stopping whenever it tarried, asking no questions, marching on in faith — so must a man deal with Christ. He must 'follow the Lamb whithersoever he goeth' (Rev. 14:4).

He that so follows Christ shall 'not walk in darkness'. He shall not be left in ignorance, like the many around him. He shall not grope in doubt and uncertainty, but shall see the way to heaven and know where he is going. He 'shall have the light of life'. He shall feel within him the light of God's countenance shining on him. He shall find in his conscience and understanding a living light which nothing can altogether quench. The lights with which many please themselves shall go out in the valley of the shadow of death and prove worse than useless. But the light that Christ gives to everyone that follows him shall never fail.

And now, where are we ourselves? Do we know? Many are living and dying in a kind of fog. Where are we going? Can we give a satisfactory answer? Hundreds go out of existence in utter uncertainty. Let us leave nothing uncertain that concerns our everlasting salvation.

For meditation: *There can be no better leader and teacher than he who is the truth and the way to God* (John 14:6).

Suggested further reading: Acts 8:9-13,18-24

In the hearing of a great multitude our Lord delivered warnings against false teachers and denounces the sins of the times in which he lived unsparingly, unflinchingly and without partiality. This was true love. This was doing the work of a physician. This was the pattern that all his ministers are intended to follow. Well might it have been for the church if ministers had always spoken out as plainly and as faithfully as their Master! Their own lives would have been made more uncomfortable, but they would have saved more souls.

Our Lord warns his disciples against hypocrisy (v. 1). This warning can never be overrated. It was delivered by our Lord more than once during his earthly ministry. It was intended to be a standing caution to the church in every age, in every part of the world. It was meant to remind us that the principles of the Pharisees are deeply ingrained in human nature and that Christians should always be on their guard against them. Pharisaism is a subtle leaven that the natural heart is always ready to receive. Once received into the heart it affects the whole character of a man's Christianity.

This plague is about us on every side. Pharisaism lives still in Romanism, Anglo-Catholicism, formalism, church adorning, sacrament worship and ceremonialism.

If we would not become Pharisees let us cultivate a heart religion. Let us realize that the God with whom we have to do looks far beyond the outward surface of our profession and that he measures us by the state of our hearts. Let us be real and true in our Christianity. Let us abhor all part-acting, affectation and semblance of devotion put on for public occasions but not felt within. It may deceive men and get us a reputation for being very religious, but it cannot deceive God (vv. 2-3). Whatever we are in religion, let us not wear a cloak or a mask.

For meditation: *How real is the Christian experience about which you sing and speak? How much is it only a doing of the done thing and a speaking of correct words?*

Suggested further reading: John 17:1-8

Let us notice in these verses what the Lord Jesus says of his enemies. He tells the Pharisees that, with all their pretended wisdom, they were ignorant of God. 'Ye neither know me nor my Father: if ye had known me, ye should have known my Father also.'

Ignorance like this is only too common. There are thousands who are conversant with many branches of human learning and can even argue and reason about religion and yet know nothing really about God. That there is such a being as God they fully admit. But his character and attributes revealed in Scripture — his holiness, his purity, his justice, his perfect knowledge, his unchangeableness — are things with which they are little acquainted. In fact, the subject of God's nature and character makes them uncomfortable and they do not like to dwell upon it.

The grand secret of knowing God is to draw near to him through Jesus Christ. Approached from this side, there is nothing that need make us afraid. Viewed from this standpoint, God is the sinner's friend. God, out of Christ, may well fill us with alarm. How shall we dare to look at so high and holy a being? God in Christ is full of mercy, grace and peace. His law's demands are satisfied. His holiness need not make us afraid. Christ, in one word, is the way and door, by which we must ever draw nigh to the Father. If we know Christ, we shall know the Father. It is his own word: 'No man cometh unto the Father but by me' (John 14:6). Ignorance of Christ is the root of ignorance of God. Wrong at the starting-point, the whole sum of a man's religion is full of error. Christ, the light of the world, is for us as well as for others, if we humbly follow him, cast our souls on him and become his disciples.

For meditation: *Biographies are rarely as revealing as autobiographies. Christ is the autobiography of God — his supreme self-revelation* (John 1:18; Col. 1:15).

Suggested further reading: Psalm 34:1-10

Christ warns us against fearing man (v. 4). But this is not all. He not only tells us whom we ought not to fear, but of whom we ought to be afraid. The manner in which the lesson is conveyed is very striking and impressive. Twice over the exhortation is enforced (v. 5).

The fear of man is one of the greatest obstacles which stand between the soul and heaven. We worry what men will think of us, what they will say of us and what they will do to us. How often these questions have turned the balance against the soul and kept men bound hand and foot by sin and the devil! Thousands would never hesitate a moment to face a lion or charge into battle who dare not face the laughter of relatives, neighbours and friends. If the fear of man is so powerful in our easy days, what in days when it costs much to follow Christ? But he says, 'Fear not.'

But what is the best remedy for the fear of man? How are we to overcome this powerful feeling and break the chains which it throws around us? There is no remedy like that which our Lord recommends. We must supplant the fear of man by a higher and a more powerful principle — the fear of God. We must look away from those who can only hurt the body to him who has all dominion over the soul. We must turn our eyes from those who can only injure us in the life that now is, to him who can condemn us to eternal misery in the life that is to come. The lesser fear must melt before the greater, the weaker before the stronger.

Christ goes on to give encouragement to persecuted believers. Nothing whatever, whether great or small, can happen to a believer without God's ordering and permission (vv. 6-7). Just as the telescope and microscope show us that there is order and design in all the works of God's hand, from the greatest planet to the least insect, so does the Bible teach us that there is wisdom, order and design in all the events of daily life. There is no such thing as chance, luck or accident in the Christian's journey through this world. All is appointed for the believer's good (Rom. 8:28).

For meditation:
Fear him, ye saints, and ye will then
Have nothing else to fear

                         (Tate and Brady).

Suggested further reading: Proverbs 1:20-33

It is possible to seek Christ in vain. Our Lord says to the unbelieving Jews, 'Ye shall seek me, and shall die in your sins.' He meant, by these words, that the Jews would one day seek him in vain.

The lesson before us is a very painful one. That such a Saviour as the Lord Jesus, so full of love, so willing to save, should ever be sought 'in vain' is a sorrowful thought. Yet so it is! A man may have many religious feelings about Christ, without any saving religion. Sickness, sudden affliction, the fear of death, the failure of usual sources of comfort — all these causes may draw out of a man a good deal of 'religiousness'. Under the immediate pressure of these he may say his prayers fervently, exhibit strong spiritual feelings and profess for a season to 'seek Christ' and be a different man. And yet all this time his heart may never be touched at all! Take away the peculiar circumstances that affected him and he may possibly return at once to his old ways. He sought Christ 'in vain', because he sought him from false motives and not with his whole heart.

Unhappily this is not all. There is such a thing as a settled habit of resisting light and knowledge, until we seek Christ 'in vain'. Scripture and experience alike prove that men may reject God until God rejects them and will not hear their prayer. They may go on stifling their convictions, quenching the light of conscience, fighting against their own better knowledge, until God is provoked to give them over and let them alone. It is not for nothing that these words are written: 'Then shall they call upon me, but I will not answer; they shall seek me early, but they shall not find me: for that they hated knowledge, and did not choose the fear of the Lord' (Prov. 1:28-29).

There is no safety but in seeking Christ while he may be found and calling on him while he is near, seeking him with a true heart and calling on him with an honest spirit.

For meditation: *Salvation is not eternally available. There is an accepted time and it is now* (2 Cor. 6:2).

Suggested further reading: Matthew 10:32-42

We must confess Christ on earth if we expect him to own us as his saved people in the last day. We must not be ashamed to let all men see that we believe in Christ, serve Christ, love Christ and care more for the praise of Christ than the praise of men.

The duty of confessing Christ is incumbent on all Christians, not martyrs only. It is not for the great occasions only, but for our daily walk through an evil world. The rich man among the rich, the labourer among labourers, the young among the young, the servant among servants — each and all must be prepared to confess their Master if they are true Christians. It needs no blowing a trumpet, no noisy boasting — nothing more than daily opportunity. If a man loves Jesus he ought not to be ashamed to let people know it.

The difficulty of confessing Christ is undoubtedly very great. It never was easy. It never will be as long as the world stands. It is sure to entail us in laughter, ridicule, contempt, mockery, enmity and persecution. The wicked dislike to see anyone better than themselves. The world that hated Christ will always hate true Christians. But whether we like it or not, whether it is hard or easy, our course is perfectly clear. In one way or another, Christ must be confessed.

The grand motive to stir us up in bold confession is forcibly brought before us. Our denial and refusal to confess now before men will mean his denial and refusal to confess before God (v. 9). He will refuse to acknowledge us as his people. He will disown us as cowards, faithless and deserters. He will not plead for us. He will not be our Advocate. He will not deliver us from wrath to come. What an awful prospect is this! How much turns on this one hinge of confessing Christ before men! Surely we ought not to hesitate for a moment. To deny Christ may get us a little of men's good opinion for a few years but at the last day will be our ruin in hell for all eternity.

For meditation: *A faith that is too weak to prompt us to confess Christ is a faith too weak to enable us to possess Christ.*

Suggested further reading: John 17:9-19

We learn how wide is the difference between Christ and the ungodly. Our Lord says to the unbelieving Jews, 'Ye are from beneath, I am from above: ye are of this world, I am not of this world.'

These words, no doubt, have a special application to our Lord Jesus Christ himself. In the highest and most literal sense, there never was but one who could truly say, 'I am from above... I am not of this world.' That one is he who came forth from the Father and was before the world — even the Son of God.

But there is a lower sense, in which these words are applicable to all Christ's living members. Compared to the thoughtless multitude around them, they are 'from above' and 'not of this world', like their Master. The thoughts of the ungodly are about things beneath; the true Christian's affections are set on things above. The ungodly man is full of this world — its cares and pleasures and profits absorb his whole attention. The true Christian, though in the world, is not of it; his citizenship is in heaven and his best things are yet to come.

The true Christian will do well never to forget this line of demarcation. If he loves his soul and desires to serve God, he must be content to find himself separated from many around him by a gulf that cannot be passed. He may not like to seem peculiar and unlike others, but it is the certain consequence of grace reigning within him. He may find it brings on him hatred, ridicule and hard speeches, but it is the cup which his Master drank and of which his Master forewarned all his disciples: 'If ye were of the world, the world would love his own: but because ye are not of the world, but I have chosen you out of the world, therefore the world hateth you' (John 15:19). Then let the Christian never be ashamed to stand alone and show his colours.

For meditation: *Being a Christian is two-sided. It involves God's knowledge of us and our departure from sin* (2 Tim. 2:19).

Suggested further reading: Acts 4:8-20

There is such a thing as an unpardonable sin (v. 10). This sin appears to be the sin of deliberately rejecting God's truth with the heart while the truth is clearly known with the head. It is a combination of light in the understanding and determined wickedness in the will. It is a sin into which, it may be feared, many constant hearers of the gospel nowadays fall by determined clinging to the world. It is a sin which is commonly accompanied by utter deadness, hardness and insensibility of heart. The man whose sins will not be forgiven is precisely the man who will never seek to have them forgiven. He might be pardoned but he will not seek to be pardoned. He is gospel-hardened and twice dead.

Let us pray that we may be delivered from a cold, speculative, unsanctified head-knowledge of Christianity. It is a rock on which thousands made shipwreck to all eternity. No heart becomes so hard as that on which the light shines but finds no admission. To be called a Christian and know the theory of the gospel and yet cleave to sin and the world with the heart is to be a candidate for the worst and lowest place in hell. It is to be as like as possible to the devil.

Christians need not be over-anxious as to what they shall say when required to speak for Christ's cause (vv. 11-12). This promise has a primary reference to those who are on trial for the faith in court, but there is a secondary sense that should not be overlooked. In the home, or among friends, or at business Christians may suddenly be called on to speak on behalf of their Master. On such occasions the believer should fall back on the Scripture now before us. We need not be alarmed, flurried, cast down or excited. If we remember the promise of Christ we have no reason to be afraid. Our faith should be in our Master that he will help us to say what we ought to say and that we shall be kept from saying what we ought not to say.

For meditation: *When we are called on to speak a word for Christ let us not be taken up with the adequacy of our eloquence and the power of our reason, but with the adequacy and power of Christ.*

Suggested further reading: Luke 16:19-31

Our Lord says to his enemies, 'If ye believe not that I am he, ye shall die in your sins.'

These solemn words are invested with peculiar solemnity when we consider from whose lips they came. Who is this that speaks of men dying 'in their sins', unpardoned, unforgiven, unfit to meet God, of men going into another world with all their sins upon them? He that says this is no other than the Saviour of mankind, who laid down his life for his sheep — the loving, gracious, merciful, compassionate Friend of sinners. It is Christ himself! Let this simple fact not be overlooked.

They are greatly mistaken who suppose that it is harsh and unkind to speak of hell and future punishment. How can such persons get over such language as that which is before us? How can they account for many a like expression which our Lord used, and specially for such passages as those in which he speaks of the 'worm that dieth not and the fire that is not quenched'? (Mark 9:46). They cannot answer these questions. Misled by a false charity and a morbid amiability, they are condemning the plain teaching of the Scripture and are wise above that which is written.

Let us settle it in our minds, as one of the great foundation truths of our faith, that there is a hell. Just as we believe firmly that there is an eternal heaven for the godly, so let us believe firmly that there is an eternal hell for the wicked. Let us never suppose that there is any want of love in speaking of hell. Let us rather maintain that it is the highest love to warn men plainly of danger and to beseech them to 'flee from the wrath to come'. It was Satan, the deceiver, murderer and liar, who said to Eve in the beginning, 'Ye shall not die' (Gen. 3:4). To shrink from telling men that except they believe they will 'die in their sins' may please the devil, but surely it cannot please God.

For meditation: *Denying reality does not change it. Mocking reality does not transform it. Disliking reality does not destroy it. Face reality and flee from wrath to come.*

Suggested further reading: Philippians 4:10-20

The passage we have read now affords a singular instance of man's readiness to bring the things of this world into the midst of his religion. One of our Lord's hearers wanted assistance with his temporal affairs (v. 13). He probably had some vague idea that Jesus was going to set up a worldly kingdom. He resolved to make an early application to him about his own pecuniary matters. When other hearers might be thinking about the world to come, this man's thoughts evidently ran upon this present life. How many gospel hearers are just like this man! How many are incessantly planning about the things of time even under the very sound of the things of eternity! Even the preaching of Christ did not arrest the attention of all his hearers. The servant must not expect his sermons to be more valued than his Master's.

There is a solemn warning given against covetousness (v. 15). There is no sin to which the heart is more prone than covetousness. It was the sin which helped to cast down the angels that fell. They were not content with their first estate (Jude 6). It was this sin that helped drive Adam and Eve out of paradise and brought death into the world (Gen. 3:1-6). They coveted and so they fell. Ever since the Fall this sin has been the fertile cause of misery and unhappiness on earth. Wars, quarrels, strifes, divisions, envyings, disputes, jealousies, hatreds of all sorts, both public and private, may nearly all be traced up to this fountain-head.

Let the warning that our Lord pronounces sink down into our hearts and bear fruit in our lives. Let us try to learn the lesson that St Paul mastered (Phil. 4:11). Let us pray for a thorough confidence in God's superintending providence over all our worldly affairs and God's perfect wisdom in all his arrangements concerning us. Happy is he who is persuaded that whatever is, is best, and has ceased from vain wishing.

For meditation: *The bigger and the better are the gods of this world. We cannot serve them and the true and living God* (Matt. 6:24).

Suggested further reading: Matthew 13:18-23

These verses show us the importance of steady perseverance in Christ's service. There were many, it seems, at this particular period, who professed to believe on our Lord and expressed a desire to become his disciples. There is nothing to show that they had true faith. They appear to have acted under the influence of temporary excitement, without considering what they were doing. And to them our Lord addresses this instructive warning: 'If ye continue in my word, then are ye my disciples indeed.'

This sentence contains a mine of wisdom. To make a beginning in religious life is comparatively easy. Not a few mixed motives assist us. The love of novelty, the praise of well-meaning but indiscreet professors, the secret self-satisfaction of feeling 'how good I am', the universal excitement attending a new position — all these things combine to aid the young beginner. Aided by them he begins to run the race that leads to heaven, lays aside many bad habits, takes up many good ones, has many comfortable frames and feelings and gets on swimmingly for a time. But when the newness of his position is past and gone, when the freshness of his feelings is rubbed off and lost, when the world and the devil begin to pull hard at him, when the weakness of his own heart begins to appear — then it is that he finds out the real difficulties of vital Christianity. Then it is that he discovers the deep wisdom of our Lord's saying now before us. It is not beginning, but 'continuing' a religious profession that is the test of true grace.

We should remember these things in forming our estimate of other people's religion. No doubt we ought to be thankful when we see anyone ceasing to do evil and learning to do well. We must not 'despise the day of small things' (Zech. 4:10). But we must not forget that to begin is one thing and to go on is quite another.

For meditation: *No athlete receives a medal for beginning a race with a sprint and then dropping out. The Christian continues to the end.*

Suggested further reading: Matthew 6:25-34

What a withering exposure our Lord makes of the folly of worldly-mindedness! He draws a picture of the rich man of this world whose mind is wholly set on earthly things. He paints him scheming and planning about his own life as if he were its master. Then he turns the picture to show God questioning the worldling. Folly is the right word for a man who thinks of nothing but his money. The man who has earthly treasure but no treasure with God is a fool.

Such characters are far from being uncommon. Thousands in every age have lived continually doing the very things which are here condemned. Thousands are doing it at this very day. They are laying up treasure on earth and thinking of nothing but how to increase it. They are continually adding to their hoards as if they could enjoy them for ever, and as if there were no death, no judgement and no world to come. And yet these are the men who are called clever, prudent and wise. Truly the Lord does not see as man sees (Isa. 55:8-9).

Let us pray for rich men. Their souls are in great danger. Even when converted the rich carry a great disadvantage. The possession of wealth has a most hardening effect on the conscience. We never know what we might do when we become rich (1 Tim. 6:10). Poverty has many disadvantages, but riches destroy far more souls than poverty.

It is true wisdom to be rich towards God. This is true providing for the time to come. This is genuine prudence. The wise man is concerned for treasure in heaven. When can it be said that a man is rich towards God? Never till he is rich in grace, faith and good works! Never till he has applied to Jesus Christ and bought of him gold tried in the fire! Never till he has a house not made with hands, eternal in the heavens! Never till he has a name inscribed in the book of life and is an heir of God and joint-heir with Jesus! Such a man is truly rich. His treasure is incorruptible. His bank never breaks. Neither man nor death can deprive him of his inheritance.

For meditation: *We may as well hold on to our possessions lightly because death's cold hand will require us to lose grip of them altogether.*

Suggested further reading: 2 Timothy 2:22-26

These verses show us the nature of true slavery. The Jews were fond of boasting, though without any just cause, that they were politically free and were not in bondage to any foreign power. Our Lord reminds them that there was another bondage to which they were giving no heed, although enslaved by it. 'He that committeth sin is the servant of sin.'

How true that is! How many on every side are thorough slaves, although they do not acknowledge it! They are led captive by their besetting corruptions and infirmities and seem to have no power to get free. Ambition, the love of money, the passion for drink, the craving for pleasure and excitement, gambling, gluttony, illicit connections — all these are so many tyrants among men. Each and all have crowds of unhappy prisoners bound hand and foot in their chains. The wretched prisoners will not allow their bondage. They will even boast sometimes that they are eminently *free*. But many of them know better. There are times when the iron enters into their souls and they feel bitterly that they are slaves.

There is no slavery like this. Sin is indeed the hardest of all taskmasters. Misery and disappointment by the way, despair and hell in the end — these are the only wages that sin pays to its servants. To deliver men from this bondage is the grand object of the gospel. To awaken people to a sense of their degradation, to show them their chains, to make them arise and struggle to be free — this is the great end for which Christ sent forth his ministers. Happy is he who has opened his eyes and found out his danger. To know that we are being led captive is the very first step towards deliverance.

For meditation: *One mark of certain types of illness is that the sufferers totally refuse to accept that they are ill and therefore avoid treatment. So it is with the sinner.*

Suggested further reading: Romans 8:28-39

This passage contains a gracious word of consolation for all true believers (v. 32). Our Lord knew the hearts of his disciples well. He knew how ready they were to be filled with fears of every description, fears because of the fewness of their number, fears because of the multitude of their enemies, fears because of the many difficulties in their way, fears because of their sense of weakness and unworthiness. He answers these many fears with one golden sentence (v. 32).

Believers are a little flock. They always have been ever since the world began. Professing servants of God have sometimes been many. But true Christians are very few. It is foolish to be surprised at this. Listen to our Lord's teaching (Matt. 7:14).

Believers have a glorious kingdom awaiting them. Here upon earth they are often mocked and ridiculed, persecuted and, like their Master, despised and rejected of men. But let us remember Paul's words (Rom. 8:18; Col. 3:4).

Believers are tenderly loved by the Father. It is 'the Father's good pleasure' to give them a kingdom. He does not receive them grudgingly, unwillingly and coldly. He rejoices over them as members of his beloved Son in whom he is well pleased. He regards them as his dear children in Christ. He sees no spot in them. Even now when he looks down on them from heaven in the midst of their infirmities he is well pleased and, hereafter, when presented before his glory he will welcome them with exceeding joy (Jude 24).

Are we members of Christ's little flock? Then surely we ought not to be afraid. There are given to us exceeding great and precious promises (2 Peter 1:4). God is ours and Christ is ours. Greater are those that are for us than all that are against us. The world, the flesh and the devil are mighty enemies. But with Christ on our side we have no cause to fear.

For meditation: *Christ has not been sent for us, nor the Spirit sent to us, so that in the end we might fail to reach our eternal home. When God appoints us to salvation he does not fail to bring us to our destiny.*

Suggested further reading: Romans 6:1-11

These verses show us, lastly, the nature of true liberty. Our Lord declares this to the Jews in one comprehensive sentence. He says, 'If the Son shall make you free, ye shall be free indeed.'

Liberty, most Englishmen know, is rightly esteemed one of the highest temporal blessings. Freedom from foreign dominion, a free constitution, free trade, a free press, civil and religious liberty — what a world of meaning lies beneath these phrases! How many would sacrifice life and fortune to maintain the things which they represent! Yet, after all our boasting, there are many so-called freemen who are nothing better than slaves. There are many who are totally ignorant of the highest, purest form of liberty. The noblest liberty is that which is the property of the true Christian. Those only are perfectly free people whom the Son of God 'makes free'. All else will sooner or later be found slaves.

Wherein does the liberty of true Christians consist? Of what is their freedom made up? They are freed from the guilt and consequences of sin by the blood of Christ. Justified, pardoned, forgiven, they can look forward boldly to the Day of Judgement, and cry, 'Who shall lay anything to our charge? Who is he that condemneth?' They are freed from the power of sin by the grace of Christ's Spirit. Sin has no longer dominion over them. Renewed, converted, sanctified, they mortify and tread down sin and are no longer led captive by it. Liberty like this is the portion of all true Christians in the day that they flee to Christ by faith and commit their souls to him. That day they become free men. Liberty like this is their portion for evermore. Death cannot stop it. The grave cannot even hold their bodies for more than a little season. Those whom Christ makes free are free to all eternity.

For meditation: *John Knox as a slave on a galley ship was freer as a Christian than John Newton as a slave-trader without Christ.*

Suggested further reading: Matthew 24:36-44

These verses contain a striking exhortation to seek treasure in heaven (v. 33) and enforce this exhortation with a mighty heart-searching principle (v. 34).

The language of this charge is doubtless somewhat figurative but the meaning is clear and unmistakable. We are to sell — to give up anything, and deny ourselves anything, which stands in the way of our soul's salvation. We are to give — to show love and kindness to everyone, and to be more ready in giving our money to relieve others than to hoard it for our own selfish ends. We are to provide ourselves treasure in heaven — making sure that our names are in the book of life, laying hold of eternal life and laying up for ourselves evidences which will bear inspection on the Day of Judgement. The man who does well for himself is the man who gives up everything for Christ's sake. He carries the cross for a few years in this world and in the world to come has everlasting life.

The true Christian has a frame of mind which is like a servant who expects his master's return (v. 36). He fulfils his duties and does nothing that he would not like to be found doing when his Master comes.

The standard of life which our Lord requires here is an exceedingly high one, but the believer should not flinch from it or be afraid. Readiness for the return of our Lord to this world implies nothing which is impossible or unattainable. It requires no angelic perfection. It requires no man to forsake his family and retire into solitude. It requires nothing more than a life of repentance, faith and holiness. A life of faith, looking unto Jesus, is required.

Are we ourselves living as if we were ready for the second coming of Christ? Well would it be if we put this question to our consciences more frequently! It might keep us back from many a false step in our daily lives. If a man cannot say from his heart, 'Come, Lord Jesus,' there must be something wrong about his soul.

For meditation: *The Thessalonians not only served God but also waited for Christ to come* (1 Thess. 1:10). *How eager are you for his coming?*

Suggested further reading: Romans 2:17-29

We are taught, for one thing, the ignorant self-righteousness of the natural man. We find the Jews pluming themselves on their natural descent from Abraham, as if that must needs cover all deficiencies: 'Abraham is our father.' We find them going even further than this and claiming to be God's special favourites and God's own family: 'We have one Father, even God.' They forgot that fleshly relationship to Abraham was useless unless they shared Abraham's grace. They forgot that God's choice of their father to be head of a favoured nation was never meant to carry salvation to the children, unless they walked in their father's footsteps. All this in their blind self-conceit they refused to see. 'We are Jews. We are God's children. We are the true church. We are in the covenant. We must be all right.' This was their whole argument!

Strange as it may seem, there are multitudes of so-called Christians who are exactly like these Jews. Their whole religion consists of a few notions neither wiser nor better than those propounded by the enemies of our Lord. They will tell you that they 'are regular church people', they 'have been baptized', they 'go to the Lord's table', but they can tell you no more. Of all the essential doctrines of the gospel they are totally ignorant. Of faith and grace and repentance and holiness and spiritual-mindedness they know nothing at all. But, forsooth! they are churchmen and so they hope to go to heaven! There are myriads in this condition. It sounds sad, but unhappily it is only too true.

Let us settle firmly in our minds that connection with a good church and good ancestors is no proof whatever that we ourselves are in a way to be saved. We need something more than this. We must be joined to Christ himself by a living faith. We must know something experimentally of the work of the Spirit in our hearts.

For meditation: *The very best religious pedigree and connections do not make up for the lack of salvation in Christ.*

Suggested further reading: Matthew 25:31-46

The Lord here teaches us the importance of doing in our Christianity. He speaks of his own return. He is comparing his disciples to servants waiting for their master's return, who each have their own work to do during his absence. He pronounces the doer blessed (v. 43).

The warning doubtless has a primary reference to ministers of the gospel. They are stewards of God's mysteries, who are especially bound to be found doing when Christ comes again. But the words contain a further lesson which all Christians would do well to consider. The lesson is the immense importance of a working, practical, diligent, useful religion.

The lesson is one that is greatly needed in the churches of Christ. We hear a great deal about people's intentions, hopes, wishes, feelings and professions. It would be well if we could hear more about people's practice. It is not the servant who is found wishing and professing, but the servant who is found doing, who is blessed.

The lesson is one which many, unhappily, shrink from giving and many more shrink from receiving. We are gravely told that to talk of working and doing is legal and brings Christians into bondage. Remarks of this kind should never move us. They savour of ignorance or perverseness. The lesson before us is not about justification but about sanctification — not about faith but about holiness. The point is not what should a man do to be saved, but what ought a saved man to do? The teaching of Scripture is clear on this point (Titus 3:8). The desire of a true Christian ought to be to be found doing.

If we love life let us resolve by God's help to be doing Christians. This is to be like Christ (Acts 10:38). This is to be like the apostles: they were men of deeds even more than words. This is to glorify God (John 15:8). This is to be useful to the world (Matt. 5:16).

For meditation: *We must not make good works 'dirty words' in our religion. For salvation good works are indeed like filthy rags (Isa. 64:6). But as products of holy living they are adornments of the gospel (Titus 2:10,14).*

Suggested further reading: Galatians 3:26 - 4:7

We are taught the true marks of spiritual sonship. Our Lord makes this point most plain by two mighty sayings. Did the Jews say, 'We have Abraham as our father'? He replies, 'If ye were Abraham's children, ye would do the works of Abraham.' Did the Jews say, 'We have one Father, even God'? He replies, 'If God were your Father, ye would love me.'

Let these two sayings of Christ sink down into our hearts. They supply an answer to two of the most mischievous, yet most common, errors of the present day. What more common, on one side, than vague talk about the universal fatherhood of God? 'All men', we are told, 'are God's children, whatever be their creed or religion; all are finally to have a place in the Father's house, where there are many mansions.' What more common, on another side, than high-sounding statements about the effect of baptism and the privileges of church membership? 'By baptism,' we are confidently told, 'all baptized people are made children of God; all members of the church, without distinction, have a right to be addressed as sons and daughters of the Lord Almighty.'

Statements like these can never be reconciled with the plain language of our Lord in the passage before us. If words mean anything, no man is really a child of God who does not love Jesus Christ. The charitable judgement of a baptismal service or the hopeful estimate of a catechism may call him by the name of a son and reckon him among God's children. But the reality of sonship to God and all its blessings, no one possesses who does not love the Lord Jesus Christ in sincerity (Eph. 6:24). In matters like these we need not be shaken by mere assertions. We may well afford to despise the charge of undervaluing the sacraments. We have only to ask one question: 'What is written?' What saith the Lord? And with this saying before us, we can only come to one conclusion: 'Where there is no love to Christ, there is no sonship to God.'

For meditation: *The right to call God 'Father' belongs to those who have Christ as Saviour.*

Suggested further reading: Luke 13:22-27

Those who neglect the duties of their calling are in awful danger (v. 46). These words apply to ministers, but also to all who occupy positions of trust. Peter's request for clarification as to whom these things applied (v. 41) received no answer.

The language which our Lord uses about slothful and unfaithful servants is peculiarly severe. Few places in the Gospels contain such strong expressions as these. The same loving Saviour, who holds out mercy to the uttermost to the penitent and believing, never shrinks from holding up the judgements of God against those who despise his counsels. Let no man deceive himself on this subject. There is a hell for one who goes on in his wickedness, no less than a heaven for a believer in Jesus.

Let us strive so to live that whenever our heavenly Master comes we may be found ready to receive him. Let us watch our hearts with a godly jealousy and beware of any disposition to lower our standard of holiness.

The greater a man's religious light, the greater is his guilt if he is not converted (vv. 47-48). The lesson of these verses is one of wide application. It demands the attention of many classes. The judgement of every man who has the Bible will be far greater than the judgement of the heathen who has never seen or read it. Every hearer of the gospel is far more guilty than the inhabitant of some dark place where nothing but semi-heathen morality is heard. Every child in a Christian family is far more blameworthy in God's sight than those who live in houses where no honour is paid to the Word of God. Let these things never be forgotten. Our judgement at the last day will be according to our light and opportunities.

What are we doing with our religious knowledge? Are we using it wisely and turning it to good account? Or are we content to know the Lord's will but not to do it? Knowledge not used and light not followed only add to our condemnation.

For meditation: *Even if a man was a walking encyclopaedia of Bible knowledge it would not save him. The Bible has to be believed and obeyed.*

Suggested further reading: Ephesians 6:10-20

We are taught in these verses the reality and character of the devil. Our Lord speaks of him as one whose personality and existence are beyond dispute. In solemn words of stern rebuke he says to his unbelieving enemies, 'Ye are of your father the devil,' led by him, doing his will and showing unhappily that you are like him. And then he paints his picture in dark colours, describing him as a 'murderer' from the beginning, as a 'liar' and the father of lies.

There is a devil! We have a mighty invisible enemy always near us, one who never slumbers and never sleeps, one who is about our path and about our bed and spies out all our ways and will never leave us till we die. He is a murderer! His great aim and object is to ruin us for ever and kill our souls. To destroy, to rob us of eternal life, to bring us down to the second death in hell are the things for which he is unceasingly working. He is ever going about, seeking whom he may devour. He is a liar! He is continually trying to deceive us by false representations, just as he deceived Eve at the beginning. He is always telling us that good is evil and evil good, truth is falsehood and falsehood truth, the broad way good and the narrow way bad. Millions are led captive by his deceit and follow him, both rich and poor, both high and low, both learned and unlearned. Lies are his chosen weapons. By lies he slays many.

These are awful things, but they are true. Let us live as if we believed them. Let us not be like many who mock and sneer and scoff and deny the existence of the very being who is invisibly leading them to hell. Let us believe there is a devil and watch and pray and fight hard against his temptations. Strong as he is, there is one stronger than he who said to Peter, 'I have prayed for thee, that thy faith fail not' (Luke 22:32) and who still intercedes at God's right hand. Let us commit our souls to him. With such a being as the devil going to and fro in the world, we never need wonder to see evil abounding. But with Christ on our side, we need not be afraid.

For meditation: *The devil deceives men into denying his existence and thereby disarms them.*

Suggested further reading: John 10:11-18

The heart of Christ was thoroughly set on finishing the work which he came into the world to do (v. 50). Though this was a baptism of suffering, wounds, agony, blood and death, none of these things moved him. The prospect of coming trouble did not deter him for a moment. He was ready and willing to endure all things in order to provide eternal redemption for his people. Zeal for the cause he had taken into hand was like a burning fire within him. To advance his Father's glory, to open the door of life to a lost world, to provide a fountain for all sin and uncleanness by the sacrifice of himself were continually the uppermost thoughts in his mind. He was pressed in spirit till this mighty work was finished.

Forever let us bear in mind that all Christ's sufferings were endured willingly, voluntarily and of his own free choice on our behalf. They were not submitted to patiently because he could not avoid them. They were not borne without a murmur simply because he could not escape them. He lived a humble life for thirty-three years simply because he loved to do so. He died a death of agony with a willing and a ready mind. Both in life and death he was carrying out the eternal plan whereby God was to be glorified and sinners saved. He carried it out with all his heart, mighty as the struggle was which it entailed upon his flesh and blood. He delighted to do God's will.

Let us not doubt that the heart of Christ in heaven remains the same (Heb. 13:8). He feels as deep an interest now in the salvation of sinners as he did formerly about dying in their stead. There is in him an infinite willingness to receive, pardon, justify and deliver the souls of men from hell. Christ is far more willing to save us than we are to be saved.

Let the recollection of our Master's burning readiness to die for us be like a glowing coal in our memories and constrain us to live for him and not to ourselves. A zealous Saviour should have zealous disciples.

For meditation: *He willingly suffered our hell that we might share his heaven. Should we not serve him with zeal on earth?*

Suggested further reading: Matthew 5:10-12

Silenced in argument, these wicked men resorted to personal abuse. To lose temper and call names is a common sign of a defeated cause.

Nicknames, insulting epithets and violent language are favourite weapons with the devil. When other means of carrying on his warfare fail, he stirs up his servants to smite with the tongue. Grievous indeed are the sufferings which the saints of God have had to endure from the tongue in every age.

The true Christian in the present day must never be surprised to find that he has constant trials to endure from this quarter. Human nature never changes. So long as he serves the world and walks in the broad way, little perhaps will be said against him. Once let him take up the cross and follow Christ and there is no lie too monstrous and no story too absurd for some to tell against him and for others to believe. But let him take comfort in the thought that he is only drinking the cup which his blessed Master drank before him. The lies of his enemies do him no injury in heaven, whatever they may on earth. Let him bear them patiently and not fret or lose his temper. When Christ was reviled, 'he reviled not again' (1 Peter 2:23). Let the Christian do likewise.

We should observe what glorious encouragement our Lord holds out to his believing people. We read that he said, 'Verily, verily, I say unto you, if a man keep my saying, he shall never see death.'

Of course, these words do not mean that true Christians shall never die. But the words do mean that they shall not be hurt by the second death, that final ruin of the whole man in hell of which the first death is only a faint type or figure (Rev. 21:8). And they do mean that the sting of the first death shall be removed from the true Christian. His flesh may fail and his bones may be racked with strong pain, but the bitter sense of unpardoned sins shall not crush him down. This is the worst part of death and in this he shall have the 'victory through our Lord Jesus Christ' (1 Cor. 15:57).

For meditation: *'I consider that our present sufferings are not worth comparing with the glory that will be revealed in us'* (Rom. 8:18).

Suggested further reading: Matthew 10:34-39

It is useless to expect universal peace and harmony from the preaching of the gospel. The disciples were probably expecting Messiah's kingdom to appear at once and for peace to begin to reign (Isa. 11:9). Our Lord saw what was in their hearts and checked their untimely expectations with a striking saying (v. 51).

There is something at first sight very startling in this saying. It seems hard to reconcile it with the angelic promise of peace (Luke 2:14). Yet startling as this saying sounds, it is one which facts have proved literally true. Peace is undoubtedly the result of the gospel wherever it is believed and received. But wherever there are hearers of the gospel who are hardened, impenitent and determined to have their sins, the very message of peace brings division. They that are resolved to live for the world will always be evil affected towards those that are resolved to serve Christ. We may lament this state of things, but we cannot prevent it. Grace and nature can no more amalgamate than oil and water. So long as men are disagreed on the first principles of religion, there can be no real cordiality among them.

Thousands of well-meaning persons nowadays are continually crying out for more 'unity' amongst Christians. To attain this they are ready to sacrifice almost anything, and to throw overboard sound doctrine, if they can secure peace. Such people would do well to remember that even gold may be bought too dear and that peace is useless if purchased at the expense of truth.

Let us never be moved by those who charge the gospel with being the cause of strife and divisions upon earth. It is not the gospel that is to blame, but the corrupt heart of man. The self-willed child refusing the medicine prescribed for its cure is at fault. So long as some men and women will not repent and believe there must be a division. To be surprised at it is the height of folly.

For meditation: *Bishop Ryle's comments on the cry for 'church unity' could have been written today. Still a look of harmony is sought and truth is the casualty. No agreement; no unity.*

Suggested further reading: Isaiah 53:1-12

Abraham had been dead and buried at least 1,850 years and yet he is said to have seen our Lord's day! How wonderful that sounds! Yet it was quite true. Not only did Abraham 'see' our Lord and talk to him when he 'appeared unto him in the plains of Mamre' the night before Sodom was destroyed (Gen. 18:1), but by faith he looked forward to the day of our Lord's incarnation yet to come and, as he looked, he 'was glad'. That he saw many things through a glass darkly we need not doubt. That he could have explained fully the whole manner and circumstances of our Lord's sacrifice on Calvary we are not obliged to suppose. But we need not shrink from believing that he saw in the far distance a Redeemer whose advent would finally make all the earth rejoice. And as he saw it, he 'was glad'.

The plain truth is that we are too apt to forget that there never was but one way of salvation, one Saviour and one hope for sinners and that Abraham and all the Old Testament saints looked to the same Christ that we look to ourselves.

How distinctly our Lord declares his own pre-existence! We read that he said to the Jews, 'Before Abraham was, I am.' Without a controversy, these remarkable words are a great deep. They contain things which we have no eyes to see through, or mind to fathom. But if language means anything, they teach us that our Lord Jesus Christ existed long before he came into the world. Before man was created, he was. In short, they teach us that the Lord Jesus was no mere man like Moses or David. He was one whose goings forth were from everlasting, the same yesterday, today and for ever, very and eternal God.

He to whom the gospel bids us come with our sins and believe for pardon and peace is no mere man. He is nothing less than very God and therefore 'able to save to the uttermost' all who come to him.

For meditation: *There is one divine Saviour for all God's people.*

Suggested further reading: Genesis 5:3-20

We know nothing of the murder of these Galileans, but they gave the Lord an opportunity of talking to men about their own souls which he did not fail to employ. He seized the event and bade his informants look within and think of their own state before God. He points them from the death of others to their own death.

How much more ready people are to talk about the deaths of others than their own death! The death of the Galileans, mentioned here, was probably a common subject of conversation in Jerusalem and all Judea. We can well believe that all the circumstances and particulars belonging to it were continually discussed by thousands who never thought of their own death. It is just the same in the present day. A murder, a sudden death, a shipwreck or a railway accident will completely occupy the minds of a neighbourhood and be in the mouth of everyone you meet. And yet these persons dislike talking of their own death and their own prospects in the world beyond the grave. Such is human nature in every age. In religion men are willing to talk of anybody's business rather than their own.

The state of our souls should always be our first concern. It is eminently true that real Christianity will always begin at home. The converted man will always think first of his own heart, his own life, his own deserts and his own sins. Does he hear of a sudden death? He will say to himself. 'Should I be found ready if this had happened to me?' Does he hear of some awful crime or deed of wickedness? He will say to himself, 'Are my sins forgiven? Have I really repented of my own transgressions?' Does he hear of worldly men running into every excess of sin? He will say to himself, 'Who has made me to differ? What has kept me from walking in the same road except the free grace of God?' Let us feel tender pity and compassion for all who suffer violence or are removed by sudden death. But let us never forget to look at home and to learn wisdom for ourselves from all that happens to others.

For meditation: *The refrain of each genealogy is the same: 'and he died'. We cannot hide from the reality of death, so we need to prepare to meet it.*

Suggested further reading: Psalm 90:1-12

We are told of a man 'who was blind from his birth'. A more serious affliction can hardly be conceived. Of all the bodily crosses that can be laid on man, without taking away life, none perhaps is greater than the loss of sight. It cuts us off from some of the greatest enjoyments of life. It shuts us up within a narrow world of our own. It makes us painfully helpless and dependent on others. In fact, until men lose their eyesight, they never fully realize its value.

Now blindness, like every other bodily infirmity, is one of the fruits of sin. If Adam had never fallen, we cannot doubt that people would never have been blind, or deaf, or dumb. The many ills that flesh is heir to, the countless pains and diseases and physical defects to which we are all liable came in when the curse came upon the earth. 'By one man sin entered into the world, and death by sin' (Rom. 5:12).

Let us learn to hate sin with a godly hatred, as the root of more than half of our cares and sorrows. Let us fight against it, mortify it, crucify it and abhor it both in ourselves and in others.

What a solemn lesson Christ gives us about the use of opportunities! He says to the disciples who asked him about the blind man, 'I must work while it is called today: the night cometh, when no man can work.'

That saying was eminently true when applied to our Lord himself. He knew well that his own earthly ministry would only last three years altogether and, knowing this, he diligently redeemed the time. He let slip no opportunity of doing works of mercy and attending to his Father's business. Morning, noon and night, he was always carrying on the work which the Father gave him to do.

The life that we now live in the flesh is our day. Let us take care that we use it well, for the glory of God and the good of our souls.

For meditation: *Our time is very short. Our daylight will soon be gone. Opportunities once lost can never be retrieved. A second lease of life is granted to no man.*

Suggested further reading: Acts 17:24-31

Our Lord strongly lays down the universal necessity of repentance (vv. 3,5). The truth here asserted is one of the foundations of Christianity. All of us are born in sin. We are fond of sin and are naturally unfit for friendship with God. Two things are absolutely necessary to the salvation of every one of us. We must repent and we must believe the gospel. Without repentance towards God and faith towards our Lord Jesus Christ no man can be saved.

The nature of true repentance is clearly and unmistakably laid down in Scripture. It begins with the knowledge of sin. It goes on to work sorrow for sin. It leads to confession of sin before God. It shows itself before man by a thorough breaking off from sin. It results in producing a habit of deep hatred for all sin. Above all, it is inseparably connected with lively faith in the Lord Jesus Christ. Repentance like this is the characteristic of all true Christians.

The necessity of repentance to salvation will be evident to all who search the Scriptures and consider the nature of the subject. Without it there is no forgiveness of sins. There never was a pardoned man who was not also a penitent. There never was one washed in the blood of Christ who did not feel, mourn, confess and hate his own sins. We could not be happy if we reached the kingdom of glory with a heart loving sin. The company of saints and angels would give us no pleasure. Our minds would not be in tune for an eternity of holiness.

Have we ourselves ever repented? Do we really know our own sinfulness? Do our sins cause us any sorrow? Have we cried to God about our sins and sought forgiveness at the throne of grace? Have we ceased to do evil and broken off from our bad habits? Do we cordially and heartily hate everything that is evil? If we have never yet repented let us begin without delay. For this we are accountable (Acts 3:19; 8:22). There is everything to encourage us to begin. If we have repented in times past let us go on repenting to the end of our lives.

For meditation: *Repentance is often reduced to a meaningless 'I'm sorry'. In fact it is a radical break with all sin.*

Suggested further reading: Matthew 28:18-20

What different means Christ used in working miracles on different occasions! In healing the blind man he might, if he had thought fit, have merely touched him with his finger, or given command with his tongue. But he did not rest content with doing so. We are told that 'He spat on the ground, and made clay of the spittle, and he anointed the eyes of the blind man with the clay.'

The Lord of heaven and earth will not be tied down to the use of any one means or instrumentality. In conferring blessings on man, he will work in his own way and will allow no one to prescribe to him.

We should observe in this passage the almighty power that Christ holds in his hands. We see him doing that which in itself was impossible. Without medicines he cures an incurable case. He actually gives eyesight to one that was born blind.

Such a miracle as this is meant to teach an old truth, which we can never know too well. It shows us that Jesus, the Saviour of sinners, 'has all power in heaven and earth'. Such mighty works could never have been done by one that was merely man. In the cure of this blind man we see nothing less than the finger of God.

Such a miracle, above all, is meant to make us hopeful about our own souls and the souls of others. Why should we despair of salvation while we have such a Saviour? Where is the spiritual disease that he cannot take away? He can open the eyes of the most sinful and ignorant and make them see things they never saw before. He can send light into the darkest heart and cause blindness and prejudice to pass away.

Surely, if we are not saved, the fault will be all our own. There lives at God's right hand one who can heal us if we apply to him. Let us take heed lest those solemn words are found true of us: 'Light is come into the world: but men loved darkness rather than light, because their deeds were evil' (John 3:19). 'Ye will not come to me, that ye might have life' (John 5:40).

For meditation: *Christ has all power in the whole universe. He is Lord of all.*

Suggested further reading: Isaiah 5:1-7

This parable is peculiarly humbling and heart-searching. The Christian who can hear it and not feel sorrow and shame as he looks at the state of Christendom must be in a very unhealthy state of soul.

We are taught that where God gives spiritual privileges he expects proportionate returns. Our Lord teaches this lesson by comparing the Jewish church of his day to a fig tree planted in a vineyard (v. 6). This was exactly the position of Israel in the world. They were separated from other nations by the Mosaic laws and ordinances no less than by the situation of their land. They were favoured with revelations from God which were granted to no other people. Things were done for them which were never done for Egypt, Nineveh, Babylon, Greece or Rome. It was only just and right that they should bear fruit to God's praise. It might reasonably be expected that there would be more faith, penitence, holiness and godliness in Israel than among the heathen. This is what God looked for (v. 6).

But we must look beyond the Jewish church if we mean to get the full benefit of the parable before us. We must look to the Christian churches. They have light, truth, doctrines and precepts of which the heathen never hear. How great is their responsibility! Is it not just and right for God to expect fruit from them? We must look to our own hearts. We live in a land of Bibles, liberty and gospel preaching. How vast are our benefits compared with others! Never let us forget that God expects some fruit.

Few things are so much forgotten by men as the close connection between privilege and responsibility. We are all ready enough to bask in our privileges and pity those not so blessed. But we are slow to remember that we are accountable to God for all that we enjoy. Let us awake to the sense of these things. As a highly blessed people and nation God looks to us to see our fruit.

For meditation: *How much do you value the Bible in your own language, a church where the truth is preached, fellow Christians with whom you can fellowship? While others long for these, do you despise them?*

Suggested further reading: Hebrews 10:19-25

These verses show us how little the Jews of our Lord's time understood the right use of the sabbath day. We read that some of the Pharisees found fault because a blind man was miraculously healed on the sabbath. They said, 'This man is not of God, because he keepeth not the sabbath day.' A good work had manifestly been done to a helpless fellow creature. A heavy bodily infirmity had been removed. A mighty act of mercy had been performed. But the blind-hearted enemies of Christ could see no beauty in the act. They called it a breach of the fourth commandment!

These would-be wise men completely mistook the intention of the sabbath. They did not see that it was 'made for man' and meant for the good of man's body, mind and soul. It was a day to be set apart from others, no doubt, and to be carefully sanctified and kept holy. But its sanctification was never intended to prevent works of necessity and acts of mercy. To heal a sick man was no breach of the sabbath day. In finding fault with our Lord for so doing, the Jews only exposed their ignorance of their own law. They had forgotten that it is as great a sin to add to a commandment as to take it away.

Here, as in other places, we must take care that we do not put a wrong meaning on our Lord's conduct. We must not for a moment suppose that the sabbath is no longer binding on Christians and that they have nothing to do with the fourth commandment. This is a great mistake and the root of great evil. Not one of the Ten Commandments has ever been repealed or put aside. Our Lord never meant the sabbath to become a day of pleasure, or a day of business, or a day of travelling and idle dissipation. He meant it to be 'kept holy' as long as the world stands. It is one thing to employ the sabbath in works of mercy, in ministering to the sick and doing good to the distressed. By the sabbath may be found out whether we love communion with God.

For meditation: *If giving God time now is a bore, why should we expect to enjoy eternity with him?*

Suggested further reading: Romans 2:1-5

It is a most dangerous thing to be unfruitful under great religious privileges. The whole parable plainly warns all professing churches that if their ministers do not preach sound doctrine and their members do not live holy lives they are in peril of destruction. God is every year observing them and taking account of their ways. Not all the forms, services and ordinances will make up for being destitute of the fruit of the Spirit. Except they repent they will be cut down.

There is a plainer warning also for all the unconverted. There are in every congregation those who hear the gospel and who hang over the brink of the pit. They have lived for years in the best part of God's vineyard and have borne no fruit. They have the gospel faithfully preached for hundreds of Sundays and yet have never embraced it, taken up the cross and followed Christ. They do not perhaps run into open sin, but they do nothing for God's glory. Myriads of such professing Christians have no idea of how near they are to destruction. Never let us forget that to be content with sitting in the congregation and hearing sermons while we bear no fruit in our lives is conduct which is most offensive to God. It provokes him to cut us off suddenly without remedy.

But what an infinite debt we all owe to God's mercy and Christ's intercession! We have the loving-kindness of God and the mediation of Christ (v. 8). Mercy has been called the darling attribute of God. Power, justice, purity, holiness, wisdom, unchangeableness are all parts of God's character and have all been manifested to the world in a thousand ways, both in his works and in his Word. But if there is one part of his perfections that he is pleased to exhibit to man more clearly than any other, it is his mercy (Micah 7:18). Mercy is even now why unconverted sinners are so long spared and not cut off in their sins. Even those who are finally lost will find that it was God's long-suffering that kept them from hell till then.

For meditation: *'The Lord is not slow in keeping his promise, as some understand slowness. He is patient with you, not wanting anyone to perish, but everyone to come to repentance'* (2 Peter 3:9).

Suggested further reading: Acts 26:9-24

We read that 'The Jews ... agreed ... that if any man did confess that Jesus was Christ, he should be put out of the synagogue.' They were determined not to believe. They were resolved that no evidence should change their minds and no proofs influence their will. They were like men who shut their eyes and tie a bandage over them and refuse to have it untied. Just as in after-times they stopped their ears when Stephen preached and refused to listen when Paul made his defence, so they behaved at this period of our Lord's ministry.

The state of mind we should always desire to possess is that of the noble-minded Bereans. When they first heard the apostle Paul preach, they listened with attention. They received the Word 'with all readiness of mind'. They 'searched the Scriptures' and compared what they heard with God's Word. 'And therefore,' we are told, 'many of them believed.' Happy are they that go and do likewise! (Acts 17:11-12).

Nothing convinces a man so thoroughly as his own senses and feelings. We read that the unbelieving Jews tried in vain to persuade the blind man whom Jesus healed that nothing had been done for him. They only got from him one plain answer: 'One thing I know, that whereas I was blind, now I see.' How the miracle had been worked, he did not pretend to explain. Whether the person who had healed him was a sinner, he did not profess to know. But that something had been done for him he stoutly maintained. He was not to be reasoned out of his senses. Whatever the Jews might think, there were two distinct facts of which he was conscious: 'I was blind; now I see.'

There is no kind of evidence so satisfactory as this to the heart of a real Christian. His knowledge may be small. His faith may be feeble. His doctrinal views may be at present confused and indistinct. But if Christ has really wrought a work of grace in his heart by his Spirit, he feels within him something that you cannot overthrow.

For meditation: *When men know God in their experience, theoretical denials of his existence count for nothing.*

Suggested further reading: Psalm 126

The parable of the sower is one of those parables which admits of a very wide application. It is being continually verified under our own eyes. Wherever the Word of God is preached and expounded and people are assembled to hear it, the sayings of our Lord in this parable are found to be true. It describes what goes on in all congregations.

The work of the preacher resembles that of the sower. Like the sower, the preacher must sow good seed if he wants to see fruit. He must sow the pure Word of God, and not the traditions of the church or the doctrines of man. Without this his labour will be in vain. He may go to and fro and seem to say much and to work much in his weekly round of ministerial duty. But there will be no harvest of souls for heaven, no living results, no conversions.

Like the sower, the preacher must be diligent. He must spare no pains. He must use every possible means to make his work prosper. He must be patient and undeterred by difficulties and discouragements. No doubt his success does not entirely depend on his labour and diligence, but without labour and diligence success will seldom be obtained (Isa. 32:20; 2 Tim. 4:2; Eccles. 11:4).

Like the sower, the preacher cannot give life. He can scatter the seed committed to his charge, but cannot command it to grow. He may offer the word of truth to the people, but he cannot make them receive it and bear fruit. To give life is God's sovereign prerogative (John 6:63; 1 Cor. 3:7).

Let these things sink deep down in to hearts. It is no light thing to be a real minister of God's Word. To be an idle, formal workman in the church is an easy business. To be a faithful sower is very hard. Preachers ought especially to be remembered in our prayers.

For meditation: *Do you expect too much of those who preach to you? Do you think it is their fault that there are so few conversions? Have you ever looked to your own responsibility? How much do you pray for their ministries to be crowned with success? How much do you waste their time and keep them from their true work? How much do you encourage them in their work? Are you a fellow labourer or a criticizing hindrance?*

Suggested further reading: Romans 8:31-39

We see in these verses how much wiser the poor sometimes are than
the rich. The man whom our Lord healed of his blindness was evidently a person of very humble condition. It is written that he was
one who 'sat and begged' (see v. 8). Yet he saw things which the
proud rulers of the Jews could not see and would not receive. He
saw in our Lord's miracle an unanswerable proof of our Lord's
divine commission. 'If this man were not of God,' he cries, 'he could
do nothing.' In fact, from the day of his cure his position was completely altered. He had eyes and the Pharisees were blind.

We see secondly in these verses how cruelly and unjustly
unconverted men will sometimes treat those who disagree with them.
When the Pharisees could not frighten the blind man who had been
cured, they expelled him from the Jewish church. Because he manfully refused to deny the evidence of his own senses, they excommu-
nicated him and put him to an open shame. They cast him out 'as a
heathen man and a publican'.

The temporal injury that such treatment did to a poor Jew was
very great indeed. It cut him off from the outward privileges of the
Jewish church. It made him an object of scorn and suspicion among
all true Israelites. But it could do no harm to his soul. That which
wicked men bind on earth is not bound in heaven. 'The curse cause-
less shall not come' (Prov. 26:2).

The children of God in every age have only too frequently met
with like treatment. Excommunication, persecution and imprisonment have generally been favourite weapons with ecclesiastical tyrants. Unable, like the Pharisees, to answer arguments, they have
resorted to violence and injustice. Let the child of God console himself with the thought that there is a true church out of which no man
can cast him and a church membership which no earthly power can
take away. He only is blessed whom Christ calls blessed and he only
is accursed whom Christ shall pronounce accursed at the last day.

For meditation: *When a man has done his worst he has failed to
destroy a single child of God* (John 10:28-29).

Suggested further reading: Hebrews 3:12 - 4:2

There are some hearers of the gospel whose hearts are like the way-side in a field (vv. 4,15). These are they who hear sermons but pay no attention to them. They go to a place of worship for form or fashion, to appear respectable before men. But they take no interest whatever in the preaching. It seems to them a mere matter of words and names and unintelligible talk. It is neither money, meat, drink, clothes nor company; and as they sit under the sound of it they are taken up with thinking of other things. It matters nothing whether it is law or gospel. It produces no more effect on them than water on a stone. At the end they go away knowing no more than when they came in.

There are myriads of professing Christians in this state of soul. There is hardly a church or chapel where a number are not to be found. Sunday after Sunday they allow the devil to catch away the good seed that is sown on the face of their hearts. Week after week they live on without faith, fear, knowledge or grace, feeling nothing, caring nothing, taking no more interest in religion than if Christ had never died on the cross at all. And in this state they often die and are buried and are lost for ever in hell. This is a mournful picture but only too true.

The seed of the gospel is plucked away from them by the devil almost as soon as it is sown. It does not sink down into their consciences. It does not make the least impression on their minds. The devil no doubt is everywhere. But nowhere perhaps is he more active than in a congregation of gospel-hearers. From him come wandering thoughts and roving imaginations, listless minds and dull memories, sleepy eyes and fidgety nerves, weary ears and distracted attentions. We shall always find the devil at church. He never stays away from public ordinances. Let us remember this and be on our guard. Heat, cold, draughts, damp, wet, rain, snow are often dreaded by churchgoers and alleged as reasons for not going to church. But Satan is the enemy they ought to fear more than all these.

For meditation: *We need to seek God to keep Satan from us and to provide us with receptive hearts as we listen to his Word preached.*

Suggested further reading: Psalm 3

We see in these verses how great is the kindness and condescension of Christ. No sooner was this poor blind man cast out of the Jewish church than Jesus finds him and speaks words of comfort. He knew full well how heavy an affliction excommunication was to an Israelite and at once cheered him with kind words. He now revealed himself more fully to this man than he did to anyone except the Samaritan woman. In reply to the question, 'Who is the Son of God?' he says plainly, 'Thou hast both seen him, and it is he that talketh with thee.'

We have here one among many beautiful illustrations of the mind of Christ. He sees all that his people go through for his sake and feels for all, from the highest to the lowest. He keeps account of all their losses, crosses and persecutions. 'Are they not all written in his book?' (Ps. 56:8). He knows how to come to their hearts with consolation in their time of need and to speak peace to them when all men seem to hate them.

We see in these verses how dangerous it is to possess knowledge, if we do not make a good use of it. The rulers of the Jews were fully persuaded that they knew all religious truth. They were indignant at the very idea of being ignorant and devoid of spiritual eyesight. 'Are we blind also?' they cried. And then came the mighty sentence: 'If ye were blind, ye should have no sin: but now ye say, We see; therefore your sin remaineth.'

When knowledge only sticks in a man's head and has no influence over his heart and life, it becomes a most perilous possession. And when, in addition to this, its possessor is self-conceited and self-satisfied and fancies he knows everything, the result is one of the worst states of soul into which man can fall. There is far more hope about him who says, 'I am a poor blind sinner and want God to teach me,' than about him who is ever saying, 'I know it, I know it, I am not ignorant,' and yet cleaves to his sins. The sin of that man 'remaineth'.

For meditation: *God requires dependence and humility, not self-sufficiency and pride.*

Suggested further reading: John 8:27-32

There are some hearers of the gospel whose hearts are like the stony ground in a field (vv. 5,16). They are those on whom preaching produces temporary impressions but no deep, lasting, abiding effect. The seed of the Word springs up immediately, as soon as they hear it, and bears a crop of joyful impressions and pleasurable emotions. But these impressions unhappily are only on the surface. Such people take pleasure in hearing sermons in which the truth is faithfully set forth. They can speak with apparent joy and enthusiasm about the sweetness of the gospel and the happiness which they experience as they listen to it. They can be moved to tears by the appeals of preachers and talk with apparent earnestness of their own inner conflicts, hopes, struggles, desires and fears. But unhappily there is no stability in their religion (v. 17). There is no real work of the Holy Spirit within their hearts. Their impressions are like Jonah's plant which came up in a night and perished in a night (Jonah 4:6-7). They fade as rapidly as they grew. Once trouble and persecution come they fall away. Their goodness proves as the morning cloud and early dew (Hosea 6:4). Their religion has no more life in it than the cut flower.

Feelings no doubt fill a most important office in our personal Christianity. Without them there can be no saving religion. Hope, joy, peace, confidence, resignation, love, fear are things which must be felt if they really exist. But it must never be forgotten that there are religious affections that are spurious and false and spring from nothing better than animal excitement. It is quite possible to feel great pleasure or deep alarm under the preaching of the gospel and yet to be utterly destitute of the grace of God. The tears of some hearers of sermons and the extravagant delight of others are no certain marks of conversion. Unless old things are passed away there is no real inner work of conversion and they are on the high road to destruction.

For meditation: *Professions of faith should make us rejoice, but continuance in the things of God is a far more important reason for joy.*

Suggested further reading: Philippians 1:12-18

We have, for one thing, in these verses a vivid picture of a false teacher of religion. Our Lord says that he is one who 'enters not by the door into the sheepfold, but climbs up some other way'.

The 'door', in this sentence, must evidently mean something far more than outward calling and commission. The Jewish teachers, at any rate, were not deficient in this point: they could probably trace up their orders in direct succession to Aaron himself. Ordination is no proof whatever that a man is fit to show others the way to heaven.

The true sense of the 'door' must be sought in our Lord's own interpretation. It is Christ himself who is 'the door'. The true shepherd of souls is he who enters the ministry with a single eye to Christ, desiring to glorify Christ, doing all in the strength of Christ, preaching Christ's doctrine, walking in Christ's steps and labouring to bring men and women to Christ. The false shepherd of souls is he who enters the ministerial office with little or no thought about Christ, from worldly and self-exalting motives, but from no desire to exalt Jesus and the great salvation that is in him. Christ, in one word, is the grand touchstone of the minister of religion. The man who makes much of Christ is a pastor after God's own heart, whom God delights to honour. The minister who makes little of Christ is one whom God regards as an impostor, as one who has climbed up to his holy office not by the door, but by 'some other way'.

Thousands of ordained men in the present day know nothing whatever about Christ, except his name. They have not entered 'the door' themselves and they are unable to show it to others.

Unconverted ministers are the dry-rot of the church. 'When the blind lead the blind' both must fall into the ditch. If we would know the value of a man's ministry, we must never fail to ask, 'Where is the Lamb? Where is the Door? Does he bring forward Christ and give him his rightful place?'

For meditation: *Your minister may have many faults (so have you!) but if he preaches Christ and loves him, treasure him.*

Suggested further reading: 1 Timothy 6:6-10

There are some hearers of the gospel whose hearts are like the thorny ground in a field (vv. 7,18). These are they who attend to the preaching of Christ's truth and to a certain extent obey it. Their understanding assents to it. Their judgement approves of it. Their conscience is affected by it. They acknowledge that it is all right and good and worthy of all reception. They even abstain from many things that the gospel condemns and adopt many habits which the gospel requires. But then they unhappily stop short. Something appears to chain them fast and they never get beyond a certain point in their religion. With everything apparently that is promising and favourable in their spiritual state, they stand still. They never come up to the full standard of New Testament Christianity. They bring no fruit to perfection. The grand secret of this condition is the world (v. 19). They allow the things of the earth to get such a hold upon their minds that they leave no room for the Word of God to do its work. However many sermons they hear, they are not bettered by them. A weekly process of truth-stifling goes on within.

The things of this life form one of the greatest dangers that beset a Christian's path. The money, the pleasures, the daily business of the world are so many traps to catch souls. Thousands of things which in themselves are innocent become, when followed to excess, little better than soul poisons and helps to hell. Open sin is not the only thing that ruins souls. In the midst of our families, and in the pursuit of our lawful callings, we have need to be on our guard. Except we watch and pray, these temporal things may rob us of heaven and smother every sermon we hear. Without a decided change we will never enter the kingdom of heaven in this state. Christ will have all our hearts. James's warning stands (James 4:4).

For meditation: *We live in a preoccupied day when so many are too busy to listen to what God has to say. But no one who is too busy to listen now will be too busy to appear before God and be damned. We can and should make time for God.*

Suggested further reading: 1 John 4:1-6

We have, for one thing, in these verses, a peculiar picture of true Christians. Our Lord describes them as sheep who 'hear the voice of a true Shepherd, and know his voice', and as 'sheep who will not follow a stranger, but will flee from him, for they know not the voice of strangers'.

The thing taught in these words is a very curious one and may seem 'foolishness' to the world. There is a spiritual instinct in most true believers, which generally enables them to distinguish between true and false teaching. When they hear unsound religious instruction, there is something within them which says, 'This is wrong.' When they hear the real truth as it is in Jesus, there is something in their hearts which responds, 'This is right.' The careless man of the world may see no difference whatever between minister and minister, sermon and sermon. The poorest sheep of Christ, as a general rule, will 'distinguish things that differ', though he may sometimes be unable to explain why.

Let us beware of despising this spiritual instinct. Whatever a sneering world may please to say, it is one of the peculiar marks of the indwelling of the Holy Ghost. As such, it is specially mentioned by St John, when he says, 'Ye have an unction from the Holy One, and ye know all things' (1 John 2:20). Let us rather pray for it daily, in order that we may be kept from the influence of false shepherds. To lose all power of distinguishing between bitter and sweet is one of the worst symptoms of bodily disease. To be unable to see any difference between law and gospel, truth and error, Protestantism and popery, the doctrine of Christ and the doctrine of man is a sure proof that we are yet dead in heart and need conversion.

For meditation: *The gospel in which the Christian rejoices is the very thing that others scorn and find offensive* (1 Cor. 1:23-24).

Suggested further reading: John 15:1-8

There are some hearers of the gospel whose hearts are like the good ground in a field (vv. 8,20). These are they who really receive Christ's truth into the bottom of their hearts, believe it implicitly and obey it thoroughly. In these the fruits of that truth will be seen — uniform, plain and unmistakable results in heart and life. Sin will be truly hated, mourned over, resisted and renounced. Christ will be truly loved, trusted in, followed and obeyed. Holiness will show itself in all their lives, in humility, spiritual-mindedness, patience, meekness and love. There will be something that can be seen. The true work of the Holy Spirit cannot be hid.

Forever let us bear in mind that this is the only religion that saves. Outward profession of Christianity and the formal use of church ordinances and sacraments never yet gave a man good hope in life, peace in death or rest in the world beyond the grave. There must be the fruit of the Spirit in our hearts and lives, or else the gospel is preached to us in vain. Those only who bear such fruits shall be found at Christ's right hand at the day of his appearing.

There will always be some fruitful hearers wherever the gospel is preached faithfully. Their numbers may very likely be few compared to the worldly around them. Their experience and degree of spiritual attainment may differ widely; some bring forth thirty, some sixty and some a hundredfold. But the fruit of the seed falling into the ground will always be of the same kind. There will always be visible repentance, visible faith in Christ and visible holiness of life. Without these things there is no saving religion.

Let us leave the parable with a deep sense of the danger and responsibility of all hearers of the gospel. There are four ways in which we may hear, and of these four only one is right. There are three kinds of hearers whose souls are in imminent peril. There is only one class of hearers who are right in the sight of God. Are we?

For meditation: *We are known by our fruits* (Matt. 7:20). *What does the fruit of your life reveal about you?*

Suggested further reading: Hebrews 10:19-25

We have in these verses a most instructive picture of Christ himself. He utters one of those golden sayings which ought to be dear to all true Christians. They apply to people as well as to ministers. 'I am the door: by me if any man enter in, he shall be saved, and shall go in and out, and find pasture.'

We are all by nature separate and far off from God. Sin, like a great barrier wall, rises between us and our Maker. The sense of guilt makes us afraid of him. The sense of his holiness keeps us at a distance from him. Born with a heart at enmity with God, we become more and more alienated from him by practice the longer we live. The very first questions in religion that must be answered are these: 'How can I draw near to God? How can I be justified? How can a sinner like me be reconciled to my Maker?'

The Lord Jesus Christ has provided an answer to these mighty questions. By his sacrifice for us on the cross, he has opened a way through the great barrier and provided pardon and peace for sinners. He has 'suffered for sin, the just for the unjust, to bring us to God'. He has opened a way into the holiest, through his blood, by which we may draw near to God with boldness and approach God without fear. And now he is able to save to the uttermost all who come unto God by him. In the highest sense he is 'the door'. No one 'can come to the Father' but by him.

Let us take heed that we use this door and do not merely stand outside looking at it. It is a door free and open to the chief of sinners: 'If any man enter in by it he shall be saved.' It is a door within which we shall find a full and constant supply for every want of our souls. We shall find that we can 'go in and out' and enjoy liberty and peace. The day comes when this door will be shut for ever and men shall strive to enter in, but not be able. Then let us make sure work of our own salvation. Let us not stand tarrying without and halting between two opinions. Let us enter in and be saved.

For meditation: *The door to heaven is still wide open. Have you yet entered in?*

Suggested further reading: 2 Timothy 3:1-15

The parable of the wheat and the tares is eminently suited to correct the extravagant expectations in which many Christians indulge as to the effect of missions abroad and of preaching the gospel at home.

The parable teaches us that good and evil will always be found together until the end of the world. It is a vast field in which wheat and tares grow side by side. The purest preaching of the gospel will not prevent this. The devil, that great enemy of souls, has always taken care to sow tares. Extreme efforts to obtain purity will do more harm than good. We run the risk of encouraging hypocrisy and breaking many a bruised reed. Those who care not what happens to the wheat, in their zeal to root up the tares, show little of the mind of Christ. The labours of our missionaries and ministers will not see the conversion of the whole world because there will always be tares.

The present mixed state of things is not to be for ever. The wheat and tares are divided at last. The Lord Jesus shall send forth his angels in the day of his second advent. Those mighty reapers shall make no mistake. They shall discern with unerring judgement between the righteous and the wicked and place everyone in his own lot. The worldly, the ungodly, the careless and the unconverted shall be cast into a furnace of fire and receive shame and everlasting contempt.

Let the ungodly man tremble when he reads this parable. Let him see in its fearful language his own certain doom unless he repents and is converted. Let him know that he is sowing misery for himself if he goes on still in neglect of God. Let him reflect that his end will be to be gathered among the bundles of tares and be burned. Surely such a prospect ought to make a man think!

Let the believer in Christ take comfort. There is happiness and safety prepared for him in the great and terrible day of the Lord. The voice of the archangel shall summon him to join a perfect church.

For meditation: *Although this world shall ever be a mixture of righteousness and evil, we look forward to a renewed universe where righteousness alone is at home* (2 Peter 3:13).

Suggested further reading: 2 Timothy 1:8-12

These verses show us, for one thing, the great object for which Christ came into the world. He says, 'I am come that [men] might have life, and that they might have it more abundantly.'

The truth contained in these words is of vast importance. They supply an antidote to many crude and unsound notions which are abroad in the world. Christ did not come to be only a teacher of new morality, or an example of holiness and self-denial, or a founder of new ceremonies, as some have vainly asserted. He left heaven and dwelt for thirty-three years on earth for far higher ends than these. He came to procure eternal life for man by the price of his own vicarious death. He came to be a mighty fountain of spiritual life for all mankind, to which sinners coming by faith might drink and, drinking, might live for evermore. By Moses came laws, rules, ordinances, ceremonies. By Christ came grace, truth and eternal life.

Important as this doctrine is, it requires to be fenced with one word of caution. We must not overstrain the meaning of our Lord Jesus Christ's words. We must not suppose that eternal life was a thing entirely unknown until Christ came, or that the Old Testament saints were in utter darkness about the world to come. The way of life by faith in a Saviour was a way well known to Abraham and Moses and David. A Redeemer and a sacrifice was the hope of all God's children from Abel down to John the Baptist, but their vision of these things was necessarily imperfect. They saw them afar off and not distinctly. They saw them in outline only and not completely. It was the coming of Christ which made all things plain and caused the shadows to pass away. Life and immortality were brought into full light by the gospel. In short, to use our Lord's own words, even those who had life had it 'more abundantly' when Christ came into the world.

For meditation: *The life that our Lord brings transforms our present life on earth and opens up a new life for ever.*

Suggested further reading: Luke 8:16-18

Mark emphasizes for us the importance of hearing and considering well what we hear (v. 24). This is a point to which our Lord evidently attaches great weight. We have seen it already brought out in the parable of the sower and it is now enforced by two statements (vv. 23-24).

Hearing the truth is one principal avenue through which grace is conveyed to the soul of man (Rom. 10:17). One of the first steps towards conversion is to receive from the Spirit a hearing ear. Seldom are men brought to repentance and faith without hearing. The general rule is that of which St Paul reminds us in Ephesians 1:13.

Let us bear this in mind when we hear preaching decried. There are many who proclaim loudly that it is of far more importance to the soul to hear liturgical forms read, and to receive the Lord's Supper, than to hear God's Word expounded. Of all such notions let us beware. Let it be a settled principle that hearing the Word is one of the foremost means of grace that God has given to man (2 Tim. 4:2).

Luke emphasizes for us the importance of right hearing — not what we hear but how (Luke 8:18). The degree of benefit which men receive from all the means of grace depends entirely on the way in which they use them. It is not good enough that we go to church and hear sermons. We may do so for fifty years and be nothing bettered but rather worse.

Would anyone know how to hear aright? Then let him lay to heart three simple rules. For one thing, we must hear with faith, believing implicitly that every word of God is true and shall stand. Without faith the Word does not profit (Heb. 4:2). For another thing we must hear with reverence, remembering that the Bible is the book of God (1 Thess. 2:13). Above all we must hear with prayer, praying for God's blessing before the sermon is preached, praying for God's blessing after the sermon is over. Here lies the great defect of the hearing of many. They ask no blessing and so they have none. The sermon passes through their minds like water through a leaky vessel and leaves nothing behind.

For meditation: *Do you prepare yourself for listening to the preached Word? If not, is this the key to so much fruitless hearing?*

Suggested further reading: Psalm 23

These verses show us one of the principal offices which Jesus Christ fills for true Christians. Twice over our Lord uses an expression which, to an Eastern hearer, would be singularly full of meaning. Twice over he says emphatically, 'I am the Good Shepherd.' It is a saying rich in consolation and instruction.

Like a good shepherd, Christ knows all his believing people. Their names, their families, their dwelling-places, their circumstances, their private history, their experience, their trials — with all these things Jesus is perfectly acquainted. There is not a thing about the least and lowest of them with which he is not familiar. The children of this world may not know Christians and may count their lives folly, but the Good Shepherd knows them thoroughly and, wonderful to say, does not despise them.

Like a good shepherd, Christ cares tenderly for all his believing people. He provides for all their wants in the wilderness of this world and leads them by the right way to a city of habitation. He bears patiently with their many weaknesses and infirmities and does not cast them off because they are wayward, erring, sick, footsore or lame. He guards and protects them against all their enemies, as Jacob did the flock of Laban, and of those that the Father has given him he will be found at last to have lost none.

Like a good shepherd, Christ lays down his life for the sheep. He did it once for all, when he was crucified for them. When he saw that nothing but his blood could deliver them from hell and the devil he willingly made his soul an offering for their sins. The merit of that death he is now presenting before the Father's throne. The sheep are saved for evermore, because the Good Shepherd died for them. This is indeed a love that passeth knowledge! 'Greater love hath no man than this, that a man lay down his life for his friends'(John 15:13).

For meditation: *When a stranger enters a field of sheep they scatter in alarm. When their own shepherd comes they are confident. They know they can trust him.*

Suggested further reading: Matthew 25:14-30

A diligent use of religious privileges is important (vv. 24-25). This principle is continually brought forward in Scripture. All that believers have is undoubtedly of grace. Their repentance, faith and holiness are all the gifts of God. But the degree to which a believer attains in grace is ever set before us as closely connected with his own diligence in the use of means and his own faithfulness in living up to the light and knowledge that he possesses. Indolence and laziness are always discouraged in God's Word. Labour and pains in hearing, reading and prayer are always represented as bringing their own reward (Prov. 13:4; 19:15).

Attention to this great principle is the main secret of spiritual prosperity. The man who makes rapid progress in spiritual attainments, who grows visibly in grace, knowledge, strength and usefulness, will always be found to be a diligent man. He leaves no stone unturned to promote his soul's well-being. He is diligent in his Bible study, diligent in his private devotions, diligent as a hearer of sermons and diligent in his attendance at the Lord's table. And he reaps according as he sows. Just as the muscles of the body are strengthened by regular exercise, so are the graces of the soul increased by diligence in using them.

We ought not only to receive knowledge but impart it to others (v. 21). A candle is not lit in order to be hidden and concealed, but to be set on a candlestick and used. Religious light is not given to a man for himself alone but for the benefit of others. We are to try to spread and diffuse our knowledge. We are to display to others the precious treasure that we have found and persuade them to seek it for themselves.

We shall all have to give an account of our use of knowledge one day. The books of God in the judgement shall show what we have done. If we have been content with a lazy, idle, do-nothing Christianity, and cared nothing what happened to others so long as we went to heaven ourselves, there will be a fearful exposure at last (v. 22).

For meditation: *Our spiritual usefulness to others will depend on our care over our own spiritual state.*

Suggested further reading: Isaiah 40:1-11

We should notice the name which Christ gives to true Christians. He uses a figurative expression which, like all his language, is full of deep meaning. He calls them 'my sheep'.

The word 'sheep', no doubt, points to something in the character and ways of true Christians. It would be easy to show that weakness, helplessness, harmlessness, usefulness are all points of resemblance between the sheep and the believer. But the leading idea in our Lord's mind was the entire dependence of the sheep upon its shepherd. Just as sheep hear the voice of their own shepherd and follow him, so do believers follow Christ. By faith they listen to his call. By faith they submit themselves to his guidance. By faith they lean on him and commit their souls implicitly to his direction. The ways of a shepherd and his sheep are a most useful illustration of the relation between Christ and the true Christian.

The expression 'my sheep' points to the close connection that exists between Christ and believers. They are his by gift from the Father, his by purchase, his by calling and choice and his by their own consent and heart-submission. In the highest sense they are Christ's property and, just as a man feels a special interest in that which he has bought at a great price and made his own, so does the Lord Jesus feel a peculiar interest in his people.

Expressions like these should be carefully treasured up in the memories of true Christians. They will be found cheering and heart-strengthening in days of trial. The world may see no beauty in the ways of a godly man and may often pour contempt on him. But he who knows that he is one of Christ's sheep has no cause to be ashamed. He has within him a 'well of water springing up into everlasting life' (John 4:14).

For meditation: *The tender care of the Shepherd for the sheep should ever be their comfort in times of weakness and trial* (Isa. 40:11).

Suggested further reading: 1 Corinthians 3:1-9

This parable sets before us the work of grace in the individual soul. We must not press the details. In this, as in many of our Lord's parables, we must carefully keep in view the main scope and object of the whole story and not stress lesser points.

As in the growth of corn, so in the work of grace, there must be a sower. The earth, as we know, never brings forth corn of itself. It is a mother of weeds but not of wheat. The hand of man must plough it and scatter the seed, or else there would never be a harvest.

The heart of man, in like manner, will never of itself turn to God, repent, believe and obey. It is utterly barren of grace. It is entirely dead towards God and unable to give itself to spiritual life. The Son of man must break it up by his Spirit and give it a new nature. He must scatter over it by the hand of his labouring ministers the good seed of the Word.

Let us mark this truth well. Grace in the heart is a new principle from outside, sent down from heaven and implanted in the soul. Left to himself no man living would ever seek God. And yet in communicating grace God ordinarily works by means. To despise the instrumentality of teachers and preachers is to expect corn where no seed has been sown.

There is much that is beyond man's comprehension and control (v. 27). The wisest farmer on earth can never explain all that takes place in a grain of wheat when he has sown it. He knows he must plant seed, but why some grains come up and others die, and the hour and minute when life shall begin to show itself, he cannot define. He sows the seed and leaves the growth to God (1 Cor. 3:7).

The workings of grace in the heart in like manner are utterly mysterious and unsearchable. We cannot explain why the Word produces effects on one person in a congregation and not on another, why one rejects the Word and another is born again, nor how the Spirit conveys life to the soul. We see results but not processes (John 3:8). As God alone gives life we must diligently work and leave success with God.

For meditation: *Where the gospel is not spread the people cannot believe it* (Rom. 10:14-15). *Do not pray for conversions if you will not spread the Word!*

Suggested further reading: John 19:5-11

These verses show us that when Christ died, he died of his own voluntary free will. He uses a remarkable expression to teach this: 'I lay down my life that I might take it again. No man taketh it from me, but I lay it down of myself. I have power to lay it down and I have power to take it again.' The point before us is of no mean importance. We must never suppose for a moment that our Lord had no power to prevent his sufferings and that he was delivered up to his enemies and crucified because he could not help it. Nothing could be further from the truth than such an idea. The treachery of Judas, the armed band of priests' servants, the enmity of scribes and Pharisees, the injustice of Pontius Pilate, the rude hands of Roman soldiers, the scourge, the nails and the spear — all these could not have harmed a hair of our Lord's head, unless he had allowed them. Well might he say those remarkable words: 'Thinkest thou that I cannot now pray to my Father, and he shall presently give me more than twelve legions of angels? But how, then, shall the Scripture be fulfilled?' (Matt. 26:53).

The plain truth is that our Lord submitted to death of his own free will, because he knew that his death was the only way of making atonement for man's sins. He poured out his soul unto death with all the desire of his heart, because he had determined to pay our debt to God and redeem us from hell. For the joy set before him he willingly endured the cross and laid down his life, in order that we, through his death, might have eternal life. His death was not the death of a martyr, who sinks at last overwhelmed by enemies, but the death of a triumphant conqueror, who knows that even in dying he wins for himself and his people a kingdom and a crown of glory.

Let us lean back our souls on these mighty truths and be thankful. If we hear his voice, repent and believe, he is our own.

For meditation: *On the day of Jesus' death Pilate thought he was in control* (John 19:10) *but our Lord knew otherwise* (John 19:11).

Suggested further reading: Philippians 3:12-21

As in the growth of corn, so in the work of grace, life manifests itself gradually. The ripe ear of wheat does not appear at once, as soon as the seed bursts forth into life. The plant goes through many stages before it arrives at perfection (v. 28). But in all these stages one great thing is true about it: even at its weakest it is a living plant.

In like manner, the work of grace goes on in the heart by degrees. The children of God are not born perfect in faith, hope, knowledge or experience. Their beginning is a day of small things. They see in part their own sinfulness and Christ's fulness and the beauty of holiness. But for all that, the weakest child in God's family is a true child of God. With all his weakness and infirmity he is alive. The seed of grace has really come up in his heart though at present it be only in the blade. He is alive from the dead — and any life is better than death (Eccles. 9:4).

Let us not despise grace because it is weak, or think that people are not converted because they are not yet as strong in the faith as St Paul. Let us remember that grace, like everything else, must have a beginning. The mightiest oak was once an acorn. The strongest man was once a babe. Better a thousand times have grace in the blade than no grace at all.

As in the growth of corn, so in the work of grace, there is no harvest till the seed is ripe. No farmer thinks of cutting his wheat when it is green. He waits till the sun, rain, heat and cold have done their appointed work and the golden ears hang down. Then, and not till then, he puts in the sickle and gathers the wheat into his barn.

God deals with his work of grace in exactly the same way. He never removes his people from this world till they are ripe and ready. He never takes them away till their work is done. They never die at the wrong time. We do not understand why some die in the midst of their usefulness, but all was done well by God in their deaths as well as in their lives. There is no chance, accident or mistake about the decease of any believer.

For meditation: *God used six days to create a formless world into an inhabitable earth. He works by process. So he does in making us like Christ* (Rom. 8:29).

Suggested further reading: Acts 19:23-41

We should notice in this passage what strifes and controversies our Lord occasioned when he was on earth. We read that 'There was a division among the Jews for his sayings,' and that 'Many of them said, He hath a devil, and is mad,' while others took an opposite view. It may seem strange, at first sight, that he who came to preach peace between God and man should be the cause of contention. But herein were his own words literally fulfilled: 'I came not to send peace, but a sword' (Matt. 10:34). The fault was not in Christ or his doctrine, but in the carnal mind of his Jewish hearers.

Let us never be surprised if we see the same thing in our own day. Human nature never changes. So long as the heart of man is without grace, so long we must expect to see it dislike the gospel of Christ. Just as oil and water, acids and alkalies, cannot combine, so in the same way unconverted people cannot really like the people of God. 'The carnal mind is enmity against God' (Rom. 8:7). 'The natural man receiveth not the things of the Spirit of God' (1 Cor. 2:14).

The servant of Christ must think it no strange thing if he goes through the same experience as his Master. He will often find his ways and opinions in religion the cause of strife in his own family. He will have to endure ridicule, hard words and petty persecution from the children of this world. He may even discover that he is thought a fool or a madman on account of his Christianity. Let none of these things move him. The thought that he is a partaker of the afflictions of Christ ought to steel him against every trial. 'If they have called the Master of the house Beelzebub, how much more shall they call them of his household' (Matt. 10:25).

One thing, at any rate, should never be forgotten. We must not allow ourselves to think the worse of religion because of the strifes and dissensions to which it gives rise. Whatever men may please to say, it is human nature, and not religion, which is to blame.

For meditation: *Our Lord divides humanity not just for time, but for eternity. Are you with him or against him?*

Suggested further reading: Zechariah 4:1-7

The mustard seed shows us the progress of professing Christianity in the world. Like a grain of mustard seed, Christ's visible church was to be small and weak in its beginnings. Weakness and apparent insignificance were undoubtedly characteristics of its beginning. Its King came as a feeble infant, born in a manger at Bethlehem, without riches, attendants, armies or power. The men that King gathered round him and appointed as his apostles were fishermen and publicans, not influential men likely to shake the world. The King's last public act was to be crucified among thieves, having been forsaken by nearly all his disciples, betrayed by one and denied by another. The King's followers offered life to the world through his death on a cross. Here is weakness and feebleness. To the eyes of man the visible church was contemptible, insignificant and powerless in its beginnings.

However, the mustard seed once planted, the visible church, was to grow and greatly increase. It began to grow on the Day of Pentecost, and grew with a rapidity which nothing can account for but the finger of God. Its growth until it took over the world must have been a marvel in the eyes of many, but this is what our Lord foretold.

The visible church has not yet done growing. Notwithstanding the melancholy apostasy of some of its branches and the deplorable weakness of others, it is still extending and expanding all over the world. The prophecy is not yet exhausted. A day shall yet come when the great Head of the church shall take his power and reign. The earth shall be filled with the knowledge of God, as the waters cover the sea (Isa. 11:9). The little seed shall become a great tree and fill the whole earth (Dan. 2:35).

Let us resolve never to despise any movement or instrumentality in the church of Christ because at first it was weak and small (Zech. 4:10). One child may be the beginning of a flourishing school, one conversion the beginning of a mighty church, one word the beginning of some blessed Christian enterprise, one seed the beginning of a rich harvest of saved souls.

For meditation: *God and one man are a majority with infinite strength.*

Suggested further reading: Isaiah 49:14-26

Christ 'knows' his people with a special knowledge of approbation, interest and affection. By the world around them they are comparatively unknown, uncared for or despised. But they are never forgotten or overlooked by Christ.

Christ 'gives' his people 'eternal life'. He bestows on them freely a right and title to heaven, pardoning their many sins and clothing them with a perfect righteousness. Money and health and worldly prosperity he often wisely withholds from them. But he never fails to give them grace, peace and glory.

Christ declares that his people 'shall never perish'. Weak as they are, they shall all be saved. Not one of them shall be lost and cast away; not one of them shall miss heaven. If they err, they shall be brought back; if they fall, they shall be raised. The enemies of their souls may be strong and mighty, but their Saviour is mightier and none shall pluck them out of their Saviour's hands.

A promise like this deserves the closest attention. If words mean anything, it contains that great doctrine, the perseverance, or continuance in grace, of true believers. That doctrine is literally hated by worldly people. No doubt, like every other truth of Scripture, it is liable to be abused. But the words of Christ are too plain to be evaded. He has said it and he will make it good: 'My sheep shall never perish.'

Whatever men may please to say against this doctrine, it is one which God's children ought to hold fast and defend with all their might. To all who feel within them the workings of the Holy Spirit, it is a doctrine full of encouragement and consolation. Once inside the ark, they shall never be cast out. Once converted and joined to Christ, they shall never be cut off from his mystical body. Hypocrites and false professors shall doubtless make shipwreck for ever, unless they repent. But true 'sheep' shall never be confounded. Christ has said it, and Christ cannot lie: 'They shall never perish.'

For meditation:
More happy, yet not more secure,
The glorified spirits in heaven

                                                    (A. M. Toplady).

Suggested further reading: Philippians 3:2-11

Men really convinced of the importance of salvation will give up everything to win Christ and eternal life. What was the conduct of the two men our Lord describes? Both were convinced that they had found a thing of great value (vv. 44,46). Both were satisfied that it was worth a great present sacrifice to make this thing their own. Others might wonder at them. Others might think them foolish for paying such a sum of money for the field and the pearl. But they knew what they were about. They were sure that they were making a good bargain.

The conduct of a true Christian is explained in this single picture! He is what he is, and does what he does in religion because he is thoroughly persuaded that it is worthwhile. He comes out from the world. He puts off the old man. He forsakes the vain companions of his past life. He gives up everything, counting them worthless. Why? Because he is convinced that Christ will make amends to him for all his sacrifices. He sees in Christ an endless treasure. He sees in Christ a precious pearl. To win Christ he will make any sacrifice. This is true faith. This is the stamp of the work of the Holy Spirit.

We have in these two parables the real clue to the conduct of many unconverted people. They are what they are in religion because they are not fully persuaded that it is worthwhile to be different. They flinch from decision. They shrink from taking up the cross. They halt between two opinions. They will not commit themselves. They will not come forward boldly on the Lord's side. Why? Because they are not convinced it will answer their needs. They are not sure that treasure is before them. They are not satisfied that the pearl is worth so great a price. They cannot yet make up their minds to 'sell all' that they might win Christ. And so too often they perish everlastingly! When a man will venture nothing for Christ's sake we must draw the conclusion that he has not got the grace of God.

For meditation: *Peter tells us that Christ is precious to those who believe* (1 Peter 2:7). *How precious is he to you?*

Suggested further reading: 1 Kings 22:7-18

We should observe the extreme wickedness of human nature. The unbelieving Jews at Jerusalem were neither moved by our Lord's miracles, nor by his preaching. They were determined not to receive him as their Messiah. Once more it is written that 'They took up stones to stone him.'

Our Lord had done the Jews no injury. He was no robber, murderer or rebel against the law of the land. He was one whose whole life was love and who 'went about doing good' (Acts 10:38). There was no fault or inconsistency in his character. There was no crime that could be laid to his charge. So perfect and spotless a man had never walked on the face of this earth. But yet the Jews hated him and thirsted for his blood. How true are the words of Scripture: 'They hated him without a cause'! (John 15:25). How just the remark of an old divine: 'Unconverted men would kill God himself if they could only get at him'!

The true Christian has surely no right to wonder if he meets with the same kind of treatment as our blessed Lord. In fact, the more like he is to his Master and the more holy and spiritual his life, the more probable is it that he will have to endure hatred and persecution. Let him not suppose that any degree of consistency will deliver him from this cross. It is not his faults, but his graces, which call forth the enmity of men. The world hates to see anything of God's image. The children of the world are vexed and pricked in conscience when they see others better than themselves. Why did Cain hate his brother Abel and slay him? 'Because,' says St John, 'his own works were evil, and his brother's righteous' (1 John 3:12). Why did the Jews hate Christ? Because he exposed their sins and false doctrines and they knew in their own hearts that he was right and they were wrong.

For meditation: *Men will put up with anything except the truth that exposes the evil of their hearts.*

Suggested further reading: Matthew 7:21-29

The preaching of the gospel was the letting down of a large net into the midst of the sea of this world. The professing church which it was to gather together was to be a mixed body. Within the fold of the net there were to be fish of every kind, both good and bad. Within the pale of the church there were to be 'Christians' of various sorts, unconverted as well as converted, false as well as true. The separation was sure to come at last, but not before the end of the world. Such was the account which the great Master gave to his disciples of the results of their gospel work.

To tell all people who are baptized that they are born again, they have the Spirit, they are members of Christ and holy, in the face of a parable such as this, is unwarrantable. Such a mode of address may flatter and please. It is not likely to profit and save. It is painfully calculated to promote self-righteousness and lull sinners to sleep. It overthrows the plain teaching of Christ and is ruinous to souls.

We may be inside the net, yet not be in Christ. The waters of baptism are poured on myriads who are never washed in the water of life. The bread and wine are eaten and drunk at the Lord's table by thousands who never feed on Christ by faith. Are we converted? Are we among the 'good fish'? That is the grand question. The net will soon be drawn to shore. The true character of man's religion will soon be exposed. There will be an eternal separation between the good fish and the bad.

Our Lord winds up these parables with a striking question (v. 51). Personal application has been called the 'soul' of preaching. A sermon without application is like a letter posted without direction. It may be well written, rightly dated and duly signed. But it is useless because it never reaches its destination.

Let us apply what we hear. Let us take to church with us not only our bodies but our minds, our reason, our hearts and our consciences. Let us often ask ourselves, 'What have I got from this sermon?'

For meditation: *What have you got from your reading this day? Are you reading in order to apply?*

Suggested further reading: Psalm 19:7-11

What high honour Jesus Christ puts on the Holy Scriptures! We find him using a text out of the Psalms as an argument against his enemies, in which the whole point lies in the single word 'gods'. And then, having quoted the text, he lays down the great principle: 'The Scripture cannot be broken.' It is as though he said, 'Wherever the Scripture speaks plainly on any subject, there can be no more question about it. The cause is settled and decided. Every jot and tittle of Scripture is true and must be received as conclusive.'

The principle here laid down by our Lord is one of vast importance. Let us grasp it firmly and never let it go. Let us maintain boldly the complete inspiration of every word of the original Hebrew and Greek Scriptures. Let us believe that not only every book of the Bible, but every chapter, and not only every chapter, but every verse, and not only every verse, but every word was originally given by inspiration of God. Inspiration, we must never shrink from asserting, extends not only to the thoughts and ideas of Scripture, but to the least words.

The principle before us, no doubt, is rudely assaulted in the present day. Let no Christian's heart fail because of these assaults. Let us stand our ground manfully and defend the principle of plenary inspiration as we would the apple of our eye. There are difficulties in Scripture, we need not shrink from conceding, things hard to explain, hard to reconcile and hard to understand. But in almost all these difficulties, the fault, we may justly suspect, is not so much in Scripture as in our own weak minds. In all cases we may well be content to wait for more light and believe that all shall be made clear at last.

The wisest course is to walk in the old path — the path of faith and humility — and say, 'I cannot give up a single word of my Bible.'

For meditation: *A small fault can render a whole machine unreliable in its work. If God's Word contains errors, how can we trust any of it?*

Suggested further reading: 2 Timothy 2:1-7

The first of these sayings was addressed to one who offered to be a disciple unconditionally and of his own accord (v. 57). That offer sounded well. It was a step in advance of many. Thousands of people heard our Lord's sermons who never thought of saying what this man said. Yet he who made this offer was evidently speaking without thought. He had never considered what belonged to discipleship. He had never counted the cost. And hence he needed the grave reply that his offer called forth (v. 58). He must weigh well what he was taking in hand. He must not suppose that Christ's service was all pleasure and plain sailing. Was he prepared for this? Was he willing to endure hardship? (2 Tim. 2:3). If not, he had better withdraw his application to be a disciple.

Let us learn from this that our Lord would have all who profess and call themselves Christians reminded that they must carry the cross. They must be ready to be despised, afflicted and tried like their Master. He would have no man enlisted on false pretences. He would have it distinctly understood that there is a battle to be fought and a race to be run, a work to be done and many things to be endured, if we propose to follow him. Salvation he is ready to bestow without money and without price. Grace by the way and glory at the end shall be given to every sinner that comes to him. But he would not have us ignorant that we will have deadly enemies: the world, the flesh, the devil, those that hate us, slander us and persecute us, if we become his disciples. He does not wish to discourage us, but he does wish us to know the truth.

Many a man begins a religious life full of warmth and zeal and by and by loses all his first love and turns back again to the world. He liked the new uniform and the pocket money and the name of a Christian soldier. He never considered the watching, warring, wounds and conflicts which Christian soldiers must endure. This need not make us afraid to begin serving Christ, but it ought to make us begin carefully, humbly and with much prayer for grace.

For meditation: *Our Lord never glibly called us to an easy life, but to serve him, though difficult, is the most worthwhile thing that anyone can do.*

Suggested further reading: Exodus 4:1-9

What importance our Lord Jesus Christ attaches to his miracles! He appeals to them as the best evidence of his own divine mission. He bids the Jews look at them and deny them if they can. 'If I do not the works of my Father, believe me not. But if I do, though ye believe not me, believe the works.'

The mighty miracles which our Lord performed during the three years of his earthly ministry are probably not considered as much as they ought to be in the present day. These miracles were not few in number. Forty times and more we read in the Gospels of his doing things entirely out of the ordinary course of nature — healing sick people in a moment, raising the dead with a word, casting out devils, calming winds and waves in an instant, walking on the water as on solid ground. These miracles were not all done in private among friends. Many of them were wrought in the most public manner under the eyes of unfriendly witnesses. We are so familiar with these things that we are apt to forget the mighty lesson they teach. They teach that he who worked these miracles must be nothing less than very God. They stamp his doctrines and precepts with the mark of divine authority. He only who created all things at the beginning could suspend the laws of creation at his will. He who could suspend the laws of creation must be one who ought to be thoroughly believed and implicitly obeyed. To reject one who confirmed his mission by such mighty works is the height of madness and folly.

Hundreds of unbelieving men, no doubt, in every age, have tried to pour contempt on Christ's miracles and to deny that they were ever worked at all. But they labour in vain. Proofs upon proofs exist that our Lord's ministry was accompanied by miracles and that this was acknowledged by those who lived in our Lord's time.

For meditation: *Our Lord did not challenge his hearers with unverifiable miracles performed miles away, but with miracles before their very eyes.*

Suggested further reading: Luke 14:25-33

The second of our Lord's sayings is addressed to one whom he invited to follow him (v. 59). The answer he received was a very remarkable one (v. 59). The thing he requested was in itself harmless. But the time at which the request was made was unseasonable. Affairs of even greater importance than a father's funeral demanded the man's immediate attention. There would always be plenty of people ready and fit to take charge of a funeral. But there was at that moment a pressing want of labourers to do Christ's work in the world. And hence the man's request drew from our Lord a solemn reply (v. 60).

Let us learn from this saying to beware of allowing family and social duties to interfere with our duty to Christ. The children of the King of kings should plainly declare by their conduct that the world to come is the greater reality which fills their thoughts. Their Master's work waits for them and their Master's work must have the chief place in their hearts.

The third of our Lord's sayings was addressed to one who volunteered to follow him but marred the grace of his offer by interposing a request (v. 61). The answer he received shows plainly that the man's heart was not yet thoroughly engaged in Christ's service, and that he was therefore unfit to be a disciple (v. 62).

We learn from this saying that it is impossible to serve Christ with a divided heart. If we are looking back to anything in the world we are not fit to be disciples. Those who look back want to go back. Jesus will not share his throne with anyone — not even our dearest relatives. He must have all our heart or none. No doubt we are to honour father and mother and love all around us. But when love to Christ and love to relatives come in collision Christ must have the preference. It may wring our hearts to go contrary to those whom we love, but such conduct may sometimes be positively necessary to our salvation.

For meditation:
The dearest idol I have known,
Whate'er that idol be,
Help me to tear it from thy throne
And worship only Thee

(Cowper).

Suggested further reading: Romans 8:18-23

Nowhere shall we find such convincing proofs of our Lord's divine power. As God, he makes the grave itself yield up its tenants. Nowhere shall we find such striking illustrations of our Lord's ability to sympathize with his people. As man, he can be touched with the feelings of our infirmities. Such a miracle well became the end of such a ministry. It was meet and right that the victory of Bethany should closely precede the crucifixion at Calvary.

These verses teach us that true Christians may be sick and ill as well as others. We read that Lazarus of Bethany was one 'whom Jesus loved' and a brother of two well-known holy women. Yet Lazarus was sick, even unto death! The Lord Jesus, who had power over all diseases, could no doubt have prevented this illness, if he had thought fit. But he did not do so. He allowed Lazarus to be sick and in pain and weary and to languish and suffer like any other man.

The lesson is one which ought to be deeply graven in our memories. Living in a world full of disease and death, we are sure to need it some day. Sickness, in the very nature of things, can never be anything but trying to flesh and blood. Our bodies and souls are strangely linked together and that which vexes and weakens the body can hardly fail to vex the mind and soul. But sickness, we must always remember, is no sign that God is displeased with us; nay, more, it is generally sent for the good of our souls. It tends to draw our affections away from this world and to direct them to things above. It sends us to our Bibles and teaches us to pray better. It helps to prove our faith and patience and shows us the real value of our hope in Christ. It reminds us betimes that we are not to live always and tunes and trains our hearts for our great change. Let us believe that the Lord Jesus loves us when we are sick no less than when we are well.

For meditation: *By miraculous healing God grants us an insight into the disease-free age to come* (Rom. 8:23). *By leaving us ill he reminds us we are part of a fallen world* (Rom. 8:18).

Suggested further reading: Hebrews 2:14-18; 4:4-16

Christ's service does not exempt his servants from storms. Here were the twelve disciples in the path of duty. They were obediently following Jesus wherever he went. They were not ashamed to give up all for his sake. Yet here we see these men in trouble, tossed up and down by a tempest and in danger of being drowned.

True Christians must not expect everything to be smooth on their journey to heaven. We must count it no strange thing if we have to endure sicknesses, losses, bereavements and disappointments just like other men. Free pardon and full forgiveness, grace by the way and glory at the end, all this our Saviour promised to give. But he has never promised that we shall have no affliction. He loves us too well to promise us that. By affliction he teaches many precious lessons which without it we should never learn. By affliction he shows us our emptiness and weakness, draws us to the throne of grace, purifies our affections, weans us from the world and makes us long for heaven. In the resurrection morn we shall thank God for every storm.

Our Lord Jesus Christ was really and truly man. When the storm began he was asleep (v. 38). He had a body exactly like our own — a body that could hunger, thirst, feel pain, be weary and need rest. After being diligent all day in his Father's work he needed repose.

Let us mark this lesson attentively. The Saviour in whom we are bid to trust is as really a man as he is God. He knows the trials of a man because he has experienced them. He knows the bodily infirmities of a man because he has felt them. He can well understand what we mean when we cry to him for help in a time of need. He is just the Saviour that men and women, with weary frames and aching heads in a weary world, require for their comfort every morning and night.

For meditation: *God does not send us through this life's afflictions without a full knowledge of our situation (Ps. 139:1-5). But in addition to his perfect knowledge he has also had experience of this life's difficulties in the person of his Son. The paths we tread he has trodden before.*

Suggested further reading: 2 Chronicles 16:11-14

Jesus Christ is the Christian's best Friend in the time of need. We read that when Lazarus was sick, his sisters at once sent to Jesus and laid the matter before him. Beautiful, touching and simple was the message they sent. They did not ask him to come at once, or to work a miracle and command the disease to depart. They only said, 'Lord, he whom thou lovest is sick,' and left the matter there, in the full belief that he would do what was best. Here was the true faith and humility of saints! Here was gracious submission of will!

The servants of Christ, in every age and climate, will do well to follow this excellent example. No doubt when those whom we love are sick, we are to use diligently every reasonable means for their recovery. We must spare no pains to obtain the best medical advice. We must assist nature in every possible manner to fight a good fight against its enemy. But in all our doing, we must never forget that the best and ablest and wisest Helper is in heaven, at God's right hand. Like afflicted Job, our first action must be to fall on our knees and worship. Like Hezekiah, we must spread our matters before the Lord. Like the holy sisters at Bethany, we must send up a prayer to Christ.

Christ loves all who are true Christians. We read that 'Jesus loved Martha, and her sister, and Lazarus.' The characters of these three good people seem to have been somewhat different.

We must not undervalue others because they are not exactly like ourselves. The flowers in a garden may differ widely and yet the gardener feels interest in all. The children of a family may be curiously unlike one another and yet the parents care for all. It is just so with the church of Christ. There are degrees of grace and varieties of grace, but the least, the weakest, the feeblest disciples are all loved by the Lord Jesus.

For meditation: *Prayerlessness in times of need undoubtedly is an affront to God* (2 Chr. 16:12).

Suggested further reading: Hebrews 11:32-38

True saving faith is often mingled with much weakness and infirmity. It is a humbling lesson but a very wholesome one. The disciples' fears (v. 38) are rooted in a lack of faith (v. 40). What a vivid picture we have here of the hearts of thousands of believers! How many have faith and love enough to follow Christ, and yet are full of fears in the hour of trial! How many have grace enough to cry, 'Lord, save us,' and yet not grace enough to lie still and believe in the darkest hour that all is well!

Let the prayer, 'Lord, increase our faith,' always form part of our daily petitions. We never perhaps know the weakness of our faith until we are placed in the furnace of trial and anxiety. Blessed and happy is that person who finds by experience that his faith can stand the fire, and that he can say with Job, 'Though he slay me, yet will I trust in him' (Job 13:15).

Our Lord, as God, has almighty power. He turns the raging storm into a calm with a few words (v. 39). The elements knew the voice of their Master and, like obedient servants, were quiet at once. With the Lord Jesus nothing is impossible. No stormy passions are so strong but he can tame them. No temper is so rough and violent but he can change it. No conscience is so disquieted but he can speak peace to it and make it calm. No man ever need despair if he will only bow down his pride and come as a humbled sinner to Christ. Christ can do miracles in his heart. No man ever need despair of reaching his journey's end if he has once committed his soul to Christ's keeping. Christ will carry him through every danger. Christ will make him conqueror over every foe. What though our relations oppose us? What though our neighbours laugh us to scorn? What though our place be hard? What though our temptations be great? It is all nothing if Christ is on our side and we are in the ship with him.

For meditation: *Faith looks beyond the circumstances to the hands which mould them for the good of the church* (Rom. 8:28).

Suggested further reading: 2 Corinthians 12:7-10

Christ knows best at what time to do anything for his people. We read that 'When he had heard that Lazarus was sick, he abode two days still in the same place where he was.' In fact, he purposely delayed his journey and did not come to Bethany till Lazarus had been four days in the grave. No doubt he knew well what was going on, but he never moved till the time came which he saw was best. For the sake of the church and the world, for the good of friends and enemies, he kept away.

The children of God must constantly school their minds to learn the great lesson now before us. Nothing so helps us to bear patiently the trials of life as an abiding conviction of the perfect wisdom by which everything around us is managed. Let us try to believe not only that all that happens to us is well done, but that it is done in the best manner, by the right instrument and at the right time. We are all naturally impatient in the day of trial. We are apt to say, like Moses, when beloved ones are sick, 'Heal her *now*, Lord, we beseech thee' (Num. 12:13). We forget that Christ is too wise a physician to make any mistakes. It is the duty of faith to say, 'My times are in thy hand. Do with me as thou wilt, how thou wilt and when thou wilt. Not my will, but thine be done.' The highest degree of faith is to be able to wait, sit still and not complain.

Let us turn from the passage with a settled determination to trust Christ entirely with all the concerns of this world, both public and private. Let us believe that he by whom all things were made at first is he who is managing all with perfect wisdom. The affairs of kingdoms, families and private individuals are all alike overruled by him. He chooses all the portions of his people. When we are sick, it is because he knows it to be for our good; when he delays coming to help us, it is for some wise reason. The hand that was nailed to the cross is too wise and loving to smite without a needs-be, or to keep us waiting for relief without a cause.

For meditation: *If God is all-wise, how can we ever think that he does not know best?*

Suggested further reading: Isaiah 42:1-9

Our Lord Jesus Christ is exceedingly patient and full of pity in dealing with his own people. We see the disciples on this occasion showing great lack of faith and giving way to most unseemly fears (v. 38). They forgot their Master's miracles and care for them in days gone by. They thought of nothing but their present peril. They awoke our Lord and accused him of lack of concern. We see our Lord dealing most gently and tenderly with them. He gives them no sharp reproof. He makes no threat of casting them off because of their unbelief. He simply asks a question (v. 40).

The Lord Jesus is full of pity and of tender mercy (Ps. 103:13). He does not deal with believers according to their sins, nor reward them according to their iniquities. He sees their weakness. He is aware of their shortcomings. He knows all the defects of their faith, hope, love and courage. And yet he will not cast them off. He bears with them continually. He loves them even to the end. He raises them when they fall. He restores them when they err. His patience, like his love, is a patience that passes knowledge. When he sees a heart right, it is his glory to pass over many a shortcoming.

Let us leave these verses with the comfortable recollection that Jesus is not changed. His heart is still the same that it was when he crossed the Sea of Galilee and stilled the storm. High in heaven at the right hand of God Jesus is still sympathizing, still almighty, still full of pity and patience towards his people. Let us be more charitable and patient towards our brethren in the faith. They may err in many things but if Jesus has received them and can bear with them surely we may bear with them too?

Let us be more hopeful about ourselves. We may be very weak, frail and unstable. But if we can truly say that we come to Christ and believe on him we may take comfort. The question for conscience to answer is not 'Are we perfect?' but 'Do we really repent and believe?'

For meditation: *Christ is ever so severe with the blatant sinner and hypocrite but there is no harshness in him towards those who are seeking to please him, yet fall.*

Suggested further reading: Hebrews 11:8-16

How mysterious are the ways in which Christ sometimes leads his people! We are told that when he talked of going back to Judaea, his disciples were perplexed. It was the very place where the Jews had lately tried to stone their Master; to return thither was to plunge into the midst of danger. These timid Galileans could not see the necessity or prudence of such a step.

Things such as these are often going on around us. The servants of Christ are often placed in circumstances just as puzzling and perplexing as those of the disciples. They are led in ways of which they cannot see the purpose and object; they are called to fill positions from which they naturally shrink and which they would never have chosen for themselves. Thousands in every age are continually learning this by their own experience. The path they are obliged to walk in is not the path of their own choice. At present they cannot see its usefulness or wisdom.

At times like these a Christian must call into exercise his faith and patience. He must believe that his Master knows best by what road his servant ought to travel and that he is leading him by the right way to a city of habitation. He may rest assured that the circumstances in which he is placed are precisely those which are most likely to promote his graces and to check his besetting sins. He need not doubt that what he cannot see now he will understand hereafter. He will find one day that there was wisdom in every step of his journey, though flesh and blood could not see it at the time. If the twelve disciples had not been taken back into Judaea, they would not have seen the glorious miracle of Bethany. If Christians were allowed to choose their own course through life, they would never learn hundreds of lessons about Christ and his grace, which they are now taught in God's ways.

For meditation:
All the way my Saviour leads me.
What have I to ask beside?

Suggested further reading: John 20:24-29

The possession of a man's body by the devil was a real and true thing in the time of our Lord's earthly ministry. It is a painful fact that there are never lacking professing Christians who try to explain away the Lord's miracles. They endeavour to account for them by natural causes and to show that they were not worked by any extraordinary power. Of all miracles there are none which they assault so strenuously as the casting out of devils. They do not scruple to deny satanic possession entirely. They tell us it was nothing more than lunacy, frenzy or epilepsy and that the idea of the devil inhabiting a man's body is absurd.

The best and simplest answer to such sceptical objections is a reference to the plain narratives of the Gospels and especially to the one before us at this moment. The facts here detailed are utterly inexplicable if we do not believe in satanic possession. It is well known that lunacy, frenzy and epilepsy are not infectious complaints and at any rate cannot be communicated to a herd of swine! And yet men ask us to believe that as soon as this man was healed two thousand swine ran violently down a steep place into the sea from a sudden impulse, without any apparent cause for their so doing! Such reasoning is the height of credulity. When men can satisfy themselves with such explanations they are in a pitiable state of mind.

Let us beware of a sceptical and incredulous spirit in all matters relating to the devil. No doubt there is much in the subject of satanic possession which we do not understand and cannot explain. But let us not therefore refuse to believe it. The eastern king who would not believe in the possibility of ice, because he lived in a hot country and had never seen it, was not more foolish than the man who refuses to believe in satanic possession because he has never seen a case himself and cannot understand it. We may be sure that upon the subject of the devil and his power we are far too likely to believe too little than too much. Unbelief about the existence and personality of Satan has often proved the first step to unbelief about God.

For meditation: *The perversity of the human heart is rarely given a clearer demonstration than when we read the 'explanations' that men make up to explain away the biblical records. Scepticism will do anything rather than believe.*

Suggested further reading: 1 Corinthians 1:26-31

How much of natural temperament clings to a believer even after conversion! We read that when Thomas saw that Lazarus was dead and that Jesus was determined, in spite of all danger, to return into Judaea, he said, 'Let us also go, that we may die with him.' There can only be one meaning in that expression: it was the language of a despairing and desponding mind, which could see nothing but dark clouds in the picture. The very man who afterwards could not believe that his master had risen again and thought the news too good to be true is just the one of the twelve who thinks that if they go back to Judaea they must all die!

Things such as these are deeply instructive and are doubtless recorded for our learning. They show us that the grace of God in conversion does not so remould a man as to leave no trace of his natural bent of character. The sanguine do not altogether cease to be sanguine, nor the desponding to be desponding, when they pass from death to life and become true Christians. They show us that we must make large allowances for natural temperament in forming our estimate of individual Christians. We must not expect all God's children to be exactly one and the same. Each tree in a forest has its own peculiarities of shape and growth and yet all at a distance look one mass of leaf and verdure. Each member of Christ's body has his own distinctive bias and yet all in the main are led by one Spirit and love one Lord. The two sisters Martha and Mary, the apostles Peter and John and Thomas were certainly very unlike one another in many respects. But they had all one point in common: they loved Christ and were his friends.

Happy is the man of whom, with all his defects, Christ says to saints and angels, 'This is our friend.'

For meditation: *Christians are aptly described as God's 'peculiar' people in a number of senses. But the important thing is to be God's!*

Suggested further reading: John 8:42-47

The passage before us is full of evidence that Satan is an awfully cruel, powerful and malicious being.

The cruelty of Satan appears in the miserable condition of the unhappy man of whose body he had possession. His home was the tombs, his nature was violent and he was like a savage (vv. 3-5). Such is the state to which the devil would bring us all if he had the power. He would rejoice to inflict upon us the utmost misery both of body and mind. Cases like this are faint types of the miseries of hell.

The power of Satan appears in the awful words which the unclean spirit used in response to our Lord (v. 9). We probably have not the faintest idea of the number, subtlety and activity of Satan's agents. We forget that he is the king over an enormous host of subordinate spirits who do his will. We should probably find, if our eyes were opened to see spirits, that they are about our paths and about our beds, and observing all our ways to an extent of which we have no conception. In private and in public, in church and in the world, there are busy enemies ever near us, of whose presence we are not aware.

The malice of Satan appears in his strange petition (v. 12). Cast forth from the man whose body they had so long inhabited and possessed, the spirits still thirsted to do mischief. Unable to injure any more an immortal soul, they desired leave to injure the dumb beasts which were feeding nearby. Such is the true character of Satan. It is the bent of his nature to harm, to kill and to destroy. No wonder that he is called Apollyon, the destroyer (Rev. 9:11).

Let us beware of giving way to the senseless habit of jesting about the devil. It is a habit which furnishes awful evidence of the blindness and corruption of human nature and one which is far too common. Well would it be for us all if we strove more to realize the power and presence of our great spiritual enemy and prayed more to be delivered from him.

For meditation: *If archangels need God's aid to oppose the devil* (Jude 9) *how much more do weak sinners!*

Suggested further reading: 2 Corinthians 5:1-10

How tenderly Christ speaks of the death of believers! He announces the fact of Lazarus being dead in language of singular beauty and gentleness: 'Our friend Lazarus sleepeth.'

Every true Christian has a Friend in heaven, of almighty power and boundless love. He is thought of, cared for, provided for, defended by God's eternal Son. He has an unfailing Protector, who never slumbers or sleeps and who watches continually over his interests. The world may despise him, but he has no cause to be ashamed. Father and mother even may cast him out, but Christ, having once taken him up, will never let him go. He is the 'friend of Christ' even after he is dead! The friendships of this world are often fair-weather friendships and fail us like summer-dried fountains, when our need is the sorest; but the friendship of the Son of God is stronger than death and goes beyond the grave. The Friend of sinners is a Friend that sticketh closer than a brother.

The death of true Christians is 'sleep' and not annihilation. It is a solemn and miraculous change, no doubt, but not a change to be regarded with alarm. They have nothing to fear for their souls in the change, for their sins are washed away in Christ's blood. The sharpest sting of death is the sense of unpardoned sin. Christians have nothing to fear for their bodies in the change; they will rise again by and by, refreshed and renewed, after the image of the Lord. The grave itself is a conquered enemy. It must render back its tenants safe and sound, the very moment that Christ calls for them at the last day.

To a mere worldly man death must needs be a terrible thing, but he that has Christian faith may boldly say, as he lays down life, 'I will lay me down in peace, and take my rest, for it is thou, Lord, that makest me dwell in safety.'

For meditation: *Do you know and believe that for you to die is gain?* (Phil. 1:21).

Suggested further reading: 1 John 3:1-8

How complete is the Lord's power and authority over the devil! We see this in the cry of an unclean spirit (v. 7). We see it in the command given and the immediate obedience that follows (v. 8). We see it in the blessed change that at once took place in him that was possessed: he was found sitting, clothed and in his right mind (v. 15). We see it in the confession of all the devils (v. 12) declaring their consciousness that they could do nothing without leave. All these things show that one mightier than Satan was there. Strong as the great enemy of man was, he was in the presence of one stronger than he. Numerous as his hosts were, he was confronted with one who could command more than twelve legions of angels. A King was present with power (Matt. 26:53; Eccles. 8:4).

The truth here taught is full of strong consolation for all true Christians. We live in a world full of difficulties and snares. We are ourselves weak and compassed with infirmity. The awful thought that we have a mighty spiritual enemy ever near us, subtle, powerful and malicious as Satan is, might well disquiet us and cast us down. But thanks be to God, we have in Jesus an almighty Friend who is able to save to the uttermost (Heb. 7:25). He has already triumphed over Satan on the cross (Col. 2:15). He will ever triumph over him in the hearts of all believers and intercede for them that their faith fail not. And he will finally triumph over Satan completely when he shall come forth at the second advent.

Are we delivered from Satan's power? He still reigns and rules in the hearts of all who are children of disobedience (Eph. 2:2-3). He is still a king over the ungodly. Have we by grace broken his bonds and escaped his hands? Have we really denounced him and all his works? Do we daily resist him and make him flee? Do we put on the whole armour of God and stand against him?

For meditation: *Let us take to heart the teaching of John* (1 John 4:4). *God has not abdicated.*

Suggested further reading: Matthew 25:31-46

How great a blessing God sometimes bestows on actions of kindness and sympathy!

It seems that the house of Martha and Mary at Bethany was filled with mourners when Jesus arrived. Many of these mourners, no doubt, knew nothing of the inner life of these holy women. Their faith, their hope, their love to Christ, their discipleship were things of which they were wholly ignorant. But they felt for them in their heavy bereavement and kindly came to offer what comfort they could. By so doing they reaped a rich and unexpected reward. They beheld the greatest miracle that Jesus ever wrought. They were eyewitnesses when Lazarus came forth from the tomb. To many of them, we may well believe, that day was a spiritual birth. The raising of Lazarus led to a resurrection in their souls. How small sometimes are the hinges on which eternal life appears to depend! If these people had not sympathized they might never have been saved.

We need not doubt that these things were written for our learning. To show sympathy and kindness to the sorrowful is good for our own souls, whether we know it or not. To visit the fatherless and widows in their affliction, to weep with them that weep, to try to bear one another's burdens and lighten one another's cares — all this will make no atonement for sin and will not take us to heaven. Yet it is healthy employment for our hearts and employment which none ought to despise. Few perhaps are aware that one secret of being miserable is to live only for ourselves and one secret of being happy is to try to make others happy and to do a little good in the world.

The saying of our Lord is too much overlooked: 'Whosoever shall give to drink unto one of these little ones a cup of cold water only in the name of a disciple, verily I say unto you, he shall in no wise lose his reward' (Matt. 10:42).

For meditation: *Sympathy is not merely to be a natural virtue. It is to be a Christian grace* (1 Cor. 12:26).

Suggested further reading: Matthew 10:11-15

The people of the region asked Christ to depart from them and their request was granted (vv. 17-18). Why did these unhappy men desire the Son of God to leave them? Why, after the amazing miracle of mercy which had just been done amongst them, did they feel no wish to know more of him who had done it? Why, in a word, did they become their own enemies, forsake their own mercies, and shut the door against the gospel? There is but one answer to these questions. They loved the world and the things of the world and were determined not to give them up. They felt convinced in their own consciences that they could not receive Christ amongst them and keep their sins, and their sins they resolved to keep. They saw, at a glance, that there was something about Jesus with which their habits of life would not agree and, having to choose between the new ways and the old ones, they refused the new and chose the old.

Why did the Lord grant their request and leave them? He did it in judgement to testify to the greatness of their sins. He did it to show how great is the wickedness of those who wilfully reject the truth. It seems an eternal law of his government that those who obstinately refuse to walk in the light shall have the light taken from them. Great is Christ's patience and long-suffering! His mercy endures for ever. His offers and invitations are wide, broad, sweeping and universal. But if men persist in refusing his counsel he has nowhere promised to persist in forcing it on them. People who have the gospel and yet refuse to obey it must not be surprised if the gospel is removed from them.

Let us take heed that we do not sin the sin of these people. Let us beware lest by coldness, inattention and worldliness we drive Jesus from our doors and compel him to forsake us entirely. Of all sins which we can sin this is the most sinful. Of all states of soul none is so fearful as to be let alone. The heart that Christ has ceased to visit is like an old wreck, high and dry on a sandbank.

For meditation: *The most terrible judgement possible on this earth is for God to leave people to themselves* (Rom. 1:24,26,28).

Suggested further reading: Galatians 2:11-14

What a strange mixture of grace and weakness is to be found even in the hearts of true believers! We see this strikingly illustrated in the language used by Martha and Mary. Both these holy women had faith enough to say, 'Lord, if thou hadst been here, my brother had not died.' Yet neither of them seems to have remembered that the death of Lazarus did not depend on Christ's absence and that our Lord, had he thought fit, could have prevented his death with a word, without coming to Bethany. Martha had knowledge enough to say, 'I know, that even now, whatsoever thou wilt ask of God, God will give it thee... I know that my brother shall rise again at the last day... I believe that thou art the Christ, the Son of God.' But even she could get no further. Her dim eyes and trembling hands could not grasp the grand truth that he who stood before her had the keys of life and death and that in her master dwelt 'all the fulness of the Godhead bodily' (Col. 2:9). She saw indeed, but through a glass darkly. She knew, but only in part. She believed, but her faith was mingled with much unbelief. Yet both Martha and Mary were genuine children of God and true Christians.

These things are graciously written for our learning. It is good to remember what true Christians really are. Many and great are the mistakes into which people fall by forming a false estimate of the Christian's character. Many are the bitter things which people write against themselves, by expecting to find in their hearts what cannot be found on this side of heaven. Let us settle it in our minds that saints on earth are not perfect angels, but only converted sinners. They are sinners renewed, changed, sanctified, no doubt, but they are yet sinners and will be till they die.

For meditation: *Where faults are seen attempts at loving restoration are to be made. Criticism is neither helpful nor meaningful if it does not aim at helping.*

Suggested further reading: James 4:13-17

The man out of whom the devils were cast asked our Lord that he might be with him, but his request was not granted (vv. 18-19). We can easily understand the request that this man made. He felt deeply grateful for the amazing mercy that he had received in being cured. He felt full of love and warm affection towards him who had so wonderfully and graciously cured him. He felt that he could never see too much of him, be too much in his company or cleave to him too closely. He forgot everything else under the influence of these feelings. Family, relations, friends, home, house, country, all seemed nothing in his eyes. He cared for nothing but to be with Christ. We cannot blame him for his feelings.

Why did the Lord Jesus refuse to grant this man's request? Why not have another disciple when he had so few? Our Lord did what he did in infinite wisdom. He did it for the benefit of the man's own soul. He saw it was far more for his good to be a witness for the gospel at home than a disciple abroad. He did it in mercy to the people who had just rejected him. He left amongst them a testimony of the truth of his own mission. He did it to teach us that there are various ways of glorifying God, in private life as well as in a public ministry, and that our first place of witness is to be our home.

From this let us learn our utter ignorance of what position is good for us in the world and the necessity of submitting our wills to the will of Christ. The place we wish to fill is not always the place best for us. The line of life that we want to take up is not always that which Christ sees as the most beneficial to our souls. The place that we are obliged to fill may be distasteful and yet necessary for our sanctification. It is better to be sent away from Christ's bodily presence by Christ himself than to remain in Christ's bodily presence without his consent. Let us ask the Lord to choose everything for us.

For meditation: *The disciples would never have chosen that Christ should leave them. But he did because he knew it was for their benefit and ours* (John 16:6-7).

Suggested further reading: Colossians 1:9-14

What need many believers have of clear views of Christ's person, office and power! This is a point which is forcibly brought out in the well-known sentence which our Lord addressed to Martha. In reply to her vague and faltering expression of belief in the resurrection at the last day, he proclaims the glorious truth: 'I am the resurrection and the life.' 'I, even I, thy Master, am he that has the keys of life and death in his hands.' And then he presses on her once more that old lesson, which she had doubtless often heard, but never fully realized: 'He that believeth in me, though he were dead, yet shall he live; and whosoever liveth and believeth in me shall never die.'

There is matter here which deserves the close consideration of all true Christians. Many of them complain of want of sensible comfort in their religion. They do not feel the inward peace which they desire. Let them know that vague and indefinite views of Christ are too often the cause of all their perplexities. They must try to see more clearly the great object on which their faith rests. They must grasp more firmly his love and power towards them that believe and the riches he has laid up for them even now in this world. We are many of us sadly like Martha. A little general knowledge of Christ as the only Saviour is often all that we possess. But of the fulness that dwells in him, of his resurrection, his priesthood, his intercession, his unfailing compassion, we have tasted little or nothing at all. They are things of which our Lord might well say to many, as he did to Martha, 'Believest thou this?'

Let us take shame to ourselves that we have named the name of Christ so long and yet know so little about him. What right have we to wonder that we feel so little comfort in our Christianity?

For meditation: *Is your great desire to know Christ above all else?* (Phil. 3:10).

Suggested further reading: 1 Thessalonians 1:4-10

Conversion is a cause of joy to a true believer. When Levi was converted he made a feast. A feast is made for laughter and merriment. Levi regarded the change in himself as an occasion for rejoicing and wished others to rejoice with him also.

Levi did right to rejoice, and if we are converted let us rejoice likewise. Nothing can happen that ought to be such an occasion of joy as conversion. It is a far more important event than being married, or coming of age, or wealth. It is the birth of an immortal soul! It is the rescue of a sinner from hell! It is being made a king and priest for evermore! It is being provided for both in time and eternity! It is adoption into the noblest and richest of all families, the family of God! Let us not heed the opinion of the world in this matter. Let us with Levi consider every fresh conversion a cause for great rejoicing. The words of the prodigal's father should be remembered (Luke 15:32).

Converted souls desire the conversion of others. When Levi was converted he made a feast and invited a large group of his friends and companions. He knew well what their souls needed, for he had been one of them. He desired to make them acquainted with that Saviour who had been merciful to himself. Having found mercy, he wanted them also to find it. Having been graciously delivered from the bondage of sin, he wished others also to be set free.

The feeling of Levi will always be the feeling of the true Christian. There is no grace in the man who cares nothing about the salvation of his fellow men. The heart that is really taught by the Holy Spirit will always be full of love and compassion. A converted man will not wish to go to heaven alone.

How is it with ourselves in this matter? Do we strive in every way to make our friends and relatives acquainted with Christ? We have many biblical examples (Num. 10:29; John 1:41; 4:39). This supplies a searching test of the real state of our souls.

For meditation: *Would you sit by while friends and relatives burned to death in a house on fire? Do you sit by while friends and relatives head for eternal fire?*

Suggested further reading: Hebrews 4:14 - 5:10

What a depth of tender sympathy there is in Christ's heart towards his people! We read that when our Lord saw Mary weeping and the Jews also weeping with her, 'He groaned in the spirit and was troubled.' We read even more than this. He gave outward expression to his feelings: he 'wept'. He knew perfectly well that the sorrow of the family of Bethany would soon be turned into joy and that Lazarus in a few minutes would be restored to his sisters. But though he knew all this, he 'wept'.

This weeping of Christ is deeply instructive. It shows us that it is not sinful to sorrow. Weeping and mourning are sadly trying to flesh and blood and make us feel the weakness of our mortal nature. But they are not in themselves wrong. Even the Son of God wept. It shows us that deep feeling is not a thing of which we need be ashamed. To be cold and stoical and unmoved in the sight of sorrow is no sign of grace. There is nothing unworthy of a child of God in tears. Even the Son of God could weep. It shows us, above all, that the Saviour in whom believers trust is a most tender and feeling Saviour. He is one who can be touched with sympathy for our infirmities. When we turn to him in the hour of trouble and pour out our hearts before him, he knows what we go through and can pity. And he is one who never changes. Though he now sits at God's right hand in heaven, his heart is still the same that it was upon earth. We have an Advocate with the Father who, when he was upon earth, could weep.

Let us strive to be men and women of a tender heart and a sympathizing spirit. If there were more Christians of this stamp and character, the church would be far more beautiful and the world would be far more happy.

For meditation: *The Christian is to become like Christ* (Rom. 8:29). *Christ has become like the Christian.*

Suggested further reading: Romans 5:6-11

One of Christ's principal offices is that of Physician. The scribes and Pharisees who criticized him for eating and drinking with publicans and sinners received a clear reply (v. 31).

The Lord Jesus did not come into the world, as some suppose. to be nothing more than a Lawgiver, a King, a Teacher and an example. Had this been all the purpose of his coming it would have been small comfort for man. Diet tables and rules for living are all very well for the convalescent, but not suitable to the man labouring under a mortal disease. A teacher and an example might be sufficient for an unfallen man like Adam in the Garden of Eden. But fallen sinners like ourselves want healing first, before we can value rules.

The Lord Jesus came into the world to be a Physician as well as a Teacher. He knew the necessities of human nature. He saw us all sick of a mortal disease, struck with the plague of sin and dying daily. He pitied us and came down to bring us divine medicine for our relief. He came to give health and cure to the dying, to heal the broken-hearted, and to offer strength to the weak. No sin-sick soul is too far gone for him. It is his glory to heal and restore life to the most desperate cases. For unfailing skill, for unwearied tenderness, for long experience of man's spiritual ailments, the great Physician of souls stands alone. Have we ever applied to him for relief?

We need to be frequently reminded that only those can receive benefit from him who will confess that they are ruined, bankrupt, hopeless, miserable sinners. Let us use this mighty truth if we have never used it before. Are we conscious of our own wickedness and sinfulness? Do we feel that we are unworthy of anything but wrath and condemnation? Then let us understand that we are the very persons for whose sake Jesus came into the world (v. 32). If we feel ourselves sinners Christ calls us to repentance.

For meditation:
Let not conscience make you linger,
Nor of fitness fondly dream.
All the fitness he requireth
Is to feel your need of him

                 (Hart).

Suggested further reading: Romans 10:13-17

These verses record one of the greatest miracles the Lord Jesus Christ ever worked and supply an unanswerable proof of his divinity. He whose voice could bring back from the grave one that had been four days dead must indeed have been very God! The miracle itself is described in such simple language that no human comment can throw light upon it. But the sayings of our Lord on this occasion are peculiarly interesting and demand special notice.

We should mark our Lord's words about the stone which lay upon the grave of Lazarus. We read that he said to those around him, when he came to the place of burial, 'Take ye away the stone.'

Now why did our Lord say this? It was doubtless as easy for him to command the stone to roll away untouched as to call a dead body from the tomb. But such was not his mode of proceeding. Here, as in other cases, he chose to give man something to do. Here, as elsewhere, he taught the great lesson that his almighty power was not meant to destroy man's responsibility. Even when he was ready and willing to raise the dead, he would not have man stand by altogether idle.

Let us treasure up this in our memories. It involves a point of great importance. In doing spiritual good to others, in training up our children for heaven, in following after holiness in our own daily walk — in all these things it is undoubtedly true that we are weak and helpless. 'Without Christ we can do nothing.' But still we must remember that Christ expects us to do what we can. 'Take ye away the stone' is the daily command which he gives us. Let us beware that we do not stand still in idleness, under the pretence of humility. Let us daily try to do what we can and in the trying Christ will meet us and grant his blessing.

For meditation: *Salvation is a work of God, but it must be preached by man and received by man. God does not leave us as passive spectators.*

Suggested further reading: Ephesians 5:25-33

Twice our Lord calls himself the 'Bridegroom' (vv. 34-35). This name, applied to our Lord, is full of instruction. It is a name peculiarly comforting and encouraging to all true Christians. It teaches the deep and tender love with which Jesus regards all sinners of mankind who believe in him. Weak, unworthy and shortcoming as they are in themselves, he feels towards them a tender affection, even as a husband does towards his wife. It teaches the close and intimate union which exists between Jesus and believers. It is something far nearer than the union of king and subject, master and servant, teacher and scholar, shepherd and sheep. It is the closest of all unions, the union of husband and wife — the indissoluble union (Matt. 19:6).

Above all, the name teaches that entire participation of all that Jesus is and has which is the privilege of every believer. Just as the husband gives to the wife his name, makes her partaker of his property, home and dignity, and undertakes all her debts and liabilities, so does Christ deal with all true Christians. He takes on himself all their sins. He declares that they are a part of himself and that he who hurts them hurts him (Acts 9:4; Matt. 25:38,45). He gives them, even in this world, such things as pass man's understanding. And he promises that in the next world they shall sit with him on the throne and go out from his presence no more.

If we know anything of true and saving religion, let us often rest our souls on this name and office of Christ. Let us remember daily that the weakest of Christ's people are cared for with a tender care that passes knowledge, and whoever hurts them is hurting the apple of Christ's eye. In this world we may be poor and contemptible and laughed at because of our religion, but if we have faith we are precious in the sight of Christ. The Bridegroom of our soul will one day plead our cause before the whole world.

For meditation: *If it is the responsibility of the Bridegroom to lavish love on the bride, it is the responsibility of the bride to be submissive to the Groom* (Eph. 5:23). *How submissive are you to Christ?*

Suggested further reading: Matthew 9:27-31

We should mark the words which our Lord addressed to Martha, when she objected to the stone being removed from the grave. The faith of this holy woman completely broke down, when the cave where her beloved brother lay was about to be thrown open. She could not believe that it was of any use. 'Lord,' she cries, 'by this time he stinketh.' And then comes in the solemn reproof of our Lord: 'Said I not unto thee that if thou wouldest believe thou shouldest see the glory of God?'

That sentence is rich in meaning. It is far from unlikely that it contains a reference to the message which had been sent to Martha and Mary, when their brother first fell sick. It may be meant to remind Martha that her Master had sent her word: 'This sickness is not unto death, but for the glory of God.' But it is perhaps more likely that our Lord desired to recall to Martha's mind the old lesson he had taught her all through his ministry, the duty of always believing. It is as though he said, 'Martha, Martha, thou art forgetting the great doctrine of faith, which I have ever taught thee. Believe, and all will be well. Fear not, only believe.'

The lesson is one which we can never know too well. How apt our faith is to break down in time of trial! How easy it is to talk of faith in the days of health and prosperity and how hard to practise it in the days of darkness, when neither sun, moon, nor stars appear! Let us lay to heart what our Lord says in this place. Let us pray for such stores of inward faith that, when our turn comes to suffer, we may suffer patiently and believe all is well. The Christian who has ceased to say, 'I must see, and then I will believe,' and has learned to say, 'I believe, and by and by I shall see,' has reached a high degree in the school of Christ.

For meditation: *Do your trials crush your faith or strengthen it?*

Suggested further reading: Ephesians 2:11-22

In religion it is worse than useless to attempt to mix things that essentially differ (vv. 36-37). These words were a parable. They were spoken with a special reference to the question which the Pharisees raised (v. 33). Our Lord evidently means that to enforce fasting amongst his disciples would be inexpedient and unseasonable. His little flock was as yet young in grace and weak in faith, knowledge and experience. They must be led on softly and not burdened at this early stage with requirements which they were not able to bear. Fasting, moreover, might be suitable to the disciples of him who was only the Bridegroom's friend, who lived in the wilderness, preached the baptism of repentance, was clothed in camel's hair and ate locusts and wild honey. But fasting was not equally suitable to him who was the Bridegroom himself, brought good news to sinners and came living like other men. In short, to require fasting of his disciples at present would be putting new wine into old bottles. It would be trying to amalgamate things that essentially differed.

The principle laid down in these little parables is one of greatest importance. It is a kind of proverbial saying and admits of a wide application. Forgetfulness of it has frequently done great harm in the church. All sorts of evils have arisen.

In the Galatian church men wished to reconcile Judaism and Christianity, to circumcise as well as to baptize. They endeavoured to keep alive the law of ceremonies and ordinances and to place it side by side with the gospel of Christ. They erred, seeking to put new wine into old bottles.

In the church after the death of the apostles, some tried to make the gospel more acceptable by mingling it with Platonic philosophy. Some laboured to recommend it by borrowing heathen forms, processions and vestments. In so doing they paved the way for Romanism.

Today thousands try to reconcile the service of Christ and the service of the world, the name of Christian with the life of the ungodly, God and mammon. But it cannot be done (Matt. 6:24).

For meditation: *Christianity is not the patching up and propping up of a crumbling way of life. It is a new way of life under new ownership.*

Suggested further reading: Hebrews 1:1-14

We should mark the words which our Lord addressed to God the Father when the stone was taken from the grave. We read that he said, 'Father, I thank thee that thou hast heard me. And I knew that thou hearest me always: but because of the people which stand by I said it, that they may believe that thou hast sent me.'

This wonderful language is totally unlike anything said by prophets or apostles when they worked miracles. In fact, it is not prayer, but praise. It evidently implies a constant mysterious communion going on between Jesus and his Father in heaven, which it is past the power of man either to explain or conceive. We need not doubt that here, as elsewhere in St John, our Lord meant to teach the Jews the entire and complete unity there was between him and his Father, in all that he did, as well as in all that he taught. Once more he would remind them that he did not come among them as a mere prophet, but as the Messiah who was sent by the Father and who was one with the Father. Once more he would have them know that as the words which he spake were the very words which the Father gave him to speak, so the works which he wrought were the very works which the Father gave him to do. In short, he was the promised Messiah, whom the Father always hears, because he and the Father are one.

Deep and high as this truth is, it is for the peace of our souls to believe it thoroughly and to grasp it tightly. Let it be a settled principle of our religion that the Saviour in whom we trust is nothing less than eternal God, one whom the Father hears always, one who in very deed is God's fellow. A clear view of the dignity of our Mediator's person is one secret of inward comfort. Happy is he who can say, 'I know whom I have believed, and that he is able to keep that which I have committed to him' (2 Tim. 1:12).

For meditation: *The Saviour who intercedes for us* (Heb. 7:25) *is always heard* (John 11:42).

Suggested further reading: Acts 4:8-12

What misery sin has brought into the world! A long-standing painful disease afflicted this woman (v. 25). Medical skill had proved unable to cure it (v. 26). After twelve long, weary years battling with disease relief seemed no nearer than at first (Prov. 13:12).

How amazing it is that we do not hate sin more! Sin is the cause of all the pain and disease in the world. God did not create man to be an ailing and suffering creature. It was sin, and nothing but sin, which brought in all the ills that flesh is heir to. It was sin to which we owe every racking pain, every loathsome infirmity and every humbling weakness to which our bodies are liable. Let us hate sin with a godly hatred.

People thronged Christ with different feelings. Only one in the crowd touched him with faith and was healed (vv. 24,27). Many followed Jesus from curiosity without deriving benefit from him. Many now go to church and receive the sacraments, but few touch Christ by faith and go home in peace.

This one woman, weary of her disease and her physicians, describes many a sinner. Such men and women have felt their sins deeply and have been sore afflicted by the thought that they are not forgiven and not fit to die. They have desired relief and peace of conscience, but have not known where to find them. They have tried many false remedies but not been helped. They have gone the rounds of all the forms of religion and wearied themselves with every imaginable man-made device for obtaining spiritual health. But all has been in vain.

Let all such take comfort in the miracle which we are now considering. Let them know that there is something that can cure them, if only they will seek it. There is one door at which they have never knocked in all their efforts to find relief. There is one Physician to whom they have never applied who never fails to heal. Let them consider the conduct of this woman in her necessity. When all other means had failed, she went to Jesus for help. Let them go and do likewise.

For meditation: *Without Christ, without hope* (Eph. 2:12).

Suggested further reading: 1 Corinthians 15:50-58

We should mark the words which our Lord addressed to Lazarus when he raised him from the grave. We read that 'He cried with a loud voice, Lazarus, come forth!' At the sound of that voice, the king of terrors at once yielded up his lawful captive and the insatiable grave gave up its prey. At once 'He that was dead came forth, bound hand and foot with grave-clothes.'

The greatness of this miracle cannot possibly be exaggerated. The mind of man can scarcely take in the vastness of the work that was done. Here, in open day and before many hostile witnesses, a man four days dead was restored to life in a moment. Here was public proof that our Lord had absolute power over the material world! A corpse, already corrupt, was made alive! Here was public proof that our Lord had absolute power over the world of spirits! A soul that had left its earthly tenement was called back from paradise and joined once more to its owner's body. Well may the church of Christ maintain that he who could work such works was 'God over all blessed for ever' (Rom. 9:5).

Let us turn from the whole passage with thoughts of comfort and consolation. Comfortable is the thought that the loving Saviour of sinners, on whose mercy our souls entirely depend, is one who has all power in heaven and earth and is mighty to save. Comfortable is the thought that there is no sinner too far gone in sin for Christ to raise and convert. He that stood by the grave of Lazarus can say to the vilest of men, 'Come forth: loose him, and let him go.' Comfortable, not least, is the thought that when we ourselves lie down in the grave, we may lie down in the full assurance that we shall rise again. The voice that called Lazarus forth will one day pierce our tombs and bid soul and body come together. 'The trumpet shall sound, and the dead shall be raised incorruptible, and we shall be changed' (1 Cor. 15:52).

For meditation: *The funerals of our loved ones only have the appearance of finality. There is a God who raises the dead.*

Suggested further reading: Romans 10:9-13

Here is a striking picture of the first beginnings of saving faith and its effect. The woman's act (v. 27) appeared a most simple one and utterly inadequate to produce any great result. But the effect of that act was marvellous. In an instant the poor sufferer was healed. One touch and she was well (vv. 27-29).

It is hard to conceive a better image of the experience of many souls than the history of this woman's cure. Hundreds could testify that, like her, they had long sought spiritual help from physicians of no value and wearied their souls by using remedies which brought no cure. At last they heard of one who healed labouring consciences and forgave sinners freely if men would only come to him by faith. The terms sounded too good to be credible, the tidings too good to be true. But like this woman they resolved to try. They came to Christ by faith, with all their sins, and to their amazement at once found relief.

For ever let it be graven on our hearts that faith in Christ is the grand secret of peace with God. Without it we shall never find inward rest, whatever we may do in religion. Without it we may go to services daily, receive the Lord's Supper every week, give our goods to the poor, give our bodies to be burned, fast, wear sackcloth, live the lives of hermits — all this we may do and still be miserable. One true believing touch of Christ is worth all these things put together. The pride of human nature may not like it! But it is true!

Our Lord greatly desires those who have received benefit from him to confess him before men. This woman was not allowed to go home once cured without her cure being noticed (vv. 30-32). There should be a public acknowledgement of mercies received. If we have found peace through his blood and been renewed by his Spirit we must not shrink from avowing it on every proper occasion. Without flinching from ridicule or persecution we should acknowledge Christ as our Master.

For meditation: *Faith is so humiliating because it requires us to receive a gift rather than make a contribution to salvation. In this way God receives all of the praise.*

Suggested further reading: Luke 16:19-31

A man four days dead was raised to life in the sight of many witnesses. The fact was unmistakable and could not be denied and yet the chief priests and Pharisees would not believe that he who did this miracle ought to be received as the Messiah. In the face of overwhelming evidence, they shut their eyes and refused to be convinced. 'This man', they admitted, 'does many miracles.' But so far from yielding to this testimony, they only plunged into further wickedness and 'took counsel to put him to death'. Great, indeed, is the power of unbelief!

Let us beware of supposing that miracles alone have any power to convert men's souls and to make them Christians. The idea is a complete delusion. To fancy, as some do, that if they saw something wonderful done before their eyes in confirmation of the gospel, they would at once cast off all indecision and serve Christ is a mere idle dream. It is the grace of the Spirit in our hearts, and not miracles, that our souls require. The Jews of our Lord's day are standing proof to mankind that men may see signs and wonders and yet remain hard as stone. It is a deep and true saying: 'If men believe not Moses and the prophets, neither would they be persuaded though one rose from the dead' (Luke 16:31).

We must never wonder if we see abounding unbelief in our own times and around our own homes. It may seem at first inexplicable to us how men cannot see the truth which seems so clear to ourselves and do not receive the gospel which appears so worthy of acceptation. But the plain truth is that man's unbelief is a far more deeply-seated disease than it is generally reckoned. It is proof against the logic of facts, against reasoning, against argument, against moral suasion. Nothing can melt it down but the grace of God. If we ourselves believe, we can never be too thankful.

For meditation: *Unbelief is not concerned with evidence. The only power to overcome it is the gift of a new heart.*

Suggested further reading: 1 Thessalonians 4:13-18

Rank places no man beyond the reach of sorrow. Jairus was a ruler with wealth, but sickness, trouble and death came to his house. We often talk as if the possession of riches was the great antidote to sorrow and as if money could secure us against sickness and death. But it is the very extreme of blindness to think so. Death stands on no ceremony. It awaits no man's leisure or convenience. All are going to the grave (Heb. 9:27). Sickness is a great leveller. Heaven is the only place where there shall be no sickness (Isa. 33:24).

The power of our Lord is almighty. That message which pierced the ruler's heart, telling him that his child was dead, did not stop the Lord for a moment. At once he cheered the fainting father's spirits (vv. 35-36). He came to the house and took the girl's hand and spoke to her (vv. 40-41). At once her heart began to beat again and the breath returned to the lifeless body (v. 42).

How wonderful was the change that took place in that house! From weeping to rejoicing, from mourning to congratulation, from death to life, how great and marvellous must have been the transition! They only can tell that who have seen death face to face and had the light of their households quenched and felt the iron entering into their own souls. They and they only can conceive what the family of Jairus must have felt when they saw their beloved one given back once more into their bosom. What a picture of what Jesus can do for dead souls! Have we a dead soul in our family? Let us call on the Lord to come and give life (Eph. 2:1).

We have in this miracle a blessed pledge of what our Lord will do in the day of his second appearing. He will call his people from the graves to part no more and die no more. Believing parents shall once again see believing children. Believing husbands shall once more see believing wives. There is to be a glorious resurrection (1 Thess. 4:14). Words of promise shall receive a fulfilment (Hosea 13:14). He that raised the daughter of Jairus still lives.

For meditation: *If we overcome our fear of death we will be bold in our living. As long as we fear what men may do to us we will be cowardly.*

Suggested further reading: Psalm 2

These rulers of the Jews said to one another, 'If we let this Christ alone we shall be ruined. If we do not stop his course and make an end of his miracles, the Romans will interfere and make an end of our nation.' Never, the event afterwards proved, was there a more short-sighted and erring judgement than this. They rushed madly on the path they had chosen and the very thing they feared came to pass. They did not leave our Lord alone, but crucified and slew him. And what happened then? After a few years, the very calamity they had dreaded took place: the Roman armies did come, destroyed Jerusalem, burned the temple and carried away the whole nation into captivity.

The Roman emperors persecuted the Christians in the first three centuries and thought it a positive duty not to let them alone. But the more they persecuted them, the more they increased. The blood of the martyrs became the seed of the church. The English Papists, in the days of Queen Mary, persecuted the Protestants and thought that truth was in danger if they were let alone. But the more they burned our forefathers, the more they confirmed men's minds in steadfast attachment to the doctrines of the Reformation. In short, the words of the second Psalm are continually verified in this world: 'The kings of the earth set themselves, and the rulers take counsel together against the Lord.' But, 'He that sitteth in the heavens shall laugh; the Lord shall have them in derision.' God can make the designs of his enemies work together for the good of his people and cause the wrath of man to praise him. In days of trouble and rebuke and blasphemy, believers may rest patiently in the Lord. The very things that at one time seem likely to hurt them shall prove in the end to be for their gain.

For meditation: *The church is indestructible because it is built by Christ* (Matt. 16:18).

Suggested further reading: Psalm 103:1-14

Strong faith in Christ may sometimes be found where it might have been least expected. Who would have thought that two blind men would have called our Lord 'Son of David'? They could not have seen the miracles he did. They could only know him by common report. But the eyes of their understanding were enlightened if their bodily eyes were dark. They saw the truth that the scribes and Pharisees did not see. They saw that Jesus of Nazareth was the Messiah. They believed that he was able to heal them.

We must never despair of anyone's salvation merely because he lives in a position unfavourable to his soul. Grace is stronger than circumstances. The life of religion does not depend merely upon outward advantages. The Holy Spirit can give faith and keep faith in active exercise without book-learning, without money and with scanty means of grace. Without the Holy Spirit a man may know all mysteries and be lost. The poor and uneducated believe while the university man is full of hardened unbelief.

Our Lord has had a great experience of disease and sickness (vv. 27,32,35). He was an eyewitness to all the ills to which the flesh is heir. He saw ailments of every kind, sort and description. He was brought into contact with every form of bodily suffering. None were too loathsome for him to attend to. None were too frightful for him to cure.

We are all living in a poor frail body. We never know what quantity of suffering we may have to watch as we sit by the bedside of dear relations and friends. We never know what racking complaint we ourselves may have to submit to before we lie down and die. But let us arm ourselves with the precious thought that Jesus is especially fitted to be the sick man's friend. The great High Priest is eminently suited to sympathize with an aching body and to look with pity on the diseased.

For meditation: *Our Lord assumes that his people will engage in the visiting of the sick* (Matt. 25:39). *Do you?*

Suggested further reading: Matthew 15:1-9

What importance bad men sometimes attach to outward ceremonial, while their hearts are full of sin! We are told that many Jews 'went up out of the country to Jerusalem, before the Passover, to purify themselves'. The most of them, it may be feared, neither knew nor cared anything about inward purity of heart. They made much ado about the washings and fastings and ascetic observances which formed the essence of popular Jewish religion in our Lord's time and yet they were willing in a very few days to shed innocent blood. Strange as it may appear, these very sticklers for outward sanctification were found ready to do the will of the Pharisees and to put their own Messiah to a violent death.

Extremes like this meeting together in the same person are, unhappily, far from uncommon. Experience shows that a bad conscience will often try to satisfy itself by a show of zeal for the cause of religion, while the 'weightier matters' of the faith are entirely neglected. The very same man who is ready to compass sea and land to attain ceremonial purity is often the very man who, if he had fit opportunity, would not shrink from helping to crucify Christ. Startling as these assertions may seem, they are abundantly borne out by plain facts.

Let us settle it firmly in our minds that a religion which expends itself in zeal for outward formalities is utterly worthless in God's sight. The purity that God desires to see is not the purity of bodily washing and fasting, of holy water and self-imposed asceticism, but purity of heart. 'Blessed are the pure in heart, for they shall see God' (Matt. 5:8).

For meditation: *Are you more concerned about what other people **think** of you, or what God **knows** about you?*

Suggested further reading: Matthew 10:11-15

Our Lord taught in his home town in the synagogue. His teaching was the same as it always was. But it had no effect on the people of Nazareth. They were astonished but their hearts were unmoved. They despised him because he was so familiar to them. They drew from our Lord his solemn remark (v. 57).

Here a melancholy page of human history is unfolded to our view. We are all apt to despise mercies if we are accustomed to them and have them cheap. The Bibles and religious books which are so plentiful in England, the means of grace of which we have such an abundant supply, the preaching of the gospel which we hear every week — all, all are liable to be undervalued. It is mournfully true that in religion, more than in anything else, familiarity breeds contempt. Men forget that truth is truth, however old and hackneyed it may sound, and despise it because it is old. Alas! by so doing they provoke God to take it away.

The chapter ends with the fearful words concerning our Lord's few miracles (v. 58). Here we see the ruinous nature of unbelief. See in this single word the secret of the everlasting ruin of multitudes of souls. They perish for ever because they will not believe. There is nothing beside in earth or heaven that prevents their salvation. Their sins, however many, might all be forgiven. The Father's love is ready to receive them. The blood of Christ is ready to cleanse them. The power of the Spirit is ready to renew them. But a great barrier interposes — they will not believe (John 5:40).

May we all be on our guard against this accursed sin. It is the old root sin which caused the fall of man. Cut down in the true child of God by the power of the Spirit, it is ever ready to bud and sprout again. There are three great enemies against which God's children should daily pray — pride, worldliness and unbelief. Of these three none is greater than unbelief.

For meditation: *When we can hear the gospel and not long that we might again be converted and respond to its call, we have grown cold to its great and marvellous truths.*

Suggested further reading: Luke 24:36-43

What abounding proofs exist of the truth of our Lord's greatest miracles! We read of a supper at Bethany, where Lazarus 'sat at the table' among the guests — Lazarus, who had been publicly raised from the dead after lying four days in the grave. No one could pretend to say that his resurrection was a mere optical delusion and that the eyes of the bystanders must have been deceived by a ghost or vision. Here was the very same Lazarus, after several weeks, sitting among his fellow men with a real material body and eating and drinking real material food. It is hard to understand what stronger evidence of a fact could be supplied. He that is not convinced by such evidence as this may as well say that he is determined to believe nothing at all.

It is a comfortable thought that the very same proofs which exist about the resurrection of Lazarus are the proofs which surround the still mightier fact, the resurrection of Christ from the dead. Was Lazarus seen for several weeks by the people of Bethany, going in and coming out among them? So was the Lord Jesus seen by his disciples. Did Lazarus take material food before the eyes of his friends? So did the Lord Jesus eat and drink before his ascension. No one, in his sober senses, who saw Jesus take 'broiled fish and a honeycomb' and eat it before several witnesses, would doubt that he had a real body (Luke 24:42).

We shall do well to remember this. In an age of abounding unbelief and scepticism, we shall find that the resurrection of Christ will bear any weight that we can lay upon it. Just as he placed beyond reasonable doubt the rising again of a beloved disciple within two miles of Jerusalem, so in a very few weeks he placed beyond doubt his own victory over the grave. If we believe that Lazarus rose again, we need not doubt that Jesus rose again also. If we believe that Jesus rose again, we need not doubt the truth of his Messiahship, the reality of his acceptance as our Mediator and the certainty of our own resurrection.

For meditation: *Surely only prejudice would reject over 500 eyewitnesses to an event?* (1 Cor. 15:6).

Suggested further reading: Romans 10:11-15

What tender compassion our Lord had for neglected souls! He saw multitudes of people while he was on earth scattered like sheep having no shepherd and he was moved with compassion. He saw them neglected by those who for the time ought to have been teachers. He saw them ignorant, hopeless, dying and unfit to die. The sight moved him to deep pity. That loving heart could not see such things and not feel.

Now what are our feelings when we see such a sight? There are many such to be seen on every side. There are millions of idolaters and heathens. There are millions of deluded Moslems, millions of superstitious Roman Catholics, thousands of ignorant Protestants. Do we feel tenderly concerned about their souls? Do we feel pity for their spiritual destitution? Do we long to see that destitution relieved? These are serious enquiries and ought to be answered. It is easy to sneer at missions to the heathen and those who work for them. But the man who does not feel for the souls of the unconverted can surely not have the mind of Christ.

There is a solemn duty incumbent upon all Christians. They should do good to the unconverted part of humanity. They are to pray for more men to be raised up for the work of the conversion of souls. It seems as if it were to be a daily part of our prayers (v. 38).

If we know anything of prayer let us make it a point of conscience never to forget this solemn charge of our Lord's. Let us settle it in our minds that it is one of the surest ways of doing good and stemming evil. Personal working for souls is good. Giving money is good. But praying is best of all. By prayer we reach him without whom work and money are alike in vain. We obtain the aid of the Holy Spirit. Money can pay agents. Universities can give learning. Congregations may elect. Elders may ordain. But the Holy Spirit alone can make ministers of the gospel and raise up workmen in the spiritual harvest who need not be ashamed. Never, never may we forget that if we would do good to the world our first duty is to pray!

For meditation:
Prayer is the Christian's vital breath,
The Christian's native air

                                               (Montgomery).

Are you even breathing?

Suggested further reading: Jeremiah 38:1-6

What unkindness and discouragement Christ's friends sometimes meet from man! We read that, at the supper in Bethany, Mary, the sister of Lazarus, anointed the feet of Jesus with precious ointment and wiped them with the hair of her head. Nor was this ointment poured on with a niggardly hand. She did it so liberally and profusely that 'The house was filled with the odour of the ointment.' She did it under the influence of a heart full of love and gratitude. She thought nothing too great and good to bestow on such a Saviour. Sitting at his feet in days gone by and hearing his words, she had found peace for her conscience and pardon for her sins. At this very moment she saw Lazarus, alive and well, sitting by her Master's side — her own brother Lazarus, whom he had brought back to her from the grave. Greatly loved, she thought she could not show too much love in return. Having freely received, she freely gave.

But there were some present who found fault with Mary's conduct and blamed her as guilty of wasteful extravagance. One especially, an apostle, a man of whom better things might have been expected, declared openly that the ointment would have been better employed if it had been sold and the price 'given to the poor'. The heart which could conceive such thoughts must have had low views of the dignity of Christ's person and still lower views of our obligations to him. A cold heart and a stingy hand will generally go together.

We must never allow ourselves to be moved from 'patient continuance in well-doing' by the unkind remarks of such persons. It is vain to expect a man to do much for Christ when he has no sense of debt to Christ. We must pity the blindness of our unkind critics and work on. He who pleaded the cause of loving Mary and said, 'Let her alone,' is sitting at the right hand of God and keeps a book of remembrance.

For meditation: *Christ's 'Well done'* (Matt. 25:23) *will more than compensate for every human rebuttal.*

Suggested further reading: Ezekiel 33:1-9

All ministers are not necessarily good men. We see our Lord choosing a Judas Iscariot to be one of his apostles. We cannot doubt that he who knew all hearts knew well the character of the men whom he chose. And he included in the lists one who was a traitor!

We shall do well to bear this fact in mind. Ministerial office does not confer the saving grace of the Holy Spirit. Ordained men are not necessarily converted men. We are not to regard them as infallible, either in doctrine or in practice. We are not to make popes or idols of them and insensibly put them in Christ's place. We are to regard them as men of like passions with ourselves, liable to the same infirmities and daily requiring the same grace. We are not to think it impossible for them to do very bad things or to expect them to be above the reach of harm from flattery, covetousness and the world. We are to prove their teaching by the Word of God and follow them so far as they follow Christ but no further. Above all, we ought to pray for them that they may be successors not of Judas Iscariot, but of James and John. It is an awesome thing to be a minister of the gospel! Ministers need many prayers.

The great work of a minister of Christ is to do good. He is sent to seek 'lost sheep' (v. 6), to proclaim good news, to relieve those who are suffering, to diminish sorrow and to increase joy (vv. 7-8). His life is meant to be one of giving rather than receiving (v. 8).

This is a high standard and a very peculiar one. The life of a minister of Christ cannot be one of ease. He must be ready to spend body and mind, time and strength in the work of his calling. Laziness and frivolity are bad enough in any profession, but worst of all in that of a watchman of souls. Ministers are not so much ordained to rule as to serve. They are not so much intended to have dominion over the church as to supply its wants and wait upon its members (2 Cor. 1:24). Happy would it be for the cause of true religion if these things were better understood!

For meditation: *It is far easier to criticize your minister than to pray for him. Do you require perfection of him while not seeking it for yourself?*

Suggested further reading: 1 Timothy 6:3-10

What desperate hardness and unbelief there is in the heart of man! Unbelief appears in the chief priests, who 'consulted that they might put Lazarus to death'. They could not deny the fact of his having been raised again. Living and moving and eating and drinking within two miles of Jerusalem, after lying four days in the grave, Lazarus was a witness to the truth of Christ's Messiahship, whom they could not possibly answer or put to silence. Yet these proud men would not give way. They would rather commit a murder than throw down the arms of rebellion and confess themselves in the wrong. No wonder that the Lord Jesus in a certain place 'marvelled' at unbelief (Mark 6:6). Well might he say, in a well-known parable, 'If they believe not Moses and the prophets, neither will they be persuaded though one rose from the dead' (Luke 16:31).

Hardness appears in Judas Iscariot who, after being a chosen apostle and a preacher of the kingdom of heaven, turns out at last a thief and a traitor. So long as the world stands, this unhappy man will be a lasting proof of the depth of human corruption. That anyone could follow Christ as a disciple for three years, see all his miracles, hear all his teaching, receive at his hand repeated kindnesses, be counted an apostle and yet prove rotten at heart in the end — all this at first sight appears incredible and impossible! Yet the case of Judas shows plainly that the thing can be. Few things, perhaps, are so little realized as the extent of the fall of man.

Let us thank God if we know anything of faith and can say, with all our sense of weakness and infirmity, 'I believe.' Let us pray that our faith may be real, true, genuine and sincere, and not a mere temporary impression, like the morning cloud and the early dew. Not least, let us watch and pray against the love of the world. It ruined one who basked in the full sunshine of privileges and heard Christ himself teaching every day.

For meditation: *How much is your heart welded to this world?*

Suggested further reading: 1 Timothy 6:11-19

The commission to the apostles contained special reference to the devil and bodily sickness (v. 1). We may fairly expect the minister to resist the devil and all his works and to keep up a constant warfare against him. We may expect him to take a special interest in all sick people, to visit them, sympathize with them and help them. In opposing the devil he must not allow drunkenness, blasphemy, uncleanness, fighting, revelling and the like to go unreproved in his congregation.

One of the principal works which the apostles were commissioned to take up was preaching (v. 7). This passage is one instance among many of the high value which the Bible everywhere sets on preaching. It is God's chosen instrument for doing good to men's souls. By it sinners are converted, enquirers led on and saints built up. A preaching ministry is absolutely essential to the health and prosperity of a visible church. The pulpit is the place where the chief victories of the gospel have been won, and no church has ever done much for the advancement of true religion in which the pulpit is neglected. A truly apostolic minister will give his best attention to his sermons. He will labour and pray to make his preaching effective and he will tell his congregation that he looks to preaching for the chief results on souls.

Our Lord charges his apostles to study simplicity of habits and contentment with such things as they have (vv. 9-10). In part these instructions applied to that particular period, but in part they have an application for all time. The leading idea that these words convey is a warning against worldliness and luxurious habits. Through personal worldliness and luxury of lives many Christian teachers have destroyed by their daily lives the whole work of their lips. They have given occasion to the enemies of the gospel to say that they love ease, money and good things more than souls. An apostolic man's affections cannot be set on money, dress, feasting and pleasure-seeking.

For meditation: *A worldly, materialistic congregation can encourage worldly materialism in its minister to their mutual destruction. Do you expect ministers and missionaries to be other-worldly while you permit yourself to be this-worldly?*

Suggested further reading: Zechariah 9:9-13

The riding into Jerusalem on an ass, which is here recorded, might seem at first sight a simple action and in no way remarkable. But when we turn to the Old Testament, we find that this very thing had been predicted by the prophet Zechariah five hundred years before (Zech. 9:9). We find that the coming of a Redeemer some day was not the only thing which the Holy Ghost had revealed to the fathers, but that even the least particulars of his earthly career were predicted and written down with precise accuracy.

Such fulfilments of prophecy as this deserve the special attention of all who love the Bible and read it with reverence. They show us that every word of Holy Scripture was given by inspiration of God. They teach us to beware of the mischievous practice of spiritualizing and explaining away the language of Scripture. We must settle it in our minds that the plain, literal meaning of the Bible is generally the true and correct meaning. Here is a prediction of Zechariah literally and exactly fulfilled. Our Lord was not merely a very humble person, as some spiritualizing interpreters would have explained Zechariah's words to mean, but he literally rode into Jerusalem on an ass. Above all, such fulfilments teach us what we may expect in looking forward to the second advent of Jesus Christ. They show us that we must look for a literal accomplishment of the prophecies concerning that second coming and not for a figurative and a spiritual one. Forever let us hold fast this great principle. Happy is that Bible-reader who believes the words of the Bible to mean exactly what they seem to mean. Such a man has got the true key of knowledge in looking forward to things to come. To know that predictions about the second advent of Christ will be fulfilled literally, just as predictions about the first advent of Christ were fulfilled literally, is the first step towards a right understanding of unfulfilled prophecy.

For meditation: *The Scriptures stand detailed study because God is a God of detailed accuracy.*

Suggested further reading: Genesis 19:12-26

Our Lord prepares his disciples to meet with impenitence and unbelief in those to whom they preach (v. 14). All involved in any evangelistic work will do well to lay this to heart. Let them not be cast down if their work seems in vain and their labour without profit. Let them remember that the very first labourers sent forth by Jesus were warned that not all would believe. Let them work on patiently and sow the good seed without fainting. Duties are theirs. Results are God's. Apostles may plant and water. The Holy Spirit alone can give spiritual life.

Our Lord states that it is a most dangerous thing to neglect the offers of the gospel (v. 15). Men are sadly apt to forget that it does not require great open sins to be sinned in order to ruin a soul for ever. They have only to go on hearing without believing, listening without repenting, going to church without going to Christ, and by and by they will find themselves in hell! We shall all be judged according to our light. We shall have to give account of our use of religious privileges. To hear of the great salvation and yet neglect it is one of the worst sins man can commit (John 16:9).

What are we doing ourselves with the gospel? Are we no more than decent and respectable in our lives, correct and moral in all the relations of life and regular in our attendance at the means of grace? Or are we really loving the truth? Is Christ dwelling in our hearts by faith? If not, we are in fearful danger. We are far more guilty than the men of Sodom who never heard the gospel at all. We are far more guilty and we may awake to find that in spite of our regularity, morality and correctness we have lost our souls for all eternity. It will not save us to have lived in the full sunshine of Christian privileges and to have heard the gospel faithfully preached every week. There must be a personal acquaintance with Christ, a personal reception of his truth. Without this the gospel only adds to our condemnation.

For meditation: *Sodom's rejection of God's morality was not half so wicked as modern man's rejection of God's Son.*

Suggested further reading: John 18:1-8

How entirely voluntary the sufferings of Christ were! It is imposs-ible not to see in the history before us that our Lord had a mysteri-ous influence over the minds and wills of all around him, whenever he thought fit to use it. Nothing else can account for the effect which his approach to Jerusalem had on the multitudes which accompa-nied him. They seem to have been carried forward by a secret con-straining power, which they were obliged to obey, in spite of the disapproval of the leaders of the nation. In short, just as our Lord was able to make winds and waves and diseases and devils obey him, so was he able, when it pleased him, to turn the minds of men according to his will.

For the case before us does not stand alone. The men of Naza-reth could not hold him when he chose to 'pass through the midst of them and go his way' (Luke 4:30). The angry Jews of Jerusalem could not detain him when they would have laid violent hands on him in the temple, but 'going through the midst of them, he passed by' (John 8:59). Above all, the very soldiers who apprehended him in the garden at first 'went backward and fell to the ground' (John 18:6). In each of these instances there is but one explanation. A divine influence was put forth. There was about our Lord during his whole earthly ministry a mysterious 'hiding of his power' (Hab. 3:4). But he had almighty power when he was pleased to use it.

Why then, did he not resist his enemies at last? Why did he not scatter the band of soldiers who came to seize him like chaff before the wind? There is but one answer. He was a willing sufferer. He did not bleed and suffer and die because he was vanquished by superior force and could not help himself, but because he loved us and re-joiced to give himself for us as our Substitute.

For meditation: *How willing was Jesus to die that we poor sinners might live!*

Suggested further reading: Ecclesiastes 3:1-8

Those who would do good to souls have need to pray for wisdom, good sense and a sound mind. Our Lord tells his disciples to be both wise and harmless (v. 16) and to flee when persecuted (v. 23).

There are few of our Lord's instructions which it is so difficult to use rightly as this. There is a line marked out for us between two extremes, but one that requires great judgement to define. To avoid persecution by holding our tongues and keeping our religion entirely to ourselves is one extreme. We are not to err in that direction. To court persecution and thrust our religion upon everyone we meet, without regard to place, time or circumstances, is another extreme. In this direction also we are warned not to err any more than in the other. We have need of wisdom.

The extreme into which most men are likely to fall in the present day is that of silence, cowardice and letting others alone. Our so-called prudence is apt to degenerate into a compromising line of conduct or downright unfaithfulness. We are only too ready to suppose that it is no good trying to do good to certain people. We excuse ourselves from efforts to benefit their souls by saying it would be indiscreet or inexpedient or would give needless offence or do positive harm. Let us all watch and be on our guard against this spirit. Laziness and the devil are often the true explanation of it. To give way to it is pleasant to flesh and blood, no doubt, and saves us from much trouble. But those who give way to it often throw away opportunities of usefulness.

On the other hand it is impossible to deny that there is such a thing as holy and righteous zeal which is not according to knowledge. It is quite possible to create much needless offence, commit great blunders, and stir up much opposition which might have been avoided by a little prudence, wise management and exercise of judgement. Our Lord does not require us to throw aside our common sense when we undertake work for him. There will be offence enough connected with our religion without our increasing it without cause. Let us live wisely (Eph. 5:15).

For meditation: *Our lives are to adorn the gospel* (Titus 2:10). *Sometimes a God-honouring life will require a closed mouth* (1 Peter 3:1).

Suggested further reading: Acts 26:19-29

A careful reader of the Gospels can hardly fail to observe that our Lord Jesus Christ's conduct at this stage of his earthly ministry is very peculiar. It is unlike anything else recorded of him in the New Testament. Hitherto we have seen him withdrawing as much as possible from public notice, retiring into the wilderness and checking those who would have brought him forward and made him a king. As a rule he did not court popular attention. He did not 'cry or strive, or cause his voice to be heard in the streets' (Matt. 12:19). Here, on the contrary, we see him making a public entry into Jerusalem, attended by an immense crowd of people and causing even the Pharisees to say, 'Behold, the world has gone after him.'

The explanation of this apparent inconsistency is not hard to find out. The time had come at last when Christ was to die for the sins of the world. The time had come when the true Passover Lamb was to be slain, when the true blood of atonement was to be shed, when Messiah was to be 'cut off' according to prophecy (Dan. 9:26), when the way into the holiest was to be opened by the true High Priest to all mankind. Knowing all this, our Lord purposely drew attention to himself. Knowing this, he placed himself prominently under the notice of the whole Jewish nation. It was only meet and right that this thing should not be 'done in a corner' (Acts 26:26). If ever there was a transaction in our Lord's earthly ministry which was public, it was the sacrifice which he offered up on the cross of Calvary. He died at the time of year when all the tribes were assembled at Jerusalem for the Passover feast. Nor was this all. He died in a week when, by his remarkable public entry into Jerusalem, he had caused the eyes of all Israel to be specially fixed upon himself.

For meditation: *Our Lord was not interested in gaining publicity for himself, but in focusing attention on his saving death.*

Suggested further reading: Acts 13:42-52

To do good to souls in this world is very hard. All who try it find this by experience. It needs a large stock of courage, faith, patience and perseverance. Satan will fight vigorously to maintain his kingdom. Human nature is desperately wicked. To do harm is easy. To do good is hard.

The Lord knew this well when he sent forth his disciples to preach the gospel for the first time. He knew what was before them, if they did not. He took care to supply them with a list of encouragements in order to cheer them when they were cast down.

Those who try to do good to souls must not expect to fare better than their great Master (v. 24). The Lord Jesus was slandered and rejected by those he came to benefit. There was no error in his teaching. There was no defect in his method of imparting instruction. Yet many hated him and called him Beelzebub (v. 25). Few believed him and cared for what he said. Surely we have no right to be surprised if we, whose best efforts are mingled with much imperfection, are treated in the same way as Christ. If we let the world alone it will probably let us alone. But if we try to do it spiritual good it will hate us as it did our Master.

Those who try to do good must look forward to the Day of Judgement with patience (v. 26). They must be content in this present world to be misunderstood, misrepresented, vilified, slandered and abused. They must not cease to work because their motives are mistaken and their characters are fiercely assailed. They must remember that all will be set right at the last day. The secrets of all hearts will then be revealed (Ps. 37:6). The purity of their intentions, the wisdom of their labours and the rightfulness of their cause shall at length be manifest to all the world. Let us work on steadily and quietly. Men may not understand us and may vehemently oppose us. But the Day of Judgement draws nigh. We shall be righted at last (1 Cor. 4:5).

For meditation: *God cannot vindicate and reward us on the Day of Judgement for work we have not done! What work are you doing for Christ?*

Suggested further reading: Hebrews 2:14-18

Who would have thought when Christ was on earth that foreigners from a distant land would have come forward in Jerusalem and said, 'Sir, we would see Jesus'? Who these Greeks were, what they meant, why they desired to see Jesus, what their inward motives were — all these are questions we cannot answer. Enough for us to know that they showed more interest in Christ than Caiaphas and all his companions. Death is the way to spiritual life and glory. 'Except a corn of wheat fall into the ground, it abideth alone; but if it die, it bringeth forth much fruit.' This sentence was primarily meant to teach the wondering Greeks the true nature of Messiah's kingdom. If they thought to see a king like the kings of this world, they were greatly mistaken. Our Lord would have them know that he came to carry a cross and not to wear a crown. He came not to live a life of honour, ease and magnificence, but to die a shameful and dishonoured death. The kingdom he came to set up was to begin with a crucifixion and not with a coronation. Its glory was to take its rise not from victories won by the sword and from accumulated treasures of gold and silver, but from the death of its King.

But this sentence was also meant to teach a wider and broader lesson still. It revealed, under a striking figure, the mighty foundation truth that Christ's death was to be the source of spiritual life to the world. From his cross and passions was to spring up a mighty harvest of benefit to all mankind. His death, like a grain of seed-corn, was to be the root of blessings and mercies to countless millions of immortal souls. In short, the great principle of the gospel was once more exhibited — that Christ's vicarious death (not his life, or miracles, or teaching, but his death) was to bring forth fruit to the praise of God and to provide redemption for a lost world.

For meditation: *Paul did not simply preach Christ, but Christ and him crucified* (1 Cor. 2:2).

Suggested further reading: 2 Corinthians 12:7-10

Those who try to do good must fear God more than man. Man can hurt the body, but there his enmity must stop. He can go no further. But God can (v. 28). We may be threatened with the loss of character, property and all that makes life enjoyable if we go on in the path of religious duty. We must not heed such threats when our course is plain. Like Daniel and his three companions, we must submit to anything rather than displease God and wound our consciences. The anger of man may be hard to bear, but the anger of God is much harder. The fear of man does indeed bring a snare, but we must make it give way to the expulsive power of a stronger principle — even the fear of God.

Those who try to do good must keep before their eyes the providential care of God over them. Nothing in the world can happen without his permission. There is no such thing in reality as chance, accident or luck. The path of duty may sometimes lead them into great danger. Health and life may seem to be imperilled if they go forward. Let them take comfort in the thought that all around them is God's hand. Their bodies, their souls, their characters are all in his safe keeping (vv. 29-31). No disease can seize them, no hand can hurt them, unless he allows. They can have the confidence of our Lord (John 19:11).

Those who try to do good should continually remember the day when they shall meet their Lord to receive their final portion. If they would have him own them and confess them before his Father's throne they must not be ashamed to own and confess him before the men of this world (vv. 32-33). To do it may cost us much. It may bring on us laughter, mockery, persecution and scorn. But let us not be laughed out of heaven. Let us recollect the great and dreadful day of account and not be afraid to show men that we love Christ and want them to know and love him also.

For meditation: *When our Lord calls us to serve him he knows all that we will face and provides all that we need to stand firm in evil days.*

Suggested further reading: Galatians 6:12-18

'He that hateth his life shall keep it.' He that would be saved must be ready to give up life itself, if necessary, in order to obtain salvation. He must bury his love of the world, with its riches, honours, pleasures and rewards, with a full belief that in so doing he will reap a better harvest, both here and hereafter. He who loves the life that now is so much that he cannot deny himself anything for the sake of his soul will find at length that he has lost everything. He, on the contrary, who is ready to cast away everything most dear to him in this life, if it stands in the way of his soul, and to crucify the flesh, with its affections and lusts, will find at length that he is no loser. In a word, his losses will prove nothing in comparison to his gains.

Truths such as these should sink deeply into our hearts and stir up self-enquiry. It is as true of Christians as it is of Christ that there can be no life without death, there can be no sweet without bitter, there can be no crown without a cross. Without Christ's death there would have been no life for the world. Unless we are willing to die to sin and crucify all that is most dear to flesh and blood, we cannot expect any benefit from Christ's death. Let us remember these things and take up our cross daily like men. Let us for the joy set before us endure the cross and despise the shame, and in the end we shall sit down with our Master at God's right hand. The way of self-crucifixion and sanctification may seem foolishness and waste to the world, just as burying good seed-corn seems waste to the child and the fool. But there never lived the man who did not find that by sowing to the Spirit he reaped life everlasting.

For meditation: *We must beware of that mentality which always talks of the sacrifices it has made for Christ. They always pale into insignificance in the light of his sacrifice.*

Suggested further reading: 2 Corinthians 11:22-28

The gospel will not cause peace and agreement wherever it comes. We are not to think it strange if the gospel rends families asunder and causes estrangement between near relations. It is sure to do so in many cases because of the deep corruption of man's heart. So long as one man believes and another remains unbelieving, so long as one is resolved to keep his sins and another desirous to give them up, the result of the preaching of the gospel must be division. For this the gospel is not to blame, but the heart of man.

There is a deep truth in all this which is constantly forgotten and overlooked. Many talk vaguely about unity and harmony and peace in the church of Christ as if they were things we ought always to expect and for the sake of which everything ought to be sacrificed. Such persons would do well to remember the words of our Lord. No doubt unity and peace are mighty blessings. We ought to seek them, pray for them and give up everything to obtain them, excepting truth and a good conscience.

True Christians must make up their minds to expect troubles in this world. Whether we are ministers or hearers, teachers or the taught, it makes little difference. We must carry a cross (v. 38). We must be content to lose even a life for Christ's sake (v. 39). We must submit to loss of man's favour, we must endure hardships, we must deny ourselves in many things, or we shall never reach heaven at last (vv. 37-39). So long as the world, the devil and our own hearts are what they are, these things must be so.

We shall find it useful to remember this lesson ourselves and to impress it on others. Few things do more harm in religion than exaggerated expectations. People look for a degree of worldly comfort in Christ's service which they have no right to expect and, not finding what they look for, are tempted to give up religion in disgust. Happy is he who understands that, though Christianity holds out a crown at the end, it brings also a cross in the way.

For meditation: *'I have told you these things, so that in me you may have peace. In this world you will have trouble. But take heart! I have overcome the world'* (John 16:33).

Suggested further reading: Matthew 5:10-12

If we profess to serve Christ, we must follow him. That expression, 'following', is one of wide signification and brings before our minds many familiar ideas. As the soldier follows his general, as the servant follows his master, as the scholar follows his teacher, as the sheep follows its shepherd, just so ought the professing Christian to follow Christ. Faith and obedience are the leading marks of real followers and will always be seen in true believing Christians. Their knowledge may be very small and their infirmities very great, their grace very weak and their hope very dim. But they believe what Christ says and strive to do what Christ commands. And of such Christ declares, 'They serve me; they are mine.'

Christianity like this receives little from man. It is too thorough, too decided, too strong, too real. To serve Christ in name and form is easy work and satisfies most people, but to follow him in faith and life demands more trouble than the generality of men will take about their souls. Laughter, ridicule, opposition, persecution are often the only reward which Christ's followers get from the world. Their religion is one 'whose praise is not of men, but of God' (Rom. 2:29).

Yet to him that followeth, let us never forget, the Lord Jesus holds out abundant encouragement: 'Where I am,' he declares, 'there also shall my servant be; if any man serve me, him will my Father honour.' Let us lay to heart these comfortable promises and go forward in the narrow way without fear. The world may cast out our name as evil and turn us out of its society, but when we dwell with Christ in glory, we shall have a home from which we can never be ejected. The world may pour contempt on our religion and laugh us and our Christianity to scorn, but when the Father honours us at the last day, before the assembly of angels and men, we shall find that his praise makes amends for all.

For meditation: *To suffer is difficult enough, but to rejoice in suffering is a Christian virtue* (Acts 5:41).

Suggested further reading: Matthew 25:31-46

Our Lord cheers us by saying that the least service done to those who work in his cause is observed and rewarded by God (v. 42). There is something very beautiful in this promise. It teaches us that the eyes of the great Master are ever upon those who labour for him and try to do good. They seem perhaps to work on unnoticed and unregarded. The proceedings of preachers, missionaries, teachers and visitors may appear trifling and insignificant compared to the movements of kings, parliaments, armies and statesmen. But they are not insignificant in the sight of God. He takes notice who opposes his servants and who helps them. He observes who is kind to them, as Lydia was to Paul (Acts 16:15), and who throws difficulties in their way, as Diotrephes did to John (3 John 9). All their daily experience is recorded as they labour in his harvest. All is written down in the great book of remembrance and will be brought to light at the last day. The chief butler forgot Joseph when he was restored to his place (Gen. 40:23). But the Lord Jesus never forgets any of his people. Listen to his words on the day of resurrection (Matt. 25:35).

Let us ask ourselves in what way we regard Christ's work and Christ's cause in the world? Are we helpers of it or hinderers? Do we in any way aid the Lord's 'prophets' and 'righteous men'? Do we assist his 'little ones'? (vv. 40-42). Do we impede his labourers or cheer them on? These are serious questions.

They do well and wisely who give 'the cup of cold water' whenever they have the opportunity. They do better still who work actively in the Lord's vineyard. May we all strive to leave the world a better world than it was when we were born! That is to have the mind of Christ.

For meditation: *There is nothing so small or insignificant done to the people of Christ that he does not note and reward. There is nothing so small or insignificant done against the people of Christ that he does not note and punish. To touch Christ's people for good or ill is to touch him. We are members of his body.*

Suggested further reading: Romans 5:12-21

We have in these verses a great doctrine indirectly proved. That doctrine is the imputation of man's sin to Christ. We see the Saviour of the world, the eternal Son of God, troubled and disturbed in mind: 'Now is my soul troubled.' We see him who could heal diseases with a touch, cast out devils with a word and command the waves and winds to obey him in great agony and conflict of spirit. Now how can this be explained?

To say, as some do, that the only cause of our Lord's trouble was the prospect of his own painful death on the cross is a very unsatisfactory explanation. At this rate it might justly be said that many a martyr has shown more calmness and courage than the Son of God. Such a conclusion is, to say the least, most revolting. Yet this is the conclusion to which men are driven if they adopt the modern notion that Christ's death was only a great example of self-sacrifice.

Nothing can ever explain our Lord's trouble of soul, both here and in Gethsemane, except the old doctrine that he felt the burden of man's sin pressing him down. It was the mighty weight of a world's guilt imputed to him and meeting on his head which made him groan and agonize and cry, 'Now is my soul troubled.' Forever let us cling to that doctrine, not only as untying the knot of the passage before us, but as the only ground of solid comfort for the heart of a Christian. That our sins have been really laid on our divine Substitute and borne by him and that his righteousness is really imputed to us and accounted ours — this is the real warrant for Christian peace. And if any man asks how we know that our sins were laid on Christ, we bid him read such passages as that which is before us and explain them on any other principle if he can. Christ has borne our sins, carried our sins, groaned under the burden of our sins, been 'troubled' in soul by the weight of our sins and really taken away our sins. This, we may rest assured, is sound doctrine; this is scriptural theology.

For meditation: *Christ had no sin but our sin for which to die* (2 Cor. 5:21).

Suggested further reading: Matthew 5:27-30

Truth has an amazing power over the conscience. Herod fears John the Baptist while he is alive (v. 20) and is troubled about him after he dies (v. 16). A friendless, solitary preacher, with no other weapon than God's truth, disturbs and terrifies a king.

Everybody has a conscience. Here lies the secret of a faithful minister's power. This is the reason why Felix trembled (Acts 24:25) when Paul the prisoner spoke before him. God has not left himself without witness in the hearts of unconverted people. Fallen and corrupt as man is, there are thoughts within him accusing or excusing, according as he lives, thoughts that will not be shut out, thoughts that can make even kings like Herod restless and afraid.

None ought to remember this so much as ministers and teachers. If they preach and teach Christ's truth they may rest assured that their work is not in vain. Children may seem inattentive in schools. Hearers may seem restless in congregations. But in both cases there is often far more going on in the conscience than our eyes see. Seeds often spring up and bear fruit when the sower, like John the Baptist, is dead or gone.

People may go far in religion and yet miss salvation by yielding to one master sin. King Herod went further than many. He feared John (v. 20). He knew he was a just and holy man (v. 20). He heard him (v. 20). But there was one thing Herod would not do. He would not cease from adultery. He would not give up Herodias. And so he ruined his soul for evermore.

Let us take warning from Herod's case. Let us keep back nothing, cleave to no favourite vice, spare nothing that stands between us and salvation. Let us often look within and make sure that there is no darling lust or pet transgression which, Herodias-like, is murdering our souls. Let us rather cut off the right hand or pluck out the right eye than go into hell-fire. Let us not be content to hear sermons and admire preachers. Let us hate wickedness (Ps. 119:128).

For meditation: *Do you hate that which is evil, or merely regret it?*

Suggested further reading: Galatians 5:13-25

We cannot fail to see in the passage before us a mighty mental struggle in our blessed Saviour. Of its depth and intensity we can probably form very little conception. But the agonizing cry, 'My soul is troubled,' the solemn question, 'What shall I say?', the prayer of suffering flesh and blood, 'Father, save me from this hour,' the meek confession, 'For this cause came I unto this hour,' the petition of a perfectly submissive will, 'Father, glorify thy name' — what does all this mean? Surely there can be only one answer. These sentences tell of a struggle within our Saviour's breast, a struggle arising from the natural feelings of one who was perfect man and as man could suffer all that man is capable of suffering. Yet he in whom this struggle took place was the holy Son of God. 'In him is no sin' (1 John 3:5). There is a fountain of comfort here for all true servants of Christ which ought never to be overlooked. Let them learn from their Lord's example that inward conflict of soul is not necessarily in itself a sinful thing. Too many, we believe, from not understanding this point, go heavily all their days on their way to heaven. They fancy they have no grace because they find a fight in their own hearts. They refuse to take comfort in the gospel because they feel a battle between the flesh and the Spirit. Let them mark the experience of their Lord and Master and lay aside their desponding fears. Let them study the experience of his saints in every age, from St Paul downwards, and understand that, as Christ had inward conflicts, so must Christians expect to have them also. To give way to doubts and unbelief, no doubt, is wrong and robs us of our peace. There is a faithless despondency, unquestionably, which is blameworthy and must be resisted, repented of and brought to the fountain for all sin that it may be pardoned. But the mere presence of fight and strife and conflict in our hearts is in itself no sin. The believer may be known by his inward warfare as well as by his inward peace.

For meditation: *Our Lord's identification with us in our humanity means that he knew inner struggles too.*

Suggested further reading: 2 Samuel 12:1-13

A faithful minister of God ought boldly to rebuke sin. John the Baptist spoke plainly to Herod about the wickedness of his life. He did not excuse himself under the plea that it was imprudent, or impolitic, or untimely, or useless to speak out. He did not say smooth things, and palliate the king's ungodliness by using soft words to describe his offence. He told his royal hearer the plain truth regardless of the consequences (v. 18).

Here is a pattern that all ministers ought to follow. Publicly and privately, from the pulpit and in private visits, they ought to rebuke all open sin and deliver a faithful warning to all who are living in it. It may give offence. It may entail immense unpopularity. With all this they have nothing to do. Duties are theirs; results are God's.

No doubt it requires much grace and courage to do this. No doubt a reprover like John the Baptist must go to work wisely and lovingly in carrying out his Master's commission and rebuking the wicked. But it is a matter in which his character for faithfulness and love are manifestly at stake. If he believes a man is injuring his soul he ought surely to tell him so. If he loves him truly and tenderly he ought not to let him ruin himself unwarned. Great as the present offence may be, in the long run the faithful reprover will generally be respected (Prov. 28:23).

How bitterly people hate a reprover when they are determined to keep their sins! Hardened and seared in conscience by her wickedness, Herodias never rested till she had procured the death of John the Baptist for his faithful testimony (v. 19). When men and women have chosen their own wicked way they dislike anyone who tries to turn them. They are irritated by opposition (1 Kings 22:8). Faithful ministers will be spoken against, hated and reviled. It is no disgrace to a minister's character to be hated by the wicked and ungodly. It is no real honour to be thought well of by everyone (Luke 6:26).

For meditation: *How do we respond to the preaching of the Word when it spotlights our sins? Anger is unproductive* (James 1:20).

Suggested further reading: 2 Peter 1:16-18

We have in these verses a great miracle exhibited. That miracle is the heavenly voice described in this passage — a voice which was heard so plainly that people said it thundered — proclaiming, 'I have glorified my name, and will glorify it again.'

This wondrous voice was heard three times during our Lord's earthly ministry. Once it was heard at his baptism, when the heavens were opened and the Holy Ghost descended on him. Once it was heard at his transfiguration, when Moses and Elias appeared for a season with him before Peter, James and John. Once it was heard here at Jerusalem in the midst of a mixed crowd of disciples and unbelieving Jews. On each occasion we know that it was the voice of God the Father. But why and wherefore this voice was only heard on these occasions we are left to conjecture. The thing was a deep mystery and we cannot now speak particularly of it.

Let it suffice us to believe that this miracle was meant to show the intimate relations and unbroken union of God the Father and God the Son throughout the period of the Son's earthly ministry. At no period during his incarnation was there a time when the eternal Father was not close to him, though unseen by man. Let us also believe that this miracle was meant to signify to bystanders the entire approval of the Son by the Father, as the Messiah, the Redeemer and the Saviour of man. That approval the Father was pleased to signify by voice three times, as well as to declare by signs and mighty deeds, performed by the Son in his name. These things we may well believe. But when we have said all, we must confess that the voice was a mystery. We may read of it with wonder and awe, but we cannot explain it.

For meditation: *God has usually revealed himself through men, but has added to this the witness of his own voice.*

Suggested further reading: 1 Peter 4:1-6

How much sin may follow on from feasting and revelling! Herod keeps his birthday with a splendid banquet (v. 21). Company, drinking and dancing fill the day. In a moment of excitement he grants a wicked girl's request to have the head of John the Baptist cut off (vv. 26-27). Next day in all probability he repented bitterly of his conduct. But the deed was done. It was too late.

This is a faithful picture of what often happens in feasting and merry-making. People do things at such seasons from heated feelings which they afterwards deeply regret. Happy are those who keep clear of such temptations and avoid giving occasion to the devil. Men never know what they may do when they once venture off of safe ground. Late hours, crowded rooms, splendid entertainments, mixed company, music, dancing — all may seem harmless to many people. But the Christian should never forget that to take part in these things is to open a wider door to temptation.

How little reward some of God's best servants receive in this world! An unjust imprisonment and a violent death were the last fruit that John the Baptist reaped in return for his labour. Like Stephen and James, he was called to seal his testimony with his blood.

Histories like these are meant to remind us that the true Christian's best things are yet to come. His rest, his wages, his reward are all on the other side of the grave. Here, in this world, he must walk by faith and not by sight; and if he looks for the praise of man he will be disappointed. Here he must sow, labour, fight and endure persecution, and if he expects an earthly reward he expects what he will not find. But this life is not all. There is to be a day of retribution. There is a glorious harvest yet to come. Heaven will make amends for all. The value of true religion is not to be measured by the things seen but the things unseen (Rom. 8:18; 2 Cor. 4:17).

For meditation: *Moses recognized that although sin was enjoyable it only lasted a short time. He learned it was better to be associated with God's people and to participate in their sufferings and gain eternal life* (Heb. 11:25).

Suggested further reading: Revelation 7:9-12

We have in these verses a great prophecy delivered. The Lord Jesus declared, 'I, if I be lifted up from the earth, will draw all men unto me.'

Concerning the true meaning of these words there can be but one opinion in any candid mind. They do not mean, as is often supposed, that if the doctrine of Christ crucified is lifted up and exalted by ministers and teachers, it will have a drawing effect on hearers. This is undeniably a truth, but it is not the truth of the text. They simply mean that the death of Christ on the cross would have a drawing effect on all mankind. His death as our Substitute and the sacrifice for our sins would draw multitudes out of every nation to believe on him and receive him as their Saviour. By being crucified for us, and not by ascending a temporal throne, he would set up a kingdom in the world and gather subjects to himself.

How thoroughly this prophecy has been fulfilled for nineteen centuries, the history of the church is an abundant proof. Whenever Christ crucified has been preached and the story of the cross fully told, souls have been converted and drawn to Christ, just as iron filings are drawn to a magnet, in every part of the world. No truth so exactly suits the wants of all children of Adam, of every colour, climate and language, as the truth about Christ crucified.

And the prophecy is not yet exhausted. It shall yet receive a more complete accomplishment. A day shall come when every knee shall bow before the Lamb that was slain and every tongue confess that he is Lord, to the glory of God the Father. He that was 'lifted up' on the cross shall yet sit on the throne of glory and before him shall be gathered all nations. Friends and foes, each in their own order, shall be 'drawn' from their graves and appear before the judgement-seat of Christ. Let us take heed in that day that we are found on his right hand!

For meditation: *All the ransomed church of God shall be saved to sin no more.*

Suggested further reading: Mark 1:32-39

When the apostles returned from their first mission as preachers they told our Lord all about it (v. 30). These words are a bright example to all who labour in the great work of doing good to souls. All such should daily tell all their proceedings to the great Head of the church. They should spread all their work before Christ and ask of him counsel, guidance, strength and help.

Prayer is the main secret of success in spiritual business. It moves him who can move earth and heaven. It brings down the promised aid of the Holy Spirit, without whom the finest sermons, the clearest teaching and the most diligent working are all in vain. It is not always those who have the most eminent gifts who are the most successful labourers for God. It is generally those who keep up closest communion with Christ and are most instant in prayer, those who pray Ezekiel's prayer (Ezek. 37:9). It is those who follow most exactly the apostles' method and give themselves to the ministry of the Word and prayer (Acts 6:4). Happy is the church that has a praying as well as a preaching ministry. The question we should ask about a new minister is not merely, 'Can he preach well?' but, 'Does he pray much for his people and his work?'

Our Lord showed great wisdom and tender consideration to the apostles when they returned (v. 31). The Lord knows well that his servants are flesh as well as spirit and have bodies as well as souls. He knows that at best they are earthen vessels compassed with many infirmities. He shows that he does not expect from them more than their bodily strength can do. He asks for what we can do and not for what we cannot do.

These words are full of deep wisdom. Our Lord knows well that his servants must attend to their own souls as well as the souls of others. He knows that a constant attendance to public work is apt to make us forget our own private soul-business. He reminds us that it is good for ministers to withdraw occasionally from public work and look within. Our hearts are to be watched jealously and time is to be made for regular self-examination and calm meditation.

For meditation: *Just as it is easier to cook for a number and easy not to bother to cook for oneself and to accept a snack rather than a meal, so it is easier to study the Scriptures to benefit others rather than for self. Biblical snacks can easily replace solid meals!*

Suggested further reading: 2 Corinthians 5:16 - 6:2

We may learn from these verses the duty of using present opportunities. The Lord Jesus says to us all, 'Yet a little while is the light with you. Walk while ye have the light, lest darkness come upon you... While ye have light believe in the light.' Let us not think that these things were only spoken for the sake of the Jews. They were written for us also, upon whom the ends of the world are come.

The lesson of the words is generally applicable to the whole professing church of Christ. Its time for doing good in the world is short and limited. The throne of grace will not always be standing; it will be removed one day and the throne of judgement will be set up in its place. The door of salvation by faith in Christ will not always be open; it will be shut one day for ever and the number of God's elect will be completed. The fountain for all sin and uncleanness will not always be accessible; the way to it will one day be barred and there will remain nothing but the lake that burns with fire and brimstone.

These are solemn thoughts, but they are true. They cry aloud to sleeping churchmen and drowsy congregations and ought to arouse great searchings of heart. 'Can nothing more be done to spread the gospel at home and abroad? Has every means been tried for extending the knowledge of Christ crucified? Can we lay our hands on our hearts and say that the churches have left nothing undone in the matter of missions? Can we look forward to the second advent with no feelings of humiliation and say that the talents of wealth and influence and opportunities have not been buried in the ground?' Such questions may well humble us when we look, on one side, at the state of professing Christendom and, on the other, at the state of the heathen world. We must confess with shame that the church is not walking worthy of its light.

For meditation: *Salvation is not something to put off till tomorrow. There is an urgency about its reception.*

Suggested further reading: Ezekiel 33:1-11

The admonition to come aside for rest is unhappily needed by few in today's church. There are but few in danger of overworking themselves and injuring their own bodies and souls by excessive attention to others! The vast majority of professing Christians are indolent and slothful, and do nothing for the world around them. There are comparatively few who need the bridle so much as the spur!

The heart of Christ was moved by the people who gathered to him (v. 34). They were destitute of teachers. They had no guides but blind Pharisees and scribes. They had no spiritual food but manmade traditions. Thousands of immortal souls stood before our Lord ignorant, helpless and on the high road to ruin. It touched the gracious heart of the Lord Jesus Christ.

Let us never forget that our Lord is the same yesterday, today and for ever. He never changes. High in heaven at God's right hand he still looks with compassion on the children of men. He still pities the ignorant and them that are out of the way. He is still willing to teach them many things. Special as his love is towards his own sheep who hear his voice, he still has a mighty general love towards all mankind — a love of real pity, a love of compassion. We must not overlook this. It is a poor theology that teaches that Christ cares for none but believers. There is warrant in Scripture for telling the chief of sinners that Jesus pities them and cares for their souls, that Jesus is willing to save them and invites them to believe and be saved.

Do we know anything of the mind of Christ? Are we like him tenderly concerned for the souls of the unconverted? Do we like him feel deep compassion for all who are yet as sheep without a shepherd? Do we care about the impenitent and ungodly near our doors? Do we care about the heathen, the Moslem, the Jew and the Roman Catholic? Do we use every means and give our money willingly to spread the gospel in the world?

For meditation: *Can you say with our Lord that you desire to gather men for the kingdom?* (Matt. 23:37).

Suggested further reading: Exodus 7:1-5

We may learn from these verses the desperate hardness of the human heart. It is written of our Lord's hearers at Jerusalem that, 'Though he had done so many miracles before them, yet they believed not on him.'

We err greatly if we suppose that seeing wonderful things will ever convert souls. Thousands live and die in this delusion. They fancy if they saw some miraculous sight, or witnessed some supernatural exercise of divine grace, they would lay aside their doubts and at once become decided Christians. It is a total mistake. Nothing short of a new heart and a new nature implanted in us by the Holy Ghost will ever make us real disciples of Christ. Without this, a miracle might raise within us a little temporary excitement, but, the novelty once gone, we should find ourselves just as cold and unbelieving as the Jews.

The prevalence of unbelief and indifference in the present day ought not to surprise us. It is just one of the evidences of that mighty foundation doctrine, the total corruption and fall of man. How feebly we grasp and realize that doctrine is proved by our surprise at human incredulity. We only half believe the heart's deceitfulness. Let us read our Bibles more attentively and search their contents more carefully. Even when Christ wrought miracles and preached sermons, there were numbers of his hearers who remained utterly unmoved. What right have we to wonder if the hearers of modern sermons in countless instances remain unbelieving? 'The disciple is not greater than his Master.' If even the hearers of Christ did not believe, how much more should we expect to find unbelief among the hearers of his ministers! Let the truth be spoken and confessed. Man's obstinate unbelief is one among many indirect proofs that the Bible is true. The clearest prophecy in Isaiah begins with the solemn question: 'Who hath believed?' (Isa. 53:1).

For meditation: *Pharaoh saw mighty miracles but repeatedly hardened his heart. 'Mere' miracles do not change hearts.*

Suggested further reading: Exodus 16:1-15

We have here a striking example of our Lord's divine power. He feeds an assembly of five thousand men with five loaves and two fishes. He makes a scanty supply of food, scarcely sufficient for the daily wants of him and his disciples, satisfy the hunger of a company as large as a Roman legion. There could be no mistake about the reality and greatness of this miracle. It was done publicly and before many witnesses. The same power which at the beginning made the world out of nothing caused food to exist which before had not existed. The circumstances of the whole event made deception impossible. Five thousand hungry men would not have agreed that they were all filled if they had not received real food. Twelve baskets of fragments would not have been taken up if real material loaves and fishes had not been miraculously multiplied. Nothing, in short, can explain the whole transaction save the finger of God (Exod. 8:19). The same hand which sent manna from heaven in the wilderness to feed Israel was the hand which made five loaves and two fishes supply the needs of five thousand men.

The miracle before us is one of many proofs that with Christ nothing is impossible. The Saviour of sinners is almighty. He calls the non-existent into being (Rom. 4:17). When he wills a thing it shall be done. When he commands a thing it shall come to pass. He can create light out of darkness, order out of disorder, strength out of weakness, joy out of sorrow and food out of nothing at all! Forever let us bless God that it is so! We might well despair when we see the corruption of human nature and the desperate hardness and unbelief of man's heart, if we did not know the power of Christ. Can any man or woman be saved? Can any child or friend ever become a true Christian? Can we ourselves win our way through to heaven? Questions like these could never be answered apart from the almighty power of Jesus. Jesus has all power in heaven and on earth. He lives in heaven for us, able to save to the uttermost, and therefore we may hope.

For meditation: *Does your life reflect unbelief's disabilities, or faith's confidence in Christ's power?*

Suggested further reading: Genesis 13:5-18

We may learn from these verses the amazing power which the love of the world has over men. We read that 'Among the chief rulers many believed on Christ; but because of the Pharisees they did not confess him, lest they should be put out of the synagogue. For they loved the praise of men more than the praise of God.'

These unhappy men were evidently convinced that Jesus was the true Messiah. Reason and intellect and mind and conscience obliged them secretly to admit that no one could do the miracles which he did unless God was with him and that the preacher of Nazareth really was the Christ of God. But they had not courage to confess it. They dared not face the storm of ridicule, if not of persecution, which confession would have entailed. And so, like cowards, they held their peace and kept their convictions to themselves.

Their case, it may be feared, is a sadly common one. There are thousands of people who know far more in religion than they act up to. They know they ought to come forward as decided Christians. They know that they are not living up to their light. But the fear of man keeps them back. They are afraid of being laughed at, jeered at and despised by the world. They dread losing the good opinion of society and the favourable judgement of men and women like themselves. And so they go on from year to year, secretly ill at ease and dissatisfied with themselves, knowing too much of religion to be happy in the world and clinging too much to the world to enjoy any religion.

Faith is the only cure for soul ailments like this. A believing view of an unseen God, an unseen Christ, an unseen heaven and an unseen judgement day — this is the grand secret of overcoming the fear of man. The expulsive power of a new principle is required to heal the disease. 'This is the victory that overcometh the world, even our faith' (1 John 5:4).

For meditation: *Lot wanted the best land for himself and got Sodom. Abram gave up his rights and received the land from God.*

Suggested further reading: Psalm 42

When the miracle of feeding the multitude was over our Lord departed into the mountain to pray (v. 46). There is something deeply instructive in this circumstance. Our Lord sought not the praise of men. After one of his greatest miracles we find him immediately seeking solitude and spending his time in prayer. He practised what he taught elsewhere (Matt. 6:6). None ever did such mighty works as he did. None ever spoke such words. None ever was so constant in prayer.

Let our Lord's conduct in this respect be our example. We cannot work miracles as he did; in this matter he stands alone. But we can walk in his steps in the matter of private devotion. If we have the Spirit of adoption we can pray. Let us resolve to pray more than we have done hitherto. Let us strive to make time and place and opportunity for being alone with God. Above all let us not only pray before we attempt work for God, but pray also after our work is done.

It would be well for us all if we examined ourselves more frequently as to our habits about private prayer. What time do we give to it in the twenty-four hours of the day? What progress can we mark, one year with another, in the fervency, fulness and earnestness of our prayers? What do we know by experience of labouring fervently in prayer? (Col. 4:12). These are humbling enquiries, but they are useful for our souls. There are few things, it may be feared, in which Christians come so far short of Christ's example as they do in the matter of prayer. Our Master's strong crying and tears, his continuing in prayer all night to God, his frequent withdrawal to private places to hold close communion with the Father are things talked of and admired rather than imitated. We live in an age of hurry, bustle and so-called activity. Men are tempted continually to cut short their private devotions and abridge their prayers. When this is the case we need not wonder that the church of Christ does little in proportion to its machinery. The church must learn to copy its Head more closely (James 4:2).

For meditation: *We blight so much of our Christian service because we are too busy in it to pray for it.*

Suggested further reading: John 14:8-11

One thing shown in these verses is the dignity of our Lord Jesus Christ. We find him saying, 'He that seeth me, seeth him that sent me. I am come a light into the world, that whosoever believeth on me should not abide in darkness.' Christ's oneness with the Father and Christ's office are clearly exhibited in these words.

Concerning the unity of the Father and the Son, we must be content to believe reverently what we cannot grasp mentally or explain distinctly. Let it suffice us to know that our Saviour was not like the prophets and patriarchs, a man sent by God the Father, a friend of God and a witness for God. He was something far higher and greater than this. He was in his divine nature essentially one with the Father and, in seeing him, men saw the Father that sent him. This is a great mystery, but a truth of vast importance to our souls. He that casts his sins on Jesus Christ by faith is building on a rock. Believing on Christ, he believes not merely on him, but on him that sent him.

Concerning the office of Christ, there can be little doubt that in this place he compares himself to the sun. Like the sun, he has risen on this sin-darkened world with healing in his wings and shines for the common benefit of all mankind. Like the sun, he is the great source and centre of all spiritual life, comfort and fertility. Like the sun, he illuminates the whole earth, and no one need miss the way to heaven, if he will only use the light offered for his acceptance.

Forever let us make much of Christ in all our religion. We can never trust him too much, follow him too closely or commune with him too unreservedly. He has all power in heaven and earth. He is able to save to the uttermost all who come to God by him. None can pluck us out of the hand of him who is one with the Father. He can make all our way to heaven bright and plain and cheerful like the morning sun cheering the traveller.

For meditation: *The Father and the Son are one* (John 10:30). *To have one is to have both* (2 John 9).

Suggested further reading: Ephesians 1:15-23

Our Saviour has absolute dominion over all created things. We see him walking on the sea as if it was dry land. Those angry waves which tossed the ship of his disciples to and fro obey the Son of God and become a solid floor under his feet. That liquid surface which was agitated by the least breath of wind bears up the feet of our Redeemer like a rock. To our poor weak minds the whole event is utterly incomprehensible. The picture of two feet walking on the sea is said by Doddridge to have been the Egyptian emblem of an impossible thing. The man of science will tell us that for material flesh and blood to walk on water is a physical impossibility. Enough for us to know that it was done. Enough for us to remember that to him who created the seas at the beginning it must have been perfectly easy to walk over their waves when he pleased.

There is encouragement here for all true Christians. Let them know that there is nothing created which is not under Christ's control. He may allow his people to be tried for a season and tossed to and fro by storms of trouble. He may be later than they wish in coming to their aid. But let them never forget that winds, waves and storms are all Christ's servants. They cannot move without his permission (Ps. 93:4).

What power Jesus can bestow on those who believe on him! To walk on the sea himself was a mighty miracle. But to enable Simon Peter to do the same was a mightier miracle still!

This shows us the great things which our Lord can do for those that hear his voice and follow him. He can enable them to do the things which at one time they would have thought impossible. He can carry them through difficulties and trials which without him they could never have dared to face. He can give them the strength to walk through fire and water unharmed and to get the better of every foe. Let us fear nothing if we are in the path of duty. The waters may seem deep. But if Jesus says, 'Come,' we have no cause to be afraid.

For meditation: *'I can do all things through Christ who strengthens me' is meant to be a principle of living, not just a motto for special occasions!* (Phil. 4:13). *But is it?*

Suggested further reading: Revelation 20:11-15

In these verses there is the certainty of a judgement to come. We find our Lord saying, 'He that rejecteth me, and receiveth not my words, hath one that judgeth him: the word that I have spoken, the same shall judge him in the last day.'

There is a last day! The world shall not always go on as it does now. Buying and selling, sowing and reaping, planting and building, marrying and giving in marriage — all this shall come to an end at last. There is a time appointed by the Father when the whole machinery of creation shall stop and the present dispensation shall be changed for another. It had a beginning and it shall also have an end. Banks shall at length close their doors for ever. Stock exchanges shall be shut. Parliaments shall be dissolved. The very sun, which since Noah's flood has done his daily work so faithfully, shall rise and set no more. Well would it be if we thought more of this day! Rent days, birthdays, wedding days are often regarded as days of absorbing interest, but they are nothing compared to the last day.

There is a judgement coming! Men have their reckoning days and God will at last have his. The trumpet shall sound. The dead shall be raised incorruptible. The living shall be changed. All, of every name and nation and people and tongue, shall stand before the judgement-seat of Christ. The books shall be opened and the evidence brought forth. Our true character will come out before the world. There will be no concealment, no evasion, no false colouring. Everyone shall give account of himself to God and all shall be judged according to their works. The wicked shall go away into everlasting fire and the righteous into life eternal.

These are awful truths! But they are truths and ought to be told. No wonder that the Roman governor Felix trembled when Paul the prisoner discoursed about 'righteousness, temperance and judgement to come' (Acts 24:25).

For meditation: *How much does the reality of judgement affect the way you live?*

Suggested further reading: Hebrews 12:1-12

Disciples can bring much trouble on themselves by unbelief. We see
Peter walking boldly on the water for a little while. But by and by
when he sees the boisterous wind he is afraid and begins to sink
(v. 30). The weak flesh gets the better of the willing spirit. He forgets the wonderful proofs of the Lord's goodness and power which
he had just received. He considered not that the same Saviour who
had enabled him to walk one step must be able to hold him up for
ever. He did not reflect that he was nearer to Christ when once on
the water than when he first left the ship. Fear took away his memory.
Alarm confused his reason. He thought of nothing but the winds and
waves and his immediate danger, and his faith gave way (v. 30).

What a picture we have here of many a believer! How many
there are who have faith enough to take the first step in following
Christ but not faith enough to go on as they began. They take fright
at the trials and dangers which seem to be in their way. They look at
the enemies and the difficulties that beset their paths. They dwell on
them more than on Jesus and at once their feet begin to sink. Their
hearts faint within them. Their hope vanishes away. Their comforts
disappear. And why is all this? Christ is not altered. Their enemies
are not greater than they were. It is just because, like Peter, they
have ceased to look to Jesus and have given way to unbelief. They
are taken up with thinking about their enemies instead of thinking
about Christ. May we lay this to heart and learn wisdom.

How merciful our Lord is to weak believers! We see him stretch-
ing forth his hand immediately to save Peter as soon as he cried out
(v. 31). He does not leave him to reap the fruit of his own unbelief.
The only word he utters is a gentle reproof (v. 31). How gentle Christ
is! He can bear with much and forgive much when he sees true grace
in a man's heart. As a mother deals gently with her child even when
wayward and froward, so Jesus deals gently with his people. He
loves and pities them, knowing their feebleness and bearing long
with them.

For meditation: *Too many of the problems of Christians arise from
looking to self and looking to circumstances rather than looking to
Christ.*

Suggested further reading: Exodus 12:1-13

The passage we have now read begins one of the most interesting portions of St John's Gospel. For five consecutive chapters we find the evangelist recording matters which are not mentioned by Matthew, Mark and Luke. We can never be thankful enough that the Holy Ghost has caused them to be written for our learning! In every age the contents of these chapters have been justly regarded as one of the most precious parts of the Bible. They have been the meat and drink, the strength and comfort of all true-hearted Christians. Let us ever approach them with peculiar reverence. The place whereon we stand is holy ground.

We should observe that the Feast of the Passover is always carefully mentioned by each Gospel writer as the precise time of the year when Jesus was crucified. It was ordered of God that it should be at this particular time for two good reasons. For one thing, the Passover lamb was the most striking and remarkable type in the whole Jewish ceremonial of Christ himself, and the history of the Passover of Christ's work of redemption. For another thing, it secured the greatest assembly of Israelites to be eyewitnesses of our Lord's crucifixion. At no time of the Jewish year were so many Jews gathered at Jerusalem. Anything that happened at the Passover would be reported by Jewish worshippers, on returning home, all over the civilized world. For these two reasons 'the Lamb of God' was slain at this feast, in spite of the priests, who said, 'Not on the feast day.'

Let us note that our Lord knew perfectly beforehand when and how he should suffer. This, whatever we may think, is a great addition to suffering. Our ignorance of things before us is a great blessing. Our Lord saw the cross clearly before him and walked straight up to it. His death was not a surprise to him, but a voluntary, foreknown thing.

For meditation: *Christ is our Passover Lamb* (1 Cor. 5:7).

Suggested further reading: Colossians 2:16-21

When our Lord was on the earth the Jewish religion was in a low and degraded state. The principal teachers of the Jewish nation found fault with disciples who ate without washing their hands (v. 2) and attached great importance to the washing of cups, pots and tables (vv. 3-4). In short, the man who paid most rigid attention to mere external observances of human invention was reckoned the holiest man!

The nation, be it remembered, in which this state of things existed, was the most highly favoured in the world. To it was given the law of Mount Sinai, the service of God, the priesthood, the covenants and the promises. Moses, Samuel, David and the prophets lived and died among its people. No nation upon earth ever had so many spiritual privileges. No nation ever mistook its privileges so fearfully and so thoroughly forsook its own mercies. From the religion of the books of Deuteronomy and Psalms to the religion of washing hands, pots and cups was a great fall! No wonder that in the time of our Lord's earthly ministry he found the people like sheep without a shepherd. External observances alone feed no consciences and sanctify no hearts.

Let the history of the Jewish church be a warning to us never to trifle with false doctrine. If we once tolerate it we never know how far it may go, or into what degraded state of religion we might at last fall. Once leave the King's highway of truth and we end up washing pots and cups like the Pharisees. There is nothing too mean, trifling or irrational for a man if he once turns his back on God's Word. There are 'churches' which never have the Scriptures read or the gospel preached. All that remains is a few unmeaning forms and the keeping of certain man-made feasts and fasts. These churches began well but have fallen into barrenness and decay. We can never be too jealous about false doctrine. A little leaven leavens the whole lump. Let us earnestly contend for the whole faith once delivered to the saints.

For meditation: *It is always difficult to get everything in its right place in the Christian life. The Pharisees were masterful in getting wrong priorities. Are you?*

Suggested further reading: John 10:25-30

Let us observe how death is spoken of here. It is taking a journey —
a going from one place to another. In the case of our Lord, it was a
return to his Father's house and a going home after finishing the
work he came to do. So a believer's death, in a lower sense, is going
home. Calvin observes, 'This definition of death belongs to the whole
body of the church. It is to the saints a passage to the Father, an inlet
to eternal life.'

It is written that 'Having loved his own which were in the world,
he loved them unto the end.' The meaning of this seems to be: 'Having always loved his own disciples and having given many proofs of
his singular affection, he now, before leaving them alone like orphans in the world, gave one more striking proof of his love by
washing their feet and thus on the last evening before his death showed
that he loved them to the very end of his ministry and was not weary
of them.'

He knew perfectly that they were going to forsake him and act
like cowards, but that did not prevent him loving them, with all their
weakness, to the very end. He knew perfectly that he was about to
suffer within twenty-four hours, but the knowledge and foresight of
it did not absorb his thoughts so as to make him forget his little flock
of followers.

The expression 'his own', applied to believers, is very noteworthy.
They are Christ's peculiar property, given to him by the Father and
his own special care as members of his body.

The expression 'which were in the world' is another great depth.
Believers are not in heaven yet and find it out to their cost. They are
in a cold, unkind, persecuting world. Let them take comfort in the
thought that Jesus knows and remembers it. 'I know thy works and
where thou dwellest' (Rev. 2:13).

For meditation: *Christ remains faithful even when we are faltering and failing.*

Suggested further reading: Hebrews 10:19-25

The religious worship that God desires is the worship of the heart (v. 6). The heart is the principal thing in the relation of husband and wife, of friend and friend, of parent and child. The heart must be the principal point to which we attend in all our relations between God and our souls. What is the first thing we need in order to be Christians? A new heart. What is the sacrifice God asks us to bring him? A broken and contrite heart. What is the true circumcision? The circumcision of the heart. What is genuine obedience? To obey from the heart. What is saving faith? To believe with the heart. Where ought Christ to dwell? In the heart by faith. What is the chief request that wisdom makes to everyone? To give her the heart (Ezek. 36:26; Ps. 51:17; Rom. 2:29; 6:17; 10:9; Eph. 3:17; Prov. 23:26).

Let us remember this in the public congregation. The bowed head and the bended knee, the grave face and rigid posture, the regular response and the formal amen — all these together do not make a spiritual worshipper. It must not content us to take our bodies to church if we leave our hearts at home. The eye of man may detect no flaw in our service. Our minister may look at us with approbation. Our neighbours may think of us as patterns of what Christians ought to be. Our voice may be heard foremost in praise and prayer. But it is all worse than nothing in God's sight if our hearts are far away. It is only wood, hay and stubble before him who discerns thoughts and reads the secrets of the inward man.

Let us remember this in our private devotions. It must not satisfy us to say good words if our hearts and lips do not go together. What does it profit us to be fluent and lengthy if our imaginations are roving far away while we are on our knees? It profits us nothing at all. God sees what we are about and rejects our offering. Heart prayers are the prayers he loves to hear. Heart prayers are the only prayers that he will answer. Our petitions may be weak and stammering and mean in our eyes. They may be presented with no fine words or well-chosen language, and might seem almost unintelligible if they were written down. But if they come from a right heart God understands them. Such prayers are his delight.

For meditation: *How much is your heart in your worship?*

Suggested further reading: 1 John 4:7-16

The love of Christ to sinners is the very essence and marrow of the gospel. That he should love us at all and care for our souls, that he should love us before we love him, or even know anything about him, that he should love us so much as to come into the world to save us, take our nature on him, bear our sins and die for us on the cross — all this is wonderful indeed! It is a kind of love to which there is nothing like among men. The narrow selfishness of human nature cannot fully comprehend it. It is one of those things which even the angels of God 'desire to look into'. It is a truth which Christian preachers and teachers should proclaim incessantly and never be weary of proclaiming.

The love of Christ to saints is no less wonderful, in its way, than his love to sinners, though far less considered. That he should bear with all their countless infirmities from grace to glory, that he should never be tired of their endless inconsistencies and petty provocations, that he should go on forgiving and forgetting incessantly and never be provoked to cast them off and give them up — all this is marvellous indeed! No mother watching over the waywardness of her feeble babe, in the days of its infancy, has her patience so thoroughly tried as the patience of Christ is tried by Christians. Yet his long-suffering is infinite. His compassions are a well that is never exhausted. His love is 'a love that passeth knowledge'.

Let no man be afraid of beginning with Christ, if he desires to be saved. The chief of sinners may come to him with boldness and trust him for pardon with confidence. This loving Saviour is one who delights to 'receive sinners' (Luke 15:2). Let no man be afraid of going on with Christ after he has once come to him and believed.

For meditation: *'There is no love like the love of Jesus.'*

Suggested further reading: Leviticus 10:1-7

Man's inventions in religion have a tendency to supplant God's Word. Three times we find this charge levelled by our Lord against the Pharisees (vv. 8,9,13). The first step of the Pharisees was to add their traditions to Scripture as useful supplements. The second was to place them on a level with the Word of God and to give them equal authority with it. The last was to honour them above Scripture and to degrade Scripture from its lawful position. This was the state of things which our Lord found when he was on the earth. Practically the traditions of man were everything and the Word of God was nothing at all. Obedience to the traditions constituted true religion. Obedience to the Scriptures was lost sight of altogether. Whenever a man takes upon him to make additions to the Scriptures, he is likely to end with valuing his own additions above Scripture itself.

We see this point brought out most strikingly in our Lord's answer to the charge of the Pharisees against his disciples (v. 9). He strikes at the system of adding anything to God's perfect Word. He exposes the mischievous tendency of this system by an example. He shows how the vaunted traditions of the Pharisees were actually destroying the authority of the fifth commandment (vv. 10-13). In short, he establishes the great truth, which ought never to be forgotten, that there is an inherent tendency in all traditions to make the Word of God ineffective. The authors of these traditions may have meant no such thing. Their intentions may have been pure. But there is a tendency in all religious institutions of mere human authority to usurp the authority of God's Word. In due course these very observances have been enjoined with more vigour than God's commandments and defended with more zeal than the authority of God's own Word. Church history is full of examples of this very procedure. Traditions are first called useful. Then they become necessary. At last they are too often made idols and all must bow down to them or be punished.

For meditation: *All Christians and churches should be reforming, but the rule for such reform must be the Word of God, not the traditions of man nor the spirit of the age.*

Suggested further reading: Jude 5-16

What deep corruption may sometimes be found in the heart of a great professor of religion! It is written that 'The devil put into the heart of Judas Iscariot, Simon's son, to betray Christ.'

This Judas, we must always remember, was one of the twelve apostles. He had been chosen by Christ himself, at the same time with Peter, James, John and their companions. For three years he had walked in Christ's society, had seen his miracles, had heard his preaching, had experienced many proofs of his loving-kindness. He had even preached himself and wrought miracles in Christ's name and when our Lord sent out his disciples two and two, Judas Iscariot no doubt must have been one of some couple that was sent. Yet here we see this very man possessed by the devil and rushing headlong to destruction.

He shows us what length a man may go in religious profession and yet turn out a rotten hypocrite at last and prove never to have been converted. He shows us the uselessness of the highest privileges unless we have a heart to value them and turn them to good account. Privileges alone without grace save nobody and will only make hell deeper. He shows us the uselessness of mere head-knowledge. To know things with our brains and be able to talk and preach and speak to others is no proof that our own feet are in the way of peace. These are terrible lessons, but they are true.

Let us never be surprised if we see hypocrisy and false profession among Christians in modern days. There is nothing new in it, nothing peculiar, nothing that did not happen even among Christ's own immediate followers and under Christ's own eyes.

For meditation: *Boastful claims do not make up for inner unreality.*

Suggested further reading: Jeremiah 7:20-29

How slow of understanding men are in spiritual things! (vv. 14,18). The corruption of human nature is a universal disease. It affects not only a man's heart, will and conscience, but his mind, memory and understanding. The very same person who is quick and clever in worldly things will often utterly fail to comprehend the simplest truths of Christianity. He will often be unable to take in the plainest reasonings of the gospel. He will see no meaning in the clearest statements of evangelical doctrine. They will sound to him either foolish or mysterious. He will listen to them like one listening to a foreign language, catching a word here or there, but not seeing the whole (1 Cor. 1:21).

We must pray daily for the teaching of the Holy Spirit if we would make progress in divine things. Without him the mightiest intellect and the strongest reasoning powers will carry us but a little way. In reading the Bible and hearing sermons everything depends on the spirit in which we read and hear. A humble, teachable, childlike frame of mind is the grand secret of success (Ps. 119:64).

The heart is the chief source of defilement and impurity in God's sight. Moral purity does not depend on washing or not washing, touching things or not touching them, eating things or not eating them (vv. 15-20). There is a deep truth in these words which is frequently overlooked. Our original sinfulness and natural inclination to evil are seldom sufficiently considered. The wickedness of men is often attributed to bad examples, bad company, peculiar temptations or the snares of the devil. It seems forgotten that every man carries within him a fountain of wickedness. We need no bad company to teach us and no devil to tempt us in order to run into sin. We have within us the beginning of every sin under heaven.

We ought to remember this in the training and education of children. The seeds of all mischief are in their hearts. It is not enough to keep them at home away from temptations. Until their heart is changed they are not safe!

For meditation: *Adam blamed Eve; Eve blamed the serpent; but the sin was theirs alone. Whom do you blame, or do you confess your sinfulness?*

Suggested further reading: Genesis 3:1-7

Verse 2 does not mean that Judas now for the first time left the faith and became an apostate. Our Lord long before had spoken of him as one that was 'a devil' (John 6:70). But it means that now at length the devil suggested into the heart of this unhappy man the atrocious idea of betraying his Master. It was the last and final heading up of his apostasy.

The word rendered 'put' is literally 'cast'. This graphically describes the way in which Satan works. He casts into the heart of those he tempts the seeds of evil. The heart is the seed-plot which he sows. Suggestion is one of his chief weapons. The sin of man consists in opening his heart to the suggestion, giving it a place and letting it sink down. This is obvious in the first temptation of Eve in the Garden of Eden.

There seems no need for regarding Judas' betrayal of his Master as anything but the wicked act of a wicked man who loved money more than his soul. The theory that he was a high-minded, impatient disciple, who wished his Master no harm, but desired to hasten his kingdom and expected him to work a miracle and save himself at the last, is ingenious, but lacks foundation. Our Lord's word applied to him, 'a devil', and the word of St John, 'a thief', appear to me to overturn the theory altogether. Judas betrayed Jesus because he loved money better than his Master. He probably did not realize the full consequence of his act. But this is often the case with wicked men.

Melanchthon shows that the three greatest marks of pity and compassion are (1) to tolerate the wicked for a season; (2) to abstain from exposing their sins as long as possible; (3) to warn them plainly and gently before leaving them for ever. All this appears in our Lord's dealings with Judas in this chapter.

For meditation: *We must never undermine the truth that Satan exists, nor underestimate his power.*

Suggested further reading: Jeremiah 17:1-10

What a black catalogue of evils the human heart contains! (vv. 21-23). Let us distinctly understand that our Lord is speaking of the human heart generally. He is not speaking of the notorious profligate only, nor of the prisoner in jail. He is speaking of all mankind. All of us, whether high or low, rich or poor, old or young, learned or unlearned — all of us have by nature such a heart as Jesus here describes. The seeds of all the evils mentioned here lie hidden within us. They may lie dormant in our hearts. They may be kept down by fear of consequences, the restraint of public opinion, the dread of discovery, the desire to be thought respectable and above all by the mighty grace of God. But every man has within him the root of every sin.

How humble we ought to be when we read these verses! We are all unclean in God's sight (Isa. 64:6). He sees in each one of us countless evils which the world never sees at all, for he reads our hearts. Surely, of all sins to which we are liable, self-righteousness is the most unreasonable and unbecoming.

How thankful we ought to be for the gospel when we read these verses! That gospel contains a complete provision for all the wants of our poor defiled natures. The blood of Christ can cleanse us from all sin (1 John 1:9). The Holy Spirit can change even our sinful hearts and keep them clean when changed. The man that does not glory in the gospel can surely know little of the plague of sin that is within him.

How watchful we ought to be when we remember these verses! What a careful guard we ought to keep over our imaginations, our tongues and our daily behaviour! At the head of the black list of our heart's contents stand 'evil thoughts'. Let us never forget that. Thoughts are the parents of words and deeds. Let us pray for grace to keep our thoughts in order and let us cry fervently and earnestly, 'Lead us not into temptation.'

For meditation: *The people who worked in concentration camps were just ordinary people who cast off restraint. But for the grace of God, none of us is far from the foulest and most wicked of deeds.*

Suggested further reading: Genesis 18:1-5

The object of verse 3 is to show the extent and depth of our Lord's infinite condescension and love to his disciples. With a full knowledge that the Father had committed all power into his hands, that he had been from eternity with God and was going back to God, knowing all the dignity and majesty of his person and office, he yet condescended to perform the most menial office and to minister like a servant to his disciples.

Wonderful as all this transaction seems and no doubt is, when we remember who our Lord was, one thing must never be forgotten. The actions here described would not seem nearly so strange to the disciples as they do to us. They were simply the courteous actions of a host who desired to show the utmost degree of hospitable attention to the guests. Thus Abraham washed the feet of the three angelic messengers (Gen. 18:4; so also 1 Sam. 25:41). In a hot country like Palestine, where people wore no stockings and the heat was very scorching to the skin, frequent washing of the feet was an absolute necessity and to wash the feet of guests was a common piece of hospitality. It is one mark of a deserving widow that she has 'washed the saints' feet' (1 Tim. 5:10). The real wonder was that such a Master, on such a solemn occasion, should do such a condescending act to such weak disciples. It was not so much the action as the doer of it that was remarkable.

After all, there was a touching fitness in our Lord's choice of an instructive action on this solemn occasion. He knew that he was leaving his disciples, like poor feeble travellers, in a weary, wicked world. He would therefore wash their feet before parting and strengthen and refresh them for their journey.

It will be observed that the work was not left unfinished and half done. Like a perfect servant, our Lord 'wiped' the feet as well as 'washed' them.

For meditation: *'The Son of man did not come to be served, but to serve'* (Mark 10:45).

Suggested further reading: John 4:27-38

True faith may sometimes be found where it is least expected. It was a Canaanite woman who cried to the Lord for mercy (v. 22). Such a prayer would have showed great faith had she lived in Bethany or Jerusalem. But when we find she lived in the region of Tyre and Sidon, such a prayer may well fill us with surprise. It ought to teach us that it is grace, not place, that makes people believers. Gehazi lived in a prophet's family but was impenitent, unbelieving and fond of the world (2 Kings 5:19-27). The little maid in Naaman's idolatrous house was a faithful witness to God (2 Kings 5:2-3). Let us not despair of anyone's soul because of the circumstances in which they are placed.

Affliction can sometimes prove a blessing to a person's soul. The Canaanite mother had no doubt been surely tried. She had seen her darling child vexed with a devil and had been unable to relieve her. But yet that trouble brought her to Christ and taught her to pray. Without it she might have lived and died in careless ignorance and never have seen Jesus at all. Surely it was good for her that she was afflicted (Ps. 119:71).

There is nothing that shows our ignorance more than impatience under trouble. We forget that every cross is a message from God and intended to do us good in the end. Trials are intended to make us think, to wean us from the world, to send us to the Bible, to drive us to our knees. Health is a good thing, but sickness is far better if it drives us to God. Anything, anything is better than living in carelessness and dying in sin.

The disciples were less compassionate and gracious than Christ himself (v. 23). There is too much of this spirit among believers. They are too ready to doubt the reality of a beginner's grace because it is small (Acts 9:26). Let us be like Christ, gentle, kind and encouraging in all our treatment of those who are seeking to be saved. Christ may keep men waiting, as he did with this woman, but he will never send them away empty.

For meditation: *Do you ever divide people into those likely to be converted and those whom you 'write off'? The grace of God can take hold of the 'chief of sinners' (1 Tim. 1:12-17).*

Suggested further reading: Luke 24:25-35

The English language here fails to give the full emphasis of the Greek. Verse 6 should be rendered: 'Dost thou, of me, wash the feet?' 'Such a one as thou art wash the feet of such a one as I am!' It is like John the Baptist's exclamation when our Lord came to his baptism: 'Comest thou to me?' (Matt. 3:14). In verse 8 one sentence would be rendered literally: 'Thou shalt never wash my feet for ever,' or 'unto eternity'.

We should notice the hasty ignorance of the apostle Peter. One moment we find him refusing to allow his Master to do such a servile work as he is about to do: 'Dost thou wash my feet? ... Thou shalt never wash my feet.' Another moment we find him rushing with characteristic impetuosity into the other extreme: 'Lord, wash not my feet only, but my hands and my head.' But throughout the transaction we find him unable to take in the real meaning of what his eyes behold. He sees, but he does not understand.

Let us gather from Peter's conduct that a man may have plenty of faith and love and yet be sadly destitute of clear knowledge. We must not set down men as graceless and godless because they are dull and stupid and blundering in their religion. The heart may often be quite right when the head is quite wrong. We must make allowances for the corruption of the understanding as well as of the will. We must not be surprised to find that the brains as well as the affections of Adam's children have been hurt by the Fall. It is a humbling lesson and one seldom fully learned except by long experience. But the longer we live, the more true shall we find it that a believer, like Peter, may make many mistakes and lack understanding and yet, like Peter, have a heart right before God and get to heaven at last.

For meditation: *Ignorance and slowness to learn are not to be confused with the absence of grace.*

Suggested further reading: 1 Timothy 2:1-8

This passage is meant to encourage us to pray for others. The woman who came to our Lord in the history now before us must doubtless have been in deep affliction. She had a beloved child possessed by an unclean spirit. She saw her in a condition in which no teaching could reach the mind and no medicine could heal the body — a condition only one degree better than death itself. She heard of Jesus and begged his help (v. 22). She prayed for one who could not pray for herself and never rested till her prayer was granted. By prayer she obtained the cure which no human means could obtain. Through the prayer of the mother the daughter was healed. On her own behalf the daughter did not speak a word, but her mother spoke for her to the Lord and did not speak in vain. Hopeless and desperate as her case appeared, she had a praying mother and where there is a praying mother there is always hope.

Few duties are so strongly recommended by scriptural example as the duty of intercessory prayer. There is a long catalogue of instances in Scripture which show the wonderful benefits that may be conferred on others by praying for them. So many of our Lord's miracles were performed in response to the requests of others. Wonderful as it may seem, God is pleased to do great things for souls when friends and relations are moved to pray for them (James 5:16).

Fathers and mothers are especially bound to remember this woman. They cannot give their children new hearts. They can give them Christian education and show them the way of life, but they cannot give them a will to choose Christ's service and a mind to love God. Yet there is one thing they can always do: they can pray for them. They can pray even for profligate sons and worldly daughters. Such prayers are heard on high. Such prayers will often bring down blessings. Never, never let us forget that the children for whom many prayers have been offered seldom finally perish. Even when they will not let us speak to them about religion, we can speak to God about them.

For meditation: *There are many people you know who will not pray for themselves. Who will pray for them if you do not?*

Suggested further reading: 2 Timothy 3:10-17

The famous saying of verse 7 stretches far beyond the literal application of the words. Primarily, of course, it means, 'This action of
mine has a meaning which in a few minutes I will explain and you
will understand, though at present it may seem to you strange and
unsuitable.' But in every age true Christians have seen a higher,
deeper, broader meaning in the words and a pious mind cannot doubt
that they were intended to bear that meaning. It supplies the key to
many things which we cannot understand in the providential government of the world, in the history of the church, in the events of
our own lives. We must make up our minds to see many things
happening which we do not know and understand now and of which
we cannot at present see the wisdom. But we must believe that 'we
shall know hereafter' the full purposes, the why and wherefore and
needs-be, of each and all. It is a golden sentence to store up in our
memories. God's eternal counsels, the wisdom of the great Head of
the church, must never be forgotten. All is going on well, even when
we think all is going on ill. When we cannot see it, we must believe.
In sickness, sorrow, bereavement, disappointment, we must summon up faith and patience and hear Christ saying to us, 'What I do
thou knowest not now, but thou shalt know hereafter.'

The 'why' and 'wherefore' of many a providence will often puzzle
and perplex us quite as much as the washing puzzled Peter. The
wisdom and fitness and necessity of many a thing will often be hidden from our eyes. There came days, long after Christ had left the
world, when Peter saw the full meaning of all that happened on the
memorable night before the crucifixion. Even so, there will be a day
when every dark page in our life's history will be explained and
when, as we stand with Christ in glory, we shall know all.

For meditation: *We have often to wait for our questions to be
answered. All we **need** to know we have revealed (2 Tim. 3:15-17).*

Suggested further reading: Luke 18:1-8

Let us persevere in praying for others! The woman whose history
we are now reading appeared at first to obtain nothing by her application to the Lord. On the contrary, our Lord's reply was discouraging (v. 24). But she did not give up in despair. She prayed on and did
not faint. She pressed her case with ingenious claims. She would
take no refusal. She pleaded for a few crumbs of mercy rather than
none at all. And through this holy insistence she succeeded. At last
she heard joyful words (v. 28).

Perseverance in prayer is of great importance. Our hearts are apt
to become cool and indifferent and to think that it is no use to draw
near to God. Our hands soon hang down and our knees become
faint. Satan is ever labouring to draw us off from prayers and filling
our minds with reasons why we may give them up. These things are
true with respect to all prayers, but they are especially true with
intercessory prayers on behalf of others. It is always far more meagre
than it ought to be. It is often attempted for a little while and then
left off. We see no immediate answer to our prayers. We see the
persons for whose souls we pray going on still in sin. We draw the
conclusion that it is useless to pray for them and allow our intercession to come to an end. But this woman prayed and did not give
up in the face of great discouragement. At last she went home rejoicing. Let us resolve by God's grace to follow her example.

Do we pray for ourselves? Let us pray for others also. Let us
beware of selfish prayers — prayers which are wholly taken up
with our own affairs and in which there is no place for other souls
besides our own. Let us name all we love before God continually.
Let us pray for all — the worst, the hardest and the most unbelieving. Let us continue praying for them year after year in spite of their
continued unbelief. While we live let us pray for others.

For meditation: *How many relatives do you have? How many do
you pray for? How many friends have you? How many do you
name before God in heartfelt intercession? What of your
neighbours?*

Suggested further reading: Hebrews 9:11-14

We need not doubt that verse 8 was meant to bear a deep and full meaning and to reach far beyond the primary application. It would be a very cold and tame exposition to say that our Lord only meant, 'Unless thy feet are washed by me tonight, thou art not one of my disciples.' It means a great deal more. Our Lord seems in effect to say, 'Thou wilt not be wise to object to the symbolical action which I am performing. Remember no one can be saved, or have any part in me and my work of redemption, unless I wash away his sins. Except I wash away thy many sins, even thou, Simon Peter, hast no part in me. I must wash every saved soul and every saved soul must be washed. Surely, therefore, it does not become thee to object to my doing an instructive and figurative act to thy feet, when I must needs do a far greater work to thy soul.'

The sentence is one of wide, deep and sweeping application. It is true of every Christian of every rank and position. To each one Christ says, 'If I wash thee not, thou hast no part in me.' It is not enough that we are churchmen, professed communicants and the like. The great question for everyone is this: 'Am I washed and justified?'

The common assertion that this 'washing' here spoken of is baptism seems to me unwarrantable. Our Lord never baptized anyone, so far as we can learn from Scripture. Where is it said that he baptized Peter? Moreover, if baptism were meant, the past tense would have been used: 'If I had not washed thee, thou wouldst have no part in me.' The washing here spoken of is something far above baptism.

No man or woman can be saved unless his sins are washed away in Christ's precious blood. Nothing else can make us clean or acceptable before God.

For meditation:
What can wash away my sin?
Nothing but the blood of Jesus.

Suggested further reading: Philippians 4:10-20

How great is the kindness and compassion of our Lord! He saw around him many people who had nothing to eat. He knew that the majority were following him from no other motive than idle curiosity and had no claim whatever to be regarded as his disciples. Yet when he saw them hungry and destitute he pitied them (vv. 1-3).

The feeling heart of our Lord appears in these words. He has compassion on those who are not his people — the faithless, the graceless, the followers of this world. He feels tenderly for them, though they know it not. He would receive them graciously and pardon them freely if they would only repent and believe on him. Let us ever beware of measuring the love of Christ by any human measure. He has, beyond doubt, a special love for his own believing people. But he has a general love of compassion even for the unthankful and the evil. His love passes knowledge (Eph. 3:19).

Let us strive to make Jesus our pattern in this as well as in everything else. Let us be kind, courteous, compassionate and full of pity to all men. Let us be ready to do good to all men, and not only to the household of faith (Matt. 5:44; Rom. 12:20).

With Christ nothing is impossible. The disciples might well ask their question (v. 4). Without the hand of him who made the world out of nothing the thing could not be. But in the almighty hands of Jesus seven loaves and a few fishes were made sufficient to satisfy four thousand men. Nothing is too hard for the Lord.

We must never allow ourselves to doubt Christ's power to supply the spiritual needs of his people. He has enough and to spare for all who trust in him. Weak, infirm, corrupt, empty as believers feel themselves, let them never despair while Jesus lives. In him there is a boundless store of mercy and grace for the use of all his believing people and ready to be bestowed on all who ask in prayer (Col. 1:19).

For meditation: *So often when we ask, 'How?' we should be asking, 'To whom shall I go but to him?' As his authority is universal (Matt. 28:18), he does not have too many problems with our 'impossibles'!*

Suggested further reading: 1 John 1:5-10

The exclamation of Peter in verse 9 is highly characteristic of the man. Impulsive, excitable, zealous, ardent, with more love than knowledge and more feeling than spiritual discernment, he is horrified at the very idea of 'having no part in Christ'. Anything rather than that! Not seeing clearly the deep meaning of his Master's words and still sticking to a carnal, literal interpretation of the word 'washing', he cries out that his Master may wash him all over, hands and head as well as feet, if an interest in Christ depends on that.

Verse 10 conveys a latent rebuke of Peter's spiritual dullness. It is as though Jesus said, 'The washing of head and hands whereof thou speakest is not needed. Even assuming that a literal washing is all I meant in saying, "If I wash thee not", it is well known that he who is washed needs only to wash his feet after a journey and is accounted clean entirely after such a partial washing. But this is far more true of the washing of pardon and justification. He that is pardoned and justified by me is entirely washed from all his sins and only needs the daily forgiveness of the daily defilement he contracts in travelling through a sinful world. Once washed, justified and accepted by me, ye are clean before God, although not all of you. There is one painful exception.'

The great practical truth contained in this sentence ought to be carefully noted and treasured up by all believers. Once joined to Christ and cleansed in his blood, they are completely absolved and free from all spot of guilt and are counted without blame before God. But, for all this, they need every day, as they walk through this world, to confess their daily failures and to sue for daily pardon. They require, in short, a daily washing of their feet, over and above the great washing of justification, which is theirs the moment they first believe.

For meditation: *Our sin needs to be confessed* (1 John 1:9).

Suggested further reading: Jeremiah 9:1-21

Unbelief causes our Lord Jesus Christ much sorrow. The Pharisees' questionings led him to sigh deeply (v. 12). There was a deep meaning in that sigh! It came from a heart which mourned over the ruin that these wicked men were bringing on their own souls. Enemies as they were, Jesus could not see them hardening themselves in unbelief without sorrow.

The feeling which our Lord Jesus Christ here expressed will always be the feeling of all true Christians. Grief over the sins of others is one true evidence of grace. The man who is really converted will always regard the unconverted with pity and concern (Ps. 119:158). This was the mind of the godly in the days of Ezekiel (Ezek. 9:4). This was the mind of Lot in Sodom (2 Peter 2:8). This was the mind of Paul (Rom. 9:2). In all these cases we see something of the mind of Christ. As the great Head feels, so the members feel. They all grieve when they see sin.

What of us? Do we know anything of likeness to Christ and fellow feeling with him? Do we feel hurt and pained, sorrowful, when we see men continuing in unbelief and sin? Do we feel grieved and concerned about the state of the unconverted? These are heart-searching questions and demand serious consideration. There are few surer marks of an unconverted heart than carelessness and indifference about the souls of others.

Finally, let us never forget that unbelief and sin are just as great a cause of grief to our Lord now as they were in his earthly days. Let us strive and pray that we might not add to that grief by any act or deed of ours. The sin of grieving Christ is one which many commit continually without thought or reflection. He that sighed over the unbelief of the Pharisees is still unchanged. Can we doubt that when he sees some persisting in unbelief at the present day he is grieved? From such sin may we be delivered!

For meditation: *Today's generation have been called the people that have forgotten how to blush. Is today's church the church that has forgotten how to sigh and weep?*

Suggested further reading: Matthew 20:20-28

What did our Lord really mean? Did he mean that we all ought literally to do the very same thing that he did? Or did he only mean that we are to imitate the spirit of his action?

The church of Rome, it is well known, puts a literal sense on our Lord's language. Once every year, about Easter, the head of the Roman church publicly washes the feet of certain poor persons got ready for the occasion. The absurdity, to say the least, of this view is evident on a moment's reflection.

It seems absurd to take our Lord's words literally and to suppose that the pope's literal washing of a few feet at Easter can supersede the duty of all Christians to do the same. It is in any case absurd to suppose that our Lord would require his disciples to perform a duty which the young and the feeble would be physically unable to do.

It is inconsistent with the general tenor of our Lord's teaching to suppose that he would ever attach so much importance to a mere bodily action. 'Bodily exercise profiteth little' (1 Tim. 4:8). A formal performance of bodily acts of religion is just the easiest thing that can be imposed on people. The thing that is really hard, and yet always required, is the service of the heart.

The true interpretation of the two verses is that which places a spiritual sense on our Lord's words. It is a practical illustration of Matthew 20:26-28. He wished to teach his disciples that they ought to be willing to wait on one another, serve one another, minister to one another, even in the least and lowest things. They should think nothing too low, or humble, or menial to undertake, if they can show love, kindness and condescension to another. Doctrinal orthodoxy without practical love and humility is utterly worthless before God.

For meditation: *Copying actions to the letter in a mimicking way is not as helpful as applying the principle of the action to each situation.*

Suggested further reading: Galatians 1:6-10

Our Lord's mind was obviously pained by the false doctrines which he saw among the Jews and the pernicious influence that they exercised. He seized the opportunity to utter a caution (v. 6), and this caution was addressed even to men like these apostles who had forsaken all for him.

Against what does our Lord warn his apostles? Against the doctrine of the Pharisees and Sadducees. The Pharisees, we are frequently told in the Gospels, were self-righteous formalists. The Sadducees were sceptics, free-thinkers and half infidels. Yet even the apostles must beware of their doctrine. Truly the best and holiest of believers may well be on his guard.

Our Lord calls their false doctrines 'leaven' (v. 6). Like leaven, they may seem a small thing compared to the whole body of truth. Like leaven, once admitted they work secretly and noiselessly. Like leaven, they would gradually change the whole nature of the religion with which they are mixed. It was not just the open danger of heresy but the hidden!

This warning was meant for all time. Our Lord knew that Pharisee doctrines and Sadducee doctrines would prove the two great wasting diseases of his churches until the end of the world. We live in a world where Pharisaism and Sadduceeism are continually striving for the mastery in the church of Christ. Some want to add to the gospel and some want to take away from it. Some would bury it and some would pare it down to nothing. Some would stifle it by heaping on it additions and some would bleed it to death by subtraction from its truths. Both parties agree in only one respect. Both would kill and destroy the life of Christianity if they succeeded in having their own way. Against both errors let us watch and pray and stand guard. Let our principle be 'the truth, the whole truth and nothing but the truth', nothing added to it and nothing taken away.

For meditation: *Our Lord knew nothing of limited inerrancy: for him the revelation that he was giving was the truth, the whole truth and nothing but the truth. A Bible with errors and a revelation with flaws are inventions of the devil, not of the Son of God.*

Suggested further reading: Philippians 2:1-8

If the only-begotten Son of God, the King of kings, did not think it beneath him to do the humblest work of a servant, there is nothing which his disciples should think themselves too great or too good to do. No sin is so offensive to God and so injurious to the soul as pride. No grace is so commended, both by precept and example, as humility. 'Be clothed with humility' (1 Peter 5:5). 'He that humbleth himself shall be exalted' (Luke 18:14). 'Let this mind be in you, which was also in Christ Jesus: who, being in the form of God, thought it not robbery to be equal with God: but made himself of no reputation, and took upon him the form of a servant, and was made in the likeness of men: and being found in fashion as a man, he humbled himself' (Phil. 2:5-8). Well would it be for the church if this very simple truth was more remembered and real humility was not so sadly rare. Perhaps there is no sight so displeasing in God's eyes as a self-conceited, self-satisfied, self-contented, stuck-up professor of religion.

Love is manifestly the other part of the great practical lesson. Our Lord would have us love others so much that we should delight to do anything which can promote their happiness. We ought to rejoice in doing kindnesses, even in little things. We ought to count it a pleasure to lessen sorrow and multiply joy, even when it costs us some self-sacrifice and self-denial. We ought to love every child of Adam so well, that if in the least trifle we can do anything to make him more happy and comfortable, we should be glad to do it. This was the mind of the Master and this the ruling principle of his conduct upon earth. There are but few who walk in his steps, it may be feared, but these few are men and women after his own heart.

For meditation: *Do other people think of you as selfish or selfless?*

Suggested further reading: 1 Peter 1:22 - 2:3

When our Lord gave his disciples the warning they were dull of understanding. They thought that the leaven of which he spoke must be the leaven of bread (v. 7). It never struck them that he was speaking of doctrine. They drew from him this sharp reproof (vv. 8,11). Believers, converted, renewed, as the disciples were, were still dull of apprehension in spiritual things. Their eyes were still dim and their perception slow in the matters of the kingdom of God.

We shall find it useful to remember what is recorded here of the disciples. It may help to correct the high thoughts which we are apt to entertain of our own wisdom and to keep us humble and lowly-minded. We must not fancy that we know everything as soon as we are converted. Our knowledge, like all our graces, is always imperfect and never so far from perfection as at our first beginning in the service of Christ. There is more ignorance in our hearts than we are at all aware of (1 Cor. 8:2).

Above all, we shall find it useful to remember what is recorded here in dealing with young Christians. We must not expect perfection in a new convert. We must not set him down as graceless and godless and a false professor because at first he sees but half a truth and commits many mistakes. His heart may be right in the sight of God, and yet, like the disciples, he may be very slow of understanding in the things of the Spirit. We must bear with him patiently and not cast him aside. We must give him time to grow in grace and knowledge and his latter end may find him ripe in wisdom like Peter and John. It is a blessed thought that Jesus, our Master in heaven, despises none of his people. Amazing and blameworthy as their slowness to learn undoubtedly is, his patience never gives way. He goes on teaching them. Let us do likewise. Let it be a rule with us never to despise the weakness and dullness of young Christians. Wherever we see a spark of true grace, however dim and mixed with infirmity, let us be helpful and kind. Let us do as we would be done by.

For meditation: *Are you self-assured in all your interpretations of Scripture or willing to learn? Are you more critical of the mistakes of others or of your own faults?*

Suggested further reading: Matthew 18:1-5

Christians must never be ashamed of doing anything that Christ has done. We read, 'Verily, I say unto you, The servant is not greater than his Lord; neither he that is sent greater than he that sent him.'

There seems little doubt that our Lord's all-seeing eye saw a rising unwillingness in the minds of the apostles to do such menial things as they had just seen him do. Puffed up with their old Jewish expectation of thrones and kingdoms in this world, secretly self-satisfied with their own position as our Lord's friends, these poor Galileans were startled at the idea of washing people's feet! They could not bring themselves to believe that Messiah's service entailed work like this. They could not yet take in the grand truth that true Christian greatness consisted in doing good to others. And hence they needed our Lord's word of warning. If he had humbled himself to do humbling work, his disciples must not hesitate to do the same.

The lesson is one of which we all need to be reminded. We are all too apt to dislike any work which seems to entail trouble, self-denial and going down to our inferiors. We are only too ready to depute such work to others and to excuse ourselves by saying, 'It is not in our way.' When feelings of this kind arise within us we shall find it good to remember our Lord's words in this passage, no less than our Lord's example. We ought never to think it beneath us to show kindness to the lowest of men. We ought never to hold our hand because the objects of our kindness are ungrateful or unworthy. Such was not the mind of him who washed the feet of Judas Iscariot as well as Peter. He who in these matters cannot stoop to follow Christ's example gives little evidence of possessing true love or true humility.

For meditation: *'I don't mind helping out but...' But what? And why?*

Suggested further reading: John 9:13-38

We do not know the reason of the peculiar means employed by our Lord in working this miracle. We see a blind man miraculously healed. We know that a word from our Lord's mouth or a touch of his hand would have been sufficient to effect a cure. But we see Jesus taking this man by the hand, leading him out of the town, spitting on his eyes, putting his hands upon him and, not till then, restoring his sight. And the meaning of all these actions is left entirely unexplained.

It is well to remember in such passages that the Lord is not tied to any one means. In the conversion of men's souls there are diversities of operation, but it is the same Spirit that converts. So in the healing of men's bodies there are varieties of agency employed by our Lord, but the same divine power effected the cure. In all his works God is sovereign.

This man was not delivered from his blindness at once, but by degrees. The Lord might have done it in a moment but he chose to do it step by step. First the man saw partially (v. 24) then completely (v. 25). In this respect this miracle stands alone.

This gradual cure is a striking illustration of the manner in which the Spirit frequently works in the conversion of souls. We are all blind and ignorant in things that concern our souls. Conversion is an illumination, a change from darkness to light, from blindness to seeing. Yet few converted people see things distinctly at first. The nature and proportion of doctrines, practices and ordinances are dimly seen and imperfectly understood. Their vision is unaccustomed to the new world into which they have been introduced. It is not till the work of the Spirit has become deeper and their experience has somewhat matured that they see all things clearly. Happy is he who has learned this lesson well and is humble and distrustful of his own judgement.

This gradual cure is also a picture of the present position of Christ's believing people in the world compared with that which is to come. We see now indistinctly; then clearly.

For meditation: *It does not matter whether a conversion is gradual or instantaneous as long as it is real!*

Suggested further reading: Romans 2:17-24

We read, 'If ye know these things, happy are ye if ye do them.' It sounds as if our Lord would warn his disciples that they would never be really happy in his service if they were content with a barren head-knowledge of duty and did not live according to their knowledge.

Nothing is more common than to hear people saying of doctrine or duty, 'We know it, we know it,' while they sit still in unbelief or disobedience. They actually seem to flatter themselves that there is something creditable and redeeming in knowledge, even when it bears no fruit in heart, character, or life. Yet the truth is precisely the other way. To know what we ought to be, believe and do, and yet to be unaffected by our knowledge, only adds to our guilt in the sight of God. To know that Christians should be humble and loving, while we continue proud and selfish, will only sink us deeper in the pit unless we awake and repent. Practice, in short, is the very life of religion. 'To him that knoweth to do good, and doeth it not, to him it is sin' (James 4:17).

Of course, we must never despise knowledge. It is in one sense the beginning of Christianity in the soul. So long as we know nothing of sin, or God, or Christ, or grace, or repentance, or faith, or conscience, we are, of course, nothing better than heathens. But we must not overrate knowledge. It is perfectly valueless unless it produces results in our conduct and influences our lives and moves our wills. In fact knowledge without practice does not raise us above the level of the devil.

Satan knows truth, but has no will to obey it and is miserable. He that would be happy in Christ's service must not only know, but do.

For meditation: *'Knowledge puffs up, but love edifies'* (1 Cor. 8:1).

Suggested further reading: Acts 17:16-21

A variety of opinions about our Lord prevailed during his earthly ministry (v. 14). One common remark applies to all these opinions. All were agreed that our Lord's doctrine was not like that of the scribes and Pharisees. All saw in him a bold witness against the evil that was in the world.

Let us never be surprised to find the same variety of opinions about Christ and his gospel in our own times. God's truth disturbs the spiritual laziness of men. It obliges them to think. It makes them begin to talk, reason, speculate, invent theories and account for its acceptance in some quarters and its rejection in others. Thousands in every age spend their time in this way and never come to the point of drawing near to God. They satisfy themselves with a miserable round of gossip about this preacher's sermons or that writer's opinions. They think 'that this man goes too far' and 'that man does not go far enough'. Some doctrines they approve. Some they disapprove. Some teachers they call 'sound' and some 'unsound'. They cannot quite make up their minds what is true and right. Year rolls on after year, and finds them in the same state — talking, criticizing, fault-finding, speculating, but never getting any further. They hover like the moth around religion but never settle down like the bee to feed on its treasures. They never boldly lay hold of Christ. They never set themselves heartily to the great business of serving God. They never take up the cross and become thorough Christians. And at last, after all their talking, they die in their sins unprepared to meet God.

Let us not be content with a religion of this kind. It will not save us to talk and speculate and bandy opinions about the gospel. The Christianity that saves is a thing personally grasped, personally experienced, personally felt and personally possessed. The Jews and modern man may find out who Christ is if they only follow our Lord's dictum (John 7:17).

For meditation: *It is possible to be always learning without believing* (2 Tim. 3:7).

Suggested further reading: Matthew 22:1-14

We are taught in these verses the perfect knowledge which Christ has of all his people. He can distinguish between false profession and true grace. The church may be deceived and rank men as apostles who are nothing better than brethren of Judas Iscariot. But Jesus is never deceived, for he can read hearts. And here he declares with peculiar emphasis, 'I know whom I have chosen.'

This perfect knowledge of our Lord Jesus Christ is a very solemn thought and one which cuts two ways. It ought to fill the hypocrite with alarm and drive him to repentance. Let him remember that the eyes of the all-seeing Judge already see him through and through and detect the lack of a wedding garment. If he would not be put to shame before assembled worlds, let him cast aside his false profession and confess his sin before it is too late. Believers, on the other hand, may think of an all-knowing Saviour with comfort. They may remember, when misunderstood and slandered by an evil world, that their Master knows all. He knows that they are true and sincere, however weak and failing. A time is coming when he will confess them before his Father and bring forth their characters clear and bright as the summer sun at noonday.

The forty-first Psalm is here shown to apply to one greater than David and one worse than Ahithophel. The ninth verse here quoted says, 'Mine own familiar friend, which did eat of my bread, hath lifted up his heel against me.' The expression implies the act of one who, like a stubborn and vicious horse, suddenly turns round against his master and kicks at him. 'This', our Lord says, 'is about to be fulfilled in the conduct of Judas Iscariot to me.'

The grand lesson that we must be prepared for much disappointment in friends and companions in this life is very plain in this passage. The less we expect from man, the better.

For meditation: *'Nothing in all creation is hidden from God's sight. Everything is uncovered and laid bare before the eyes of him to whom we must give account'* (Heb. 4:13).

Suggested further reading: 1 Peter 2:4-10

What a noble confession Peter makes in this passage! (v. 16). At first sight a careless reader might see nothing remarkable in this passage. He might think it extraordinary that they should call forth such a strong commendation from the Lord. But such thoughts arise from ignorance and inconsideration. Men forget that it is a widely different thing to believe in Christ's mission when we live in the midst of professing Christians and to believe in it when we dwell in the midst of hardened and unbelieving Jews. The glory of Peter's confession lies in this, that he made it when few were with Christ and many were against him. He made it when the rulers of his nation, the scribes, the priests and Pharisees were all opposed to his Master. He made it when our Lord was in the form of a servant without wealth, royal dignity or any marks of a king.

We shall do well to copy that hearty zeal and affection that Peter here displayed. We are perhaps too inclined to underrate this holy man because of his occasional instability and his thrice repeated denial of his Lord. This is a great mistake. With all his faults, Peter was a true-hearted, fervent, single-minded servant of Christ. Zeal like Peter's, with all its problems, is better than sluggishness, luke-warmness and torpor in the service of Christ.

Does our Lord's reply mean that Peter himself was to be the foundation on which Christ's church was to be built? (v. 18). Such an interpretation seems exceedingly improbable. To speak of an erring, fallible child of Adam as the foundation of the spiritual temple is very unlike Scripture. No reason can be given why our Lord did not say, 'I will build my church on you,' instead of upon 'this rock'. The true meaning of 'the rock' appears to be the truth of our Lord's Messiahship which Peter had just confessed. He is rightly called rock because he has confessed the truth on which, as a rock, the church is built.

For meditation: *Peter had no doubt who the foundation-stone of the church is* (1 Peter 2:4-8). *We are built on Christ the God-man.*

Suggested further reading: Matthew 10:5-15

We are taught in these verses the true dignity of Christ's disciples. The world may despise and ridicule the apostles because they care more for works of love and humility than the pursuits of the world. But the Master bids them remember their commission and not be ashamed. They are God's ambassadors and have no cause to be cast down. 'Verily, verily,' he declares, 'he that receiveth whomsoever I send receiveth me, and he that receiveth me receiveth him that sent me.'

The doctrine here laid down is full of encouragement. It ought to cheer and hearten all who lay themselves out to do good and specially to do good to the fallen and the poor. Work of this kind gets little praise from men and they who give themselves up to it are often regarded as miserable enthusiasts and meet with much opposition. Let them, however, work on and take comfort in the words of Christ which we are now considering. To spend and be spent in trying to do good makes a man far more honourable in the eyes of Jesus than to command armies or amass a fortune. The few who work for God in Christ's way have no cause to be ashamed. Let them not be cast down if the children of the world laugh and sneer and despise them. A day comes when they will hear the words: 'Come, ye blessed children of my Father, inherit the kingdom prepared for you' (Matt. 25:34).

Let us note that it is no light matter to reject and despise a faithful minister of Christ. A weak and ignorant servant may carry a message for a royal master and, for his master's sake, ought not to be lightly esteemed. Contempt for Christ's ministers, when they are really faithful, is a bad symptom in a church or nation.

For meditation: *Do you give your minister joy before God?* (Heb. 13:17).

Suggested further reading: John 10:22-30

The church which our Lord promises to build (v. 18) is not the visible church of any one nation, country or place. It is the whole body of believers of every age, tongue and people, who are washed in Christ's blood, clothed in Christ's righteousness, renewed by Christ's Spirit, joined by faith to Christ under its one Head, Christ (Col. 1:18). It is the one true church, not of a particular class, group, denomination or party, but the one true church of God's elect.

Our Lord promised that the power of Satan would never destroy the people of Christ (v. 18). The body of Christ shall never perish or decay. Though often persecuted, afflicted and distressed, it shall never come to an end. It shall outlive the wrath of its persecutors. Visible churches may come to an end. But the true church never dies. Every member of it shall be brought safe to glory (John 10:28).

Our Lord promised Peter the keys of the kingdom (v. 19). The idea that this means Peter was given the right to admit souls to heaven is preposterous. Such an office is the special prerogative of Christ (Rev. 1:18). The true meaning of the promise seems to be that Peter was to have the special privilege of first opening the door of salvation to the Jews at Pentecost (Acts 2:14) and the Gentiles in the house of Cornelius (Acts 10:28). He threw open the door of faith as he preached (Acts 15:7).

Does the promise that Peter could bind and loose (v. 19) mean that he was given the power to forgive sins and absolve sinners? Such an idea is derogatory to Christ's special office as our great High Priest. Peter and the apostles never used this power but always referred men to Christ. The true meaning of this promise appears to be that Peter and his fellow apostles were to be especially commissioned to teach with authority the way of salvation. They were to declare authoritatively whose sins were forgiven. They were inspired to lay down rules and regulations for the guidance of the church on disputed questions. The decision of the Council of Jerusalem is one such event (Acts 15:19).

For meditation: *Peter had no pretensions about himself* (1 Peter 5:1) *but always exalted Christ* (1 Peter 5:4).

Suggested further reading: Job 6:1-13

The subject of the verses before us is a very painful one. They describe the last scene between our Lord Jesus Christ and the false apostle Judas Iscariot. They contain the last words which passed between them before they parted for ever in this world. They never seem to have met again on earth, excepting in the garden when our Lord was taken prisoner. Within a short time both the holy Master and the treacherous servant were dead. They will never meet again in the body till the trumpet sounds and the dead are raised and the judgement is set and the books are opened. What an awful meeting will that be!

What trouble our Lord Jesus went through for the sake of our souls! We are told that, shortly after washing the disciples' feet, he 'was troubled in spirit, and said, One of you shall betray me'.

This expression applied to our Lord is peculiar to St John. We find it only in his Gospel, here and at 11:33 and 12:27. Here it seems to mean principally the pain and sorrow which our Lord experienced on seeing one of his own chosen apostles about to betray him. In addition to this, it probably includes that peculiar agony and distress of soul which our Lord was subject to under the presence of a world's sin laid upon him and which we see intensified in the Garden of Gethsemane.

Let it be noted, that, of all the Gospel writers, John is the one who dwells most fully on the divine nature of our Lord and also is the one who describes most fully the reality of his human affections.

Observe that to be troubled and disturbed in mind is not in itself sinful. How foolish were the Stoic philosophers, who taught that a wise man is never disturbed in mind!

For meditation: *Neither physical sickness nor mental distress are necessarily sinful. We must not condemn the innocent.*

Suggested further reading: Isaiah 53

Our Lord's prediction of his own coming death shows us that his death was a voluntary act of his own free will, the result of the eternal counsels of the blessed Trinity. He saw Calvary and the cross before him all the days of his earthly ministry and went up to them willingly, knowingly and with full consent.

Peter, although a true disciple of Christ, showed much spiritual ignorance in trying to dissuade our Lord from suffering on the cross (v. 22). He did not see the full purpose of our Lord's coming into the world. His eyes were blinded to the necessity of our Lord's death. He actually did what he could to prevent that death taking place at all! And yet we know that Peter was a converted man.

These things are meant to teach us that we must not regard good men as infallible because they are good men, nor yet suppose they have no grace because their grace is weak and small. One brother might possess singular gifts but he is a man liable to great mistakes. Another brother's knowledge may be scanty. He may err in word and deed. But has he faith and love towards Christ? If so, let us deal patiently with him.

There is no doctrine of Scripture so important as Christ's atoning death. We cannot have clearer proof than the language used by our Lord in rebuking Peter. He addresses him by the awful name 'Satan', as if he was an adversary and doing the devil's work in trying to prevent his death. He dismisses him from his presence and warns him that his mind is not in favour of the things of God (v. 23). Stronger words than these never fell from our Saviour's lips. The error so rebuked must have been a mighty error indeed.

The truth is that our Lord would have us regard the crucifixion as the central truth of Christianity. Right views of his death and the benefits resulting from it lie at the foundation of Bible religion.

For meditation: *A man may be saved with wrong views on many subjects but not without a true faith in the saving death of Christ.*

Suggested further reading: Psalm 22:1-11

The whole length and breadth and depth of our Master's troubles during his earthly ministry are far beyond the conception of most people. His death and suffering on the cross were only the heading up and completion of his sorrows. But all throughout his life, partly from the general unbelief of the Jews, partly from the special hatred of the Pharisees and Sadducees, partly from the weakness and infirmity of his few followers, he must have been in a peculiar degree 'a man of sorrows and acquainted with grief' (Isa. 53:3).

But the trouble before us was a singular and exceptional one. It was the bitter sorrow of seeing a chosen apostle deliberately becoming an apostate, a backslider and an ungrateful traitor. That it was foreseen sorrow from the beginning we need not doubt, but sorrow is not less acute because long foreseen. That it was a peculiarly cutting sorrow is very evident. Nothing is found so hard for flesh and blood to bear as ingratitude. Even a poet of our own has said that it is 'sharper than a serpent's tooth to have a thankless child'. Absalom's rebellion seems to have been David's heaviest trouble and Judas Iscariot's treachery seems to have been one of the heaviest trials of the Son of David. When he saw it drawing near, he was 'troubled in spirit'.

Passages like these should make us see the amazing love of Christ to sinners. How many cups of sorrow he drained to the dregs in working out our salvation, beside the mighty cup of bearing our sins! They show us how little reason we have for complaining when friends fail us and men disappoint us. If we share our Master's lot, we have no cause to be surprised. Above all, they show us the perfect suitableness of Christ to be our Saviour. He can sympathize with us. He has suffered himself and can feel for those who are ill-used and forsaken.

For meditation: *'Judas' is a synonym for treachery, a term of utter contempt.*

Suggested further reading: Romans 8:17-25

The disciples could not bear the thought of crucifixion. They dreamed of worldly honours and temporal rewards in their Master's service. They did not understand that true Christians, like Christ, must be made perfect through sufferings. Hence our Lord's solemn teaching.

If men follow Christ they must make up their minds to trouble and self-denial (v. 24). It is good for us to see this point clearly. The flesh must be crucified daily. The devil must be resisted daily. The world must be overcome daily. There is a warfare to be waged and a battle to be fought. All this is the inseparable accompaniment of true religion. Heaven is not to be won without it. Never was there a truer word than the old saying: 'No cross, no crown!'

There is nothing so precious as a man's soul (v. 26). Our Lord teaches this lesson by asking one of the most solemn questions that the New Testament contains, which ought to sound in our ears like a trumpet whenever we are tempted to neglect our eternal interests. He reminds us that there is nothing so precious as a man's soul. There is nothing that money can buy, or man can give, to be named in comparison with our souls. The world and all that is in it is temporal. It is all fading, perishing and passing away. The soul is eternal. That one single word 'eternal' is the key to the whole question. Let it sink down deeply into our hearts.

The Second Coming is the time when Christ's people shall receive their rewards (v. 27). Our Lord knows the heart of man. He knows how soon we are ready to be discouraged. He therefore holds out a gracious promise reminding us that when he comes we shall receive good things. The bitter must come before the sweet, the cross before the crown, humiliation before glory, but it shall come.

We have seen the necessity of taking up our cross and denying ourselves. Have we? We have heard of the value of a soul. Do we live as if we believed it? We have heard of Christ's second advent. Do we anticipate it with joy?

For meditation: *It is easy to desire Christianity's benefits without facing its cost. But only those who die with Christ can live with him.*

Suggested further reading: James 2:21-23

We notice from verse 22 that the first effect of our Lord's declaration seems to have been silence. Like men stunned and amazed, the disciples looked at one another in astonishment. The thing announced was the last thing they expected to hear.

Let us note that neither here nor afterwards does any suspicion appear to have fallen on Judas. For anything we can see, he looked as good as Peter, James and John, and as unlikely to betray his Master. The length to which hypocrisy can go is very awful.

To understand verse 23 we must remember the customs of the East in the time of our Lord about the position and attitude of the guests at a meal. They did not sit, but reclined.

The disciple that Jesus loved was John, the writer of this Gospel. It is the first time he speaks of himself in this way and the expression occurs afterwards four times (John 19:26; 20:2; 21:7,20).

The Greek word rendered 'loved' deserves notice. It signifies the higher, nobler and more refined kind of love. There are two words in the Greek language translated 'love' in the New Testament.

Let it be noted that the general special love with which our Lord loves all his disciples did not prevent his having a particular love for one individual. Why he specially loved John we are not told. Gifts certainly do not appear so much in John as grace. But it is worth noticing that love seems more the characteristic of John than of any disciple and that in this he showed more of the mind of Christ. It is quite clear that special friendship for one individual is quite consistent with love for all.

It is noteworthy that, of all the writers of the New Testament, none goes so deep and reveals so much of the hidden things of God as he who lay in the bosom of Christ.

For meditation: *What greater title could be given than 'the disciple that Jesus loved'?*

Suggested further reading: 2 Peter 1:12-18

We have in these verses a striking pattern of the glory in which Christ and his people will appear when he comes the second time. There can be little doubt that this was one of the main objects of this vision. It was meant to encourage the disciples by giving them a glimpse of good things yet to come. That 'face shining as the sun' and 'raiment white as the light' were intended to give the disciples some idea of the majesty in which Jesus will appear to the world when he comes the second time. The corner of the veil was lifted up to show them the Master's true dignity. They were taught that if he did not yet appear in the guise of a King it was only because the time for putting on royal apparel was not yet come. This is what Peter says (2 Peter 1:16).

We have reason to thank God for this vision. We are often tempted to give up Christ's service because of the cross and affliction which it entails. We see few with us and many against us. We find our names cast out as evil, and all manner of evil said of us because we believe and love the gospel. Year after year we see our companions in Christ's service removed by death, and we feel as if we knew little about them except that they are gone to an unknown world and that we are left alone. All these things are trying to flesh and blood. No wonder that the faith of believers sometimes languishes and their eyes fail while they look for their hope.

Let us see in the story of the transfiguration a remedy for such doubting thoughts as these. The vision of the holy mount is a gracious pledge that glorious things are in store for the people of God. Their crucified Saviour shall come again in power and great glory. His saints shall all come with him and are in safe keeping until that happy day. We may wait patiently (Col. 3:4).

Part of this glory was actually seen by the three competent witnesses on the mount. One of them records this fact (John 1:14). Such witnesses may surely be believed.

For meditation: *Bodily weakness shall be laid aside when heavenly glory becomes ours* (Phil. 3:21).

Suggested further reading: Romans 2:1-10

The characteristic forwardness and zeal of Peter come out strikingly (v. 24). None seems so excited by our Lord's announcement as he is. None is so anxious to know of whom our Lord can be speaking. He cannot wait silently like the others. He makes a sign to John to ask privately who it can be. A fisherman by early training, like John, he was probably intimate with him and could make himself understood by signs.

In verse 25 the idea is evidently of one moving and leaning towards another, so as to get closer to him and whisper a question, so as not to be heard or observed. That this is what John did is evident. It is plain that he did not say out aloud, 'Lord, who is it?'

The action by which our Lord told John he would indicate the traitor to him was probably so common at an Eastern banquet that no one at the table would remark anything about it. That it was a common way of eating is shown by Ruth 2:14. Hengstenberg observes that by this act of kindness and attention Jesus 'would touch the heart of Judas once more, if haply he might be susceptible of better emotions'. That our Lord's answer was whispered is evident. No one seems to have noticed it, except John.

The word 'gave' is literally 'gives' in the present tense, showing the immediate action which followed our Lord's reply to John's question.

Here, as elsewhere, it is noteworthy that John specially calls Judas 'the son of Simon', in order to make it quite clear what Judas it was who did this foul deed.

Bengel remarks, 'How very near to Jesus was Judas on this occasion! But in a short time after, by what a wide gulf did glory separate Jesus from Judas, and destruction separate Judas from Jesus!'

For meditation: *Even God is finally impatient with the stubbornly impenitent.*

Suggested further reading: Matthew 22:23-33

All true believers who have been removed from this earth are safe. We are told that Moses and Elijah appeared visibly with Christ in glory (v. 3). They were seen in a bodily form. They were heard talking with our Lord. Fourteen hundred and eighty years had rolled on since Moses died and was buried. More than nine hundred years had passed away since Elijah went up to heaven. Yet here they are seen alive by Peter, James and John.

Let us lay a firm hold on this part of the vision. It deserves close attention. We must all feel, if we ever think at all, that the state of the dead is a wonderful and mysterious subject. One after another we bury them out of our sight. We lay them in narrow beds and see them no more and their bodies become dust. But will they really live again? Shall we really see them any more? Will the grave really give back the dead at the last day? These questions will occasionally cross our minds.

Now we have in the transfiguration the clearest evidence that the dead will rise again. We find two men appearing on earth in their bodies, who had long been separate from the land of the living, and in them we have a pledge of the resurrection of all. All that have ever lived upon the earth will again be called to life and render up their account. No one will be found missing. There is no such thing as annihilation. All that have ever fallen asleep in Christ will be found in safe keeping — patriarchs, prophets, apostles, martyrs — down to the humblest servant of God in our own day. Though unseen to us, they all live to God (Luke 20:38). Their spirits live as surely as we live ourselves, and will hereafter appear in glorified bodies as surely as Moses and Elijah in the mount. These are indeed solemn thoughts! There is a resurrection and men like Felix may well tremble (Acts 24:25). There is a resurrection, and men like Paul might well rejoice (2 Cor. 4:13-14). Our brethren and sisters in Christ are in safe keeping. They are not lost. They are gone before.

For meditation: *Christians are not forbidden to grieve for those who die in the Lord. But the nature of their grief is different to those who die outside of the Lord. They do not grieve as those without hope* (1 Thess. 4:13).

Suggested further reading: Genesis 3:1-6

Let us mark in these verses the power and malignity of our great enemy the devil. We are told in the beginning of the chapter that he 'put it into the heart' of Judas to betray our Lord. We are told here that he 'entered into' him. First he suggests; then he commands. First he knocks at the door and asks permission to come in; then, once admitted, he takes complete possession and rules the whole inward man like a tyrant.

Let us take heed that we are not 'ignorant of Satan's devices'. He is still going to and fro in the earth, seeking whom he may devour. He is about our path and about our bed and spies out all our ways. Our only safety lies in resisting him at the first and not listening to his first advances. For this we are all responsible. Strong as he is, he has no power to do us harm, if we cry to the stronger one in heaven and use the means which he has appointed. It is a standing principle of Christianity and will ever be found true: 'Resist the devil, and he will flee from you' (James 4:7).

Once let a man begin tampering with the devil and he never knows how far he may fall. Trifling with the first thoughts of sin, making light of evil ideas when first offered to our hearts, allowing Satan to talk to us and flatter us and put bad notions into our hearts — all this may seem a small matter to many. It is precisely at this point that the road to ruin often begins. He that allows Satan to sow wicked thoughts will soon find within his heart a crop of wicked habits. Happy is he who really believes that there is a devil and, believing, watches and prays daily that he may be kept from his temptations.

For meditation: *We can believe Satan has too much power and dishonour God, or believe he has too little and be defeated by him.*

Suggested further reading: Hebrews 3:1-6

There is here a remarkable testimony of the infinite superiority of Christ over all others. This is a point which is brought out strongly by the voice from heaven which his disciples heard. Peter, bewildered by the heavenly vision and not knowing what to say, proposed to build three tabernacles, one for Christ, one for Elijah and one for Moses (v. 4). He seemed in fact to place the law-giver and the prophet side by side with his divine Master, as if all three were equal. At once, we are told, the proposal was rebuked in a marked manner. A cloud covered Moses and Elijah and they were seen no more (v. 5). A voice at the same time came forth from the cloud repeating the solemn words made use of at our Lord's baptism (v. 5; Matt. 3:17). That voice was meant to teach Peter that there was one there far greater than Moses or Elijah. Moses was a faithful servant of God. Elijah was a bold witness for the truth. But Christ was far above either one or the other. He was the Saviour to whom the law and the prophets were continually pointing. He was the true Prophet whom all were commanded to hear (Deut. 18:15). Moses and Elijah were great men in their day. But Peter and his companions were to remember that in nature, dignity and office they were far below Christ. He was the true sun; they were stars depending daily on his light. He was the root; they were the branches. He was the Master; they were the servants. Their goodness was all derived; his was original and his own. Let them honour Moses and the prophets as holy men. But if they would be saved, they must take Christ alone for their Master, and glory only in him (v. 5).

Let no man usurp the office of Christ. The best of men are only men at their very best. Patriarchs, prophets, apostles, martyrs, fathers, Reformers, Puritans — all, all are sinners who need a Saviour, holy, useful and honourable in their place, but sinners after all. They must never be allowed to stand between us and Christ. The sum and substance of saving religion is to 'hear Christ'.

For meditation: *The views of Calvin, Luther and any great men of God must always be tested by the statements of Christ.*

Suggested further reading: Hebrews 10:26-39

Let us mark in these verses the extreme hardness which comes over the heart of a backsliding professor of religion. This is a thing which is most painfully brought out in the case of Judas Iscariot. One might have thought that the sight of our Lord's trouble and the solemn warning, 'One of you shall betray me,' would have stirred the conscience of this unhappy man. But it did not do so. One might have thought that the solemn words, 'That thou doest, do quickly,' would have arrested him and made him ashamed of his intended sin. But nothing seems to have moved him. Like one whose conscience was dead, buried and gone, he rises and goes out to do his wicked work and parts with his Lord for ever.

The extent to which we may harden ourselves by resisting light and knowledge is one of the most fearful facts in our nature. We may become past feeling, like those whose limbs are mortified before they die. We may lose entirely all sense of fear, or shame, or remorse and have a heart as hard as the nether millstone, blind to every warning and deaf to every appeal. It is a sore disease, but one which unhappily is not uncommon among professing Christians. None seem so liable to it as those who, having great light and privilege, deliberately turn their backs on Christ and return to the world. Nothing seems likely to touch such people, but the voice of the archangel and the trump of God.

Let us watch jealously over our hearts and beware of giving way to the beginnings of sin. Happy is he who feareth always and walks humbly with his God. The strongest Christian is the one who feels his weakness most and cries most frequently, 'Hold thou me up, and I shall be safe' (Ps. 119:117; Prov. 28:14).

For meditation: *Persistence in sin is a guaranteed road to disaster.*

Mark 9:14-29
(Matthew 17:14-20; Luke 9:37-43)

Suggested further reading: John 15:1-5

How dependent Christ's disciples are on the company of their Master and on his help! When our Lord comes down from the mount, he finds his little flock in confusion. His nine apostles were besieged by a party of malicious scribes and baffled in an attempt to heal one possessed by a devil. The very disciples who a short time before had done many miracles and cast out many devils now met with a case too hard for them. They were learning by humbling experience that without Christ they could do nothing (John 15:5). It was a useful lesson, no doubt, and overruled to their spiritual good, but it was a bitter lesson at that time. How much we learn from such lessons! We do not love to learn that we can do nothing without Christ.

We need not look far to see many illustrations of this truth in the history of God's people in every age. The very men who at one time have done great exploits in the cause of the gospel at another time have failed entirely and proved weak and unstable as water. Some great Reformers temporarily recanted under pressure. The holiest and best of Christians have nothing to glory of. Their strength is not their own. They have nothing that they have not received. They have only to provoke the Lord to leave them for a season and they will soon discover that their power is gone. Like Samson when his hair was shorn, they become weak like other men.

Let us learn a lesson of humility from the failure of the disciples. Let us strive every day to realize our need of the grace and the presence of Christ. With him we may do all things (Phil. 4:13). With him we may overcome the greatest temptations. Without him the least may overcome us. Every morning we need to pray that he will not leave us to ourselves but that his presence might go with us, for we do not know what will happen in any day.

For meditation: *Every action in the Christian life is either in the flesh or in the Spirit, with God's aid or without it. To face Satan in the flesh is to face him disarmed and vulnerable. To face him in the Spirit is to have Christ on our side.*

Suggested further reading: Matthew 19:23-30

The statement that 'Judas had the bag' shows the position he occupied among the apostles. He was so far from being suspected that he had the charge of the common store of money.

The supposition of some that Jesus told Judas to 'buy the things needed against the feast' shows clearly that our Lord did not work miracles in order to procure the necessaries required by himself and his disciples. Christians must buy and sell like other people and must manage their money affairs with prudence and economy. It shows how little the disciples realized that their Master's death was close at hand.

The supposition of others that Jesus told Judas to 'give something to the poor' shows plainly what was our Lord's custom in the matter of almsgiving. He sanctified and adorned the practice of caring for the poor by his own example. This passage and Galatians 2:10 deserve careful consideration.

Let us mark the snares which attend the possession, fingering and handling of money. The man who has care of the money in our Lord's little company of followers is the very man who makes shipwreck of his soul for ever through the love of money. 'Give me neither poverty nor riches,' should be a Christian's frequent prayer (Prov. 30:8).

The hasty departure of Judas as soon as our Lord had given him the morsel and spoken the remarkable words already commented on may easily be explained. He saw at once that our Lord knew all his plot and dreaded exposure. His conscience condemned him and he dared no longer sit in our Lord's company. He, at any rate, understood what our Lord meant, if nobody else did. He felt himself detected and discovered and for very shame got up and went away.

It is curious and noteworthy that John, at all events, must have known Judas to be the traitor and yet he seems to have said nothing.

For meditation: *No one has ever successfully served God and money* (Matt. 6:24).

Suggested further reading: Romans 7:14-25

Faith and unbelief can be mixed together in the same heart. The words of the child's father set this truth before us in a touching way (v. 24).

We see in those words a vivid picture of the heart of many a true Christian. Few indeed are to be found among believers in whom trust and doubt, hope and fear, do not exist side by side. Nothing is perfect in a child of God so long as he is in the body. His knowledge, love and humility are all more or less defective and mingled with corruption. And as it is with other graces, so it is with his faith. He believes and yet has about him a remainder of unbelief.

What shall we do with our faith? We must use it. Weak, trembling, doubting, feeble as it may be, we must use it. We must not wait till it is great, perfect and mighty, but like the man before us turn it to account and hope that one day it will be more strong.

What shall we do with our unbelief? We must resist it and pray against it. We must not allow it to keep us back from Christ. We must take it to Christ, as we take all other sins and infirmities, and cry to him for deliverance.

Happy are those who know something of these truths. The world is ignorant of them. Faith and unbelief, doubts and fears are all foolishness to the natural man. But let the true Christian study these things well and thoroughly understand them. It is of the utmost importance to our comfort to know that a true believer may be known by his inward warfare as well as his inward peace.

We notice that Christ has complete dominion over Satan and all his agents. The spirit who was too strong for the disciples is immediately cast out by the Master. He speaks with almighty authority and Satan is obliged to obey (v. 25). Greater is he that is for us than all that is against us. Satan is strong, busy, active and malicious. But Jesus is stronger.

For meditation: *Our inward struggle with sin is an evidence that sin has something to struggle with and is not at home.*

Suggested further reading: Isaiah 53

The crucifixion brought glory to the Father. It glorified his wisdom, faithfulness, holiness and love. It showed him wise in providing a plan whereby he could be just and yet the justifier of the ungodly. It showed him faithful in keeping his promise that the seed of the woman should bruise the serpent's head. It showed him holy in requiring his law's demands to be satisfied by our great Substitute. It showed him loving, in providing such a Mediator, such a Redeemer and such a Friend for sinful man as his co-eternal Son.

The crucifixion brought glory to the Son. It glorified his compassion, his patience and his power. It showed him most compassionate, in dying for us, suffering in our stead, allowing himself to be counted sin and a curse for us and buying our redemption with the price of his own blood. It showed him most patient, in not dying the common death of most men, but in willingly submitting to such horrors and unknown agonies as no mind can conceive, when with a word he could have summoned his Father's angels and been set free. It showed him most powerful in bearing the weight of all a world's transgressions and vanquishing Satan and despoiling him of his prey.

Forever let us cling to these thoughts about the crucifixion. Let us remember that painting and sculpture can never tell a tenth part of what took place on the cross. Crucifixes and pictures at best can only show us a human being agonizing in a painful death. But of the length and breadth and depth and height of the work transacted on the cross, of God's law honoured, man's sins borne, sin punished in a substitute, free salvation bought for man — of all this they can tell nothing. Yet all this lies hid under the crucifixion. No wonder St Paul cries, 'God forbid that I should glory, save in the cross of our Lord Jesus Christ' (Gal. 6:14).

For meditation: *Humans delight in strength. God saved us through weakness* (2 Cor. 13:4).

Suggested further reading: Psalm 8

The Lord has perfect knowledge of all that is said and done in this world. It is evident that our Lord was not present when the men came to Peter with their question and received his answer (vv. 24-25). And yet no sooner had Peter come into the house than our Lord spoke (v. 25). He showed that he was as well acquainted with the conversation as if he had been listening or standing by.

There is something unspeakably solemn in the thought that the Lord Jesus knows all things. There is an eye that sees our daily conduct. There is an ear that hears all our daily words. All things are naked and opened to the eyes of him with whom we have to do (Heb. 4:13). Concealment is impossible. Hypocrisy is useless. We may deceive ministers. We may impose upon our relations and neighbours. But the Lord sees us through and through. We cannot deceive Christ.

We ought to endeavour to make practical use of this truth. We should strive to live as in the Lord's sight and, like Abraham, to 'walk before him' (Gen. 17:1). Let it be our daily aim to say nothing we would not like Christ to hear and to do nothing we would not like Christ to see. Let us measure every difficult question by the simple test as to right and wrong: 'How would I behave if Jesus was standing by my side?' Such a standard is not extravagant or absurd. It is a standard that interferes with no duty or relation of life. It interferes with nothing but sin. Happy is he who tries to realize his Lord's presence and to do all and say all as unto Christ.

The Lord has almighty power over all creation. He makes a fish his paymaster. He makes a dumb creature bring the tribute money to meet the collector's demand. We see a literal fulfilment of the psalmist's words (Ps. 8:6-8).

Here is demonstrated the majesty and greatness of the Lord. Only he who first created could at his will command the obedience of all his creatures (Col. 1:16-18).

For meditation: *If creatures obey his will because he made them, Christians should obey his will because he saved them. Of all creatures none should be more obedient than the saved sinner.*

Suggested further reading: John 17:20-26

This is the only time our Lord ever calls his disciples his children. It was evidently a term of affection and compassion, like the language of a father speaking to children whom he is about to leave alone as orphans in the world: 'My believing followers, whom I love and regard as my children.' Observe that the expression is not used till Judas has gone away. Unbelievers are not to be addressed as Christ's children.

'Yet a little while and I am with you,' seems to mean, 'I am only staying a very little longer with you. The time is short. The hour approaches when we must part. Give me your best attention while I talk to you for the last time before I go.'

It is not clear what 'You will seek me,' means. Of course, it cannot refer to the time after the resurrection when the disciples were fully convinced that the Lord had risen. Much less can it refer to the time after the ascension. I can only suppose it means, 'After my death ye shall be perplexed, amazed and confounded for a little season, wanting me, seeking me, wishing for me and wondering where I am gone. The very moment the little child is left alone by mother or nurse, it begins to cry after her and want her. So will it be with you.'

The closing words of verse 33 applied to the Jews meant that Jesus was going to a place where spiritually and morally the Jews were unfit to go and in their impenitent state could not go. The words applied to the disciples only meant that Jesus was going into a world where they could not follow him till they died. They were remaining on earth and he was going to heaven.

Hengstenberg observes that this is the only place in which Jesus ever spoke to his disciples concerning 'the Jews'. Elsewhere he uses the expression in speaking to the Samaritan woman (John 4:22) and before Caiaphas and Pilate.

For meditation: *Where unbelievers cannot go, believers surely shall* (John 17:24).

Suggested further reading: Romans 13:1-7

Our Lord was willing to make concessions rather than give offence. He might have justly claimed exemption from the payment of tribute money. He, who was the Son of God, might fairly have been excused from paying for the maintenance of his Father's house. He who was greater than the temple (Matt. 12:6) might have shown good cause for declining to contribute to the support of the temple. But our Lord does not do so. He claims no exemption. He desires Peter to pay the money demanded. At the same time he declares his reason (v. 27). A miracle is worked rather than offend a tax collector.

Our Lord's example in this case deserves the attention of all who profess and call themselves Christians. It teaches us plainly that there are matters in which Christ's people ought to sink their own opinions and submit to requirements of which they may not thoroughly approve rather than give offence and hinder the gospel of Christ. God's rights we undoubtedly ought never to give up; but we may sometimes safely give up our own. It may sound very fine and heroic to be always standing out tenaciously for our rights. But it may well be doubted, in the light of such a passage as this, whether such tenacity is always wise and shows the mind of Christ. There are occasions when it shows more grace in a Christian to submit than to resist.

Let us remember this passage as citizens and subjects. We may not like all the political measures of our rulers. We may disapprove of some of the taxes they impose. But the grand question after all is: 'Will it do any good to the cause of religion to resist the powers that be? Are their measures really injuring our souls?' If not, let us avoid acting in a way that will offend them.

As members of society there may be usages and customs in our circle which to us as Christians are tiresome, useless and unprofitable. But are they matters of principle? Do they injure our souls? Will religion be profited if we do not comply? Let us beware of false scruples.

For meditation: *Paul avoided doing anything that would hinder the gospel* (1 Cor. 9:12). *Do you?*

Suggested further reading: 1 John 3:10-15

What great importance our Lord Jesus attaches to the grace of brotherly love! Almost as soon as the false apostle had left the faithful eleven, comes the injunction, 'Love one another.' Immediately after the sad announcement that he would leave them soon, the commandment is given: 'Love one another.' It is called a 'new' commandment, not because it had never been given before, but because it was to be more honoured, to occupy a higher position, to be backed by a higher example than it ever had been before. Above all, it was to be the test of Christianity before the world. 'By this shall all men know that ye are my disciples, if ye have love one to another.'

Let us take heed that this well-known Christian grace is not merely a notion in our heads, but a practice in our lives. Of all the commands of our Master, there is none which is so much talked about and so little obeyed as this. Yet, if we mean anything when we profess to have charity and love towards all men, it ought to be seen in our tempers and our words, our bearing and our doing, our behaviour at home and abroad, our conduct in every relation of life. Specially it ought to show itself forth in all our dealings with other Christians. We should regard them as brethren and sisters and delight to do anything to promote their happiness. We should abhor the idea of envy, malice and jealousy towards a member of Christ and regard it as a downright sin. This is what our Lord meant when he told us to love one another.

Christ's cause in the earth would prosper far more than it does if this simple law was more honoured. There is nothing that the world understands and values more than true love.

For meditation: *Do your neighbours **see** that you love your fellow Christians?*

Suggested further reading: Luke 18:9-14

We are here taught the necessity of conversion and of conversion manifested by childlike humility. The disciples came to the Lord with a question (v. 1) as men half enlightened and full of carnal expectations. They received an answer well calculated to awaken them from their day-dream, an answer containing a truth which lies at the very foundation of Christianity (v. 2).

Let these words sink down deeply into our hearts. Without conversion there is no salvation. We all need an entire change of nature. Of ourselves we have neither faith, nor fear, nor love towards God. We must be born again (John 3:3-8). Of ourselves we are utterly unfit to dwell in God's presence. Heaven would be no heaven to us if we were not converted. It is true of all ranks, classes and orders of mankind. All are born in sin and are children of wrath, and all, without exception, need to be born again and made new creatures. A new heart must be given to us and a new spirit put within us. Old things must pass away and all things must become new.

Would we know whether we really are converted? Would we know the test by which we must try ourselves? The surest mark of true conversion is humility. If we have received the Holy Spirit we shall show it by a meek and childlike spirit. Like children we shall think humbly of our own strength and wisdom and be very dependent on our Father in heaven. Like children we shall not seek great things in this world, and having food and clothing and a Father's love, we shall be content. Truly this is a heart-searching test! It exposes the unsoundness of many a so-called conversion. It is easy to convert from one party to another, from one sect to another, from one set of opinions to another set of opinions. Such conversions save no one's soul. What we all want is a conversion from pride to humility, from high thoughts of ourselves to low thoughts, from self-conceit to self-abasement, from the mind of the Pharisee to the mind of the publican (Luke 18:9-14). This alone is true conversion.

For meditation: *'Humble yourselves before the Lord, and he will lift you up'* (James 4:10).

Suggested further reading: 1 John 4:7-11

There can be no mistake about these words. Love was to be the grand characteristic, the distinguishing mark of Christ's disciples.

Let us note that our Lord does not name gifts, or miracles, or intellectual attainments, but love, the simple grace of love, a grace within reach of the poorest, lowliest believer, as the evidence of discipleship. No love, no grace, no regeneration, no true Christianity!

Let us note what a heavy condemnation this verse pronounces on sectarianism, bigotry, narrow-mindedness, party-spirit, strife, bitterness, needless controversy between Christian and Christian.

Let us note how far from satisfactory is the state of those who are content with sound doctrinal opinions and orthodox correct views of the gospel, while in their daily life they give way to ill-temper, ill-nature, malice, envy, quarrelling, squabbling, bickering, surliness, passion, snappish language and crossness of word and manner. Such persons, whether they know it or not, are daily proclaiming that they are not Christ's disciples. It is nonsense to talk about justification and regeneration and election and conversion and the uselessness of works, unless people can see in us practical Christian love.

In verse 36, as elsewhere, the forward, impulsive spirit of Peter prompts him to ask anxiously what our Lord meant by talking of going: 'Whither goest thou?' Can we doubt, however, that in this question he was the spokesman of all?

How very little the disciples had ever comprehended our Lord's repeated saying that he must be taken prisoner, be crucified and die, we see in this place. Often as he had told them he must die, they had never realized it and are startled when he talks of going away. It is marvellous how much religious teaching men may have and yet not take it in, receive or believe it, especially when it contradicts preconceived notions.

For meditation: *Do your fellow Christians know that you love them?*

Suggested further reading: Galatians 2:11-21

It is a great sin to put stumbling-blocks in the way of believers (v. 7).
We put offences or stumbling-blocks in the way of men's souls whenever we do anything to keep them back from Christ, or to turn them
out of the way of salvation, or to disgust them with true religion. We
may do it by what we say or how we live, and this is a great sin. It is
awful to think of the amount of harm that can be done by one inconsistent professor of religion. He gives a handle to the infidel. He
supplies the worldly man with an excuse for remaining undecided.
He checks the enquirer after salvation. He discourages the saints.
He is, in short, a sermon on behalf of the devil. This is what Nathan
accused David of being (2 Sam. 12:14).

Future punishment after death is a reality (vv. 8-9). The meaning of the words is clear and unmistakable. There is a place of unspeakable misery in the world to come to which all who die impenitent and unbelieving must inevitably be consigned. There is revealed
in Scripture a 'fiery indignation' (Heb. 10:27), which sooner or later
will devour all God's adversaries. The same sure Word that holds
out a heaven to all who repent and are converted holds out a hell for
the ungodly. Men have arisen who use the devil's old argument (Gen.
3:4). Let none of their reasonings move us. The God of love is also
a God of justice. No lips have ever spoken so clearly about hell as
those of Christ himself. There is such a thing as the wrath of the
Lamb (Rev. 6:17).

God sets a high value on the least and lowest of believers (v. 14).
These words are meant for the encouragement of all true Christians
and not for the little children only. Their connection to a parable
leaves this beyond doubt (vv. 12-13). They are meant to show us
that the Lord Jesus is a Shepherd who cares tenderly for every soul
committed to his charge. The youngest, the weakest, the sickliest of
the flock is as dear to him as the strongest. They shall not perish. He
will carry them through every difficulty. He will defend them against
every enemy (John 17:9). With such a Shepherd who needs fear
being cast away?

For meditation: *If an apostle's inconsistencies needed rebuke lest
he stumble others, how much more do we need rebuke? But are we
willing to receive it?*

Suggested further reading: 1 Corinthians 10:1-13

It is not unlikely, as Cyril observes, that these words, 'Thou shalt follow me,' pointed to the manner of Peter's death by crucifixion. He was to walk in his Master's steps and enter heaven by the same road.

Verse 37 shows how little Peter realized what our Lord fully meant and the nearness of his death on the cross: 'Why cannot I follow thee now? Where is the place thou art going to on earth, where I am not willing and ready to follow thee? I love thee so much and am so determined to cling to thee, that I am ready to lay down my life rather than be separate from thee.'

These words were well meant and Peter never doubted, perhaps, that he could stand to them. But he did not know his own heart. There was more feeling than principle in his declaration. He did not see all that was in himself. Let us note the mischief of self-ignorance. Let us pray for humility. Let us beware of overconfidence in our own courage and steadfastness. Pride goeth before a fall.

The meaning of our Lord's answer to Peter appears to be 'Wilt thou really and truly lay down thy life for me? Thou little knowest thy own weakness and feebleness. I tell thee in the most solemn answer that this very night, before the cock crow, before sunrise, thou, even thou, wilt deny three times that thou knowest me. So far from laying down thy life, thou wilt try to save thy life by cowardly denying that thou hast anything to do with me.'

Let us note the wonderful foreknowledge of our Lord. What an unlikely thing it seemed that such a professor should fall so far and so soon. Yet our Lord foresaw it all!

Let us note the wonderful kindness and condescension of Jesus. He knew perfectly well the weakness and feebleness of his chief disciple and yet never rejected him and even raised him again after his fall. Christians should be men of very pitiful and tender feelings towards weak brethren.

For meditation: *Self-confidence is a cliff from which many fall very far.*

Suggested further reading: Philippians 1:12-19

The man whom John saw was doing a good work, no doubt. He was warring on the same side as the apostles, beyond question. But this did not satisfy John. He did not work in the company of the apostles. He did not fight alongside them. And therefore John had forbidden him. But hear what the great Head of the church decides (vv. 39-40).

Here is a golden rule indeed, and one that human nature sorely needs and has too often forgotten. Men of all branches of Christ's church are apt to think that no good can be done in the world except by their own party and denomination. They are so narrow-minded that they cannot conceive the possibility of working on any other pattern but that which they follow. They make an idol of their own peculiar ecclesiastical machinery and can see no merit in any other. They are like Joshua who wanted to forbid Eldad and Medad (Num. 11:28).

To this intolerant spirit we owe some of the blackest pages of church history. Christians have repeatedly persecuted Christians for no better reason than that given here by John.

Let us be on our guard against this feeling. It is only too near the surface of our hearts. Let us study to realize that liberal, tolerant spirit which Christ here commends and be thankful for good works wheresoever and by whomsoever done. Let us beware of the slightest inclination to stop and check others merely because they do not choose to adopt our plans and work by our sides. We may think that our fellow Christians are mistaken in some points. We may fancy that more would be done for Christ if they would join us and if all worked in the same way. But all this must not prevent us from rejoicing if the works of the devil are destroyed and souls are saved. Is our neighbour warring against Satan? Is he really trying to labour for Christ? This is the grand question. Better a thousand times that the work should be done by other hands than not done at all. Happy is he who knows something of the spirit of Moses (Num. 11:29) and Paul (Phil. 1:18).

For meditation: *How much of the 'I, only I am left' mentality is in you? Do you need reminding that the Lord has preserved for himself many others?*

Suggested further reading: John 14:7-27

Our Lord's great object throughout this and the two following chapters seems clear and plain. He desired to comfort, stablish and build up his downcast disciples. He saw their 'hearts were troubled' from a variety of causes — partly by seeing their Master 'troubled in spirit' (13:21), partly by hearing that one of them should betray him, partly by the mysterious departure of Judas, partly by their Master's announcement that he should only be a little time longer with them and that at last they could not come with him and partly by the warning addressed to Peter that he would deny his Master thrice. For all these reasons this little company of weak believers was disquieted and cast down and anxious. Their gracious Master saw it and proceeded to give them encouragement: 'Let not your heart be troubled.'

Hengstenberg gives the following list of the grounds of comfort which the chapter contains, in systematic order, which well deserve attention.

1. The first encouragement is that to the disciples of Christ heaven is sure (vv. 2-3).

2. The second encouragement is that disciples have in Christ a certain way to heaven (vv. 4-11).

3. The third encouragement is that disciples need not fear that with the departure of Christ his work will cease (vv. 12-14).

4. The fourth encouragement is that in the absence of Christ disciples will have the help of the Spirit (vv. 15-17).

5. The fifth encouragement is that Christ will not leave his people for ever, but will come back again (vv. 18-24).

6. The sixth encouragement is that the Spirit will teach the disciples and supply their want of understanding when left alone (vv. 25-26).

7. Finally, the seventh encouragement is that the legacy of peace will be left to cheer them in their Master's absence (v. 27).

For meditation: *God never forgets to comfort his people and care for them* (Ps. 121:4).

Suggested further reading: Philippians 3:17 - 4:3

How admirable the rules laid down by our Lord are for the healing of differences among brethren! If we have unhappily received any injury from a fellow member of Christ's church the first step to be taken is to visit him alone and tell him his fault. He may have injured us unintentionally, as Abimelech did Abraham (Gen. 21:26). His conduct may admit of explanation, like that of the tribes of Reuben, Gad and Manasseh when they built an altar as they returned to their own land (Josh. 22:24). At any rate, this friendly, faithful, straightforward way of dealing is the most likely course to win a brother if he is to be won (Prov. 25:15). Who can tell but he may admit his fault and make reparation?

If, however, this course of proceedings fails to produce any good effect a second step is to be taken. We are to take one or two with us and tell our brother his fault in their presence and hearing. Who can tell but his conscience may be stricken when he finds his misconduct made known and he may be ashamed and repent? If not, we shall at all events have the testimony of witnesses that we did all we could to bring our brother to a right mind and that he deliberately refused, when appealed to, to make amends.

Finally, if this second course of proceeding proves useless we are to refer the whole matter to the Christian congregation of which we are part. Who can tell but the heart may be moved by fear of public exposure if unmoved by private remonstrances? If not, there remains but one view to take of the brother's case — we must sorrowfully regard him as one who has shaken off all Christian principles and will be guided by no higher motives than a heathen or publican.

What a knowledge is shown here of human nature! Nothing does so much harm to the cause of religion as the quarrels of Christians. No stone should be left unturned, no trouble spared, to prevent their being dragged before the public.

For meditation: *If we are not willing to follow through the procedure set out by our Lord, our grievances cannot be important enough to share with anyone else. Seek reconciliation or be silent. Never gossip or slander.*

Suggested further reading: Philippians 4:1-7

Heart trouble is the commonest thing in the world. No rank or class or condition is exempt from it. No bars or bolts or locks can keep it out. Partly from inward causes and partly from the mind, partly from what we love and partly from what we fear, the journey of life is full of trouble. Even the best of Christians have many bitter cups to drink between grace and glory. Even the holiest saints find the world a vale of tears.

Faith in the Lord Jesus is the only sure medicine for troubled hearts. To believe more thoroughly, trust more entirely, rest more unreservedly, lay hold more firmly, lean back more completely — this is the prescription which our Master urges on the attention of all his disciples. No doubt the members of that little band which sat round the table at the Last Supper had believed already. They had proved the reality of their faith by giving up everything for Christ's sake. Yet what does their Lord say to them here? Once more he presses on them the old lesson, the lesson with which they first began: 'Believe! Believe more! Believe on me!' (Isa. 26:3).

Never let us forget that there are degrees in faith and that there is a wide difference between weak and strong believers. The weakest faith is enough to give a man a saving interest in Christ and ought not to be despised, but it will not give a man such inward comfort as a strong faith. Vagueness and dimness of perception are the defect of weak believers. They do not see clearly what they believe and why they believe. In such cases more faith is the one thing needed. Like Peter on the water, they need to look more steadily at Jesus and less at the waves and wind.

For meditation: *When our mind is fixed on God our heart can be at peace* (Isa. 26:3).

Suggested further reading: 1 Corinthians 5:1-13

We have a clear argument in these verses for the exercise of discipline in the Christian congregation. Our Lord commands disagreements between Christians which cannot otherwise be settled to be referred to the decision of the church to which they belong. It is evident from this that he intends every congregation of professing Christians to take cognizance of the moral conduct of its members. He intends every congregation to have the power of excluding disobedient and refractory members from participation in its ordinances. He says not a word about temporal punishment and civil disabilities. Spiritual penalties are the only penalty that he permits the church to inflict, and when rightly inflicted they are not lightly regarded. It can never be right that all sorts of people, however wicked or ungodly, should be allowed to come to the table of the Lord, no man forbidding. It is the bounden duty of every Christian to use his influence to prevent such a state of things. An increasingly high standard of qualification for church membership will always be found one of the best evidences of a prosperous church.

Christ holds out gracious encouragement to those who meet in his name (v. 20). This saying is a striking proof of our Lord's divinity. God alone can be in more places than one at the same time.

There is comfort in these words for all who love to meet together for religious purposes. At every assembly for public worship, at every gathering for prayer and praise, at every missionary meeting, at every Bible study, the King of kings is present, Christ himself attends. We may often be disheartened by the small number who are present on such occasions compared to those who meet for worldly ends. But at all such meetings we have the company of Christ himself.

There is a solemn rebuke in these words for all who neglect the public worship of God. They turn their backs on the society of the Lord of lords. They miss the opportunity of meeting Christ himself.

For meditation: *Verse 20 proves that we cannot worship Christ as well by staying at home as by going to church.*

Suggested further reading: 2 Corinthians 5:1-11

Heaven is 'a Father's house', the house of that God of whom Jesus says, 'I go to my Father, and your Father.' It is, in a word, home, the home of Christ and Christians. This is a sweet and touching expression. Home, as we all know, is the place where we are generally loved for our own sakes, and not for our gifts or possessions, the place where we are loved to the end, never forgotten and always welcome. This is one idea of heaven. Believers are in a strange land and at school in this life. In the life to come they will be at home.

Heaven is a place of 'mansions', of lasting, permanent and eternal dwellings. Here in the body we are in lodgings, tents and tabernacles, and must submit to many changes. In heaven we shall be settled at last and go out no more. 'Here we have no continuing city' (Heb. 13:14). Our house not made with hands shall never be taken down.

Heaven is a place of 'many mansions'. There will be room for all believers and room for all sorts, for little saints as well as great ones, for the weakest believer as well as for the strongest. The feeblest child of God need not fear there will be no place for him. None will be shut out but impenitent sinners and obstinate unbelievers.

Heaven is a place where Christ himself shall be present. He will not be content to dwell without his people: 'Where I am, there ye shall be also.' We need not think that we shall be alone and neglected. Our Saviour, our elder Brother, our Redeemer, who loved us and gave himself for us, shall be in the midst of us for ever. What we shall see and whom we shall see in heaven, we cannot fully conceive yet, while we are in the body. But one thing is certain: we shall see Christ.

For meditation: *When the Christian leaves his body in the grave he is at home with the Lord* (2 Cor. 5:8).

Suggested further reading: Romans 12:9-21

The Lord Jesus lays down the general rule that we ought to forgive others to the uttermost. He does so by giving a reply (v. 22) to Peter's question (v. 21). The rule laid down here must, of course, be interpreted with sober-minded qualification. Our Lord does not mean that offences against the law of the land and the good order of society are to be passed over in silence. He does not mean that we are to allow people to commit thefts and assaults with impunity. All that he means is that we are to study a general spirit of mercy and forgiveness towards our brethren. We are to bear much and put up with much rather than quarrel. We are to overlook much and submit to much rather than have any strife. We are to lay aside everything like malice, strife, revenge and retaliation. Such feelings are only fit for heathens. They are utterly unworthy of a disciple of Christ.

What a happy world this would be if this rule of our Lord's was more known and more obeyed! How many of the miseries of mankind are occasioned by disputes, quarrels, lawsuits and an obstinate tenacity about what men call their 'rights'! How many of them might be avoided if men were more willing to forgive and more desirous of peace! Let us never forget that a fire cannot go on burning without fuel. Just in the same way it takes two to make a quarrel. Let us resolve that by God's grace of these two we will never be one. Let us resolve to return good for evil, blessing for cursing, and so melt down enmity and change our foes into friends (Rom. 12:20). It was a fine feature in Archbishop Cranmer's character that if you did him an injury he was sure to be your friend.

Would we grow in grace ourselves and become more holy in all our ways, works and words? Let us remember this passage — nothing so grieves the Holy Spirit and brings spiritual darkness over the soul as giving way to a quarrelsome and unforgiving temper (Eph. 4:30-32).

For meditation: *Are you nursing a grudge against anyone? Is it not time to put it to death and to recognize that your begrudging spirit is just as sinful as that which caused you offence in the actions of another?*

Suggested further reading: Titus 2:11-14

We have in this passage a solid ground for expecting good things to come. The evil heart of unbelief within us is apt to rob us of our comfort about heaven. 'We wish we could think it was all true.' 'We fear we shall never be admitted into heaven.' Let us hear what Jesus says to encourage us.

One cheering word is this: 'I go to prepare a place for you.' Heaven is a prepared place for a prepared people: a place which we shall find Christ himself has made ready for true Christians. He has prepared it by procuring a right for every sinner who believes to enter in. None can stop us and say we have no business there. He has prepared it by going before us as our Head and Representative and taking possession of it for all the members of his mystical body. As our Forerunner he has marched in, leading captivity captive, and has planted his banner in the land of glory. He has prepared it by carrying our names with him as our High Priest into the holy of holies and making angels ready to receive us. They that enter heaven will find they are neither unknown nor unexpected.

Another cheering word is this: 'I will come again and receive you unto myself.' Christ will not wait for believers to come up to him, but will come down to them, to raise them from their graves and escort them to their heavenly home. As Joseph came to meet Jacob, so will Jesus come to call his people together and guide them to their inheritance. The second advent ought never to be forgotten. Great is the blessedness of looking back to Christ coming the first time to suffer for us, but no less great is the comfort of looking forward to Christ coming the second time, to raise and reward his saints.

For meditation: *Do you love Christ's appearing?* (2 Tim. 4:8).

Suggested further reading: Luke 23:26-34

It is clear from this parable that one motive for forgiveness ought to be the recollection that we all need forgiveness at God's hands ourselves. Day after day we are coming short in many things, 'leaving undone what we ought to do and doing what we ought not to do'. Day after day we require mercy and pardon. Our neighbour's offences against us are mere trifles compared with our offences against God. Surely it ill becomes poor erring creatures like us to be extreme in marking what is done amiss by our brethren or to be slow to forgive it.

Another motive for forgiving others ought to be the recollection of the Day of Judgement and the standard by which we shall all be tried in that day. There will be no forgiveness in that day for unforgiving people (v. 35). Such people will be unfit for heaven. They would not be able to value a dwelling-place to which mercy is the only title and in which mercy is the eternal subject of song. Surely if we mean to stand at the right hand when Jesus sits on the throne of his glory we must learn while we are on earth to forgive.

Let these truths sink down deeply into our hearts. It is a melancholy fact that there are few Christian duties so little practised as that of forgiveness. It is sad to see how much bitterness, unmercifulness, spite, hardness and unkindness there is among men. Yet there are few duties so strongly enforced in the New Testament as is this duty, and few the neglect of which so clearly shuts a man out of the kingdom of God.

Would we give proof that we are at peace with God, washed in Christ's blood, born of the Spirit and made children of God by grace and adoption? Let us remember this passage. Like our Father in heaven let us be forgiving. Has any man injured us? Let us this day forgive him. Would we do good to the world? Would we have any influence on others and make them see the beauty of true religion? Let us remember this passage.

For meditation: *What are the number and quality of men's sins against you in comparison with the quantity and quality of your sins against God?*

Suggested further reading: Psalm 119:97-104

How much better Jesus speaks of believers than they speak of themselves! He says to his disciples, 'Ye know whither I go, and ye know the way.' And yet Thomas at once breaks in with the remark: 'We know neither the whither nor the way.' The apparent contradiction demands explanation. It is more seeming than real.

Certainly, in one point of view, the knowledge of the disciples was very small. They knew little before the crucifixion and resurrection compared to what they might have known and little compared to what they afterwards knew after the Day of Pentecost. About our Lord's purpose in coming into the world, about his sacrificial death and substitution for us on the cross, their ignorance was glaring and great. It might well be said that they 'knew in part' only and were children in understanding.

And yet, in another point of view, the knowledge of the disciples was very great. They knew far more than the great majority of the Jewish nation and received truths which the scribes and Pharisees entirely rejected. Compared to the world around them, they were in the highest sense enlightened. They knew and believed that their Master was the promised Messiah, the Son of the living God, and to know him was the first step towards heaven. All things go by comparison. Before we lightly esteem the disciples because of their ignorance, let us take care that we do not underrate their knowledge. They knew more precious truth than they were aware of themselves. Their hearts were better than their heads.

The plain truth is that all believers are apt to undervalue the work of the Spirit in their own souls and to fancy they know nothing because they do not know everything.

For meditation: *If you know Christ you know more than the worldly-wise* (Ps. 119:99-100).

Suggested further reading: Matthew 5:43-48

A certain Samaritan village refused our Lord hospitality, so James and John made their strange proposal (vv. 53-54). Here was zeal indeed, and zeal of a most plausible kind, zeal for the honour of Christ! Here was zeal justified and supported by a scriptural example, and that example no less a person than Elijah! But it was not a zeal according to knowledge. The two disciples forgot that circumstances alter cases and that punishments should always be proportioned to offences. They meant well but they greatly erred.

Facts like this are carefully recorded for our learning. It is possible to have much zeal for Christ but to exhibit it in the most unholy and unchristian ways. It is possible to mean well and have good intentions and yet to make most grievous mistakes in our actions. It is possible to fancy that we have Scripture on our side and to support our conduct by scriptural quotations, and yet to commit serious errors. It is clear as daylight that it is not enough to be zealous and well meaning. Very grave faults are frequently committed with good intentions. Zeal without knowledge is an army without a general and a ship without a rudder. We must pray to handle rightly and apply properly the Scriptures.

Our Lord gives a solemn rebuke to persecution carried on under the colour of religion (v. 55). Uncourteous behaviour was not to be met with violence. The mission of the Son of Man was to do good, but never harm. His kingdom was to be extended by patient continuance in well-doing and by meekness and gentleness in suffering, but never by violence and severity.

Religious wars and persecutions have disgraced the annals of church history because men have sought to deal with men's errors by persecution. Carnal weapons (2 Cor. 10:4) are not ours. We appeal to the will and conscience. Our arguments are not the sword, fire and prison, but doctrines, precepts and texts.

For meditation: *The state is given the sword of punishment. The church is given the sword of the Spirit, the Word of God. The two are to remain separate.*

Suggested further reading: Acts 4:8-12

'I am the way, the truth, and the life.' The fulness of these precious words can probably never be taken in by man. He that attempts to unfold them does little more than scratch the surface of a rich soil.

Christ is 'the way' — the way to heaven and peace with God. He is not only the guide and teacher and lawgiver, like Moses; he is himself the door, the ladder and the road through whom we must draw near to God. He has opened the way to the tree of life, which was closed when Adam and Eve fell, by the satisfaction he made for us on the cross. Through his blood we may draw near with boldness and have access with confidence into God's presence.

Christ is 'the truth' — the whole substance of true religion which the mind of man requires. Without him the wisest heathen groped in gross darkness and knew nothing about God. Before he came even the Jews saw 'through a glass darkly' and discerned nothing distinctly under the types, figures and ceremonies of the Mosaic law. Christ is the whole truth and meets and satisfies every desire of the human mind.

Christ is 'the life' — the sinner's title to eternal life and pardon, the believer's root of spiritual life and holiness, the surety of the Christian's resurrection life. He that believeth on Christ hath everlasting life. He that abideth in him, as the branch abides in the vine, shall bring forth much fruit. He that believeth on him, though he were dead, yet shall he live. The root of all life, for soul and for body, is Christ.

Forever let us grasp and hold fast these truths. To use Christ daily as the way, to believe Christ daily as the truth, to live on Christ daily as the life — this is to be a well-informed, a thoroughly furnished and an established Christian.

For meditation: *If I have Christ, what need I more?*

Suggested further reading: Ephesians 5:23-33

In the days when our Lord was upon earth divorces were permitted amongst the Jews for the most trifling and frivolous reasons. The practice, though tolerated by Moses to prevent worse evils, such as cruelty and murder, had gradually become an enormous abuse and no doubt led to much immorality (Mal. 2:14-16). The remark made by our Lord's disciples shows the deplorably low state of public feeling on the subject (v. 10).

Our Lord brings forward a widely different standard for the guidance of his disciples. He first founds his judgement on the original institution of marriage (vv. 4-5). He then backs up the quotation by his own solemn words (v. 6). And finally he brings in the grave charge of breaking the seventh commandment against marriages contracted after a divorce for light and frivolous reasons (v. 9).

The importance of the whole subject on which our Lord pronounces judgement can hardly be overrated. The marriage relation lies at the very root of the social system of the nations. It is a fact clearly ascertained that polygamy and permission to obtain divorce on slight grounds have a direct tendency to promote immorality.

It becomes all those who are married or purpose marriage to ponder this passage well. Of all relations of life none ought to be regarded with such reverence and none taken in hand so cautiously as that of husband and wife. In no relationship is so much earthly happiness to be found if entered upon discreetly, advisedly and in the fear of God. In none is so much misery to be found if entered into unadvisedly, lightly, wantonly and without thought.

In the matter of marriage let three rules be observed. Firstly, marry only in the Lord and after prayer for God's approval and blessing. Secondly, do not expect too much of marriage. Two sinners are involved, not two angels. Thirdly, strive first and foremost for each other's sanctification (Eph. 5:25-26).

For meditation: *Marriages have to be worked at. They do not prosper automatically.*

Suggested further reading: Revelation 20:11-15

The Lord Jesus shuts out all ways of salvation but himself. 'No man,' he declares, 'no man cometh unto the Father but by me.'

'Coming to the Father' in this place means coming to him in a friendly relation for peace and comfort now in this life. 'By me' is literally 'through me, as a door, a gate, a road, a path, an entrance. It is an expression which would be peculiarly expressive to the Jews, taught from their childhood to draw near to God only through the priests.

It avails nothing that a man is clever, learned, highly gifted, amiable, charitable, kind-hearted and zealous about some sort of religion. All this will not save his soul if he does not draw near to God by Christ's atonement and make use of God's own Son as his Mediator and Saviour. God is so holy that all men are guilty and debtors in his sight. Sin is so sinful that no mortal man can make satisfaction for it. There must be a mediator, a ransom-payer, a redeemer, between ourselves and God, or else we can never be saved. There is only one door, one bridge, one ladder, between earth and heaven — the crucified Son of God. Whosoever will enter in by that door may be saved, but to him who refuses to use that door the Bible holds out no hope at all. Without shedding of blood there is no remission.

Let us beware, if we love life, of supposing that mere earnestness will take a man to heaven, though he know nothing of Christ. The idea is a deadly and ruinous error. Sincerity will never wipe away our sins. It is not true that every man will be saved by his own religion, no matter what he believes, so long as he is diligent and sincere. We must not pretend to be wiser than God. Christ has said, and Christ will stand to it, 'No man cometh unto the Father but by me.'

For meditation: *Is your name in the Lamb's book of life?*

Suggested further reading: 2 Timothy 4:6-18

All those involved in the work of the gospel should notice our Lord's emphasis on the importance of prayer and intercession (v. 2). Prayer is one of the best and most powerful means of helping forward the cause of Christ in the world. It is a means within the reach of all who have the Spirit of adoption. Not all believers have money to give, great intellectual gifts, or influence among men, but all believers can pray for the success of the gospel daily. Many and marvellous are the answers to prayer which are recorded for our learning in the Bible.

Prayer is one of the principal weapons which those who are in gospel work ought to use. Ministers must give themselves to prayer as well as the ministry of the Word if they would be true successors of the apostles (Acts 6:4). Not only must the sword of the Spirit be used, but prayer with supplication (Eph. 6:17-18). This is the way to win a blessing on the ministry. This is the way to procure helpers to carry on Christ's work. Only God can raise up labourers to do a work amongst souls.

In giving his charge to his seventy disciples our Lord warned them of the perilous nature of the work in which they were going to be engaged. He does not keep back from them the dangers and trials which are before them. He does not enlist them under false pretences, prophesy smooth things, or promise them unvarying success. He tells them plainly what they must expect (v. 3).

These words, no doubt, had a special reference to the lifetime of those to whom they were spoken. We see their fulfilment in the many persecutions described in the Acts of the Apostles. But we must not conceal from ourselves that the words describe a state of things which may be seen at this very day. So long as the church stands believers will be sheep among wolves. They must look for no favour from unconverted people, for they will find none. The words of John and Paul stand true (1 John 3:13; 2 Tim. 3:12).

For meditation: *How much do you support your work and that of others with prayer? How much are you willing to suffer in the promotion of the Lord's work, or do you want success with ease?*

Suggested further reading: Isaiah 9:1-7

The seventh verse contains a deep saying, like every saying which handles the mysterious union of the Father and the Son in St John's Gospel. The meaning seems to be: 'If you had rightly, properly and perfectly known me, as the divine Messiah, in all the fulness of my nature, you would then have known more of that Father to whom I am inseparably united. No one can rightly know me without knowing the Father, because I and the Father are one. Understand from this time forward that in knowing me you know the Father and in seeing me see the Father, so far as the Father can be seen and known by man.'

Sayings like these are full of deep mystery. We have no eyes to see their meaning fully, no line to fathom it, no language to express it, no mind to take it in. We must be content to believe when we cannot explain and to admire and revere when we cannot interpret. Let it suffice us to know and hold that the Father is God and the Son is God and yet that they are one in essence though two distinct persons — ineffably one and yet ineffably distinct. These are high things and we cannot attain to a full comprehension of them.

Let us, however, take comfort in the simple truth that Christ is very God of very God, equal with the Father in all things and one with him. He who loved us and shed his blood for us on the cross and bids us trust him for pardon is no mere man like ourselves. He is 'God over all, blessed for ever' and able to save to the uttermost the chief of sinners. Though our sins be as scarlet, he can make them white as snow. He that casts his soul on Christ has an almighty Friend — a Friend who is one with the Father and very God.

For meditation: *Christ is Emmanuel, 'God with us'* (Matt. 1:23). *He is not far off but near.*

Suggested further reading: Hebrews 11:13-16

The Lord charged his seventy disciples to have a thorough devotion to their work. They were to abstain from every appearance of covetousness, love of money or luxury (v. 4). They were to behave like men who had no time to waste on the empty compliments and conventional courtesies of the world (v. 4). Servants of Christ are to beware of allowing the world to eat up their time and thoughts and to hinder them in their spiritual work. These words teach us that care about money and excessive attention to the courtesies of life are mighty snares in the way of Christ's labourers, into which they can easily fall.

Let us strive to show the men of this world that we have no time for their mode of living. Let us show them that we find life too precious to be spent in perpetual feasting, visiting, calling and the like, as if there were no death, judgement or life to come. Let our principle be that of Nehemiah (Neh. 6:3).

The Lord charged the seventy to have a simple-minded and contented spirit. They were to avoid fickleness in their work, moving from one place to another looking for the best food! (v. 7). Simplicity in food and household arrangements, and a readiness to put up in any accommodation, should mark the man of God. Once let a man get a reputation for being fond of eating and drinking and worldly comforts, and his usefulness as a minister is at an end. The sermon about 'things unseen' will produce little effect when the life preaches the importance of the 'things which are seen'.

All believers ought to be reminded of the necessity for simpleness and unworldliness in daily life. We must beware of thinking too much about our meals, our furniture, our houses and all those many things that concern the life of this body. We must strive to live like men whose first thoughts are about the immortal soul. We must pass through this world like men who are not yet at home and are not overmuch troubled about the food and lodging they meet with on the road.

For meditation: *Do not merely admire the self-sacrifice of others for the gospel; copy it!*

Suggested further reading: Exodus 33:12 - 34:9

We are not told Philip's motive in making this request. Perhaps, like Moses, he and the other disciples had a pious desire to see a more full vision and revelation of God's glory, as an authentication of their Master's divine mission. 'Show me thy glory' (Exod. 33:18). Perhaps Philip's petition is recorded to show how little clear knowledge the apostles yet had of their Master's nature and how little they realized that he and the Father were one: 'If we could only see once for all the divine being whom thou dost call the Father, it would be sufficient. We should be satisfied and our doubts would be removed.' At any rate we have no right to think that Philip spoke like the unbelieving Jews, who always pretended to want signs and wonders. Whatever sense we put on the words, we must carefully remember not to judge Philip too harshly. Living as we do in the twentieth century, amidst light and creeds and knowledge, we can have faint ideas of the extreme difficulty that must have been felt by the disciples in fully realizing their Master's nature, in the days when he was 'in the form of a servant' and under a veil of poverty, weakness and humiliation.

Melanchthon remarks that Philip's petition represents the natural wish of man in every age. Men feel an inward craving everywhere to see God.

Our Lord's answer is undoubtedly a gentle rebuke. The expression 'so long time' is noteworthy when we remember that Philip was one of the very first disciples whom Jesus called (see John 1:43). The meaning seems to be: 'After three long years, Philip, dost thou not yet thoroughly know and understand who I am?'

Our Lord's reply can only mean, 'He that hath thoroughly seen me with the eye of faith and realized that I am the eternal Son, the divine Messiah, hath seen as much of my Father, whose express image I am, as mortal man can comprehend.' There is so close and intimate a union between persons in the Trinity that he who sees the Son sees the Father.

For meditation: *We can know no more of God than is seen in the Lord Jesus.*

Suggested further reading: 2 Thessalonians 1:5-10

What a simple message the Lord gave his disciples to proclaim! (v. 9). It may be doubted whether the modern way of teaching Christianity is sufficiently simple. It is a certain fact that deep reasoning and elaborate arguments are not the weapons by which God is generally pleased to convert souls. Simple plain statements, boldly and solemnly made, and made in such a manner that they are evidently felt and believed by him who makes them, seem to have the most effect on hearts and consciences. Parents and teachers of the young, ministers and missionaries and district visitors would do well to remember this. We need not be so anxious as we often are about fencing, proving, demonstrating and reasoning out the doctrines of the gospel. Not one soul in a hundred was ever brought to Christ in this fashion. We want more simple, plain, solemn, earnest, affectionate statements of simple gospel truth. We may safely leave such statements to take care of themselves. They are arrows from God's quiver and will often pierce hearts that have not been touched by the most eloquent gospel sermons.

How sinful it is to reject the offers of the gospel! (vv. 12-15). The guilt of the cities where our Lord had preached and worked miracles was greater than the guilt of wicked heathen cities. Declarations like this are particularly awful. They throw light on truths that men are peculiarly apt to forget. They teach us all will be judged according to their spiritual light and that from those who have enjoyed most religious privileges most will be required. Man is responsible for the state of his own soul. Those who reject the gospel and remain impenitent and unbelieving are not merely objects of pity and compassion, but deeply guilty and blameworthy in God's sight. God called but they refused. God spoke to them but they would not regard.

Let us beware of unbelief. We have only to sit still and do nothing when the gospel is pressed for our acceptance and we shall find ourselves one day in hell. No sin makes less noise, but none so surely damns the soul as unbelief.

For meditation: *There is no escape for those who neglect salvation* (Heb. 2:3).

Suggested further reading: Mark 6:1-6

Verse 10 means: 'The words that I speak to you, I speak not independently of the Father, and the works that I do, I do not do them independently of the Father. The Father, who dwells in me, speaks in me and works in me. My words are words given me to speak and my works are works given me to do in the eternal counsel between the Father and the Son. Both in speaking and working, I and my Father are one. What I speak he speaks and what I work he works.'

The whole difficulty of the verse arises from forgetting the close and mysterious and indissoluble union between the persons of the Trinity. How little we realize the fulness of the expression, 'The Father dwelleth in me'!

Direct instruction follows the rebuke of the preceding verse. Our Lord repeats for the benefit, not of Philip only, but of all the eleven, the great doctrine he had so often taught them: 'Once more, I say, Believe, all of you, my words, when I say that I and the Father are so closely united that I am in him and he in me.' The word rendered 'believe' in this verse is in the plural number. Our Lord does not address Philip only, but the whole company of the apostles.

What an example we have here of the necessity of repeating instruction over and over again! Our Lord had evidently taught these things before to the eleven and yet they had either not understood or not remembered.

Our Lord condescends to the weakness of the disciples: 'If you will not believe the close union of myself and the Father because of my word, believe it because of the works I work. They are such works as no one could work of himself and without the Father.'

Let us carefully observe how our Lord here, as elsewhere, specially names his works, or miracles, as testimonies of his nature and divine mission. To leave out miracles in the list of the evidences of Christianity is a great mistake.

For meditation: *Only one thing is more amazing than the miraculous — the unbelief of those who see it.*

Suggested further reading: 2 Corinthians 12:1-10

How ready Christians are to be puffed up with success! (v. 17). There was much false fire in their joy when the seventy returned from their mission. There was evidently self-satisfaction in the report of achievements.

The lesson is one which all who work for Christ should mark and remember. Success is what all faithful labourers in the gospel field desire. Whether at home or abroad, they long for success. All long to see Satan's kingdom pulled down and souls converted to God. We cannot wonder. The desire is right and good. Let it, however, never be forgotten that the time of success is a time of danger to the Christian's soul. The very hearts that are depressed when all things seem against them are often unduly exalted in the day of prosperity. Few men are like Samson and can kill a lion without telling others about it (Judg. 14:6). Paul warns of pride in the successful novice (1 Tim. 3:6). Most of Christ's labourers probably have as much success as their souls can bear.

Let us pray much for humility, and especially for humility in our days of peace and success. When everything around us seems to prosper and all our plans work well, when family trials and sicknesses are kept from us and the course of our worldly affairs runs smooth, when our daily crosses are light and all within and without is like a morning without clouds — then, then is the time when our souls are in danger! Then is the time when we have need to be doubly watchful over our own hearts. Then is the time that seeds of evil are sown in us by the devil which may one day astound us by their growth and strength. There are few Christians who can carry a full cup with a steady hand. There are few whose souls prosper in their days of uninterrupted success. We are ready to think that our own might and our own wisdom have procured us the victory. In the midst of our triumphs let us cry to God for humility.

For meditation: *As blessing is the sovereign gift of God* (1 Cor. 3:6) *only God should receive praise for it.*

Suggested further reading: Colossians 1:19-23

Our Lord says, 'He that believeth on me, the works that I do shall he do also; and greater works than these shall he do; because I go unto my Father.'

The full meaning of this promise is not to be sought in the miracles which the apostles wrought after Christ left the world. Such a notion seems hardly borne out by facts. We read of no apostle walking on the water, or raising a person four days dead, like Lazarus. What our Lord has in view seems to be the far greater number of conversions, the far wider spread of the gospel, which would take place under the ministry of the apostles than under his own teaching. That this was the case, we know from the Acts of the Apostles. We read of no sermon preached by Christ under which three thousand were converted in one day, as they were on the Day of Pentecost. In short, 'greater works' mean more conversions. There is no greater work possible than the conversion of a soul.

Let us admire the condescension of our Master in allowing to the ministry of his weak servants more success than to his own. Let us learn that his visible presence is not absolutely necessary to the progress of his kingdom. He can help forward his cause on earth quite as much by sitting at the right hand of the Father and sending forth the Holy Ghost, as by walking to and fro in the world. Let us believe that there is nothing too hard or too great for believers to do, so long as their Lord intercedes for them in heaven. Let us work on in faith and expect great things, though we feel weak and lonely, like the disciples. Our Lord is working with us and for us, though we cannot see him. It was not so much the sword of Joshua that defeated Amalek as the intercession of Moses on the hill (Exod. 17:11).

For meditation: *Our Lord taught a few people with limited success. In one generation after him the whole world had heard the gospel* (Col. 1:23).

Suggested further reading: Matthew 7:21-28

Gifts and the power of working miracles are very inferior to grace (v. 20). It was doubtless an honour and a privilege to be allowed to cast out devils. The disciples were right to be thankful. But it was a far higher privilege to be converted and pardoned men and to have their names written in the register of saved souls.

The distinction drawn between grace and gifts is one of deep importance and often sadly overlooked in the present day. Gifts are often unduly valued by those who possess them and unduly admired by those who possess them not. These things ought not to be so. Men forget that gifts without grace save no one's soul and are characteristic of Satan himself. Grace, on the contrary, is an everlasting possession and, lowly and despised as its possessor might be, will land him safe in glory. He that has gifts without grace is dead in sins, however splendid his gifts may be. But he that has grace without gifts is alive to God, however unlearned and ignorant he may appear (Eccles. 9:4).

Let the religion we aim to possess be a religion in which grace is the main thing. Let it not satisfy us to have gifts and knowledge. These things are all well in their own way. They are not to be undervalued. They have their use. But these things are not the grace of God and will not deliver us from hell. Let us never rest till we have the witness of the Spirit within us that we are washed, sanctified, justified in the name of the Lord Jesus and by the Spirit (1 Cor. 6:11). Let us seek to know that our names are written in heaven and that we are really one with Christ and Christ in us. Let us seek to show by our meekness, love, faith and spiritual-mindedness that we are children of God. This is true religion. These are the real marks of saving Christianity. Without such marks a man may have an abundance of gifts and turn out nothing better than a follower of Judas Iscariot, the false apostle, and go to hell. With such marks a man may be like Lazarus, poor and despised on earth, and have no gifts at all. But his name is written in heaven.

For meditation: *It is much easier to look at a person's activities than to look at his life. But it is the life that counts.*

Suggested further reading: 1 John 5:10-15

'Whatsoever ye shall ask in my name, that will I do... If ye shall ask anything in my name, I will do it.'

These words are a direct encouragement to the simple, yet great, duty of praying. Everyone who kneels daily before God and from his heart 'says his prayers' has a right to take comfort in these words. Weak and imperfect as his supplications may be, so long as they are put in Christ's hands and offered in Christ's name, they shall not be in vain. We have a Friend at court, an Advocate with the Father, and if we honour him by sending all our petitions through him, he pledges his word that they shall succeed. Of course, it is taken for granted that the things we ask are for our souls' good and not mere temporal benefits. 'Anything' and 'whatsoever' do not include wealth and money and worldly prosperity. These things are not always good for us and our Lord loves us too well to let us have them. But whatever is really good for our souls, we need not doubt we shall have, if we ask in Christ's name.

How is it that many true Christians have so little? How is it that they go halting and mourning on the way to heaven and enjoy so little peace and show so little strength in Christ's service? The answer is simple and plain. 'They have not, because they ask not.' They have little because they ask little. They are no better than they are, because they do not ask their Lord to make them better. Our languid desires are the reason of our languid performances. We are not straitened in our Lord, but in ourselves. Happy are they who never forget the words: 'Open thy mouth wide, and I will fill it' (Ps. 81:10). He that does much for Christ and leaves his mark in the world will always prove to be one who prays much.

For meditation: *What do you not have because you do not ask, or because you ask with wrong motives?* (James 4:2-3).

Suggested further reading: 1 Peter 1:8-12

We have here the one instance on record of our Lord Jesus Christ rejoicing (v. 21). And what was the cause of our Lord's joy? The conversion of souls. It was the reception of the gospel by the weak and lowly among the Jews, when the wise and prudent were rejecting it. Our Lord saw much in this world to grieve him, not least the obstinate blindness and unbelief of the majority, but when he saw a few believing his heart was refreshed. Let Christians follow his example.

We see the sovereignty of God in saving sinners (v. 21). Why some around us are converted and some are not we cannot possibly explain. We can only acknowledge the words of our Lord (v. 21) and remember that God's sovereignty does not destroy man's responsibility. The same God who does all things according to the counsel of his will addresses us as accountable creatures, as beings whose blood will be upon their own heads if they are lost.

The wisdom of this world often makes people proud and increases their natural enmity to the gospel. Nothing so blinds our eyes to the beauty of the gospel as the vain, delusive idea that we are not so wicked and ignorant as some men are and that we have a character that will bear inspection. To see that we are bad and ignorant is the first step to being really good and having saving knowledge.

Our Lord speaks of his own majesty and dignity (v. 22) as no patriarch, apostle or saint could. He is distinct from the Father and yet entirely one with him, knowing him in an unspeakable manner.

Those who hear the gospel have peculiar privileges (vv. 23-24). The full significance of these words will probably never be understood by Christians until the last day. We have probably a most faint idea of the enormous advantages enjoyed by believers who have lived since Christ came into the world. The difference between the knowledge of an Old Testament believer looking forward to Christ and a New Testament believer looking back is the difference of twilight and noon, of winter and summer, of a child and a full-grown man.

For meditation: *We are privileged in knowledge. Do we use our privilege to the full?*

Suggested further reading: Galatians 5:16-26

Here we have a direct practical exhortation: 'If ye really love me, prove your love not by weeping and lamenting at my departure, but by striving to do my will when I am gone. Doing, and not crying, is the best proof of love.' The commandments here mentioned must include all the Lord's moral teaching while on earth and specially such rules and laws as he had laid down in the Sermon on the Mount.

In this verse our Lord had in view the disposition of his disciples to give way to grief and distress at his leaving them and to forget that the true test of love was not useless and barren lamentation, but practical obedience to their Master's commands.

Let us notice how our Lord speaks of 'my commandments'. We never read of Moses or any other servant of God using such an expression. It is the language of one who was one with God the Father and had power to lay down laws and make statutes for his church.

Our Lord says, 'I will pray the Father, and he shall give you another Comforter … even the Spirit of truth.'

This is the first time that the Holy Ghost is mentioned as Christ's special gift to his people. Of course, we are not to suppose that he did not dwell in the hearts of all the Old Testament saints.

No one ever served God acceptably, from Abel downwards, without the grace of the Holy Ghost. John the Baptist was 'filled' with him. But he was given with peculiar influence and power to believers when the New Testament dispensation came in and this is the special promise of the passage before us.

It can only mean that he shall come with more fulness, influence, grace and manifestation than he did before.

One principal point is the mention of all the three persons in the blessed Trinity, the Son praying, the Father giving, the Spirit comforting.

For meditation: *We are not only commanded to obey; we are also given the Holy Spirit to equip us to obey.*

Suggested further reading: Acts 16:25-34

This solemn question that was addressed to our Lord (v. 25) was evidently not from a correct motive. He only asked the question to tempt the Lord and to provoke him to say something on which his enemies might lay hold. Yet the question he propounded was undoubtedly one of the deepest importance.

It is a question which deserves the principal attention of every man, woman and child on earth. We are all sinners — dying sinners, and sinners going to be judged after death. The questions that all people should put to themselves, and never rest till they find an answer, are 'How shall our sins be pardoned? With what shall we come before God? How shall we escape the damnation of hell? Where shall we flee from the wrath to come? What must we do to be saved?'

The question of this man is one that few care to consider. Thousands are constantly enquiring, 'What shall we eat? What shall we drink? How shall we be clothed? How can we get money? How can we enjoy ourselves? How can we prosper in the world?' Few, very few, will ever give a moment's thought to the salvation of their souls. They hate the subject. It makes them uncomfortable. They turn from it and put it away. But our Lord's saying remains faithful and true (Matt. 7:13). Let us not be ashamed of putting the lawyer's question to our own souls.

Our Lord places high honour on the Bible as the rule of faith and practice to which the lawyer is to turn (v. 26). He does not say that he should turn to the Jewish church, or the scribes, Pharisees and priests, or the tradition of the elders. He takes a far simpler course, sending his questioner to the Old Testament.

The principle contained in these words is one of the foundation principles of Christianity. Let the Bible, the whole Bible and nothing but the Bible, be the rule of our faith and practice. It matters nothing how beautiful and clever sermons or religious books may appear. Are they in the smallest degree contrary to Scripture? Then they are rubbish and poison. The Scripture is the rule, gauge and measure of religious truth.

For meditation: *Scripture provides all we need to know for salvation and sanctification. How are we using this bountiful provision?*

Suggested further reading: 1 John 1:5 - 2:1

The word 'Comforter' is the same that is translated 'Advocate' and applied to Christ himself in 1 John 2:1. This word aptly expresses the office of the Spirit as pleading our cause and making intercession for the saints and helping them in prayer and preaching (see Rom. 8:26; Matt. 10:19-20).

The Holy Ghost is spoken of as 'a person'. To apply the language before us to a mere influence or inward feeling is an unreasonable strain of words.

We should never speak of him as a mere 'influence', or dishonour him by calling him 'it'.

The Holy Ghost is given to the church of the elect, 'to abide with them' until Christ comes the second time. He is meant to supply all the needs of believers and to fill up all that is wanting while Christ's visible presence is removed. He is sent to abide with and help them until Christ returns.

The Holy Ghost is called 'the Spirit of truth'. It is his special office to apply truth to the hearts of Christians, to guide them into all truth and to sanctify them by the truth.

The Holy Ghost is said to be one whom 'the world cannot receive and does not know'. His operations are in the strongest sense foolishness to the natural man. The inward feelings of conviction, repentance, faith, hope, fear and love, which he always produces, are precisely that part of religion which the world cannot understand.

The Holy Ghost is said to 'dwell in' believers and to be known of them. They know the feelings that he creates and the fruits that he produces, though they may not be able to explain them, or see at first whence they come. But they all are what they are — new men, new creatures, light and salt in the earth, compared to the worldly — by the indwelling of the Holy Ghost.

Let us never rest till we feel and know that he dwells in us. 'If any man have not the Spirit of Christ, he is none of his' (Rom. 8:9).

For meditation: *Is the fruit of the Spirit in evidence in your life?* (Gal. 5:22-23).

Suggested further reading: 1 John 4:7-21

The Jews in our Lord's time possessed a clear knowledge of their duty to God and man. The lawyer's reply to our Lord (v. 27) was well spoken. A clearer description of daily practical duty could not be given by the most thoroughly instructed Christian in the present day. Let this not be forgotten.

The words of the lawyer are very instructive in two points of view. They throw a strong light on two subjects about which many mistakes abound. For one thing, they show how great were the privileges of religious knowledge which the Jews enjoyed under the Old Testament compared to the heathen world. A nation which possessed such principles of duty as those now before us was immeasurably in advance of Greece and Rome. For another thing, the lawyer's words show us how much clear head-knowledge a person may possess while his heart is full of wickedness. Here is a man who talks of loving God with all his soul and loving his neighbour as himself, while he is actually tempting Christ and trying to do him harm, and while he is anxious to justify himself and make himself out to be a charitable man! Let us ever beware of this kind of religion. Clear knowledge in the head, when accompanied by determined impenitence of heart, is a most dangerous state of soul. Our Lord blesses doing, not knowing (John 13:17).

Let us not forget to apply the high standard of duty which it contains to our own heart and to prove our own selves. Do we love God with all our heart, and soul, and mind, and strength? Do we love our neighbour as ourselves? Where is the person that could say with perfect truth, 'I do'? Where is the man that ought not to lay his hand on his mouth when he hears these questions? Truly we are all guilty in this matter! The best of us, however holy we may be, comes far short of perfection. We are taught our need of Christ's blood and righteousness. Let us seek grace to make these principles rule in our lives.

For meditation: *In difficult days it is our love that determines whether we stand by someone. Will your love for God cause you to stand or fall in days of persecution?*

Suggested further reading: Titus 2:11-15

Now what is the 'coming' here spoken of? It is only fair to say that this is a disputed point among Christians. Many refer it to our Lord's coming to his disciples after his resurrection. Many refer it to his invisible coming into the hearts of his people by the grace of the Holy Spirit. Many refer it to his coming by the outpouring of the Holy Ghost on the Day of Pentecost. It may well be doubted, however, whether any one of these three views conveys the full meaning of our Lord's words: 'I will come.'

The true sense of the expression appears to be the second personal coming of Christ at the end of the world. It is a wide, broad, sweeping promise, intended for all believers, in every age, and not for the apostles alone: 'I will not stay always in heaven. I will one day come back to you.' It is like the message which the angels brought to the disciples after the ascension: 'This same Jesus shall come in like manner as ye have seen him go' (Acts 1:11). It is like the last promise which winds up the book of Revelation: 'Surely I come quickly' (Rev. 22:20). Just in the same way, the parting consolation held out to believers the night before the crucifixion is a personal return: 'I will come.'

Let us settle it in our minds that all believers are comparatively 'orphans' and children in their minority, until the second advent. Our best things are yet to come. Faith has yet to be exchanged for sight and hope for certainty. Our peace and joy are at present very imperfect. They are as nothing to what we shall have when Christ returns. For the return let us look and long and pray. Let us place it in the forefront of all our doctrinal system, next to the atoning death and the interceding life of our Lord. The highest style of Christians are the men who look for and love the Lord's appearing (2 Tim. 4:8).

For meditation: *'Absence makes the heart grow fonder.' Does each year of waiting for our Lord's second coming make him dearer to you?*

Suggested further reading: James 2:14-26

How rare and uncommon is true brotherly love! This is a lesson which stands out prominently on the face of the narrative before our eyes. Our Lord tells us of a traveller who fell among thieves and was left naked, wounded and half dead on the road. He then tells us of a priest and a Levite who, one after the other, came travelling that way, saw the poor wounded man, but gave him no help. Both were men who from their office and profession ought to have been ready and willing to do good to one in distress. But both in succession were too selfish or too unfeeling to offer the slightest assistance. They doubtless reasoned with themselves that they knew nothing of the wounded traveller, that he had perhaps got into trouble by his own misconduct, that they had no time to stop to help him and that they had enough to do to mind their own business without troubling themselves with strangers. And the result was that, one after another, they both passed by on the other side.

We have in this striking description an exact picture of what is continually going on in the world. Selfishness is the leading characteristic of the great majority of mankind. That cheap charity that costs no more than a trifling subscription or contribution is common enough. But that self-sacrificing kindness of heart which cares not what trouble is entailed, so long as good can be done, is a grace which is rarely met with. There are still thousands in trouble who can find no friend or helper. And there are still hundreds of 'priests and Levites' who see them, but pass by on the other side.

Let us beware of expecting much from the kindness of man. If we do, we shall certainly be disappointed. The longer we live, the more clearly we see that few people care for others except from interested motives, and that unselfish, disinterested, pure brotherly love is as scarce as diamonds and rubies. How thankful we ought to be that the Lord Jesus Christ is not like man! His kindness and love are unfailing. He never disappoints any of his friends.

For meditation: *The institutionalized charity of the welfare state cannot replace the personal love of an interested person.*

Suggested further reading: Colossians 3:1-4

Christ's life secures the life of his believing people. He says, 'Because I live ye shall live also.' There is a mysterious and indissoluble union between Christ and every true Christian. The man that is once joined to him by faith is as closely united as a member of the body is united to the head. So long as Christ, his Head, lives, so long he will live. He cannot die unless Christ can be plucked from heaven and Christ's life destroyed. But this, since Christ is very God, is totally impossible! 'Christ being raised from the dead, dieth no more: death hath no more dominion over him' (Rom. 6:9). That which is divine, in the very nature of things, cannot die.

Christ's life secures the continuance of spiritual life to his people. They shall not fall away. They shall persevere unto the end. The divine nature of which they are partakers shall not perish. The incorruptible seed within them shall not be destroyed by the devil and the world. Weak as they are in themselves, they are closely knit to an immortal Head and not one member of his mystical body shall ever perish.

Christ's life secures the resurrection life of his people. Just as he rose again from the grave, because death could not hold him one moment beyond the appointed time, so shall all his believing members rise again in the day when he calls them from the tomb. The victory that Jesus won, when he rolled the stone away and came forth from the tomb, was a victory not only for himself, but for his people. If the Head rose, much more shall the members.

Truths like these ought to be often pondered by true Christians. The careless world knows little of a believer's privileges. It sees little but the outside of him. It does not understand the secret of his present strength and of his strong hope of good things to come. And what is that secret? Invisible union with an invisible Saviour in heaven! Each child of God is invisibly linked to the throne of the Rock of Ages. When that throne can be shaken, and not till then, we may despair. But Christ lives and we shall live also.

For meditation: *The believer is secure as long as Christ lives.*

Suggested further reading: Acts 9:36-42

The only person who helped the wounded traveller of whom we are reading was a certain Samaritan. This man was one of a nation who had 'no dealings' with the Jews (John 4:9). He might have excused himself by saying that the road from Jerusalem to Jericho was through Jewish territory and that cases of distress ought to be dealt with by the Jews. But he does nothing of the sort. He sees a man stripped of his clothes and lying half dead. He asks no questions but at once has compassion on him. He makes no difficulties but at once gives aid. Our Lord requires his example to be followed (v. 37).

Now if these words mean anything, a Christian ought to be ready to show kindness and brotherly love to everyone that is in need. Our kindness must not merely extend to our families, friends and relations. We must love all men and be kind to all, whenever occasion requires. We must beware of an excessive strictness in scrutinizing the past lives of those who need our aid. Are they in real trouble? Are they in real distress? Do they really want help? Then according to the teaching of this parable we ought to be ready to assist them. We should regard the whole world as our parish and the whole race of mankind as our neighbours. We should seek to be the friend of everyone who is oppressed, or neglected, or afflicted, or sick, or in prison, or poor, or an orphan, or a heathen, or starving, or dying. We should exhibit such worldwide friendship, no doubt, wisely, discreetly and with good sense, but of such friendship we need never be ashamed. The ungodly may sneer at it as extravagance and fanaticism. But we need not mind that. To be friendly to all men in this way is to show something of the mind that was in Christ.

How few Christians seem to remember that such a parable was ever written! What an enormous amount of stinginess, meanness, ill-nature and suspicion there is to be seen in the church! How seldom we see a man who is really kind, feeling, generous, liberal and good-natured except to himself and his children!

For meditation: *What difference do your good works make to the non-Christian world around you?*

Suggested further reading: 1 Corinthians 13:8-12

Full and perfect knowledge of divine things will never be attained by believers until the second advent. Our Lord says, 'At that day,' the day of his coming, 'ye shall know that I am in my Father, and ye in me, and I in you.'

The best of saints knows but little so long as he is in the body. The fall of our father Adam has corrupted our understandings, as well as our consciences, hearts and wills. Even after conversion we see through a glass darkly and on no point do we see so dimly as on the nature of our own union with Christ and the Father. These are matters in which we must be content to believe humbly and like little children, to receive on trust the things which we cannot explain.

But it is a blessed and cheering thought that when Christ comes again, the remains of ignorance shall be rolled away. Raised from the dead, freed from the darkness of this world, no longer tempted by the devil and tried by the flesh, believers shall see as they have been seen and know as they have been known. We shall have light enough one day. What we know not now, we shall know hereafter.

Let us rest our souls on this comfortable thought, when we see the mournful divisions which rend the church of Christ. Let us remember that a large portion of them arise from ignorance. We know in part and therefore misunderstand one another. A day comes when Lutherans shall no longer wrangle with Zwinglians, nor Calvinist with Arminian, nor churchman with dissenter. That day is the day of Christ's second coming. Then and then only will the promise receive its complete fulfilment: 'At that day ye shall know.'

For meditation: *The most knowledgeable Christian on earth is still only in the nursery school of knowledge.*

Suggested further reading: 1 John 3:11-18

We are told in this parable in what manner and to what extent we are
to show kindness and love to others. We are told that the Samaritan's compassion towards the wounded traveller was not confined
to feelings and passive impressions. He took much trouble to give
him help. He acted as well as felt. He spared no pains and expense
in befriending him. Stranger as the man was, he went to him, bound
up his wounds, set him on his own beast, brought him to an inn and
took care of him. He also provided for his care in the future (v. 35).
Our Lord calls us to follow this example (v. 37).

This parable teaches us that the kindness of a Christian towards
others should not be in word and in tongue only but in deed and in
truth. His love should be a practical love, a love which entails on
himself sacrifice and self-denial, both in money, time and trouble.
His love should be seen not merely in his talking but his acting, not
merely in his profession but in his practice. He should think it no
misspent time to work as hard in doing good to those who need help
as others work in trying to get money. He should not be ashamed to
toil as much to make the misery of this world smaller as those toil
who indulge in their pleasurable sports all day. He should have a
ready ear for every tale of sorrow and a ready hand to help everyone
in affliction so long as he has the power. Such brotherly love the
world may not understand. The returns of gratitude that such love
meets with may be few and small. But to show such brotherly love
is to walk in the steps of Christ and to reduce to practice the parable
of the Good Samaritan.

What are we ourselves? What are we doing, each in his own
sphere, to prove that this mighty parable is one of the rules of our
daily life? What are we doing for the heathen at home and abroad?
What are we doing to help those who are troubled in mind, body and
estate? There are many such in our world all around us. What are
we doing for them? Anything or nothing at all?

For meditation: *Christians are sometimes criticized for being so
heavenly-minded that they are no earthly use. True heavenly-
mindedness is, however, very much involved with the needs of this
world. Are you?*

Suggested further reading: 1 John 1:8 - 2:6

Keeping Christ's commandments is the best test of love to Christ. Burgon observes, 'This amounts to a declaration that the sad hearts and weeping eyes of the apostles would not be accepted by their Lord as any proof of their love. Obedience was the test he chose.'

This is a lesson of vast importance and one that needs continually pressing on the attention of Christians. It is not talking about religion, and talking fluently and well too, but steadily doing Christ's will and walking in Christ's ways, that is the proof of our being true believers. Good feelings and desires are useless if they are not accompanied by action. They may even become mischievous to the soul, induce hardness of conscience and do positive harm. Passive impressions which do not lead to action gradually deaden and paralyse the heart. Living and doing are the only real evidence of grace. Where the Holy Spirit is, there will always be a holy life. A jealous watchfulness over tempers, words and deeds, a constant endeavour to live by the rule of the Sermon on the Mount — this is the best proof that we love Christ.

Of course, such maxims as these must not be wrested and misunderstood. We are not to suppose for a moment that 'keeping Christ's commandments' can save us. Our best works are full of imperfection. When we have done all we can, we are feeble and unprofitable servants. 'By grace are ye saved through faith ... not of works' (Eph. 2:8). But while we hold one class of truths, we must not forget another. Faith in the blood of Christ must always be attended by loving obedience to the will of Christ. What the Master has joined together, the disciple must not put asunder. Do we profess to love Christ? Then let us show it by our lives. The apostle who said, 'Thou knowest that I love thee!' received the charge: 'Feed my lambs.' That meant, 'Do something. Be useful; follow my example' (John 21:17).

For meditation: *It takes little effort to talk about religion, but to live it is another matter.*

Suggested further reading: Matthew 6:25-33

What a snare to our souls the cares of the world may be if allowed to take up too much attention! It is plain from the passage before us that Martha allowed her concern to provide a suitable meal for the Lord to carry her away. Her excessive zeal for temporal provisions made her forget for a time her zeal for her soul (v. 40). By and by her conscience pricked her when she found herself alone serving tables and saw her sister sitting at Jesus' feet and hearing his Word. Under the pressure of a conscience ill at ease her temper became ruffled and sin within her broke out into open complaint (v. 40). In so saying this holy woman sadly forgot what she was and to whom she was speaking. She brought down upon herself a solemn rebuke and had to learn a lesson which probably made a lasting impression.

The fault of Martha should be a perpetual warning to all Christians. If we desire to grow in grace and to enjoy soul prosperity we must beware of the cares of the world. Except we watch and pray they will insensibly eat up our spirituality and bring leanness on our souls. It is not open sin or flagrant breaches of God's commandments alone that lead men to eternal ruin. It is far more frequently an excessive attention with things lawful in themselves. Our families, our business, our daily work, our household affairs, our socializing — all, all may become snares to our hearts and may draw us away from God. We may go down to the pit of hell from the very midst of lawful things.

Let us take heed to ourselves in this matter. If we love life we must hold the things of this world with a very loose hand and beware of allowing anything to have the first place in our hearts, excepting God. Let us mentally write 'poison' on all temporal good things. Used in moderation they are blessings for which we ought to be thankful. Permitted to fill our minds and trample upon holy things, they become a curse. Profits and pleasures are dearly purchased if in order to obtain them we thrust aside eternity from our thoughts, abridge our Bible readings, become careless hearers of the gospel and shorten our prayers.

For meditation: *Those who are too busy for God in life are never too busy to meet him in judgement.*

Suggested further reading: Romans 9:14-26

There is a special love of God the Father which is peculiarly set on believers, over and above the general love of pity and compassion with which he regards all mankind. In the highest sense God is a 'Father' to none but those who love Christ.

Verse 21 is another encouragement to the man who strives to keep Christ's commandments. Christ will specially love that man and will give him special manifestations of his grace and favour, invisibly and spiritually. He shall feel and know in his own heart comforts and joys that wicked men and inconsistent professors know nothing of. That the 'manifesting' of himself here spoken of is a purely unseen and spiritual thing is self-evident. It is one of those things which can only be known by experience and is only known by holy and consistent Christians.

We should carefully observe here that Christ does more for the comfort of some of his people than he does for others. Those who follow Christ most closely and obediently will always follow him most comfortably and feel most of his inward presence. It is one thing, as St John says, to know Christ, another to know that we know him (1 John 2:3).

In verse 24 the same great principle already taught is laid down again from the negative side. Where there is no obedience to Christ, there is no love. Nothing can be more plain than our Lord's repeated warnings that practical obedience, keeping his commandments and sayings, doing his will, is the only sure test of love to him. Without this obedience, profession, talk, knowledge, churchmanship, yea, even feeling, conviction, weeping and crying are all worthless things.

Verse 24 is to remind the disciples of the authority and dignity of our Lord's sayings and commandments. They are not his words only, but his Father's. He that despises them despises the Father and he that honours them by obedience honours the Father.

For meditation: *It is a believer's privilege to say, 'He loved me'* (Gal. 2:20).

Suggested further reading: 2 Corinthians 4:10 - 5:1

Like the wise physician who sees the disease which is preying on his client and applies the remedy, our Lord gives a solemn rebuke to his servant Martha (v. 41). He told her that one thing was needful (v. 42). How true that saying! The longer we live in the world, the more true it will appear. The nearer we come to the grave, the more thoroughly we shall assent to it. Health, money, lands, rank, prosperity are all well in their way, but they cannot be called needful. Without them thousands are happy in the world and reach the world to come. The 'many things' which men and women are really struggling for are not really necessities. The grace of God which brings salvation is the one thing needful. In earthly trials and persecutions let us remember that if Christ is ours we have all and abound.

Our Lord highly commended Mary's choice (v. 42). His words have a meaning for all Christ's believing people in every part of the world. They were meant to encourage all true Christians to be single-eyed and wholehearted, to follow the Lord fully and walk closely with God, to make soul business immeasurably their first business, and to think comparatively little of the things of this world.

The true Christian's portion is the grace of God. It is the only portion that really deserves the name of 'good'. It is the only good thing which is substantial, satisfying, real and lasting. It is good in sickness and good in health, good in youth and good in old age, good in adversity and good in prosperity, good in life and good in death, good in time and good in eternity. No circumstance and no position can be imagined in which it is not good for man to have the grace of God.

The true Christian's possession shall never be taken from him. He alone, of all mankind, shall never be stripped of his inheritance. Kings must one day leave their palaces and rich men their money and lands. But the poorest saint on earth has a treasure of which he will never be deprived. The grace of God goes to the grave and is resurrected with him.

For meditation: *What good will it be for a man if he gains the whole world, yet forfeits his soul? Or what can a man give in exchange for his soul?* (Matt. 16:26).

Suggested further reading: Genesis 22:15-18

There are special comforts laid up for those who love Christ and prove it by keeping his words. This, at any rate, seems the general sense of our Lord's language: 'My Father will love him and we will come unto him and make our abode with him.'

The full meaning of this promise, no doubt, is a deep thing. We have no line to fathom it. It is a thing which no man can understand except he that receives and experiences it. But we need not shrink from believing that eminent holiness brings eminent comfort with it and that no man has such sensible enjoyment of his religion as the man who, like Enoch and Abraham, walks closely with God. There is more of heaven on earth to be obtained than most Christians are aware of. 'The secret of the Lord is with them that fear him, and he will show them his covenant.' 'If any man hear my voice and open the door, I will come in to him, and sup with him, and he with me' (Ps. 25:14; Rev. 3:20). Promises like these, we may be sure, mean something, and were not written in vain.

How is it, people often ask, that so many professing believers have so little happiness in their religion? How is it that so many know little of 'joy and peace in believing' and go mourning and heavy-hearted towards heaven? The answer to these questions is a sorrowful one, but it must be given. Few believers attend as strictly as they should to Christ's practical sayings and words. There is far too much loose and careless obedience to Christ's commandments. There is far too much forgetfulness that, while good works cannot justify us, they are not to be despised. Let these things sink down into our hearts. If we want to be eminently happy, we must strive to be eminently holy.

Let us note the condescension of the Father and the Son and the high privileges of a believer. No matter how poor and lowly a man may be, if he has faith and grace, he has the best of company and friends. Christ and the Father dwell in his heart and he is never alone and cannot be poor. He is the temple of Father, Son and Holy Ghost.

For meditation: *Does God bless you because you have obeyed?* (Gen. 22:16).

Suggested further reading: Psalm 122

Sickness was no excuse with this woman for tarrying from God's house. In spite of suffering and infirmity she found her way to the place where the day and the Word were honoured and where the people of God met together. And truly she was blessed in her deed! She found a rich reward in all her pains. She came sorrowing and went home rejoicing! The conduct of this suffering Jewess may well put to shame many a strong and healthy professing Christian. How many in the full enjoyment of bodily vigour allow the most frivolous excuses to keep them away from the house of God! How many think it a great matter if they attend the public worship of God once on Sunday and regard a second attendance as a needless excess of zeal akin to fanaticism! How few know anything of David's spirit! (Ps. 122:1). Yet if we cannot enjoy a few hours in God's service once a week in this world it is plain that we could not enjoy an eternity in his service in the world to come. Too many have no heart for God's service.

What almighty power our Lord has! With Christ nothing is impossible. This healing can provide comfort to sin-sick souls. Christ can soften hearts which seem as hard as the millstone. He can bend stubborn wills which have long been set on self-pleasing, sin and the world. He can create, transform, renew, break down, build and quicken with irresistible power. There are no incurable cases with Christ. Let us never despair about the salvation of others for as long as we live. Let us name them before the Lord day and night and cry to him on their behalf. Let us have Job's belief (Job 42:2).

Our Lord defended the right observance of the sabbath day. The criticism of the synagogue ruler brought down his sharp rebuke (vv. 14-15). If it was allowable to tend to the wants of beasts on the sabbath, how much more to human creatures! Works of necessity and mercy were not prohibited on the sabbath. The sabbath was made for man's benefit, not his hurt.

For meditation: *Do you hate those times when you are prevented from being with God's people in the worship of God? If not, why not?*

Suggested further reading: 1 Corinthians 2:9-15

Let us note how distinctly the Holy Spirit is spoken of here as a person and not an influence. Let us note how the Father sends the Spirit, but also sends him in Christ's name and with a special reference to Christ's work.

One part of the Holy Ghost's work is to teach and to bring things to remembrance. It is written: 'The Comforter shall teach you all things, and bring all things to your remembrance.'

To confine this promise to the eleven apostles, as some do, seems a narrow and unsatisfactory mode of interpreting Scripture. It appears to reach far beyond the Day of Pentecost and the gift of writing inspired books of God's holy Word. It is safer, wiser and more consistent with the whole tone of our Lord's last discourse to regard the promise as the common property of all believers, in every age of the world. Our Lord knows the ignorance and forgetfulness of our nature in spiritual things. He graciously declares that when he leaves the world, his people shall have a Teacher and Remembrancer.

Are we sensible of spiritual ignorance? Do we feel that at best we know in part and see in part? Do we desire to understand more clearly the doctrines of the gospel? Let us pray daily for the help of the 'teaching' Spirit. It is his office to illuminate the soul, to open the eyes of the understanding and to guide us into all truth. He can make dark places light and rough places smooth.

Do we find our memory of spiritual things defective? Do we complain that, though we read and hear, we seem to lose as fast as we gain? Let us pray daily for the help of the Holy Ghost. He can bring things to our remembrance. He can make us remember 'old things and new'. He can keep in our minds the whole system of truth and duty and make us ready for every good word and work.

For meditation: *Are you confident of your own understanding of Scripture, or do you seek God's help?*

Suggested further reading: Isaiah 55:1-5

We do not know who the enquirer was. He may have been a self-righteous Jew trained to believe that there was no hope for the uncircumcised and no salvation for any but the children of Abraham. He may have been an idle trifler with religion who was ever wasting his time on curious and speculative questions. In any case, we must all feel that he asked a question of deep and momentous importance.

He that desires to know the number of the saved in this present dispensation need only turn to the Bible and his curiosity will be satisfied. The Sermon on the Mount gives the answer (Matt. 7:14). The world around him will teach a man that the ways of many are not the ways of the Word of God and that few are saved. This is an awful state of affairs which our souls naturally turn away from. But Scripture and facts combine to shut us up to it. Salvation to the uttermost is offered to men. All things are ready on God's part. Christ is willing to receive sinners; but sinners are not willing to come to Christ. And hence few are saved.

Our Lord gave a striking exhortation in response to the question. He thought it not good to gratify curiosity with a direct reply. He chose rather to press home on him, and all around him, their own immediate duty. In minding their own souls they would soon find the question answered. In striving to enter in at the strait gate they would soon find whether the saved were many or few.

Whatever others may do in religion, the Lord would have us know that our duty is clear. We are to wait for nobody. We are not to enquire what other people are doing and whether many of our relatives and friends are serving Christ. The unbelief and indecision of others will be no excuse at the last day. We must never follow a multitude to do evil. If we go to heaven alone we must resolve by God's grace to go. We are responsible for exertion. We are not to sit still in sin and worldliness waiting for the grace of God. We are to draw near to him. The command is express and unmistakable (v. 24).

For meditation: *To love your neighbour as yourself you must first love yourself. To be concerned for your neighbour's salvation while neglecting your own is crass stupidity and sin.*

Suggested further reading: Isaiah 26:3-12

Let us notice Christ's last legacy to his people. We find him saying, 'Peace I leave with you, my peace I give unto you; not as the world giveth give I unto you.'

Peace is Christ's peculiar gift — not money, not worldly ease, not temporal prosperity. These are at best very questionable possessions. They often do more harm than good to the soul. They act as clogs and weights to our spiritual life. Inward peace of conscience, arising from a sense of pardoned sin and reconciliation with God, is a far greater blessing. This peace is the property of all believers, whether high or low, rich or poor.

The peace which Christ gives he calls 'my peace'. It is specially his own to give, because he bought it by his own blood, purchased it by his own substitution and is appointed by the Father to dispense it to a perishing world. Just as Joseph was sealed and commissioned to give corn to the starving Egyptians, so is Christ specially commissioned, in the counsels of the eternal Trinity, to give peace to mankind.

The peace that Christ gives is not given as the world gives. What he gives, the world cannot give at all, and what he gives is given neither unwillingly, nor sparingly, nor for a little time. Christ is far more willing to give than the world is to receive. What he gives, he gives to all eternity and never takes away. He is ready to give abundantly above all that we can ask or think. 'Open thy mouth wide,' he says, 'and I will fill it' (Ps. 81:10).

Who can wonder that a legacy like this should be backed by the renewed emphatic charge: 'Let not your heart be troubled, neither let it be afraid'? There is nothing lacking on Christ's part for our comfort, if we will only come to him, believe and receive. The chief of sinners has no cause to be afraid. If we will only look to the one true Saviour, there is medicine for every trouble of heart. Half our doubts and fears arise from dim perceptions of the real nature of Christ's gospel.

For meditation: *The condition attached to the promise of Philippians 4:7 is found in Philippians 4:6.*

Suggested further reading: Matthew 25:1-13

Here we have a description of a day of awful solemnity (v. 25). The Day of Judgement and the Second Coming of Christ are described. A day is coming on the earth when the long-suffering of God towards sinners shall have an end. The door of mercy, which has been open so long, shall be shut. The throne of grace shall be removed and the throne of judgement shall be set up in its place. All that are found impenitent and unbelieving shall be thrust out for ever from God's presence. Men shall find that the Lamb does have wrath (Rev. 6:16).

A day is coming when believers in Christ shall receive a full reward. The Master of the great house in heaven shall call his servants together and give to each a crown of glory that does not fade. They shall sit down with the patriarchs and rest for ever from warfare and work. They shall be shut in with Christ, saints and angels in the kingdom of God, and sin, death, sorrow, the world and the devil shall be eternally shut out.

When on the day of his second coming many desire to enter they will find no admission (v. 25). Their earnest pleas will be unavailing (vv. 26-27). Religious profession and formal knowledge of Christ will save none who have served sin and the world.

This prophecy reveals that men may see what is right when it is too late for them to be saved. There is a time coming when many will repent too late and believe too late, sorrow for sin too late and begin to pray too late, be anxious about salvation too late and long for heaven too late. Myriads shall wake up in another world and be convinced of truths which on earth they refused to believe. Earth is the only place in God's creation where there is any infidelity. Hell itself is nothing but truth known too late.

Let us set a right estimate on things around us. Money, pleasure, rank and greatness occupy the first place now in the world. Praying, believing, holy living and acquaintance with Christ are despised and ridiculed and held very cheap. But there is a change coming one day! Let us be prepared for that change.

For meditation: *Part of the arrogance of man and the delusion of Satan is to think that he can come to God tomorrow, but for so many tomorrow never comes.*

Suggested further reading: Philippians 2:5-11

Verse 28 presents two difficulties.

1. What did our Lord mean by saying, 'My Father is greater than I'? I answer that the words of the Athanasian Creed contain the best reply. Christ is no doubt 'equal to the Father as touching his Godhead and inferior to the Father as touching his manhood'. The enemies of the doctrine of Christ's divinity forget that Trinitarians maintain the humanity of Christ as strongly as his divinity and never shrink from admitting that, while Christ as God is equal to the Father, as man he is inferior to the Father. And it is in this sense that he here says truly, 'My Father is greater than I.' It was specially spoken of the time of his incarnation and humiliation. When the Word was 'made flesh', he took on him 'the form of a servant' (Phil. 2:7). This was temporary inferiority.

2. But what did our Lord mean by saying that the disciples ought to rejoice at his going to the Father *because* 'The Father is greater than I'? This is a hard knot to untie and has received different solutions. My own impression is that the meaning must be something of this kind: 'Ye ought to rejoice at my going to the Father, because in so going I shall resume that glory which I had with him before the world was and which I laid aside on becoming incarnate. Here on earth, during the thirty-three years of my incarnation, I have been in the form of a servant and dwelling in a body as one inferior to my Father. In leaving this world I go to take up again the equal glory and honour which I had with the Father before my incarnation and to lay aside the position of inferiority in which I have tabernacled here below. I go to be once more almighty with the Almighty and to share once more my Father's throne, as a person in that Trinity in which "none is afore or after other, none is greater or less than another". I go to receive the kingdom and honour which in eternal counsels the Father has prepared for the Son, and on this account, if you really knew and understood all, you would rejoice at my going.'

For meditation: *'For you know the grace of our Lord Jesus Christ, that though he was rich, yet for your sakes he became poor, so that you through his poverty might become rich'* (2 Cor. 8:9).

Suggested further reading: Isaiah 46:8-13

Our Lord teaches us how entirely our times are in God's hands by his reply to those who would encourage him to depart because Herod would kill him. His time was not yet come for leaving the world. His work was not yet finished. Until that time came it was not in the power of Herod to hurt him.

These words demand the attention of all true Christians. We do well to copy the frame of mind exhibited. Our Lord knew what was ahead in a way that we cannot. Nevertheless the lesson stands. We ought to possess a spirit of calm, unshaken confidence about things to come. We should study to have a heart not afraid of evil tidings, but quiet, steady and trusting in the Lord (Ps. 112:7).

We are not intended to be idle fatalists, like the Moslems, or cold, unfeeling statues like the Stoics. We are not to neglect the use of means or to omit all prudent provision for an unseen future. To neglect means is fanaticism, not faith. But still, when we have done all, we should remember that duties are ours and events are God's. We should therefore endeavour to leave things to come in God's hands and not to be over-anxious about health, family, money or plans. To cultivate this frame of mind would add immensely to our peace. How many of our cares and fears are about things that never come to pass!

The very hairs of believers' heads are numbered. Their steps are ordered by the Lord. All things are working together for their good. When they are afflicted it is for their profit. When they are sick it is for some wise purpose. All things are said to be theirs — life, death, things present and things to come (Matt. 10:30; Ps. 37:23; Rom. 8:28; Heb. 12:10; John 11:4; 1 Cor. 3:22). There is no such thing as chance, luck or accident in the life of a believer. There is one thing needful in order to make a believer calm, quiet, unruffled and undisturbed in every circumstance. That one thing is faith in active exercise. For such faith let us pray.

For meditation: *While some of us are more temperamentally disposed to worry, faith does not depend on temperament.*

Suggested further reading: 1 Peter 1:15-19

Let us observe Christ's perfect holiness. We find him saying, 'The prince of this world cometh and hath nothing in me.' The meaning of these remarkable words admits of only one interpretation. Our Lord would have his disciples know that Satan, 'the prince of this world', was about to make his last and most violent attack on him. He was mustering all his strength for one more tremendous onset. He was coming up with his utmost malice to try the Second Adam in the Garden of Gethsemane and on the cross of Calvary. But our blessed Master declares, 'He hath nothing in me.' 'There is nothing he can lay hold on. There is no weak and defective point in me. I have kept my Father's commandment and finished the work he gave me to do. Satan, therefore, cannot overthrow me. He can lay nothing to my charge. He cannot condemn me. I shall come forth from the trial more than conqueror.'

Let us mark the difference between Christ and all others who have been born of woman. He is the only one in whom Satan has found 'nothing'. He came to Adam and Eve and found weakness. He came to Noah, Abraham, Moses, David and all the saints and found imperfection. He came to Christ and found 'nothing' at all. He was a Lamb 'without blemish and without spot', a suitable sacrifice for a world of sinners, a suitable Head for a redeemed race.

Let us thank God that we have such a perfect, sinless Saviour, that his righteousness is a perfect righteousness and his life a blameless life. In ourselves and our doings we shall find everything imperfect and if we had no other hope than our own goodness we might well despair. But in Christ we have a perfect, sinless Representative and Substitute. Well may we say, with the triumphant apostle, 'Who shall lay anything to our charge?' (Rom. 8:33). Christ hath died for us and suffered in our stead. In him Satan can find nothing. We are hidden in him. The Father sees us in him, unworthy as we are, and for his sake is well pleased.

For meditation: *'Such a high priest meets our need — one who is holy, blameless, pure, set apart from sinners, exalted above the heavens'* (Heb. 7:26).

Suggested further reading: Ezekiel 33:1-11

Our Lord's language about Jerusalem most forcibly brings out his compassion towards sinners (v. 34). He knew the wickedness of that city. He knew what crimes had been committed there in times past. He knew what was coming on at the time of his crucifixion. Yet he would have gathered her (v. 34).

It grieves the Lord Jesus to see sinners going on in their wickedness (Ezek. 33:11). Let all unconverted people remember this! It is not enough that they grieve godly ministers, friends, neighbours and parents. There is one higher than all these that they grieve by their conduct. They are daily grieving Christ.

The Lord Jesus is willing to save sinners (2 Peter 3:9; 1 Tim. 2:4). This is a mighty principle of the gospel and one which sorely perplexes narrow-minded and shallow theologians. But the Scriptures are clear (v. 34). The will of poor hardened sinners is the cause why they are lost for evermore. Christ would save them, but they will not be saved.

Let the truth before us sink down into our hearts. Let us thoroughly understand that if we die in our sins and go to hell our blood will be upon our own heads. We cannot blame God the Father, Jesus the Redeemer, nor the Holy Spirit the Comforter. The promises of the gospel are wide, broad and general. The readiness of Christ to save sinners is unmistakably declared. If we are lost we have none to find fault with but ourselves (John 5:40).

Let us not be more systematic than Scripture. Our salvation is wholly of God. Let that never be forgotten. None but the elect shall finally be saved. No one will come unless drawn by the Father (John 6:44). But our ruin, if we are lost, will be wholly of ourselves. These two truths are a deep mystery. Our minds are too feeble to understand now. But we shall understand it hereafter. God's sovereignty and man's responsibility shall appear perfectly harmonious one day. In the meantime, whatever we doubt let us never doubt Christ's infinite willingness to save sinners.

For meditation: *Men love to iron out problems, but in dealing with God we must ever remember he is too great for our minds to grasp fully. His ways and thoughts are different to ours* (Isa. 55:8-9).

Suggested further reading: Matthew 11:25-27

Verse 31 is a somewhat dark and obscure passage. The meaning is probably something of this kind: 'I do all I am doing now and go to the cross voluntarily, though innocent, that the world may have full proof that I love the Father who sent me to die, and am willing to go through everything which he has commanded me to go through. Innocent as I am, and without one spot of sin that Satan can lay to my charge, I willingly go forward to the cross, to show how I love the Father's will and am determined to do it by dying for sinners.'

We ought not to leave the closing portion of this wonderful chapter without noticing one striking feature in it. That feature is the singular frequency with which our Lord uses the expression 'my Father' and 'the Father'. In the last five verses we find it four times. In the whole chapter it occurs no fewer than twenty-two times. In this respect the chapter stands alone in the Bible.

The reason of this frequent use of the expression is a deep subject. Perhaps the less we speculate and dogmatize about it the better. Our Lord was one who never spoke a word without a meaning and we need not doubt there was a meaning here. Yet may we not reverently suppose that he desired to leave on the minds of his disciples a strong impression of his entire unity with the Father? Seldom does our Lord lay claim to such high dignity and such power of giving and supplying comfort to his church as in this discourse. Was there not, then, a fitness in his continually reminding his disciples that in all his giving he was one with the Father and did nothing without the Father? This, at any rate, seems a fair conjecture. Let it be taken for what it is worth.

For meditation: *Thoroughness of knowledge is a key to intimacy in relationships.*

Suggested further reading: Daniel 6:1-5

Our Lord accepted the hospitality of those who were not his disciples (v. 1). How did the Lord conduct himself at the Pharisee's table? He first defended the true observance of the sabbath day (vv. 1-6), he then expounded the nature of true humility (vv. 7-11), then explained the character of true hospitality (vv. 12-14) and finally delivered a striking parable to them (vv. 15-24). All this was done in a most wise, calm and dignified manner. His speech was edifying and appropriate (Col. 4:6). The perfection of our Lord's conduct appears on this as on all other occasions. He always said the right thing, at the right time and in the right way. He never forgot for a moment who he was and where he was.

What an example is set for Christians here! Do we go among non-Christians watchfully and prayerfully, with a firm resolution to carry our Master and our Master's business with us? The house from which Christ is deliberately excluded is not the house for us, but where we can carry on conversation with the unconverted we should go. There are two questions we should put to ourselves in reference to this subject: 'Do I in company spend all my time in light and worldly conversation?' and 'Do I endeavour to follow, however feebly, the example of Christ?' So long as we can take Christ with us, we shall come to no harm.

How our Lord was watched by his enemies! (v. 1). They watched for some word or deed on which they could build an accusation, but they found none. Our blessed Lord was ever harmless, holy, undefiled and separate from evil. Perfect indeed must that life have been in which they, his bitterest enemies, could find no flaw, or blemish, or spot, or wrinkle, or any such thing!

Servants of Christ will also be watched. If they make a slip here in word or deed, or act inconsistently, it will not be forgotten. Let us live holy lives before God and men. By God's grace it can be done and we can receive the testimony given to Daniel (Dan. 6:5).

For meditation: *We are so to live that our opponents must make up slander against us if they are to accuse us, because no real accusations can be made to stick* (1 Peter 2:15).

Suggested further reading: Ephesians 5:25-33

The general lesson of each parable is the main thing to be noticed. The minor details must not be tortured and pressed to an excess in order to extract a meaning from them. The mistakes into which Christians have fallen by neglecting this rule are neither few nor small.

We are meant to learn from these verses that the union between Christ and believers is very close. He is 'the Vine' and they are 'the branches'. The union between the branch of a vine and the main stem is the closest that can be conceived. It is the whole secret of the branch's life, strength, vigour, beauty and fertility. Separate from the parent stem, it has no life of its own. The sap and juice that flow from the stem are the origin and maintaining power of all its leaves, buds, blossoms and fruit. Cut off from the stem, it must soon wither and die.

The union between Christ and believers is just as close and just as real. In themselves believers have no life or strength or spiritual power. All that they have of vital religion comes from Christ. They are what they are and feel what they feel and do what they do, because they draw out of Jesus a continual supply of grace, help and ability. Joined to the Lord by faith and united in mysterious union with him by the Spirit, they stand and walk and continue and run the Christian race. But every jot of good about them is drawn from their spiritual Head, Jesus Christ.

The thought before us is both comfortable and instructive. Believers have no cause to despair of their own salvation and to think they will never reach heaven. Let them consider that they are not left to themselves and their own strength. Their root is Christ and all that there is in the root is for the benefit of the branches. Because he lives, they shall live also. Worldly people have no cause to wonder at the continuance and perseverance of believers. Weak as they are in themselves, their Root is in heaven and never dies. 'When I am weak,' said Paul, 'then am I strong' (2 Cor. 12:10).

For meditation: *'But he who unites himself with the Lord is one with him in spirit'* (1 Cor. 6:17).

Suggested further reading: Job 42:1-6

Our Lord asserts the lawfulness of doing works of mercy on the sabbath day (v. 5). The qualification that our Lord puts on the requirements of the fourth commandment is evidently founded on Scripture, reason and common sense. The sabbath was made for man, not man for the sabbath; for his benefit, not for his injury; for his advantage, not for his hurt. The interpretation of God's law respecting the sabbath was never intended to be strained so far as to interfere with charity, kindness and the real needs of human nature.

Our Lord teaches the value of humility in two ways. He advises guests at a wedding to take the lowest place (v. 10) and sets out one of his oft-repeated principles (v. 11). Humility may well be called the queen of Christian graces. To know our own sinfulness and weakness, and to feel our need of Christ, is the very beginning of saving religion. It is a grace which has always been a distinguishing feature in the character of the saints of every age. It is a grace within the reach of every Christian. All have not money to give away. All have not time and opportunities for working directly for Christ. All have not gifts of speech, tact and knowledge in order to do good in the world. But all converted men should labour to adorn the doctrine they profess by humility. If they can do nothing else, they can strive to be humble.

Would we know the root and spring of humility? One word describes it. The root of humility is right knowledge. The man who really knows himself and his own heart, who knows God and the infinite majesty of his holiness, who knows Christ and the price at which he was redeemed — that man will never be a proud man. He will count himself, like Jacob, unworthy of the least of all God's mercies. Like Job he will see his own vileness. Like Paul he will esteem himself the chief of sinners (Gen. 32:10; Job 40:4; 1 Tim. 1:15). Ignorance, nothing but sheer ignorance, of self, of God and of Christ, is the real secret of pride. He is the wise man who knows himself, and he who knows himself will find nothing within him to make him proud.

For meditation: *A sinner saved by grace who is proud is a contradiction in terms.*

Suggested further reading: Matthew 7:15-23

There are false Christians as well as true ones. There are 'branches in the vine' which appear to be joined to the parent stem and yet bear no fruit. There are men and women who appear to be members of Christ and yet will prove finally to have had no vital union with him.

There are myriads of professing Christians in every church whose union with Christ is only outward and formal. Some of them are joined to Christ by baptism and church membership. Some of them go even further than this and are regular communicants and loud talkers about religion. But they all lack the one thing needful. Notwithstanding services and sermons and sacrament, they have no grace in their hearts, no faith, no inward work of the Holy Spirit. They are not one with Christ and Christ in them. Their union with him is only nominal and not real. They have 'a name to live', but in the sight of God they are dead.

Christians of this stamp are aptly represented by branches in a vine which bear no fruit. Useless and unsightly, such branches are only fit to be cut off and burned. They draw nothing out of the parent stem and make no return for the place they occupy. Just so will it be at the last day with false professors and nominal Christians. Their end, except they repent, will be destruction. They will be separated from the company of true believers and cast out, as withered, useless branches, into everlasting fire. They will find at last, whatever they thought in this world, that there is a worm that never dies and a fire that is not quenched.

The fruits of the Spirit are the only satisfactory evidence of a man being a true Christian. The disciple that 'abides in Christ', like a branch abiding in the vine, will always bear fruit. Repentance towards God, faith towards our Lord Jesus Christ, holiness of life and conduct — these are what the New Testament calls 'fruit'. Where these things are wanting, it is vain to talk of possessing dormant grace and spiritual life.

For meditation: *'But the fruit of the Spirit is love, joy, peace, patience, kindness, goodness, faithfulness, gentleness and self-control. Against such things there is no law'* (Gal. 5:22-23).

Suggested further reading: Matthew 25:31-46

Our Lord lays on us the duty of caring for the poor by telling the Pharisee whom not to invite and whom to invite to his feasts (vv. 12-13). The precept contained in these words must evidently be interpreted with considerable limitation. Hospitality to our friends and relatives is not wrong, nor is indiscriminate giving to the poor correct, as other Scriptures show. But when we have said that, we must let this parable teach us its truths. The Lord does place upon us the solemn duty of caring for our poorer brothers, aiding and not neglecting them in times of need.

There are always needy people around us (Deut. 15:11). A little help conferred judiciously upon the poor will often add immensely to their happiness and take away immensely from their worries. That stinginess that condemns all charity to the poor is not in line with the mind of our Lord. His references to Judgement Day have reference to the poor (Matt. 25:42) and the apostolic church had the same concern (Gal. 2:10).

There is a great importance in looking to the resurrection of the dead. The poor cannot repay, but there is a resurrection of repayment (v. 14). There is a resurrection after death. Let this never be forgotten. The life that we live here in the flesh is not all. The visible world around us is not the only world with which we have to do. All is not over when the last breath is drawn and men and women are carried to their long home in the grave. The trumpet shall one day sound and the dead shall be raised: those that have done good to the resurrection of life, and those that have done evil to the resurrection of damnation.

Let us strive to live like men who believe in a resurrection and a life to come and desire to be always ready for another world. So living, we shall look forward to death with calmness. We shall feel that there remains some better portion for us beyond the grave. We shall take patiently all that we bear in this world and wait for all to be rectified one day. The Judge of all the earth shall do right (Gen. 18:25). Are you ready for that day?

For meditation: *A life lived in the light of eternity is a life with new priorities and which is distinctive in an earth-bound world.*

Suggested further reading: Hebrews 12:4-13

God will often increase the holiness of true Christians by his providential dealings with them. 'Every branch,' it is written, 'that beareth fruit, he purgeth it, that it may bear more fruit.'

The meaning of this language is clear and plain. Just as the vine-dresser prunes and cuts back the branches of a fruitful vine, in order to make them more fruitful, so does God purify and sanctify believers by the circumstances of life in which he places them.

Trial, to speak plainly, is the instrument by which our Father in heaven makes Christians more holy. By trial he calls out their passive graces and proves whether they can suffer his will as well as do it. By trial he weans them from the world, draws them to Christ, drives them to the Bible and prayer, shows them their own hearts and makes them humble. This is the process by which he 'purges' them and makes them more fruitful. The lives of the saints in every age are the best and truest comment on the text. Never, hardly, do we find an eminent saint, either in the Old Testament or the New, who was not purified by suffering and, like his Master, a 'man of sorrows'.

Clement of Alexandria and many writers in all ages remark on this verse that the vine branch which is not sharply pruned is peculiarly liable to run to wood and bear no fruit.

Let us learn to be patient in the days of darkness, if we know anything of vital union with Christ. Let us remember the doctrine of the passage before us and not murmur and complain because of trials. Our trials are not meant to do us harm, but good. God chastens us 'for our profit, that we may be partakers of his holiness' (Heb. 12:10). Fruit is the thing that our Master desires to see in us and he will not spare the pruning-knife if he sees we need it. In the last day we shall see that all was well done.

For meditation: *The cleansing of a wound may be painful but it is necessary for health.*

Suggested further reading: John 6:35-56

We do not know who prompted our Lord to teach this parable, but it is far from unlikely that he who made this remark (v. 15) was one of that class of people who wish to go to heaven but never get any further. Our Lord took the opportunity to remind him that men may have the kingdom of God offered to them, may wilfully neglect it and be lost for ever.

God has made a great provision for men's souls (v. 16). The gospel provides a full supply of everything that sinners need in order to be saved. We are all naturally starving, empty, helpless and ready to perish. Forgiveness of all sin, peace with God, justification of the person and sanctification of the heart, grace by the way and glory in the end are the gracious provision which God has prepared for our souls. There is nothing that sin-laden souls could wish for, or weary consciences require, which is not spread before men in rich abundance in Christ. Christ, in one word, is the sum and substance of the great supper. He is so presented to us in his own teaching (John 6:35-36).

The offers and invitations of the gospel are most broad and liberal. The invitation is made (v. 17). There is nothing lacking on God's part for the salvation of man. If man is not saved, the fault is not on God's side. The Father is ready to receive all who come to him by Christ. The Son is ready to cleanse all from their sins who apply to him by faith. The Spirit is ready to come to all who ask for him. There is an infinite willingness in God to save man if only man is willing to be saved.

There is the fullest warrant for sinners to draw near to God by Christ. The word 'Come' is addressed to all without exception. Our Lord speaks to those who are labouring and heavy laden (Matt. 11:28). Our Lord speaks to those who are thirsty (John 7:37). Our Lord speaks to those who are poor and hungry (Isa. 55:1). No man shall ever be able to say he had no encouragement to seek salvation (John 6:37).

For meditation:
There's a way back to God from the dark paths of sin,
There's a door that is open and you may go in
— but will you? Or must our Lord say of you what he said of others? (John 5:40).

Suggested further reading: Hebrews 6:4-12

In verse 5 our Lord gives encouragement to the disciples to keep up the habit of close union with him. This is the secret of bearing 'much fruit' and being an eminently holy and useful Christian. The experience of every age of the church proves the truth of this saying. The greatest saints have always lived nearest to Christ.

Do we not see here that there is a difference in the degrees of fruitfulness to which Christians attain? Is there not a tacit distinction here between 'fruit' and 'much fruit'?

With regard to the closing words of verse 5, the marginal rendering gives our Lord's meaning more completely: 'Severed from me, separate from me, you have no strength and can do nothing. You are lifeless as a branch cut off from the parent stem.'

In verse 6 the consequences of not abiding in Christ, of refusing to live the life of faith in Christ, are here described under a terrible figure. The end of such false professors will be like the end of fruitless and dead branches of a vine. Sooner or later they are cast out of the vineyard as withered, useless things and gathered as firewood to be burned. Such will be the last end of professing Christians who turn their backs on Jesus and bear no fruit to God's glory. They will finally come to the fire that is never quenched in hell.

These are awful words. They seem, however, to apply specially to backsliders and apostates, like Judas Iscariot. There must be about a man some appearance of professed faith in Christ, before he can come to the state described here. Doubtless there are those who seem to depart from grace and to go back from union with Christ, but we need not doubt in such cases that the grace was not real, but seeming, and the union was not true, but fictitious.

For meditation: *'I'm a believer and can live as I like' is the philosophy of the presumptuous, not the words of the assured.*

Suggested further reading: Hebrews 3:7 - 4:2

Many who receive gospel invitations refuse to accept them (v. 18). One trivial excuse followed another. In one point they were all agreed: they would not come.

We have in this part of the parable a vivid picture of the reception which the gospel is continually meeting wherever it is proclaimed. Thousands are continually doing what the parable describes. They are invited to come to Christ and they will not come. It is not ignorance of religion that ruins many men's souls. It is lack of will to use knowledge, or love of this present world. It is not open profligacy that fills hell. It is excessive attention to things which in themselves are lawful. It is not avowed dislike of the gospel which is so much to be feared. It is that procrastinating, excuse-making spirit which is always ready with a reason why Christ cannot be served today. No excuse can justify a man in refusing God's invitation and not coming to Christ.

God earnestly desires the salvation of souls and would have all means used to procure the acceptance of the gospel (vv. 21,23). The meaning of these words can admit of little dispute. They surely justify us in asserting the exceeding love and compassion of God towards sinners. His long-suffering is inexhaustible. If some will not receive the truth he will have others invited in their stead. His pity for the lost is no feigned or imaginary thing. He is infinitely willing to save souls.

Above all, the words justify every preacher and teacher of the gospel in employing all possible means to awaken sinners and turn them from their sins. If they will not come to us in public we must visit them in private. If they will not attend our preaching in the congregation we must be ready to preach from house to house. We must even not be ashamed to use a gentle violence. We must deal with many an unconverted man as one half asleep. We must press the gospel on him again and again. We must deal with him as a man about to commit suicide. Men may sneer at such zeal as fanaticism but we must compel them to come in (v. 23).

For meditation: *Is your soul stirred by a passion for the lost, or is it insensitive and indifferent?*

Suggested further reading: Psalm 91

Our Lord declares, 'If ye abide in me, and my words abide in you, ye shall ask what ye will, and it shall be done unto you.' This is a distinct promise of power and success in prayer. And what does it turn upon? We must 'abide in Christ' and Christ's words must 'abide in us'.

To abide in Christ means to keep up a habit of constant close communion with him, to be always leaning on him, resting on him, pouring out our hearts to him and using him as our Fountain of life and strength, as our chief Companion and best Friend. To have his words abiding in us is to keep his sayings and precepts continually before our memories and minds and to make them the guide of our actions and the rule of our daily conduct and behaviour.

Christians of this stamp, we are told, shall not pray in vain. Whatever they ask they shall obtain, so long as they ask things according to God's mind. No work shall be found too hard and no difficulty insurmountable. Asking they shall receive and seeking they shall find. Such men were Martin Luther, the German Reformer, and our own martyr, Bishop Latimer. Such a man was John Knox, of whom Queen Mary said that she feared his prayers more than an army of twenty thousand men. It is written in a certain place: 'The effectual fervent prayer of a righteous man availeth much' (James 5:16).

Now, why is there so little power of prayer like this in our own time? Simply because there is so little close communion with Christ and so little strict conformity to his will. Men do not 'abide in Christ' and therefore pray in vain. Christ's words do not abide in them, as their standard of practice, and therefore their prayers seem not to be heard. They ask and receive not, because they ask amiss. Let this lesson sink down into our hearts. He that would have answers to his prayers must carefully remember Christ's directions. We must keep up intimate friendship with the great Advocate in heaven, if our petitions are to prosper.

For meditation: *Do you have not because you ask not?* (James 4:2).

Suggested further reading: Matthew 10:37-39

True Christians must be ready if need be to give up everything for Christ's sake (v. 26). Our Lord did not mean us to understand that it is the duty of Christians to hate their relatives. This would have been to contradict the fifth commandment. He only meant that those who follow him must love him with a deeper love than even their nearest and dearest connections, or their own lives. He did not mean that it is an essential part of Christianity to quarrel with our relatives and friends. But he did mean that if the claims of our relatives and friends and the claims of Christ come into collision, the claims of relatives must give way. We must choose rather to displease those we love most upon earth than to displease him who died for us on the cross.

The demand which our Lord makes upon us here is peculiarly stringent and heart-searching. Yet it is a wise and necessary one. Experience shows, both in the church at home and the mission-field abroad, that the greatest foes to a man's soul are sometimes those of his own house. It sometimes happens that the greatest hindrance to an awakened conscience is the opposition of relatives and friends. Ungodly fathers cannot bear to see their sons taking up new views of religion. Worldly mothers are vexed to see their daughters avoiding this world's gaieties. A collision of opinion takes place frequently as soon as grace enters into a family. In such situations the true Christian must be willing to offend his family rather than offend Christ.

It is a heavy cross to disagree with those we love, and especially about spiritual things. But if this cross be laid upon us we must remember that firmness and decision are true kindness. It can never be true love to relatives to do wrong in order to please them. Best of all, firmness accompanied by gentleness and consistency, in the long run of life, often brings its own reward. Thousands of Christians will bless God at the last day that they had relatives and friends who chose to displease them rather than Christ, and so led them to consider their own souls.

For meditation: *We are not to oppose our relatives and friends for our own sakes, to get our own way, but only for Christ's sake, to walk in his way.*

Suggested further reading: 1 John 3:21-24

Our Lord declares, 'Herein is my Father glorified, that ye bear much fruit; so shall ye be my disciples.' The meaning of this promise seems to be that fruitfulness in Christian practice will not only bring glory to God, but will supply the best evidence to our own hearts that we are real disciples of Christ.

Assurance of our own interest in Christ and our consequent eternal safety is one of the highest privileges in religion. To be always doubting and fearing is miserable work. Nothing is worse than suspense in any matter of importance and above all in the matter of our souls. He that would know one of the best receipts for obtaining assurance should diligently study Christ's words now before us. Let him strive to bear much fruit in his life, his habits, his temper, his words and his works. So doing, he shall feel the 'witness of the Spirit' in his heart and give abundant proof that he is a living branch of the true Vine. He shall find inward evidence in his own soul that he is a child of God and shall supply the world with outward evidence that cannot be disputed.

Would we know why so many professing Christians have little comfort in their religion and go fearing and doubting along the road to heaven? The question receives a solution in the saying of our Lord we are now considering. Men are content with a little Christianity and a little fruit of the Spirit and do not labour to be holy in all manner of conversation. They must not wonder if they enjoy little peace, feel little hope and leave behind them little evidence. The fault lies with themselves. God has linked together holiness and happiness and what God has joined together we must not think to put asunder.

The feeling of one eternal person in the Trinity to another person is a thing into which we cannot enter. Yet even such is the love of Christ towards those who believe in him — a vast, wide, deep, unmeasurable love that passeth knowledge and can never be fully comprehended by man (v. 9).

For meditation: *Where there is little real holiness there can be little real happiness.*

Suggested further reading: Hebrews 6:4-12

Those who are thinking of following Christ should be warned to count the cost. This is a lesson intended for the multitudes who followed our Lord without thought and consideration, and was enforced by examples drawn from building (vv. 28-30) and war (vv. 31-32). It is a lesson which will be found useful in every age of the church.

Our Lord did not use this language to discourage men from becoming his disciples or to make the gate of life more narrow than it is. Rather he spoke as he did to prevent men following him lightly and inconsiderately, from mere animal feeling or temporary excitement, who in time of temptation would fall away. He knew that nothing does so much harm to the cause of true religion as backsliding, and nothing causes so much backsliding as enlisting disciples without letting them know what they are taking in hand. He had no desire to swell the number of his disciples by admitting soldiers who would fail in the hour of need. For this reason he raised a warning voice.

Too often people are built up in self-deception and encouraged to think that they are converted when in reality they are not converted at all. Feelings are supposed to be faith. Convictions are supposed to be grace. These things ought not to be so. By all means let us encourage the first beginnings of religion in the soul. But let us never urge people forward without telling them what true Christianity entails. Never let us hide from them the battle and the toil.

In a lesson that is intimately connected with the preceding one our Lord teaches us how miserable is the condition of backsliders and apostates (vv. 34-35). The consequences of neglecting to count the cost, of making a profession of religion and turning back from it, are as salt which has lost its savour and become useless. Such a man can be told nothing he has not heard. He has turned from the only God and Saviour, and is a case well-nigh desperate (Heb. 6:4-6). Let us never be afraid of beginning to serve Christ but, having begun, let us pray for grace to persevere.

For meditation: *Those who turn from the only God and Saviour there is are spiritually shipwrecked because if they will not have the only salvation provided they must perish.*

Suggested further reading: Deuteronomy 8:1-10

Our Lord declares, 'If ye keep my commandments, ye shall abide in my love.' The meaning of this promise is near akin to that of the preceding one. The man who makes conscience of diligently observing Christ's precepts is the man who shall continually enjoy a sense of Christ's love in his soul.

Of course, we must not misunderstand our Lord's words when he speaks of 'keeping his commandments'. There is a sense in which no one can keep them. Our best works are imperfect and defective and when we have done our best we may well cry, 'God be merciful to me a sinner.' Yet we must not run into the other extreme and give way to the lazy idea that we can do nothing at all. By the grace of God we may make Christ's laws our rule of life and show daily that we desire to please him. So doing, our gracious Master will give us a constant sense of his favour and make us feel his face smiling on us, like the sun shining on a fine day. 'The secret of the Lord is with them that fear him and he will show them his covenant' (Ps. 25:14).

Lessons like these may be legal to some and bring down much blame on those who advocate them. Such is the narrow-mindedness of human nature that few can look on more than one side of truth! Let the servant of Christ call no man his master. Let him hold on his way and never be ashamed of diligence, fruitfulness and jealous watchfulness, in his obedience to Christ's commands. These things are perfectly consistent with salvation by grace and justification by faith, whatever anyone may say to the contrary.

Let us hear the conclusion of the whole matter. The Christian who is careful over his words and tempers and works will generally be the most happy Christian. 'Joy and peace in believing' will never accompany an inconsistent life. It is not for nothing that our Lord concludes the passage: 'These things have I spoken unto you that your joy might be full.'

For meditation: *Do you delight yourself in God's commandments?* (Ps. 119:47).

Suggested further reading: Philippians 2:5-8

Our Lord's enemies criticized him for welcoming sinners (vv. 1-2). Our Lord took up their reproach and showed by his parables that he was emphatically the sinner's Friend.

Our Lord's three parables are all meant to illustrate one and the same truth. They all throw strong light on Christ's willingness to save sinners. Christ's love is an active, working love. Just as the shepherd did not sit still bewailing his lost sheep, and the woman did not sit bewailing her lost money, so our blessed Lord did not sit still in heaven pitying sinners. He left the glory which he had with the Father, and humbled himself to be made in the likeness of man. He came down to the world to seek and save that which was lost. He never rested till he had made atonement for transgressions, brought in everlasting righteousness, provided eternal redemption and opened a door of life to all who are willing to be saved.

Christ's love is a self-denying love. The shepherd brought his lost sheep home on his shoulders rather than leave it in the wilderness. The woman lit a candle, swept the house, searched diligently and spared no pains till she found her lost money. And just so Christ did not spare himself when he undertook to save sinners (John 15:13; Heb. 12:2).

Christ's love is a deep and mighty love. Just as the shepherd rejoiced to find his sheep and the woman to find her money, so does the Lord Jesus rejoice to save sinners. It is a real pleasure to him to pluck them from the burning. His whole life was devoted to this end. It is still his delight to show mercy.

What encouragement our Lord holds out to repentance! (v. 10). However wicked a man may have been, in the day that he really turns from his wickedness and comes to God by Christ, God is well pleased. God has no pleasure in the death of him that dies, and God has pleasure in true repentance. An open door is set before the sinner. A free pardon awaits him (1 John 1:9).

For meditation: *Christ loves sinners before they repent. It is not repentance that causes him to love, but love that causes men to repent.*

Suggested further reading: 1 Corinthians 13:1-7

We should observe how our Lord speaks of the grace of brotherly love. He returns to it a second time, though he has already spoken of it in the former part of his discourse. He would have us know that we can never think too highly of love, attach too much weight to it, labour too much to practise it. Truths which our Master thinks it needful to enforce on us by repetition must needs be of first-class importance.

He commands us to love one another. 'This is my commandment.' It is a positive duty laid on our consciences to practise this grace. We have no more right to neglect it than any of the ten precepts given on Mount Sinai.

He supplies the highest standard of love: 'Love one another, as I have loved you.' No lower measure must content us. The weakest, the lowest, the most ignorant, the most defective disciple is not to be despised. All are to be loved with an active, self-denying, self-sacrificing love. He that cannot do this, or will not try to do it, is disobeying the command of his Master.

A precept like this should stir up in us great searchings of heart. It condemns the selfish, ill-natured, jealous, ill-tempered spirit of many professing Christians with a sweeping condemnation. Sound views of doctrine and knowledge of controversy will avail us nothing at last, if we have known nothing of love. Without charity we may pass muster very well as churchmen but without charity we are no better, says St Paul, than 'sounding brass and tinkling cymbal' (1 Cor. 13:1). Where there is no Christ-like love, there is no grace, no work of the Spirit and no reality in our religion. Blessed are they that do not forget Christ's commandment! They are those who shall have right to the tree of life and enter the celestial city. The unloving Christian is unmeet for heaven.

For meditation: *The Christian has a responsibility of love towards all men, but especially towards his fellow believers.*

Suggested further reading: Romans 3:9-18

We see in this parable a man following the natural bent of his own heart (vv. 11-13). We have in these words a faithful portrait of the mind with which we are all born. This is our likeness. We are naturally proud and self-willed. We have no pleasure in fellowship with God. We depart from him and go afar. We spend our time, strength, faculties and affections on things that cannot profit. The covetous man does it in one way, the slave of lusts and passions in another, the lover of pleasure in another. In one point they are all agreed. Like sheep we all naturally 'go astray and turn every one to his own way' (Isa. 53:6). In the younger son's first conduct we see the natural heart.

He that knows nothing of these things has yet much to learn. He is spiritually blind. The eyes of his understanding need to be opened. The worst ignorance in the world is not to know ourselves. Happy is he who has been delivered from the kingdom of darkness and been made acquainted with himself.

The young man found out that the ways of sin are hard by bitter experience. Our Lord shows the younger son spending all his property and reduced to need, obliged to take a job and feed swine, so hungry that he is ready to eat pig's food and is cared for by none.

These words describe a common case. Sin is a hard master and the servants of sin always find it out sooner or later to their cost. Unconverted people are never really happy. Under a profession of high spirits and cheerfulness they are often ill at ease with themselves. Thousands of them are sick at heart, dissatisfied with themselves, weary of their own ways and thoroughly uncomfortable (Ps. 4:6; Isa. 57:21).

Sin's ways are hard ways, however loudly unconverted people may deny it (Prov. 13:15). The secret wretchedness of natural man is exceedingly great. There is a famine within, however much they try to conceal it. They are in need. They reap what they sow and are not profited by their sins (Gal. 6:8; Rom. 6:21).

For meditation: *Just as the drunkard's pleasure is followed by the hangover, so sin always extracts its price.*

Suggested further reading: 1 John 3:11-18

The frequent repetition of this command teaches the vast importance of Christian charity and the great rarity of it. How anyone can pretend to Christian hope who is ignorant of Christian love, it is hard to understand. He that supposes he is right in the sight of God, because his doctrinal views are correct, while he is unloving in his temper and sharp, cross, snappish and ill-natured in the use of his tongue, exhibits wretched ignorance of the first principles of Christ's gospel. The crossness, spitefulness, jealousy, maliciousness and general disagreeableness of many high professors of 'sound doctrine' are a positive scandal to Christianity. Where there is little love there can be little grace.

In verse 13 our Lord teaches what should be the measure and degree of the love which Christians should have to one another. It should be a self-sacrificing love, even to death, as his was. He proved the greatness of his love by dying for his friends and even for his enemies (Rom. 5:6-8). It would be impossible for love to go further. There is no greater love than willingness to lay down life for those we love. Christ did this and Christians should be willing to do the same.

Let us note here that our Lord clearly speaks of his own death as a sacrificial and propitiatory death. Even his friends need a substitute to die for them.

Verse 14 seems closely connected with the preceding one. 'You are the friends for whom I lay down my life, if you do whatever things I command you.' We are not to dream that we are Christ's friends, if we do not habitually practise his commands. Very striking is it to observe how frequently our Lord returns to this great principle, that obedience is the great test of vital Christianity and doing the real mark of saving faith. Men who talk of being 'the Lord's people', while they live in sin and neglect Christ's plain commands, are in the broad way that leads to destruction.

For meditation: *What evidence have your fellow Christians that you have passed from death to life?* (1 John 3:14).

Suggested further reading: Ephesians 2:1-10

In this parable we see a man awaking to a sense of his natural state and resolving to repent (vv. 17-19). The thoughts of thousands are vividly painted in these words. Thousands have reasoned in this way and are saying things like this to themselves every day. And we must be thankful when we see such thoughts arise. Thinking is not a change of heart, but it may be the beginning of it. Conviction is not conversion, but it is one step, at any rate, in a right direction. The ruin of many people's souls is simply this, that they never think at all!

One caution, however, must always be given. Men must beware that they do not stop short in thinking. Good thoughts are all very well, but they are not saving Christianity. If the younger son had never got beyond thinking he might have been kept from home to the day of his death.

He turned to God with true repentance and faith (vv. 18-20). His good intentions were carried into practice and he unreservedly confessed his sin. These words are a lifelike outline of true repentance and conversion. The man in whose heart a true work of the Holy Spirit has begun will never be content with thinking and resolving. He will break off from sin. He will come out from its fellowship. He will cease to do evil. He will learn to do well. He will turn to God in humble prayer. He will confess his iniquities. He will not attempt to excuse his sins. He will be like David (Ps. 51:3) and the publican (Luke 18:13). Let us beware of false repentance. Action and change of life are the essence of true repentance.

This penitent man was received readily, pardoned freely and completely accepted with God (vv. 20-24). More deeply affecting words than these were never written. To comment seems needless. It is like gilding refined gold and painting the lily. They show in great broad letters the infinite love of the Lord Jesus towards sinners. He receives sinners. With him and his mercy sinners ought to begin when they first desire salvation. On him and his mercy saints ought to live when they have been taught to repent and believe (Gal. 2:20).

For meditation:
Jesus ready stands to save you
... He is able.
He is willing; doubt no more

(Hart).

Suggested further reading: James 2:14-24

Having used the word 'friends', our Lord tells his disciples that he has used that word purposely to cheer and encourage them. 'Observe that I call you friends. I do so intentionally. I no longer call you servants, because the servant from his position knows not all his master's mind and is not in his confidence. But to you I have revealed all the truths which my Father sent me to teach the world and have kept nothing back. I may therefore justly call you friends.'

This is indeed a glorious privilege. To know Christ, serve Christ, follow Christ, obey Christ, work in Christ's vineyard, fight Christ's battles — all this is no small matter. But for sinful men and women like ourselves to be called 'friends of Christ' is something that our weak minds can hardly grasp and take in. The King of kings and Lord of lords not only pities and saves all them that believe in him, but actually calls them his 'friends'. We need not wonder, in the face of such language as this, that St Paul should say, 'The love of Christ ... passeth knowledge' (Eph. 3:19).

Let the expression before us encourage Christians to deal familiarly with Christ in prayer. Why should we be afraid to pour out all our hearts and unbosom all our secrets, in speaking to one who calls us his 'friends'? Let it cheer us in all the troubles and sorrows of life and increase our confidence in our Lord. 'He that hath friends', says Solomon, 'will show himself friendly' (Prov. 18:24). Certainly our great Master in heaven will never forsake his 'friends'. Poor and unworthy as we are, he will not cast us off, but will stand by us and keep us to the end. David never forgot Jonathan and the Son of David will never forget his people. None so rich, so strong, so independent, so well off, so thoroughly provided for as the man of whom Christ says, 'This is my friend!'

For meditation:
And will this sovereign King of glory condescend,
And will he write his name my Father and my Friend?

Suggested further reading: Matthew 9:9-13

How unkind and ill-natured are the feelings of self-righteous men towards sinners! This is a lesson that our Lord conveys to us by describing the conduct of the elder brother of the prodigal son. He shows him as angry and finding fault because of the rejoicings over his brother's return. He shows him complaining that his father treated the returning prodigal too well and that he himself had not been treated as well as his merits deserved. He shows him utterly unable to share in the joy which prevailed when his younger brother came home and giving way to ill-natured and envious feelings.

This elder brother is an exact picture of the Jews of our Lord's time. They could not bear the idea of their Gentile younger brother being made partaker of their privileges. They would have excluded him from God's favour. They steadily refused to see the Gentiles as fellow heirs and partakers of Christ with themselves.

This elder brother is an exact type of the scribes and Pharisees of our Lord's time. They objected that our Lord received sinners and ate with them. They murmured because he opened the door of salvation to publicans and prostitutes. They would have been better pleased if our Lord had confined his ministry to them and their party and had left the ignorant and sinful entirely alone. Our Lord painted their picture here.

This elder brother is a type of many in the church of Christ today. There are thousands on every side who hate a free, full, unfettered gospel to be preached. They complain that ministers throw the doors open too wide, that grace leads to loose living. This is the elder brother's voice.

Let us beware of this spirit infecting our own hearts. It arises partly from ignorance. Men begin by not seeing their own sinfulness and unworthiness and then they fancy that they are much better than others and that nobody is worthy to be put by their side. It arises from lack of love. They cannot take pleasure in others being saved. If a man understands gospel forgiveness and that all stand by grace and are all debtors, and that what we have we have received, he will not be the elder brother.

For meditation: *Do you see the gospel as for 'nice' young people, or for ruffians, too? Is it for the 'ladies' of Soho as well as the ladies of refinement?*

Suggested further reading: 2 Timothy 1:8-12

Our Lord speaks of the doctrine of election. He says, 'Ye have not chosen me, but I have chosen you ... that ye should go and bring forth fruit.' The choosing here mentioned is evidently twofold. It includes not only the election to the apostolic office, which was peculiar to the eleven, but the election to eternal life, which is the privilege of all believers. To this last 'choosing', as it specially concerns ourselves, we may profitably direct our attention.

Election to eternal life is a truth of Scripture which we must receive humbly and believe implicitly. Why the Lord Jesus calls some and does not call others, quickens whom he will and leaves others alone in their sins, these are deep things which we cannot explain. Let it suffice us to know that it is a fact. God must begin the work of grace in a man's heart, or else a man will never be saved. Christ must first choose us and call us by his Spirit, or else we shall never choose Christ. Beyond doubt, if not saved, we shall have none to blame but ourselves. But if saved, we certainly trace up the beginning of our salvation to the choosing grace of Christ. Our song to all eternity will be that which fell from the lips of Jonah: 'Salvation is of the Lord' (Jonah 2:9).

Election is always to sanctification. Those whom Christ chooses out of mankind, he chooses not only that they may be saved, but that they may bear fruit, and fruit that can be seen. All other election beside this is a mere vain delusion and a miserable invention of man. It was the faith and hope and love of the Thessalonians which made St Paul say, 'I know your election of God' (1 Thess. 1:4). Where there is no visible fruit of sanctification, we may be sure there is no election.

Armed with such principles as these, we have no cause to be afraid of the doctrine of election. Like any other truth of the gospel, it is liable to be abused and perverted. But to a pious mind it is a doctrine 'full of sweet, pleasant and unspeakable comfort'.

For meditation: *We are Christians not by chance but by divine choice.*

Suggested further reading: Acts 11:19-26

The conversion of any soul ought to be an occasion of joy to all who see it. Our Lord shows this by the words he puts into the mouth of the prodigal's father (v. 32).

The lesson of these words was primarily meant for the scribes and Pharisees. If their hearts had been in a right state they would never have murmured at our Lord for receiving sinners. They would have remembered that the worst of publicans and sinners were their own brethren, and that if they were different it was grace that made them so. They would have been glad to see such helpless wanderers returning to the fold. They would have been thankful to see them as brands plucked from the burning, and not cast away for ever. Of all these feelings, unhappily, they knew nothing. Wrapped in their own self-righteousness, they murmured and found fault when in reality they ought to have thanked God and rejoiced.

This lesson is one that we shall all do well to lay to heart. Nothing ought to give us such true pleasure as the conversion of souls. It makes angels rejoice in heaven. It ought to make Christians rejoice on earth. What if those converted were lately the vilest of the vile? What if they served sin and Satan for many years and wasted their substance in riotous living? It matters nothing. Has grace come into their hearts? Are they truly penitent? Have they come back to their Father's house? Are they new creatures in Christ Jesus? Are the dead made alive and the lost found? If these questions can be answered satisfactorily we ought to rejoice and be glad. Let the worldly, if they please, mock and sneer at such conversions. Let the self-righteous, if they will, murmur and find fault and deny the reality of all great and sudden changes. But let the Christian who reads the words of Christ in this chapter remember them and act upon them. Let them thank God and be merry. Let them praise God that one more soul is saved. The man who can take a deep interest in politics, field sports, money-making or farming, but none in conversion of souls, is not a true Christian.

For meditation: *Are you a sceptic about conversions? Is it so long since you led anyone to Christ that you doubt that it can be done?*

Suggested further reading: Hebrews 11:32-38

We are shown in this passage what true Christians must expect to meet in this world — hatred and persecution. If the disciples looked for kindness and gratitude from man, they would be painfully disappointed. They must lay their account to be ill-treated like their Master. 'The world hateth you. Be not moved or surprised. If they have persecuted me, they will also persecute you; if they have kept my saying, they will keep yours also.'

Facts, painful facts in every age, supply abundant proof that our Lord's warning was not without cause. Persecution was the lot of the apostles and their companions wherever they went. Not more than one or two of them died quietly in his bed. Persecution has been the lot of true believers throughout the twenty Christian centuries of history. The doings of Roman emperors and Roman popes, the Spanish Inquisition, the martyrdoms of Queen Mary's reign — all tell the same story. Persecution is the lot of all really godly people at this very day. Ridicule, mockery, slander, misrepresentation still show the feelings of unconverted people against the true Christian. As it was in St Paul's day, so it is now. In public and in private, at school and at college, at home and abroad, 'All that will live godly in Christ Jesus shall suffer persecution' (2 Tim. 3:12). Mere churchmanship and outward profession are a cheap religion, of course, and cost a man nothing. But real vital Christianity will always bring with it a cross.

To know and understand these things is of the utmost importance to our comfort. Nothing is so mischievous as the habit of indulging false expectations. Let us realize that human nature never changes, that 'The carnal mind is enmity against God' and against God's image in his people. Let us settle it in our minds that no holiness of life or consistency of conduct will ever prevent wicked people hating the servants of Christ, just as they hated their blameless Master. Let us remember these things and then we shall not be disappointed.

For meditation: *Expect nothing from men but great things from God.*

Suggested further reading: Luke 12:13-21

The steward, whom our Lord describes, is not set before us as a pattern of morality. He is distinctly called unjust (v. 8). The Lord never meant to sanction dishonesty and unfair dealing between man and man. The steward broke the eighth commandment. His master was struck with his cunning and forethought when he heard of it and 'commended' him as a shrewd and far-seeing man. But there is no proof that his master was pleased with his conduct. This man was not praised by Christ. His treatment of his master was wrong. The purpose of the parable is not to commend his dishonesty.

The parable teaches the wisdom of providing against coming evil. The conduct of the unjust steward when he received notice to quit was undeniably clever. Dishonest as he was in striking off from the bills of debtors anything that was due to his master, he certainly by doing so made friends. Wicked as he was, he had an eye to the future. Disgraceful as he was, he provided well for himself. He did not sit still in idleness and see himself reduced to poverty without a struggle. When he lost one home he secured another.

What a striking contrast between the steward's conduct about his earthly prospects and the conduct of most men about their souls! In this general point of view, and in this only, the steward sets an example for us all to follow. Like him we should look far forward to things to come. Like him we should provide against the day when we have to leave our present habitation. We should secure a heavenly home when this earthly home must be laid aside. The diligence of worldly men about the things of time should put to shame the coldness of professing Christians about the things of eternity.

Our Lord also teaches us the great importance of strict faithfulness about little things (v. 10). Little things are the best test of character. Unfaithfulness about little things is a symptom of a bad state of heart. The man who has not been dealing faithfully with money in this world can never be one who has true riches in heaven (vv. 11-12). Doctrinal soundness will not cover over swindling and dishonest practices!

For meditation: *To be prepared for eternity is the all-important issue. But preparedness for tomorrow's world will have moral consequences in today's life.*

Suggested further reading: Matthew 10:16-25

We are shown in this passage two reasons for patience under the persecution of this world. Each is weighty and supplies matter for much thought.

For one thing, persecution is the cup of which Christ himself drank. Faultless as he was in everything, in temper, word and deed, unwearied as he was in works of kindness, always going about doing good, never was anyone so hated as Jesus was to the last day of his earthly ministry. Scribes and high priests, Pharisees and Sadducees, Jews and Gentiles united in pouring contempt on him and opposing him and never rested till he was put to death.

Surely this simple fact alone should sustain our spirits and prevent our being cast down by the hatred of man. Let us consider that we are only walking in our Master's footsteps and sharing our Master's portion. Do we deserve to be better treated? Are we better than he? Let us fight against these murmuring thoughts. Let us drink quietly the cup which our Father gives us. Above all, let us often call to mind the saying: 'Remember the word that I spake unto you, The servant is not greater than his Master.'

For another thing, persecution helps to prove that we are children of God and have treasure in heaven. It supplies evidence that we are really born again, that we have grace in our hearts and are heirs of glory: 'If ye were of the world, the world would love his own: but because ye are not of the world, therefore the world hateth you.' Persecution, in short, is like the goldsmith's hallmark on real silver and gold; it is one of the marks of a converted man.

Let us nerve our minds with this cheering thought, when we feel ready to faint and give way under the world's hatred. No doubt it is hard to bear and the more hard when our conscience tells us we are innocent. But, after all, let us never forget that it is a token for good. It is a symptom of a work begun within us by the Holy Ghost, which can never be overthrown.

For meditation: *Men only persecute what they fear.*

Suggested further reading: Matthew 19:16-24

It is useless to attempt to serve God with a divided heart (v. 13). The truth here propounded by our Lord appears at first sight too obvious to admit of being disputed. And yet the very attempt which is here declared to be useless is constantly being made by many in the matter of their souls. Thousands on every side are continually trying to do the thing which Christ pronounces impossible. They are endeavouring to be friends of the world and friends of God at the same time. Their consciences are so far enlightened that they feel they must have some religion. But their affections are so chained down to earthly things that they never come up to the mark of being true Christians. And hence they live in a state of constant discomfort. They have too much religion to be happy in the world and too much of the world in their hearts to be happy in religion. In short they waste their time in labouring to do that which cannot be done. They are striving to serve God and mammon.

He that desires to be a happy Christian will do well to ponder our Lord's sayings in this verse. There is perhaps no point on which the experience of all God's saints is more uniform than this, that decision is the secret of comfort in Christian service. It is the half-hearted Christian who brings up the evil report of the good land. The more thoroughly we give ourselves to Christ, the more sensibly we shall feel within the peace of God that passes all understanding (Phil. 4:7). The more entirely we live, not to ourselves, but to him who died for us, the more powerfully shall we realize what it is to have joy and peace in believing. If it is worthwhile to serve Christ at all, let us serve him with all our heart, soul, mind and strength. Life, eternal life, after all, is the matter at stake, no less than happiness. If we cannot make up our minds to give up everything for Christ's sake, we must not expect Christ to own us at the last day. He will have all our hearts or none. Friendship with the world is enmity with God (James 4:4). The end of undecided and half-hearted Christians is to be cast out for ever.

For meditation: *A key description of the Christian in the Scriptures is the servant of Christ. Service involves loyal, obedient duties.*

Suggested further reading: 2 Thessalonians 2:5-12

Our Lord reminds the eleven of the things he had said before, when he first sent them out to preach (Matt. 10:24; Luke 6:40). He had always told them that they must not expect to be better treated than he had been himself. He quotes the proverbial saying that 'A servant must not expect to fare better than his master.' 'Did they persecute me? Then they will persecute you. Did they keep, mind and attend to my teaching? As a rule the greater part did not, and you must expect the same.' Wrong expectations are one great cause of Christians feeling troubled and perplexed.

Our Lord here tells his disciples that he himself was the cause of all the enmity and hatred they would meet with. They would be hated on account of their Master, more than on account of themselves.

It may be some comfort to a persecuted Christian to think that it is for his Master's sake that he is ill-used. He is 'filling up that which is behind of the afflictions of Christ' (Col. 1:24). He is bearing the 'reproach of Christ' (Heb. 11:26).

Dark ignorance was the great cause of the conduct of the unbelieving Jews. They did not rightly know God the Father who had sent Christ into the world. They did not know that Christ was the Messiah whom the Father had promised to send. In this state of ignorance they blindly persecuted Christ and his disciples.

This judicial blindness and hardness of the Jewish nation in the time of our Lord and his apostles is a thing that ought to be carefully observed by all Bible readers (see Acts 3:17; 13:27; 28:25-27; 1 Cor. 2:8; 2 Cor. 3:14). It was a peculiar judicial blindness, we must remember, to which the whole nation was given over, like Pharaoh, as a final punishment for many centuries of idolatry, wickedness and unbelief. Nothing but this seems thoroughly to account for the extraordinary unbelief of many of our Lord's hearers.

For meditation: *When we toy with unbelief God may leave us to sink in it.*

Suggested further reading: Isaiah 8:11-20

How widely different is the estimate set on things by man from that which is set on things by God! Our Lord declares this in a severe rebuke which he addresses to the covetous Pharisees who derided him (v. 15).

The truth of this solemn saying appears on every side of us. We have only to look round the world and mark the things on which men set their affections in order to see it proved in a hundred ways. Riches, honours, rank and pleasure are the chief objects for which the greater part of mankind are living. Yet these are the very things which God declares to be vanity, and of the love of which he warns us to beware! Praying, Bible reading, holy living, repentance, faith, communion with God, are things for which few care at all. Yet these are the very things which God in his Bible is ever urging to our attention! The disagreement is glaring, painful and appalling. What God calls good, man calls evil! What God calls evil, man calls good!

Whose words, after all, are true? Whose estimate is correct? Whose judgement will stand at the last day? By whose standard will all be tried before they receive their eternal sentence? Before whose bar will the current opinions of the world be tested and weighed at last? These are the only questions that ought to influence our conduct, and to these questions the Bible returns a plain answer. The counsel of the Lord alone shall stand for ever. The word of Christ alone shall judge man at the last day. By that word let us live. By that word let us measure everything and every person in this world. It matters nothing what man thinks. What does the Lord say? It matters nothing what it is fashionable and customary to think. Let God be true and every man a liar (Rom. 3:4). The more entirely we are of one mind with God, the better we are prepared for the Judgement Day. To love what God loves, to hate what God hates, to approve what God approves is the highest style of Christianity. The moment we find ourselves honouring anything which in the sight of God is lightly esteemed, we may be sure there is something wrong with our souls.

For meditation: *The church needs to regain the title 'the people of one book'.*

Suggested further reading: Amos 9:7-10

We should observe how our Lord speaks of the misuse of religious privileges. It intensifies man's guilt and will increase his condemnation. He tells his disciples that if he had not 'spoken' and 'done' among the Jews things which none ever spoke or did before, 'they had not had sin'. By this, we must remember, he means, 'They had not been so sinful and so guilty as they are now.' But now they were utterly without excuse. They had seen Christ's works and heard Christ's teaching and yet remained unbelieving. What more could be done for them? Nothing — absolutely nothing! They wilfully sinned against the clearest possible light and were of all men most guilty.

Let us settle it down as a first principle in our religion that religious privileges are in a certain sense very dangerous things. If they do not help us towards heaven, they will only sink us deeper into hell. They add to our responsibility. 'To whomsoever much is given, of him shall much be required' (Luke 12:48). He that dwells in a land of open Bibles and preached gospel and yet dreams that he will stand in the judgement day on the same level with an untaught Chinese is fearfully deceived. He will find to his own cost, except he repents, that his judgement will be according to his light. The mere fact that he had knowledge and did not improve it will of itself prove one of his greatest sins. 'He that knew his Master's will and did it not, shall be beaten with many stripes' (Luke 12:47).

Well would it be for all professing Christians in England, if this point was more thoroughly considered! Nothing is more common than to hear men taking comfort in the thought that they 'know what is right', while at the same time they are evidently unconverted and unfit to die. They rest in that unhappy phrase, 'We know it, we know it,' as if knowledge could wash away all their sins, forgetting that the devil has more knowledge than any of us and yet is no better for it. Let the burning words of our Lord in the passage now before us sink down into our hearts and never be forgotten.

For meditation: *If ignorance does not excuse sin, then knowledge makes it worse.*

Suggested further reading: Psalm 73:1-17

A man's worldly condition is no test of his state in the sight of God.
The Lord Jesus decribes to us two men, of whom one was very rich,
and the other was very poor. The one ate plenty. The other was a
mere beggar who had nothing that he could call his own. And yet of
these two men the poor man had grace and the rich man had none.
The poor man lived by faith and walked in the steps of Abraham.
The rich man was a thoughtless, selfish worldling, dead in trespasses and sins.

Let us not give way to the common idea that men are to be valued according to their income and that the man who has most money
is the one who ought to be the most highly esteemed. There is no
authority for this notion in the Bible. The general teaching of Scripture is flatly opposed to it. Riches and noble birth are not marks of
God's people (1 Cor. 1:26; Jer. 9:24). Wealth is no mark of God's
favour. Poverty is no mark of God's displeasure. Those whom God
justifies and glorifies are seldom the rich of this world. If we would
measure men as God measures them we must value them according
to grace.

Death is the common end to which all classes of men must come.
The trials of the beggar and the feasting of the rich man alike ceased
at last. There came a time when both of them died (Eccles. 3:20).
Death is a great fact that all acknowledge but very few seem to
realize. Most men eat, drink, talk and plan as if they were going to
live upon earth for ever. The true Christian must be on guard against
this spirit. Against murmuring, discontent and envy in a state of
poverty, and pride, self-sufficiency and arrogance in a state of wealth,
there are few better antidotes than the remembrance of death. Death
stopped the beggar's bodily needs. Death stopped the rich man's
feasting for ever.

For meditation: *Job's friends made the great mistake of associat-
ing bodily weakness and financial ruin with the displeasure of God.
In fact God 'trusted' Job with these disasters because he knew that
Job would demonstrate his steadfast faith even under the most difficult of circumstances.*

Suggested further reading: Acts 5:1-11

We should observe in these verses how our Lord speaks of the Holy Ghost.

He speaks of him as a person. He is 'the Comforter' who is to come; he is one sent and 'proceeding'; he is one whose office it is to 'testify'. These are not words that can be used of a mere influence or inward feeling. So to interpret them is to contradict common sense and to strain the meaning of plain language. Reason and fairness require us to understand that it is a personal being who is here mentioned, even he whom we are justly taught to adore as the Third Person in the blessed Trinity.

Again, our Lord speaks of the Holy Ghost as one whom he 'will send from the Father' and one 'who proceedeth from the Father'. These are deep sayings, no doubt, so deep that we have no line to fathom them. The mere fact that for centuries the Eastern and Western churches of Christendom have been divided about their meaning should teach us to handle them with modesty and reverence. One thing, at all events, is very clear and plain. There is a close and intimate connection between the Spirit, the Father and the Son. Why the Holy Ghost should be said in this verse to be *sent* by the Son and to *proceed* from the Father, we cannot tell. But we may quietly repose our minds in the thought expressed in an ancient creed that 'In this Trinity none is afore or after other: none is greater or less than another.' 'Such as the Father is, such is the Son and such is the Holy Ghost.' Above all, we may rest in the comfortable truth that in the salvation of our souls all three persons in the Trinity equally cooperate. It was God in Trinity who said, 'Let us create,' and it is God in Trinity who says, 'Let us save.'

Forever let us take heed to our doctrine about the Holy Spirit. Let us make sure that we hold sound and scriptural views of his nature, his person and his operations. A religion which entirely leaves him out and gives him no place is far from uncommon. Let us beware that such a religion is not ours.

For meditation: *Our religion is to be Christ-centred but it is not to despise the Father or the Spirit.*

Suggested further reading: James 5:1-11

The souls of believers are especially cared for by God in the hour of death (v. 22). There is something very comforting in these words. We know very little of the state or feelings of the dead. When our own last hour comes and we lie down to die we shall be like those who journey into an unknown country. But it may satisfy us to know that all who fall asleep in Jesus are in good keeping. They are not houseless, homeless wanderers between the hour of death and the hour of resurrection. They are at rest in the midst of friends with all who have had the like faith as Abraham. They have no lack of anything. Best of all, they are 'with Christ' (Phil. 1:23).

Hell is real and eternal. The Lord Jesus' words could not be clearer (vv. 23-24). He gives us an awful picture of the rich man's longing for a drop of water to cool his tongue and of the gulf between him and Abraham which could not be passed. There are few more fearful passages in the whole Bible than this. And he whose lips spoke these words is one who delights in mercy, let it be remembered!

The certainty and endlessness of the future punishment of the wicked are truths which we must hold fast and never let go. From the day when Satan first said to Eve that she would not die, there never have been men lacking to deny them. Let us not be deceived. There is a hell for the impenitent as well as a heaven for believers. There is wrath to come for all who do not obey the gospel (2 Thess. 1:8). From that wrath let us flee to the great hiding-place, Jesus Christ the Lord.

Unconverted men find out the value of a soul after death when it is too late. The rich man desired that Lazarus might be sent to his five brethren who were yet alive, to prevent them going to hell. While he lived he had done nothing for their spiritual good. They had probably been his companions in worldliness and, like him, had neglected their souls entirely. When he is dead he finds out too late the folly of which they had all been guilty.

For meditation: *How often in this life we say, 'If only...' and are sure we would have been different if... Hell is a groaning 'if only' with no escape.*

Suggested further reading: Acts 10:39-43

We should observe how our Lord speaks of the special office of the apostles. They were to be his witnesses in the world: 'Ye also shall bear witness.'

The expression is singularly instructive and full of meaning. It taught the eleven what they must expect their portion to be, so long as they lived. They would have to bear testimony to facts which many would not believe and to truths which the natural heart would dislike. They would often have to stand alone, a few against many, a little flock against a great multitude. None of these things must move them. They must count it no strange thing to be persecuted, hated, opposed and discredited. They must not mind it. To witness was their grand duty, whether men believed them or not. So witnessing, their record would be on high, in God's book of remembrance, and so witnessing, sooner or later, the Judge of all would give them a crown of glory that fadeth not away.

Let us never forget, as we leave this passage, that the position of the apostles is that which, in a certain sense, every true Christian must fill, as long as the world stands. We must all be witnesses for Christ. We must not be ashamed to stand up for Christ's cause, to speak out for Christ and to persist in maintaining the truth of Christ's gospel. Wherever we live, in town or in country, in public or in private, abroad or at home, we must boldly confess our Master on every opportunity. So doing, we shall walk in the steps of the apostles, though at a long interval. So doing, we shall please our Master and may hope at last that we shall receive the apostles' reward.

For meditation: *Enthusiasm for politics and false religion soon opens men's mouths. Shall love for Christ shut ours?*

Suggested further reading: John 5:39-47

The change that will come over the minds of unconverted men after death is one of the most fearful points in their future condition. They will see, know and understand a hundred things to which they were blind while they were alive. They will discover, like Esau, they have bartered away eternal happiness for a mere 'mess of pottage'. There is no infidelity, scepticism or unbelief after death. Hell is truth known too late.

The greatest miracles would have no effect on men's hearts if they will not believe God's Word. The rich man thought otherwise (vv. 27-28). He argued that the sight of one who came from another world would surely make them feel their need, though the old familiar words of Moses and the prophets had been heard in vain. The reply of Abraham is solemn and instructive (v. 31).

The principle laid down in these words is of deep importance. The Scriptures contain all that we need to know in order to be saved, and a messenger from the world beyond the grave could add nothing to them. It is not more evidence that is wanted in order to make men repent, but more heart and will to make use of what they already know. The dead could tell us nothing more than the Bible contains if they rose from their graves to instruct us. After the first novelty of their testimony was worn away we should care no more for their words than the words of any other. This wretched waiting for something which we have not, and neglect of what we have, is the ruin of thousands of souls. Faith, simple faith in the Scriptures which we already possess, is the first thing needful to salvation. The man who has the Bible and can read it, and yet waits for more evidence before he becomes a decided Christian, is deceiving himself. Except he awakens from his delusion, he will die in his sins.

For meditation: *Constantly we are told that it is the rediscovery of the miraculous that will change the apathy of the world into belief. Abraham's clear words deny it. Men who do not want to believe can and do explain away every piece of evidence presented to them.*

Suggested further reading: Luke 14:25-33

In leaving chapter 15 let us not fail to note how systematically our
blessed Master gave his disciples instruction on three most important points. The first was their relation to himself. They were to
abide in close union with him, like branches in a vine. The second
was their relation to one another. They were to love one another
with a deep, self-sacrificing love, like their Master's. The third was
their relation to the world. They were to expect its hatred, not be
surprised at it; to bear it patiently and not be afraid of it.

Chapter 16 is a direct continuation of the last chapter, without
break or pause. Our Lord's object in this first verse is to cheer and
revive the minds of the apostles and to prevent them being discouraged by the persecution of the unbelieving Jews. 'I have spoken the
things which I just been speaking, in order to obviate the de-
pressing effect of the treatment you will receive. Lest you should be
stumbled and offended by the conduct of your enemies, I have told
you the things you have just heard.'

Stier remarks that 'these things' include both the warning of the
world's hatred and the promise of the witnessing Spirit. Foreknowledge of the world's hatred would prevent the disciples being surprised and disappointed. The promise of the Spirit would cheer and
encourage.

How great a stumbling-block it often is to young and unestablished
Christians to find themselves persecuted and ill-used for their religion, it is needless to point out. Our Lord knew this and took care to
arm the eleven apostles with warnings. He never kept back the cross,
or concealed the difficulties in the way to heaven.

For meditation: *No one and nothing is to have a greater call on
our allegiance than our Lord.*

Suggested further reading: Romans 2:17-24

It is a great sin to put stumbling-blocks in the way of other men's souls (vv. 1-2). When do men make others stumble? When do they cause offences to come? They do it, beyond doubt, whenever they persecute believers or endeavour to turn them from Christ. But this, unhappily, is not all. Professing Christians do it whenever they bring discredit on their religion by inconsistencies of temper, word or deed. We do it whenever we make our Christianity unlovely in the eyes of the world by conduct not in keeping with our profession. The world may not understand the doctrines and principles of believers. But the world is very keen-sighted about their practice.

The sin against which our Lord warns us was the sin of David (2 Sam. 12:14). It was the sin of which Paul charges the Jews (Rom. 2:24). It is the sin which he frequently entreats Christians to beware (1 Cor. 10:32).

The subject is a deeply searching one. The sin which our Lord brings before us is unhappily very common. The inconsistencies of professing Christians too often supply men with an excuse for neglecting religion altogether. An inconsistent believer, whether he knows it or not, is daily doing harm to souls. His life is a positive injury to the gospel.

Let us often ask ourselves whether we are doing harm or good in the world. We cannot live to ourselves if we are Christians. The eyes of many will always be upon us. Men will judge far more by what they see than by what they hear. If they see the Christian contradicting by his practice what he professes to believe they are justly stumbled and offended. For the world's sake, as well as our own, let us strive to be eminently holy. Let us endeavour to make our religion beautiful in the eyes of men and to adorn the gospel of Christ in all things. Anything is better than doing harm to souls. The cross of Christ will give offence. Let us not increase that offence by carelessness in our daily lives.

For meditation: *What sort of representative for Christ are you? Do you bring him joy or incite him to disown you?*

Suggested further reading: Acts 5:27-42

We find our Lord delivering a remarkable prophecy. He tells his disciples that they will be cast out of the Jewish church and persecuted even unto death: 'They shall put you out of the synagogues: yea, the time cometh, that whosoever killeth you will think that he doeth God service.'

How strange that seems at first sight! Excommunication, suffering and death are the portion that the Prince of peace predicts to his disciples. So far from receiving them and their message with gratitude, the world would hate them, despitefully use them and put them to death. And, worst of all, their persecutors would actually persuade themselves that it was right to persecute and would inflict the cruellest injuries in the sacred name of religion.

How true the prediction has turned out! Like every other prophecy of Scripture, it has been fulfilled to the very letter. The Acts of the Apostles show us how the unbelieving Jews persecuted the early Christians. The pages of history tell us what horrible crimes have been committed by the popish Inquisition. The annals of our own country inform us how our holy Reformers were burned at the stake for their religion by men who professed to do all they did from zeal for pure Christianity. Unlikely and incredible as it might seem at the time, the great Prophet of the church has been found in this, as in everything else, to have predicted nothing but literal truth.

Let it never surprise us to hear of true Christians being persecuted, in one way or another, even in our own day. Human nature never changes. Grace is never really popular. The quantity of persecution which God's children have to suffer in every rank of life, even now, if they confess their Master, is far greater than the thoughtless world supposes. They only know it who go through it, at school, at college, in the counting-house, in the barrack-room, on board the ship. Those words shall always be found true: 'All that will live godly in Christ Jesus shall suffer persecution' (2 Tim. 3:12).

For meditation: *Men may put Christians out of their societies but God preserves them for his new universe.*

Suggested further reading: Hebrews 11:1-6

The apostles made an important request (v. 5). We do not know the secret feelings from which this request sprang. Perhaps the hearts of the apostles failed within them as they heard one weighty lesson after another fall from the Lord's lips. Perhaps the thoughts arose in their minds: 'Who is sufficient for these things? Who can follow such a lofty standard of practice? Who can receive such high doctrines?' These, however, are only conjectures. But their important request is plain.

Faith is the root of saving religion (Heb. 11:6). It is the hand by which the soul lays hold on Christ, and is united to him and saved. It is the secret of all Christian comfort and spiritual prosperity. According to a man's faith will be his peace, his hope, his strength, his courage, his decision and his victory over the world. When the apostles made request about faith they did well, and wisely.

Faith is a grace that admits of degrees. It does not come to full strength and perfection as soon as it is planted in the heart by the Holy Spirit. There is 'little' faith and 'great' faith. There is 'weak' faith and 'strong' faith. Both are spoken of in the Scriptures. Both are to be seen in the experience of God's people. The more faith a Christian has, the more happy, holy and useful he will be. To promote the growth and progress of faith should be the daily prayer and endeavour of all who love life.

Have we any faith at all? This, after all, is the first question which the subject should raise in our hearts. Saving faith is not mere repetition of the creed. Thousands weekly repeat sound doctrine who know nothing of real believing (2 Thess. 3:2). True faith is not natural to man. It comes down from heaven. It is the gift of God. If we have any faith let us pray for more of it. It is a bad sign of a man's spiritual state when he is satisfied to live on old stock and does not hunger and thirst to grow in grace.

For meditation: *Our world is blinded by its self-confident self-sufficiency. The Christian is the person who sees his dependence and trusts.*

Suggested further reading: Hebrews 10:32-39

We find our Lord explaining his special reason for delivering the prophecy just referred to, as well as all his discourse. 'These things,' he says, 'I have spoken unto you, that ye should not be offended.'

Well did our Lord know that nothing is so dangerous to our comfort as to indulge false expectations. He therefore prepared his disciples for what they must expect to meet with in his service. Forewarned, forearmed! They must not look for a smooth course and a peaceful journey. They must make up their minds to battles, conflicts, wounds, opposition, persecution and perhaps even death. Like a wise general, he did not conceal from his soldiers the nature of the campaign they were beginning. He told them all that was before them, in faithfulness and love, that when the time of trial came, they might remember his words and not be disappointed and offended. He wisely forewarned them that the cross was the way to the crown.

To count the cost is one of the first duties that ought to be pressed on Christians in every age. It is no kindness to young beginners to paint the service of Christ in false colours and to keep back from them the old truth: 'Through much tribulation we must enter the kingdom of God.' By prophesying smooth things and crying 'Peace', we may easily fill the ranks of Christ's army with professing soldiers. But they are just the soldiers, who, like the stony-ground hearers, in time of tribulation will fall away and turn back in the day of battle. No Christian is in a healthy state of mind who is not prepared for trouble and persecution. He that expects to cross the troubled waters of this world and to reach heaven with wind and tide always in his favour knows nothing yet as he ought to know. We never can tell what is before us in life. But of one thing we may be very sure: we must carry the cross if we would wear the crown. Let us grasp this principle firmly and never forget it. Then, when the hour of trial comes, we shall 'not be offended'.

For meditation: *When Christianity costs little, its truths are held to lightly and its practices treated without seriousness.*

Suggested further reading: Philippians 3:1-9

Our Lord delivers a heavy blow to self-righteousness. Look at what he says to his apostles! (v. 10). We are all naturally proud and self-righteous. We think far more highly of ourselves, our deserts and our character than we have any right to do. It is a subtle disease which manifests itself in a hundred different ways. Most men can see it in other people. Few will allow its presence in themselves. Seldom will a man be found, however wicked, who does not secretly flatter himself that there is somebody worse than he is. Seldom will a saint be found who at seasons is not tempted to be satisfied and pleased with himself. There is such a thing as pride that wears the cloak of humility. There is not a heart on earth that does not contain a piece of the Pharisee's character.

To give up self-righteousness is absolutely needful to salvation. He that desires to be saved must confess that there is no good thing in him and that he has no merit, no goodness, no worthiness of his own. He must be willing to renounce his own righteousness and to trust in the righteousness of another, even Christ the Lord. Once pardoned and forgiven, we must travel the daily journey of life under a deep conviction that we are unprofitable servants. At our best we only do our duty and have nothing to boast of. And even when we do our duty it is not by our own power and might that we do it but by the strength that is given to us by God. Claim upon God we have none. Right to expect anything from God we have none. Worthiness to deserve anything from God we have none. All that we have we have received. All that we are we owe to God's distinguishing grace.

What is the true cause of self-righteousness? It all arises from ignorance. We see neither ourselves, nor our lives, nor God, nor the law of God, as we ought. Once let the light of grace shine into a man's heart, and the reign of self-righteousness is over.

For meditation: *Our self-assessment is always flattering. The assessment made of us by others is less flattering but still too good. Only God sees us as we really are. We need to see ourselves through his eyes.*

Suggested further reading: Luke 6:17-26

Our Lord warns the eleven that they must not be surprised if even death was the final result of discipleship. There would be no length of persecution to which their enemies would not go. 'The hour comes when he who has killed you will think that in so doing he offers God an acceptable service.'

How true this has proved, the history of all religious persecution has abundantly showed. Who can doubt that Saul before his conversion was sincere? 'I verily thought that I ought to do many things contrary to the name of Jesus of Nazareth' (Acts 26:9). The extent to which conscience may be blinded, until a man actually thinks that he is doing a godly deed, when in reality he is committing a huge sin, is one of the most painful phenomena in human nature.

Let us never forget that religious earnestness alone is no proof that a man is a sound Christian. Not all zeal is right; it may be a zeal without knowledge. Let us pray that we may have light as well as zeal.

Once more our Lord repeats his reasons for telling the disciples what they must expect. 'I have told you what treatment you will receive, in order that you may not be surprised when the time of trial comes, but may remember that I foretold you all, and not be cast down. Nothing unforeseen, nothing unpredicted, you will feel, happens to us. Our Master told us it would be so.'

Our Lord adds the reason why he had not dwelt on these trials before: 'I did not tell you so much of these things at the beginning of your discipleship, because I was with you, and would not disturb your minds with painful tidings while you were learning the first principles of the gospel. But now that I am about to leave you, it is needful to forewarn you of things you are likely to meet with.'

For meditation: *If everyone speaks well of us, it probably indicates that our version of the gospel has little to say about their sin.*

Suggested further reading: Psalm 130

How earnestly men can cry for help when they feel their need of it! (v. 13). It is difficult to conceive of any condition more thoroughly miserable than that of men afflicted with leprosy. They were cast out from society. They were cut off from all communion with their fellows. The lepers in this passage were aware of their wretchedness. They stood afar off but they did not stand idly by doing nothing. They felt acutely the deplorable state of their bodies. They found words to express their feelings. They cried earnestly for relief when a chance of relief appeared in sight. Their conduct throws much light on prayer.

How is it that many never pray at all? How is it that many are content to repeat a form of words but never pray with their hearts? How is it that dying men and women, with souls to be lost or saved, can know so little of real, hearty, businesslike prayer? The answer to these questions is short and simple. The bulk of mankind have no sense of sin. They do not feel their spiritual disease. They are not conscious that they are lost and guilty and hanging over the brink of hell. When a man finds out his soul's ailment he soon learns to pray. Like the lepers, he finds words to express his needs.

How is it that many true believers often pray so coldly? What is the reason that their prayers are so feeble, wandering and lukewarm? The answer once more is very plain. Their sense of need is not as deep as it ought to be. They are not truly alive to their own weakness and helplessness and so they do not cry fervently for mercy and grace. Let us remember these things.

Help meets men in the path of obedience (v. 14). Our Lord neither touched them nor prescribed means. Yet healing power accompanied the words he spoke. Relief met the afflicted company as soon as they obeyed his command. Surely this teaches us the wisdom of simple, childlike obedience to every word which comes from the mouth of Christ. It does not become us to stand still, reason and doubt when our Master's commands are plain and unmistakable (John 7:17).

For meditation: *'I need Thee every hour'*

(Hawks).

Suggested further reading: Genesis 50:15-20

Our Lord's words seem to convey a reproof to the disciples for not enquiring more earnestly about the heavenly home to which their Master was going. Peter, no doubt, had said with vague curiosity, 'Whither goest thou?' (John 13:36); but his question had not originated in a desire to know the place, so much as in surprise that his Lord was going at all. Our Lord seems here to say, 'If your hearts were in a right frame, you would seek to understand the nature of my going and the place to which I go.'

Let us observe that the disciples, with all their grace, were slow to use their opportunities and to seek the knowledge which they might have obtained. They had not because they asked not.

The minds of the eleven were absorbed and overwhelmed with sorrow at the thought of their Master going and they could think of nothing else. Instead of seizing the little time that was left, in order to learn more from his lips about his place and work in heaven, they were completely taken up with sorrow and could think of nothing else but their Master's departure.

We should do well to mark how mischievous overmuch sorrow is and to seek grace to keep it in proper control. No affection, if uncontrolled, so disarranges the order of men's minds and unfits them for the duties of their calling.

We can well suppose that our gracious Lord saw the minds of his disciples crushed at the idea of his leaving them. Little as they realized his full meaning, on this, as well as on other occasions, they evidently had a vague notion that they were about to be left, like orphans, in a cold and unkind world, by their almighty Friend. Their hearts quailed and shrank back at the thought. Most graciously does our Lord cheer them by words of deep and mysterious meaning. He tells them that his departure, however painful it might seem, was not an evil, but a good. They would actually find it was not a loss, but a gain. His bodily absence would be more useful than his presence.

For meditation: *We do not always see the wisdom of God's ways.*

Suggested further reading: Psalm 92

What a rare thing thankfulness is! Of all the ten lepers whom Christ healed there was only one who turned back and gave him thanks. The words that fell from our Lord's lips upon this occasion are very solemn (v. 17).

The lesson before us is humbling, heart-searching and deeply instructive. The best of us are far too like the nine lepers. We are more ready to pray than to praise, and more disposed to ask God for what we have not than to thank him for what we have. Murmurings, complainings and discontent abound on every side of us. Few indeed are to be found who are not continually hiding their mercies under a bushel and setting their needs and trials on a hill. These things ought not to be so. But all who know the church and the world must confess that they are true. The widespread thanklessness of Christians is a disgrace of our day. It is a plain proof of our little humility.

Let us pray for a daily thankful spirit. It is the spirit which God loves and delights to honour. David and Paul were eminently thankful men. It is the spirit that has marked all the brightest saints in every age of the church. It is the spirit which is the very atmosphere of heaven. Angels and 'just men made perfect' are always blessing God. It is the spirit that is the source of happiness on earth. If we would be anxious for nothing we must make our requests known to God, not only with prayer and supplications, but with thanksgiving (Phil. 4:6).

Above all, let us pray for a deeper sense of our own sinfulness, guilt and undeserving. This, after all, is the true secret of a thankful spirit. It is the man who daily feels his debt to grace, and daily remembers that in reality he deserves nothing but hell, who will be daily blessing and praising God. Thankfulness is a flower which will never bloom excepting upon a root of deep humility.

For meditation: *Perhaps of all the prayers that are prayed, none is prayed with less feeling than the giving of thanks before food. Is it not because in fact we so often feel not one iota of thankfulness for God's provision?*

Suggested further reading: Isaiah 44:1-5

If Christ had not died, risen again and ascended up into heaven, it is plain that the Holy Ghost could not have come down with special power on the Day of Pentecost and bestowed his manifold gifts on the church. Mysterious as it may be, there was a connection in the eternal counsels of God between the ascension of Christ and the outpouring of the Spirit.

If Christ had remained bodily with the disciples, he could not have been in more places than one at the same time. The presence of the Spirit whom he sent down would fill every place where believers were assembled in his name, in every part of the world.

If Christ had remained upon earth and not gone up into heaven, he could not have become a high priest for his people in the same full and perfect manner that he became after his ascension. He went away to sit down at the right hand of God and to appear for us in our human nature glorified, as our Advocate with the Father.

Finally, if Christ had always remained bodily with his disciples, there would have been far less room for the exercise of their faith and hope and trust than there was when he went away. Their graces would not have been called into such active exercise and they would have had less opportunity of glorifying God and exhibiting his power in the world.

After all there remains the broad fact that after the Lord Jesus went away and the Comforter came down on the Day of Pentecost, the religion of the disciples became a new thing altogether. The growth of their knowledge and faith and hope and zeal and courage was so remarkable that they were twice the men they were before. They did far more for Christ when he was absent than they had ever done when he was present. What stronger proof can we require that it was expedient for them that their Master should go away?

For meditation: *A world without a Calvary and a world without a Pentecost are now equally inconceivable.*

Suggested further reading: Matthew 24:23-27

The kingdom of God is utterly unlike the kingdoms of this world (v. 20). Our Lord means that its approach and presence were not to be marked by outward signs of dignity. Those who expected to observe anything of this kind were to be disappointed. They would wait and watch for such a kingdom in vain, while the real kingdom would be in the midst of them without their knowing it (v. 21).

The expression which our Lord here uses decribes exactly the beginning of his spiritual kingdom. It began in a manger in Bethlehem without the knowledge of the great, the rich and the wise. It appeared suddenly in the temple at Jerusalem and none but Simeon and Anna recognized its King. It was received thirty years after by none but a few fishermen and publicans in Galilee. The rulers and Pharisees had no eyes to see it. The King came to his own and his own received him not. All this time the Jews professed to be waiting for his kingdom. But they were looking in the wrong direction. They were waiting for signs that they had no warrant for expecting. The kingdom of God was actually in the midst of them! Yet they could not see it!

The second coming of our Lord will be a very sudden event (v. 24). Of the precise day and hour of that event we know nothing. But whenever it might take place, one thing at least is clear — it will come on the world suddenly without previous notice (Matt. 24:44; 1 Thess. 5:2).

This suddenness of Christ's advent is a solemn thought. It ought to make us study a continual preparedness of mind. Our heart's desire and endeavour should be to be always ready to meet our Lord (Rev. 16:15). Those who denounce the doctrine of the second coming as speculative, fanciful and unpractical would do well to reconsider the subject. The doctrine was not so regarded in the days of the apostles. In their eyes patience, hope, diligence, moderation, personal holiness etc. were inseparably linked with the expectation of our Lord's return.

For meditation: *The Thessalonians turned to serve the living God and to wait for his Son from heaven* (1 Thess. 1:9-10). *You may be serving, but are you also waiting?*

Suggested further reading: Isaiah 32:14-20

When our Lord in this passage speaks of the Holy Spirit 'coming', we must take care that we do not misunderstand his meaning. On the one hand, we must remember that the Holy Ghost was in all believers in the Old Testament days, from the very beginning. No man was ever saved from the power of sin and made a saint, except by the renewing of the Holy Ghost. Abraham and Isaac and Samuel and David and the prophets were made what they were by the operation of the Holy Ghost. On the other hand, we must never forget that after Christ's ascension the Holy Ghost was poured down on men with far greater energy as individuals and with far wider influence on the nations of the world at large than he was ever poured out before. It is this increased energy and influence that our Lord has in view in the verses before us. He meant that after his own ascension the Holy Ghost would 'come' down into the world with such a vastly increased power that it would seem as if he had 'come' for the first time and had never been in the world before.

The difficulty of rightly explaining the wondrous sayings of our Lord in this place is undeniably very great. It may well be doubted whether the full meaning of his words has ever been entirely grasped by man and whether there is not something at the bottom which has not been completely unfolded. The common, superficial explanation that our Lord only meant that the work of the Spirit in saving individual believers is to convince them of their own sins, of Christ's righteousness and of the certainty of judgement at last will hardly satisfy thinking minds. It is a short-cut and superficial way of getting over Scripture difficulties. It contains excellent and sound doctrine, no doubt, but it does not meet the full meaning of our Lord's words. It is truth, but not the truth of the text. It is not individuals here and there whom he says the Spirit is to convince, but the world.

For meditation: *The Spirit strives even with those who ultimately are condemned* (Gen. 6:3).

Suggested further reading: Genesis 19:15-26

What a fearful picture the Lord paints of the state of things at his second coming! (v. 26). We are not left to conjecture the character of Noah's days. We are told distinctly that men were entirely taken up with eating, drinking, marrying, buying, selling, planting and building, and would attend to nothing else. The flood came at last in Noah's day and all drowned except those in the ark. The fire fell from heaven in Lot's day and destroyed all except Lot, his wife and his daughters. And our Lord declares most plainly that like things will happen when he comes at the end of the world (vv. 28-30; 1 Thess. 5:3).

Let us take heed to ourselves and beware of the spirit of the world. It is not enough to do as others and buy, sell, plant, build, eat, drink, marry as if we were born for nothing else. Exclusive attention to these things may ruin us as thoroughly as open sin. We must come out from the world and be separate. We must dare to be peculiar. We must escape for our lives like Lot. We must flee to the ark like Noah. This is safety.

What a solemn warning our Lord gives against unsound profession! (v. 32). Lot's wife went far in religious profession. She was the wife of a righteous man. She was connected with Abraham through him. She fled with her husband from Sodom in the day when he escaped for his life by God's command. But Lot's wife was not really like her husband. Though she fled with him, she left her heart behind her. She wilfully disobeyed the strict injunction that the angel had laid upon her. She looked back towards Sodom and was at once struck dead. She was turned into a pillar of salt and perished in her sins.

Lot's wife is meant to be a warning to all professing Christians. There are many who go to a certain length in religion. They conform to the outward ways of Christian relatives and friends. They say the right words. But the world is in their hearts and their hearts are in the world. In the day of sifting, their unsoundness will be exposed to all the world.

For meditation: *Do not love the world or anything in the world... The world and its desires pass away, but the man who does the will of God lives for ever* (1 John 2:15-17).

Suggested further reading: Acts 2:37-47

Our Lord probably meant to show us what the Holy Ghost would do to the world of unbelieving Jews. He would convince them 'of sin and righteousness and judgement'.

He would convince the Jews of *'sin'*. He would compel them to feel and acknowledge in their own minds that in rejecting Jesus of Nazareth they had committed a great sin and were guilty of gross unbelief.

He would convince the Jews of *'righteousness'*. He would press home on their consciences that Jesus of Nazareth was not an impostor and a deceiver, as they had said, but a holy, just and blameless person, whom God had owned by receiving up into heaven.

He would convince the Jews of *'judgement'*. He would oblige them to see that Jesus of Nazareth had conquered, overcome and judged the devil and all his host and was exalted to be a Prince and a Saviour at the right hand of God.

That the Holy Ghost did actually so convince the Jewish nation after the Day of Pentecost is clearly shown by the Acts of the Apostles. It was he who gave the humble fishermen of Galilee such grace and might in testifying of Christ that their adversaries were put to silence. It was his reproving and convincing power which enabled them to 'fill Jerusalem with their doctrine'. Not a few of the nation, we know, were savingly convinced, like St Paul, and 'a great company of priests' became obedient to the faith. Myriads more, we have every reason to believe, were mentally convinced, if they had not courage to come out and take up the cross. The whole tone of the Jewish people towards the end of the Acts of the Apostles is unlike what it is at the beginning. A vast reproving and convincing influence, even where not saving, seems to have gone over their minds. Surely this was partly what our Lord had in view on these verses when he said, 'The Holy Ghost shall reprove and convince.'

For meditation: *By the means of a single sermon the Holy Spirit converted 3,000 unbelieving Jews. His power has not changed.*

Suggested further reading: Matthew 13:47-50

What an awful separation there will be when Christ comes again! Our Lord describes this separation by a striking picture (vv. 34-35). The meaning of these expressions is clear and plain. The day of Christ's second advent shall be the day when good and evil, converted and unconverted, shall at length be divided into two distinct bodies. The wheat and the tares shall no longer grow side by side. The good fish and the bad fish shall at length be sorted into two bodies. The angels shall come forth and gather together the godly, that they may be rewarded, and leave the wicked behind to be punished. 'Converted or unconverted' will be the only subject of enquiry. It will matter nothing that people have worked together, slept together and lived together for many years. They will be dealt with at last according to their religion. Those members of the family who have loved Christ will be taken up to heaven, and those who have loved the world will be cast down into hell. Converted and unconverted shall be separated for evermore when Jesus comes again.

Let us lay these things to heart. He that loves his relatives and friends is especially bound to consider them. If those whom he loves are true servants of Christ, let him know that he must cast in his lot with them if he would not one day be parted from them for ever. If those whom he loves are yet dead in trespasses and sins, let him know that he must work and pray for their conversion lest he should spend eternity separated from them. Life is the only time for such work. Life is fast ebbing away from us all. Partings, separations and the breaking up of families are at all times painful things. But all the separations that we see now are nothing compared to those which will be seen when Christ comes again.

For meditation: *The gospel proclaims a unity in Christ but a division from that which is outside of Christ. Every Christian is cut off from the world to the church, from sin to God. Paul expresses the reality of this division in a severe saying* (1 Cor. 16:22).

Suggested further reading: Ephesians 2:11-22

Our Lord probably meant to foretell what the Holy Ghost would do for the whole of mankind, both Gentiles as well as Jews.

He would reprove in every part of the earth the current ideas of men about sin, righteousness and judgement, and convince people of some far higher ideas on these points than they had before acknowledged. He would make men see more clearly the nature of sin, the need of righteousness, the certainty of judgement. In a word, he would insensibly be an Advocate and convincing pleader for God throughout the whole world and raise up a standard of morality, purity and knowledge, of which formerly men had no conception.

That the Holy Ghost actually did so in every part of the earth, after the Day of Pentecost, is a simple matter of fact. The unlearned and lowly Jews, whom he sent forth and strengthened to preach the gospel after our Lord's ascension, 'turned the world upside down' and in two or three centuries altered the habits, tastes and practices of the whole civilized world. The power of the devil received a decided check. Even infidels dare not deny that the doctrines of Christianity had an enormous effect on men's ways, lives and opinions, when they were first preached and that there were no special graces or eloquence in the preachers that can account for it. In truth, the world was 'reproved and convinced' in spite of itself, and even those who did not become believers became better men. Surely this also was partly what our Lord had in view when he said to his disciples, 'When the Holy Ghost comes, he shall convince the world of sin, and righteousness, and judgement.'

For meditation: *Through the work of Christ and the Holy Spirit the Jews and the Gentiles have found salvation.*

Suggested further reading: Matthew 7:7-11

Our Lord gives us the purpose of the parable (v. 1). These words are closely connected with the solemn words of the preceding chapter concerning the solemn advent. It is prayer without fainting during the long weary interval between his first and second advents which Jesus is urging his disciples to keep up.

Our Lord conveys the great importance of prayer by telling the story of the friendless widow who obtained justice from a wicked magistrate by virtue of sheer persistence (vv. 2-5).

The subject of prayer ought always to be interesting to Christians. Prayer is the very life breath of true Christianity. Here it is that religion begins. Here it flourishes. Here it decays. Prayer is one of the first evidences of conversion (Acts 9:11). Neglect of prayer is a sure road to a fall (Matt. 26:40-41). Whatever throws light on the subject of prayer is for our soul's health.

Let it then be graven deeply on our minds that it is far more easy to begin a habit of prayer than it is to keep it up. The fear of death, some temporary pricking of conscience, some excited feelings may make a man begin praying after a fashion. But to go on praying requires faith. We are apt to become weary and to give way to the suggestion of Satan that it is of no use. And then comes the time when the parable before us ought to be carefully remembered.

Do we ever feel a secret inclination to hurry our prayers, or shorten our prayers, or become careless about our prayers, or omit our prayers altogether? Let us be sure, when we do, that is a direct temptation from the devil. He is trying to sap and undermine the very citadel of our souls and to cast us down to hell. Let us resolve to pray on steadily, patiently, perseveringly and let us never doubt that it does us good. However long the answer may be in coming, still let us pray on. Whatever sacrifice and self-denial it may cost us, still let us pray on. Whatever we make time for, let us make time for prayer (1 Thess. 5:17; Col. 4:2).

For meditation: *Prayer is not something that is automatic. It requires simple self-discipline. The only way to persist in prayer is to pray on.*

Suggested further reading: Psalm 119:17-24

'The Spirit of truth', says our Lord to his weak and half-informed followers, 'shall guide you into all truth.' That promise was for our sakes, no doubt, as well as for theirs. Whatever we need to know for our present peace and sanctification, the Holy Ghost is ready to teach us. All truth in science, nature and philosophy, of course, is not included in this promise. But into all spiritual truth that is really profitable and that our minds can comprehend and bear, the Holy Spirit is ready and willing to guide us. Then let us never forget, in reading the Bible, to pray for the teaching of the Holy Ghost. We must not wonder if we find the Bible a dark and difficult book, if we do not regularly seek light from him by whom it was first inspired. In this, as in many other things, 'we have not because we ask not'.

Verse 13 is meant to show the close and intimate union existing between the Spirit and the two other persons in the blessed Trinity. 'He shall not speak from himself, independently of me and my Father. He shall only speak such things as he shall hear from us.'

The phrases 'speak' and 'hear' are both accommodations to man's weakness. The Spirit does not literally 'speak' or literally 'hear'. It must mean, 'His teachings and guidings shall be those of one who is in the closest union with the Father and the Son.'

He shall 'glorify Christ'. He shall continually teach and lead and guide disciples to make much of Christ. Any religious teaching which does not tend to exalt Christ has a fatal defect about it. It cannot be from the Spirit.

The object of verse 15 seems to be to show the entire unity between Father, Son and Holy Spirit in the revelation of truth made to man. 'The Holy Spirit shall show you things concerning me, and yet things at the same time concerning the Father because all things that the Father hath are mine.'

For meditation: *Are your prayers for God's help in reading the Scriptures formal or real?*

Suggested further reading: Romans 11:1-5

God has an elect people on earth who are under his special care (vv. 7-8). Election is one of the deepest truths of Scripture. It is clearly and beautifully stated in the Seventeenth Article of the Church of England: 'It is the everlasting purpose of God, whereby, before the foundations of the world were laid, he hath decreed by his counsels, secret to us, to deliver from curse and damnation those whom he hath chosen in Christ out of mankind and to bring them by Christ to everlasting salvation.' This testimony is true (Titus 2:8).

Election is a truth which should call forth praise and thanksgiving from all Christians. Except God had chosen and called them, they would never have chosen and called on him. Except he had chosen them of his own good pleasure, without respect to any goodness that is theirs, there would never have been anything in them to make them worthy of his choice. The worldly and the carnal-minded may rail at the doctrine of election. The false professor may abuse it (Jude 4). But the believer who knows his own heart will ever bless God for election. He will confess that without election there would be no salvation.

But what are the marks of election? By what tokens shall a man know whether he is one of God's elect? These marks are clearly laid down in Scripture. Election is inseparably connected with faith in Christ and conformity to his image (Rom. 8:29-30). It was when Paul saw the working faith, the patient hope and the labouring love of the Thessalonians that he knew their election of God (1 Thess. 1:3-4). Above all we have a plain mark in the passage that is before us. God's elect are a people who cry unto him day and night (v. 7). They are essentially a praying people. No doubt there are many people whose prayers are formal and hypocritical. But one thing is clear — a prayerless man must never be called one of God's elect. Let that never be forgotten.

For meditation:
Chosen not for good in me,
Wakened up from wrath to flee,
Hidden in the Saviour's side,
By the Spirit sanctified,
Teach me, Lord, on earth to show
By my love how much I owe

(M'Cheyne).

Suggested further reading: Song of Solomon 5:2-6

Christ's absence from the earth will be a time of sorrow to believers, but of joy to the world. It is written: 'Ye shall weep and lament, but the world shall rejoice.' To confine these words to the single point of Christ's approaching death and burial appears a narrow view of their meaning. Like many of our Lord's sayings on the last evening of his earthly ministry, they seem to extend over the whole period of time between his first and second advents.

Christ's personal absence must needs be a sorrow to all true-hearted believers. 'The children of the bride-chamber cannot but fast when the bridegroom is taken from them.' Faith is not sight. Hope is not certainty. Reading and hearing are not the same as beholding. Praying is not the same as speaking face to face. There is something, even in the hearts of the most eminent saints, that will never be fully satisfied as long as they are on earth and Christ is in heaven. So long as they dwell in a body of corruption and see through a glass darkly, so long as they behold creation groaning under the power of sin and all things not put under Christ — so long their happiness and peace must needs be incomplete.

Yet this same personal absence of Christ is no cause of sorrow to the children of this world. It was not to the unbelieving Jews, we may be sure. When Christ was condemned and crucified, they rejoiced and were glad. They thought that the hated reprover of their sins and false teaching was silenced for ever. It is not to the careless and the wicked of our day, we may be sure. The longer Christ keeps away from this earth and lets them alone, the better will they be pleased. 'We do not want this Christ to reign over us' is the feeling of the world. His absence causes them no pain. Their so-called happiness is complete without him. All this may sound very painful and startling. But where is the thinking reader of the Bible who can deny that it is true? The world does not want Christ back again and thinks that it does very well without him. What a fearful waking up there will be by and by!

For meditation: *Do you feel the loss of Christ's presence?*

Suggested further reading: Isaiah 65:1-5

The sin which our Lord denounces is self-righteousness (v. 9). We are all naturally self-righteous. It is the family disease of all the children of Adam. From the highest to the lowest, we think more highly of ourselves than we ought to. We secretly flatter ourselves that we are not so bad as some and that we have something to recommend us to the favour of God (Prov. 20:6). We forget the plain testimony of Scripture (James 3:2; Eccles. 7:20; Job 15:14).

The true cure for self-righteousness is self-knowledge. Once let the eyes of our understanding be opened by the Spirit, and we shall talk no more of our own goodness. Once let us see what there is in our own hearts and what the holy law of God requires, and self-conceit will die.

The prayer of the Pharisee (vv. 11-12) is condemned by the Lord. One great defect stands out on the face of this prayer, a defect so glaring that even a child might mark it. It exhibits no sense of sin and need. It contains no confession and no petition, no acknowledgement of guilt and emptiness, no supplication for mercy and grace. It is a mere boastful recital of fancied merits accompanied by an uncharitable reflection on a brother sinner. It is a proud, high-minded profession, destitute alike of penitence, humility and love. In short, it hardly deserves to be called prayer at all.

No state of soul can be conceived so dangerous as that of the Pharisee. Never are men's bodies in such desperate plight as when mortification and insensibility set in. Never are men's hearts in such a desperate and hopeless condition as when they are not sensible of their own sins. He that would not make shipwreck on this rock must beware of measuring himself by his neighbours. What is the significance of being better than other men, when we consider what we all are in God's sight? (Job 9:3). In all our self-examination let us not try to compare ourselves with other men. Let us look at the requirements of God alone.

For meditation: *We are used to being addressed as 'brethren and sisters'. How would we like sermons to begin, 'My dear fellow sinners with wicked hearts and lives'?*

Suggested further reading: 2 Thessalonians 1:3-10

Christ's personal return shall be a source of boundless joy to his believing people. It is written: 'I will see you again, and your heart shall rejoice, and your joy no man taketh from you.' Once more we must take care that we do not narrow the meaning of these words by tying them down to our Lord's resurrection. They surely reach much further than this. The joy of the disciples when they saw Christ risen from the dead was a joy soon obscured by his ascension and withdrawal into heaven. The true joy, the perfect joy, the joy that can never be taken away, will be the joy which Christ's people will feel when Christ returns the second time, at the end of this world.

The second personal advent of Christ, to speak plainly, is the one grand object on which our Lord, both here and elsewhere, teaches all believers to fix their eyes. We ought to be always looking for and 'loving his appearing', as the perfection of our happiness and the consummation of all our hopes (2 Peter 3:12; 2 Tim. 4:8). That same Jesus who was taken up visibly into heaven shall also come again visibly, even as he went. Let the eyes of our faith be always fixed on this coming. It is not enough that we look *backwards* to the cross and rejoice in Christ dying for our sins, and *upwards* to the right hand of God and rejoice in Christ's interceding for every believer. We must do more than this. We must look *forwards* to Christ's return from heaven to bless his people and to wind up the work of redemption. Then, and then only, will the prayer of twenty centuries receive its complete answer: 'Thy kingdom come. Thy will be done on earth as it is in heaven.' Well may our Lord say that in that day of resurrection and reunion our 'hearts shall rejoice'. 'When we awake up after his likeness we shall be satisfied' (Ps. 17:15).

For meditation: *Are you looking forward to the Lord's second coming?*

Suggested further reading: Psalm 51

The publican's prayer receives the commendation of our Lord. That prayer was in every respect the very opposite of that of the Pharisee. His whole demeanour and prayer are stamped with our Lord's approbation (vv. 13-14).

The excellence of the publican's prayer consists in five things. Firstly, it was a real petition. A prayer that only contains thanksgiving and profession and asks nothing is essentially defective. It may be suitable for angels, but sinners need to petition God.

Secondly, it was a direct personal prayer. The publican did not speak about his neighbours, but himself. Vagueness and generality are the great defects of most men's religion. To get out of 'we', 'our' and 'us', into 'I', 'my' and 'me' is a great step towards heaven.

Thirdly, it was a humble prayer, a prayer which put self in the right place. The publican confessed plainly that he was a sinner. This is the very ABC of saving Christianity. We never begin to be good till we can feel and say that we are bad.

Fourthly, it was a prayer in which mercy was the chief thing desired and faith in God's covenant mercy, however weak, was displayed. Mercy is the first thing we must ask for in the day we begin to pray. Mercy and grace must be the subject of our daily petitions at the throne of grace until the day we die.

Fifthly, the publican's prayer was one which came from his heart. He was deeply moved in uttering it. He smote upon the breast like one who felt more than he could express. Such prayers are the prayers which are God's delight. A broken and contrite spirit he will not despise (Ps. 51:17).

Let these things sink deep into our hearts. He that has learned to feel his sins has great reason to be thankful. Happy indeed is he who is not ashamed to sit by the side of the publican! Our Lord gives high praise to such humility (v. 14).

For meditation: *We do not speak to an equal when we pray, nor to an inferior, but to an almighty, sinless, sin-hating God. Do our prayers reflect this?*

Suggested further reading: Isaiah 64:1-8

We learn in these verses that while Christ is absent believers must ask much in prayer. It is written: 'Hitherto have ye asked nothing in my name: ask and ye shall receive, that your joy may be full.'

We may well believe that up to this time the disciples had never realized their Master's full dignity. They had certainly never understood that he was the one Mediator between God and man, in whose name and for whose sake they were to put up their prayers. Here they are distinctly told that henceforward they are to 'ask in his name'. Nor can we doubt that our Lord would have all his people, in every age, understand that the secret of comfort during his absence is to be instant in prayer. He would have us know that if we cannot see him with our bodily eyes any longer, we can talk with him and through him have special access to God. 'Ask, and ye shall receive,' he proclaims to all his people in every age, 'and your joy shall be full.'

Let the lesson sink down deeply into our hearts. Of all the list of Christian duties there is none to which there is such abounding encouragement as prayer. It is a duty which concerns all. High and low, rich and poor, learned and unlearned — all must pray. It is a duty for which all are accountable. All cannot read, or hear, or sing, but all who have the Spirit of adoption can pray. Above all, it is a duty in which everything depends on the heart and motive within. Our words may be feeble and ill-chosen and our language broken and ungrammatical and unworthy to be written down. But if the heart be right, it matters not. He that sits in heaven can spell out the meaning of every petition sent up in the name of Jesus and can make the asker know and feel that he receives.

'If we know these things, happy are we if we do them.' Let prayer in the name of Jesus be a daily habit with us every morning and evening of our lives. Keeping up that habit, we shall find strength for duty, comfort in trouble, guidance in perplexity, hope in sickness and support in death.

For meditation: *Does Isaiah 64 reflect your prayer life?*

Suggested further reading: 2 Timothy 1:3-5; 3:10-15

Our Lord instructs us with respect to little children by both word and deed, by both precept and example. These were evidently tender infants, too young to receive instruction, but not too young to receive benefit by prayer. The disciples seem to have thought them beneath their Master's notice and rebuked those that brought them (v. 13). But this brought forth a solemn declaration from the Head of the church (v. 14).

There is something deeply interesting both in the language and action of our Lord on this occasion. We know the weakness and feebleness both in body and mind of a little infant. Of all creatures born into the world none is so helpless and dependent. We know who it was who took such notice of infants and found time in his busy ministry among grown men and women to put his hands on them and pray. It was the eternal Son of God, the great High Priest, the King of kings, by whom all things consist, the brightness of the Father's glory and the express image of his person (Heb. 7:3; Rev. 19:16; Col. 1:17; Heb. 1:3).

Let us learn from these verses that the Lord Jesus cares tenderly for the souls of little children. It is probable that Satan especially hates them. It is certain that Jesus especially loves them. Young as they are, they are not beneath his thoughts and attention. That mighty heart of his has room for the baby in its cradle as well as the king upon his throne. He regards each one as possessing within its little body an undying principle that will outlive the pyramids of Egypt and see sun and moon quenched at the last day.

Let us attempt great things in the religious instruction of children. Let us begin from their very earliest years to deal with them as having souls to be lost or saved and strive to bring them to Christ. Let us make them acquainted with the Bible as soon as they can understand anything. Let us pray for them and with them and teach them to pray for themselves. We may rest assured that Jesus looks with pleasure on such endeavours, and such endeavours are not in vain.

For meditation: *Many modern Christians think 'children's work' can be done by just anyone. Would our Lord have agreed?*

Suggested further reading: Matthew 7:7-11

Clear knowledge of God the Father is one of the foundations of the Christian religion. Our Lord says to his disciples, 'The time cometh when I shall show you plainly of the Father.' He does not say, we should mark, 'I will show you plainly about myself.' It is the Father whom he promises to show.

The wisdom of this remarkable saying is very deep. There are few subjects of which men know so little in reality as the character and attributes of God the Father. It is not for nothing that it is written: 'No man knoweth the Father save the Son, and he to whomsoever the Son shall reveal him' (Matt. 11:27). 'The only begotten Son which is in the bosom of the Father, he hath declared him' (John 1:18). Thousands fancy they know the Father because they think of him as great and almighty and all-hearing and wise and eternal, but they think no further. To think of him as just and yet the justifier of the sinner who believes in Jesus, as the God who sent his Son to suffer and die, as God in Christ reconciling the world unto himself, as God specially well-pleased with the atoning sacrifice of his Son, whereby his law is honoured — to think of God the Father in this way is not given to most men. No wonder that our Master says, 'I will show you plainly of the Father.'

Let it be part of our daily prayers that we may know more of 'the only true God', as well as of Jesus Christ whom he has sent. Let us beware alike of the mistakes which some make, who speak of God as if there was no Christ, and of the mistakes which others make, who speak of Christ as if there was no God. Let us seek to know all three persons in the blessed Trinity and give to each one the honour due to him.

For meditation: *Christianity is no mere Jesus cult. The Son has come to make the Father known* (John 1:18).

Suggested further reading: Acts 24:10-25

A person may have desires after salvation and yet not be saved. Here is one who in a day of abounding unbelief comes of his own accord to Christ. He comes not to have a sickness healed. He comes not to plead about a child. He comes about his own soul. He opens his conversation with a frank question (v. 16). Surely we might have thought this is a promising case — not a prejudiced ruler or Pharisee, but a hopeful enquirer. Yet soon he goes away sorrowful (v. 22), and we never read a word to show that he was ever converted!

We must not forget that good feelings alone in religion are not the grace of God. We may know the truth intellectually. We may often be pricked in conscience. We may have religious affections awakened within us, have many anxieties of souls and shed many tears. But all this is not conversion. It is not the genuine saving work of the Holy Spirit.

Unhappily this is not all that must be said on this point. Not only are good feelings alone not grace, but they are even positively dangerous, if we content ourselves with them and do not act as well as feel. It is a profound remark that passive impressions often repeated gradually lose all their power. Actions often repeated produce a habit in man's mind. Feelings often indulged in, without leading to corresponding actions, will finally exercise no influence at all.

Let us apply this lesson to our own state. Perhaps we know what it is to feel religious fears, wishes and desires. Let us beware that we do not rest in them. Let us never be satisfied till we have the witness of the Spirit in our hearts that we are actually born again and new creatures. Let us never rest until we know that we have actually repented and laid hold on the hope that is set before us in the gospel. It is good to feel. But it is far better to be converted.

For meditation: *The old proverb that 'The road to hell is paved with good intentions' is full of tragic truth. There are too many who dismiss salvation until a more convenient time. They may tremble under the Word, but they do not believe.*

Suggested further reading: Hebrews 6:9-12

Anton paraphrases, 'Ye need not so think of my intercession as if the Father were not himself well disposed, but must first be coerced into kindness. No! He himself loveth you and himself ordained my intercession.'

We should notice here how graciously our Lord acknowledges the grace there was in the disciples, with all their weakness. When myriads of Jews regarded Jesus as an impostor, the eleven loved him and believed in him. Jesus never forgets to honour grace, however much it may be mingled with infirmity.

How weak was the faith and love of the apostles! How soon, in a very few hours, they were buried under a cloud of unbelief and cowardice! These very men whom Jesus commends for loving and believing, before the morning sun arose forsook him and fled. Yet, weak as their graces were, they were real and true and genuine. They were graces which hundreds of learned priests and scribes and Pharisees never attained and, not attaining, died miserably in their sins.

Let us take great comfort in this blessed truth. The Saviour of sinners will not cast off them that believe in him, because they are babes in faith and knowledge. He will not break the bruised reed or quench the smoking flax. He can see reality under much infirmity and where he sees it, he is graciously pleased. The followers of such a Saviour may well be bold and confident. They have a Friend who despises not the least member of his flock and casts out none who come to him, however weak and feeble, if they are only true.

For meditation: *God never forgets anything that we do, however insignificant it is.*

Suggested further reading: Acts 5:1-11

An unconverted person is often profoundly ignorant on spiritual subjects. Our Lord referred this enquirer to the law. Seeing that he speaks so boldly about 'doing', he tries him by a command well calculated to draw out the real state of his heart (v. 17). At once the young man makes a confident assertion (v. 20). So utterly ignorant is he of the spirituality of God's statutes that he never doubts that he has perfectly fulfilled them. He seems thoroughly unaware that the commandments apply to the thoughts and the words as well as to the deeds, and that if God were to enter into judgement with him he could not answer him. How dark must his mind have been as to the nature of God's law! How low must his ideas have been as to the holiness which God requires!

It is a melancholy fact that such ignorance is only too common amongst professing Christians. Thousands of them know no more of the leading doctrines of Christianity than the heathen. Thousands fill churches weekly, who are utterly in the dark as to the full extent of man's sinfulness. They cling obstinately to the notion that somehow their own actions can save them. They are as blind as if they had never heard truth at all (1 Cor. 2:14).

One idol cherished in the heart may ruin a soul for ever. Our Lord detected the weak point in this man's character. It turns out that, with all his wishes and desires after eternal life, there was one thing that he loved better than his soul, and that was his money. He is weighed in the balances and found wanting. He goes away sorrowful (v. 22).

We have one more proof of the truth of Scripture (1 Tim. 6:10). We must place this man in our memories alongside Judas, Ananias and Sapphira, and learn to beware of covetousness. How many near to the kingdom stick fast because they are fond of money? What of us? Have we given up our idols? Is there no secret sin to which we still cling? Is there nothing or no person that we are privately loving more than Christ and our souls? Spiritual idolatry keeps many from Christ (1 John 5:21).

For meditation:
The dearest idol I have known,
Whate'er that idol be,
Help me to tear it from thy throne
And worship only thee

(Cowper).

Suggested further reading: Luke 8:11-15

'When Christ came forth from the Father, he so came into the world as never to leave the Father, and he so left the world and went unto the Father as never to leave the world' (see v. 28).

The words of the disciples seem to be a reference to our Lord's statement in the twenty-fifth verse that the time was coming when he would no more speak in proverbs, but show them plainly concerning the Father. The eleven appear to catch at that promise. 'Even now thou art speaking to us more plainly than we have ever heard thee speaking before, and not in figurative language.'

Verse 29 is a peculiar verse. It is hard to see what there was in our Lord's statement in verse 28 to carry such conviction to the minds of the eleven and to make them see things about their Master so much more clearly than they had seen them before. But the precise reason why words affect men's minds and lay hold on their attention at one time and not at another is a deep mystery and hard to explain. The very same truths which a man hears from one mouth and is utterly unimpressed come home to him with such power from another mouth that he will declare he never heard them before! Nay, more, the very same speaker who is heard without attention one day is heard another day teaching the very same things with the deepest interest by the same hearers and they will tell you they never heard them before!

Our Lord warns the eleven of their self-ignorance. They thought they believed. They did not doubt their own faith. Let them not be too confident. They would soon find they had an evil root of unbelief within. Never do we find our Lord flattering his disciples. Warnings against self-confidence need to be continually pressed on believers. Nothing is so deceptive as feeling and excitement in religion. We know not the weakness of our hearts.

For meditation: *We should never confuse religious enthusiasm with religious conviction.*

Suggested further reading: Revelation 18:4-19

Riches bring an immense danger on the souls of those that possess them. Our Lord states this (v. 23) and supports it by a proverbial expression (v. 24). Few of our Lord's statements seem more startling than this. Few run more counter to the opinions and prejudices of the world. Few are so little believed. Yet this saying is true and to be accepted. Riches, which all desire to obtain, for which men labour and toil and become grey before their time, are a most perilous possession. They often inflict great injury on the soul. They lead men into many temptations. They engross men's thoughts and affections. They bind heavy burdens on the heart and make the way to heaven even more difficult than it naturally is.

Let us beware of the love of money. It is possible to use it well and do good with it. But, for one who makes a right use of money, there are thousands who make a wrong use of it and do harm both to themselves and others. Let the worldly man, if he will, make an idol of money and count him happy who has most of it. But let the Christian who professes to have 'treasure in heaven' set his face like a flint against the spirit of the world in this matter. Let him not worship gold. He is not the best man in God's eyes who has most money, but he who has most grace.

However, the Holy Spirit can incline even the richest of men to seek treasure in heaven (v. 26). He can dispose even kings to cast their crowns at the feet of Jesus and count all things but loss for the sake of the kingdom of God. Proof upon proof is given us of this in the Bible. Abraham, Moses, Job, David, Jehoshaphat, Hezekiah, Josiah — all were wealthy men, but they loved the Lord's favour more than earthly greatness. They show us that faith can grow in the most unlikely soil.

Let us hold fast this doctrine and never let it go. No man's place or circumstances shut him out from the kingdom of God. Let us never despair of anyone's salvation. No doubt rich people require special grace and are exposed to special temptations. But the Lord of Abraham, Moses, Job and David has not changed. He who saved them in spite of their riches can save others, too.

For meditation: *The god of money does not save from hell.*

Suggested further reading: Isaiah 43:1-7

In this sentence our Lord reveals to his confident hearers the amazing fact that they, even they, would in a very short time forsake him, desert him, run away and fail in faith altogether. 'Behold!' he begins, to denote how wonderful it was, 'the hour cometh, yea, is now come. This very night, before the sun rises, the thing is immediately going to take place. Ye shall be scattered, like sheep fleeing from a wolf, one running one way and another another, every man going off to his own things, his own friends, or his own house, or his own place of refuge. Ye shall leave me alone. You will actually allow me to be taken off by myself as a prisoner to the high priests and to Pontius Pilate and not so much as one of you will stand by me.'

How little the best of believers know of their own hearts, or understand how they may behave in times of trial! If any men were ever fully and fairly warned of their coming failure, the disciples were. We can only suppose that they did not understand our Lord, or did not realize the magnitude of the trial coming on them, or fancied that he would work some miracle at the last moment for his deliverance.

Our Lord reminds his disciples that their desertion would not deprive him of all comfort: 'And yet, when you are scattered, and have left me, I am not entirely alone, because the Father is always with me.'

We need not doubt that one great need of the sentence was to teach the disciples where they must look themselves in their own future trials. They must never forget that God the Father would always be near them and with them, even in the darkest times. A sense of God's presence is one great source of the comfort of believers. The last promise in Matthew before the ascension was: 'I am with you always, even unto the end of the world' (Matt. 28:20).

For meditation: *Even in his darkest and loneliest times the believer has the promises of Hebrews 13:5-6.*

Suggested further reading: Matthew 10:37-42

What immense encouragement the gospel offers to those who give up everything for Christ's sake! We are told that Peter asked our Lord what he and the other apostles, who had forsaken all for his sake, should receive in return (v. 27). He obtained a most gracious reply. A full return shall be given to those who have made sacrifices for Christ's sake.

There is something very cheering in this promise. Few in the present day in this land are ever required to forsake homes, relations and lands on account of their religion. Yet there are few true Christians who have not much to go through in one way or another if they are really faithful to the Lord. The offence of the cross is not yet ceased. There can be laughter, ridicule, mockery and family persecution. The favour of the world is often forfeited, places and situations are often imperilled by a conscientious adherence to the demands of the gospel of Christ. All who are exposed to trials of this kind may take comfort in the promise of these verses. Jesus foresaw their need and intended these words to be their consolation.

We may rest assured that no man shall ever be a real loser by following Christ. The believer may seem to suffer a loss for a while when he first begins the life of a devoted Christian. He may be much cast down by the afflictions that are cast upon him on account of his religion. But let him rest assured that he will never find himself a loser in the long run. Christ can raise up friends for us who shall more than compensate for those we lose. Christ can open hearts and homes to us far more warm and hospitable than those that are closed against us. Above all, Christ can give us peace of conscience, inward joy, bright hopes and happy feelings which shall far outweigh every pleasant earthly thing that we have cast away for his sake. He has pledged his royal word that it shall be so. None ever found that word fail. Let us trust it and not be afraid.

For meditation: *God does not always make up our loss immediately. Sometimes we must wait for eternity to receive good from his hand, but ultimately we shall receive it.*

Suggested further reading: Psalm 42

Christ is the true source of peace. We read that our Lord winds up all his discourse with these soothing words: 'These things have I spoken unto you, that ye might have peace.' The end and scope of his parting address, he would have us know, is to draw us nearer to himself as the only fountain of comfort. He does not tell us that we shall have no trouble in the world. He holds out no promise of freedom from tribulation while we are in the body. But he bids us rest in the thought that he has fought our battle and won a victory for us. Though tried and troubled and vexed with things here below, we shall not be destroyed. 'Be of good cheer,' is his parting charge, 'Be of good cheer; I have overcome the world.'

John Huss, the famous martyr who was burned at Constance, is said to have drawn special comfort from this passage during the lonely imprisonment which preceded his death.

Let us lean back our souls on these comfortable words and take courage. The storms of trial and persecution may sometimes beat heavily on us, but let them only drive us closer to Christ. The sorrows and losses and crosses and disappointments of our life may often make us feel sorely cast down, but let them only make us tighten our hold on Christ. Armed with this very promise let us, under every cross, come boldly to the throne of grace that we may obtain mercy and find grace to help in time of need. Let us often say to our souls, 'Why art thou cast down, and why art thou disquieted?' And let us often say to our gracious Master, 'Lord, didst not thou say, "Be of good cheer"? Lord, do as thou hast said, and cheer us to the end.'

For meditation: *Meditation upon the character of God is a great cure for depression.*

Suggested further reading: Romans 4:16-25

In the calling of the nations to the professed knowledge of himself God exercises free, sovereign and unconditional grace. He calls the families of the earth into the visible church at his own time and in his own way. We see this truth in the history of God's dealings with the world. We see the children of Israel called and chosen to be God's people in the very beginning of the day. We see some of the Gentiles called at a later period by the preaching of the apostles. We see others being called in the present age by the labours of missionaries. We still see others uncalled, 'unhired' (v. 7). Why is this? We cannot tell. We only know that God loves to hide pride from the churches. He will never allow the older branches of his church to look contemptuously at the younger. The gospel holds out the same pardon and peace through Christ as in Bible times.

In the saving of individuals, as well as in the calling of nations, God acts as a Sovereign and gives no account in these matters (Rom. 9:15). This is a truth we see illustrated on every side in the church of Christ. We see a young man like Timothy labouring for the rest of his life for the Lord. We see an old man at the end of his life plucked like a brand from the burning on the edge of eternity. And yet the whole tenor of the gospel leads us to believe that both of these men are equally saved. Both are equally forgiven before God. Both are equally washed in Christ's blood and clothed in Christ's righteousness. Both are equally justified, accepted and will be found at Christ's right hand on the last day.

There can be no doubt that this doctrine sounds strange to the ignorant and inexperienced Christian. It confounds the pride of human nature. It leaves the self-righteous man no room to boast. It is a levelling, humbling doctrine and gives occasion to many a murmur. It is impossible to reject it unless we reject the whole Bible. True faith in Christ, though it be a day old, like that of the dying thief, justifies a man before God as completely as the faith of a lifelong servant of God like Timothy.

For meditation: *Biblical salvation leaves no place for human boasting.*

Suggested further reading: Hebrews 5:7-10

Henry remarks that this was a prayer after sermon, a prayer after sacrament, a family prayer, a parting prayer, a prayer before a sacrifice, a prayer which was a specimen of Christ's intercession.

We have here the only long prayer of the Lord Jesus which the Holy Ghost has thought good to record for our learning. That he often prayed we know well; but this is the only prayer reported. We have many of his sermons, parables and conversations, but only this prayer.

We have here the prayer of one who spake as never man spake and prayed as never man prayed, the prayer of the Second Person in the Trinity to the Father, the prayer of one whose office it is, as our High Priest, to make intercession for his people.

We have a prayer offered up by the Lord Jesus on a specially interesting occasion, just after the Lord's Supper, just after a most striking discourse, just before his betrayal and crucifixion, just before the disciples forsook him and fled, just at the end of his earthly ministry.

We have here a prayer which is singularly full of deep and profound expressions, so deep, indeed, that we have no line to fathom them. The wisest Christian will always confess that there are things here which he cannot fully explain.

The Bible reader who attaches no weight to such considerations as these must be in a very strange state of mind.

Augustine remarks, 'The prayer which Christ made for us, he hath also made known to us. Being so great a Master, not only what he saith in discoursing to the disciples, but also what he saith to the Father in praying for them is their edification.'

Calvin remarks, 'Doctrine has no power, unless efficacy is imparted to it from above. Christ holds out an example to teachers, not to employ themselves only in sowing the Word, but by mingling prayers with it to implore the assistance of God, that his blessing may render their labour fruitful.'

For meditation: *If Christ needed to pray, how much more do you?*

Suggested further reading: Hebrews 12:1-4

Our Lord made a clear announcement of his own approaching death
(vv. 18-19). The Lord Jesus knew from the beginning what was
before him. The treachery of Judas Iscariot, the fierce persecution
of the chief priests and scribes, the unjust judgement, the delivery to
Pontius Pilate, the mocking, the scourging, the crown of thorns, the
cross, the hanging between two malefactors, the nails, the spear —
all were spread before his mind like a picture.

How great an aggravation of suffering foreknowledge is, those
who have lived in prospect of some fearful surgical operation know!
Yet none of these things moved the Lord (Isa. 50:5-6). He saw Calvary
in the distance all his life through and yet walked calmly up to it
without turning to the right hand or the left. Surely there was never
sorrow like unto his sorrow or love like his love.

The Lord Jesus was a voluntary sufferer. When he died on the
cross it was not because he had no power to prevent it. He suffered
intentionally, deliberately and of his own free will (John 10:18). He
knew that without the shedding of his own blood there could be no
forgiveness of sins. He knew that he was the Lamb of God who
must die to take away the sin of the world. He knew that his death
was the appointed sacrifice which must be offered up to make reconciliation for iniquity. Knowing all this, he went willingly to the
cross. His heart was set on finishing the mighty work he came into
the world to do. He was well aware that all hinged on his own death
and that without that death his miracles and preaching would have
done comparatively nothing for the world. No wonder that he pressed
on his disciples the fact that he must die. Blessed and happy are
those who know the real meaning and importance of the sufferings
of Christ!

For meditation: *Our Lord knew that he not only had physical and
mental sufferings to endure, but spiritual sufferings also. He who
hated sin was to have sin reckoned to him and be treated as if he
had sinned. He who knows how much God hates sin knows he must
endure that wrath.*

Suggested further reading: Philippians 2:5-11

The 'hour' here named is the hour appointed in God's eternal counsels for the sacrifice of the death of Christ and the final accomplishment of his atonement. That time, which had been promised by God and expected by saints for 4,000 years ever since Adam's fall, had at length arrived and the seed of the woman was actually about to bruise the serpent's head by dying as man's Substitute and Redeemer. Up to this night 'The hour was not yet come' (John 7:30; 8:20); and till it had come, our Lord's enemies could not hurt him. Now, at last, the hour had come and the sacrifice was ready.

Let us remember, though in a far lower sense, that believers are all immortal till their hour is come, and till then they are safe and cannot be harmed by death.

The glory of God and his attributes is the grand end of all creation and of all God's arrangements and providences. Nothing brings such glory to God as the completion of the redeeming work of Christ, by his death, resurrection and ascension into heaven. Our Lord seems to me to ask that his death may at once take place, that he through death may be taken up to glory and that there the justice, holiness, mercy and faithfulness of the Father may be glorified and exhibited to all creation and many souls be at once saved and glorify the divine wisdom and power.

Augustine remarks, 'Some take the Father's glorifying the Son to consist in this, that he spared him not, but delivered him up for us all. But if he be said to be glorified by passion, how much more by resurrection? For in the passion it is more his humility than his glory that is shown forth, as the apostle says in Philippians 2:7-11.'

For meditation: *All that God does he does for his own glory, for there is no greater motive than this, even for him!*

Suggested further reading: Romans 8:12-17

Ignorance and faith may be found mixed even in true-hearted Christians. In making her strange petition (v. 21) the mother of James and John seems to have forgotten all he had just been saying about his sufferings. Her eager mind can think of nothing but his glory. His plain warnings about crucifixion seem to have been thrown away on her sons. Their thoughts were full of nothing but the throne and day of power. There was much faith in their request, but much more of infirmity. There was something to be commended in that they could see in Jesus of Nazareth a coming King. But there was also much to blame because they could not see that he was about to be crucified before he could reign. Truly the flesh lusts against the Spirit in all God's children (Gal. 5:17).

There are many Christians who are like this woman and her sons. They have faith and some knowledge, but there are many truths of which they are deplorably ignorant. But we must learn to deal gently with such people. We must reflect that James and John became pillars in the church. A believer may begin his course in much darkness and yet finally prove a man mighty in the Scriptures.

Our Lord gave this ignorant request a solemn rebuke (v. 22). They had asked to share in their Master's reward but they had not considered that they must first be partakers of their Master's sufferings (1 Peter 4:13). They had forgotten that those who would stand with Christ in glory must also carry the cross.

Do we ever make the same mistake as the sons of Zebedee? We ask that our souls may be saved and go to heaven when we die. It is a good request indeed. But are we prepared to take up the cross, to give up the world, to put off the old man and to put on the new, to fight, to labour, to run so as to obtain? Or do we know not what we ask? We ask to be made holy. But are we willing to be made holy by affliction, bereavement, loss, sickness and sorrow? Or do we not know what we ask? Let us beware of thoughtless, rash petitions.

For meditation: *Biblical Christianity is costly, not a sunny cruise on a calm sea.*

Suggested further reading: Ephesians 1:3-14

We have a glorious account of our Lord Jesus Christ's office and dignity. We read that the Father has 'given him power over all flesh, that he should give eternal life'. The keys of heaven are in Christ's hands. The salvation of every soul of mankind is at his disposal.

There is a twofold giving of men to the Son by the Father. One is eternal, in the purpose of his grace, and this is mainly meant here. The other is in time, when the Father by his Spirit draws men to Christ (John 6:44). All the elect are given from eternity to the Son, to be redeemed by his blood, and all the redeemed are in due time drawn by the Father to the Son, to be kept to eternal life.

The Son gives 'eternal life' to none but those who are 'given to him', in the everlasting counsels of the Trinity, from all eternity. Who these are man cannot say. 'Many of the given ones,' says Traill, 'do not for a long time know it.' All are invited to repent and believe, without distinction. No one is warranted in saying, 'I was not given to Christ and cannot be saved.' But that the last day will prove that none are saved except those given to Christ by the Father is clear and plain.

The phrase 'eternal life' includes everything that is necessary to the complete salvation of a soul — the life of justification, sanctification and final glory.

Poole remarks, 'We need not ascend up to heaven to search the rolls of the eternal counsels. All whom the Father hath given to Christ shall come to Christ and not only receive him as Priest, but give themselves up to be ruled and quickened by him. By such a receiving of Christ we shall know whether we are of the number of those that are given to Christ.'

For meditation: *Every believer is a love gift to Christ from the Father from all eternity.*

Suggested further reading: 1 John 1:5 - 2:6

There may be pride, jealousy and love of pre-eminence even amongst true disciples of Christ (v. 24). Pride is one of the oldest and most mischievous of sins. By it the angels fell (Jude 6). Through pride Adam and Eve were seduced into eating forbidden fruit. They were not content and thought they would be as 'gods' (Gen. 3:5). From pride the saints of God receive their greatest injuries after conversion.

A life of self-denying kindness to others is the true secret of greatness in the kingdom of Christ (v. 26). The standard of the world and the standard of the Lord Jesus are indeed widely different. They are more than different. They are flatly contradictory one to the other. Amongst the children of this world he is thought the most great who has most land, most money, most servants, most rank and most earthly power. Amongst the children of God he is reckoned greatest who does most to promote the spiritual and temporal happiness of his fellow creatures. True greatness consists not in receiving, but giving; not in selfish absorption of good things, but in imparting good to others; not in being served, but in serving; not in sitting still and being ministered to, but in going about and ministering to others. The angels of God see far more beauty in the work of the missionary than in the victories of generals, the political speeches of statesmen or the council chambers of kings. Let us seek true greatness (Acts 20:35).

The Lord Jesus is the true Christian's example (v. 28). Not only has the Lord God provided those who follow after holiness with the clearest of precepts, the best of motives and the most encouraging of promises, but he has supplied them with the most perfect pattern and example in the life of his Son. By that life he bids us walk (1 Peter 2:21). He is the model after which we must strive to mould our tempers, our words and our works in this evil world. How he would have spoken and behaved is the key to how we should speak and behave. How humbling this truth is! (1 John 2:6).

For meditation: *We are only to imitate others in so far as they imitate Christ* (1 Cor. 11:1).

Suggested further reading: Hebrews 8:7-12

Verse 3 is mercifully given to us by our Lord as a description of saved souls: 'The secret of possessing eternal life, of being justified and sanctified now and glorified hereafter, consists simply in this: in having a right saving knowledge of the one true God and of that Jesus Christ whom he has sent to save sinners.' In short, our Lord declares that he who rightly knows God and Christ is the man who possesses eternal life.

Of course, we must distinctly understand that mere head-knowledge, like that of the devil, is not meant by our Lord in this verse. The knowledge he means is a knowledge which dwells in the heart and influences the life. A true saint is one who 'knows the Lord'. To know God on the one hand — his holiness, his purity, his hatred of sin — and to know Christ on the other hand — his redemption, his mediatorial office, his love to sinners — are the two grand foundations of saving religion.

Right knowledge, after all, lies at the root of all vital Christianity, as light was the beginning of creation. We need to be 'renewed in knowledge' (Col. 3:10). We must know what we believe and we cannot properly worship an unknown God. 'Do we know God?' and 'Do we know Christ aright?' are the two great questions to be considered. God known out of Christ is a consuming fire and will fill us with fear only. Christ known without God will not be truly valued; we shall see no meaning in his cross and passion. To see clearly at the same time a holy, pure, sin-hating God and a loving, merciful, sin-atoning Christ is the very ABC of comfortable religion. In short, it is life eternal to know rightly God and Christ. 'To know God without Christ', says Newton, 'is not to know him savingly.'

God out of Christ is a consuming fire; God not worshipped in Christ is an idol; all hopes of acceptance out of Christ are vain dreams.

For meditation: *To have eternal life after death is the consequence of having eternal life now.*

Suggested further reading: Genesis 32:22-32

What wisdom there is in using every opportunity for getting good for our souls! These blind men sat by the wayside. Had they not done so they would never have been healed. Jesus never returned to Jericho again. Let us see in this simple fact the importance of diligence in the use of the means of grace. Let us never neglect the house of God, the Word of God, prayer, assembling with God's people. These things will not save us without the grace of the Holy Spirit. But it is just in the use of these things that souls are converted and saved. They are the ways in which Jesus walked. We do not wait in idleness but go where he is.

There is a value in pains and perseverance in seeking Christ. These blind men were rebuked by the multitude that accompanied our Lord (v. 31). But they were not to be silenced in any way. They felt their need of help. They cared nothing for the opposition they received. They cried all the more (v. 31). Nor are we to be deterred by opposition, or discouraged by difficulties, when we begin to seek the salvation of our souls (Luke 18:1). We must press our petitions at the throne of grace (Gen. 32:26). Friends, relatives and neighbours may say unkind things and reprove our earnestness. We may meet with coldness and lack of sympathy where we might have looked for help. But let none of these things move us. If we desire to have our sins forgiven let us press on.

How gracious the Lord Jesus is to those who seek him! (v. 32). He stood still, called the blind men, kindly asked them their petition, heard it and did as they requested (vv. 32-34). We see here the mercifulness of Christ's heart towards men. The Lord Jesus is not only a mighty Saviour, but merciful, kind and gracious to a degree our minds cannot conceive. His love passes knowledge (Eph. 3:19). Like Paul, let us pray that we might know more of that love. We need it when we first begin our Christian course as babes in grace. We need it as we travel along the narrow way, often erring, often stumbling and cast down. We shall need it when we go into the valley of the shadow of death. Let us grasp the love of Christ firmly and keep it daily before our minds.

For meditation: *Has Christ yet rejected any who come to him?*

Suggested further reading: Hebrews 10:11-14

The meaning of these words I take to be this: 'I have now glorified thee during my life on earth by keeping thy law perfectly, so that Satan can find no defect or blemish in me, by witnessing faithfully to thy truth in opposition to the sins and false teaching of the Jews, by showing thee and thy mind towards man in a way that was never known before.'

Christ alone, of all born of woman, could say literally, 'I have finished the work thou gavest me to do.' He did what the first Adam failed to do and all the saints in every age fail to do: he kept the law perfectly and by so keeping it brought in everlasting righteousness for all them that believe. Yet here is the model we ought to keep before our eyes continually. We must aim to finish the work our Father appoints for us, whether great or small.

Musculus remarks that true godly obedience is to be seen not merely in doing such work as we arbitrarily take up, but in doing such work as God appoints us to do.

The glory which the Son had with the Father, in the time before the creation of the world, is a matter passing our comprehension. But the pre-existence of Christ, the doctrine that Father and Son are two distinct persons and the equal glory of the Father and the Son are at any rate taught here very plainly. It seems perfectly impossible to reconcile the verse with the Socinian theory that Christ was a mere man, like David or Paul, and did not exist before he was born at Bethlehem.

Let us also learn the practical lesson that a prayer for glory comes best from those who have done work upon earth for God. A lazy wish to go to glory without working is not according to Christ's example.

For meditation: *The crown follows the race. It is not for the non-starter or the person who gives up* (Heb. 10:35).

Suggested further reading: John 7:45-52

No one is too bad to be saved or beyond the power of Christ's grace. We are told of a wealthy tax collector becoming a disciple of Christ. A more unlikely event we cannot well imagine! We see the camel passing through the eye of the needle and the rich man entering the kingdom of God (Matt. 19:23-24). We see a plain proof that all things are possible with God. We see a covetous tax collector transformed into a generous Christian.

The door of hope that the gospel reveals to sinners is very wide open. Let us leave it as open as we find it. We should never be afraid to maintain that Christ is able to save to the uttermost (Heb. 7:25), and that the vilest of sinners may be forgiven freely if they will only come to him. We should offer the gospel boldly to the worst and the wickedest (Isa. 1:18). Such doctrine may seem to the worldly as foolish and a licence for evil. But such doctrine is the gospel of him who saved Zacchaeus at Jericho. There are no incurables under the gospel. Any sinner may be healed if he will only come to Christ.

A soul's salvation may turn on little and insignificant things. Curiosity, and only curiosity, seems to have been the motive of Zacchaeus' mind (v. 3). That curiosity once aroused, Zacchaeus was determined to gratify it. Rather than not see Jesus, he ran along the road and climbed up a tree. Upon that little action, as far as man's eyes can see, hinged the salvation of his soul.

We must never despise the day of small things (Zech. 4:10). We must never reckon anything little that concerns the salvation of a soul. The ways by which the Holy Spirit leads men and women are wonderful and mysterious. He is often beginning a heart-work that shall stand for eternity when a looker-on observes nothing marvellous. Whenever we see little signs let us be hopeful. Let us not look on a man coldly because his motives are poor. It is far better to hear the gospel from wrong motives than not to hear it at all. He may go on to receive Christ.

For meditation: *The excitement of living as Christians is that a simple word or action can be the very thing God will use to bring someone else to himself.*

Suggested further reading: Revelation 7:1-8

Believers are 'given' to Christ by the Father, according to an ever-lasting covenant made and sealed long before they were born, and taken out from the world by the calling of the Spirit in due time. They are the Father's peculiar property, as well as the property of the Son. They were of the world and nowise better than others. Their calling and election out of the world to be Christ's people, and not any foreseen merit of their own, is the real foundation of their character.

These are deep things, things to be read with peculiar reverence, because they are the words of the Son addressed to the Father and handling matter about believers which the eternal Trinity alone can handle with positiveness and certainty. Who those are who are given to Christ by the Father we can only certainly know by outward evidences. But that all believers are so given by the Father, predestined, elect, chosen, called by an everlasting covenant and their names and exact number known from all eternity, is truth which we must reverently believe and never hesitate to receive. So long as we are on earth, we have to do with invitations, promises, commands, evidences and faith, and God's election never destroys our responsibility. But all true believers, who really repent and believe and have the Spirit, may fairly take comfort in the thought that they were known and cared for and given to Christ by an eternal covenant, long before they knew Christ or cared for him. It is an unspeakable comfort to remember that Christ cares for that which the Father had given him.

Our Lord continues the description of his disciples and names things about them which may be seen by men as well as God. He says, 'They have kept, or observed, or attended to, the word of the gospel, which thou didst send them by me. While others would not attend to or keep that word, these eleven men had hearing ears and attentive hearts and diligently obeyed thy message.' Practical obedience is the first great test of genuine discipleship.

For meditation: *'For those God foreknew he also predestined to be conformed to the likeness of his Son ... those he justified, he also glorified'* (Rom. 8:29-30).

Suggested further reading: Acts 26:12-20

A more striking instance than that before us of Christ's free compassion towards sinners and Christ's power to change hearts is impossible to conceive. Unasked, our Lord stops and speaks to Zacchaeus. Unasked, he offers himself to be a guest at his house. Unasked, he sends into the heart of a tax collector the renewing grace of the Spirit and puts him among the very children of God.

It is impossible that with such a passage before us we will exalt too highly the grace of our Lord Jesus. We cannot maintain too strongly that there is in him an infinite readiness to receive and an infinite ability to save sinners. Above all, we cannot hold too firmly that salvation is not of works but of grace. If ever there was a soul that was saved without having done anything to deserve it, that soul was the soul of Zacchaeus. Let us grasp these doctrines firmly and never let them go. Their price is above rubies. Grace, free grace, is the only thought that gives men rest in a dying hour. Let us proclaim these doctrines confidently to everyone to whom we speak about spiritual things. Let us bid them come to Jesus Christ, just as they are, and not wait in vain hope that they can make themselves fit and worthy to come.

Converted sinners will always give evidence of their conversion. There was reality in Zacchaeus' speech (v. 8). There was unmistakable proof that Zacchaeus was a new creature. When a wealthy Christian begins to distribute his riches and an extortioner begins to make restitution, we may well believe that old things have passed away and that all things are become new (2 Cor. 5:17). Zacchaeus does not speak of future intentions. He does not say, 'I will', but 'I do'. Freely pardoned, raised from death to life, Zacchaeus felt that he could not begin to show too soon whose he was and whom he served.

He that desires to give proof that he is a believer should walk in the steps of Zacchaeus. Let him, like him, thoroughly renounce the sins which have formerly most easily beset him. Let him follow the Christian graces that formerly he has habitually neglected.

For meditation: *What evidences of conversion are there in your life?*

Suggested further reading: Luke 21:1-4

What a gracious account we have of our Lord Jesus Christ's disciples! We find our Lord himself saying of them, 'They have kept thy word ... they have known that all things thou hast given me are of thee ... they have received thy words ... they have known surely that I came out from thee ... they have believed that thou didst send me.'

These are wonderful words when we consider the character of the eleven men to whom they were applied. How weak was their faith! How slender their knowledge! How shallow their spiritual attainments! How faint their hearts in the hour of danger! Yet a very little time after Jesus spoke these words they all forsook him and fled and one of them denied him three times with an oath. No one, in short, can read the four Gospels with attention and fail to see that never had a great master such weak servants as Jesus had in the eleven apostles. Yet these very weak servants were the men of whom the gracious Head of the church speaks here in high and honourable terms.

The lesson before us is full of comfort and instruction. It is evident that Jesus sees far more in his believing people than they see in themselves, or than others see in them. The least degree of faith is very precious in his sight. Though it be no bigger than a grain of mustard seed, it is a plant of heavenly growth and makes a boundless difference between the possessor of it and the man of the world. Wherever the gracious Saviour of sinners sees true faith in himself, however feeble, he looks with compassion on many infirmities and passes by many defects. It was even so with the eleven apostles. They were weak and unstable as water, but they believed and loved their Master when millions refused to own him.

For meditation: *Our Lord loves to praise his children.*

Suggested further reading: 2 Corinthians 5:1-10

In this parable we are told the present position of our Lord (v. 12). When the Lord Jesus left the world he ascended into heaven as a conqueror, leading captivity captive. He is there sitting at the right hand of God, doing the work of a High Priest for all his believing people, and ever making intercession for them. But he will not sit there always. He will come forth from the holy of holies to bless his people. When Christ returns the kingdoms of this earth shall become his.

All professing Christians are compared to servants who have been left in charge of money by an absent master with strict instructions to use that money well (v. 13). The countless privileges which Christians enjoy compared to others are like money given to them by Christ for which they must one day give account. Our responsibility is far greater than that of those who have never heard the gospel. Much has been given to us and much will be required.

Are we living like men who know to whom they are indebted and to whom they must one day give account? This is the only life worthy of a reasonable being. The best answer we can give to those who invite us to plunge into worldliness and frivolity is the Master's commandment which is before us. Let us tell them that we will not consent because we are looking for the coming of the Lord. We must be busy until he comes.

A certain reckoning awaits all professing Christians (v. 15). There is a day coming when the Lord Jesus Christ shall judge his people and give to everyone according to his works. The course of this world shall not always go on as now. Disorder, confusion, false profession and unpunished sin shall not always cover the face of the earth. The Judge shall sit on his throne. High and low, rich and poor, gentle and simple will all at length give an account to God. Let this thought exercise an influence on our hearts and lives. The time for wickedness to triumph is short. Let us judge ourselves so that we shall not be condemned and let us live in the light of the judgement (1 Cor. 11:31; James 2:12).

For meditation: *Let our one ambition in life or death be to please Christ.*

Suggested further reading: Deuteronomy 4:5-8

In verse 9 our Lord begins that part of his prayer which is specially intercessory and proceeds to name things which he asks for his disciples, from this point down to the end of the chapter. It may be convenient to remember that the things he asks may be divided under four heads. He prays that his disciples may be kept, sanctified, united and be with him in glory. Four more important things cannot be desired for believers.

The Lord Jesus does things for his believing people which he does not do for the wicked and unbelieving. He helps their souls by special intercession. He says, 'I pray for them: I pray not for the world, but for them which thou hast given me.'

The doctrine before us is one which is specially hated by the world. Nothing gives such offence and stirs up such bitter feeling among the wicked as the idea of God making any distinction between man and man and loving one person more than another. Yet the world's objections to the doctrine are, as usual, weak and unreasonable. Surely a little reflection might show us that a God who regarded good and bad, holy and unholy, righteous and unrighteous, with equal complacency and favour would be a very strange kind of God!

Of course, like every other gospel truth, the doctrine before us needs careful statement and scriptural guarding. On the one hand, we must not narrow the love of Christ to sinners, and on the other, we must not make it too broad. It is true that Christ loves all sinners and invites all to be saved, but it is also true that he specially loves the 'blessed company of all faithful people' whom he sanctifies and glorifies. It is true that he has wrought out a redemption *sufficient* for all mankind and offers it freely to all, but it is also true that his redemption is *effectual* only to them that believe.

For meditation: *As the husband has a special love reserved exclusively for his wife, so Christ has a special love for his people.*

Suggested further reading: Revelation 6:12-17

All true Christians shall certainly be rewarded. Our Lord tells us that those who are found to have been faithful servants shall receive honour and dignity. Each shall receive a reward proportioned to his diligence.

The people of God receive little apparent recompense in this present time. Their names are often cast out as evil. They enter the kingdom of God through much tribulation. Their good things are not in this world. The gain of godliness does not consist in earthly rewards, but in inward peace, hope and joy in believing. But they shall have an abundant recompense one day. They shall receive wages far exceeding what they have done for Christ. They shall find, to their amazement, that for everything they have done and borne for their Master, their Master will pay them back a hundredfold. Let us often look to the good things that are yet to come.

All unfaithful professing Christians shall be exposed at the last day. We are told of a faithless servant, his useless arguments in his own defence and of his final ruin for not using the knowledge that he confessedly possessed.

Let us never forget the end to which all ungodly people are coming. Sooner or later, the unbeliever and the impenitent will be put to shame before the whole world, stripped of the means of grace and hope of glory, and cast down to hell. There will be no escape at the last day. False profession and formality will fail to abide the fire of God's judgement. Grace, and grace only, shall stand. Men will discover at last that there is such a thing as the wrath of the Lamb. The excuses with which so many content their consciences now shall prove unavailing at the bar of Christ. The possessors of buried talents and misused privileges will discover at last that it would have been good for them never to have been born. These are solemn things. Who shall stand in the great day when the Master requires an account? Listen to Peter's appropriate words (2 Peter 3:14).

For meditation: *An opportunity passed is an opportunity lost and unable to be recalled.*

Suggested further reading: 1 Timothy 2:1-6

Christ is the Mediator between God and man, but it is also true that he intercedes actively for none but those that come unto God by him. Hence it is written: 'I pray for them: I pray not for the world.'

This special intercession of the Lord Jesus is one grand secret of the believer's safety. He is daily watched and thought for and provided for with unfailing care by one whose eye never slumbers and never sleeps. Jesus is 'able to save them to the uttermost who come unto God by him, because he ever liveth to make intercession for them' (Heb. 7:25). They never perish, because he never ceases to pray for them and his prayer must prevail. They stand and persevere to the end, not because of their own strength and goodness, but because Jesus intercedes for them. When Judas fell never to rise again, while Peter fell but repented and was restored, the reason of the difference lay under those words of Christ to Peter: 'I have prayed for thee, that thy faith fail not' (Luke 22:32).

The true servant of Christ ought to lean back his soul on the truth before us and take comfort in it. It is one of the peculiar privileges and treasures of a believer and ought to be well known. However much it may be wrested and abused by false professors and hypocrites, it is one which those who really feel in themselves the workings of the Spirit should hold firmly and never let go. Well says the judicious Hooker, 'No man's condition is so safe as ours: the prayer of Christ is more than sufficient both to strengthen us, be we never so weak; and to overthrow all adversary power, be it never so strong and potent.'

For meditation: *'So they took away the stone. Then Jesus looked up and said, "Father, I thank you that you have heard me. I knew that you always hear me, but I said this for the benefit of the people standing here, that they may believe that you sent me"'* (John 11:41-42).

Suggested further reading: Hebrews 6:9-12

What honour Christ loves to put on those that honour him! The woman who poured a box of precious ointment on him did it no doubt out of reverence and affection for him. She had received soul benefit from him and she considered no mark of honour too costly to bestow on him in return. But this deed of hers called forth disapprobation from some who saw it. They called it 'waste'. They said it might have been better to sell the ointment and give the money to the poor. At once our Lord rebuked these cold-hearted fault-finders. He commended the woman and accepted her work and approved of it. Then he made his striking prediction about her action (v. 13).

We see in this little incident how perfectly our Lord knew things to come and how easy it is for him to confer honour. The prophecy concerning this woman is fulfilled before our very eyes. Wherever the Gospel of Matthew is read the deed that she did is known. The deeds and titles of many a king, emperor and general are as completely forgotten as if written in the sand. But the grateful act of this one humble Christian woman is recorded in Bibles in hundreds of languages all over the globe. The praise of man is but for a few days; the praise of Christ endureth for ever. The pathway to lasting honour is to honour Christ.

We see in this incident a blessed foretaste of things that will yet take place in the Day of Judgement. In that great day no honour done to Christ on earth shall be found to have been forgotten. The speeches of orators, the exploits of warriors, the works of poets and painters shall not be mentioned in that day. But the least work of the least Christian done for Christ or his members shall be found written in a book of everlasting remembrance. Not a single kind word or deed, not a cup of cold water or a box of ointment shall be omitted from the record. Men may call sacrifices for Christ's sake 'waste' — waste of time, waste of money, waste of strength. But the eye of Christ is on us. He notes these things and is well pleased. Let us continue in them (1 Cor. 15:58).

For meditation: *When our Christian service is not appreciated by men let us remember that it is not done for them but for Christ. He appreciates it.*

Suggested further reading: Philippians 1:1-6

The 'son of perdition', of course, refers to Judas Iscariot, the traitor, the only one of the apostles who was lost and cast away in hell. The name given to Judas is a strong Hebraism and means 'a person worthy of perdition, or only fit to be lost and cast away, by reason of his wickedness'. David says to Saul's servants, 'Ye are worthy to die,' or, as the margin says, 'sons of death' (1 Sam. 26:16). Again he says to Nathan, 'The man that hath done this thing shall surely die,' or, 'is a son of death' (2 Sam. 12:5; see also Ps. 79: 11; Matt. 13:38; Luke 16:8). It is a tremendously strong expression to come from the lips of our merciful and loving Saviour. It shows the desperate helplessness of anyone who, living in great light and privileges like Judas, misuses his opportunities and deliberately follows the bent of his own sinful inclinations. He becomes the 'child of hell' (Matt. 23:15).

A question of very grave importance arises out of the words before us. Did our Lord mean that Judas was originally one of those that the Father 'gave to him' and was primarily a true believer? Did he therefore fall away from grace?

I maintain that the 'but' in the text is not an 'exceptive' word, but an 'adversative' one. I hold the right meaning to be: 'Those whom thou gavest me I have kept, and out of them not one is lost. But there is one man who is lost, even Judas, the son of perdition; not one who was ever given to me, but one whom I declared long ago to be a "devil", a man whose hardened heart fitted him for destruction.'

Our Lord does not mean, 'Not one of those given to me is lost *except* the son of perdition.' What he does mean is: 'Not one *of those given to me* is lost. On the other hand, and in contrast, Judas, a man not given to me, a graceless man, is lost.'

For meditation:
The work that his goodness began,
The arm of his strength will complete

(Toplady).

Suggested further reading: John 21:15-17

Our Lord Jesus Christ has perfect knowledge. We see him sending two of his disciples to a village and telling them what they will find and where, what they will see and hear, with as much confidence as if the whole transaction had been previously arranged. In short, he speaks like one to whom all things are naked and open, like one whose eyes are in every place, like one who knew things unseen as well as seen.

An attentive reader will observe the same thing in other parts of the Gospel. We are told in one place that he knew the thoughts of his enemies (Matt. 12:25). We are told in another that he knew what was in a man (John 2:25). Yet again he knew which of them believed and who would betray him from the beginning (John 6:64). Knowledge like this is a peculiar attribute of God. Passages like this are meant to remind us that the man Christ Jesus is not only man. He is also God blessed for ever (Rom. 9:5).

The thought of Christ's perfect knowledge should alarm sinners and awaken them to repentance. The great Head of the church knows them and all their doings. The Judge of all sees them continually and marks down all their ways. There is no darkness where the workers of iniquity can hide themselves (Job 34:22). If they go into the secret room, the eyes of Christ are there. If they privately scheme villainy and plot wickedness, Christ knows it and observes it. If they speak secretly against the righteous, Christ hears. They may deceive men all their life long but they cannot deceive Christ. A day comes when God judges their secrets (Rom. 2:16).

The thought of Christ's perfect knowledge should comfort all true-hearted Christians and quicken them to increased diligence in good works. The Master's eye is always upon them. He knows where they live, what are their daily trials and who are their companions. There is not a word in their mouths or a thought in their hearts but Jesus knows it completely. Let them take comfort and courage. He knows (John 21:17).

For meditation: *His knowledge encompasses everything. His sovereignty controls it all. Yesterday, today and tomorrow are safe with him.*

Suggested further reading: 1 Kings 19:1-9

Christ does not wish his believing people to be taken out of the world, but to be kept from the evil of it.

We need not doubt that our Lord's all-seeing eye detected in the hearts of his disciples an impatient desire to get away from this troubled world. Few in number and weak in strength, surrounded on every side by enemies and persecutors, they might well long to be released from the scene of conflict and to go home. Even David had said in a certain place, 'Oh, that I had wings like a dove, then would I flee away and be at rest!' (Ps. 55:6). Seeing all this, our Lord has wisely placed on record this part of his prayer for the perpetual benefit of his church. He has taught us the great lesson that he thinks it better for his people to remain in the world and be kept from its evil than to be taken out of the world and removed from the presence of evil altogether.

Nor is it difficult on reflection to see the wisdom of our Lord's mind about his people, in this as in everything else. Pleasant as it might be to flesh and blood to be snatched away from conflict and temptation, we may easily see that it would not be profitable. How could Christ's people do any good in the world, if taken away from it immediately after conversion? How could they exhibit the power of grace and make proof of faith and courage and patience, as good soldiers of a crucified Lord? How could they be duly trained for heaven and taught to value the blood and intercession and patience of their Redeemer, unless they purchased their experience by suffering? Questions like these admit of only one kind of answer. To abide here in this vale of tears, tried, tempted, assaulted and yet kept from falling into sin, is the surest plan to promote the sanctification of Christians and to glorify Christ.

For meditation: *The Lord does not promise to preserve us **from** trouble, but **through** troubles.*

Suggested further reading: Acts 26:12-26

Our Lord's last entry into Jerusalem was very public. He rode on an ass like a king visiting his capital city, or a conqueror returning in triumph to the native land. A multitude of rejoicing disciples surrounded him as he rode into the city. The whole history is strikingly unlike the general tenor of our Lord's life. On other occasions we see him withdrawing from public observation, retiring into the wilderness, charging those whom he healed to tell no one what was done. On the present occasion all is changed. Reserve is completely thrown aside. He seems to court public notice. He appears desirous that all should see him and should mark, note and observe what he did.

The reasons for our Lord's conduct at the crisis of his ministry are clear and plain. He knew that the time had come when he was to die for sinners on the cross. His work as the great Prophet, so far as his earthly ministry was concerned, was almost finished and completed. His work as the sacrifice for sin and substitute for sinners remained to be accomplished. Before giving himself up as a sacrifice he desired to draw the attention of the whole Jewish nation to himself. The Lamb of God was about to be slain. The great sin offering was about to be killed. It was fitting that all the eyes of Israel should be fixed upon him.

For ever let us bless God that the death of the Lord was so widely known and so public an event. Had he been suddenly stoned by a mob or privately beheaded, there would have been those who would have denied he died at all. The wisdom of God so ordered events that such a denial was rendered impossible. Whatever men may think of the doctrine of Christ's atoning death, they can never deny the fact that Christ died. Publicly he rode into Jerusalem. Publicly he was seen and heard until the day he was betrayed. Publicly he was led forth and condemned. Publicly he was led forth to Calvary and nailed to the cross. His death was public. It could not be denied and it was the life of the world (John 6:51).

For meditation: *The great events of Christianity did not take place 'in a corner' but openly. Christianity is rooted in history.*

Suggested further reading: 1 Thessalonians 4:1-8

In verse 17 our Lord proceeds to name the second thing he asks for his disciples in prayer. Preservation was the first thing and sanctification the second. He asks his Father to make the disciples more holy, to lead them on to higher degrees of holiness and purity. He asks him to do it 'through the truth', by bringing truth to bear more effectually and powerfully on their hearts and consciences and inner man. And to prevent mistake as to what he meant by truth, he adds, 'Thy Word, thy revealed Word, is the truth that I mean.'

No doubt the word 'sanctify' originally and primarily means 'set apart, separate for religious uses'; and it might be used of a vessel, a house, or an animal. But inasmuch as in human beings this separation is principally evidenced by holiness and godliness of life and character, the secondary sense of 'sanctify' is 'to make holy', and holy and godly people are 'sanctified'. This I hold to be the meaning here most decidedly. It is a prayer for the increased holiness and practical godliness of Christ's people. In short, the petition comes to this: 'Separate them more and more from sin and sinners, by making them more pure, more spiritually-minded and more like thyself.'

It is a prayer that the Father would make his people more holy, more spiritual, more pure, more saintly in thought and word and deed, in life and character. Grace had done something for the disciples already — called, converted, renewed and changed them. The great Head of the church prays that the work of grace may be carried higher and further and that his people may be more thoroughly sanctified and made holy in body, soul and spirit — in fact, more like himself.

Surely we need not say much to show the matchless wisdom of this prayer. More holiness is the very thing to be desired for all servants of Christ. Holy living is the great proof of the reality of Christianity.

For meditation: *'Since we have these promises, dear friends, let us purify ourselves from everything that contaminates body and spirit, perfecting holiness out of reverence for God'* (2 Cor. 7:1).

Suggested further reading: Matthew 23:33-39

The tenderness and compassion of our Lord towards sinners is great (v. 41). He knew well the character of the inhabitants of Jerusalem. Their cruelty, their stubbornness, their obstinate prejudice against the truth, their pride of heart were not hidden from him. He knew well what they were going to do to him within a few days. His unjust judgement, his delivery to the Gentiles, his sufferings, his crucifixion were all spread out distinctly before his mind's eye. And yet, knowing all this, our Lord pitied Jerusalem.

We err greatly if we suppose that Christ cares for none but his own believing people. He cares for all. His heart is wide enough to take an interest in all mankind. His compassion extends to every man, woman and child on earth. He has a love of general pity for the man who is going on still in his wickedness, as well as a love of special affection for the sheep who hear his voice and follow him. He is not willing that any should perish, but that all should come to repentance. Hardened sinners are fond of making excuses for their conduct. But they will never be able to say that Christ was not merciful and was not ready to save.

We know but little of true Christianity if we do not feel a deep concern about the souls of unconverted people. A lazy indifference about the spiritual state of others may doubtless save us much trouble. To care nothing whether our neighbours are going to heaven or hell is no doubt the way of the world. But a man of this spirit is very unlike David, who wept profusely because of the disobedience of the people (Ps. 119:136). Paul also knew what it was to feel deeply the impenitence of his people (Rom. 9:2). Above all, our Lord felt tenderly about wicked people. The disciples of Christ ought to have the same feelings as their Master.

For meditation: *There is a perverseness in our hearts that means that whereas we do everything within our power to keep our loved ones from physical harm, we shrink from keeping our loved ones from eternal damnation. Yet which is worse?*

Suggested further reading: 2 Peter 1:3-11

Four great principles may be gathered from verse 17.

1. The importance of sanctification and practical godliness. Our Lord specially asks it for his people. Those that despise Christian life and character and think it of no importance, so long as they are sound in doctrine, know very little of the mind of Christ. Our Christianity is worth nothing, if it does not make us value and seek practical sanctification.

2. The wide difference between justification and sanctification. Justification is a perfect and complete work obtained for us by Christ, imputed to us and external to us, as perfect and complete the moment we believe as it can ever be, and admitting of no degrees. Sanctification is an inward work wrought in our hearts by the Holy Spirit and never quite perfect so long as we live in this body of sin. The disciples needed no prayer for justification; they were completely justified already. They did need prayer for their sanctification, for they were not completely sanctified.

3. Sanctification is a thing that admits of growth; else why should our Lord pray, 'Sanctify them'? The doctrine of imputed sanctification is one that I can find nowhere in the Word of God. Christ's imputed righteousness I see clearly, but not an imputed holiness. Holiness is a thing imparted and inwrought, but not imputed.

4. The Word is the great instrument by which the Holy Ghost carries forward the work of inward sanctification. By bringing that Word to bear more forcibly on mind and will and conscience and affection, we make the character grow more holy. Sanctification from without by bodily austerities and asceticism and a round of forms, ceremonies and outward means is a delusion. True sanctification begins from within. Here lies the immense importance of regularly reading the written Word and hearing the preached Word. It surely, though insensibly, promotes our sanctification. Believers who neglect the Word will not grow in holiness and victory over sin.

For meditation: *The life of holiness is a walking tract able to be read by all.*

Suggested further reading: Matthew 11:20-24

There is a religious ignorance that is sinful and blameworthy (v. 44). Jerusalem might have known that the times of the Messiah had come and that Jesus of Nazareth was the Messiah. But she would not know. Her rulers were wilfully ignorant. They would not calmly examine evidences and impartially consider great plain facts. Her people would not see the 'signs of the times'. Therefore judgement was to come on Jerusalem to the uttermost. Her wilful ignorance left her without excuse.

We learn, then, that all ignorance is not excusable. When men might know truth but refuse to know it, their guilt is very great in the sight of God. If from indolence or prejudice we will not know, our lack of knowledge will ruin our souls. This should rid us of the notion that ignorance will excuse everyone who dies in ignorance and that he will be pardoned because he knew no better. Wilful ignorance will never be allowed as a plea in a man's favour. On the contrary, it will add to his guilt.

God is sometimes pleased to give men special opportunities and invitations. Jerusalem had a special season of God's coming to her (v. 44). The Son of God himself visited her. The mightiest miracles that man had ever seen were done around her. The most wonderful preaching that was ever preached was within her walls. The days of our Lord's ministry were the clearest calls to repentance and faith that any city ever received. They were calls so marked, peculiar and unlike any other calls that Jerusalem had ever received that it seemed impossible that they should ever be disregarded. But they were disregarded! Our Lord declares this disregard was one of Jerusalem's principal sins.

There seems no doubt that churches, nations and even individuals are sometimes visited with special manifestations of God's presence and that neglect of such manifestations is the turning-point in their spiritual ruin. Let us learn not to ignore convictions or quench the workings of conscience. We may be throwing away our last chance of salvation.

For meditation: *'Once the owner of the house gets up and closes the door, you will stand outside knocking and pleading, "Sir, open the door for us." But he will answer, "I don't know you or where you come from"'* (Luke 13:25).

Suggested further reading: Ephesians 5:25-33

Calvin remarks, 'As the apostles were not destitute of grace, we ought to infer from Christ's words that sanctification is not instantly completed in us on the first day, but that we make progress in it through the whole course of our life.'

The connection between verse 18 and the preceding one seems to me to be this: 'I ask for the increased sanctification of my disciples, because of the position they have to occupy on earth. Just as thou didst send me to be thy Messenger to this sinful world, so have I now sent them to be my messengers to the world. It is therefore of the utmost importance that they should be holy — the holy messengers of a holy Master — and so stop the mouths of their accusers.' Believers are Christ's witnesses and the character of a witness should be spotless and blameless. For this reason our Lord specially prays that his disciples may be 'sanctified'.

Verse 19 is a rather hard passage. In one sense, of course, our Lord needed no sanctification. He was always perfectly holy and without sin. I believe, with Chrysostom, the meaning must be: 'I consecrate myself and offer myself up as a sacrifice and a priest, for one special reason, to say nothing of others: in order that these my disciples may be sanctified by the truth and made a holy people.' Is it not as good as saying, 'The sanctification no less than the justification of my people is the end of my sacrifice. I want to have a people who are sanctified as well as justified. So much importance do I attach to this that this is one principal reason why I now offer myself to die as a sacrifice'? The same idea seems to lie in the text: 'He gave himself for us that he might redeem us from all iniquity, and purify unto himself a peculiar people.' And again: 'Christ loved the church and gave himself for it, that he might sanctify it' (Titus 2:14; Eph. 5:26; 1 Peter 2:24).

For meditation: *There was no limit to Christ's self-giving for the church. How can the church hold back anything from him?*

Suggested further reading: Hebrews 11:1-6

This whole transaction was an emblem of spiritual things. The withered fig tree spoke to the Jewish church. Rich in the leaves of formal religion, but barren of all fruits of the Spirit, that church was in fearful danger at the very time this withering took place. Well would it have been for the Jewish church if it had had eyes to see its peril!

The withered fig tree speaks to all the branches of Christ's visible church in every age and in every part of the world. There is a warning against an empty profession of Christianity unaccompanied by sound doctrine and holy living which some of those branches would have done well to lay to heart.

Above all the withered fig tree speaks to all carnal, hypocritical, false-hearted Christians. Well would it be for all who have a name that lives, while in reality they are dead, if they would only see their own faces in the glass of this passage.

Baptism, the Lord's Supper, church membership and a diligent use of all the outward means of Christianity will not save our souls. They are leaves, nothing but leaves. Without fruit they add to our condemnation. Like the fig leaves of Adam and Eve, they will not hide the nakedness of our souls from the eye of an all-seeing God. We must bear fruit or be lost for ever.

The Lord teaches the immense importance of faith by his sayings (vv. 22-24). His promise (v. 24) must of course be taken with a reasonable qualification. It assumes that the believer will ask things which are not sinful and which are in accordance with the will of God.

Confidence in God's power and will to help every believer in Christ and in the truth of every word that God has spoken is the grand secret of success and prosperity in our religion. It is the very root of saving Christianity. Do we wish to grow in grace and make progress in religion? Let us pray daily for more faith.

For meditation: *However beautiful things outward may be, it is always the heart that matters most.*

Suggested further reading: Ephesians 4:1-6

In verse 20 and the three following verses our Lord proceeds to name another thing that he prays for his people. He asks that they may be 'one'. He had already named this on behalf of the eleven apostles. But he takes occasion now to enlarge the prayer and to include others besides the eleven — the whole company of future believers. 'I now pray also for all who shall believe on me through the preaching of my disciples in all future time, and not for my eleven apostles only.' All believers needed preservation and sanctification in every age, but none so much as the eleven, because they were the first to attack the world and bear the brunt of the battle. In some respects it was more easy to be 'one' at the first beginnings of the church, and harder to be kept and 'sanctified'. As the church grew, it would be more difficult to keep unity. The want of unity and consequent strife among English Christians in the last 300 years has been a miserable example of the enormous damage that believers may do their Master's cause.

Let us mark how wide was the scope of our Lord's intercessory prayer. He prayed not only for present, but for future believers. So should it be with our prayers. We may look forward and pray for believers yet to be born, though we may not look back and pray for believers who are dead.

George Newton observes what an encouragement it should be to us in praying for others, for a child or a friend, to remember that perhaps Christ is asking him or her of God too. He here prays for those who did not yet believe, but were to believe one day.

Let us mark how the 'word' preached is mentioned as the means of making men believe. Faith cometh by hearing. The church which places sacraments above the preaching of the Word will have no blessing of God, because it rejects God's order.

For meditation: *Do you attempt in any way to show your unity with other true believers or are you an isolated island of self-satisfaction?*

Suggested further reading: Malachi 2:17 - 3:5

Our Lord found his Father's house in a state which too truly shad-owed forth the general condition of the whole Jewish church — everything out of order and out of course. He found the courts of that holy building disgracefully profaned by worldly transactions. Trading, buying and selling were actually going on within its walls. There stood dealers ready to supply the Jew who came from distant countries with any sacrifice he wanted. There sat the money-changer ready to change foreign money for the current coin of the land. Bull-ocks, sheep, goats and pigeons were there exposed for sale, as if the place had been a market. The jingling of money might there be heard, as if these holy courts had been a bank or exchange. Such were the scenes that met our Lord's eyes. He saw it with holy indignation and acted (v. 12). There was no resistance, for men knew that he was right. There was no objection, for all felt that he was only reforming a notorious abuse which had been basely permitted for the sake of gain. Well might his words sound in the ears of the astonished trad-ers as they fled from the temple (v. 13).

Let us see in our Lord's conduct on this occasion a striking type of what he will do when he comes again the second time. He will purify his church as he purified the temple. He will cleanse it from everything that defiles and works iniquity and cast every worldly professor out of it. He will allow no worshipper of money or lover of gain to have a place in that final glorious temple.

May we all strive to live daily in the expectation of that coming! May we judge ourselves, that we might not be condemned and cast out in that searching and sifting day! We should often study the word of Malachi (Mal. 3:2).

For meditation: *Because there is corruption in the heart of man, there is a corrupting influence at work in man's religion. The church needs constantly to be returning to the Word of God to judge itself and to reform itself according to what it finds there. Tradition is often a corruption of God's original institution. 'Back to the Bible' must be our watchword.*

Suggested further reading: 1 John 2:28 - 3:3

Jesus prays that his people may at last be with him and behold his glory. 'I will,' he says, 'that those whom thou hast given me, be with me where I am: that they may behold my glory.'

This is a singularly beautiful and touching conclusion to our Lord's remarkable prayer. We may well believe that it was meant to cheer and comfort those who heard it and to strengthen them for the parting scene which was fast drawing near. But for all who read it even now, this part of his prayer is full of sweet and unspeakable comfort.

We do not see Christ now. We read of him, hear of him, believe in him and rest our souls in his finished work. But even the best of us, at our best, walk by faith and not by sight, and our poor halting faith often makes us walk very feebly in the way to heaven. There shall be an end of all this state of things one day. We shall at length see Christ as he is and know as we have been known. We shall behold him face to face and not through a glass darkly. We shall actually be in his presence and company and go out no more. If faith has been pleasant, much more will sight be, and if hope has been sweet, much more will certainty be. No wonder that when St Paul has written, 'We shall ever be with the Lord,' he adds, 'Comfort one another with these words' (1 Thess. 4:17-18).

We know little of heaven now. Our thoughts are all confounded when we try to form an idea of a future state in which pardoned sinners shall be perfectly happy. 'It does not yet appear what we shall be' (1 John 3:2). But we may rest ourselves on the blessed thought that after death we shall be 'with Christ'.

For meditation: *How much of your desire for heaven is a longing to be free from trouble, and how much is it a desire for the presence of Christ?*

Suggested further reading: John 1:19-28

The enemies of truth are ever ready to question the authority of all who do more good than themselves. The chief priests have not a word to say about our Lord's teaching or against his life or conduct. The point on which they fasten is his commission.

The same charge has often been made against the servants of God when they have striven to check the progress of ecclesiastical corruption. It is the old weapon by which the children of this world have often laboured to stop the progress of revivals and reformation. It is the weapon that was often brandished in the face of Reformers, Methodists and Puritans in their day. Too many care nothing for the manifest blessing of God on a man's work if he is not sent forth by their own sect or party. It matters nothing to them that some humble labourer in God's harvest can point to numerous conversions of souls through his instrumentality. They consider his success nothing: they demand his commission. What he does is not important. It is his authority to do it that matters!

With consummate wisdom our Lord replied to the question. This answer of our Lord was no evasion. His counter question was an answer to their enquiry. He knew that they dare not deny that John the Baptist was a man sent from God. He knew that, this being granted, he only needed to remind them of John's testimony to himself. Our Lord's question was a home thrust to their consciences. If they once conceded the divine authority of John's mission, they must also concede the divine authority of his own. Let us pray for like wisdom in the defence that we give of the truth.

In the parable of the sons the Lord holds out immense encouragement to those who repent. One son, like the profligate tax collectors, for some time flatly refused obedience, but afterwards repented and went. The other, like the formal Pharisees, pretended willingness to go, but in reality went not. It was the son like the tax collector who obeyed. It is not our initial profession and response that matters, but whether we actually repent and obey.

For meditation: *'Not everyone who says to me, "Lord, Lord," will enter the kingdom of heaven, but only he who does the will of my Father who is in heaven'* (Matt. 7:21).

Suggested further reading: 1 Corinthians 1:10-17

We can ask no stronger proof of the value of unity among Christians and the sinfulness of division than the great prominence which our Master assigns to the subject in this passage. How painfully true it is that in every age divisions have been the scandal of religion and the weakness of the church of Christ! How often Christians have wasted their strength in contending against their brethren, instead of contending against sin and the devil! How repeatedly they have given occasion to the world to say, 'When you have settled your own internal differences we will believe!' All this, we need not doubt, the Lord Jesus foresaw with prophetic eye. It was the foresight of it which made him pray so earnestly that believers might be 'one'.

 Let the recollection of this part of Christ's prayer abide in our minds and exercise a constant influence on our behaviour as Christians. Let no man think lightly, as some men seem to do, of schism, or count it a small thing to multiply sects, parties and denominations. These very things, we may depend, only help the devil and damage the cause of Christ. 'If it be possible, as much as lieth in us, let us live peaceably with all men' (Rom. 12:18). Let us bear much, concede much and put up with much, before we plunge into secessions and separations. They are movements in which there is often much false fire. Let rabid zealots who delight in sect-making and party-forming rail at us and denounce us if they please. We need not mind them. So long as we have Christ and a good conscience, let us patiently hold on our way, follow the things that make for peace and strive to promote unity. It was not for nothing that our Lord prayed so fervently that his people might be 'one'.

For meditation: *Let us make every effort to be in harmony with our fellow believers. Are we not members of one spiritual family?*

Suggested further reading: Romans 9:1-5

God is pleased to bestow distinguishing privileges on some nations. He chose Israel to be a peculiar people to himself. He separated them from the other nations of the earth and bestowed on them countless blessings. He gave them revelations of himself while all the rest of the earth was in darkness. He gave them the law, the covenants, the oracles of God, while all the world besides was left alone. In short, God dealt with the Jews as a man deals with a piece of land which he fences out and cultivates, while all the fields around are left untilled and waste. The vineyard of the Lord was the house of Israel (Isa. 5:7).

And have we no privileges? Beyond doubt we have many. We have the Bible and liberty for everyone to read it. We have the gospel and permission for everyone to hear it. We have spiritual mercies in abundance denied to many men in many nations. How thankful we ought to be!

What a bad use nations sometimes make of their privileges! When the Lord separated the Jews from other people he had a right to expect that they would serve him and obey his laws. Where a man has taken pains with a vineyard he has a right to expect fruit. But Israel rendered not a due return for all God's mercies. They mingled with the heathen and learned their works. They hardened themselves in sin and unbelief. They turned aside after idols. They kept not God's ordinances. They despised God's temple. They refused to listen to his prophets. They ill used those whom he sent to call them to repentance. And finally they brought their wickedness to a height by killing the Son of God himself.

And what are we doing with our privileges? Truly that is a serious question and one that ought to make us think! It may well be feared that we are not, as a nation, living up to our light or walking worthy of the mercies we have. Must we not confess with shame that millions amongst us seem utterly without God in the world? Must we not acknowledge that in many a town and village Christ seems hardly to have a disciple and the Bible seems hardly to be believed? Are we provoking God as did the Jews?

For meditation: *No nation has been so blessed of God in past centuries as our own. What fruit of that blessing is there today? Why so little?*

Suggested further reading: Ephesians 3:14-21

It is well to remember that the church, whose unity the Lord desires and prays for, is not any particular or visible church, but the church which is his body, the church of the elect, the church which is made up of true believers and saints alone.

The unity which our Lord prays for is not unity of forms, discipline, government and the like, but unity of heart and will and doctrine and practice. Those who make uniformity the chief subject of this part of Christ's prayer entirely miss the mark. There may be uniformity without unity, as in many visible churches on earth now. There may be unity without uniformity, as between godly Episcopalians and godly Presbyterians. Uniformity no doubt may be a great help to unity, but it is not unity itself.

The unity which our Lord prays about here is that true, substantial, spiritual, internal heart unity which undoubtedly exists among all members of Christ of every church and denomination. It is the unity which results from one Holy Ghost having made the members of Christ what they are. It is unity which makes them feel more of one mind with one another than with mere professors of their own party. It is unity which is the truest freemasonry on earth. It is unity which shakes the world and obliges it to confess the truth of Christianity. For the continued maintenance of this unity and an increase of it, our Lord seems to me in this prayer specially to pray. And we need not wonder. The divisions of mere worldly professors are of little moment. The divisions of real true believers are the greatest possible injury to the cause of the gospel. If all believers at this moment were of one mind and would work together, they might soon turn the world upside down. No wonder the Lord prayed for unity.

For meditation: *It is easy to confuse schemes for church union which unite heretics and believers with the true unity of all true believers.*

Suggested further reading: Amos 2:6 - 3:2

The fruit that the Lord receives from his vineyard in this land is disgracefully small compared with what it ought to be. We should note what an awful reckoning God sometimes makes with nations and churches which make a bad use of their privileges.

A time came when the long-suffering of God towards the Jews had an end. Forty years after our Lord's death the cup of their iniquity was at length full and they received a heavy chastisement for their sins in the destruction of Jerusalem and its temple. They themselves were scattered over the face of the earth and the kingdom removed from them (v. 43).

And will the same thing ever happen to us? Will the judgements of God come down upon this nation because of her unfaithfulness under so many mercies? Who can tell? Only God knows. But history tells us that judgements have come on many churches and nations. Where are the early African and Eastern churches? They are run over by Islam and destroyed. At all events it becomes all believers to intercede much on behalf of our country. Nothing offends God so much as the neglect of privileges. Much has been given to us and much will be required.

What power conscience has even in wicked men! The chief priests and elders at last discovered that our Lord's parable was especially meant for them. The point of its closing words was too sharp to escape.

There are many hearers in every congregation who are exactly in the position of these unhappy men. They know that what they hear Sunday after Sunday is all true. They know that they are wrong themselves and that every sermon condemns them. But they have neither will nor courage to acknowledge this. They are too proud and too fond of the world to confess their past mistakes and to take up the cross and follow Christ. Let us all beware of this awful state of mind. The last day will prove that there was more going on in the consciences of hearers than was at all known to preachers. Tens of thousands will be found to have been convicted by their own conscience and yet to have died unconverted.

For meditation: *Do not neglect your freedom to hear the Word preached, nor suppress the strivings of your conscience. Listen to both.*

Suggested further reading: Genesis 3:1-7

Henry observes, 'The office of the priest was to teach and pray and offer sacrifice. Christ, after teaching and praying, applies himself to make atonement. He had said all he had to say as a prophet. He now addresses himself to his work as a priest.'

The Cedron here mentioned is the same as the Kidron named more than once in the Old Testament. The word 'brook' means, literally, a 'winter torrent', and this, according to all travellers, is precisely what the Kidron is. Excepting in winter, or after rains, it is merely the dry bed of a watercourse. It lies on the east side of Jerusalem, between the city and the Mount of Olives. It is the same Kidron which David passed over weeping when obliged to flee from Jerusalem by the rebellion of Absalom (2 Sam. 15:23). It is the same Kidron by the side of which Asa burnt the idol of his mother Maachah (2 Chr. 15:16), and into which Josiah cast the dust of the idolatrous altars which he destroyed (2 Kings 23:12).

Lampe says that the way by which our Lord left the city was the way by which the scapegoat, Azazel, was annually sent out into the wilderness on the great Day of Atonement.

Bishop Andrews says that 'The first breach made by the Romans, when Titus took Jerusalem, was at the brook Cedron, where they took Christ.'

There can be little doubt that this garden is the same as the 'place called Gethsemane'.

Almost all commentators notice the curious fact that the fall of Adam and Eve took place in a garden, and Christ's passion also began in a garden, and the sepulchre where Christ was laid was in a garden, and the place where he was crucified was in a garden (John 19:41).

Augustine remarks, 'It was fitting that the blood of the Physician should there be poured out, where the disease of the sick man first commenced.'

For meditation: *Even the new universe will contain a river in a garden* (Rev. 22:1-2).

Suggested further reading: Romans 13:1-7

Our Lord was accosted by his enemies with flattering language
(v. 16). How well these Pharisees and Herodians talked! What smooth
and honeyed words were these! They thought no doubt that by smooth
words and fair speeches they would throw our Lord off guard (Ps.
55:21).

It becomes all professing Christians to be much on their guard
against flattery. We mistake greatly if we suppose that persecution
and hard usage are the only weapons in Satan's armoury. That crafty
foe has other weapons for doing us mischief which he knows how to
work well. He knows how to poison souls by the world's seductive
kindness when he cannot frighten them by fiery dart and sword. Let
us not be ignorant of his devices. By peace he destroys many.

Samson and Solomon were not ruined by foreign armies, but by
women. Hezekiah was not ruined by invading forces, but by the
flattery of future opponents. Peace often ruins nations far more than
war. The sun makes the traveller cast off his protective garments far
sooner than the north wind. Let us beware of the flatterer. When
Judas betrayed his Lord it was with a kiss.

What marvellous wisdom our Lord showed in his reply! Had our
Lord simply replied that it was lawful to pay tribute, they would
have denounced him to the people as one who dishonoured the privileges of Israel and considered the children of Abraham no longer
free but subjects to a foreign power. Had he, on the other hand,
replied that it was not lawful to pay tribute they would have denounced him to the Romans as a mover of sedition and a rebel against
Caesar, who refused to pay his taxes. But our Lord's conduct and
answer baffled them.

The principle laid down is of deep importance. The Christian
should obey the government under which he lives in all matters temporal. The Christian must obey his God in all matters spiritual. No
temporal loss, no civil disability, no displeasure of the powers that
be must ever tempt him to do things which Scripture plainly forbids.

For meditation: *Christianity does not require us to draw away
from this life's order in society, but to be God-fearing citizens. Are
you paying all your taxes?*

Suggested further reading: Daniel 6:10-11

Verse 2 tells us that this garden was a place where our Lord and his disciples were in the habit of assembling together when they went up to Jerusalem at the great Jewish feasts. At such seasons the crowd of worshippers was very great, and many had to content themselves with such shelter as they could find under trees, or rocks, in the open air. This is what Luke means when he says, 'At night he went out and abode in the mount that is called the Mount of Olives' (Luke 21:37). Excepting at the celebration of the first Lord's Supper, we have no mention of our Lord ever being in any *house* in Jerusalem.

The fact that the traitor Judas 'knew the place', while our Lord deliberately went there, shows three things. One is that our Lord went to his death willingly and voluntarily; he went to the 'garden', knowing well that Judas was acquainted with the place. Another thing is that our Lord was in the habit of going to this garden so 'often' that Judas felt sure he would be found there. Another thing is that the heart of Judas must have been desperately hard, when, after so many seasons of spiritual refreshment as he must have seen in this garden, he could use his knowledge for the purpose of betraying his Master. He 'knew the place', because he had often heard his Master teaching and praying there. He knew it from spiritual associations and yet turned his knowledge to wicked ends!

May we not learn from this verse that there is nothing to be ashamed of, nothing wrong, in loving one place more than another and choosing one place more than another for communion with God? Even our blessed Lord had one special place near Jerusalem, more than other places, to which he often resorted. The common idea of some that it matters not where or in what place we worship and that it is unspiritual and wrong to care for one seat in church more than another can hardly be reconciled with this verse.

For meditation: *To have special places and times for prayer is not wrong as long as we avoid superstition.*

Suggested further reading: Exodus 3:1-6

Absurd, sceptical objections to Bible truths are ancient things. The
Sadducees wished to show the absurdity of the doctrine of the resurrection and the life to come and so invented a story and asked a
question to bring the doctrine into contempt. They meant to insinuate that there must be confusion, strife and unseemly disorder if,
after death, men and women were to live again. Supposed cases are
one of the favourite strongholds in which an unbelieving mind loves
to entrench itself. Such a mind will often set up a shadow of its own
imagining and fight with it as if it were the truth. Such a mind will
often refuse to look at the overwhelming mass of plain evidence by
which Christianity is supported and will fasten on some one difficulty which it fancies is unanswerable. Such was the ploy of the
Sadducees.

Our Lord brings forward a remarkable text to prove the reality
of the life to come (Exod. 3:6) and adds his own comment (v. 32).
At the time when Moses heard these words Abraham, Isaac and
Jacob had been dead and buried many years. Two centuries had
passed since Jacob, the last of the three, was carried to his tomb.
And yet God spoke of them as still being his people and of himself
as still being their God. He said not, 'I was their God', but 'I am'.
Those who have passed away from our eyes live in the eyes of God
and will one day be raised to be sentenced. There is no such thing as
annihilation. It is a miserable delusion. The sun, moon and stars, the
solid mountains and the deep sea will one day come to nothing. But
the weakest babe of the poorest man will live for evermore in another
world. May we never forget this!

We know but little of the life to come. Perhaps our clearest ideas
of it are drawn from considering what it will not be, rather than
what it will be. It is a state in which we shall hunger no more nor
thirst any more. Sickness, pain and disease will not be known. Wasting, old age and death will have no place. Marriages, births and a
constant succession of inhabitants will be no more needed. Like angels
we shall serve God perfectly, unhesitatingly and unweariedly.

For meditation: *When God becomes our God he does so for ever
and ever.*

Suggested further reading: Matthew 16:13-23

Verse 4 shows our Lord's perfect foreknowledge of everything that was about to happen to him. Never was there a more willing, deliberate and voluntary sufferer than our Lord. The best of martyrs, like Ridley and Latimer, did not know for certain up to the moment of their deaths that something might not occur to alter the mind of their persecutors and save their lives. Our Lord knew perfectly well that his death was sure, by the determinate counsel and foreknowledge of God.

Ford quotes a saying of Pinart that 'What rendered Christ's sufferings most terrible was the perfect foreknowledge he had of the torments he should endure. From the first moment of his life he had present to his mind the scourge, the thorns, the cross and the agonizing death which awaited him. Saw he a lamb in the meadow or a victim in the temple, the sight reminded him that he was the Lamb of God and that he was to be offered up a sacrifice.'

Our Lord came forward from that part of the garden where he was and did not wait for the party of Judas to find him. On the contrary, he suddenly showed himself and met them face to face. The effect of this action alone must have been startling to the soldiers. They would feel at once that they had to do with no common person.

Henry remarks, 'When the people would have forced him to take a crown and wished to make him a king, he withdrew and hid himself (John 6:15). But when they came to force him to his cross he offered himself. He came to this world to suffer and went to the other world to reign.'

Jesus himself was the first to speak and did not wait to be challenged or commanded to surrender. This sudden question no doubt would take the party of Judas by surprise and prepare the way for the mighty miracle which followed. The soldiers must needs have felt, 'This is not the language or manner of a malefactor or a guilty man.'

For meditation: *The terror of the cross for Christ included knowing what would happen. The mercy of God to us is to hide the future from us.*

Suggested further reading: 1 John 4:7-21

How high is our Lord's standard of duty to God and man! The question propounded by the scribe was a very wide one. If he expected an answer pointing him to some outward form and ceremony, he was surprised. He heard solemn words (vv. 29-31).

How striking is our Lord's description of the feeling with which we ought to regard both God and our neighbour! We are not merely to obey the one and to abstain from injuring the other. In both cases we are to give far more than this. We are to give love, the strongest of all affections and the most comprehensive. A rule like this includes everything. It makes all petty details unnecessary. Nothing will be intentionally lacking where there is love.

How striking is the measure in which we should love God and our neighbour! We are to love God better than ourselves, with all the powers of our inward man. We cannot love him too well. We are to love our neighbour as ourselves and deal with him in all respects as we would like him to deal with us. The marvellous wisdom of this distinction is clear and plain. We may easily err in our affections to others either by thinking too little or too much of them. We therefore need the rule to love them as ourselves, neither more nor less. We cannot err in our affection towards God in the matter of excess. He is worthy of all we can give him. We are therefore to love him with all our heart.

Happy is the man who strives to frame his life according to these rules and who uses them to try every difficulty of conscience that happens to besiege us as to right and wrong. From this standard of duty we learn how great is the need in which we all stand of the atonement and mediation of our Lord Jesus Christ. Where is anyone who can say that he has perfectly loved God and perfectly loved man? Where is the person who must not plead guilty when tried by such a law as this? The man who has the clearest view of God's requirements will have the highest sense of the value of Christ's atoning blood.

For meditation: *How much easier it would be if God's commands said, 'Do not hate'! The call to love is positive.*

Suggested further reading: 1 Corinthians 10:1-13

We should notice in these verses the exceeding hardness of heart to which a backsliding professor may attain. We are told that Judas, one of the twelve apostles, became guide to them that took Jesus. We are told that he used his knowledge of the place of our Lord's retirement, in order to bring his deadly enemies upon him, and we are told that when the band of men and officers approached his Master in order to make him prisoner, Judas 'stood with them'. Yet this was a man who for three years had been a constant companion of Christ, had seen his miracles, had heard his sermons, had enjoyed the benefit of his private instruction, had professed himself a believer, had even worked and preached in Christ's name! 'Lord,' we may well say, 'what is man?' From the highest degree of privilege down to the lowest depth of sin, there is but a succession of steps. Privileges misused seem to paralyse the conscience. The same fire that melts wax will harden clay.

Let us beware of resting our hopes of salvation on religious knowledge, however great, or religious advantages, however many. We may know all doctrinal truth and be able to teach others and yet prove rotten at heart and go down to the pit with Judas. We may bask in the full sunshine of spiritual privileges and hear the best of Christian teaching and yet bear no fruit to God's glory and be found withered branches of the vine, only fit to be burned. 'Let him that thinketh he standeth take heed lest he fall' (1 Cor. 10:12). Above all, let us beware of cherishing within our hearts any secret besetting sin, such as love of money or love of the world. One faulty link in a chain-cable may cause a shipwreck. One little leak may sink a ship. One allowed and unmortified sin may ruin a professing Christian. Let him that is tempted to be a careless man in his religious life consider these things and take care. Let him remember Judas Iscariot. His history is meant to be a lesson.

For meditation: *The higher we rise, the greater our privileges and the further our fall.*

Suggested further reading: Matthew 13:36-43

A man may go far in religion and yet not be a true disciple of Christ. The scribe in the passage before us was evidently a man of more knowledge than most of his equals. He saw things which many Pharisees and scribes never saw at all. His own words are a strong proof of this (vv. 32-33). These words are remarkable in themselves and doubly remarkable when we remember who the speaker was and the generation amongst whom he lived. No wonder our Lord responded as he did (v. 34).

But we must not shut our eyes to the fact that we are nowhere told that this man became one of our Lord's disciples. On this point there is a mournful silence. The parallel passage in Matthew throws not a gleam of light on his case. The other parts of the New Testament tell us nothing about him. We are left to draw the painful conclusion that, like the young rich man, he could not make up his mind to give up all and follow Christ; or that, like the chief rulers elsewhere mentioned, he loved the praise of men more than the praise of God (John 12:43). In short, though not far from the kingdom, he probably never entered into it and died outside it.

Cases like that of this scribe are unhappily far from being uncommon. There are thousands on every side who, like him, see much and know much of religious truth and yet live and die undecided. There are few things which are so much overlooked as the length to which people may go in religious attainments and yet never be converted and be saved. May we all mark out this man's case and take care!

Let us beware of resting our hopes of salvation on mere intellectual knowledge. We live in days when there is a great danger of doing so. Education makes children acquainted with many things in religion. But education will not make Christians. We must not only know the leading doctrines of the gospel with our heads but receive them into our hearts and be guided by them in our lives. To rest satisfied with being not far from the kingdom is to be shut out for evermore from it.

For meditation: *Has the truth that is in your head sunk into your heart and taken hold of your life?*

Suggested further reading: 1 Corinthians 9:15-23

We should notice in these verses the entire voluntariness of Christ's sufferings. We are told that the first time that our Lord said to the soldiers, 'I am he', they 'went backward, and fell to the ground'. A secret invisible power, no doubt, accompanied the words. In no other way can we account for a band of hardy Roman soldiers falling prostrate before a single unarmed man. A real miracle was wrought, though few had eyes to see it. At the moment when our Lord seemed weak, he showed that he was strong.

Let us carefully remember that our blessed Lord suffered and died of his own free will. He did not die because he could not help it; he did not suffer because he could not escape. All the soldiers of Pilate's army could not have taken him, if he had not been willing to be taken. They could not have hurt a hair of his head, if he had not given them permission. But here, as in all his earthly ministry, Jesus was a willing sufferer. He had set his heart on accomplishing our redemption. He loved us and gave himself for us, cheerfully, willingly, gladly, in order to make atonement for our sins. It was 'the joy set before him' which made him endure the cross and despise the shame and yield himself up without reluctance into the hands of his enemies.

We should notice in these verses our Lord's tender care for his disciples' safety. Even at this critical moment, when his own unspeakable sufferings were about to begin, he did not forget the little band of believers who stood around him. He remembered their weakness. He knew how little fit they were to go into the fiery furnace of the high priest's palace and Pilate's judgement hall. He mercifully makes for them a way of escape: 'If ye seek me, let these go their way.' It seems most probable that here also a miraculous influence accompanied his words. At any rate, not a hair of the disciples' heads was touched. While the Shepherd was taken, the sheep were allowed to flee away unharmed.

For meditation: *It is better to serve God voluntarily than out of necessity.*

Suggested further reading: Psalm 110

How much there is about Christ in the Old Testament Scriptures! Our Lord desires to expose the ignorance of the Jewish teachers about the true nature of the Messiah. He does it by referring to a passage in the book of Psalms and by showing that the Pharisees did not rightly understand it. The Old Testament Scriptures testify of Christ (John 5:39). They were intended to teach men about Christ by types, figures and prophecies till he himself should appear on the earth. Christ is undoubtedly to be found in every part of the Law and the Prophets, but especially in the Psalms.

Let us beware of undervaluing or despising the Old Testament. In its place and proportion the Old Testament is just as valuable as the New. There are probably many rich passages in that part of the Bible which have never yet been fully explored. There are deep things about Jesus in it, which many walk over like hidden gold-mines, not knowing the treasures beneath their feet. Let us reverence all the Bible. All is given by inspiration and all is profitable. One part throws light upon another and no part can be neglected without loss and damage to our souls.

The scribes and Pharisees were no doubt familiar with the psalm quoted but they could not explain its application. It could only be explained by conceding the pre-existence and divinity of the Messiah. This the Pharisees would not concede. Their only idea of Messiah was for him to be a man like themselves. Their ignorance of the Scriptures, of which they pretended to know more than others, and their low, carnal view of the true nature of Christ were thus exposed at one and the same time. But what do we think of Christ? What do we think of his person and his work? What do we think of his life and death for us on the cross? What do we think of his resurrection, ascension and intercession? Can we truly say that he is 'my Redeemer, my Saviour, my Shepherd and my Friend'?

For meditation: *When we consider that the only Bible of the early Christians was the Old Testament, and that from it they proved so much about Christ, are we not ashamed that it is such a closed book to us?*

Suggested further reading: Matthew 5:38-48

Peter's impetuous temperament comes out in the action before us. Impulsive, earnest, zealous and inconsiderate of consequences, he acted hastily and his zeal soon cooled down and was changed into fear. It is not those who are for a time most demonstrative and fervent whose religion is deepest. John never smote with the sword, but John never denied his Lord and was at the foot of the cross when Christ died.

Whether the ear was cut off entirely, or only so cut as to hang down by the skin, may be left to conjecture. In any case we know that it gave occasion for the last miracle of bodily cure which our Lord ever wrought. Luke tells us that he 'touched' the ear and it was instantaneously healed. To the very end of his ministry our Lord did good to his enemies and gave proof of his divine power. But his hardened enemies gave no heed. Miracles alone convert no one. As in the case of Pharaoh, they only seem to make some men harder and more wicked.

We cannot doubt that Peter meant to kill Malchus with this blow, which was probably aimed at his head. His own agitation probably and the special interposition of God alone prevented him taking away the life of another and endangering his own life and that of his fellow disciples.

Musculus remarks how entirely Peter seems to have forgotten all his Master's frequent predictions that he would be delivered to the Gentiles and be condemned to death, and acts as if he could prevent what was coming. It was clearly an impulsive act, done without reflection. Zeal not according to knowledge often drives a man into foolish actions and makes work for repentance.

The gospel is not to be propagated or maintained by carnal weapons, or by smiting and violence. Matthew adds the solemn words: 'All they that take the sword shall perish with the sword.' How needful the rebuke and how true the comment have often been proved by the history of the church of Christ. The appeal to the sword can rarely be justified and has often recoiled on the head of its promoters.

For meditation: ' *"Put your sword back in its place," Jesus said to him, "for all who draw the sword will die by the sword" ' (Matt. 26:52).*

Suggested further reading: Ephesians 4:11-16

This chapter in one respect is the most remarkable in the four Gospels. It contains the last words that our Lord spoke within the walls of the temple. Those last words consist of a withering exposure of the scribes and Pharisees and a sharp rebuke of their doctrines and practices. Knowing full well that his time on earth was drawing to a close, our Lord no longer keeps back his opinion of the leading teachers of the Jews. Knowing that he would soon leave his followers alone, like sheep among wolves, he warns them plainly against the false shepherds by whom they are surrounded.

The whole chapter is a signal example of boldness and faithfulness in denouncing error. It is a striking proof that it is possible for the most loving heart to use the language of stern reproof. Above all, it is an awful evidence of the guilt of unfaithful teachers. No sins are as sinful as theirs in the sight of Christ.

Our Lord sets out the duty of distinguishing between the office of a false teacher and his example. Rightly or wrongly, the scribes and Pharisees occupied the position of the chief public teachers of religion amongst the Jews (v. 2). However unworthily they filled their office, it entitled them to respect as having authority. But while their office was to be respected, their bad lives were not to be copied. And although their teaching was to be adhered to in so far as it followed the Word of God, it was not to be observed in contradiction to that Word. They were to be heard when they taught what Moses taught, and no longer.

The duty here placed before us is one of great importance. There is a constant tendency to run into extremes. If we do not regard the office of the minister with idolatrous veneration we are apt to treat it with indecent contempt. Against both extremes we need to be on our guard. However much we may disapprove of a minister's practice or teaching, we must never forget to respect his office. The example of Paul is worthy of being copied (Acts 23:5).

For meditation: *A rejection of the office of pastor and teacher because of its abuse is a path to anarchy. Where all teach, nothing is taught.*

Suggested further reading: Exodus 9:27-35

We should mark, for one thing, the amazing hardness of unconverted men. We see this in the conduct of the men by whom our Lord was taken prisoner. Some of them most probably were Roman soldiers and some of them were Jewish servants of the priests and Pharisees. But in one respect they were all alike. Both parties saw our Lord's divine power exhibited when they 'went backward, and fell to the ground'. Both saw a miracle, according to St Luke's Gospel, when Jesus touched the ear of Malchus and healed him. Yet both remained unmoved, cold, indifferent and insensible, as if they had seen nothing out of the common way.

The degree of hardness and insensibility of conscience to which men may attain, when they live twenty or thirty years without the slightest contact with religion, is something awful and appalling. God and the things of God seem to sink out of sight and disappear from the mind's eye. The world and the things of the world seem to absorb the whole attention. In such cases we may well believe miracles would produce little or no effect, as in the case before us. The eye would gaze on them, like the eye of a beast looking at a romantic landscape, without any impression being made on the heart. He who thinks that seeing a miracle would convert him into a thorough Christian has got much to learn.

Let us not wonder if we see cases of hardness and unbelief in our own day and generation. Such cases will continually be found among those classes of mankind who, from their profession or position, are completely cut off from means of grace. Twenty or thirty years of total irreligion, without the influence of Sunday, Bible or Christian teaching, will make a man's heart hard as the nether millstone. His conscience at last will seem dead, buried and gone. He will appear past feeling. Painful as these cases are, we must not think them peculiar to our own times. They existed under Christ's own eyes and they will exist until Christ returns.

.

For meditation: *'The heart is deceitful above all things and beyond cure. Who can understand it?'* (Jer. 17:9).

Suggested further reading: Matthew 6:1-8

Inconsistency, ostentation and love of pre-eminence among professors of religion are especially displeasing to Christ. The Pharisees were full of that inconsistency that said one thing and did another (v. 3). They required from others what they did not practise themselves.

They did everything they did to be seen by men (v. 5). They had their phylacteries — or strips of parchment with texts written on them, which many Jews wore on their clothes — made of an excessive size. They had the borders of their garments, which Moses told the Israelites to wear as a remembrance of God, made of an extravagant width (Num. 15:38; Matt. 23:5). All this was done to attract notice and to make people think how holy they were.

Their love of pre-eminence caused them to want the best seats on public occasions and to want flattering titles addressed to them (vv. 6-7). All these things our Lord holds up to reprobation. Against all he would have us watch and pray. These are soul-ruining sins (John 5:44). Christians must never give to men the titles and honours due to God alone and to his Christ (vv. 8-10).

Our Lord does not here forbid us to esteem ministers highly for their work's sake (1 Thess. 5:13; 1 Cor. 4:15). But still we must be careful that we do not give ministers a place and honour which do not belong to them. We must never allow them to come between us and Christ. The very best are not infallible. They are not priests who can atone for us. They are not mediators who can undertake to manage our soul's affairs with God. They are men like us, needing the same cleansing blood, the same renewing Spirit, men set apart to a high and holy calling, but still, after all, only men. Human nature, alas, always prefers a visible minister to an invisible Christ.

Nor must the minister, or any Christian, desire to be great in the eyes of men, but rather great in the eyes of Christ. His aim must be not so much to rule the church as to serve it, not a master but a servant.

For meditation: *How much do you seek man's praise for your Christian life and service, or do you look to God alone for approval?*

Suggested further reading: Isaiah 45:1-6

In the time when our Lord Jesus was on earth, the office of the high priest among the Jews was filled up with the utmost disorder and irregularity. Instead of the high priest being high priest for life, he was often elected for a year or two and then deposed and his office given to another. There were often living at one time several priests who had served the office of high priest and then ceased to hold it, like sheriffs or mayors among ourselves. In the case before us Annas appears, after ceasing to be high priest himself, to have lived in the same palace with his son-in-law Caiaphas and to have assisted him as an assessor and adviser in the discharge of his duties, which from his age and official experience he would be well qualified to do. Remembering this, we may understand our Lord being 'led away to Annas first', and then passed on by him to Caiaphas.

The gross inconsistency of the Jews in making such ado about the law of Moses, while they permitted and tolerated such entire departures from its regulations about the high priest's office, is a curious example of what blindness unconverted men may exhibit.

Henry remarks, 'It was the ruin of Caiaphas that he was high priest that year, and so became a ringleader in putting Christ to death. Many a man's advancement has lost him his reputation, and he would not have been dishonoured if he had not been preferred and promoted.'

Let us not forget that this was the very Caiaphas who, after the raising of Lazarus, had said publicly that it was expedient that one man should die for the people. Behold how he is made the unconscious instrument of bringing that saying to pass, though in a widely different sense from that which he intended!

Let us note how the great wicked men of this world — the Sennacheribs and Neros and Bloody Marys and Napoleons — are used by God as his saws and axes and hammers to do his work and carry out the building of his church, though they are not themselves in the least aware of it. Indeed Caiaphas helps forward the one great sacrifice for the sins of the world!

For meditation: *'And we know that in all things God works for the good of those who love him, who have been called according to his purpose'* (Rom. 8:28).

Suggested further reading: Luke 18:9-14

The sin of hypocrisy is odious in the sight of Christ. Our Lord teaches this by exposing some of the notorious practices of the scribes — their ostentatious manner of dressing, their love of the honour and praise of man rather than of God, their love of money disguised under a pretended concern for widows and their long protracted public devotions intended to make men think them eminently godly. And he winds up all by a solemn declaration (v. 40).

Of all the sins into which men can fall none seem so exceedingly sinful as false profession and hypocrisy. At all events, none have drawn from our Lord's mouth such strong language and heavy denunciations. It is bad enough to be led away captive by open sin to serve various lusts and pleasures. But it is even worse to have a religion in pretence while in reality we serve the world. Let us beware of falling into this abominable sin. Whatever we do in religion, let us never wear a cloak. Let us be real, honest, thorough and sincere in our Christianity. We cannot deceive an all-seeing God. We may take in poor, short-sighted man by a little talk and profession and a few cant phrases and an affectation of devoutness. But God is not mocked. He is a discerner of the thoughts and intents of the heart. His all-seeing eye pierces through the paint, varnish and tinsel which cover the unsound heart.

One thing, however, need never be forgotten in connection with the subject of hypocrisy. Let us not flatter ourselves that because some make a false profession of religion others need not make any profession at all. This is a common delusion and one against which we must guard. It does not follow that, because some bring religion into contempt by professing what they do not really believe and feel, we should bring religion into contempt by a cowardly silence that keeps religion out of sight. Let us rather be doubly careful to adorn our doctrine by our lives. Let us show the world that there is true coin as well as counterfeit.

For meditation: *Let us rob men of the jibe that those who go to church are hypocrites by lives that prove they are liars.*

Suggested further reading: Isaiah 53

We see the Son of God taken prisoner and led away bound like a malefactor, arraigned before wicked and unjust judges, insulted and treated with contempt. And yet this unresisting prisoner had only to will his deliverance and he would at once have been free. He had only to command the confusion of his enemies, and they would at once have been confounded. He knew all these things, and yet condescended to be treated as a malefactor without resisting.

To suffer for those whom we love and who are in some sense worthy of our affections is suffering that we can understand. To submit to ill-treatment quietly when we have no power to resist is submission that is both graceful and wise. But to suffer voluntarily when we have the power to prevent it, and to suffer for a world of unbelieving and ungodly sinners, unasked and unthanked — this is a line of conduct which passes man's understanding. Never let us forget that this is the peculiar beauty of Christ's sufferings, when we read the wondrous story of his cross and passion. He was led away captive and dragged before the high priest's bar, not because he could not help himself, but because he had set his whole heart on saving sinners, by bearing their sins, by being treated as a sinner and by being punished in their stead. He was a willing prisoner, that we might be set free. He was willingly arraigned and condemned, that we might be absolved and declared innocent. 'He suffered for sins, the just for the unjust, that he might bring us unto God' (1 Peter 3:18). 'Though he was rich, yet for our sakes he became poor, that we through his poverty might be rich' (2 Cor. 8:9). 'He was made sin for us who knew no sin, that we might be made the righteousness of God in him' (2 Cor. 5:21). Surely if there is any doctrine of the gospel which needs to be clearly known, it is the doctrine of Christ's voluntary substitution. He suffered and died willingly and unresistingly, because he knew that he had come to be our Substitute and by substitution to purchase our salvation.

For meditation: *'He himself bore our sins in his body on the tree, so that we might die to sins and live for righteousness; by his wounds you have been healed'* (1 Peter 2:24).

Suggested further reading: 2 Corinthians 8:1-9

Self-denying liberality in giving is pleasing to Christ. This is a lesson that is taught us in a striking manner by our Lord's commendation of a certain poor widow. His judgement on the gifts of the rich and the gift of this poor woman (vv. 43-44) shows that he looks not merely at the amount given, but also at the ability of the giver, not merely at the quantity contributed, but at the motive and heart of the contributor.

There are few of our Lord's sayings so overlooked as this one. There are thousands who remember all his doctrinal discourses and yet contrive to forget this incident in his earthly ministry. The proof of this is to be seen in the meagre and sparing contributions which are yearly made by the church to do good in the world. The proof is seen in the miserably small incomes of all the missionary societies in proportion to the wealth of all the churches. The proof is to be seen in the long lists of those who contribute a trivial amount regularly when they could give so much more. The stinginess of professing Christians in all matters which concern God and religion is one of the crying sins of the day and one of the signs of the times. The givers to Christ's cause are but a small section of the visible church. Not one twentieth of the church knows what it is to be 'rich towards God' (Luke 12:21). The vast majority spend pounds on themselves and pence on Christ.

Let us mourn over this state of things and pray God to amend it. Let us pray to him to open men's eyes and awake men's hearts and stir up a spirit of liberality. Above all, let us each do our own duty and give liberally and gladly to every Christian object while we can. There will be no giving when we are dead. Let us give as those who remember that Christ's eyes are upon us. He still sees exactly what each gives and knows how much exactly is left behind. Above all let us give as disciples of a crucified Christ who gave himself for us body and soul, on the cross. Freely we have received. Let us freely give.

For meditation: *It is so easy for us to condemn those of whom we read in the Scriptures who loved their money and rejected Christ. What does our giving say about us?*

Suggested further reading: 1 Kings 13:7-24

The first flight and running away of the disciples is passed over entirely by John. He simply mentions that Peter followed his Master, though at a distance, lovingly anxious to see what was done to him, yet not bold enough to keep near him like a disciple. Anyone can see that the unhappy disciple was under the influence of very mixed feelings. Love made him ashamed to run away and hide himself. Cowardice made him afraid to show his colours and stick by his Lord's side. Hence he chose a middle course — the worst, as it happened, that he could have followed. After being self-confident when he should have been humble and sleeping when he ought to have been praying, he could not have done a more foolish thing than to flutter round the fire and place himself within reach of temptation. It teaches the foolishness of man when his grace is weak. No prayer is more useful than the familiar one: 'Lead us not into temptation.' Peter forgot it here.

At first Peter stood outside the door of the palace, not daring to go in. It is a little detail in the story of his fall which the three other Gospel writers omit to mention. Again we see in him the mixture of good and bad feelings, cowardice and love contending for the mastery. Happy would it have been for him if he had stayed outside the door!

Rollock remarks that when Peter found the door shut, he ought not to have stood there, but to have gone away. 'It was by God's providence the door was shut. He got a warning then to leave off, but would not. These impediments, cast in our way when we purpose to do a thing, should not be idly looked at, but should make us carefully try the deed, whether it be lawful.'

Let us mark what mistakes even the best believers make in dealing with their brethren. John thought it would be a kind and useful thing to bring Peter into the high priest's house. He was perfectly mistaken and was unintentionally one link in the chain of causes which led to his fall. People may harm each other with the best intention.

For meditation: *Beware of causing others to sin.*

Suggested further reading: 2 Timothy 3:1-9

We have in these verses the charges of our Lord against the Jewish teachers ranged under eight heads. Standing in the midst of the temple, with a listening crowd around him, he publicly denounces the main errors of the scribes and Pharisees in unsparing terms. Eight times he uses the solemn expression, 'Woe to you'. Seven times he calls them 'hypocrites'. Twice he speaks of them as blind guides, twice as fools and blind, once as serpents and a generation of vipers. Let us mark that language well. It teaches us a solemn lesson. It shows how utterly abominable the spirit of the scribes and Pharisees is in God's sight, in whatever form it may be found.

The first woe in the list is directed against the systematic opposition of the scribes and Pharisees to the progress of the gospel (v. 13). They rejected the warning voice of John the Baptist. They refused to acknowledge Jesus as the Messiah when he appeared amongst them. They tried to keep back Jewish enquirers. They would not believe the gospel themselves and they did all in their power to stop others believing it. This was a great sin.

The second woe in the list was directed against the covetousness and self-aggrandizing spirit of the scribes and Pharisees. They imposed on the credulity of weak and unprotected women by an affectation of great devoutness until they were regarded as their spiritual directors. They scrupled not to abuse the influence thus unrighteously obtained to their own temporal advantage and, in a word, to make money out of religion. This again was a great sin (v. 14).

The third woe in the list is directed against the zeal of the scribes and Pharisees for making partisans (v. 15). They laboured incessantly to make men join their party and adopt their opinions. They did this from no desire to benefit men's souls in the least or to bring them to God. They only did it to swell the ranks of their sect and to increase the number of their adherents and their own importance. Their religious zeal arose from sectarianism and not from love of God.

For meditation: *What are your motives in wanting to see men saved in your church?*

Suggested further reading: James 5:1-6

Verse 19 describes the first judicial examination that our Lord underwent. He was questioned concerning 'his disciples' — that is, who they were, how many, what position they occupied and what were their names; and concerning 'his doctrine' — that is, what were the principal points or truths of his creed, what were the peculiar things he called on man to believe. The object of this preliminary inquiry seems manifest. It was meant to elicit some admission from our Lord's mouth, on which some formal charge of heresy and blasphemy before the Sanhedrin might be founded.

Verse 20 contains a calm, dignified statement from our Lord of the general course of his ministry. He had done nothing in a clandestine or underhand way. He had always spoken openly 'to the world' and not confined his teaching to any one class. He had always taught publicly in synagogues and in the temple where the Jews resorted. He had said nothing privately and secretly, as if he had any cause to be ashamed of it.

The verse is mainly remarkable for the strong light it throws on our Lord's habit of teaching throughout the three years of his ministry. It shows that he was eminently a public teacher, kept back no part of his message from any class of the population and proclaimed it with equal boldness in every place. There was nothing whatever of reserve about his gospel. This is his own account and we therefore know that it is correct. 'I have spoken in the most public manner and taught in the most public places and done nothing in a corner.'

The boldness and dignity of our Lord's reply to Annas in verse 23 are very noteworthy. They are an example to all Christians of the courageous and unflinching tone which an innocent defendant may justly adopt before the bar of an unrighteous judge. 'The righteous is bold as a lion.'

For meditation: *In the face of abuse and hostility, we have our Lord's example to follow.*

Suggested further reading: Matthew 15:1-9

The fourth woe in the list is directed against the doctrines of the scribes and Pharisees about oaths (vv. 16-22). They drew subtle distinctions between one kind of oath and another. They taught the Jesuitical tenet that some oaths were binding on men while others were not. They attached greater importance to oaths sworn by the gold offered to the temple than to oaths sworn by the temple itself. By so doing they brought the third commandment into contempt, and by making men overrate the value of alms and oblations advanced their own interests. This again was a great sin.

The fifth woe in the list is directed against the practice of the scribes and Pharisees to exalt trifles in religion above serious things, to put the last things first and the first things last. They made great ado about tithing mint and other garden herbs, as if they could not be too strict in their obedience to God's law. And yet at the same time they neglected great plain duties such as justice, charity and honesty (v. 23). This again was a great sin.

The sixth and seventh woes in the list possess too much in common to be divided. They are directed against a general characteristic in the religion of the scribes. They set outward purity and decency above inward sanctification and purity of heart. They made it their duty to cleanse the outsides of their cups and platters, but neglected their own inward man. They were like whitened sepulchres, clean and beautiful externally, but within full of all corruption. This also was a great sin (vv. 25-28).

The last woe in this list is directed against the affected veneration of the scribes and Pharisees for the memory of the dead saints. They built their tombs and garnished their sepulchres, and yet their own lives proved that they were of one mind with those who killed the prophets. Their own conduct was evidence that they liked dead saints better than living ones (vv. 29-32). The very men that pretended to honour prophets could see no beauty in a living Christ. This also was a great sin.

For meditation: *Each of these eight woes is peculiarly applicable to the corruptions of Roman Catholicism.*

Suggested further reading: Acts 23:1-5

One of the attendants standing by rudely interrupts our Lord by striking him and coarsely taxing him with impertinence and disrespect in so speaking as he had spoken to the high priest.

Stier remarks that this was the first blow which the holy body of Jesus received from the hands of sinners.

We may learn from this circumstance what a low, degraded and disorderly condition the Jewish courts of ecclesiastical law must have been in at this period, when such a thing as publicly striking a prisoner could take place and when violence could be shown to a prisoner in a full court of justice for answering boldly for himself. It supplies strong evidence of the miserably fallen state of the whole Jewish nation, when such an act could be done under the very eyes of a judge. Nothing is a surer index of the real condition of a nation than the conduct of its courts of justice and its just or unjust treatment of prisoners. The sceptre had clearly fallen from Judah and rottenness was at the core of the nation, when the thing mentioned in this verse could happen. Our Lord's assailant evidently held that a prisoner must never reply to his judge, however unjust or corrupt the judge might be.

Our Lord's reply to him who smote is a calm and dignified reproof: 'If I have spoken wickedly, bear witness in a just and orderly way becoming a court of law, but do not strike me. If, on the contrary, I have spoken well, what reasonable cause canst thou allege for striking me, either here or out of court?'

Let us note that our Lord's conduct at this point teaches that his maxim, 'If anyone smite thee on thy right cheek, turn to him the other also' (Matt. 5:39), is a maxim which must be taken with reserve and is not of unlimited application. There may be times when, in defence of truth and for the honour of justice, a Christian must firmly protest against violence and publicly refuse to countenance it by tame submission.

For meditation: *Is there not an interesting contrast between our Lord and Paul on trial?* (John 18:23; Acts 23:3).

Suggested further reading: Matthew 7:15-23

This passage shows us how deplorable the state of the Jewish nation was when our Lord was on the earth. When such were the teachers what must have been the miserable darkness of the taught! Truly the iniquity of Israel had come to the full. It was high time indeed for the Sun of Righteousness to arise and the gospel to be preached.

Let us learn from the whole passage how abominable hypocrisy is in the sight of God. These scribes and Pharisees are charged not with being thieves and murderers but being hypocrites to the very core. Whatever we are in our religion, let us resolve never to wear the cloak of hypocrisy. Let us by all means be honest and real.

Let us learn how awfully dangerous is the position of an unfaithful minister. It is bad enough to be blind ourselves. It is a thousand times worse to be a blind guide. Of all men none is so culpably wicked as an unconverted minister, and none will be judged so severely. It is a solemn saying about such a one: 'He resembles an unskilful pilot: he does not perish alone.'

Finally, let us beware of supposing from this passage that the safest course is to make no profession at all. This is to run into a dangerous extreme. It does not follow that there is no such thing as true profession because some men are hypocrites. It does not follow that all money is bad because there is some counterfeit coin. Let not hypocrisy prevent us from confessing Christ or move us from our steadfastness if we have confessed him. Let us press on, looking unto Jesus, resting on him and praying daily to be kept from error as David did (Ps. 119:80).

Such is the melancholy picture which our Lord gives of Jewish teachers. Let us turn from the contemplation of it with sorrow and humiliation. It is a fearful exhibition of the morbid anatomy of human nature.

For meditation: *We should pray for ourselves and those who teach us, that grace might be granted so that what is preached is practised and the gospel is not brought into disrepute by our inconsistencies.*

Suggested further reading: Galatians 2:11-16

The apostle stood among the crowd of his Master's enemies and warmed himself like one of them, as if he had nothing to think of but his bodily comfort, while his beloved Master stood in a distant part of the hall, cold and a prisoner. Who can doubt that Peter, in his miserable cowardice, wished to appear one of the party who hated his Master and thought to conceal his real character by doing as they did? And who can doubt that while he warmed his hands he felt cold, wretched and comfortless in his own soul? 'The backslider in heart is filled with his own ways.'

How many do as others do and go with the crowd, while they know inwardly they are wrong!

A second time we find the unhappy apostle telling a lie and this time it is added emphatically: 'He denied it.' The further a backslider goes, the worse he becomes. The first time he seems to have said quietly, 'I am not.' The second time he flatly 'denied'. Even an apostle can fall into being a liar!

The third denial, we know from the other Gospels, was more loud and emphatic than any and was made with cursing and swearing! The further a man falls, the heavier his fall.

Calvin remarks on the course of a backslider, 'At first the fault will not be very great; next, it becomes habitual; and at last, after the conscience has been laid asleep, he who has accustomed himself to despise God will think nothing unlawful, but will dare to commit the greatest wickedness.'

As long as the world stands, Peter's fall will be an instructive example of what even a great saint may come to if he neglects to work and pray, of the mercy of Christ in restoring such a backslider and of the honesty of the Gospel writers in recording such a history.

For meditation:
Prone to wander, Lord, I feel it;
Prone to leave the God I love

(Robinson).

Suggested further reading: Luke 10:1-16

These verses form a conclusion to our Lord's address on the scribes and Pharisees. We learn that God takes notice of the treatment which his messengers and ministers receive and will one day pay it back. The Jews as a nation had often given the servants of God most shameful usage. They had often dealt with them as enemies because they told them the truth. Some they had persecuted, some they had scourged and some they had even killed (v. 34). They thought perhaps that no account would be required of their conduct. But our Lord tells them they are all mistaken. There was an eye that saw their actions. There was a hand that registered all the innocent blood they shed in the books of everlasting remembrance. The dying words of Zacharias would be found after eight hundred and fifty years not to have fallen to the ground (2 Chron. 24:22). Yet a few years and there would be such an inquisition for blood at Jerusalem as the world had never seen. The holy city would be destroyed. The nation which had murdered and destroyed so many prophets would itself be wasted by famine, pestilence and the sword. And even those that escaped would be scattered to the four winds and become fugitives. Well might our Lord speak as he did! (v. 36).

It is good for us to mark this lesson well. We are too apt to think that 'bygones are bygones' and that things which to us are past and done and old will never be raked up again. But we forget that with God one day is as a thousand years and that the events of a thousand years ago are as fresh in his sight as the events of this very hour. God will require an account of the treatment of his saints — all in every age. The world will yet see that God judges righteously (Ps. 58:11).

Present persecutors should know that all who injure, ridicule, mock or slander others on account of religion commit a great sin. Christ takes notice of everyone who persecutes his neighbour because he is better than himself, or because he prays, reads his Bible and thinks about his soul (Zech. 2:8).

For meditation: *As pains in the body send signals to the brain, so pains in Christ's body send messages to the Head.*

Suggested further reading: Matthew 23:23-28

We should notice the false conscientiousness of our Lord's wicked enemies. We are told that the Jews who brought Christ before Pilate would not go into 'the judgement hall, lest they should be defiled, but that they might eat the passover'. That was scrupulosity indeed! These hardened men were actually engaged in doing the wickedest act that mortal man ever did. They wanted to kill their own Messiah. And yet at this very time they talked of being 'defiled' and were very particular about the Passover!

The conscience of unconverted men is a very curious part of their moral nature. While in some cases it becomes hardened, seared and dead, until it feels nothing, in others it becomes morbidly scrupulous about the lesser matters of religion.

Let us pray that our consciences may always be enlightened by the Holy Ghost and that we may be kept from a one-sided and deformed Christianity. A religion that makes a man neglect the weightier matters of daily holiness and separation from the world and concentrate his whole attention on forms, sacraments, ceremonies and public services is, to say the least, very suspicious. It may be accompanied by immense zeal and show of earnestness, but it is not sound in the sight of God. The Pharisees paid tithe of mint, anise and cummin, and compassed sea and land to make proselytes, while they neglected 'judgement, mercy and faith' (Matt. 23:23). The very Jews who thirsted for Christ's blood were the Jews who feared the defilement of a Roman judgement hall and made much ado about keeping the Passover! Let their conduct be a beacon to Christians as long as the world stands. That religion is worth little which does not make us say, 'I esteem all thy commandments concerning all things to be right, and I hate every false way' (Ps. 119:128). That Christianity is worthless which makes us compound for the neglect of heart religion and practical holiness by an extravagant zeal for man-made ceremonies or outward forms.

For meditation: *Christianity is more than keeping a set of minor rules.*

Suggested further reading: Ezekiel 33:1-11

Though our Lord exposed his enemies' unbelief, yet he showed that he loved and pitied them to the last. God often takes great pains with ungodly men. He sent the Jews messengers (v. 34). He gave them repeated warnings. He sent them message after message. He did not allow them to go on sinning without rebuke. They could never say they were not told when they did wrong.

This is the way that God generally deals with unconverted men. He does not cut them off in their sins without a call to repentance. He knocks at the door of their hearts by sicknesses and afflictions. He assails their consciences by sermons or by the advice of friends. He summons them to consider their ways by opening the grave before their eyes and taking away from them their idols. They often know not what it all means. They are often blind and deaf to all his gracious messages. But they will see his hand at last, though perhaps too late. They will discover that they too, like the Jews, had prophets and wise men and scribes sent to them. There was a voice in every providence that said to them that they should turn and not die (Ezek. 33:11).

Those who are lost for ever are lost through their own fault. The words of our Lord are very remarkable (v. 37). There is something peculiarly deserving of notice in this expression. It throws light on a mysterious subject and one that is often darkened by human explanations. It shows that Christ has feelings of pity for many who are not saved and that the grand secret of man's ruin is want of will. Impotent as man is by nature, unable to think a good thought of himself, without power to turn himself to faith and call upon God, he still appears to have a mighty ability to ruin his own soul. Powerless as he is to do good, he is still powerful to do evil. The seat of impotence is his will. A will to repent and believe no man can give himself, but a will to reject Christ and have his own way every man possesses by nature. This lack of will will prove his destruction (John 5:40; Acts 7:51; Hos. 13:9).

For meditation: *We love sin. God forbid that he should allow us what we naturally want. Rather let us have new God-given desires.*

Suggested further reading: Romans 13:1-7

Our Lord's main object in saying, 'My kingdom is not of this world,' was to inform Pilate's mind concerning the true nature of his kingdom and to correct any false impression he might have received from the Jews. He tells him that he did not come to set up a kingdom which would interfere with the Roman government. He did not aim at establishing a temporal power, to be supported by armies and maintained by taxes. The only dominion he exercised was over men's hearts and the only weapons that his subjects employed were spiritual weapons. A kingdom which required neither money nor servants for its support was one of which the Roman emperors need not be afraid. In the highest sense it was a kingdom 'not of this world'.

But our Lord did not intend to teach that the kings of this world have nothing to do with religion and ought to ignore God altogether in the government of their subjects. No such idea, we may be sure, was in his mind. He knew perfectly well that it was written, 'By me kings reign' (Prov. 8:15), and that kings are as much required to use their influence for God as the meanest of their subjects. He knew that the prosperity of kingdoms is wholly dependent on the blessing of God and that kings are as much bound to encourage righteousness and godliness as to punish unrighteousness and immorality. To suppose that he meant to teach Pilate that, in his judgement, an infidel might be as good a king as a Christian, and a man like Gallio as good a ruler as David or Solomon, is simply absurd.

Let us carefully hold fast the true meaning of our Lord's words in these latter days. Let us never be ashamed to maintain that no government can expect to prosper which refuses to recognize religion, which deals with its subjects as if they had no souls and cares not whether they serve God, or Baal, or no god at all. Such a government will find, sooner or later, that its line of policy is suicidal and damaging to its best interests. No doubt the kings of this world cannot make men Christians by laws and statutes. But they can encourage and support Christianity and they will do so if they are wise.

For meditation: *'I urge, then, first of all, that requests, prayers, intercession and thanksgiving be made for everyone … that we may live peaceful and quiet lives in all godliness and holiness'* (1 Tim. 2:1-2).

Suggested further reading: John 4:21-26

The words of our Lord about the temple must have sounded strange and startling in Jewish ears in a way that our minds can hardly conceive. They were spoken of a building that every Israelite regarded with almost idolatrous veneration. They were spoken of a building that contained the holy of holies and furniture formed on a pattern given by God himself. They were spoken of a building associated with most of the principal names in Jewish history — with David, Solomon, Hezekiah, Josiah, Isaiah, Jeremiah, Ezra and Nehemiah. They were spoken of a building to which every devout Jew turned his face in every quarter of the world when he offered up his daily prayers (1 Kings 8:44; Jonah 2:4; Dan. 6:10). But they were words spoken advisedly. They were spoken in order to teach us that mighty truth that the true glory of a place of worship does not consist in outward adornments. The Lord sees differently to man (1 Sam. 16:7). Man looks at the outward appearance of a building. The Lord looks for spiritual worship and the presence of the Holy Spirit. In the temple at Jerusalem these things were utterly lacking and therefore Jesus Christ could take no pleasure in it.

Professing Christians will do well to remember our Lord's words in the present day. It is fitting and right beyond doubt that buildings set apart for Christian worship should be worthy of the purpose for which they are used. Whatever is done for Christ ought to be well done. The house in which the gospel is preached, the Word of God read, and prayer offered up ought to lack nothing that can make it comely and substantial. But let it never be forgotten that the material part of a Christian church is by far the least important part of it. The fairest combinations of marble, stone, wood and painted glass are worthless in God's sight unless there is truth in the pulpit and grace in the congregation. The dens and caves in which the early Christians used to meet were probably far more beautiful in the eyes of Christ than the noblest cathedral that was ever erected by man. The temple in which the Lord delights most is a broken and contrite heart renewed by the Holy Spirit.

For meditation: *Without the truth in their pulpits, the most beautiful buildings are simply historical museums.*

Suggested further reading: Proverbs 8:1-11

We are told that when our Lord spoke of the truth, the Roman governor replied, 'What is truth?' We are not told with what motive this question was asked, nor does it appear on the face of the narrative that he who asked it waited for an answer. It seems far more likely that the saying was the sarcastic, sneering exclamation of one who did not believe that there was any such thing as 'truth'. It sounds like the language of one who had heard, from his earliest youth, so many barren speculations about 'truth' among Roman and Greek philosophers that he doubted its very existence. 'Truth indeed! What is truth?'

There are multitudes in every Christian land whose state of mind is just like that of Pilate. Hundreds are continually excusing their own irreligion by the specious plea that, like the Roman governor, they cannot find out 'what is truth'. They point to the endless controversies of Romanists and Protestants, of High Churchmen and Low Churchmen, of churchmen and dissenters, and pretend to say that they do not understand who is right and who is wrong. Sheltered under this favourite excuse, they pass through life without any decided religion and in this wretched, comfortless state, too often die.

But is it really true that truth cannot be discovered? Nothing of the kind! God never left any honest diligent enquirer without light and guidance. Pride is one reason why many cannot discover truth. They do not humbly go down on their knees and earnestly ask God to teach them. Laziness is another reason. They do not honestly take pains and search the Scriptures. The followers of unhappy Pilate, as a rule, do not deal fairly and honestly with their consciences. Their favourite question, 'What is truth?', is nothing better than a pretence and an excuse. The words of Solomon will be found true as long as the world stands: 'If thou criest after knowledge, and liftest up thy voice for understanding; if thou seekest her as silver, and searchest for her as for hid treasures; then shalt thou understand the fear of the Lord, and find the knowledge of God' (Prov. 2:4-5). No man ever followed that advice and missed the way to heaven.

For meditation: *'Jesus answered, "I am the way and the truth and the life. No one comes to the Father except through me" '* (John 14:6).

Suggested further reading: 1 John 2:18-27

The very first words of this discourse are a warning against deception (v. 4). A more needful warning than this cannot be conceived. Satan knows well the value of prophecy and has ever laboured to bring the subject into contempt. How many false Christs and false prophets arose before the destruction of Jerusalem, the works of Josephus abundantly prove. In how many ways the eyes of man are continually blinded in the present day as to things to come, it might easily be shown. Let us watch and be on our guard.

Let no man deceive us as to the leading facts of unfulfilled prophecy by telling us that they are impossible, or as to the manner in which they will be brought to pass, telling us that it is improbable and contrary to past experience. Let no man deceive us as to the time when unfulfilled prophecies will be accomplished. On all these matters let the plain meaning of Scripture be our guide. Let us frankly allow that there are many things that we will not understand, but still hold our ground tenaciously, believe much, wait long and not doubt that one day all will be made clear.

The prophecies concerning the nations (vv. 6-8) no doubt received a partial fulfilment in the days when Jerusalem was taken by the Romans and the Jews were led into captivity. It was a season of unparalleled desolation to Judea and the countries round about her, a struggle which for bloodshed, misery and tribulation has never been equalled since the world began. But the words before us have yet to receive a more complete accomplishment. They describe the time which shall immediately precede the second advent of our Lord.

Let us dismiss from our minds the idea that the nations will ever give up wars entirely before the Lord comes. So long as the devil is the prince of this world, and the hearts of men are unconverted, so long there must be strife and fighting. But ministers and missionaries will call out a witnessing people who shall serve Christ in every land.

For meditation: *While deceivers increase and worsen, Christians are to follow the Scriptures* (2 Tim. 3:13-17).

Suggested further reading: 2 Corinthians 10:1-5

We should notice in these verses the account that our Lord gives of his own mission. He says, 'To this end was I born, and for this cause came I into the world, that I should bear witness unto the truth.'

Of course, we are not to suppose our Lord meant that this was the only end of his mission. No doubt he spoke with special reference to what he knew was passing through Pilate's mind. He did not come to win a kingdom with the sword and to gather adherents and followers by force. He came armed with no other weapon but 'truth'. To testify to fallen man the truth about God, about sin, about the need of a Redeemer, about the nature of holiness, to declare and lift up before man's eyes this long lost and buried 'truth', was one great purpose of his ministry. He came to be God's witness to a lost and corrupt world. That the world needed such a testimony, he does not shrink from telling the proud Roman governor. And this is what St Paul had in view when he tells Timothy that 'Before Pontius Pilate Christ witnessed a good confession' (1 Tim. 6:13).

The servants of Christ in every age must remember that our Lord's conduct in this place is meant to be their example. Like him, we are to be witnesses to God's truth, salt in the midst of corruption, light in the midst of darkness, men and women not afraid to stand alone and to testify for God against the ways of sin and the world. To do so may entail on us much trouble and even persecution. But the duty is clear and plain. If we love life, if we would keep a good conscience and be owned by Christ at the last day, we must be 'witnesses'. It is written: 'Whosoever shall be ashamed of me and of my words in this adulterous and sinful generation, of him also shall the Son of man be ashamed, when he cometh in the glory of his Father with the holy angels' (Mark 8:38).

For meditation: *The old saying, 'The truth will out,' is as true of real Christianity as of hidden sin.*

Suggested further reading: Matthew 24:9-14

With respect to his own disciples Christ does not prophesy smooth things and promise them an uninterrupted course of temporal comfort, but rather a great variety of persecutions and difficulties. These words began to be fulfilled in the days of the apostles and have continued to be fulfilled ever since.

Let it be a settled principle in our minds that the true Christian must always enter the kingdom of God through much tribulation (Acts 14:22). His best things are yet to come. This world is not his home. If we are faithful and decided servants of Christ, the world will certainly hate us as it hated our Master. In one way or another, grace will always be persecuted. No consistency of conduct, however faultless, no kindness and amiability of character will exempt the believer from the world's dislike as long as he lives. It is foolish to be surprised at this. It is part of the cross and we must bear it patiently (1 John 3:13; John 15:18-19).

Christ gave a gracious promise to his disciples (v. 18). Our blessed Lord knew well the hearts of the disciples. He saw that the prophecy he had just spoken might well make them faint, and so he supplies them with his cheering word of encouragement.

The promise before us is wide and comprehensive and one which is the property of believers in every age. A literal interpretation of it is clearly impossible. It cannot apply to the bodies of disciples. To say that would be contradictory to the fact that James and other apostles died violent deaths. A figurative interpretation must evidently be placed upon the words. They form a proverbial saying. They teach us that, whatever the sufferings of a disciple of Christ, his best things can never be injured. His life is hid with Christ in God. His treasure in heaven can never be touched. His soul is beyond the reach of harm. Even his weak body shall be raised again and made like his Saviour's glorious body at the last day. We may lose much by serving Christ but we will never lose our souls.

For meditation: *Nothing in heaven, earth or hell can remove God's love from those who trust in him* (Rom. 8:37-39).

Suggested further reading: 2 Timothy 1:1-7

It is quite possible that the fame and character of Jesus had reached Pilate's ears long before he was brought before him. It is hard to suppose that such miracles as our Lord wrought would never be talked of within the palace of the chief ruler of Judaea. The raising of Lazarus must surely have been reported among his servants. Our Lord's triumphal entry into Jerusalem, attended by myriads of people shouting, 'Blessed is the King,' must surely have been noted by the soldiers and officers of Pilate's guard. Can we wonder that all this made him regard our Lord with something like awe? Wicked men are often very superstitious.

The pitiable and miserable character of Pilate, the Roman governor, begins to come into clear light from this point. We see him a man utterly destitute of moral courage, knowing what was right and just in the case before him, yet afraid to act on his knowledge; knowing that our Lord was innocent, yet not daring to displease the Jews by acquitting him; knowing that he was doing wrong and yet afraid to do right. 'The fear of man bringeth a snare' (Prov. 29:25). Wretched and contemptible are those rulers and statesmen whose first principle is to please the people, even at the expense of their own consciences, and who are ready to do what they know to be wrong rather than offend the mob! Wretched are those nations which for their sins are given over to be governed by such statesmen! True godly rulers should lead the people and not be led by them, should do what is right and leave consequences to God. A base determination to keep in with the world at any price and a slavish fear of man's opinion were leading principles in Pilate's character. There are many like him. Nothing is more common than to see statesmen evading the plain line of duty and trying to shuffle responsibility on others, rather than give offence to the mob. This is precisely what Pilate did here. The spirit of his reply to the Jews is: 'I had rather not be troubled with the case. Cannot you settle it yourselves, without asking me to interfere?'

For meditation: *Christians are not called to be timid, but bold in the Spirit* (Acts 4:31).

Suggested further reading: Daniel 9:20-27

One main subject of this part of our Lord's prophecy is the taking of Jerusalem by the Romans. That great event took place about forty years after the words we have now read were spoken. A full account of it is to be found in the writings of Josephus. Those writings are the best comment on our Lord's words. They are a striking proof of the accuracy of every minute part of his predictions. The horrors and miseries the Jews endured throughout the siege of their city exceed anything on record.

It surprises some to find so much importance attached to the taking of Jerusalem. They would rather regard the whole chapter as unfulfilled. Such persons forget that Jerusalem and the temple were the heart of the old Jewish dispensation. When they were destroyed the old Mosaic system came to an end. The daily sacrifice, the yearly feasts, the altar, the holy of holies, the priesthood were all essential parts of revealed religion till Christ came, but no longer. When he died upon the cross their work was done. They were dead and it only remained that they should be buried. But it was not fitting that this should be done quietly. The ending of a dispensation given with as much solemnity as at Mount Sinai might well be expected to be marked with peculiar solemnity. The destruction of the holy temple, where so many saints had seen shadows of the good things to come, might well be expected to form a subject of prophecy. The Lord Jesus especially predicts the desolation of the holy place. The great High Priest describes the end of the dispensation which had been a schoolmaster to bring men to himself.

Flight from danger may sometimes be the positive duty of a Christian (v. 16). The servant of Christ undoubtedly is not to be a coward. He is to be willing to die if needs be for the truth. But the servant of Christ is not to run into danger unless it comes in the line of duty. He is not to be ashamed to use reasonable means to provide for his personal safety when no good is done by dying at his post. We must avoid being rash, as well as being cowards, avoiding the stopping of our usefulness by being over-hot and well as being over-cold!

For meditation: *God destroys that which fails to fulfil its function.*

Suggested further reading: 2 Corinthians 5:14-21

Verse 40 describes the complete failure of Pilate's notable plan, by which he hoped to satisfy the Jews and yet release Jesus. The fierce and bigoted party of Caiaphas would not listen to his proposal for a moment. They declared they would rather have Barabbas, a notorious prisoner in the hands of the Romans, released than Jesus. Nothing would content them but our Lord's death. Barabbas, we know from St Luke (23:19), was a murderer as well as a robber. The Jews were asked to decide whether the holy Jesus or the vile criminal should be let go free and released from prison. Such was their utter hardness, bitterness, cruelty and hatred of our Lord that they actually declare they would rather have Barabbas set free than Jesus! Nothing, in short, would satisfy them but Christ's blood. Thus they committed the great sin which Peter charges home on them not long after: 'Ye denied Jesus in the presence of Pilate, when he was determined to let him go... Ye denied the Holy One and the Just, and desired a murderer to be granted unto you' (Acts 3:13-14). They publicly declared that they liked a robber and a murderer better than Christ!

We have here a lively illustration of the great Christian doctrine of substitution. Barabbas, the real criminal, is acquitted and let go free. Jesus, innocent and guiltless, is condemned and sentenced to death. So is it in the salvation of our souls. We are all by nature like Barabbas and deserve God's wrath and condemnation; yet he was accounted righteous and set free. The Lord Jesus Christ is perfectly innocent and yet he is counted a sinner, punished as a sinner and put to death that we may live. Christ suffers, though guiltless, that we may be pardoned. We are pardoned, though guilty, because of what Christ does for us. We are sinners and yet counted righteous. Christ is righteous and yet counted a sinner. Happy is that man who understands this doctrine and has laid hold on it by faith for the salvation of his own soul.

For meditation:
Because the sinless Saviour died,
My sinful soul is counted free

                                                       (Bancroft).

Suggested further reading: Romans 8:31-39

God's elect are always special objects of God's care (vv. 22,24). Those whom God has chosen to salvation by Christ are those whom God especially loves in this world. They are the jewels among mankind. He cares more for them than for kings on their thrones if kings are not converted. He hears their prayers. He orders all the events of the nations and the consequences of wars for their good and their sanctification. He keeps them by his Spirit. He allows neither man nor devil to pluck them out of his hand. Whatever tribulation comes on the world, God's elect are safe. May we never rest till we know that we are of this blessed number! When Paul saw the faith, hope and love of the Thessalonians, then he knew their election of God (1 Thess. 1:4).

In Luke 21:24 a period is foretold during which Jerusalem was to be given over into the hands of Gentile rulers and the Jews were to have no dominion over their ancient city. A fixed period is likewise foretold which was the time in which the Gentiles were to enjoy privileges and occupy a position something like that of Israel in ancient days. Both days are one day to end. Jerusalem is once more to be restored to its ancient inhabitants. The Gentiles because of their hardness and unbelief are to be stripped of their privileges and endure the judgement of God. Their dominion shall crumble away and their vaunted institutions shall fall to pieces. The Jews shall be restored.

Whenever the second advent of Christ takes place, it shall be a very sudden event (v. 27). This is a practical truth that we should ever keep before our minds. That our Lord Jesus will come again in person we know from the Scriptures. That he will come in a time of tribulation we know. But the precise period, the year, the month, the day, the hour are all hidden things. We only know that it will be a very sudden event. Our plain duty then is to live always prepared for his return. Let us walk by faith, not by sight. Let us believe in Christ, serve Christ, follow Christ and love Christ. So living, whenever Christ may return, we will be ready for him.

For meditation: *In 1948 the Jews returned to Israel and in 1967 retook Jerusalem.*

Suggested further reading: Leviticus 16:18-22

The cruel injury inflicted on our Lord's body was a punishment sometimes so painful and violent that the sufferer died under it. As to Pilate's reason for inflicting this punishment on our Lord, there seems little doubt. He secretly hoped that this tremendous scourging in the Roman fashion would satisfy the Jews and that after seeing Jesus beaten, bleeding and torn with rods, they would be content to let him go free. As usual he was double-minded, cruel and deceitful. He tried to please the Jews by ill-treating our Lord as much as possible and at the same time he hoped to please his own conscience a little by not putting him to death. He told the Jews, indeed, according to Luke's account, what he wanted: 'I will chastise him and release him' (Luke 23:16). How entirely this weak design failed we shall see by and by.

The importance of this particular portion of our Lord's sufferings is strongly shown by the fact that Isaiah specially says, 'By his stripes we are healed,' and that St Peter specially quotes that text in his first epistle (Isa. 53:5; 1 Peter 2:24). Our Lord himself particularly foretold that he would be scourged (Luke 18:32).

We see his complete and perfect substitution for sinners. He, the innocent sin-bearer, wore the crown of thorns, that we, the guilty, might wear a crown of glory. Vast is the contrast which there will be between the crown of glory that Christ will wear at his second advent and the crown of thorns which he wore at this first coming.

It was, moreover, a striking symbol of the consequences of the Fall being laid on the head of our divine Substitute. In Leviticus it is written that Aaron shall lay his hands 'upon the head of the live goat, and confess over him all the iniquities of the children of Israel, and all their transgression in all their sins, putting them upon the head of the goat' (Lev. 16:21).

For meditation:
The head that once was crowned with thorns,
Is crowned with glory now

(Kelly).

Suggested further reading: 1 Thessalonians 4:13-18

In this part of the prophecy our Lord deals with his own second coming to judge the world. When the Lord Jesus returns to this world, he shall come with peculiar glory and majesty (v. 30). Before his presence the very planets shall be darkened and shaken (v. 29).

The second personal coming of our Lord shall be as different as possible from the first. He came the first time as a man of sorrows and acquainted with grief. He was born in a manger in Bethlehem in lowliness and humiliation. He took on him the form of a servant and was despised and rejected by men. He was betrayed into the hands of wicked men, condemned by an unjust judgement, mocked, scourged, crowned with thorns and at last crucified between two thieves. He shall come the second time as the King of all the earth with all royal majesty. The princes and great men of this world shall themselves stand before his throne to receive an eternal sentence. Before him every mouth shall be stopped and every knee bow and every tongue shall confess that Jesus Christ is Lord. May we all remember this. Whatever ungodly men may do now, there will be no scoffing, no jesting at Christ, no infidelity at the last day. The servants of Jesus may well wait patiently. Their Master shall one day be acknowledged as King of kings by the whole world.

These verses teach us that when Christ returns he will first take care of his believing people (v. 31). In the Day of Judgement true Christians shall be perfectly safe. Not a hair of their heads shall fall to the ground. Not one bone of Christ's mystical body shall be broken. There was an ark for Noah in the day of the flood. There was a Zoar for Lot when Sodom was destroyed. There shall be a hiding-place for all believers in Jesus when the wrath of God at last bursts on this wicked world. Those mighty angels who rejoiced in heaven when each sinner repented shall gladly catch up the people of Christ to meet him in the air. Believers may look forward to that awful day without fear.

For meditation: *Are you waiting for him?* (Heb. 9:28).

Suggested further reading: 2 Corinthians 11:23-29

A mock royal robe was thrown over our Lord's shoulders in order to show how ridiculous and contemptible was the idea of his kingdom. The colour 'purple' was doubtless meant to be a derisive imitation of the well-known imperial purple, the colour worn by emperors and kings. Some have thought that this robe was only an old soldier's cape, such as a guardhouse would easily furnish. Some, with more show of probability, have thought that this 'robe' must be the 'gorgeous robe' which Herod put on our Lord, mentioned by St Luke when he sent him back to Pilate (Luke 23:11), a circumstance which John has not recorded. In any case we need not doubt that the 'robe' was some shabby, cast-off garment. It is worth remembering that this brilliant colour, scarlet or purple, would make our blessed Lord a most conspicuous object to every eye, when he was led through the streets from Herod, or brought forth from Pilate's house to the assembled multitude of Jews. Once more we should call to mind the symbolical nature of this transaction also. Our Lord was clothed with a robe of shame and contempt, that we might be clothed with a spotless garment of righteousness and stand in white robes before the throne of God.

The words of the soldiers were spoken in contemptuous imitation of the words addressed to a Roman emperor, on his assuming imperial power: 'Hail, Emperor! *Ave Imperator!'* Let us not fail to remark at this point that ridicule, scorn and contempt were one prominent portion of our blessed Master's sufferings. Anyone who knows human nature must know that few things are more difficult to bear than ridicule, especially when we know that it is undeserved and when it is for religion's sake. Those who have to endure such ridicule may take comfort in the thought that Christ can sympathize with them, for it is a cup which he himself drank to the very dregs. Here again he was our Substitute. He bore contempt that we might receive praise and glory at the last day.

For meditation: *'But I am a worm and not a man, scorned by men and despised by the people. All who see me mock me; they hurl insults, shaking their heads: "He trusts in the Lord; let the Lord rescue him. Let him deliver him, since he delights in him" '* (Ps. 22:6-8).

Suggested further reading: 2 Peter 3:1-14

Some understand 'this generation' to mean true believers (v. 34), but I understand it to mean that until Christ returns the Jews will always remain a separate people. The continued existence of the Jews as a distinct nation is undeniably a great miracle. It is one of those evidences of the truth of the Bible that the infidel can never overthrow. For most of their history since A.D. 70 they have been without a land, without a king, without a government, scattered and dispersed over the world. The Jews are never absorbed among the people of the countries where they live like people of other nations, but live alone. Nothing can account for this but the finger of God. The Jewish nation stands before the world as a crushing answer to infidelity and a living book of evidence that the Bible is true. But we ought not to regard the Jewish people only as a witness that the Bible is true. We should see in them a continual pledge that the Lord Jesus is coming again. Like the Lord's Supper, they witness to the reality of the second advent as well as of the first.

Our Lord's predictions will certainly be fulfilled (v. 35). Our Lord knew well the natural unbelief of human nature. He knew that scoffers would arise in the last days saying, 'Where is the promise of his coming?' (2 Peter 3:4). He knew that when he came faith would be rare on the earth. He saw how many would contemptuously reject the solemn predictions he had just been delivering as improbable, unlikely and absurd. He warns us against all such sceptical thoughts with a caution of peculiar solemnity. He tells us that, whatever man may say or think, his words shall be fulfilled in their season and shall not pass away unaccomplished. May we all lay to heart this warning. We live in an unbelieving age. Few believed the report of our Lord's first coming and few believe the report of his second. Let us beware of this infection and believe to the saving of our souls. We are not reading cunningly devised fables, but deep and momentous truths. May God give us a heart to believe them.

For meditation: *Are you weary with waiting for his coming, or do you still feel a sense of expectancy?*

Suggested further reading: 1 Peter 2:21-25

The Roman governor went forth outside the palace where he lived to the Jews, who were waiting to hear the result of his private interview with our Lord. We must remember that, under the influence of hypocritical scrupulosity, they would not go inside the Gentile governor's house, lest they should be 'defiled', and were therefore waiting in the court outside. Now Pilate comes out of his palace and speaks to them. The words of the verse seem to show that Pilate came out first and that our Lord was led out behind him. 'Behold, I am bringing him outside again, that you may know that I can find no fault or cause of condemnation in him, and no ground for your charge that he is a stirrer up of sedition and a rebel king. He is only a weak, harmless fanatic, who lays claim to no kingdom of this world, and I bring him forth to you as a poor, contemptible person worthy of scorn, but not one that I can pronounce worthy of death. I have examined him myself and I inform you that I can see no harm in him.'

It seems to me quite plain that Pilate's private interview with our Lord had completely satisfied the governor that he was a harmless, innocent person and made him feel a strong desire to dismiss him unhurt, and he secretly hoped that the Jews would be satisfied when they saw the prisoner whom they had accused brought out beaten and bruised and treated with scorn and contempt, and that they would not press the charge any further. How thoroughly this cowardly double-dealing man was disappointed and what violence he had to do to his own conscience, we shall soon see.

It is very noteworthy that the expression, 'I find no fault in him,' is used three times by Pilate, in the same Greek words, in St John's account of the passion (John 18:38; 19:4-6). It was meet and right that he who had the chief hand in slaying the Lamb of God, the sacrifice for our sins, should three times publicly declare that he found no spot or blemish in him. He was proclaimed a Lamb without spot or fault, after a searching examination, by him that slew him.

For meditation: *'You disowned the Holy and Righteous One and asked that a murderer be released to you'* (Acts 3:14).

Suggested further reading: 2 Thessalonians 1:5-10

When our Lord returns the world will be in the same condition as it was in the days of Noah's flood (v. 37). When the flood came men were found absorbed in their worldly pursuits and utterly regardless of Noah's repeated warnings. They saw no likelihood of a flood. They would not believe that there was any danger. But at last the flood came suddenly and took them all away. All that were not with Noah in the ark were drowned. They were all swept away to their last account, unpardoned, unconverted and unprepared to meet God. So it shall be when Christ returns (v. 37).

The days of Noah are the true type of the days when Christ shall return. Millions will be found thoughtless, unbelieving, godless, Christless, worldly and unfit to meet their Judge. Let us take heed that we are not found among them.

An awful separation will take place when the Lord Jesus comes again (vv. 40-41). The godly and ungodly, at present, are all mingled together. In the congregation and in the place of worship, in the city and in the field, the children of God and the children of the world are side by side. But it shall not be so always. In the day of our Lord's return there shall at length be a division. In a moment, in the twinkling of an eye, at the last trumpet, each party shall be separated from the other for evermore. Wives shall be separated from husbands, parents from children, brothers from sisters, masters from servants, preachers from hearers. There shall be no time for parting words or a change of mind when the Lord appears. All shall be taken as they are and reap as they have sown. Believers shall be caught up to glory, honour and eternal life. Unbelievers shall be left behind to shame and everlasting contempt. Blessed and happy are those who are of one heart in following Christ. Their union alone shall never be broken. It shall last for evermore. Who can describe the happiness of those who are taken when the Lord returns? Who can imagine the misery of those who are left behind?

For meditation: *Will you be taken or left behind? The answer lies in your reception or rejection of the gospel.*

Suggested further reading: Leviticus 24:10-16

The 'law' referred to by the Jews is probably Leviticus 24:16. But it is curious that 'stoning' is the punishment there mentioned and not a word is said of crucifixion. This they do not tell Pilate. There is, perhaps, more fulness in the expression 'a law' than appears at first. It may mean, 'We Jews have a law given us by man from God, which is our rule of faith in religion. It is a law, we know, not binding on Gentiles, but it is a law which we feel bound to obey. One of the articles of that law is that "He that blasphemeth the name of the Lord shall be stoned." We ask that this article may be enforced in the case of this man. He has blasphemed by calling himself the Son of God and he ought to be put to death. We, therefore, demand his life.' There certainly seems an emphasis in the Greek on the word 'we', as if it meant 'we Jews', in contradistinction to Gentiles.

The expression 'Son of God' meant far more to a Jewish mind that it does to us. We see in John 5:18 that the Jews considered that when our Lord said that God was his Father he made himself 'equal with God'. See also John 10:33. One thing at any rate is very clear: whatever Socinians may say, our Lord distinctly laid claim to divinity and the Jews distinctly understood him to mean that he was God as well as man.

Cyril well remarks that if the Jews had dealt justly, they would have told the Gentile ruler that the person before him had not only claimed to be the Son of God, but had also done many miracles in proof of his divinity.

Rollock observes, 'Look, what blinds them! The Word of God, that should make them see, blinds them so that they use it to their ruin. The best things in the world, yea the Word of God itself, serve to wicked men for nothing else but their induration. The more they read, the blinder they are. And why? Because they abuse the Word and make it not a guide to direct their affections and actions.'

For meditation: *'For to us a child is born, to us a son is given, and the government will be on his shoulders. And he will be called Wonderful Counsellor, Mighty God, Everlasting Father, Prince of Peace'* (Isa. 9:6).

Suggested further reading: Romans 13:11-14

We have a practical duty of watchfulness in the prospect of Christ's second coming (vv. 42,44). This is a point which our blessed Master frequently presses on our notice. We hardly ever find him dwelling on the second advent without adding an injunction to watch. He knows the sleepiness of our nature. He knows how soon we forget the most solemn subjects in religion. He knows how unceasingly Satan labours to obscure the glorious doctrine of his coming again. He arms us with heart-searching exhortations to keep awake if we would not be ruined for evermore. May we all have an ear to hear them.

True Christians ought to live like watchmen. The day of the Lord comes as a thief in the night. They should always be on their guard. They should behave like the sentry on guard duty in an enemy's land. They should resolve by God's grace not to sleep on duty. The statement of Paul deserves many a thought (1 Thess. 5:6).

True Christians ought to live like good servants whose master is not at home. They should strive to be always ready for their Master's return. They should never give way to the feeling that their Master delays his coming. They should seek to keep their hearts in such a frame that whenever Christ appears they may at once give him a warm and loving reception. There is a vast depth in our Lord's words in verse 46. We may well doubt whether we are true believers in Jesus if we are not ready to have our faith changed into sight at any time.

Let us close this chapter with solemn feelings. The things we have been reading call loudly for great searchings of heart. Let us seek to make sure that we are in Christ and have an ark of safety when the day of wrath breaks on the world. Let us strive to live so that we receive the Lord's commendation and are not cast off for evermore. Let us dismiss from our minds the idea that unfulfilled prophecy is speculative and not practical. John sees a future hope as placing on us a very real present duty (1 John 3:2-3).

For meditation: *Whatever we do not understand about the detail of future events, his coming is sure and something to be prepared for.*

Suggested further reading: Romans 2:12-16

In verse 8 we see Pilate in a different frame of mind. This new charge of blasphemy against our Lord threw a new light over his feelings. He began to be really frightened and uncomfortable. The thought that the meek and gentle prisoner before him might after all be some superior being, and not a mere common man, filled his weak and ignorant conscience with alarm. What if he had before him some god in human form? What if it should turn out that he was actually inflicting bodily injuries on one of the gods? As a Roman he had doubtless heard and read many stories, drawn from the heathen mythology of Greece and Rome, about gods coming down to earth and appearing in human form. Perhaps the prisoner before him was one! The idea raised new fears in his mind. Already he had been made very uncomfortable about him. Our Lord's calm, dignified and majestic demeanour had doubtless made an impression. His evident innocence of all guilt and the extraordinary malice of his enemies, whose characters Pilate most likely knew well, had produced an effect. His own wife's dream had its influence. Even before the last charge of the Jews, the Roman judge had been awestruck and secretly convinced of our Lord's innocence and anxious to have him set free and actually 'afraid' of his prisoner. But when he heard of his being the 'Son of God', he was made more afraid.

Can we doubt for a moment that he must have heard many accounts of our Lord's ministry and specially of his miracles and astonishing power over the sick and the dead? Can we doubt that he heard of the raising of Lazarus at Bethany within a walk of Jerusalem? Remembering all this, we may well suppose that he regarded the whole case brought before him by the Jews with much anxiety from the very first and we can well understand that when he heard that Jesus was 'the Son of God', he was more than ever alarmed. Unprincipled rulers have an uneasy position.

For meditation: *To suppress conscience is always sinful.*

Suggested further reading: Jude 14-25

The Second Coming of Christ will find his church a mixed body, containing evil as well as good. The professing church is compared to ten virgins (v. 1). All of them had lamps, but only five had oil in their vessels to feed their lamps. All of them professed to have one object in view, but five only were truly wise and the rest were foolish. The visible church is in just the same condition. All its members are baptized in the name of Christ, but not all hear his voice and follow him. All are called Christians and profess to be of the Christian religion, but not all have the grace of the Spirit in their hearts, and really are what they profess to be. Our own eyes tell us that it is so now. The Lord tells us it will be so when he comes again.

Let us mark this description well. It is a humbling picture. After all our preachings and prayings, all our visiting and teachings, our missionary exertions at home and abroad, many will be found at the last spiritually dead! The wickedness and unbelief in human nature is a subject about which we all have much to learn!

Christ's second coming, whenever it may be, will take all men by surprise. The cry announcing the bridegroom's arrival was at midnight when all the virgins were slumbering and sleeping (vv. 5-6). It will be just the same when Jesus returns to this world. He will find the vast majority of mankind unbelieving and unprepared. He will find the vast majority of believing people in a sleepy and indolent state of soul. Business will be going on in town and country just as it does now. Politics, trading, farming, buying, selling, pleasure-seeking will take up men's attention just as they do now. Rich men will still be eating sumptuously and poor men will still be murmuring and complaining. Churches will still be full of divisions and wrangling about trifles and theological controversies will still be raging. Ministers will still be calling men to repent and congregations still putting off the day of decision. In the midst of all this Jesus Christ shall appear. The startled world shall stand before its King.

For meditation: *On that day only gospel believing will matter, not mere hearing.*

Suggested further reading: Ecclesiastes 3:1-8

Our Lord's silence, when this appeal was made to him by Pilate, is very striking. Hitherto he had spoken freely and replied to questions; now he refused to speak any more. The reason of our Lord's silence must be sought in the state of Pilate's soul. He deserved no answer and therefore got none. He had forfeited his title to any further revelation about his prisoner. He had been told plainly the nature of our Lord's kingdom and the purpose of our Lord's coming into the world and been obliged to confess publicly his innocence. And yet, with all this light and knowledge, he had treated our Lord with flagrant injustice, scourged him, allowed him to be treated with the vilest indignities by his soldiers and held him up to scorn, knowing in his own mind all the time that he was a guiltless person. He had, in short, sinned away his opportunities, forsaken his own mercies and turned a deaf ear to the cries of his own conscience. Hence our Lord would have nothing more to do with him and would tell him nothing more. 'He gave him no answer.'

Here, as in many other cases, we learn that God will not force conviction on men and will not compel obstinate unbelievers to believe and will not always strive with men's consciences. Most men, like Pilate, have a day of grace and an open door put before them. If they refuse to enter in, and choose their own sinful way, the door is often shut and never opened again. There is such a thing as a 'day of visitation', when Christ speaks to men. If they will not hear his voice and open the door of their hearts, they are often let alone, given over to a reprobate mind and left to reap the fruit of their own sins. It was so with Pharaoh and Saul and Ahab, and Pilate's case was like theirs. He had his opportunity and did not choose to use it, but preferred to please the Jews at the expense of his conscience and to do what he knew was wrong. We see the consequence. Our Lord will tell him nothing more.

For meditation: *'Do not give dogs what is sacred; do not throw your pearls to pigs. If you do, they may trample them under their feet, and then turn and tear you to pieces'* (Matt. 7:6).

Suggested further reading: Revelation 20:15 - 21:7

When the Lord comes again many will find out the value of saving religion too late (v. 8). Too late they asked for oil (v. 8), went to buy (v. 10) and sought admission (v. 11). All these expressions are striking emblems of things to come. Let us take heed that we do not find them true by experience to our own eternal ruin.

We may settle it in our minds that there will be an entire change of opinion one day as to the necessity of decided Christianity. At present many care nothing about it. They have no sense of sin. They have no love towards Christ. They know nothing of being born again. Repentance, faith, grace and holiness are mere words and names to them. They are subjects which they either dislike or about which they feel no concern. But all this state of things will come to an end one day. Knowledge, conviction, the value of a soul, the need of a Saviour, shall all burst on men's minds one day like a flash of lightning. But, alas! it will be too late. It will be too late to be 'buying oil' when the Lord returns. The mistakes that are not found out till that day are irretrievable.

When Christ returns true Christians shall receive a rich reward for all they have suffered for their Master's sake (v. 10). True Christians shall alone be found ready at the second advent. Washed in the blood of atonement, clothed in Christ's righteousness, renewed by the Spirit, they shall meet their Lord with boldness, and sit down at the marriage supper of the Lamb to go out no more. Surely this is a blessed prospect!

They shall be with their Lord, with him who loved them and gave himself for them, with him who bore with them and carried them through their earthly pilgrimage, with him whom they loved truly and faithfully on earth although with much weakness and many a tear.

The door shall be shut at last on all pain and sorrow, on an ill-natured and wicked world, on a tempting devil, on doubts and fears — shut, to be opened again no more.

For meditation: *Eternity with Christ tomorrow must be preceded by a life with Christ now.*

Suggested further reading: Daniel 4:24-27

We see the imperious, fierce, haughty, arrogant temper of the Roman governor breaking out. Accustomed to see prisoners cringing before him and willing to do anything to obtain his favour, he could not understand our Lord's silence. He addresses him in a tone of anger and surprise combined: 'Why dost thou not answer my question? Dost thou know what thou art doing in offending me? Dost thou not know that thou art at my mercy and that I have power to crucify thee or release thee, according as I think right?' I can see no other reasonable construction that can be put on Pilate's words. The idea that he was only persuading our Lord and gently reminding him of his own power seems utterly unreasonable and inconsistent with the following verse.

This high-minded claim to absolute power is one which ungodly great men are fond of making. It is written of Nebuchadnezzar: 'Whom he would he slew, and whom he would he kept alive; and whom he would he set up, and whom he would he put down' (Dan. 5:19). Yet even when such men boast of power, they are often like Pilate, mere slaves and afraid of resisting popular opinion. Pilate talked of 'power to release', but he knew in his own mind that he was afraid and so unable to exercise it.

Our Lord's reply to Pilate may be paraphrased thus: 'Thou speakest of power. Thou dost not know that both thou and the Jews are only tools in the hand of a higher Being and that thou couldst have no power whatever against me, if it were not given thee by God. This, however, thou dost not understand and art therefore less guilty than the Jews. The Jews who delivered me into thine hand do know that all power is from God. Thus their knowledge makes them more guilty than thou. Both thou and they are committing a great sin, but their sin is a sin against knowledge and thine is comparatively a sin of ignorance. You are both unconsciously mere instruments in the hand of God and you could do nothing against me, if God did not permit and overrule it.'

For meditation: *'I said, "You are 'gods'; you are all sons of the Most High." But you will die like mere men; you will fall like every other ruler'* (Ps. 82:6-7).

Suggested further reading: 1 Corinthians 10:31 - 11:1

Whereas vigilance is the keynote of the first parable about the virgins, diligence is the emphasis of this parable. The story of the virgins calls on the church to watch. The story of the talents calls on the church to work.

All professing Christians have received something from God (v. 14). The word 'talents' is an expression that has been curiously turned aside from its original meaning. It is generally applied to none but people of remarkable ability or gifts. They are called 'talented people'. Such a use of the expression is a pure modern invention. In the sense that our Lord used the word in this parable, it applies to all baptized persons without distinction. We all have talents in the sight of God.

Anything by which we may glorify God is a talent. Our gifts, our influence, our money, our knowledge, our health, our time, our strength, our senses, our reason, our intellect, our memory, our affections, our privileges as members of Christ's church, our advantages as possessors of the Bible — all, all are talents. Whence came these things? What hand bestowed them? Why are we what we are? Why are we not the worm that crawls upon the earth? There is only one answer to that question. All that we have is a loan from God. We are God's stewards. We are God's debtors. Let this thought sink deeply into our hearts.

Many make a bad use of the privileges and mercies they receive from God (v. 18). This man represents a large class of mankind. To hide our talent is to neglect opportunities of glorifying God when we have them. The Bible-despiser, the prayer-neglecter, the unbelieving, the sensual, the earthly-minded, the trifler, the thoughtless, the pleasure-seeker, the money-lover, the covetous, the self-indulgent — all, all alike are burying their Lord's money in the ground. They all have light that they do not use. They might all be better than they are. But they are daily robbing God. Like Belshazzar of old, they fail to glorify God (Dan. 5:23).

For meditation: *How are you using your gifts and abilities? Are you using them to glorify God?*

Suggested further reading: 1 Thessalonians 2:1-6

We see the Jews stopping Pilate short, in his weak efforts to get our Lord released, by an argument which they well knew would weigh heavily on a Roman mind. They tell him plainly that they will accuse him to Caesar, the Roman emperor, as a governor unfriendly to the imperial interests. 'You are no friend to Caesar if you let off this prisoner. Everyone who sets himself up as a king, be his kingdom what it may, is usurping part of Caesar's authority and is a rebel. If you pass over this man's claim to be a king and set him at liberty, we shall complain of you to Caesar.' This was a settling and clinching argument. Pilate knew well that his own government of Judaea would not bear any investigation. He also knew well the cold, suspicious, cruel character of Tiberius Caesar, the Emperor of Rome, which is specially mentioned by Tacitus and Suetonius, the Roman historians, and he might well dread the result of any appeal to him from the Jews. From this moment all his hopes of getting rid of this anxious case and letting our Lord go away unharmed were dashed to the ground. He would rather connive at a murder to please the Jews than allow himself to be charged with neglect of imperial interests and unfriendliness to Caesar.

It is hard to say which was the more wretched and contemptible sight at this point of the history — Pilate trampling on his own conscience to avoid the possible displeasure of an earthly monarch, or the Jews pretending to care for Caesar's interests and warning Pilate not to do anything unfriendly to him! It was a melancholy exhibition of cowardice on the one side and duplicity on the other and the whole result was a foul murder!

Men like Pontius Pilate, who are always trimming and compromising, led by popular opinion instead of leading popular opinion, afraid of doing right if it gives offence, ready to do wrong if it makes them personally popular — such men are the worst governors that a country can have. They are often God's heavy judgement on a nation because of a nation's sins.

For meditation: *Are you a man-pleaser or a God-pleaser?*

Suggested further reading: James 1:22-25

All professing Christians must one day have a reckoning with God (v. 19). There is a judgement before us all. Words have no meaning in the Bible if there is none. It is mere trifling with Scripture to deny it. There is a judgement before us according to our works — certain, strict and unavoidable. High or low, rich or poor, learned or unlearned, we shall all have to stand at the bar of God to receive our eternal judgement. There will be no escape. Concealment will be impossible. We and God must at last meet face to face. We shall have to render an account of every privilege that was granted us and of every ray of light that we enjoyed. We shall find that we are dealt with as accountable and responsible creatures and that to whomsoever much is given much is required. Let us remember this every day that we live.

True Christians will receive an abundant reward in the day of reckoning. The servants who used their Master's money well were commended (vv. 21,23). These words are full of comfort to all believers and may well fill us with wonder and surprise. The best of Christians is but a frail, poor creature and needs the blood of the atonement every day that he lives. But the least and lowest of Christ's servants will find that his labour is not in vain in the Lord. He will discover to his amazement that his Master's eye saw more beauty in his efforts to please him than he ever saw himself. He will find that every hour spent in Christ's service and every word spoken on Christ's behalf has been written in a book of remembrance. Let believers remember this and take courage.

All unfruitful members of Christ's church will be condemned and cast away at the Day of Judgement (vv. 26-30). There will be no excuse for the professing Christian who is unconverted at the last day. The ruin of his own soul will be found to be his own fault. The words of our Lord that he knew (v. 26) will ring loudly in his ears and prick him in his heart. Thousands live without Christ and without conversion and pretend that they cannot help it. They are not doing what they can.

For meditation: *God does not look for a knowledge of our duty but the doing of it.*

Suggested further reading: 1 Timothy 2:1-7

That our blessed Lord, the eternal Word, should have meekly submitted to be led out after this fashion, as a gazing-stock and an object of scorn, with an old purple robe on his shoulders and a crown of thorns on his head, his back bleeding from scourging and his head from thorns, to feast the eyes of a taunting, howling, bloodthirsty crowd, is indeed a wondrous thought! Truly, 'Though he was rich, yet for our sakes he became poor' (2 Cor. 8:9). Since the world began, the sun never shone on a more surprising spectacle both for angels and men.

'Behold the man.' This famous sentence, so well known as *'Ecce Homo'* in Latin, admits of two views being taken of it. Pilate may have spoken it in contempt: 'Behold the man you accuse of setting himself up as a king! See what a weak, helpless, contemptible creature he is.' Or else Pilate may have spoken it in pity: 'Behold the poor feeble man whom you want me to sentence to death. Surely your demands may be satisfied by what I have done to him. Is he not punished enough?' Perhaps both views are correct. In any case there can be little doubt that the latent feeling of Pilate was the hope that the Jews, on seeing our Lord's miserable condition, would be content and would allow him to be let go. In this hope, again, we shall find he was completely deceived.

Pilate probably threw a strong emphasis on the expression 'man', indicative of contempt. This may have led to the Jews saying so strongly in the seventh verse that the prisoner 'made himself the Son of God' and claimed to be divine and not a mere 'man', as Pilate had said. He probably also meant the Jews to mark that he said, 'Behold the man,' not 'your king', but a mere common man.

We see in verse 15 the complete failure of Pilate's secret scheme for avoiding the condemnation of our Lord. The pitiful sight of the bleeding and despised prisoner had not the effect of softening down the feelings of his cruel enemies. They would not be content with anything but his death and the moment he appeared they raised the fierce cry: 'Crucify him, crucify him.'

For meditation: *'A man of sorrows.'*

Suggested further reading: Acts 17:26-31

Jesus Christ himself will be the Judge in the last day (v. 31). The same Jesus who was born in the manger of Bethlehem and took upon him the form of a servant, who was despised and rejected by men, and often had nowhere to lay his head, who was condemned by the princes of this world, beaten, scourged and nailed to the cross — that same Jesus shall himself judge the world when he comes in his glory. To him the Father has committed all judgement (John 5:22). To him at last every knee shall bow and every tongue confess that he is Lord (Phil. 2:10-11).

Let believers think of this and take comfort. He that sits upon the throne in the great and dreadful day will be their Saviour, their Shepherd, their High Priest, their elder Brother, their Friend. When they see him they will have no cause to be alarmed.

Let unconverted people think of this and be alarmed! Their Judge will be that very Christ whose gospel they now despise and whose gracious invitations they refuse to hear. How great will be their confusion at last if they go on in unbelief and die in their sins! To be condemned by anyone in the Day of Judgement will be awful. But to be condemned by him who would have saved them will be awful indeed. Well may the psalmist say, 'Kiss the Son, lest he be angry' (Ps. 2:12).

All nations will be judged in the last day (v. 32). All that have ever lived will one day give an account of themselves at the bar of Christ. All must obey the summons of the great King and come forward to receive their sentence. Those who would not come to worship Christ on earth will find that they must come to his great court when he returns to earth.

All that are judged will be divided into two great classes. There will no longer be any distinction between kings and subjects, masters or servants, dissenters or churchmen. There will be no mention of rank or denomination, for the former things will have passed away. Grace or no grace, conversion or no conversion, faith or no faith will be the only distinctions at the last day. All that are found in Christ will be placed on his right with the sheep and the rest on his left with the goats.

For meditation: *Will you be on the right or the left? There is no centre position for men.*

Suggested further reading: Matthew 10:37-39

Our Lord had to bear his cross when he went forth from the city to Golgotha. We need not doubt that there was a deep meaning in all this circumstance. For one thing, it was part of that depth of humiliation to which our Lord submitted as our Substitute. One portion of the punishment imposed on the vilest criminals was that they should carry their own cross when they went to execution, and this portion was laid upon our Lord. In the fullest sense he was reckoned a sinner and counted a curse for our sakes. For another thing, it was a fulfilment of the great type of the sin-offering of the Mosaic law. It is written that 'The bullock for the sin-offering, and the goat for the sin-offering, whose blood was brought in to make atonement in the holy place, shall one carry forth without the camp' (Lev. 16:27). Little did the blinded Jews imagine, when they madly hounded on the Romans to crucify Jesus outside the gates, that they were unconsciously perfecting the mightiest sin-offering that was ever seen. It is written: 'Jesus, that he might sanctify the people with his own blood, suffered without the gate' (Heb. 13:12).

Like our Master, we must be content to go forth 'without the camp', bearing his reproach. We must come out from the world and be separate and be willing, if need be, to stand alone. Like our Master, we must be willing to take up our cross daily and to be persecuted both for our doctrine and our practice.

To wear material crosses as an ornament, to place material crosses on churches and tombs — all this is cheap and easy work and entails no trouble. But to have Christ's cross in our hearts, to carry Christ's cross in our daily walk, to know the fellowship of his sufferings, to be made conformable to his death, to have crucified affections and live crucified lives — all this needs self-denial and Christians of this stamp are few and far between.

For meditation: *Christianity provides a cross, not a cushion.*

Suggested further reading: James 2:14-26

The last judgement will be a judgement according to evidence. The works of men are the witnesses that shall be brought forward and above all their works of charity. The question to be ascertained will not merely be what we said but what we did — not merely what we professed but what we practised. Our works unquestionably will not justify us. We are justified by faith without the deeds of the law. But the truth of our faith will be tested by our lives. Faith that does not have works is dead, being alone (James 2:26).

The last judgement will be a judgement that will bring joy to all true believers. They will hear precious words (v. 34). They will be owned and confessed by their Master before his holy angels and his Father. They shall find that the wages he gives to his faithful servants are nothing less than a kingdom. The least, lowest and poorest of the family of God shall have a crown of glory and be a king.

The last judgement will be a judgement that will bring confusion on all unconverted people. They will hear awful words (v. 41). They will be disowned by the great Head of the church before the assembled world. They will find that as they would sow to the flesh, so of the flesh they must reap corruption. They would not hear Christ's invitations to come to him, so he will send them away. They would not carry his cross and so they can have no place in his kingdom.

The last judgement will be a judgement that will strikingly bring out the characters both of the lost and the saved. They on the right hand, who are Christ's sheep, will be clothed with humility. They will marvel to hear their works brought forward and commended. They on the left, who are not Christ's sheep, will still be blind and self-righteous. They will not be conscious of any neglect of Christ. Let this thought sink deep down into our hearts. Characters of earth will prove an everlasting possession in the world to come. Men will rise again with the same heart that they die.

For meditation: *Are you self-confident before God or humble? He only exalts the humble.*

Suggested further reading: Psalm 22:12-18

They crucified him. This famous mode of execution is so well known to everyone that little need be said of it. The common mode of inflicting it, in all probability, was to strip the criminal, to lay him on the cross on his back, to nail his hands to the two extremities of the cross-piece, or fork of the cross, to nail his feet to the upright piece, or principal stem of the cross, then to raise the cross on end and drop it into a hole prepared for it and then to leave the sufferer to a lingering and painful death. It was a death which combined the maximum of pain with the least immediate destruction of life. The agony of having nails driven through parts so full of nerves and sinews as the hands and feet must have been intense. Yet wounds of the hands and feet are not mortal and do not injure any great leading blood-vessel. Hence a crucified person, even in an eastern climate, exposed to the sun, might live two or three days, enduring extreme pain, without being relieved by death, if he was naturally a very strong man and in vigorous health. This is what we must remember our blessed Lord went through, when we read, 'They crucified him'. To a sensitive, delicate-minded person, it is hard to imagine any capital punishment more distressing. This is what Jesus endured willingly for us sinners. Hanging, as it were, between earth and heaven, he exactly fulfilled the type of the brazen serpent which Moses lifted up in the wilderness (John 3:14).

When we remember, beside all this, that our Lord's head was crowned with thorns, his back torn with savage scourging and his whole system weighed down by the mental and bodily agony of the sleepless night following the Lord's Supper, we may have some faint idea of the intensity of his sufferings.

There was the inexpressible misery of gradually increasing and lingering anguish.

For meditation: *The incomparable sufferings of our Lord are well captured by the weeping prophet's description of destroyed Jerusalem (Lam. 1:12).*

Suggested further reading: Hebrews 9:24-28

The state of things after the judgement is changeless and without end. The misery of the lost and the blessedness of the saved are both alike for ever. The eternity of God and of heaven and hell all stand on the same foundation. As surely as God is eternal, so surely is heaven an endless day without night, and hell an endless night without day.

Who shall describe the blessedness of eternal life? It passes the power of man to conceive. It can only be measured by contrast and comparison: an eternal rest after warfare and conflict, the eternal company of saints after buffeting with an evil world, an eternally glorious and painless body after struggling with weakness and infirmity and an eternal sight of Jesus after only hearing and believing. All this is blessedness indeed.

Who shall describe the misery of eternal punishment? It is something utterly indescribable and inconceivable: the eternal pain of body, the eternal sting of an accusing conscience, the eternal society of none but the wicked, the devil and his angels, the eternal remembrance of opportunities neglected and Christ despised, the eternal prospect of a weary, hopeless future. All this is misery indeed. It is enough to make our ears tingle and our blood run cold. And yet this picture is nothing compared to the reality.

Having spoken of his own coming in glory and of the judgement and its accompaniments, our Lord, without pause or interval, goes on to speak of his crucifixion (v. 2). While the marvellous predictions of his final glory were yet ringing in their ears, he tells them once again of his sufferings. He reminds them that he must die as a sin offering before he can reign as a king.

We can never attach too much importance to the atoning work of Christ. It is the leading fact of the Word of God. Without it the gospel is an arch without a keystone, a fair building without a foundation, a solar system without a sun. Let us make much of our Lord's second coming but let us not think more of this than of the atonement on the cross.

For meditation: *Most of the sects concentrate on the Second Coming and downgrade the first. Do not make the same mistake!*

Suggested further reading: Zechariah 9:9-13

Our Lord was crucified as a king. The title placed over our Lord's head made this plain and unmistakable. The reader of Greek or Latin or Hebrew could not fail to see that he who hung on the central cross of the three on Golgotha had a royal title over his head. The overruling hand of God so ordered matters that the strong will of Pilate overrode for once the wishes of the malicious Jews. In spite of the chief priests, our Lord was crucified as 'the King of the Jews'.

It was meet and right that so it should be. Even before our Lord was born, the angel Gabriel declared to the Virgin Mary, 'The Lord God shall give unto him the throne of his father David, and he shall reign over the house of Jacob for ever, and of his kingdom there shall be no end' (Luke 1:32-33). Almost as soon as he was born there came wise men from the East, saying, 'Where is he that is born King of the Jews?' (Matt. 2:2). The very week before the crucifixion, the multitude who accompanied our Lord at his triumphal entry into Jerusalem had cried, 'Blessed is the King of Israel that cometh in the name of the Lord' (John 12:13). The current belief of all godly Jews was that when Messiah, the Son of David, came he would come as a king. A kingdom of heaven and a kingdom of God was continually proclaimed by our Lord throughout his ministry. A King indeed he was, as he told Pilate, of a kingdom utterly unlike the kingdoms of this world, but for all that a true King of a true kingdom and a Ruler of true subjects. As such he was born. As such he lived. As such he was crucified. And as such he will come again and reign over the whole earth, King of kings and Lord of lords.

Let us take care that we ourselves know Christ as our King and that his kingdom is set up within our hearts. They only will find him their Saviour at the last day who have obeyed him as King in this world. Let us cheerfully pay him that tribute of faith and love and obedience which he prizes far above gold.

For meditation: *The power of Satan was broken by a crucified King* (Col. 2:15).

Suggested further reading: Ezekiel 34:1-10

High offices in the church do not prevent the holders of them from great blindness and sin. The first step in putting Christ to death was taken by the religious teachers of the Jewish nation. The very men who ought to have welcomed the Messiah were the men who conspired to kill him (v. 2). The very pastors who should have rejoiced in the appearing of the Lamb of God had the chief hand in slaying him. They claimed to be lights of the blind (Rom. 2:19). They belonged to the tribe of Levi. Most of them were direct descendants from Aaron. Yet they were the very men who crucified the Lord of glory! With all their boasted knowledge they were far more ignorant than the few Galilean fishermen who followed Christ.

Let us beware of attaching an excessive importance to ministers of religion because of their office. Orders and rank confer no exemption from error. The greatest heresies have been sown and the greatest practical errors introduced into the church by ordained men. Respect is undoubtedly due to high official position. Order and discipline ought not to be forgotten. The teaching and counsel of regularly appointed teachers ought not to be lightly refused. But there are limits beyond which we must not go. We must never suffer the blind to lead us into the ditch. We must never allow modern 'chief priests and scribes' to lead us into crucifying Christ afresh. We must try all teachers according to the Word of God. It matters little who says a thing in religion, but it matters greatly what is said (Isa. 8:20).

The second step towards our Lord's crucifixion was the treachery of one of the twelve apostles (vv. 3-4). These words are peculiarly awful. To be tempted by Satan is bad enough. To be sifted, buffeted, led captive by him is truly terrible. But when Satan enters into a man he indeed becomes a child of hell. An apostle became a traitor.

For meditation: *Anyone who listens to the 'theologians' quoted on the radio and television will realize that the religious hierarchy has not changed. Corruption marks their words and works. Give attention to men who are biblical in their teaching and godly in their lives. Do not be impressed by titles and clothes.*

Suggested further reading: Genesis 3:8-13

Verse 21 brings out the feeling which the sight of Pilate's title excited in the minds of the chief priests. They were annoyed and angry. They did not like the idea of this crucified criminal being publicly declared 'the King of the Jews'. They detected the latent scorn and irony which guided Pilate's hands and lay at the bottom of his mind. They did not like so public an announcement that they had crucified their own king and wanted 'no king but Caesar'. They were vexed at the implied reflection on themselves. Besides this, they were probably uncomfortable in conscience. Hardened and wicked as they were, they had, many of them, we may be sure, a secret conviction, which they vainly tried to keep down, that they were doing a wrong thing and a thing which by and by they would find it hard to defend either to themselves or others. Hence they tried to get Pilate to alter the title and to make it appear that our Lord was only a pretended king — an impostor who 'said that he was king'.

The hard, haughty, imperious character of the wicked Roman governor comes out forcibly in these words. They show his contempt for the Jews. He was glad to hold them up to scorn and contempt, as a people who crucified their own king. It is likely enough that between his wife and his own conscience and the chief priests, the Roman governor was vexed, worried and irritated and savagely resolved not to gratify the Jews any further in any matter. He had gone as far as he chose in allowing them to murder an innocent and just person. He would not go an inch further. He now made a stand and showed that he could be firm and unyielding and unbending when he liked. It is no uncommon thing to see a wicked man, when he has given way to the devil and trampled on his conscience in one direction, trying to make up for it by being firm in another.

For meditation: *Men will go to any lengths to justify themselves, but will shun repentance.*

Suggested further reading: 1 Timothy 6:3-10

Judas Iscariot ought to be a standing beacon to the church of Christ. This man, be it remembered, was one of the Lord's chosen apostles. He followed our Lord during the whole course of his ministry. He forsook all for Christ's sake. He heard Christ preach and saw Christ's miracles. He preached himself. He spoke like other apostles. There was nothing about him to distinguish him from Peter, James and John. He was never suspected of being unsound at heart. And yet this man turns out at length to be a hypocrite, betrays his Master, helps his enemies to deliver him up to death and dies himself 'a son of perdition' (John 17:12). These are fearful things, but they are true.

Let the recollection of Judas Iscariot constrain every professing Christian to pray much for humility. Let us often say the psalmist's words (Ps. 139:23). At best we have but a faint conception of the deceitfulness of our own hearts. The lengths to which men may go in religion and yet be without grace is far greater than we suppose.

The secret of this wretched man's fall was the enormous power of the love of money (vv. 5-6). Judas was fond of money. He had doubtless heard our Lord's warnings against covetousness (Luke 12:15). But he had either forgotten it or given it no heed. Covetousness was the rock on which he made shipwreck, and covetousness was the ruin of his soul. Money is one of the choicest weapons of Satan for spoiling professors of religion. For money a chosen apostle sold the best and most loving of masters! Let us be content with what we have (Heb. 13:5). We never know what we might do if we became suddenly rich.

We cannot doubt that the time of our Lord's crucifixion was overruled by God. His perfect wisdom and controlling power arranged that the Lamb of God should die at the very time when the Passover lamb was being slain (v. 7). The death of Christ was the fulfilment of the Passover. He was the true sacrifice to which every Passover lamb had pointed for over fifteen hundred years. The safety which the Passover lamb provided for Israel, his blood more abundantly provided for all who believe in him.

For meditation: *God can only pass over sin when it is covered by Christ's blood.*

Suggested further reading: Zechariah 3:1-5

The soldiers having now finished their bloody work, having nailed our Lord to the cross, put the title over his head and reared the cross on end, proceeded to do what they probably always did — to divide the clothes of the crucified criminal among themselves. In most countries the clothes of a person put to death by the law are the perquisite of the executioner. So it was with our Lord's clothes. They had most likely first stripped our Lord naked, before nailing his hands and feet to the cross, and had laid his clothes on one side till they had finished their work. They now turned to the clothes and, as they had done many a time on such occasions, proceeded to divide them.

We are told that the conduct of the soldiers was a precise fulfilment of a prophecy delivered a thousand years before (Ps. 22:18). That prophecy foretold not only that Messiah's garments should be parted and distributed, but that men should 'cast lots for his vesture'. Little did the four rough Roman soldiers think that they were actually supplying evidence of the truth of the Scriptures! They only saw that our Lord's 'coat' was a good and serviceable garment, which it was a pity to rend, or tear, and therefore they agreed to cast lots who should have it. And yet, in so doing, they added to the great cloud of witnesses who prove the divine authority of the Bible. Men little consider that they are all instruments in God's hand for accomplishing his purposes.

Our Lord was treated, we should observe, just like all common criminals — stripped naked and his clothes sold under his eyes, as one dead already and cast off by man.

It is noteworthy that in this, as in many other things, our Lord was, in striking manner, our Substitute. He was stripped naked and reckoned and dealt with as a guilty sinner, in order that we might be clothed with the garment of his perfect righteousness and reckoned innocent.

For meditation: *God even makes the small malicious acts of man's spite serve him.*

Suggested further reading: John 13:1-17

The sin before us is a very old one. Ambition, self-esteem and self-conceit lie deep at the bottom of all men's hearts and often in the hearts where they are least expected. Thousands fancy that they are humble, who cannot bear to see an equal more favoured and honoured than themselves. Few indeed can be found who rejoice heartily in a neighbour's promotion over their own heads. The quantity of envy and jealousy in the world is a glaring proof of the prevalence of pride. Men would not envy a brother's advancement if they had not a secret thought that their own merit was greater than his.

Let us live on our guard against this sore disease if we make any profession of serving Christ. The harm that is done to the church of Christ is far beyond calculation. Let us learn to take pleasure in the prosperity of others and be content with the lowest place for ourselves. The rule given to the Philippians should be often before our eyes (Phil. 2:3), as should the example of John the Baptist (John 3:30).

Our Lord tells his disciples that the worldly standard of greatness was the exercise of lordship and authority (v. 25). But he gives them a definition quite different (v. 26) and an example to follow (v. 27).

Usefulness in the church and world, a humble readiness to do anything and put our hands to any good work, a cheerful willingness to fill any post, however unpleasant, if we can only promote holiness and happiness in the world, these are the true tests of Christian greatness. The hero in Christ's army is not the man who has rank, title, dignity, chariots, horsemen and fifty men to run before him, but the man who is kind to all, tender to all, thoughtful for all, with a hand to help all and a heart to feel for all. It is the man who spends and is spent to make the vice and misery of the world less, to bind up the broken-hearted, to befriend the friendless, to cheer the sorrowful, to enlighten the ignorant and to raise the poor. He who ministers to the needs of a sin-burdened world is greater than all who have learning or gifts or money.

For meditation: *Are you willing to be a nobody for Christ's sake?*

Suggested further reading: Luke 8:1-3

A wonderfully striking incident is recorded in this and the two following verses, which is not found in the other three Gospels. St John tells us that at this awful moment, Mary, the mother of Jesus, and other women — two if not three — stood by the cross on which our Lord hung. 'Love is strong as death' and even amidst the crowd of taunting Jews and rough Roman soldiers these holy women were determined to stand by our Lord to the last and to show their unceasing affection to him. When we remember that our Lord was a condemned criminal, peculiarly hated by the chief priests and executed by Roman soldiers, the faithfulness and courage of these holy women can never be sufficiently admired. As long as the world stands, they supply a glorious proof of what grace can do for the weak and of the strength that love to Christ can supply. When all men but one forsook our Lord, more than one woman boldly confessed him. Women, in short, were the last at the cross and the first at the tomb.

Mary, the mother of our Lord (never called the 'Virgin Mary' in Scripture) was there. Who can doubt that when she saw her Son hanging on the cross, she must have realized the truth of old Simeon's prophecy: 'A sword shall pierce through thine own soul also'? (Luke 2:35).

Why the fierce enemies of our Lord among the Jews and the rough Roman soldiers permitted these holy women to stand undisturbed by the cross is a question we have no means of deciding. Possibly the centurion who superintended the execution may have felt some pity for the little weeping company of weak women. Who can tell but his kindness was a cup of cold water which was repaid him a hundredfold? He said before the day ended, 'Truly this was the Son of God' (Matt. 27:54).

For meditation: *The Scriptures give Christian women much usefulness in supporting roles in the church and home. Their relation to men is one of functional difference, not of inferiority.*

Suggested further reading: Revelation 2:8-11

There is something very striking in the words of praise that our Lord gives to his disciples (v. 28). We know the weakness and infirmity of our Lord's disciples during the whole period of his earthly ministry. We find him frequently reproving their ignorance and lack of faith. He knew full well that within a couple of hours they were all going to forsake him. But here we find him graciously dwelling on one good point in their conduct and holding it up to the perpetual notice of the church. They had been faithful to their Master notwithstanding their faults. Their hearts had been right, whatever had been their mistakes. They had clung to him in the day of his humiliation when the great and noble were against him.

Let us rest our souls on this comfortable thought that the mind of Christ is always the same. If we are true believers, let us know that he looks at our graces more than at our faults, that he pities our infirmities and that he will not deal with us according to our sins. Never had a master such poor, weak servants as Christ has, but never had servants such a compassionate and tender Master as Christ! Surely we cannot love him too much. We may come short in many things. We may fail in knowledge, faith, courage and patience. We may stumble many times. But one thing let us always do. Let us love the Lord Jesus with heart, soul, mind and strength. Let us cleave to him with purpose of heart. Let our affirmation be that of Peter (John 21:15).

What a glorious promise our Lord holds out to his faithful disciples! (vv. 29-30). We may not perhaps know the full meaning of the promise. Enough for us to know that our Lord promised his eleven faithful ones glory, honour and rewards far beyond anything they had done for him. The wages he gives his believing people far outweigh what has been done. Their least desires to do good will be found recorded. Their weakest efforts to glorify him will be found written in a book of remembrance. Not a cup of cold water shall miss its reward.

For meditation: *Just as the smallest pain in the body is noted by the brain, so the smallest act done for Christ is recorded by the Head.*

Suggested further reading: Philippians 2:1-4

We are told that even in the awful agonies of body and mind which our Lord endured, he did not forget her of whom he was born. He mercifully remembered her desolate condition and the crushing effect of the sorrowful sight before her. He knew that, holy as she was, she was only a woman and that, as a woman, she must deeply feel the death of such a son. He therefore commended her to the protection of his best-loved and best-loving disciple in brief and touching words. 'Woman,' he said, 'behold thy son! Then saith he to the disciple, Behold thy mother! And from that hour that disciple took her unto his own home.'

We surely need no stronger proof than we have here that Mary, the mother of Jesus, was never meant to be honoured as divine, or to be prayed to, worshipped and trusted in as the friend and patroness of sinners. Common sense points out that she who needed the care and protection of another was never likely to help men and women to heaven, or to be in any sense a mediator between God and man! It is not too much to say, however painful the assertion, that of all the inventions of the church of Rome, there never was one more utterly devoid of foundation, both in Scripture and reason, than the doctrine of Mary-worship.

Let us turn from points of controversy to a subject of far more practical importance. Let us take comfort in the thought that we have in Jesus a Saviour of matchless tenderness, matchless sympathy, matchless consideration for the condition of his believing people. Let us never forget his words: 'Whosoever shall do the will of God, the same is my brother, and my sister and my mother' (Mark 3:35). The heart that even on the cross felt for Mary is a heart that never changes. Jesus never forgets any that love him and even in their worst estate remembers their need. No wonder that Peter says, 'Casting all your care upon him, for he careth for you' (1 Peter 5:7).

For meditation: *Even in death our Lord put others first.*

Suggested further reading: Mark 9:42-49

Let us learn from these verses the hopeless condition of all who die unconverted. The words of our Lord on this subject are peculiarly solemn (v. 24).

This saying admits of only one interpretation. It teaches plainly that it is better never to live at all than to live without faith and to die without grace. To die in this state is to be ruined for evermore. It is a fall from which there is no rising. It is a loss which is utterly irretrievable. There is no change in hell. The gulf between hell and heaven is one that no man can pass.

This saying could never have been used if there was any truth in the doctrine of universal salvation. If it really was true that all would sooner or later reach heaven, and hell sooner or later would be emptied of inhabitants, it never could be said that it was 'good for a man that he had never been born'. Hell itself would lose its terrors if it had an end. Hell itself would be endurable if after millions of ages there was a hope of freedom and heaven. But universal salvation will find no foothold in Scripture. The teaching of the Word of God is plain and express on the subject. There is a worm that never dies and a fire that is not quenched (Mark 9:48). Except a man is born again, he will one day wish he had never been born.

Let us grasp this truth firmly and never let it go. There are always persons who dislike the reality and eternity of hell. We live in a day when a morbid charity induces many to exaggerate God's mercy and downgrade his justice, and when false teachers are talking of a love of God lower even than hell. Let us resist such teaching with a holy jealousy and abide by the doctrine of Holy Scripture. Let us not be ashamed to walk in the old paths and to believe that there is an eternal God, an eternal heaven and an eternal hell. Once depart from this belief and we admit the thin edge of the wedge of scepticism and may at last deny the doctrine of the gospel.

For meditation: *Denying facts does not change them. Wishful thinking is another term for vain hopes.*

Suggested further reading: Luke 16:19-24

Nothing in the details of our Lord's death, we must always remember, was accidental or by chance. Every part of the great sacrifice for sin was foreordained and arranged in the eternal counsels of the Trinity, even to the words which he was to speak on the cross.

The expression 'I thirst' was chiefly used, I believe, in order to afford a public testimony of the reality and intensity of his bodily sufferings and to prevent anyone supposing, because of his marvellous calmness and patience, that he was miraculously free from suffering. On the contrary, he would have all around him know that he felt what all severely wounded persons, and especially what all crucified persons, felt — a burning and consuming thirst. So that when we read that 'He suffered for sins,' we are to understand that he really and truly suffered.

Henry observes, 'The torments of hell are represented by a violent thirst in the complaint of the rich man who begged for a drop of water to cool his tongue. To that everlasting thirst we had all been condemned if Christ had not suffered on the cross, and said, "I thirst." '

It is very noteworthy that even in the roughest, hardest kind of men, like these heathen soldiers, there is sometimes a tender and compassionate spot in the breast. According to Matthew's account the cry, 'I thirst,' must have followed soon after the cry, 'My God, my God, why hast thou forsaken me?' This exhibition of great mental and bodily agony combined, in my opinion, touched the feelings of the soldiers and one of them at least ran to give our Lord vinegar. We should remember this in dealing with men. Even the worst have often a soft place, if we can find it out, in their inward nature.

For meditation: *Our Lord entered fully into the deepest experiences of human suffering, so as to be made like us.*

Suggested further reading: 1 Corinthians 11:23-34

The right meaning of our Lord's words (v. 26) has divided the church of Christ. It has caused volumes of controversial theology to be written. But we must not shrink from decided opinions on this subject because theologians have disputed and differed.

The plain meaning of our Lord's words appears to be: 'This bread represents my body. This wine represents my blood.' He did not mean that the bread he gave to his disciples was really and literally his body. He did not mean that the wine he gave them was really and literally his blood. Let us lay firm hold on this interpretation. It may be supported by several grave reasons.

The conduct of the disciples at the Lord's Supper forbids us to believe that the bread they received was Christ's body and the wine Christ's blood. They were all Jews taught from their infancy that it was sinful to eat flesh with the blood (Deut. 12:23-25). Yet they were not startled by our Lord's words as if they perceived a change in the bread and wine.

Our own senses forbid us to believe that there is any change in the bread and the wine. Our own taste tells us that they are really and literally what they appear to be. Things above our reason the Bible requires us to believe, but not what contradicts our senses.

Our Lord's true human nature forbids us to believe that his body can be in more than one place at one time. If our Lord's body could sit at table and at the same time be eaten by the disciples it is perfectly clear that it is not a human body like our own. But this we must not allow for one moment. It is the glory of Christianity that our Redeemer is perfect man as well as perfect God.

The language in which our Lord spoke made it quite unnecessary to interpret his words literally. The Bible is full of similar expressions. Our Lord speaks of himself as a 'door' and a 'vine' and we know that he is using emblems and figures. There is therefore no inconsistency in his using figurative language in instituting the Supper.

For meditation: *If the bread and the wine are the body and the blood then Christians are cannibals!*

Suggested further reading: Hebrews 10:1-14

Our Lord having now given plain proof that he had endured intense bodily suffering and that, like any other human sufferer, he could appreciate a slight relief of thirst, such as the vinegar afforded, proceeded to utter one of his last and most solemn sayings: 'It is finished.'

This remarkable expression, in the Greek, is one single word in a perfect tense: 'It has been completed.' It stands here in majestic simplicity, without note or comment from St John, and we are left entirely to conjecture what the full meaning of it is. For nineteen hundred years Christians have explained it as they best can and some portion of its meaning in all likelihood has been discovered. Yet it is far from unlikely that such a word, spoken on such an occasion, by such a person, at such a moment, just before death, contains depths which no one has ever completely fathomed. Some meanings there are, which no one perhaps will dispute, belonging to this grand expression which I will briefly mention. No one single meaning, we may be sure, exhausts the whole phrase. It is rich, full and replete with deep truths.

Our Lord meant that his great work of redemption was finished. He had, as Daniel foretold, 'finished transgression, made an end of sin, made reconciliation for iniquity, and brought in everlasting righteousness' (Dan. 9:24). After thirty-three years, since the day when he was born in Bethlehem, he had done all, paid all, performed all, suffered all that was needful to save sinners and satisfy the justice of God. He had fought the battle and won it and in two days would give proof of it by rising again.

Our Lord meant that God's determinate counsel and fore-will concerning his death was now accomplished and finished. All that had been appointed from all eternity that he should suffer, he had now suffered.

For meditation: *We rejoice in an accomplished salvation that needs nothing but to be received.*

Suggested further reading: Hebrews 9:11-14, 24-28

The ordinance of the Lord's Supper has been regarded as something mysterious and past understanding. But the more simple our views of its purpose, the more scriptural they are likely to be.

The Lord's Supper is not a sacrifice. There is no offering up of anything but prayers, praises and thanksgiving. From the day that Jesus died there needs be no more offering for sin. By one offering he perfected for ever them that are sanctified (Heb. 10:14). Priests, altars and sacrifices all ceased to be necessary when the Lamb of God offered up himself. Their office came to an end. Their work was done.

The Lord's Supper has no power to confer benefit to anyone who does not come to it with faith. The mere formal act of eating the bread and wine is unprofitable unless it is done with a right heart. It is eminently an ordinance for the living soul, and not the dead; for the converted, not the unconverted.

The Lord's Supper was ordained for a continual remembrance of the sacrifice of Christ's death until he comes again. The benefits it confers are spiritual, not physical. Its effects must be looked for in the inward man. It was intended to remind us by the visible, tangible emblems of bread and wine that the offering of Christ's body and blood for us on the cross is the only atonement for sin and the life of a believer's soul. It was meant to help our poor weak faith to closer fellowship with our crucified Saviour and to assist us in spiritually feeding on Christ's body and blood. It is an ordinance for redeemed sinners and not for unfallen angels. By receiving it we publicly declare our sense of guilt and need of a Saviour, our trust in Jesus, and our love to him, our desire to live upon him and our hope to live with him. Using it in this spirit, we shall find our faith increased, our repentance deepened, our hope brightened and our love enlarged, our besetting sins weakened and our graces strengthened. It will draw us nearer Christ.

For meditation: *To remember him regularly is necessary for sinners who so easily forget such great grace as has been shown them.*

Suggested further reading: Hebrews 9:11-14

Our Lord meant that he had finished the work of keeping God's holy law. He had kept it to the uttermost, as our Head and Representative, and Satan had found nothing in him. He had magnified the law and made it honourable by doing perfectly all its requirements. 'Woe unto us,' says Burkitt, 'if Christ had left but one farthing of our debt unpaid. We must have lain in hell insolvent to all eternity.'

Our Lord meant that he had finished the types and figures of the ceremonial law. He had at length offered up the perfect sacrifice, of which every Mosaic sacrifice was a type and symbol, and there remained no more need of offerings for sin. The old covenant was finished.

Our Lord meant that he had finished and fulfilled the prophecies of the Old Testament. At length, as the seed of the woman, he had bruised the serpent's head and accomplished the work which Messiah was engaged by covenant to come and perform.

Our Lord meant that his sufferings were finished. Like his apostle, he had 'finished his course'. His long life of pain and contradiction from sinners and, above all, his intense sufferings as bearer of our sins on Gethsemane and Calvary were at last at an end. The storm was over and the worst was passed. The cup of suffering was at last drained to the very dregs.

Luther remarks, 'In this word, "It is finished," will I comfort myself. I am forced to confess that all *my* finishing of the will of God is imperfect, piecemeal work, while yet the law urges on me that not so much as one tittle of it must remain unaccomplished. Christ is the end of the law. What it requires, Christ has performed.'

For meditation: *He left no work undone that was necessary to our full and eternal salvation.*

Suggested further reading: 1 Corinthians 11:27-34

The character of the first communicants is a point full of comfort and instruction. The little company to which the bread and wine were first administered by our Lord was composed of apostles, those chosen to accompany him during his earthly ministry. They were poor and unlearned men who loved Christ, but were weak alike in faith and knowledge. They knew but little of the full meaning of their Master's sayings and doings. They knew but little of the frailty of their own hearts. They thought they were ready to die with Jesus, and yet that very night they all forsook him and fled. All this our Lord knew perfectly well. The state of their hearts was not hid from him. And yet he did not keep them back from the Lord's Supper.

We are thus shown plainly that we must not make great knowledge and great strength of grace indispensable qualifications for communicants. A man may know but little, and be no better than a child in spiritual strength, but he is not on that account to be kept away from the Lord's table. Does he really feel his sins? Does he really love Christ? Does he really desire to serve him? If this is so, we ought to encourage and receive him. Doubtless we must do all we can to exclude unworthy communicants. But we must take heed that we do not reject those whom Christ has not rejected. There is no wisdom in being more strict than Christ and his apostles.

What is our own conduct with respect to the Lord's Supper? Do we turn away from it when it is administered? If so, how can we justify our conduct? It will not do to say that it is not a necessary ordinance. To say so is to pour contempt on Christ himself and declare that we do not obey him. It will not do to say that we feel unworthy to come to the Lord's table. To say so is to declare that we are unfit to die and unprepared to meet God. These are solemn considerations. All non-communicants should ponder them well. Do we come to the Lord's table? Do we come with humility and faith, understanding what we are doing?

For meditation: *Those for whom Christ has died should remember him for his work at Calvary with renewed repentance and faith, prayer and praise.*

Suggested further reading: Hebrews 9:22-28

Above all, let us never forget, as we read of Christ's death, that he died for our sins, as our Substitute. His death is our life. He died that we might live. We who believe on Christ shall live for evermore, sinners as we are, because Christ died for us, the innocent for the guilty. Satan cannot drag us away to everlasting death in hell. The second death cannot harm us. We may safely say, 'Who can condemn me, or slay my soul? I know well that I deserve death and that I ought to die because of my sins. But then my blessed Head and Substitute died for me and when he died, I, his poor weak member, was reckoned to die also. Get thee behind me, Satan, for Christ was crucified and died. My debt is paid and thou canst not demand it twice over.' Forever let us bless God that Christ 'gave up the ghost' and really died upon the cross, before myriads of witnesses. That 'giving up the ghost' was the hinge on which all our salvation turned. In vain Christ's life and miracles and preaching, if Christ had not at last died for us! We needed not merely a teacher, but an atonement and the death of a substitute. The mightiest transaction that ever took place on earth since the fall of man was accomplished when Jesus 'gave up the ghost'. The careless crowd around the cross saw nothing but the common death of a common criminal. But in the eyes of God the Father the promised payment for a world's sin was at last effected and the kingdom of heaven was thrown wide open to all believers. The finest pictures of the crucifixion that artists have ever painted give a miserably insufficient idea of what took place when Jesus 'gave up the ghost'. They can show a suffering man on a cross, but they cannot convey the least notion of what was really going on — the satisfaction of God's broken law, the payment of sinners' debt to God and the complete atonement for a world's sin.

For meditation: *God will not require double payment for sin — first from Christ, then from us.*

Suggested further reading: 1 Corinthians 10:1-13

The Lord well foreknew the weakness and infirmity of his disciples. He tells them plainly what they were going to do (v. 27). He tells Peter in particular of the astounding sin which he was about to commit (v. 30). Yet our Lord's knowledge did not prevent his choosing these twelve disciples to be his apostles. He allowed them to be his intimate friends and companions, knowing perfectly well what they would one day do. He granted them the mighty privilege of being continually with him and hearing his voice with a clear foresight of the melancholy weakness and lack of faith which they would exhibit at the end of his ministry. This is a remarkable fact and deserves to be had in continual remembrance.

Let us take comfort in the thought that the Lord Jesus does not cast off his believing people because they have failures and imperfections. He knows what they are. He takes them, as the husband takes the wife, with all their blemishes and defects and, once joined to him by faith, will never put them away. He is a merciful and compassionate High Priest. It is his glory to pass over the transgressions of his people and to cover their many sins. He knew what they were before conversion — wicked, guilty and defiled; yet he loved them. He knows what they will be after conversion — weak, erring and frail; yet he loves them. He has undertaken to save them, notwithstanding all their shortcomings, and what he has undertaken he will carry through.

How much ignorant self-confidence may be found in the hearts of professing Christians! The apostle Peter could not think it possible that he would ever deny his Lord (vv. 29,31). The other disciples were of the same opinion (v. 31). Yet what did all this confident boasting come to? Twelve hours did not pass away before all the disciples forsook our Lord and fled. Their loud professions were all forgotten. The present danger swept all their promises of fidelity clean away. So little do we know how we shall act in a particular position until we are placed in it! So much do present circumstances alter our feelings! We need humility and the sustaining grace of God to keep us from sin.

For meditation: *'Better to be lowly in spirit and among the oppressed than to share plunder with the proud'* (Prov. 16:19).

Suggested further reading: Revelation 1:12-18

The order of the famous seven sayings was as follows:

1. 'Father, forgive them; for they know not what they do.'
2. 'Today shalt thou be with me in paradise.'
3. 'Woman, behold thy son! ... Behold thy mother.'
4. 'My God, my God, why hast thou forsaken me?'
5. 'I thirst.'
6. 'It is finished.'
7. 'Father, into thy hands I commend my spirit.'

In order to understand verse 30 aright, there is one point concerning our Lord's death which must be carefully remembered. His death was entirely a voluntary act on his part. In this one respect his death was unlike that of a common man, and we need not wonder at it when we consider that he was God and man in one person. The final separation between body and soul in his case could not take place until he willed it and all the power of Jews and Romans together could not have effected it against his will. We die because we cannot help it; Christ died because he willed to die and not until the moment arrived when he saw it best. He said himself, 'No man taketh life from me, but I lay it down of myself. I have power to lay it down, and I have power to take it again' (John 10:18). As a matter of fact, we know that our Lord was crucified about nine o'clock in the morning and that he died about three o'clock in the afternoon of the same day. Mere physical suffering would not account for this. A person crucified in full health was known sometimes to linger on alive for three days! It is evident therefore that our Lord willed to give up the ghost in the same day that he was crucified, for some wise reason. This reason, we can easily suppose, was to secure the fullest publicity for his atoning death. He died in broad daylight, in the sight of myriads of spectators, and thus the reality of his death could never be denied. This voluntariness and free choice of his death and of the hour of his death, in my judgement, lie at the bottom of the verse before us.

For meditation: *Only God has the power of life and death —*
Jehovah-Jesus exercised this power.

Suggested further reading: Psalm 130

Why do we find our Lord so sorrowful (v. 37) and his words so full
of distress? (v. 38). Why do we see him going apart from his disciples and falling on his face, and crying to his Father with strong
cries and a thrice-repeated prayer? Why is the almighty Son of God,
who had worked so many miracles, so heavy and disquieted? Why
is Jesus, who came into the world to die, so like one ready to faint at
the approach of death?

There is but one reasonable answer to these questions. The weight
that pressed down on our Lord's soul was not the fear of death and
its pains. Thousands have endured the most agonizing sufferings of
body and died without a groan, and so, no doubt, might our Lord
have. But the real weight that bowed down our Lord was the weight
of the sin of the world which seems now to have pressed down upon
him with peculiar force. It was the burden of our guilt imputed to
him which was now laid upon him as on the head of a scapegoat.
How great that burden must have been, no heart of man can conceive. It is only known to God.

We see that Christ himself prayed when his soul was sorrowful.
All true Christians ought to do the same. Trouble is a cup that all
must drink in this world of sin (Job 5:7). We cannot avoid it. Of all
creatures none is so vulnerable as man. Our bodies, our minds, our
families, our business, our friends are all so many doors through
which trial will come in. The holiest saints can claim no exemption
from it. Like their Master, they are often 'men of sorrows'.

But what is the first thing to be done in time of trouble? We must
pray. Like Job, we must fall down and worship (Job 1:20). Like
Hezekiah, we must spread our matters before God (2 Kings 19:14).
The first person we must turn to for help must be our God. We must
tell our Father in heaven all our sorrow. We must believe confidently that nothing is too trivial or minute to be laid before him, so
long as we do it in entire submission to his will. It is the mark of
faith to keep nothing back from our best Friend.

For meditation: *Christ hated sin with a perfect hatred. Yet he bore
it for our sakes.*

Suggested further reading: Isaiah 46:8-13

The 'breaking of the legs' of crucified criminals, in order to des-patch them, seems to have been a common accompaniment of this barbarous mode of execution, when it was necessary to make an end of them and get them out of the way. In asking Pilate to allow this breaking of the legs, they did nothing but what was usual. But for anything we can see, the thing would not have been done if the Jews had not asked. The verse supplies a wonderful example of the way in which God can make the wickedest men unconsciously carry out his purposes and promote his glory. If the Jews had not interfered this Friday afternoon, for anything we can see, Pilate would have allowed our Lord's body to hang upon the cross till Sunday or Mon-day and perhaps to see corruption. The Jews procured our Lord's burial the very day that he died and thus secured the fulfilment of his famous prophecy: 'Destroy this temple of my body, and in three days I will raise it up' (John 2:19). If he had not been buried till Sunday or Monday, he could not have risen again the third day after his death. As it was, the Jews managed things so that our Lord was laid in the grave before the evening of Friday and was thus enabled to fulfil the famous type of Jonah and give the sign he had promised to give of his Messiahship, by lying three days in the earth and then rising again the third day after he died. All this could not have hap-pened if the Jews had not interfered and got him taken from the cross and buried on Friday afternoon! How true it is that the wickedest enemies of God are only axes and saws and hammers in his hands and are ignorantly his instruments for doing his work in the world! The restless, busy meddling of Caiaphas and his companions was actually one of the causes that Christ rose the third day after death and his Messiahship was proved. Pilate was their tool, but they were God's tools! The Romans, in all probability, would have left our Lord's body hanging on the cross till sun and rain had putrefied and consumed it, had such a thing been possible.

For meditation: *Even the enemies of God ultimately fulfil his purpose and assure his victory.*

Suggested further reading: James 4:13-17

Entire submission to the will of God should become one of our chief aims in this world. The words of our Lord are a beautiful example of the spirit that we should follow after in this matter (v. 39).

A will unsanctified and uncontrolled is one great cause of unhappiness in life. It may be seen in little infants. It is born with us. We all like our own way. We wish and want many things and forget that we are entirely ignorant of our own good and unfit to choose for ourselves. Happy is he who has learned to have no wishes and in every state to be content. It is a lesson which we are slow to learn and, like Paul, we must learn it not in the school of mortal man, but of Christ (Phil. 4:11).

Would we know whether we are born again and growing in grace? Let us see how it is with us in the matter of our wills. Can we bear with disappointment? Can we patiently put up with unexpected trials and vexations? Can we see our pet plans and darling schemes crossed without murmuring and complaint? Can we sit still and suffer calmly as well as go up and down and work actively? These are the things that ought to prove whether or not we have the mind of Christ. It ought never to be forgotten that warm feelings and joyful frames are not the truest evidences of grace. A mortified will is a far more valuable possession.

There is great weakness even in true disciples of Christ against which they have need to watch and pray (vv. 40-41). There is a double nature in all believers. Converted, renewed, sanctified as they are, they still carry about with them a mass of indwelling corruption, a body of sin (Rom. 7:21-23). The experience of all true Christians in every age confirms this. They find within two contrary principles and a continual strife between the two. To these two principles our Lord alludes (v. 41). He does not excuse this weakness. Rather he uses it as an argument for watchfulness and prayer. The very fact that we are weak should stir us to greater prayer.

For meditation: *The Christian should no longer ask, 'What do I want?' but 'What does Christ want?'*

Suggested further reading: Zechariah 12:10 - 13:1

We are told that 'One of the soldiers with a spear pierced his side, and forthwith came there out blood and water.' This incident, small as it may seem at first sight, supplies probable proof that the heart of our blessed Lord was pierced and that life was consequently extinct. He did not merely faint, or swoon away, or become insensible, as some have dared to insinuate. His heart actually ceased to beat and he actually died. Great indeed was the importance of this fact. We must all see, on a moment's reflection, that without a real death there could be no real sacrifice, that without a real death there could be no real resurrection and that without a real death and real resurrection, the whole of Christianity is a house built on sand and has no foundation at all. Little indeed did that reckless Roman soldier dream that he was a mighty helper of our holy religion, when he thrust his spear into our Lord's side.

That the 'blood and water' mentioned in this place had a deep spiritual meaning, we can hardly doubt. St John himself seems to refer to them in his First Epistle as highly significant: 'This is he that came by water and blood' (1 John 5:6).

The true meaning of the blood and water is probably to be sought in the famous prophecy of Zechariah, where he says, 'In that day there shall be a fountain opened to the house of David, and to the inhabitants of Jerusalem, for sin and uncleanness' (Zech. 13:1). When was that fountain so truly and really opened as in the hour when Christ died? What emblem of atonement and purification was so well known to the Jews as blood and water? Why then should we hesitate to believe that the flow of 'blood and water' from our Lord's side was a significant declaration to the Jewish nation that the true fountain for sin was at length thrown open and that henceforth sinners might come boldly to Christ for pardon and wash and be clean? Let us make sure that we ourselves are 'washed and made white in the blood of the Lamb' (Rev. 7:14).

For meditation: *The blood of Jesus Christ cleanses us from every sin* (1 John 1:7).

Suggested further reading: 2 Corinthians 10:1-6

What gracious condescension marked our Lord's relationships with his disciples! We have this proved by a deeply touching circumstance at the moment of our Lord's betrayal. When Judas Iscariot undertook to guide the multitude to the place where his Master was, he gave them a sign by which they might distinguish Jesus in the dim moonlight from his disciples (vv. 48-49). That simple fact reveals the affectionate terms on which the disciples associated with our Lord. It is a universal custom in Eastern countries, when friend meets friend, to greet one another with a kiss (Exod. 18:7; 1 Sam. 20:41). It would seem therefore that when Judas kissed our Lord he only did what the apostles were accustomed to do when they met their Master after an absence.

Let us draw comfort from this little circumstance for our own souls. Our Lord Jesus Christ is a most gracious and condescending Saviour. He is not an austere man, repelling sinners and keeping them at a distance. He is not a being so different to us in nature that we must regard him with awe rather than affection. He would have us rather regard him as an elder Brother and a beloved Friend.

Our Lord condemns those who think to use carnal weapons in defence of him and his cause (vv. 51-52). The sword has a lawful office of its own. It may be used righteously in the defence of nations against oppression. It may be positively necessary to use it to prevent confusion, plunder and rapine on earth. But the sword is not to be used in the propagation and maintenance of the gospel. Christianity is not to be enforced by bloodshed, and belief in it extorted by force. Happy would it have been for the church if this sentence had been more frequently remembered! There are few countries in Christendom where the mistake has not been made of attempting to change men's religious opinions by compulsion, penalties, imprisonment or death. No wars have been so bloody as those which have arisen out of a clash of religious opinions. The weapons of Christian warfare are not carnal but spiritual (2 Cor. 10:4).

For meditation: *Christ's blood has been shed for us. Our blood may be shed for him. But we do not shed the blood of those who do not believe.*

Suggested further reading: Matthew 5:17-20

Three several predictions are specially mentioned, in Exodus, Psalms and Zechariah, which received their accomplishment at the cross. Others, as every well-informed Bible-reader knows, might easily be added. All combine to prove one and the same thing. They prove that the death of our Lord Jesus Christ at Golgotha was a thing foreseen and predetermined by God. Hundreds of years before the crucifixion, every part of the solemn transaction was arranged in the divine counsels and the minutest particulars were revealed to the prophets. From first to last it was a thing foreknown and every portion of it was in accordance with a settled plan and design. In the highest, fullest sense, when Christ died, he 'died according to the Scriptures' (1 Cor. 15:3).

We need not hesitate to regard such fulfilments of prophecy as strong evidence of the divine authority of God's Word. The prophets foretell not only Christ's death, but the particulars of his death. It is impossible to explain so many accomplishments of predicted circumstances upon any other theory. To talk of luck, chance and accidental coincidence as sufficient explanation is preposterous and absurd. The only rational account is the inspiration of God. The prophets who foretold the particulars of the crucifixion were inspired by him who foresees the end from the beginning, and the books they wrote under his inspiration ought not to be read as human compositions, but divine. Great indeed are the difficulties of all who pretend to deny the inspiration of the Bible. It really requires more unreasoning faith to be an infidel than to be a Christian. The man who regards the repeated fulfilments of minute prophecies about Christ's death, such as the prophecies about his dress, his thirst, his pierced side and his bones, as the result of chance and not of design must indeed be a credulous man.

For meditation: *All the promises of God find their confirmation and fulfilment in Christ* (2 Cor. 1:20).

Suggested further reading: John 10:14-18

Our Lord submitted to be made a prisoner of his own free will. He was not taken captive because he could not escape. It would have been easy for him to scatter his enemies to the four winds if he had seen fit (v. 53). In these words we see the secret of his voluntary submission to his foes. He came on purpose to fulfil the types and promises of the Old Testament Scriptures and, by fulfilling them, to provide salvation for the world. He came intentionally to be the true Lamb of God, the Passover Lamb. He came to be the scapegoat on whom the iniquities of the people were laid. His heart was set on accomplishing this great work. It could not be done without the hiding of his power for a time. To do it he became a willing sufferer. He was taken, tried, condemned and crucified entirely of his own free will.

There is much encouragement in this. The willing sufferer will surely be a willing Saviour. The almighty Son of God, who allowed men to bind him and lead him away when he might have prevented them with a word, must surely be full of readiness to save the souls that flee to him. Once more then, let us learn to trust him and not be afraid.

How little Christians know the weakness of their own hearts until they are tried! We have a mournful illustration of this in the conduct of our Lord's disciples. The disciples forgot their confident assertions of a few hours before. They forgot that they had declared their willingness to die with their Master. They forgot everything but the danger that stared them in the face. The fear of death overcame them (v. 56).

How many professing Christians have done the same! How many under the influence of excited feelings have promised that they would never be ashamed of Christ! They have come away from the communion table or a striking sermon full of zeal and love and ready to dismiss those who caution them against backsliding. And yet in a few days these feelings have cooled down and passed away. A trial has come and they have fallen before it. They have forsaken Christ. Let us be humble and self-abased. Let us cultivate a spirit of lowliness and self-distrust.

For meditation: *He willingly endured for us; shall we not willingly endure for him?*

Suggested further reading: Matthew 13:31-35

The Greek word rendered 'secretly' is literally 'a concealed' disciple — a past participle. The expression teaches the interesting fact that there were Jews who secretly believed that Jesus was the Messiah and yet had not courage to confess him before his crucifixion. We are distinctly told in John 12:42 that 'Many of the chief rulers believed, but did not confess Christ, because of the Pharisees.' But the character given of them, that 'They loved the praise of men more than the praise of God,' is so condemnatory that we may well doubt whether Joseph was one of these. Want of physical or moral courage was probably the flaw in his character. It is only fair to remember that, as 'a rich man and a counsellor', he had far more to sacrifice and far more opposition to encounter than poor fishermen or publicans would have. His backwardness to confess Christ cannot, of course, be defended. But his case teaches us that there is sometimes more spiritual work going on in men's minds than appears. We must not set down everyone as utterly graceless and godless, who is not bold and outspoken at present. We must charitably hope that there are some secret disciples, who at present hold their tongues and say nothing, and yet, like Joseph, will one day come forward and be courageous witnesses for Christ. All is not gold that glitters and all is not dross that now looks dirty and makes no show. We must be charitable and hope on. His case should also teach us the great power of that mischievous principle, the fear of man. Open sin kills its thousands, but the fear of man its tens of thousands. Let us watch and pray against it. Faith is the grand secret of victory over it. Like Moses, we must ever live as those who 'see him that is invisible' (Heb. 11:27). And to faith must be added the expulsive power of a new principle, the fear of God. 'I fear God,' said holy Col. Gardiner, 'and there is none else that I need fear.'

For meditation: *Just as a little fear can cripple, so a little faith can make us courageous.*

Suggested further reading: 1 Peter 2:21-25

Our Lord declared his own Messiahship and his future coming in glory to the Jewish council. The unconverted Jew can never tell us that his forefathers were left in ignorance that Jesus was the Messiah. Our Lord's answer to the solemn adjuration of the High Priest is a sufficient reply (v. 64). He declares that they would yet see that very Jesus of Nazareth whom they arraigned at their bar appear in majesty as King of kings (Rev. 1:7).

The last word spoken by our Lord to the Jews was a warning prediction about his own second coming. He tells them plainly that they will yet see him in glory. But he spoke to deaf ears. Unbelief, prejudice and self-righteousness covered them as a thick cloud. Never was there such an instance of spiritual blindness!

How much our Lord endured before the council from ridicule, mockery and false witness! Falsehood and ridicule are old and favourite weapons of the devil (John 8:44). All through our Lord's earthly ministry we see these weapons continually employed against him. He was called a glutton, a wine-bibber and a friend of publicans and sinners. He was held up to contempt as a Samaritan. The closing scene of his life was only in keeping with the past tenor of it. Satan stirred up his enemies to add insult to injury. No sooner was he pronounced guilty than every sort of mean indignity was heaped upon him (vv. 67-68).

How amazing and strange it all sounds! How wonderful that the holy Son of God should have voluntarily submitted to such indignities to redeem such miserable sinners as we are! How amazing, no less, that every part of these insults was foretold seven hundred years before they were inflicted! (Isa. 50:6).

Let it never surprise us if we have to endure mockery, ridicule and false reports because we belong to Christ. The disciple is not greater than his Master, nor the servant than his Lord. If lies and insults were heaped upon our Saviour, we need not wonder if the same weapons are constantly used against his people. It is one of Satan's great devices to blacken the character of godly men and bring them into contempt.

For meditation: *Let us guard our tongues against destructive gossip.*

Suggested further reading: 1 Corinthians 1:26-31

There are some true Christians in the world of whom very little is known. The case of Joseph of Arimathaea teaches this very plainly. Here is a man named among the friends of Christ, whose very name we never find elsewhere in the New Testament and whose history, both before and after this crisis, is completely withheld from the church. He comes forward to do honour to Christ when the apostles had forsaken him and fled. He cares for him and delights to do him service even when dead — not because of any miracle which he saw him do, but out of free and gratuitous love. He does not hesitate to confess himself one of Christ's friends at a time when Jews and Romans alike had condemned him as a malefactor and put him to death. Surely the man who could do such things must have had strong faith! Can we wonder that, wherever the gospel is preached, throughout the whole world, this pious action of Joseph is told of as a memorial of him?

Let us hope and believe that there are many Christians in every age who, like Joseph, are the Lord's hidden servants, unknown to the church and the world, but well known to God. Even in Elijah's time there were seven thousand in Israel who had never bowed the knee to Baal, although the desponding prophet knew nothing of it. Perhaps, at this very day, there are saints in the back streets of some of our great towns, or in the lanes of some of our country parishes, who make no noise in the world and yet love Christ and are loved by him. Ill-health, or poverty, or the daily cares of some laborious calling render it impossible for them to come forward in public, and so they live and die comparatively unknown. Yet the last day may show an astonished world that some of these very people, like Joseph, honoured Christ as much as any on earth and that their names were written in heaven. After all, it is special circumstances that bring to the surface special Christians. It is not those who make the greatest show in the church who are always found the fastest friends of Christ.

For meditation: *Most Christians are not famous in this life, but fame matters far less than faithfulness.*

Suggested further reading: Galatians 2:11-16

How small and gradual are the steps by which men may go down into great sins! The various steps are clearly marked out by the Gospel writers in Peter's fall. The first step was proud self-confidence. Though all men denied Christ, yet he never would! He was ready to go with Christ both to prison and death! The second step was indolent neglect of prayer. When his Master told him to pray, lest he should enter into temptation, he gave way to drowsiness and was found asleep. The third step was vacillating indecision. When the enemies of Christ first came upon him, Peter first fought, then ran away, then turned again and then finally followed him afar off. The fourth step was mingling with bad company. He went into the high priest's house and sat among the servants by the fire, trying to conceal his religion and hearing and seeing all manner of evil. The fifth and last step was the natural consequence of the preceding four. He was overwhelmed with fear when suddenly charged with being a disciple. The snare was round his neck. He could not escape. He plunged deeper into error than ever. He denied his blessed Master three times. The mischief, let it be remembered, had been done before. The denial was only the disease coming to a head. Let us beware of the beginnings of backsliding, however small, for a believer may backslide very far.

Peter was a chosen apostle of Christ. He had enjoyed greater spiritual privileges than most men in the world. He had received the Lord's Supper and the teaching of the upper room (John 13-17). He had been plainly warned of his danger. He had protested most loudly what he was going to do. Yet this very man denied his gracious Master, and that repeatedly and after intervals giving him space for reflection. He denied him once, twice, three times! The best and highest saint is a poor, weak creature even at his best times. Whether he knows it or not, he carries within him an almost boundless capacity of wickedness, however fair and decent his outward conduct may seem. There is no enormity of sin into which he may not run if he does not watch and pray and find himself upheld by the grace of God.

For meditation: *If the best of us needs to take care lest he falls, how much more the weaker of us!*

Suggested further reading: Acts 12:25 - 13:13

There are some servants of Christ whose latter end is better than their beginning. The case of Nicodemus teaches that lesson very plainly. The only man who dared to help Joseph in his holy work of burying our Lord was one who at first 'came to Jesus by night' and was nothing better than an ignorant enquirer after truth. At a later period in our Lord's ministry we find this same Nicodemus coming forward with somewhat more boldness and raising in the council of the Pharisees the question: 'Doth our law judge any man, before it hear him, and know what he doeth?' (John 7:51). Finally, we see him in the passage before us ministering to our Lord's dead body and not ashamed to take an active part in giving to the despised Nazarene an honourable burial. How great the contrast between the man who timidly crept into the Lord's lodging to ask a question and the man who brought a hundred pounds' weight of myrrh and aloes to anoint his dead body! Yet it was the same Nicodemus.

We shall do well to store up these things in our minds and to remember the case of Nicodemus in forming our estimate of other people's religion. We must not condemn others as graceless and god-less, because they do not see the whole truth at once and only reach decided Christianity by slow degrees. The Holy Ghost always leads believers to the same foundation truths and into the same highway to heaven. In these there is invariable uniformity. But the Holy Ghost does not always lead believers through the same experience, or at the same rate of speed. In this there is much diversity in his oper-ations. He that says conversion is a needless thing and that an unconverted man may be saved is undoubtedly under a strange de-lusion, but he that says that no one is converted except he becomes a full-blown and established Christian in a single day is no less under a delusion.

For meditation: *John Mark soon deserted Paul* (Acts 13:13), *but later proved so useful* (2 Tim. 4:11). *A bad beginning saw a good ending.*

Suggested further reading: Psalm 51

The infinite mercy of our Lord Jesus Christ is brought out forcibly by a fact that is only recorded in Luke's Gospel. We are told that after Peter's third denial, 'The Lord turned, and looked upon Peter' (v. 61). Those words are deeply touching. Surrounded by blood-thirsty and insulting enemies, in the full prospect of horrible out-rages, an unjust trial and a painful death, the Lord Jesus yet found time to think kindly of his poor erring disciple. Even then he would have Peter know he did not forget him. Sorrowfully, no doubt, but not angrily, he turned and looked at Peter. There was a deep mean-ing in that look. It was a sermon that Peter never forgot.

The love of Christ towards his people is a deep well which has no bottom. There is about it a mine of compassion, patience and readiness to forgive sin, of whose riches we have but a faint concep-tion. Let us not be afraid to trust that love when we first feel our sins. Let us never be afraid to go on trusting it after we have believed.

How bitter sin is to believers when they have fallen into it and discovered their fall! Peter's bitter weeping (v. 62) shows that he had found out the truth of Jeremiah's words (Jer. 2:19). He felt keenly the truth of Solomon's saying (Prov. 14:14) and could no doubt have repeated the words of Job (Job 42:6).

Sorrow like this, let us always remember, is an inseparable com-panion of true repentance. Here lies the grand distinction between repentance unto salvation and unavailing remorse. Remorse can make a man miserable, like Judas Iscariot, but it can do no more. It does not lead him to God. Repentance makes a man's heart soft and his conscience tender and shows itself in a real turning to a Father in heaven. The falls of the man who professes Christianity, yet has no grace, are falls from which there is no rising again. But the fall of a true saint always ends in deep contrition, self-abasement and amend-ment of life. Let us not make Peter's fall an excuse for our sin, but let us learn from his sad experience to watch and pray lest we fall into temptation.

For meditation: *God always picks up the Christian who stumbles* (Ps. 37:23-24).

Suggested further reading: 2 Timothy 4:9-18

The conduct of Joseph deserves our praise and admiration and his name will be held in honour by the church of Christ, in consequence of it, as long as the world stands. Whatever Joseph was at first, he shone brightly at last. 'The last are first' sometimes. Let us see what he did.

1. Joseph honoured Christ when our Lord's own apostles had forsaken him. He showed more faith and courage than his nearest and dearest friends.

2. Joseph honoured Christ when it was a dangerous thing to do him honour. To come forward and avow respect for one condemned as a malefactor, for one cast out by the high priests and leaders of the Jews, to say practically, 'I am Christ's friend,' was bold indeed. St Mark particularly says, 'He went in boldly unto Pilate' (Mark 15:43), showing plainly that it was an act of uncommon courage.

3. Joseph honoured Christ when he was a lifeless corpse and to all appearance could do nothing for him. It was not when Jesus was doing miracles and preaching wonderful sermons, but when there remained nothing of him but a dead body, that he came forward and asked leave to bury him.

Why Joseph's 'fear' departed and he acted with such marvellous boldness now is a question which we have no means of settling. But reason points out that in all probability he had been an eyewitness of much that had happened this eventful day. He had possibly stood within a short distance of the cross and seen all that took place and heard every one of our Lord's seven sayings. The miraculous darkness for three hours and the earthquake must have arrested his attention. Surely it is not presumptuous to conjecture that all this must have had a mighty effect on Joseph's soul and made him resolve at once to cast fear away and avow himself openly one of Christ's friends.

For meditation: *Even when all men desert us, our Lord stands with us.*

Suggested further reading: Hebrews 12:14-17

Judas gives us a plain proof of the innocence of our Lord with respect to every charge laid against him. If there was any living witness who could give evidence against our Lord, Judas Iscariot was the man. A chosen apostle of our Lord, a constant companion in all his journeyings, a hearer of all his teaching, both in private and public, he must have known if our Lord had done any wrong, either in word or deed. A deserter from our Lord's company, a betrayer of him into the hands of his enemies, it was his interest, for his own character's sake, to prove Jesus guilty. It would extenuate and excuse his own conduct if he could make out that his former Master was an offender and an impostor.

Why then did Judas Iscariot not come forward? Why did he not stand forth before the Jewish council and specify his charges, if he had any to make? Why did he not venture to accompany the chief priests to Pilate and prove to the Romans that Jesus was a malefactor? There is but one answer to these questions. Judas did not come forward as a witness because his conscience would not let him. Bad as he was, he knew he could prove nothing against Christ. Wicked as he was, he knew well that his Master was holy, harmless, innocent, blameless and true. Let this never be forgotten. The absence of Judas Iscariot at our Lord's trial is one among many proofs that our Lord was without blemish, a sinless man.

There is such a thing as repentance which is too late. His repentance (v. 3) and confession (v. 4) were not unto salvation. This is a point which deserves special attention. It is a common saying that 'It is never too late to repent.' That saying is no doubt true if repentance is true, but unhappily late repentance is often not genuine. It is possible for a man to feel his sins and be sorry for them, to be under strong convictions of guilt and express deep remorse, to be pricked in conscience and exhibit much distress of mind, and yet, for all this, not to repent with his heart. Present danger or the fear of death may account for all his feelings, and the Holy Spirit may have done no work whatever in the soul.

For meditation: *Those who say that they will put off repentance until later usually put it off for ever.*

Suggested further reading: 1 Corinthians 15:1-11

Concerning the evidences of Christ's resurrection — the proofs that he actually did rise again from the grave with his body — it is most remarkable to observe how full and various they are. He was seen at least eleven times after he rose again, at different times of day, in different ways and by different witnesses.

The order of Christ's eleven appearances between his resurrection and ascension, I believe to be as follows:

1. to Mary Magdalene alone (Mark 16:9; John 20:14);
2. to certain women returning from the sepulchre (Matt. 28:9-10);
3. to Simon Peter alone (Luke 24:34);
4. to two disciples going to Emmaus (Luke 24:13);
5. to ten apostles at Jerusalem and some other disciples, Thomas being absent (John 20:19);
6. to eleven apostles at Jerusalem, Thomas being present (John 20:26-29);
7. to seven disciples fishing at the sea of Tiberias (John 21:1);
8. to eleven apostles on a mountain in Galilee and perhaps some others with them (Matt. 28:16);
9. to above five hundred brethren at once (1 Cor. 15:7);
10. to James only (1 Cor. 15:7);
11. to all the apostles and probably some others on Mount Olivet at his ascension.

He was seen first by one woman alone, then by several women together, then by one man, then by two men and each time in the open air. Then he was seen by ten disciples in the evening in a room, then by eleven disciples again in a room and afterwards on five different occasions, at one of which no less than five hundred people were present. Those to whom he appeared touched him, talked with him and saw him eat and drink (Matt. 28:9; John 20:27; Luke 24:42). Nor must it be forgotten that all who saw him were most unwilling at first to believe and most slow to credit the report of his resurrection. Yet they were all finally convinced!

For meditation: *Few historical events are as well documented as the resurrection of our Lord.*

Suggested further reading: 2 Peter 2:17-22

Judas teaches us how little comfort ungodliness brings a man in the end. We are told that he cast down the thirty pieces of silver, for which he had sold his Master, in the temple and went away in bitterness of soul. That money was dearly earned. It brought him no pleasure even when he had it, just as Scripture says (Prov. 10:2).

Sin is, in truth, the hardest of all masters. In its service there are plenty of fair promises, but an utter dearth of performance. Its pleasures are but for a season. Its wages are sorrow, remorse, self-accusation and, too often, death. They that sow to the flesh do indeed reap corruption (Gal. 6:7-8).

Are we tempted to commit sin? Let us remember the words of Scripture (Num. 32:23) and resist the temptation. Let us be sure that sooner or later, in this life or the life to come, in this world or in the Judgement Day, sin and the sinner will meet face to face and have a bitter reckoning. Let us be sure that of all trades sin is the most unprofitable. Shameful sin brings no benefits (Rom. 6:21).

To what a miserable end a man may come if he has great privileges and does not use them rightly! What an awful death Judas died! (v. 5). An apostle of Christ, a former preacher of the gospel, a companion of Peter and John, commits suicide and rushes into God's presence unprepared and unforgiven.

Let us never forget that no sinners are so sinful as sinners against light and knowledge. None are so provoking to God. It is a solemn saying of Bunyan's that 'None fall so deep into the pit as those who fall backward.' Solomon teaches the same (Prov. 29:1). May we all strive to live up to our light. There is such a thing as sin against the Holy Spirit. Clear knowledge of truth in the head, combined with deliberate love of sin in the heart, go a long way towards it.

For meditation: *'Judas' has become a term for treachery. Judas betrayed Christ for money; other Judases have done so for other gods. Have you a god that is coming between you and Christ and that might lead you to desert him for it?*

Suggested further reading: 1 Corinthians 15:12-28

Concerning the importance of Jesus Christ's resurrection from the dead, it would be hard to speak too strongly. It is a cardinal article of the Christian faith, second to none in value. It is the grand proof that he was the promised Messiah whom the prophets had foretold. It is the one great sign which he named to the Jews when asked to give convincing evidence of his divine mission — the sign of the prophet Jonas, the rebuilding of the temple after destruction (Matt. 12:39; John 2:19-21). If he did not rise again after three days they were not to believe him. It is the completion of the work of redemption which he came into the world to accomplish. It proved that the ransom was accepted and the victory over sin and death obtained. Christ 'was delivered for our offences, and raised again for our justification' (Rom. 4:25). 'We are begotten again unto a lively hope, by the resurrection of Jesus Christ from the dead' (1 Peter 1:3). If he had not risen again, our hope would have been a huge uncertainty. It is a fact which has the closest connection with the spiritual life and position before God of all believers. They are counted by God as 'risen with Christ' and they should regard themselves as partakers of Christ's resurrection life and sitting in heavenly places. Not least, it is the pledge and assurance of our own resurrection at the last day. We need not fear death and look at the grave with despair, when we remember that Jesus Christ rose again in the body. As surely as the Head rose, so shall the members be raised. Let these points never be forgotten. When we think of them we may understand why the apostles, in their preaching and epistles, dwell so much upon the resurrection. Well would it be if modern Christians thought more about it. Myriads seem unable to look at anything in the gospel except the sacrifice and death of Christ and altogether pass over his resurrection.

For meditation: *The resurrection is God's great statement that he is satisfied with the penalty our Lord paid for our sin.*

Suggested further reading: Psalm 35:1-18

False accusations were laid to the charge of our Lord Jesus Christ. The Jews accused him of various subversive activities (v. 2). In all this indictment we know that there was not a word of truth. It was nothing but an ingenious attempt to enlist the feeling of a Roman governor against our Lord.

False witness and slander are two of the favourite weapons of the devil. He was a liar from the beginning and is still the father of lies (John 8:44). When he finds that he cannot stop God's work, his next device is to blacken the character of God's servants and to destroy the value of their testimony. With this weapon he assaulted David, Elijah and Jeremiah (Ps. 35:11; 1 Kings 18:17; Jer. 38:4). With this weapon he assaulted the apostles (Acts 24:5; 17:6). With this weapon he assaulted our Lord throughout his ministry (Luke 7:34; John 8:48). Here in these verses we find him plying his old weapon to the very last. Jesus is arraigned before Pilate upon charges which are utterly untrue.

The servant of Christ must never be surprised if he has to drink of the same cup as his Lord. When he who was holy, harmless and undefiled was foully slandered, who can expect to escape? (Matt. 10:25). Nothing is too bad to be reported against a saint. Perfect innocence is no fence against enormous lying, calumny and misrepresentation. The most blameless character will not secure us against false tongues. We must bear the trial patiently. It is part of the cross of Christ. We must sit still, lean back on God's promises and believe that in the long run the truth will prevail (Ps. 37:6-7).

What meekness and lowliness the Lord showed in the face of these accusations! Though the charges against him were false and he knew no sin, he was content to endure the contradiction of sinners against himself. Let us learn from our Saviour's example to suffer patiently and not to complain, giving way to irritation and ill temper in trial.

For meditation: *The law of the world is to 'give as good as you get'. The example of Christ is to seek no revenge and retaliation but to leave God to sort things out.*

Suggested further reading: Luke 7:36-50

Those who love Christ most are those who have received most benefit from him. The first whom St John names among those who came to Christ's sepulchre is Mary Magdalene. The history of this faithful woman, no doubt, is hidden in much obscurity. We are distinctly told that she was one out of whom the Lord had cast 'seven devils' (Mark 16:9; Luke 8:2) — one who had been subjected in a peculiar way to Satan's possession — and one whose gratitude to our Lord for deliverance was a gratitude that knew no bounds. In short, of all our Lord's followers on earth, none seem to have loved him so much as Mary Magdalene. None felt that they owed so much to Christ. None felt so strongly that there was nothing too great to do for Christ. Hence, as Bishop Andrews beautifully puts it, 'She was last at his cross and first at his grave. She stayed longest *there* and was soonest *here*. She could not rest till she was up to seek him. She sought him while it was yet dark, even before she had light to seek him by.' In a word, having received much, she loved much, and loving much, she did much, in order to prove the reality of her love.

How is it that many, whose faith and grace it would be uncharitable to deny, work so little, give so little, say so little, take so little pains to promote Christ's cause and bring glory to Christ in the world? These questions admit of only one answer. It is a low sense of debt and obligation to Christ which is the account of the whole matter. Where sin is not felt at all, nothing is done, and where sin is little felt, little is done. The man who is deeply conscious of his own guilt and corruption and deeply convinced that without the blood and intercession of Christ he would sink deservedly into the lowest hell, this is the man who will spend and be spent for Jesus and think that he can never do enough to show forth his praise.

For meditation: *The depth of our self-giving reflects the depth of our love.*

Suggested further reading: Acts 24:22-26

Strange and mingled motives influence the hearts of unconverted men. Herod's attitude and hopes with regard to our Lord are remarkable (v. 8). Herod was a sensual worldly man, the murderer of John the Baptist, a man living in foul adultery with his brother's wife. Such a man we might suppose would have no desire to see Christ. But Herod had an uneasy conscience. The blood of God's murdered saints no doubt often rose before his eyes and destroyed his peace. The fame of our Lord's preaching and miracles had penetrated even into his court. It was said that another witness against sin had risen up, who was even more faithful and bold than John the Baptist, and who confirmed his teaching by works which even the power of kings could not perform. These rumours made Herod restless and uncomfortable. No wonder that his curiosity was stirred and he 'desired to see Christ'.

It may be feared that there are many great and rich men like Herod in every age of the church, men without God, without faith and living only for themselves. They generally live in an atmosphere of their own, flattered, fawned upon and never told the truth about their souls, haughty, tyrannical and knowing no will but their own. Yet even these men are sometimes conscience-striken and afraid. God raises up some bold witness against their sins whose testimony reaches their ears. At once their curiosity is stirred. They feel found out and are ill at ease. They flutter around his ministry like a moth around the candle and seem unable to keep away from it even while they do not obey it. They praise his talents and openly profess their admiration of his power. But they never get any further. Like Herod, their conscience produces within them a morbid curiosity to see and hear God's witnesses. But, like Herod, their heart is linked to the world by chains of iron. Tossed to and fro by storms of ungovernable lust or passions, they are never at rest while they live, and after all their fitful struggles of conscience they die at length in their sins.

For meditation: *No one was ever saved by merely being curious about the gospel. More than a passing interest or infatuation is needed.*

Suggested further reading: Galatians 3:26 - 4:7

There are widely different temperaments in different believers. This is a point which is curiously brought out in the conduct of Peter and John, when Mary Magdalene told them that the Lord's body was gone. We are told that they both ran to the sepulchre, but John, the disciple whom Jesus loved, outran Peter and reached the empty grave first. Then comes out the difference between the two men. John, of the two more gentle, quiet, tender, reserved, retiring, deep-feeling, stooped down and looked in, but went no further. Peter, more hot and zealous and impulsive and fervent and forward, cannot be content without going down into the sepulchre and actually seeing with his own eyes. Both, we may be sure, were deeply attached to our Lord. The hearts of both, at this critical juncture, were full of hopes and fears and anxieties and expectations all tangled together. Yet each behaves in his own characteristic fashion. We need not doubt that these things were intentionally written for our learning.

Let us learn from the case before us to make allowances for wide varieties in the inward character of believers. To do so will save us much trouble in the journey of life and prevent many an uncharitable thought. Let us not judge brethren harshly and set them down in a low place, because they do not see or feel things exactly as we see and feel, and because things do not affect or strike them just as they affect and strike us. The flowers in the Lord's garden are not all of one colour and one scent, though they are all planted by one Spirit. The subjects of his kingdom are not all exactly of one tone and temperament, though they all love the same Saviour and are written in the same book of life. The church of Christ has some in its ranks who are like Peter and some who are like John, and a place for all and a work for all to do. Let us love all who love Christ in sincerity and thank God that they love him at all. The great thing is to love Jesus.

For meditation: *Variations in ability, background and race are not to overrule our oneness in Christ.*

Suggested further reading: John 11:45-57

Let us learn from Herod's case to pity great men. With all their greatness and apparent splendour, they are often thoroughly miserable within. Costly clothes often cover hearts which are utter strangers to peace. That man knows not what he is wishing who wishes to be a rich man. Let us pray for rich men as well as pity them. They carry weight in the race for eternal life. If they are saved it is only by the greatest miracles of God's grace. Our Lord's words are very solemn (Matt. 19:24).

How easily and readily unconverted men can agree in disliking Christ! By sending our Lord to Herod, Pilate and Herod became friends again. We know not the cause of their enmity. It was probably some petty quarrel such as will arise amongst great men as well as small. But whatever the cause of enmity, it was laid aside when a common object of contempt, fear or hatred was brought before them. Whatever else they disagreed about, Pilate and Herod could agree to despise and persecute Christ.

This incident before us is a striking emblem of a state of things which may always be seen in the world. Men of the most discordant opinions can unite in opposing truth. Teachers of the most opposite doctrines can make common cause in fighting against the gospel. In the days of our Lord the Pharisees and the Sadducees might be seen combining their forces to entrap Jesus of Nazareth and put him to death. In our own time we sometimes see Romanists and Socinians, infidels and idolaters, worldly pleasure lovers and bigoted ascetics, the friends of so-called liberal views and the most determined opponents of change ranked together against evangelical religion. One common hatred binds them together. They hate the cross of Christ (Acts 4:27). All hate each other very much but they hate Christ more.

For meditation: *It does not matter what the sect calls itself. Whether it is Roman Catholicism, the Jehovah's Witnesses Movement, the Mormons or liberalism, while all disagree greatly with each other, all are agreed in opposing salvation by faith in the death of Christ alone. Salvation by grace alone, by faith alone, through Christ alone is the common point of opposition that unites them all.*

Suggested further reading: Matthew 28:11-15

Peter found in the empty tomb the clearest evidence of a deliberate, orderly and calmly done transaction. The linen clothes, in which our Lord's body had been wrapped, were lying by themselves. The napkin which had been tied round his head was rolled up by itself in another place, separate from the linen clothes. There were no symptoms of hurry, haste or fear. All had been done decently and in order. Everything that Peter saw contradicted the idea that the body had been stolen. No thief would have taken so much trouble about the clothes and napkin. In fact the person who had removed the body, whoever it was, must have entailed on himself needless labour, if he removed it as a dead corpse, by unwrapping the linen clothes in which the corpse was buried. The easiest plan would have been to carry away the body just as he found it, wrapped up in linen. Why were the linen clothes taken off and left behind? Why were the removers of the body so careful to take away nothing but the body? Questions like these must have sorely perplexed Peter's mind. The body, he saw plainly, was gone. But there was something in the whole appearance of things which he could not understand.

Chrysostom observes, 'The linen cloths lying was a sign of the resurrection. For neither if any person had removed the body, would they, before doing so, have stripped it; nor if any had stolen it, would they have taken the trouble to remove the napkin and roll it up and lay it in a place by itself. They would have taken the body as it was. On this account, John tells us by anticipation that it was buried with much myrrh, which glues linen to the body not less firmly than lead, in order that when thou hearest that the napkin lay apart, thou mayest not endure those who say he was stolen. A thief would not have been so foolish as to spend so much time on a superfluous matter.'

For meditation: *The only armoury the Jewish leaders had against the **fact** of the resurrection was their lies.*

Suggested further reading: 1 Corinthians 4:1-5

These verses describe the appearance of our Lord before Pontius
Pilate, the Roman governor. That sight must have been amazing to
the angels of God. He who will one day judge the world allowed
himself to be judged and condemned, though he had done no violence, neither was any deceit in his mouth (Isa. 53:9). He from whose
lips Pilate and Caiaphas will one day receive their eternal sentence
suffered silently an unjust sentence to be passed on him. Those silent sufferings fulfilled the words of Isaiah (Isa. 53:7). To those
silent sufferings believers owe all their peace and hope. Through
them they will have boldness in the Day of Judgement who in themselves would have nothing to say.

How pitiful is the condition of an unprincipled great man! Pilate
appears to have been inwardly satisfied that our Lord had done
nothing worthy of death. He knew why they had handed our Lord
over to him (v. 18). Both his judges bore striking testimony to his
innocence (Luke 23:14-15). Left to his own unbiased judgement,
Pilate would probably have dismissed the charges against our Lord
and let him go free.

But Pilate was the governor of a jealous and turbulent people.
His great desire was to procure favour with them and please them.
He cared little how much he sinned against God and conscience, so
long as he had the praise of man. Though willing to save our Lord's
life, he was afraid to do it if it offended the Jews. And so, after a
feeble attempt to divert the fury of the people from Jesus to Barabbas,
and a feebler attempt to satisfy his own conscience by washing his
hands publicly before the people, he at last condemned one whom he
himself called 'a just person' (v. 24). He rejected the strange and
mysterious warning that his wife sent to him after her dream. He
stifled the remonstrances of his own conscience and delivered the
Lord over to be crucified (v. 26).

How many people know that their acts are wrong, but they fear
being laughed at and cannot bear being unpopular! Like dead fish
they float with the tide. The praise of man is the idol before which
they bow down and to that idol they sacrifice conscience, inward
peace and their souls.

For meditation: *How much weight do you put on what other people
think? Do you sin to keep friends?*

Suggested further reading: Acts 18:24-28

We are taught in these verses that there may be much ignorance even in true believers. This is a point which is brought out here with singular force and distinctness. John himself, the writer of this Gospel, records of himself and his companion Peter, 'As yet they knew not the Scripture, that he must rise again from the dead.' How truly wonderful this seems! For three long years these two leading apostles had heard our Lord speak of his own resurrection as fact and yet they had not understood him. Again and again, he had staked the truth of his Messiahship on his rising from the dead and yet they had never taken in his meaning. We little realize the power over the mind which is exercised by wrong teaching in childhood and by early prejudices imbibed in our youth. Surely the Christian minister has little right to complain of ignorance among his hearers, when he marks the ignorance of Peter and John under the teaching of Christ himself.

After all, we must remember that true grace, and not head knowledge, is the one thing needful. We are in the hands of a merciful and compassionate Saviour, who passes by and pardons much ignorance when he sees 'a heart right in the sight of God'. Some things indeed we must know and without knowing them we cannot be saved. Our own sinfulness and guilt, the office of Christ as a Saviour, the necessity of repentance and faith — such things as these are essential to salvation. But he that knows these things may, in other respects, be a very ignorant man. In fact, the extent to which one man may have grace together with much ignorance, and another may have much knowledge and yet no grace, is one of the greatest mysteries in religion and one which the last day alone will unfold. Let us then seek knowledge and be ashamed of ignorance. But above all let us make sure that, like Peter and John, we have grace and right hearts.

For meditation: *We are to rebuke perversity but to instruct ignorance* (Titus 1:9).

Suggested further reading: John 3:16-21

Let us learn from the conduct of the Jews on this occasion the desperate wickedness of human nature. The behaviour of Pilate afforded the chief priests and elders an opportunity of reconsidering what they were about. The difficulties he raised about condemning our Lord gave time for second thoughts. But there were no second thoughts in the minds of our Lord's enemies. They pressed on with their wicked deed. They rejected the compromise Pilate offered. They actually preferred a felon named Barabbas to Jesus. They would head up all by recklessly taking on themselves all the guilt of our Lord's death (v. 25).

What had our Lord done that the Jews should hate him so? He was no robber or murderer, no blasphemer of their God, or reviler of their prophets. He was one whose life was love (Acts 10:38). He was innocent of any transgression against God or man. And yet the Jews hated him and never rested till he was dead! They hated him because he told them the truth. They hated him because he testified that their works were evil. They hated the light because it made their own darkness visible. In a word, they hated Christ because he was righteous and they were wicked, because he was holy and they were unholy, because he testified against sin and they were determined to keep their sins and not let them go.

There are few things so little believed and realized as the corruption of human nature. Men fancy that if they saw a perfect person they would love and admire him. They flatter themselves that it is the inconsistency of professing Christians which they dislike and not their religion. They forget that when a really perfect man was on earth in the person of the Son of God he was hated and put to death.

Let us never be surprised at the wickedness there is in the world. Let us mourn over it and labour to make it less, but let us never be surprised at its extent. There is nothing that the heart of man is not capable of conceiving, or the hand of man of doing. As long as we live let us mistrust our own hearts (Jer. 17:9).

For meditation: *'The world cannot hate you, but it hates me because I testify that what it does is evil'* (John 7:7).

Suggested further reading: Ruth 1:15-18

Those who love Christ most diligently and perseveringly are those who receive most privileges from Christ's hand. It is a touching fact, and one to be carefully noted, that Mary Magdalene would not leave the sepulchre when Peter and John went away to their own home. Love to her gracious Master would not let her leave the place where he had been laid. Where he was now she could not tell. What had become of him she did not know. But love made her linger about the empty tomb where Joseph and Nicodemus had lately laid him. Love made her honour the last place where his precious body had been seen by mortal eyes. And her love reaped a rich reward. She saw the angels whom Peter and John had never observed. She actually heard them speak and had soothing words addressed to her. She was the first to see our Lord after he rose from the dead, the first to hear his voice, the first to hold conversation with him. Can anyone doubt that this was written for our learning? Wherever the gospel is preached throughout the world, this little incident testifies that those who honour Christ will be honoured by Christ.

As it was in the morning of the first Easter Day, so will it be as long as the church stands. The great principle contained in the passage before us will hold good until the Lord comes again. All believers have not the same degree of faith, or hope, or knowledge, or courage, or wisdom, and it is vain to expect it. But it is a certain fact that those who love Christ most fervently and cleave to him most closely will always enjoy most communion with him and feel most of the witness of the Spirit in their hearts. It is precisely those who wait on the Lord, in the temper of Mary Magdalene, to whom the Lord will reveal himself most fully and make them know and feel more than others. To know Christ is good, but to 'know that we know him' is far better.

For meditation: *True devotion cannot be driven away from the one who is loved.*

Suggested further reading: Matthew 24:15-25

To the women who were following him as he was led away to be crucified our Lord gave prophetic warning (vv. 28-31). These words must have sounded peculiarly terrible to the ears of a Jewish woman. To her it was always a disgrace to be childless. The idea of a time coming when it would be a blessing to have no children must have been a new and tremendous thought to her mind. And yet within fifty years this prediction of Christ was literally fulfilled. The siege of Jerusalem by the Romans under Titus brought down on all the inhabitants of the city the most horrible sufferings from famine and pestilence that can be conceived. Women are actually reported to have eaten their own children through lack of food during the siege. Upon none did the last judgement sent upon the Jewish nation fall so heavily as upon the wives, mothers and little children.

Let us beware of supposing that the Lord Jesus holds out to man nothing but mercy, pardon, love and forgiveness. Beyond all doubt he is plenteous in mercy. There is mercy with him like a mighty stream. He delights in mercy. But we must never forget that there is justice with him as well as mercy. There are judgements preparing for the impenitent and unbelieving. There is wrath revealed in the gospel for those that harden themselves in wickedness. The same cloud that was bright to Israel was dark to the Egyptians (Exod. 14:20). The same Lord Jesus who invites the labouring and heavy laden to come to him and rest declares most plainly that unless a man repents he will perish, and that he who does not believe shall be damned (Luke 13:3; Mark 16:16). The same Saviour who now holds out his hands to the disobedient and gainsaying will come one day in flaming vengeance on those who know not God and who obey not the gospel (2 Thess. 1:8). Christ is indeed most gracious. But the day of grace must come to an end at last. An unbelieving world will find at length, as Jerusalem did, that there is judgement with God as well as mercy. Wrath long accumulated falls most heavily.

For meditation: *To reject Christ is to reject the only Saviour. Without Christ, without hope.*

Suggested further reading: Isaiah 49:14-23

We see in these verses that the fears and sorrows of believers are often quite needless. We are told that Mary stood at the sepulchre weeping, and wept as if nothing could comfort her. She wept when the angels spoke to her. 'Woman,' they said, 'why weepest thou?' She was weeping still when our Lord spoke to her. 'Woman,' he also said, 'why weepest thou?' And the burden of her complaint was always the same: 'They have taken away my Lord, and I know not where they have laid him.' Yet all this time her risen Master was close to her, with 'body, flesh and bones, and all things pertaining to the perfection of man's nature'. Her tears were needless. Her anxiety was unnecessary. Like Hagar in the wilderness, she had a well of water by her side, but she had not eyes to see it.

What thoughtful Christian can fail to see that we have here a faithful picture of many a believer's experience? How often we are anxious when there is no just cause for anxiety! How often we mourn over the absence of things which in reality are within our grasp and even at our right hand! Two-thirds of the things we fear in life never happen at all and two-thirds of the tears we shed are thrown away and shed in vain. Let us pray for more faith and patience and allow more time for the full development of God's purposes. Let us believe that things are often working together for our peace and joy, which seem at one time to contain nothing but bitterness and sorrow. Old Jacob said at one time of his life, 'All these things are against me' (Gen. 42:36), yet he lived to see Joseph again, rich and prosperous, and to thank God for all that had happened. If Mary had found the seal of the tomb unbroken and her Master's body lying cold within, she might well have wept! The very absence of the body, which made her weep, was a token for good and a cause of joy for herself and all mankind.

For meditation: *Most of what we fear will happen never in fact occurs. Much of what does happen is not as terrible as we thought it would be.*

Suggested further reading: Acts 7:54-60

When our Lord was crucified his first words were words of gracious intercession (v. 34). His own racking agony of body did not make him forget others. The first of his seven sayings on the cross was a prayer for the souls of his murderers. His prophetical office he had just exhibited by remarkable prediction. His kingly office he was about to exhibit by opening the door of paradise to the penitent thief. His priestly office he now exhibited by interceding for others, even those who crucified him.

The fruits of this marvellous prayer will never be fully seen until the day when the books are opened and the secrets of all hearts are revealed. We have probably not the least idea how many of the conversions to God which took place during the first six months after the crucifixion were the direct reply to this marvellous prayer. Perhaps this prayer was the first step to the penitent thief's repentance. Perhaps it was one means of affecting the centurion (v. 47) and the people who smote their breasts (v. 48). Perhaps the three thousand on the Day of Pentecost, foremost it may be at one time amongst our Lord's murderers, owed their conversion to that prayer. The day will declare it. There is nothing secret that shall not be revealed. This only we know: that the Father always hears the Son (John 11:42).

Let us see in our Lord's intercession for those who crucified him one more proof of Christ's infinite love to sinners. The Lord Jesus is indeed full of pity, most compassionate and gracious. None are too wicked for him to care for. None are too far gone in sin for his almighty heart to take an interest in their souls. He wept over unbelieving Jerusalem. He heard the prayer of the dying thief. He stopped under the tree to call the publican Zacchaeus. He came down from heaven to turn the heart of the persecutor Saul. Love like this is a love that passes knowledge. The vilest of sinners can apply to a Saviour like this without fear. He prayed for his murderers from the cross.

For meditation: *How much real love is there in your heart for others, especially the difficult people you know?*

Suggested further reading: Hebrews 1:5-14

Mary saw figures in white sitting inside the grave. They evidently looked like men, but they were in reality angels, two of those mysterious ministering spirits whom the Bible teaches us God is pleased to employ on great occasions. An angel announced the coming birth of John the Baptist and of Christ himself. Angels told the shepherds that Christ was born. Angels ministered to our Lord after the temptation and an angel strengthened him in Gethsemane. And now also angels appeared in the day of our Lord's resurrection. They first announced that he was born and they again, after thirty-three years, announced that he was risen.

The whole subject of angels is very deep and mysterious and one about which we must beware of holding anything that is not revealed. But the case before us teaches one or two wonderful things, which we should do well to remember.

It is clear that angels were at the tomb, when the party of women arrived there, after Mary Magdalene had run to tell Peter and John. It is equally clear that they were not to be seen when Peter and John ran to the grave on hearing Mary's report. Not one word do we read of their seeing angels. Yet it is equally clear that when Mary Magdalene looked in, after Peter and John went away, she saw two angels and talked with them.

These are very deep things. They prove plainly that the angels of God appear and disappear, are visible or invisible, instantaneously and supernaturally, according as God commissions them. In short, they are beings of a totally different nature to our own and are in all the conditions of their constitution totally unlike us. For anything we know, they were in the tomb when Peter and John inspected it, but at that moment were invisible. For anything we know, they are now very near us every minute of our existence and doing God's will concerning us, though we are utterly unaware of their presence.

For meditation:
The hosts of God encamp around
The dwellings of the just

(Tate and Brady).

Suggested further reading: 2 Corinthians 7:8-12

We are told that two malefactors were crucified together with our Lord, one on his right hand and one on his left. Both were equally near to Christ. Both saw and heard all that happened during the six hours that he hung on the cross. Both were dying men and suffering acute pain. Both alike were wicked sinners and needed forgiveness. Yet one died in his sins as he had lived, hardened, impenitent and unbelieving. The other repented, believed, cried to Jesus for mercy and was saved.

A fact like this should teach us humility. We cannot account for it. We can only use our Lord's words (Matt. 11:26). How it is that under precisely the same circumstances one man is converted and another remains dead in sins, why the same sermon is heard by one man with perfect indifference and sends another home to pray and seek Christ, why the same gospel is hid to one and revealed to another — all these are questions which we cannot possibly answer. We only know that it is so, and it is useless to deny it. One thief was saved, that no sinner might despair, but only one, so that no sinner might presume.

The unvarying character of repentance is seen in the sinner's salvation. Thousands look at the broad fact that the thief was saved in the hour of death and look no further. They do not look at the distinct and well-defined evidences of repentance which fell from his lips before he died.

The first notable step in the thief's repentance was his concern about his companion's wickedness in reviling Christ (v. 40). The second step was a full acknowledgement of his own sin (v. 41). The third step was an open confession of Christ's innocence (v. 41). The fourth step was faith in Christ's power and will to save him (v. 42). The fifth step was prayer. He cried to Jesus hanging on the cross and asked him even then to think upon his soul. The sixth and last step was humility. He mentions no great thing. Enough for him if he is remembered by Christ. Though this thief's time was short for giving proof of his conversion it was time well used.

For meditation: *Deathbed repentance is a rare thing. Now is the time for salvation.*

Suggested further reading: Psalm 103:8-18

We are here told how our Lord at last revealed himself to this faithful disciple, after her patience, love and boldness had been fully proved. Little as she had shown herself able to understand the great truth of her Saviour's resurrection, she had at any rate shown that none loved him more, or clung to him more tenaciously, than she did. And she had her reward. One single word was enough to open her eyes, to let the whole truth shine in upon her mind and to reveal the great fact that her Saviour was not dead but alive and that he had won a victory over the grave. Speaking in his usual well-known voice, our Lord addressed her by her name — the name by which, no doubt, he had often addressed her before. That single word touched a spring, as it were, and opened her eyes in a moment. Need we doubt that at once the whole world seemed turned upside down to the astonished woman, and that under the influence of such an amazing revulsion of feeling as that much-loved voice must have caused, her mind could only find expression in one passionate word — 'Rabboni', or Master?

The boundless compassion of our Lord Jesus Christ to his believing people comes out wonderfully in this verse. He can be touched with the feeling of our infirmities. He knows how weak our bodily frame is and how much excessive sorrow can unnerve and stupefy our minds. He can pass over much darkness of understanding, much slowness of comprehension, when he sees real, genuine, hearty, bold, persevering, thorough love to himself and his person. We see this prominently brought out in his dealing with Mary Magdalene, when he revealed himself to her. He graciously pardons her forgetfulness of his oft-repeated declaration that he would rise again after his death, pities her deep sorrow and abundantly rewards her love. These things are written for our learning. Jesus never changes.

For meditation: *The Father and the Son are ever full of pity towards their weak and erring people.*

Suggested further reading: 2 Corinthians 5:1-10

If we search the Bible from Genesis to Revelation we shall not find a more striking proof that Christ is able to save to the uttermost. The time when the thief was saved was the hour of our Lord's greatest weakness. He was hanging on the cross in agony. Yet even then he had the power to hear and grant a sinner's petition.

The man whom our Lord saved was a wicked sinner at the point of death, with nothing in his past life to recommend him and nothing notable in his present position but a humble prayer. Yet he was shown mercy.

Do you want proof that salvation is of grace and not of works? We have it in the case before us. The dying thief was nailed hand and foot to the cross. He could literally do nothing to save his own soul. Yet even he, through Christ's infinite grace, was saved. He had the assurance of Christ's word.

Do we want proof that sacraments and ordinances and church membership are not essential to salvation? The dying thief is the proof. He repented, believed and was saved. The same is true for the vilest sinner today.

How near a dying believer is to rest and glory! The word 'today' (v. 43) contains a body of divinity. It tells us that the very moment a believer dies his soul is in happiness and in safe keeping. His full redemption is not yet come. His perfect bliss will not begin before the resurrection morning. But there is no mysterious delay, no season of suspense, no purgatory between his death and a state of reward. In the day that he breathes his last he goes to paradise. In the hour that he departs he is with Christ (Phil. 1:23).

Let us remember these things when our believing friends fall asleep in Jesus. We must not sorrow for them as those who have no hope. While we are sorrowing they are rejoicing. While we are putting on our mourning and weeping at their funerals they are safe and happy with the Lord. For ourselves to die is a solemn thing. But if we die in the Lord then we need not doubt that to die is gain.

For meditation: *Do you, like the thief, think yourself worth nothing more than a place in Christ's thoughts? Such humility Christ rewards.*

Suggested further reading: Matthew 17:1-8

What low and earthly thoughts of Christ may creep into the mind of a true believer! It seems impossible to gather any other lesson from the solemn words which our Lord addressed to Mary Magdalene, when he said, 'Touch me not; for I am not yet ascended to my Father.' No doubt the language is somewhat mysterious and ought to be delicately and reverently handled. Yet it is only reasonable to suppose that the first surprise and the reaction from great sorrow to great joy was more than the mind of Mary could bear. She was only a woman, though a holy and faithful woman. It is highly probable that, in the first excess of her joy, she threw herself at our Lord's feet and made greater demonstrations of feeling than were seemly or becoming. Very likely she behaved too much like one who thought all must be right if she had her Lord's bodily presence and all must be wrong in his bodily absence. This was not the highest style of faith. She acted, in short, like one who forgot that her Master was God as well as man. She made too little of his divinity and too much of his humanity. And hence she called forth our Lord's gentle rebuke: 'Touch me not! There is no need of this excessive demonstration of feeling. I am not yet ascending to my Father for forty days; your present duty is not to linger at my feet, but to go and tell my brethren that I have risen. Think of the feelings of others as well as of your own.'

After all, we must confess that the fault of this holy woman was one into which Christians have always been too ready to fall. In every age there has been a tendency in the minds of many to make too much of Christ's bodily presence and to forget that he is not a mere earthly friend, but one who is 'God over all, blessed for ever', as well as man. Let us be content to have Christ dwelling in our hearts by faith and present when two or three are met in his name and to wait for the real presence of Christ's body till he comes again.

For meditation: *We cannot always live in great experiences of the reality of Christ, but we can always know he is with us, however we may feel.*

Suggested further reading: Isaiah 53

There is a deep mystery in our Lord's words recorded by Matthew
(v. 46), which no mortal man can fathom. No doubt they were not
wrung from our Lord by mere bodily pain. Such an explanation is
entirely unsatisfactory and dishonourable to our blessed Saviour.
They were meant to express the real pressure on his soul of the
enormous burden of a world's sins. They were meant to show how
truly and literally he was our Substitute, was made sin, and a curse
for us, and endured God's righteous anger against a world's sins in
his own person. At that awful moment the iniquity of us all was laid
on him to the uttermost. It pleased the Lord to bruise him and to put
him to grief (Isa. 53:10). He bore our sins. He carried our transgressions. Heavy must have been that burden, real and literal must
have been our Lord's substitution for us when he, the eternal Son of
God, could speak of himself as for a time 'forsaken'. We have no
stronger proof of the sinfulness of sin nor the vicarious nature of
our Lord's sufferings than his cry (v. 46). It should stir us to hate sin
and encourage us to trust in Christ.

There is something mysterious, no doubt, in our Lord's words as
recorded by Luke (23:46) which we have no line to fathom. He who
spoke these words was God as well as man. His divine and human
nature were inseparably united. His divine nature, of course, could
not die. He died of his own free will, voluntarily (John 10:17-18).
His death was in some respects dissimilar to ours.

There is a sense, however, in which our Lord's words supply a
true lesson to all Christians. They afford an example of how we
ought to die. Like our Master we should not be afraid to confront
the king of terrors. We should regard him as a vanquished enemy
whose sting has been taken away by Christ's death. We should think
of him as a foe who can hurt the body for a little season and after
that do no more. We should await his approaches with calmness and
patience, with the spirit of a Paul (2 Tim. 1:12) and a Stephen (Acts
7:59).

For meditation: *Through his death Christ liberates us from the
fear of death* (Heb. 2:15).

Suggested further reading: Hebrews 2:10-13

When our Lord speaks of God as 'My Father and my God', he seems, as usual, to point to the close and intimate union which he always declared to exist between himself and the first person in the Trinity. 'The God and Father of our Lord Jesus Christ' (1 Peter 1:3) is a kindred expression. He does not, we should observe, say, 'I ascend unto *our* Father', etc., but '*my* Father and *your* Father'. He thus shows that there is a certain distinction between his relation to the Father and ours. Believers are not naturally sons of God; they only become so by grace, by adoption and by virtue of union with Christ. Christ, on the contrary, is in his nature the Son of God.

How kindly and graciously our Lord speaks of his disciples! He bids Mary Magdalene carry a message to them as 'his brethren'. It was but three days before that they had all forsaken him shamefully and fled. Yet this merciful Master speaks as if all was forgiven and forgotten. His first thought is to bring back the wanderers, to bind up the wounds of their consciences, to reanimate their courage, to restore them to their former place. This was indeed a love that passeth knowledge. To trust deserters and to show confidence in backsliders was a compassion which man can hardly understand. So true is that word of David: 'Like as a father pitieth his children, so the Lord pitieth them that fear him. For he knoweth our frame; he remembereth that we are dust' (Ps. 103:13-14).

Let us leave the passage with the comfortable reflection that Jesus Christ never changes. He is the same yesterday, today and for ever. As he dealt with his erring disciples in the morning of his resurrection, so will he deal with all who believe and love him, until he comes again. When we wander out of the way, he will bring us back. When we fall, he will raise us again.

For meditation:
Though for good we render ill,
He accounts us brethren still

(Newton).

Suggested further reading: Hebrews 9:1-14

At the hour of our Lord's death the curtain which separated the holy
of holies from the rest of the temple was split from top to bottom. Of
all the wonderful signs that accompanied our Lord's death none was
more significant than this. The midday darkness for three hours must
needs have been a startling event. The earthquake which rent the
rocks must have been a tremendous shock. But there was a meaning
in the sudden rending of the veil from top to bottom which must
have pricked the heart of any intelligent Jew.

The rending of the veil proclaimed the termination and passing
away of the ceremonial law. It was a sign that the old dispensation
of sacrifices and ordinances was no longer needed. Its work was
done. Its earthly high priest, mercy-seat, sprinkling of blood, offering up of incense and Day of Atonement were no longer needed now
the true High Priest, the Lamb of God, had appeared and been slain.
The figures and shadows were no longer wanted. May we all remember this! To set up an altar and a sacrifice and a priesthood now
is to light a candle at noonday!

That rending of the veil proclaimed the opening up of the way of
salvation to all mankind. The way into the presence of God was
unknown to the Gentile and only seen dimly by the Jew until Christ
died. But Christ having now offered up a perfect sacrifice and obtained eternal redemption, the darkness and mystery have passed
away. All are invited to draw near to God with boldness and approach him with confidence by faith in Jesus. A door was thrown
open and a way of life set before the whole world. May we all remember this! From the time that Jesus died the way of peace was
never meant to be shrouded in mystery. There was to be no reserve.
The gospel was the revelation of a mystery which had been hid for
ages and generations. To clothe religion now with mystery is to mistake the grand characteristic of Christianity.

For meditation: *Any altar set up now, any priest appointed, any
sacrifice made is a denial of the adequacy of the work of Christ.
Roman Catholicism sets up all three.*

Suggested further reading: Romans 5:1-11

Our Lord greeted the apostles when he first met them after his resurrection. Twice over he addressed them with the kindly words: 'Peace be unto you.' We may dismiss as untenable, in all probability, the cold and cautious suggestion that this was nothing better than an unmeaning phrase of courtesy. He who 'spake as never man spake' said nothing without meaning. He spoke, we may be sure, with special reference to the events of the last few days and with special reference to their future ministry. 'Peace' and not blame, 'peace' and not fault-finding, 'peace' and not rebuke was the first word which this little company heard from their Master's lips after he left the tomb.

It was meet and right and fitting that it should be so, and in full harmony with things that had gone before. 'Peace on earth' was the song of the heavenly host when Christ was born. Peace and rest of soul was the general subject that Christ continually preached for three years. Peace, and not riches, had been the great legacy which he had left with the eleven the night before his crucifixion. Surely it was in full keeping with all the tenor of our Lord's dealings that, when he revisited his little company of disciples after his resurrection, his first word should be 'Peace'. It was a word that would soothe and calm their minds.

Peace, we may safely conclude, was intended by our Lord to be the keynote to the Christian ministry. That same peace which was so continually on the lips of the Master was to be the grand subject of the teaching of his disciples. Peace between God and man through the precious blood of atonement, peace between man and man through the infusion of grace and charity — to spread such peace as this was to be the work of the church. Any form of Christianity which burns men at the stake, in order to promote its own success, carries about with it the stamp of an apostasy.

For meditation: *Our Lord Jesus Christ is the Prince of Peace* (Isa. 9:6).

Suggested further reading: Romans 2:12-16

We see the power of conscience in the case of the centurion and the people who saw Christ die. The centurion glorified God and declared the righteousness of Christ (v. 47). The people who had come together to the sight smote their breasts and went away (v. 48).

We do not know exactly the nature of the feelings here described. We do not know the extent to which they went or the after-fruit which they brought forth. One thing at all events is clear: the Roman officer felt convinced that he had been superintending an unrighteous action and crucifying an innocent person. The gazing crowd were pricked to the heart by a sense of having aided, countenanced and abetted a grievous wrong. Both Jew and Gentile left Calvary that evening heavy-hearted, self-condemned and ill at ease.

Great indeed is the power of conscience! Mighty is the influence which it is able to exercise on the hearts of men! It can strike terror into the minds of monarchs on their thrones. It can make multitudes tremble and shake before a few bold friends of truth like a flock of sheep. Blind and mistaken as conscience often is, unable to convert man or lead him to Christ, it is still a most blessed part of man's constitution, and the best friend in the congregation that the preacher of the gospel has. Listen to Paul (2 Cor. 4:2).

He that desires inward peace must beware of quarrelling with his conscience. Let him rather use it well, guard it jealously, hear what it has to say and reckon it his friend. Above all, let him pray daily that his conscience might be enlightened by the Holy Spirit and cleansed by the blood of Christ. The words of John are very significant (1 John 3:21). The man is doing well who can affirm what Paul claimed (Acts 24:16).

Let us turn from the story of the crucifixion praising God for the confidence that it gives with respect to the ground of our pardon. Our sins may be great and many, but the payment made by our great Substitute far outweighs them all.

For meditation: *Only the blood of Christ can cleanse the conscience* (Heb. 9:14).

Suggested further reading: 2 Thessalonians 2:9-12

We should observe in these verses the remarkable evidence which our Lord supplied of his own resurrection. He graciously appealed to the senses of his trembling disciples. He showed them 'his hands and his side'. He bade them see with their own eyes that he had a real material body and that he was not a ghost or a spirit. 'Handle me and see,' were his first words, according to St Luke. 'A spirit hath not flesh and bones, as ye see me have.'

Even in the glory of heaven, according to Revelation, John saw him appear as a 'Lamb that had been slain' (Rev. 5:6). I think we need not doubt that when he ascended up into heaven, those wounds went with him and are a perpetual witness to angels that he has actually suffered for man's sins. When we see his real presence in the day of his appearing, we shall see 'the man Christ Jesus' and see the marks of his crucifixion.

Great indeed was the condescension of our blessed Master in thus coming down to the feeble faith of the eleven apostles! But great also was the principle which he established for the use of his church in every age until he returns. That principle is that our Master requires us to believe nothing that is contrary to our senses. Things *above* our reason we must expect to find in a religion that comes from God, but not things contrary to reason. To require people to believe that men have the quickening power of the Holy Spirit, when our eyes tell us they are living in habitual carelessness and sin, or that the bread and wine in the Lord's Supper are Christ's real body and blood, when our senses tell us they are still bread and wine — this is to require more belief than Christ ever required of his disciples. It is to require that which is flatly contradictory to reason and common sense. Such requisitions Christ never made. Let us not try to be wiser than our Lord.

For meditation: *Belief in the supernatural is conviction as to God's power, not gullibility.*

Suggested further reading: Hebrews 9:24-28

Christ has some disciples of whom little is known. We know nothing of Joseph except what is here told us. At no former period of our Lord's ministry does he ever come forward. His reason for not openly joining the disciples before we cannot explain. But here, at the eleventh hour, this man is not afraid to show himself one of our Lord's disciples and friends. At the very time when the apostles had forsaken Jesus, Joseph is not ashamed to show his love and respect. Others had confessed him while he was living and doing miracles. It was reserved for Joseph to confess him when he was dead.

The history of Joseph is full of instruction and encouragement. It shows us that Christ has friends of whom the church knows nothing or little, friends who profess less than some do, but friends who in real love and affection are second to none. It shows us that events may bring out grace in quarters where at present we do not expect it, and that the cause of Christ may one day have supporters of whose existence we are at present not aware.

The reality of Christ's death is placed beyond dispute by the circumstances surrounding his burial. Those who took his body from the cross and wrapped it in linen could not have been deceived. Their own senses must have been a witness to the fact that they handled a corpse.

The importance of the reality of Christ's death is that without it there would be no comfort in the gospel. Nothing short of his death could have paid man's debt to God. His incarnation, sermons, miracles and sinless obedience to the law would have availed nothing if he had not died. The penalty threatened to the first Adam had to be paid by the second.

Let us bless God that our Redeemer's death is beyond dispute. The centurion who stood by the cross, the friend who laid the body in the grave, the priests who sealed up the tomb, the soldiers who guarded the sepulchre all witness that Jesus is actually dead. The great Sacrifice was really offered. The debt has been paid.

For meditation: *The reality of his death is necessary for our salvation but death could not hold him!*

Suggested further reading: Mark 1:35-39

Our Lord proceeds to tell the disciples the work which he now wished them to do, but in general terms. He meant to send them forth into the world to be his ministers, messengers and witnesses, even as the Father had sent him into the world to be his messenger and witness (Heb. 3:1; John 18:37). As he had gone up and down preaching the gospel, testifying against the evil of the world and proclaiming rest and peace to the heavy laden, so he intended them to go up and down, as soon as he had ascended up into heaven. In short, he at once prepared their minds for the work which was before them. They were to dismiss from their minds the idea that the day of ease and reward had come, now that their Master had risen and was with them once more. So far from that being the case, their real work was now to begin. He himself was about to leave the world and he meant them to take his place. And one purpose for which he appeared among them was to give them their commission.

The repetition of the salutation, 'Peace be unto you,' is very noteworthy. I cannot doubt that it was specially intended to cheer and comfort and animate the disciples. Glad as they doubtless were to see the Lord, we may easily believe that they were frightened and overcome by a mixture of feelings, and the more so when they re-membered how they had behaved when they had last seen their Lord. Jesus read the condition of their hearts and mercifully made assur-ance doubly sure by repeating the gracious words: 'Peace be unto you.' As Joseph said to Pharaoh, 'The thing was doubled,' in order to make it sure and prevent the possibility of mistake.

Augustine says, 'The iteration is confirmation. It is the "peace upon peace" promised by the prophet' (Isa. 57:19).

For meditation: *'God only had one Son and he made him a preacher.'*

Suggested further reading: Romans 8:26-39

God can make the devices of wicked men work round to his glory. We are taught this by the conduct of the priests and Pharisees after our Lord was buried. The restless enmity of these unhappy men could not sleep even when the body of Jesus was in the grave. They called to mind his words, which they remembered he had said about rising again. They resolved, as they thought, to make that rising again impossible. They went to Pilate. They obtained from him a guard of Roman soldiers. They set a watch over the tomb of our Lord. They placed a seal upon the stone. They did all they could to make the sepulchre secure.

They little thought what they were doing. They little thought that they were unwittingly providing the most complete evidence of the truth of Christ's coming resurrection. They were actually making it impossible to prove that there was any deception or imposition. Their seal, their guard, their precautions were all to become in a few hours witnesses that Christ had risen. They might as well have tried to stop the tides of the sea, or to prevent the sun rising, as to prevent Jesus coming from the tomb. They were taken in their own craftiness. Their own devices became instruments to show forth God's glory.

The history of the church of Christ is full of examples of a similar kind. The very things that have seemed most unfavourable to God's people have often turned out to be for their good. What harm did the persecution surrounding Stephen do to the church? It sent the Word everywhere (Acts 8:4). What harm did imprisonment do to Paul? It gave him time to write his letters which are now read all over the world. What harm have the great and bloody persecutions done? The blood of the martyrs has become the seed of the church. What harm does difficulty ever do to God's people? It only drives them nearer to Christ. It only makes them cling more closely to the throne of grace and the Bible.

For meditation: *In days of difficulty it is not the difficult circumstances that are to fill our minds but the unchanging purpose of God. God intends to work everything together to the blessing and advantage of his people. We trust God, not sight.*

Suggested further reading: Ezekiel 37:1-14

The action of our Lord, 'He breathed on them,' is one that stands completely alone in the New Testament and the Greek word is nowhere else used. On no occasion but this do we find the Lord 'breathing' on anyone. Of course, it was a symbolical action and the only question is: 'What did it symbolize and why was it used?' My own belief is that the true explanation is to be found in the account of man's creation in Genesis. There we read, 'The Lord God formed man of the dust of the ground, and *breathed* into his nostrils the breath of life; and man became a living soul' (Gen. 2:7). Just as there was no life in man until God breathed into him the breath of life, so I believe our Lord taught the disciples, by this action of breathing on them, that the beginning of all ministerial qualification is to have the Holy Spirit breathed into us, and that, until the Holy Ghost is planted in our hearts, we are not rightly commissioned for the work of the ministry.

I do not, however, feel sure that this view completely exhausts the meaning of our Lord when he breathed on the disciples. I cannot forget that they had all forsaken their Master the night that he was taken prisoner, fallen away from their profession and forfeited their title to confidence as apostles. May we not therefore reasonably believe that this breathing pointed to a *revival of life* in the hearts of the apostles and to a restoration of their privileges as trusted and commissioned messengers, notwithstanding their grievous fall? I cannot help suspecting that this lesson was contained in the action of breathing. It not only symbolized the infusion for the first time of special ministerial gifts and graces. It also symbolized the restoration to complete power and confidence in their Master's eyes, even after their faith had so nearly breathed its last and given up the ghost. The first symptom of returning life, when a man is recovered from drowning, is his beginning to breathe again. To set the lungs breathing, in such cases, is the first aim of a skilful doctor.

For meditation: *God's breath gives life to that which is dry and dead — this is revival!*

Suggested further reading: Mark 16:1-8

The principal subject of these verses is the resurrection of our Lord Jesus Christ from the dead. It is one of those truths which lie at the very foundation of Christianity and has therefore received special attention in the Gospels. All four evangelists relate minutely how our Lord was crucified. All four describe with no less clearness that he rose again.

We need not wonder that so much importance is attached to our Lord's resurrection. It is the seal and headstone of the great work of redemption which he came to do. It is the crowning proof that he has paid the debt which he undertook to pay on our behalf, won the battle which he fought to deliver us from hell and is accepted as Surety and Substitute by our Father in heaven. Had he never come forth from the prison of the grave, how could we ever have been sure that our ransom had been fully paid? (1 Cor. 15:17). Had he never risen from his conflict with the last enemy, how could we have felt confident that he has overcome death and him that had the power of death, that is, the devil? (Heb. 2:14). But thanks be to God, we are not left in doubt. The Lord Jesus really rose again for our justification (Rom. 4:25). True Christians are born again unto a living hope by the resurrection of Jesus Christ from the dead (1 Peter 1:3). We have Paul's boldness to know that we cannot be condemned because Christ is risen (Rom. 8:34).

We have reason to be very thankful that this wonderful truth of our religion is so clearly and fully proved. It is a striking circumstance that of all the facts of our Lord's earthly ministry none is so incontrovertibly established as the fact that he rose again. The wisdom of God, who knows the unbelief of human nature, has provided a great cloud of witnesses on the subject. Never was there a fact that the friends of Christ were so slow to believe as his resurrection. Never was there a fact that his enemies were so keen to disprove. Yet in spite of the unbelief of friends and the enmity of foes, the fact was thoroughly established.

For meditation: *The wages of sin is death. If a man dies and then lives again, he proves that the wages are paid. There is no more penalty to pay.*

Suggested further reading: Ephesians 1:15-23

The words, 'Receive ye the Holy Ghost,' are almost as deep and mysterious as the action of breathing. They can only signify, 'I bestow on you the Holy Ghost.' But in what sense the Holy Ghost was bestowed is a point that demands attention and we must beware that we do not run into error.

Our Lord, in my opinion, must have meant, 'Receive the Holy Ghost as the Spirit of knowledge and understanding.' He must have meant that he now conferred on them a degree of light and knowledge of divine truth, which hitherto they had not possessed. They had been greatly deficient in light and knowledge up to this time. With all their faith and love towards our Lord's person, they had been sadly ignorant of many things and particularly of the true purpose of his coming and the necessity of his death and resurrection. 'Now,' says our Lord, 'I bestow on you the Spirit of knowledge. Let the time past suffice to have seen through a glass darkly. Receive the Holy Ghost, open your eyes and see all things clearly.' In fact, I believe the words point to the very thing which St Luke says our Lord did on this occasion: 'Then opened he their understanding, that they might understand the Scriptures' (Luke 24:45). Light was the first thing made in the day of creation. Light in the heart is the first beginning of true conversion. And light in the understanding is the first thing required in order to make a man an able minister of the New Testament. Our Lord was commissioning his first ministers and sending them out to carry on his work. He begins by giving them light and knowledge: 'Receive ye the Holy Ghost. I commission you this day, and confer on you the office of ministers. And the first gift I confer on you is spiritual knowledge.' That this is the true view of the words is proved to my own mind by the extraordinary difference in doctrinal knowledge which from this day the apostles exhibited.

For meditation: *Without the Holy Spirit we cannot receive God's truth* (1 Cor. 2:14-15).

Suggested further reading: Luke 7:36-50

The conduct of Mary Magdalene and the other Mary shows the power of strong love to Christ (vv. 1-2). We may well believe that their actions required no small courage. To visit the grave in the dim twilight of an eastern daybreak would try most women under any circumstances. But to visit the grave of one who had been put to death as a common malefactor and to rise early to show honour to one whom their nation had despised, this was a mighty boldness indeed. Yet these are the kind of acts that show the difference between weak faith and strong faith — between weak feeling and strong feeling towards Christ. These holy women had tasted of our Lord's pardoning mercies. Their hearts were full of gratitude to him for light, hope, comfort and peace. They were willing to risk all consequences in testifying to their affection for their Saviour. So true are Solomon's words (S. of S. 8:6-7).

Why is it that we see so little of this strong love to Jesus among Christians of this present day? How is it that we seldom meet with saints who will face any danger and go through fire and water for Christ's sake? There is only one answer. It is the weak faith and the low sense of obligation to Christ which so widely prevail. A low and feeble sense of sin will always produce a low and feeble sense of the value of salvation. A slight sense of our debt to God will always be attended by a slight sense of what we owe for our redemption. It is the man who feels much forgiven who loves much (Luke 7:47).

The difficulties that Christians fear (v. 3) will sometimes disappear as they approach them (v. 4). How often believers are oppressed and cast down by anticipation of evils, and yet, in time of need, find the thing they feared removed and the 'stone rolled away'! A large proportion of a saint's anxieties arise from things which never really happen. We look forward to all the possibilities of the journey to heaven and imagine all sorts of crosses and obstacles. We carry mentally tomorrow's crosses as well as today's. And often we find our alarms were groundless. Let us go forward in faith, not fear.

For meditation: *No problems, real or imagined, can dissuade the man who loves Christ from obeying him.*

Suggested further reading: Acts 13:26-38

Our Lord in this place solemnly commissioned his apostles to go into all the world and preach the gospel as he had preached it. He also conferred on them the power of declaring with peculiar authority whose sins were forgiven and whose sins were not forgiven. That this is precisely what the apostles did is a simple matter of fact, which anyone may verify for himself by reading the book of the Acts. When Peter proclaimed to the Jews, 'Repent ye, and be converted,' and when Paul declared at Antioch of Iconium, 'To you is the word of this salvation sent,' 'Through this man is preached the forgiveness of sins, and by him all that believe are justified,' they were doing what this passage commissioned the apostles to do. They were opening with authority the door of salvation and inviting with authority all sinners to enter in by it and be saved (Acts 3:19; 13:26-28).

Whatever some may please to say, there is not a single instance to be found in the Acts of any apostle granting absolution after confession. Above all, there is not a trace in the two Pastoral Epistles to Timothy and Titus of such confession and absolution being recommended or thought desirable. In short, whatever men may say about private ministerial absolution, there is not a single precedent for it in God's Word.

Let us leave the whole passage with a deep sense of the importance of the minister's office when that office is duly exercised according to the mind of Christ. No higher honour can be imagined than that of being Christ's ambassadors and proclaiming in Christ's name the forgiveness of sins to a lost world. But let us ever beware of investing the ministerial office with one jot more of power and authority than Christ conferred upon it. To treat ministers as being in any sense mediators between God and man is to rob Christ of his prerogative, to hide saving truth from sinners and to exalt ordained men to a position which they are totally unqualified to fill.

For meditation: *Ministers are neither priests nor prophets, but proclaimers.*

Suggested further reading: Ephesians 1:15-23

Christ rose from the dead with glory and majesty (v. 2). We need not suppose that our blessed Lord needed the help of any angel when he came forth from the grave. We need not doubt for a moment that he rose again by his own power (John 2:19; 10:18). But it pleased God that his resurrection should be accompanied and followed by signs and wonders. It seemed good that the earth should shake and a glorious angel appear when the Son of God arose from the dead a Conqueror.

We have in our Lord's resurrection a type and pledge of the resurrection of his believing people. The grave could not hold him beyond the appointed time, and it shall not be able to hold them. A glorious angel was a witness of the rising, and glorious angels shall be the messengers who shall gather believers when they rise again. He rose with a renewed body, and yet a body, real, true and material, and so shall his people have a glorious body and be like their Head (1 John 3:2).

Let us take comfort in this thought. Trial, sorrow and persecution are often the portion of God's people. Sickness, weakness and pain often hurt and wear their poor earthly body. But their good time is yet to come. Let them wait patiently and they shall have a glorious resurrection. When we die and where we are buried and what kind of funeral we have does not matter. The great question is: 'How shall we rise again?'

What terror Christ's enemies felt at the resurrection! (v. 4). Those hardy Roman soldiers, though not unused to dreadful sights, saw a sight that made them quail. Their courage melted at once at the appearance of one angel of God.

Here is a type and emblem of things yet to come. What will the ungodly do at the last day? What will they do when they see all the dead, both small and great, coming forth from their graves and all the angels of God assembled around the great white throne? What fears and terrors will possess their souls when they find at length that they can no longer avoid God's presence and must meet him face to face!

For meditation: *Will resurrection day be a day of terror for you or of joy?*

Suggested further reading: Hebrews 10:19-25

How much Christians may lose by not regularly attending the assemblies of God's people! Thomas was absent the first time that Jesus appeared to the disciples after his resurrection and consequently Thomas missed a blessing. Of course, we have no certain proof that the absence of the apostle could not admit of explanation. Yet, at such a crisis in the lives of the eleven, it seems highly improbable that he had any good reason for not being with his brethren and it is far more likely that in some way he was to blame. One thing, at any rate, is clear and plain. By being absent he was kept in suspense and unbelief a whole week, while all around him were rejoicing in the thought of a risen Lord. It is difficult to suppose that this would have been the case if there had not been a fault somewhere. It is hard to avoid the suspicion that Thomas was absent when he might have been present.

We shall all do well to remember the charge of the apostle Paul: 'Forsake not the assembling of yourselves together, as the manner of some is' (Heb. 10:25). Never to be absent from God's house on Sundays without good reason, never to miss the Lord's Supper when administered in our own congregation, never to let our place be empty when means of grace are going on, this is one way to be a growing and prosperous Christian. The very sermon that we needlessly miss may contain a precious word in season for our souls. The very assembly for prayer and praise from which we stay away may be the very gathering that would have cheered and established and quickened our hearts. We little know how dependent our spiritual health is on little, regular, habitual helps and how much we suffer if we miss our medicine. The wretched argument that many attend means of grace and are no better for them should be no argument to a Christian. It may satisfy those who are blind to their own state and destitute of grace, but it should never satisfy a real servant of Christ.

For meditation: *If you have no appetite for God's Word and people* ***now***, *why should things be different later?*

Suggested further reading: Matthew 28:1-7

Matthew and Luke combine to give us different elements of the angelic message. Matthew records the words of comfort that were addressed to the friends of Christ (Matt. 28:5). These words were spoken with a deep meaning. They were meant to cheer the hearts of believers in every age in the prospect of the resurrection. They were intended to remind us that true Christians have no cause for alarm, whatever may come on the world. The Lord shall appear in the clouds of heaven and the earth shall be burned up. The graves shall give up the dead that are in them and the last day shall come. The judgement shall be set and the books shall be opened. The angels shall sift the wheat from the chaff and divide between the good fish and the bad. But in all this there is nothing that need make believers afraid. Clothed in the righteousness of Christ, they shall be found without spot and blameless. Safe in the one true ark, they shall not be hurt when the flood comes on the earth. Then shall the wicked and unbelieving appreciate the truth of the psalmist's words (Ps. 33:12).

Luke records that the angel reminded the women of their Master's words in Galilee foretelling his death and resurrection (vv. 6-7). Then they remembered his words (v. 8). They had heard them but made no use of them. Now after many days they called them to mind.

Dullness of memory is a common spiritual disease. It is one of the proofs of our corrupt condition. Even after men have been renewed by the Holy Spirit their readiness to forget the promises and precepts of the gospel is continually bringing them into trouble. They hear many things which they ought to store up in their hearts but seem to forget as fast as they hear. And then, perhaps after many days, affliction brings them up to their recollection and at once it flashes across their mind that they heard them long ago. The true cure for a dull memory in religion is to get deeper love towards Christ and affections more thoroughly set on things above. We do not readily forget the things we love and which we constantly set before our eyes.

For meditation: *'I have hidden your word in my heart that I might not sin against you'* (Ps. 119:11).

Suggested further reading: 2 Corinthians 5:1-10

The unbelief of Thomas, expressed in this famous sentence, was a sad fault in a good man, which cannot be explained away. He refused to believe the testimony of ten competent witnesses, who had seen Christ in the body with their own eyes. He refused to believe the testimony of ten true friends and brethren, who could have no object in deceiving him. He passionately declares that he will not believe, unless he himself sees and touches our Lord's body. He presumes to prescribe certain conditions which must be fulfilled before he can credit the report of his brethren. He uses singularly emphatic language to express his scepticism: 'Others may believe if they like; but I shall not and will not believe until I see and touch for myself.' All this was very sad and very sinful. Thomas might have remembered that at this rate nothing could ever be proved by witnesses, and that he himself, as a teacher, could never expect men to believe him. His case shows us how foolishly and weakly a believer may speak sometimes and how, under the influence of depression and doubt, he may say things of which afterwards he is heartily ashamed.

After all, the case of Thomas is not an uncommon one. Some people are so strangely constituted that they distrust everybody, regard all men as liars and will believe nothing except they can see it all and work it all out for themselves. They have a rooted dislike to receive anything on trust or from the testimony of others and must always go over the ground for themselves. In people of this kind, though they know it not, there is often a vast amount of latent pride and self-conceit and it is almost ludicrous to observe how entirely they forget that the business of daily life could never go on, if we were always doubting everything which we could not see for ourselves. Nevertheless they exist in the church and always will exist and the case of Thomas shows what trouble they bring on themselves.

For meditation: *There is an arrogance in the demand for personal proof when the evidence is provided by God himself!*

Suggested further reading: John 20:24-29

Matthew tells us that our Lord appeared in person to the women who had come to do honour to his body. Last at the cross and first at the tomb, they were the first privileged to see him after he rose. And he gave them the commission to carry the news to his disciples. His first thought is for his scattered flock (v. 10).

There is something deeply touching in these words, 'My brethren.' They deserve a thousand thoughts. Weak, frail, erring as the disciples were, Jesus still calls them brethren. He comforts them as Joseph did his brethren who had sold him, saying, 'I am your brother Joseph.' Much as they had come short of their profession, sadly as they had yielded to the fear of man, they are still his brethren. Glorious as he was in himself, a Conqueror over death, hell and the grave, the Son of God is still meek and lowly of heart. He calls his disciples 'brethren'.

Let us turn from this verse with comfortable thoughts if we know anything of true religion. Let us see in these words of Christ an encouragement to trust and not be afraid. Our Saviour is one who never forgets his people. He pities their infirmities. He does not despise them. He knows their weakness and yet does not cast them away. Our great High Priest is also our elder brother.

How slow of belief the first disciples were on the subject of Christ's resurrection! Luke records that the disciples initially rejected the women's report (Luke 24:11). In spite of the plainest declarations from their Master's own lips that he would rise again on the third day, in spite of the distinct testimony of five or six witnesses that the sepulchre was empty and the angels had told them that he was risen, in spite of the manifest impossibility of accounting for the empty tomb on any other supposition than that of a miraculous resurrection — in spite of all this, these eleven faithless ones would not believe. Perhaps we marvel at their unbelief. But what of us? Do we believe or disbelieve the same evidence? Strong faith is indeed a rare thing!

For meditation: *Even in their times of doubt and faithlessness, God's people are still Christ's brethren. He never forsakes those who have trusted in him.*

Suggested further reading: Romans 2:1-4

Verse 26 describes how Jesus was graciously pleased to appear again to the company of the apostles, for the express purpose of convincing and satisfying the mind of Thomas.

He came when the disciples were 'within'. That means that they were assembled in a room and probably in the same house where they had assembled before. The conviction and reproof of a weak disciple was a thing which was mercifully transacted in private and among friends. We cannot doubt, moreover, that at this period the disciples would hardly dare to assemble in the open air anywhere about Jerusalem. The rumour that they stole the body of our Lord would still be rife in the city and they might well feel the necessity of caution.

He came when 'Thomas was with them'. That means that he timed his visit so that not one of the apostles was missing. He knew exactly who were assembled and where they were assembled and he ordered his appearance accordingly. It should be a great comfort to believers to remember that their Lord's eye is always upon them and that he knows exactly in what place and in what company they are.

He came when the doors were shut. That means that he appeared exactly under the same circumstances under which he appeared a week before, in an evening, when the doors were carefully closed for fear of the Jews. Thus, as on the previous Sunday, he suddenly, without a moment's notice, stood in the midst of the assembled disciples.

He came with the same gracious salutation with which he had appeared before. Once more, the first word that fell from his lips is: 'Peace be unto you.' Thomas was there. The disciple who made his emphatic declaration of unbelief might well expect to hear some word of rebuke. But our Lord makes no exception. He saw Thomas and well knew all that Thomas had said, and yet to him, as well as to the other ten, he once more says, 'Peace.'

For meditation: *God is constantly exercising patience towards undeserving men.*

Suggested further reading: Malachi 3:13-18

What encouragement is given to believers in these verses to speak to one another about Christ! We are told of two disciples walking together on the road to Emmaus and talking of their Master's crucifixion. And then there follow remarkable words (v. 15).

Conference on spiritual subjects is a most important means of grace. As iron sharpeneth iron, so does exchange of thoughts with brethren sharpen a believer's soul. It brings down a special blessing on all who make a practice of it. The striking words of Malachi were meant for the church in every age (Mal. 3:16-17).

What do we know of spiritual conversations with other Christians? Perhaps we read our Bibles and pray in private and use public means of grace. It is all well, very well. But if we stop short here we neglect a great privilege and have yet much to learn. The Scriptures exhort us to provoke one another to love and good works and exhort and edify one another (Heb. 10:24; 1 Thess. 5:11).

Have we no time for spiritual conversation? Let us think again. The quantity of time wasted on frivolous, trifling and unprofitable talk is fearfully great. Do we find nothing to say on spiritual subjects? Do we feel tongue-tied and dumb on the things of Christ? Surely if this is the case there must be something wrong within. A heart right in the sight of God will generally find words (Matt. 12:34).

Let us learn a lesson from the two travellers to Emmaus. Let us speak of Jesus when we are sitting in our houses and when we are walking by the way whenever we find a disciple to speak to (Deut. 6:7). If we believe that we are journeying to heaven, where Christ will be the central object of every mind, let us begin to learn the manners of heaven while we are still on earth. So doing we shall often have one with us whom our eyes will not see, but one who will make our hearts burn within us by blessing the conversation.

For meditation: *'But I tell you that men will have to give account on the day of judgement for every careless word they have spoken'* (Matt. 12:36).

Suggested further reading: 2 Peter 3:8-16

How kind and merciful Christ is to dull and slow believers! It is hard to imagine anything more tiresome and provoking than the conduct of Thomas, when even the testimony of ten faithful brethren had no effect on him and he doggedly declared, 'Except I see with my own eyes and touch with my own hands, I will not believe.' But it is impossible to imagine anything more patient and compassionate than our Lord's treatment of this weak disciple.

He does not reject him, or dismiss him, or excommunicate him. He comes again at the end of a week and apparently for the special benefit of Thomas. He deals with him according to his weakness, like a gentle nurse dealing with a froward child: 'Reach hither thy finger, and behold my hands; reach hither thy hand, and thrust it into my side.' If nothing but the grossest, coarsest, most material evidence could satisfy him, even that evidence was supplied. Surely this was a love that passeth knowledge and a patience that passeth understanding.

A passage of Scripture like this, we need not doubt, was written for the special comfort of all true believers. The Holy Ghost knew well that the dull and the slow and the stupid and the doubting are by far the commonest type of disciples in this evil world. The Holy Ghost has taken care to supply abundant evidence that Jesus is rich in patience as well as compassion and that he bears with the infirmities of all his people. Let us take care that we drink into our Lord's spirit and copy his example. Let us never set down men in a low place, as graceless and godless, because their faith is feeble and their love is cold. Let us remember the case of Thomas and be very pitiful and of tender mercy. Our Lord has many weak children in his family, many dull pupils in his school, many raw soldiers in his army, many lame sheep in his flock. Yet he bears with them all and casts none away.

For meditation: *Although God may chasten his people for their follies, he does so in order not to condemn them with the world* (1 Cor. 11:32).

Suggested further reading: Matthew 13:10-17

The two disciples did not recognize Christ as he joined them (v. 16). Let it be noted here that Mark mentions that he appeared in another form (Mark 16:12). This circumstance would account for their not recognizing him. At the same time it is clear that in some miraculous way the eyes of the disciples were restrained from seeing aright. We have a similar miracle in 2 Kings 6:17-20. Like Joseph of old, our Lord did not reveal himself to his brethren, but tried them by his delay to see what was in their hearts.

Cleophas' response to our Lord's query shows how public and well known the Lord's crucifixion was. He implies that only a person living in total solitariness would have failed to have heard what had happened (v. 18). The description that they gave of Christ as a 'prophet' shows the exceeding dimness of the disciples' apprehension of our Lord's divinity and atonement, in spite of the fact that God had borne him witness by signs and wonders and the people by their testimony to him (Acts 2:22; John 12:17).

We are told that the disciples confessed frankly that their expectations had been disappointed by the crucifixion of Christ (v. 21). A temporal redemption of the Jews by a conqueror seemed to have been the redemption that they looked for. A spiritual redemption by a sacrificial death was an idea which their minds could not thoroughly take in.

Ignorance like this at first sight is truly astounding. We cannot be surprised at the sharp rebuke which fell from our Lord's lips (v. 25). Yet ignorance like this is deeply instructive. It shows how little cause we have to wonder at the ignorance that obscures the minds of the careless. Myriads around us are just as ignorant of the significance of Christ's sufferings as the travellers to Emmaus. As long as the world stands, the cross will seem foolishness to the natural man. Let us bless God that there may be true grace hidden under much intellectual ignorance. Clear and accurate knowledge is helpful but not necessary to salvation. A readiness to be led into truth by the Lord is.

For meditation: *When God intervened in Saul's life he wanted to know more about Christ (Acts 9:5) and more about his duty (Acts 22:10).*

Suggested further reading: Psalm 8

To come into the world at all, and take a body on him, to allow that body to be scourged, crowned with thorns, nailed to the cross and laid in the grave — all this, beyond doubt, was astonishing condescension. But when the victory over sin and death was won, and he had taken on him his resurrection body, to come to a doubting, sceptical disciple and bid him touch him, put his finger into the nail-prints on his hands and put his hand into the great wound in his side — all this was a condescension which we can never sufficiently admire and adore.

The last sentence of the verse is a rebuke and an exhortation at the same time. It would have been more literally rendered, 'Be not an unbeliever, but a believer.' It is not merely a reproof to Thomas for his scepticism on this particular occasion, but an urgent counsel to be of a more believing turn of mind for time to come: 'Shake off this habit of doubting, questioning and discrediting everyone. Give up thine unbelieving disposition. Become more willing to believe and trust and give credit to testimony for time to come.' No doubt the primary object of the sentence was to correct and chastise Thomas for his sceptical declaration on the preceding Sunday. But I believe our Lord had in view the further object of correcting Thomas's whole character and directing his attention to his besetting sin. How many there are among us who ought to take to themselves our Lord's words! How faithless we often are and how slow to believe!

Let us not fail to observe our Lord's perfect knowledge of all that passed on the previous Sunday, of all that the apostles had said and of the sceptical declaration which Thomas had made.

Let us observe our Lord's thorough acquaintance with the special faults and besetting sins of every one of his people. He saw that Thomas's defect was his unbelief and so he says, 'Be not faithless, but believing.'

For meditation: *Although God is almighty and sovereign, he condescends to meet men at the place of their need.*

Suggested further reading: Hebrews 7:26-28

The disciples believed many of the things that the prophets had spoken, but not all. They believed the predictions of Messiah's glory but not of Messiah's sufferings. Many in the modern world err in like manner, believing part but not all of Scripture (v. 25).

Our Lord briefly states the whole truth about the expected Messiah (v. 26). He was one who was to suffer first and afterwards to reign, to be cut off first and afterwards have a kingdom, to be led as a Lamb to the slaughter first and afterwards to divide the spoil as a Conqueror.

Many a commentator has remarked on verse 27 that it would have been a blessing to the church if it had possessed the exposition which our Lord here gave. For wise reasons it has been withheld from us. But it is probable that we have at best very inadequate ideas of the fulness of our Lord's exposition. Judging from the use he made of Scripture during his earthly ministry, he saw probably many things concerning himself which we fail to discover.

The Old Testament is full of Christ because Christ was the substance of every Old Testament sacrifice ordained in the law of Moses. Christ was the true Deliverer and King of whom all the judges and deliverers in Jewish history were types. Christ was the coming Prophet greater than Moses whose glorious advent filled the pages of the prophets. Christ was the true Seed of the woman who was to bruise the serpent's head, the true Seed in whom all nations were to be blessed, the true Shiloh to whom the people were to be gathered, the true Brazen Serpent, the true Scapegoat, the true Lamb to which every daily offering pointed, the true High Priest of which every descendant of Aaron was a picture. These things, or something like them, we need not doubt were some of the things which our Lord expounded on the way to Emmaus.

Let it be a settled principle in our minds in reading the Bible that Christ is the central Sun of the whole book. So long as we keep him in view we shall never greatly err in looking for spiritual knowledge.

For meditation: *Without Christ, the Old Testament is a mass of untied loose ends.*

Suggested further reading: Revelation 22:7-9

Christ was addressed by a disciple as 'God', without prohibition or rebuke on his part. The noble exclamation which burst from the lips of Thomas, when convinced that his Lord had risen indeed — the noble exclamation, 'My Lord and my God' — admits of only one meaning. It was a distinct testimony to our blessed Lord's divinity. It was a clear, unmistakable declaration that Thomas believed him, whom he saw and touched that day, to be not only man, but God. Above all, it was a testimony which our Lord received and did not prohibit and a declaration which he did not say one word to rebuke. When Cornelius fell down at the feet of Peter and would have worshipped him, the apostle refused such honour at once: 'Stand up; I myself also am a man' (Acts 10:26). When the people of Lystra would have done sacrifice to Paul and Barnabas, 'They rent their clothes and ran in among the people ... saying, Sirs, why do ye these things? We also are men of like passions with you' (Acts 14:14-15). But when Thomas says to Jesus, 'My Lord and my God,' the words do not elicit a syllable of reproof from our holy and truth-loving Master. Can we doubt that these things were written for our learning?

Let us settle it firmly in our minds that the divinity of Christ is one of the grand foundation-truths of Christianity and let us be willing to go to the stake rather than let it go. Unless our Lord Jesus is very God of very God, there is an end of his mediation, his atonement, his advocacy, his priesthood, his whole work of redemption. These glorious doctrines are useless blasphemies, unless Christ is divine. Forever let us bless God that the divinity of our Lord is taught everywhere in the Scriptures and stands on evidence that can never be overthrown.

He is God and therefore is 'able to save to the uttermost all who come unto God by him'.

For meditation: *Do you always remember that Jesus is God in your dealings with him?*

Suggested further reading: James 4:1-10

We are told that when the disciples drew nigh to Emmaus our Lord made as though he would have gone further (v. 28). It seems surprising that anyone can stumble at the expression before us or can find ground for supposing that our Lord meant to deceive. Our Lord used the readiest and most natural means to draw out the feelings of the disciples to see if they were weary of his conversation.

They were not weary of him but constrained him to stay with them (v. 29). Cases like this are not uncommon in Scripture. Our Lord sees it good for us to prove our love by withholding mercies till we ask for them. He does not always force his gifts upon us unsought and unsolicited. He loves to draw out our desires and compel us to exercise our spiritual affections by waiting for our prayers. He dealt so with Jacob at Peniel. He desires to go and is constrained to stay (Gen. 32:26). Abraham, Gideon and Manoah all detained God (Gen. 18:3; Judg. 6:18; 13:15). The story of the Canaanite mother, the story of the healing of the two blind men at Jericho, the story of the nobleman at Capernaum, the parables of the unjust judge and the friend at midnight are all meant to teach us the same lesson. All show that our Lord loves to be entreated of his people and that those who would have much must ask much and even use a holy violence.

Let us act on this principle in all our prayers if we know anything of prayer. Let us ask much and ask often and lose nothing for lack of asking. Let us not be like the Jewish king who smote three times on the ground and then stayed his hand (2 Kings 13:18). Let us rather remember the words of David's psalm (Ps. 81:10). It is the man who puts a holy constraint on Christ in prayer who enjoys much of Christ's manifested presence.

For meditation: *Is it true of you that you receive so little from God because you ask for so little? Faith involves an earnest seeking after God in the conviction that he rewards earnest seekers* (Heb. 11:6).

Suggested further reading: Job 38:1-18

Nothing is more common nowadays than to hear people say that they decline to believe things above their reason, that they cannot believe what they cannot entirely understand in religion, that they must see everything clearly before they can believe. Such talk as this sounds very fine and is very taking with young persons and superficially educated people, because it supplies a convenient reason for neglecting vital religion altogether. But it is a style of talking which shows a mind either proud, or foolish, or inconsistent.

In matters of science, what sensible man does not know that we must begin by believing much which we do not understand, taking many positions on trust and accepting many things on the testimony of others? Even in the most exact science, the scholar must begin with axioms and postulates. Faith and trust in our teachers is the very first condition of acquiring knowledge. He that begins his studies by saying, 'I shall not believe anything which I do not see clearly demonstrated from the very first,' will make very little progress.

In the daily business of life, what sensible man does not know that we take many important steps on no other ground than the testimony of others? Parents send sons to Australia, New Zealand, China and India, without ever having seen these countries, in faith that the report about them is dependable and true. Probability, in fact, is the only guide of most parts of our life.

In the face of such facts as these, where is the common sense of saying, as many rationalists and sceptics now do, that in such a mysterious matter as the concern of our souls, we ought to believe nothing that we do not see and ought to receive nothing as true which will not admit of mathematical demonstration?

For meditation: *Much (perhaps most) of your knowledge is truth received by you on the basis of the testimony of other witnesses.*

Suggested further reading: 1 Corinthians 15:1-11

Our Lord's disappearance from the sight of his disciples shows plainly that his resurrection body was a body in a wonderful way different from the common body of a man. It was a real material body with true flesh and blood. But it was a body capable of moving, appearing and disappearing after a manner that we cannot explain. We may fairly suppose that it was a pattern of what our bodies will be after they are raised from the dead. They will be true bodies, material and real, but bodies endued with capacities of which we now know nothing.

The burning of the disciples' hearts within them (v. 32) is a strong expression to indicate the warmth and delight of their feelings as they listened to our Lord's exposition of the Scriptures (Ps. 39:4; Jer. 20:9).

It may be well to mention the eleven distinct appearances of our Lord after his resurrection. He appeared:

1. to Mary Magdalene alone (Mark 16; John 20:14);
2. to the women returning from the sepulchre (Matt. 28:9-10);
3. to Simon Peter alone (Luke 24:34);
4. to the two disciples going to Emmaus (Luke 24:13-35);
5. to the apostles at Jerusalem except Thomas (John 20:19);
6. to the apostles including Thomas (John 20:26,29);
7. at the sea of Tiberias (John 21:1);
8. to the eleven disciples in Galilee (Matt. 28:16);
9. to over five hundred brethren at once (1 Cor. 15:6);
10. to James only (1 Cor. 15:7);
11. to all the apostles at the ascension (Luke 24:51).

Three times we are told that the disciples touched him after he rose (Matt. 28:9; Luke 24:39; John 20:27). Twice we are told that he ate with them (Luke 24:42; John 21:12-13).

For meditation: *These witnesses were willing to suffer and die for the sake of testifying to the resurrection of Christ. If they had made up the story of the resurrection we cannot expect that they would all have continued teaching it whatever the personal cost. But because it happened they would suffer anything rather than deny it. Do you share their conviction?*

Suggested further reading: Matthew 16:1-4

The would-be wise man of modern times says, 'I dislike any religion which contains any mystery. I must first see and then I will believe.' Christianity replies, 'You cannot avoid mystery, unless you go out of the world. You are only asked to do with religion what you are always doing with science. You must first believe and then you will see.' The cry of the modern sceptic is: 'If I could see, I would believe.' The answer of the Christian ought to be: 'If you would only believe and humbly ask for divine teaching, you would soon see.'

There are hundreds of people in this latter age of the world who tell us they can believe nothing which is above their reason and that they want stronger evidences of the truth of the doctrine and fact of Christianity than probability. Like Thomas, they must first see before they believe. But what an extraordinary fact it is that the very men who say all this are continually acting all their lives on no better evidence than probability! They are continually doing things on no other ground than the report of others and their own belief that this report is probably true. The very principle on which they are incessantly acting, in the affairs of their bodies, their families and their money, is the principle on which they refuse to act in the affairs of their souls! In the things of this world they believe all sorts of things which they have not seen and only know to be probable and act on their belief. In the things of the eternal world they say they can believe nothing which they do not see and refuse the argument of probability altogether. Never, in fact, was there anything so unreasonable and inconsistent as rationalism, so called! No wonder that our Lord laid down, for the benefit of Thomas and the whole church, that mighty principle: 'Blessed are they that have not seen and yet have believed.'

For meditation: *The world says that 'Seeing is believing.' God says that 'Believing is seeing.'*

Suggested further reading: Matthew 5:38-48

Our Lord introduced himself to the disciples with singularly gracious words (v. 36). This was a wonderful saying when we consider the men to whom it was addressed. It was addressed to eleven disciples who three days before had shamefully forsaken their Master and fled. They had broken their promises. They had forgotten their professions of readiness to die for their faith. They had been scattered every man to his own and left their Master to die alone. One of them had even denied him three times. All of them had proved backsliders and cowards. And yet behold the return that the Master makes to his disciples! Not a word of rebuke is spoken. Not a single sharp saying fails from his lips. Calmly and quietly he appears in the midst of them and begins by speaking of peace.

We see in this one touching saying that the love of Christ 'passeth knowledge'. It is his glory to pass over a transgression. He delights in mercy. He is far more willing to forgive than men are to be forgiven and far more ready to pardon than men are to be pardoned. There is in his almighty heart an infinite willingness to put away transgressions. Though our sins have been as scarlet, he is ever ready to make them as white as snow, to blot them out, to cast them behind his back, to bury them in the depths of the sea, to remember them no more. All these are scriptural phrases intended to convey the same great truth. The natural man is continually stumbling at them and refusing to understand them. At this we need not wonder. Free, full and undeserved forgiveness to the uttermost is not the manner of man. But it is the manner of Christ.

Where is the sinner, however great his sin, who need be afraid of applying to such a Saviour as this? In the hand of Jesus there is mercy enough and to spare. Where is the backslider, however far he may have fallen, who need be afraid of returning? Christ is willing to raise and restore the very worst. Where is the professing Christian who ought not to be forgiving towards his brethren? The Saviour's words were full of peace.

For meditation: *If Christ gives us peace with God when we have sinned so greatly, will we be unforgiving towards others?*

Suggested further reading: Hebrews 11:1-6

Have you got this faith? If you have, you will find it possible to refuse seeming good and choose seeming evil. You will think nothing of today's losses, in the hope of tomorrow's gains. You will follow Christ in the dark and stand by him to the very last. If you have not, I warn you, you will never war a good warfare and 'so run as to obtain'. You will soon be offended and turn back to the world.

Above all this, there must be a real abiding faith in the Lord Jesus Christ. The life that you live in the flesh you must live by the faith of the Son of God. There must be a settled habit of continually leaning on Jesus, looking unto Jesus, drawing out of Jesus and using him as the manna of your soul. You must strive to be able to say, 'To me to live is Christ.' 'I can do all things through Christ which strengtheneth me' (Phil. 1:21; 4:13).

This was the faith by which the old saints obtained a good report. This was the weapon by which they overcame the world. This made them what they were.

This was the faith that made Noah go on building his ark, while the world looked on and mocked; and Abraham give the choice of the land to Lot, and dwell on quietly in tents; and Ruth cleave to Naomi, and turn away from her country and her gods; and Daniel continue in prayer, though he knew the lions' den was prepared; and the three children refuse to worship idols, though the fiery furnace was before their eyes; and Moses forsake Egypt, not fearing the wrath of Pharaoh. All these acted as they did because they believed. They saw the difficulties and troubles of this course. But they saw Jesus by faith and above them all, and they pressed on. Well may the apostle Peter speak of faith as 'precious faith' (2 Peter 1:1).

For meditation: *Have you eternal life by faith in Jesus, God's Son?*

Suggested further reading: Matthew 15:16-20

Our Lord's disciples were terrified at this appearance and could not believe that it was the Lord himself. We are not told in what manner the Lord entered the room where the disciples were. We know from John's words that the doors were shut (John 20:19) for fear of the Jews. Whether our Lord passed through the doors miraculously without opening them or whether he opened them miraculously, as the angel did when he brought Peter out of prison, we cannot tell (Acts 12:10). In either case there was a miracle. In any case the appearance was sudden and instantaneous.

It is striking to remark, both here (v. 37) and elsewhere in Scripture, how invariably the appearance of any supernatural being, or any inhabitant of another world, appears to strike terror into the heart of man. It seems an instinct of human nature to be afraid of such occasions and is a strong indirect proof of man's utter inability to meet God in peace without a mediator. If man is afraid of spirits and ghosts what would man feel if he saw God himself?

Here as elsewhere our Lord shows his knowledge of the inward man (v. 38). The reasonings and questionings of the apostles were all known to him. Instead of commanding his disciples to believe that he was risen from the dead, as he might have fairly done, he deals gently with his weak disciples and gives them the teaching that they are able to bear. We must copy our Lord when dealing with weak disciples. Like him we must be patient and long-suffering. Like him we must condescend to their feebleness of faith and treat them as tenderly as little children in order to bring them into the right way. We must not cast off men because they do not see everything at once. We must not despise the most humble and childish of means if only we can persuade men to believe. Such dealing may require much patience. But he who cannot condescend to deal with the young, the ignorant and the uneducated has not the mind of Christ. We need to remember Paul's words more frequently (1 Cor. 9:22).

For meditation: *Any person who takes the work of communicating the gospel seriously must learn to deal with people where they are, not where they ought to be.*

Suggested further reading: Acts 4:8-13

We should observe, for one thing, in these verses the poverty of the first disciples of Christ. We find them working with their own hands, in order to supply their temporal wants, and working at one of the humblest of callings — the calling of a fisherman. Silver and gold they had none, lands and revenues they had none and therefore they were not ashamed to return to the business to which they had, most of them, been trained. Striking is the fact that some of the seven here named were fishing when our Lord first called them to be apostles and again fishing when he appeared to them almost the last time. We need not doubt that to the minds of Peter, James and John the coincidence would come home with peculiar power.

The poverty of the apostles goes far to prove the divine origin of Christianity. These very men who toiled all night in a boat, dragging about a cold wet net and taking nothing, these very men who found it necessary to work hard in order that they might eat — these very men were some of the first founders of the mighty church of Christ which has now overspread one-third of the globe. These were they who went forth from an obscure corner of the earth and turned the world upside down. These were the unlearned and ignorant men who boldly confronted the subtle systems of ancient philosophy and silenced its advocates by the preaching of the cross. These were the men who at Ephesus and Athens and Rome emptied the heathen temples of their worshippers and turned away multitudes to a new and better faith. He that can explain these facts, except by admitting that Christianity came down from God, must be a strangely incredulous man. Reason and common sense lead us to only one conclusion in the matter. Nothing can account for the rise and progress of Christianity but the direct interposition of God.

For meditation: *Is the most striking thing about you that you have 'been with Jesus'?*

Suggested further reading: 1 John 1:14

To prove his resurrection to his disciples the Lord does not issue a command. He stoops even lower than this. He appeals to the bodily senses of the eleven. He bids them touch him with their own hands and satisfy themselves that he was a material being and not a spirit or ghost (v. 39).

A mighty principle is stored up in these circumstances which we shall do well to store up in our hearts. Our Lord permits us to use our senses in testing a fact or an assertion in religion. Things above our reason we must expect to find in Christianity. But things contradictory to reason and our own senses our Lord would have us know we are not meant to believe. A doctrine that contradicts our senses is not a doctrine which came from him who bade the eleven touch his hands and feet.

Let us remember this when dealing with the Roman Catholic doctrine of a change in the bread and the wine at the Lord's Supper. There is no such change at all. Our own eyes and our own tongues tell us that the bread is bread and the wine is wine, after consecration as well as before. Our Lord never requires us to believe what is contrary to our senses. The doctrine of transubstantiation is therefore false and unscriptural.

Let us remember this when dealing with the doctrine of baptismal regeneration. There is no inseparable connection between baptism and the new birth of a man's heart. Our own eyes and senses tell us that myriads of baptized people have not the Spirit of God, are utterly without grace and are servants of the devil and the world. Our Lord never requires us to believe what is contrary to our senses. The doctrine that rebirth invariably accompanies baptism is therefore undeserving of credit. It is vile error to say that there is grace where there is no grace to be seen.

Not only then was his body real, because subject to senses, but his eating and drinking were real, not a mere optical illusion, or apparent eating and drinking. If angels appearing to Abraham could eat (Gen. 18:8) so did the resurrected Son of God (v. 43).

For meditation: *Something that appears to be one thing but is in fact another is deceptive. Deception is of Satan* (John 8:44) *not of God.*

Suggested further reading: 1 Corinthians 12:12-26

Once more, on this deeply interesting occasion, we see Peter and John side by side in the same boat, and once more, as at the sepulchre, we see these two good men behaving in different ways. When Jesus stood on the shore, in the dim twilight of the morning, John was the first to perceive who it was and to say, 'It is the Lord,' but Peter was the first to spring into the water and to struggle to get close to his Master. In a word, John was the first to see, but Peter was the first to act. John's gentle loving spirit was quickest to discern, but Peter's fiery, impulsive nature was quickest to stir and move. And yet both were believers, both were true-hearted disciples, both loved the Lord in life and were faithful to him unto death. But their natural temperaments were not the same.

Let us never forget the practical lessons before us. As long as we live, let us diligently use it in forming our estimate of believers. Let us not condemn others as graceless and unconverted, because they do not see the path of duty from our standpoint, or feel things exactly as we feel them. 'There are diversities of gifts, but the same Spirit' (1 Cor. 12:4). The gifts of God's children are not bestowed precisely in the same measure and degree. Some have more of one gift and some have more of another. Some have gifts which shine more in public and some which shine more in private. Some are more bright in a passive life and some are more bright in an active one. Yet each and all the members of God's family, in their own way and in their own season, bring glory to God. Martha was 'careful and troubled about much serving', when Mary 'sat at the feet of Jesus and heard his word' (Luke 10:39-40). Yet there came a day at Bethany when Mary was crushed and prostrated by overmuch sorrow and Martha's faith shone more brightly than her sister's (John 11:20-28). Nevertheless both were loved by our Lord.

For meditation: *What application does Luke 9:49-50 have to your attitudes to fellow Christians?*

Suggested further reading: 1 Corinthians 2:6-16

Our Lord turned to his disciples and told them that they now were seeing actually fulfilled the words which he had so often spoken to them when he told them that his sufferings must be accomplished. Whereas then they could not believe that he was actually going to suffer and rise again, now they could see it was true (v. 44). He was about to fulfil, and had already fulfilled, the predictions made concerning him in the Old Testament. The Jews divided the Old Testament under three headings: the Law of Moses, the Prophets and the Psalms (v. 44).

The words of verse 45 must not be misapprehended. We are not to suppose that the disciples knew nothing about the Old Testament up to this time and that the Bible is a book which no ordinary person can expect to understand. We are simply to understand that Jesus showed his disciples the full meaning of many passages that had hitherto been hidden from their eyes. Above all, he showed the true interpretation of many prophetical passages concerning the Messiah.

We all need a like enlightenment of our understandings (1 Cor. 2:14). Pride, prejudice and love of the world blind our intellects and throw a veil over the eyes of our minds in the reading of the Scriptures. We see the words but do not thoroughly understand them until we are taught from above.

He that desires to read his Bible with profit must first ask the Lord Jesus to open the eyes of his understanding by the Holy Spirit. Human commentaries are useful in their way. The help of good and learned men is not to be despised. But there is no commentary to be compared with the teaching of Christ. A humble and prayerful spirit will find a thousand things in the Bible that the proud, self-conceited student will utterly fail to discern.

For meditation: *The man who needs no help is implying that he has all the wisdom that a man can have and that God cannot have given insights to others. But the man who never thinks for himself in submission to the Holy Spirit is just plain lazy!*

Suggested further reading: 1 Corinthians 15:35-49

Here, as in other places, we find an unanswerable proof that our Lord rose again with a real material body and a proof seen by seven grown-up men with their own eyes at one and the same time. We see him sitting, talking, eating, drinking on the shore of the lake of Galilee and to all appearance for a considerable time. The morning sun of spring shines down on the little party. They are alone by the well-known Galilean lake, far away from the crowd and noise of Jerusalem. In the midst sits the Master, with the nail-prints in his hands — the very Master whom they had all followed for three years and one of them, at least, had seen hanging on the cross. They could not be deceived. Will anyone pretend to say that stronger proof could be given that Jesus rose from the dead? Can anyone imagine better evidence of a fact? That Peter was convinced and satisfied we know. He says himself to Cornelius, '[We] did eat and drink with him after he rose from the dead' (Acts 10:41). Those who in modern times say they are not convinced may as well say that they are determined not to believe any evidence at all.

Let us all thank God that we have such a cloud of witnesses to prove that our Lord rose again. The resurrection of Christ is the grand proof of Christ's divine mission. He told the Jews they need not believe he was the Messiah, if he did not rise again the third day. The resurrection of Christ is the top-stone of the work of redemption. It proved that he finished the work he came to do and, as our Substitute, had overcome the grave. The resurrection of Christ is a miracle that no infidel can explain away. Men may carp and cavil at Balaam's ass and Jonah in the whale's belly, if they please, but till they can prove that Christ did not rise again we need not be moved. Above all, the resurrection of Christ is the pledge of our own. As the grave could not detain the Head, so it shall not detain the members.

For meditation: *What does Luke 16:31 teach about the nature of unbelief?*

Suggested further reading: Acts 10:34-43

Our Lord speaks of his own death in a remarkable manner. He does not speak of it as a thing to be lamented, but as a necessity (v. 46). The death of Christ was necessary to our salvation. His flesh and blood were offered for the life of the world (John 6:51). Without the death of Christ, so far as we can see, God's law would never have been satisfied, sin could never have been pardoned, man could never have been justified before God and God could never have shown mercy to man. The cross of Christ was the solution of a mighty difficulty. It untied a vast knot. It enabled God to be just and the justifier of the ungodly (Rom. 3:26). It enabled man to draw near to God with boldness and to feel that though a sinner he might have hope. Christ by suffering as a Substitute in our stead, the just for the unjust, has made a way by which we can draw near to God. We may freely acknowledge that in ourselves we are guilty and deserve death. But we may boldly plead that one has died for us and that for his sake, believing on him, we claim life and acquittal. Faith will look deeper into the death of Christ than to see cruel martyrdom. Faith sees the payment of man's enormous debt to God and the complete salvation of all who believe.

Repentance and the forgiveness of sins are the first things which ought to be pressed on the attention of every man, woman and child throughout the world. All ought to be taught the necessity of repentance. Without repentance and conversion none can enter the kingdom of God. All ought to be told of God's readiness to forgive everyone who believes on Christ. All are by nature guilty and condemned. But anyone may obtain by faith in Jesus free, full and immediate pardon. All not least ought to be reminded continually that repentance and remission of sins are inseparably linked together. A man impenitent is a man unforgiven.

Repentance and the forgiveness of sins are not mere elementary truths and milk for babies. The highest standard of sanctity is nothing more than a continual growth in practical knowledge of these two points.

For meditation: *He that would have Christ must leave his sin.*

Suggested further reading: Philippians 3:3-11

A true Christian is not a mere baptized man or woman. He is something more. He is not a person who only goes, as a matter of form, to a church or chapel on Sundays and lives all the rest of the week as if there was no God. Formality is not Christianity. Ignorant lip-worship is not true religion. The Scripture speaketh expressly: 'They are not all Israel which are of Israel' (Rom. 9:6). The practical lesson of those words is clear and plain. All are not true Christians who are members of the visible church of Christ.

The true Christian is one whose religion is in his heart and life. It is felt by himself in his heart. It is seen by others in his conduct and life. He feels his sinfulness, guilt and badness, and repents. He sees Jesus Christ to be that divine Saviour whom his soul needs and commits himself to him. He puts off the old man, with his corrupt and carnal habits, and puts on the new man. He lives a new and holy life, fighting habitually against the world, the flesh and the devil. Christ himself is the cornerstone of his Christianity. Ask him in what he trusts for the forgiveness of his many sins, and he will tell you — in the death of Christ. Ask him in what righteousness he hopes to stand innocent at the Judgement Day, and he will tell you it is the righteousness of Christ. Ask him by what pattern he tries to frame his life, and he will tell you that it is the example of Christ.

But, beside all this, there is one thing in a true Christian which is eminently peculiar to him. That thing is love to Christ. Knowledge, faith, hope, reverence, obedience are all marked features in a true Christian's character. But his picture would be very imperfect if you omitted his 'love' to his divine Master. He not only knows, trusts and obeys. He goes further than this — he loves.

For meditation: *Is 'love' the word that most adequately sums up your attitude to Christ?*

Suggested further reading: Acts 2:14-41

The first place at which the disciples were to begin preaching was at Jerusalem (v. 47). This is a striking fact and one full of instruction. It teaches us that none are reckoned too wicked for salvation to be offered to them and that no degree of spiritual disease is beyond the reach of the gospel remedy. Jerusalem was the wickedest city on earth when our Lord left the world. It was the city that had stoned the prophets and killed those whom God had sent to it to call it to repentance. It was a city full of pride, unbelief, self-righteousness and desperate hardness of heart. It was a city that had just crowned its transgressions by crucifying the Lord of glory. And yet Jerusalem was the place where the first proclamation of repentance and pardon was to be made. The command of Christ was plain.

We see in these wondrous words the length, breadth, depth and height of Christ's compassion towards sinners. We must never despair of anyone being saved, however bad and profligate he may have been. We must open the door of repentance to the chief of sinners. We must invite the worst of men to repent, believe and live. It is the glory of our Great Physician that he can heal incurable cases. The things that seem impossible to men are possible with Christ.

The result of first preaching at Jersualem shows that the command was not without cause. The greatest triumph ever won by the gospel, perhaps, was the conversion of three thousand Jerusalem hearers on the Day of Pentecost (Acts 2:41).

The other lesson was that the offer of salvation should always be made to the Jews first. Hardened and unbelieving as they were, they were still beloved for the sake of the fathers (Rom. 11:28). The Acts of the Apostles in too many instances to quote, as well as Paul in his letter to the Romans (Rom. 1:16), show how faithfully the apostles discharged the duty of preaching to the Jews. The duty of Christians to care specially for the souls of Jews seems plainly pointed out.

For meditation: *What does 'to the Jew first'* (Rom. 1:16; 2:9) *mean for today?*

Suggested further reading: 1 Corinthians 16:19-24

'Faith towards our Lord Jesus Christ' is an expression which many Christians are familiar with. Let it never be forgotten that love is mentioned by the Holy Ghost in almost as strong terms as faith. Great as the danger is of him 'that believeth not', the danger of him that 'loveth not' is equally great. Not believing and not loving are both steps to everlasting ruin.

Hear what St Paul says to the Corinthians: 'If any man love not the Lord Jesus Christ, let him be Anathema Maranatha' (1 Cor. 16:22). St Paul allows no way of escape to the man who does not love Christ. He leaves him no loophole or excuse. A man may lack clear head-knowledge and yet be saved. He may fail in courage and be overcome by the fear of man, like Peter. He may fall tremendously, like David, and yet rise again. But if a man does not love Christ, he is not in the way of life. The curse is yet upon him. He is on the broad road that leadeth to destruction.

Hear what St Paul says to the Ephesians: 'Grace be with all them that love our Lord Jesus Christ in sincerity' (Eph. 6:24). The apostle is here sending his good wishes and declaring his good will to all true Christians. Many of them, no doubt, he had never seen. Many of them in the early churches, we may be very sure, were weak in faith and knowledge and self-denial. How, then, shall he describe them in sending his message? What words can he use which will not discourage the weaker brethren? He chooses a sweeping expression which exactly describes all true Christians under one common name. All had not attained to the same degree, whether in doctrine or practice. But all loved Christ in sincerity.

Hear what our Lord Jesus Christ himself says to the Jews: 'If God were your Father, ye would love me' (John 8:42). No love to Christ — then no sonship to God!

For meditation: *What do you think of Christ? This remains for all eternity the crucial question.*

Suggested further reading: Acts 1:1-8

Believers, and especially ministers, are called to be witnesses (v. 48). Stier remarks, 'It is not the Lord's will to appoint and send forth orators, or enthusiasts, or even simple teachers, but before all, and in all, witnesses.'

If we are true disciples of Christ we must bear a continual testimony in an evil world. We must testify to the truth of our Master's gospel, the graciousness of our Master's heart, the happiness of our Master's service, the excellence of the rules of life given by our Master, and the enormous dangers and wickedness of the ways of the world. Such testimony will doubtless bring down upon us the displeasure of man. The world will hate us, as it did our Master, because we testify of it that its deeds are evil (John 7:7). Such testimony will doubtless be believed by few comparatively and will be thought by many offensive and extreme. But the duty of a witness is to bear his testimony whether he is believed or not. If we bear a faithful testimony we have done our duty, although, like Noah and Elijah and Jeremiah, we stand alone.

What do we know of this witnessing character? What kind of testimony do we bear? What evidence do we give that we are disciples of a crucified Saviour and, like him, are not of this world? (John 17:14). What marks do we show of belonging to him who said, 'I came that I should bear witness of the truth'? (John 18:37). Happy is he who can give a satisfactory answer to these questions and whose life declares plainly that he seeks a country (Heb. 11:14).

The promise of the Father is the Holy Spirit whom the Father had promised in the Old Testament prophecies and who came down at the Day of Pentecost (Isa. 44:3; Joel 2:28; Jer. 31:33; Ezek. 36:27). Let it be noted that the Lord here speaks of sending the Holy Spirit. We see in this his equality and unity with God the Father. We also see that the Holy Spirit is a Person. The words 'I send' can only be used of a person.

For meditation: *By lip and life we are bearing a testimony — but to what and to whom?*

Suggested further reading: Galatians 2:20 - 3:14

A true Christian loves Christ for all he has done for him. He has suffered in his stead and died for him on the cross. He has redeemed him from the guilt, the power and the consequences of sin by his blood. He has called him by his Spirit to self-knowledge, repentance, faith, hope and holiness. He has forgiven all his many sins and blotted them out. He has freed him from the captivity of the world, the flesh and the devil. He has taken him from the brink of hell, placed him in the narrow way and set his face towards heaven. He has given him light instead of darkness, peace of conscience instead of uneasiness, hope instead of uncertainty, life instead of death. Can you wonder that the true Christian loves Christ?

And he loves him, besides, for all that he is still doing. He feels that he is daily washing away his many shortcomings and infirmities and pleading his soul's cause before God. He is daily supplying all the needs of his soul and providing him with an hourly provision of mercy and grace. He is daily leading him by his Spirit to a city of habitation, bearing with him when he is weak and ignorant, raising him up when he stumbles and falls, protecting him against his many enemies, preparing an eternal home for him in heaven. Can you wonder that the true Christian loves Christ?

Does the debtor in jail love the friend who unexpectedly and undeservedly pays all his debts, supplies him with fresh capital and takes him into partnership with himself? Does the prisoner in war love the man who, at the risk of his own life, breaks through the enemies' lines, rescues him and sets him free? Does the drowning sailor love the man who plunges into the sea, dives after him, catches him by the hair of his head and by a mighty effort saves him from a watery grave? In the same way, and upon the same principles, a true Christian loves Jesus Christ.

For meditation: *There is no love or self-giving greater than that of God in Christ* (Rom. 5:6-8).

Suggested further reading: Philippians 2:5-11

We have here some of the last words spoken by our Lord Jesus Christ upon earth — words so remarkable that they demand and deserve our attention, all of it.

God has put great honour on our Lord Jesus Christ (v. 18). This is a truth that is declared by Paul to the Philippians (Phil. 2:9). It is a truth that in no wise takes away from the true notion of Christ's divinity, as some have ignorantly supposed. It is simply a declaration that, in the counsels of the eternal Trinity, Jesus, as Son of Man, is appointed heir of all things, that he is the Mediator between God and man, that the salvation of all who are saved is laid upon him and that he is the great fountain of mercy, grace, life and peace. It was for this joy set before him that he endured the cross (Heb. 12:2).

Let us embrace the truth reverently and cling to it firmly. Christ is he who has the keys of death and hell. Christ is the anointed Priest who can alone absolve sinners. Christ is the fountain of living waters in whom alone we can be cleansed. Christ is the Prince and Saviour who alone can give repentance and remission of sins. In him all fulness dwells. He is the way, the door, the light, the life, the Shepherd, the altar of refuge. He that has the Son has life, and he that has not the Son has not life. May we all strive to understand this. No doubt men may easily think too little of God the Father and God the Spirit, but no man ever thought too much of Christ.

Jesus lays on his disciples not to confine their knowledge to themselves but to communicate it to others (v. 19). They were not to suppose that salvation was revealed only to the Jews but to make it known to all the world. They were to strive to make disciples of all nations, and to tell the whole earth that Christ had died for sinners. This injunction is still in force. It is still the bounden duty of every disciple to do all he can in person and in prayer to make others acquainted with Jesus.

For meditation: *Jesus is Lord! Are you letting the world know?*

Suggested further reading: 1 Samuel 20:1-17

This love to Christ is the inseparable companion of saving faith. A faith of devils, a mere intellectual faith, a man may have without love, but not that faith which saves. Love cannot usurp the office of faith. It cannot justify. It does not join the soul to Christ. It cannot bring peace to the conscience. But where there is real justifying faith in Christ there will always be heart love to Christ. He that is really forgiven is the man who will really love (Luke 7:47). If a man has no love to Christ, you may be sure he has no faith.

Love to Christ is the mainspring of work for Christ. There is little done for his cause on earth from sense of duty, or from knowledge of what is right and proper. The heart must be interested before the hands will move and continue moving. Excitement may galvanize the Christian's hands into a fitful and spasmodic activity. But there will be no patient continuance in well-doing, no unwearied labour in missionary work at home or abroad, without love. The nurse in a hospital may do her duty properly and well, may give the sick man his medicine at the right time, may feed him, minister to him and attend to all his wants. But there is a vast difference between that nurse and a wife tending the sick-bed of a beloved husband, or a mother watching over a dying child. The one acts from a sense of duty; the other from affection and love. The one does her duty because she is paid for it; the other is what she is because of her heart. It is just the same in the matter of the service of Christ. The great workers of the church, the men who have led forlorn hopes in the mission-field and turned the world upside down, have all been eminently lovers of Christ.

Many great Christians have left a mark on the world. And what was the common feature of their characters? They all loved Christ. They not only held a creed. They loved a person, even the Lord Jesus Christ.

For meditation: *If Jonathan could work for David even though he was the heir to the throne and David a mere soldier, shall not we, mere sinners, work for our Master out of love?*

Suggested further reading: Acts 8:26-40

Jesus requires a public profession of those who believe his gospel. He tells his disciples to baptize those whom they have received as disciples (v. 19).

It is very difficult to conceive, when we read this last command of our Lord's, how men can avoid the conclusion that baptism is necessary when it may be had. It seems impossible to explain the word that we have here of any but an outward ordinance to be administered to all who join his church. That outward baptism is not absolutely necessary to salvation the case of the penitent thief shows. He went to paradise unbaptized. That outward baptism alone often confers no benefit the case of Simon Magus plainly shows (Acts 8:13,21). But that baptism is a matter of entire indifference and need not be used at all is an assertion which seems at variance with our Lord's words in this place.

The plain practical lesson of the words is the necessity of a public confession of faith in Christ. It is not enough to be a secret disciple. We must not be ashamed to let men see whose we are and whom we serve. We must not behave as if we did not like to be thought Christians, but take up our cross and confess our Master before the world. Our Lord's words are very solemn (Mark 8:38).

Jesus requires obedience from those who profess to be his disciples (v. 20). This is a searching expression. It shows the uselessness of a mere name and form of Christianity. It shows that they are only to be counted true Christians who live in practical obedience to his Word and strive to do the things that he has commanded. The water of baptism and the bread and wine of the Lord's Supper alone will save no man's soul. It profits nothing that we go to a place of worship and hear Christ's ministers and approve of the gospel if our religion goes no further than this. What are our lives? What is our daily conduct? Do we strive to copy Christ's example? Do we seek to do the things that he commanded? Obedience is the only proof of reality.

For meditation: *Enmity with God is revealed by disobedience* (Rom. 8:7), *friendship with Christ by obedience* (John 15:14).

Suggested further reading: Revelation 5

Love to Christ is the point which we ought specially to dwell upon, in teaching religion to children. That he loved them even to his death and that they ought to love him in return is a creed which meets the span of their minds.

Love to Christ is the common meeting-point of believers of every branch of Christ's church on earth. Whether Episcopalian or Presbyterian, Baptist or Independent, Calvinist or Arminian, Methodist or Moravian, Lutheran or Reformed, Established or Free — here at least they are agreed. About forms and ceremonies, about church government and modes of worship, they often differ widely. But on one point, at any rate, they are united. They have all one common feeling towards him on whom they build their hope of salvation. They love the Lord Jesus Christ in sincerity (Eph. 6:24). Many of them, perhaps, are ignorant of systematic divinity and could argue but feebly in defence of their creed. But they all know what they feel towards him who died for their sins. 'I cannot speak much for Christ, sir,' said an old uneducated Christian woman to Dr Chalmers, 'but if I cannot speak for him, I could die for him!'

Love to Christ will be the distinguishing mark of all saved souls in heaven. The multitude which no man can number will all be of one mind. Old differences will be merged in one common feeling. Old doctrinal peculiarities, fiercely wrangled for upon earth, will be covered over by one common sense of debt to Christ. Luther and Zwingli will no longer dispute. Wesley and Toplady will no longer waste time in controversy. Churchmen and dissenters will no longer bite and devour one another. All will find themselves joining with one heart and voice in that hymn of praise: 'Unto him that loved us, and washed us from our sins in his own blood, and hath made us kings and priests unto God and his Father; to him be glory and dominion for ever and ever. Amen' (Rev. 1:5-6).

For meditation:
Names and sects and parties fall:
Thou, O Christ, art all in all

(Wesley).

Suggested further reading: John 14:15-27

Our Lord makes solemn mention of the blessed Trinity when he bids the disciples to baptize in the name of the Father, the Son and the Holy Spirit (v. 19).

This is one of those great plain texts which directly teach the mighty doctrine of the Trinity. It speaks of the Father, Son and Holy Spirit as three distinct Persons and speaks of all three as coequal. Such as the Father is, such is the Son and such is the Holy Spirit. And yet these three are one.

This truth is a great mystery. Let it be enough to receive it and believe it and let us ever abstain from all attempts at explanation. It is childish folly to refuse assent to things that we do not understand. We are poor crawling worms of a day and know little at our best about God and eternity. Suffice it for us to receive the doctrine of the Trinity in unity with humility and reverence and to ask no vain questions. Let us believe that no sinful soul could be saved without the work of all three Persons of the blessed Trinity and let us rejoice that Father, Son and Holy Spirit, who co-operated to make man, do always co-operate to save him. Here let us pause. We may receive practically what we cannot explain theoretically.

The Lord Jesus closes his words with a gracious promise (v. 20). It is impossible to conceive words more comforting, strengthening, cheering and sanctifying than these. Though left alone like orphan children in a cold, unkind world, the disciples must never think they were deserted. Their Master would be ever 'with them'. Though commissioned to do a work as that of Moses when sent to Pharaoh, they are not to be discouraged. Their Master would certainly be with them. No words could be more suited to those to whom they were first spoken. No words could be imagined more consolatory to believers in every age of the world.

For meditation: *God himself is with us — in us, around us, over us. We who believe are enveloped in his protective, loving presence.*

Suggested further reading: Psalm 116

Three times we find the apostle saying, 'Thou knowest that I love thee.' Once we are told that he said, 'Thou knowest all things.' Once we have the touching remark made that he was 'grieved to be asked the third time'. We need not doubt that our Lord, like a skilful physician, stirred up this grief intentionally. He intended to prick the apostle's conscience and to teach him a solemn lesson. If it was grievous to the disciple to be questioned, how much more grievous must it have been to the Master to be denied!

The answer that the humbled apostle gave is the one account that the true servant of Christ in every age can give of his religion. Such a one may be weak and fearful and ignorant and unstable and failing in many things, but at any rate he is real and sincere. Ask him whether he is converted, whether he is a believer, whether he has grace, whether he is justified, whether he is sanctified, whether he is elect, whether he is a child of God — ask him any one of these questions and he may perhaps reply that he really does not know! But ask him whether he loves Christ and he will reply, 'I do.' He may add that he does not love him as much as he ought to do, but he will not say that he does not love him at all. The rule will be found true with very few exceptions. Wherever there is true grace, there will be a consciousness of love towards Christ.

What, after all, is the great secret of loving Christ? It is an inward sense of having received from him pardon and forgiveness of sins. Those love much who feel much forgiven. He that has come to Christ with his sins and tasted the blessedness of free and full absolution, he is the man whose heart will be full of love towards his Saviour. The more we realize that Christ has suffered for us and paid our debt to God and that we are washed and justified through his blood, the more we shall love him for having loved us and given himself for us.

For meditation: *What would you add to David's statement: 'I love the Lord because...'?*

Suggested further reading: Hebrews 4:14-16

All true Christians should lay hold upon the promise of Christ's unending presence and keep it in mind (v. 20). Christ is with us always. Christ is with us wherever we go. He came to be 'Emmanuel, God with us' (Matt. 1:23) when he first came into the world. He declares that he is ever 'Emmanuel', God with us, when he comes to the end of his earthly ministry and is about to leave the world. He is with us daily to pardon and forgive. He is with us daily to sanctify and strengthen. He is with us daily to defend and to keep, to lead and to guide. He is with us in sorrow and with us in joy. He is with us in sickness and with us in health. He is with us in life and with us in death. He is with us in time and with us in eternity.

What stronger consolation could believers desire than this? Whatever happens, they are at least never completely friendless and alone. Christ is ever with them. They may look into the grave and say with David, 'Though I walk through the valley of the shadow of death I will fear no evil, for thou art with me' (Ps. 23:4). They may look beyond the grave and say with Paul, 'We shall ever be with the Lord' (1 Thess. 4:17). He has said it and he will stand by it. He is always with us even to the end of the world (v. 20). He has promised never to leave us or forsake us (Heb. 13:5). We could ask nothing more. It is everything to be a real Christian. None have such a King, such a Priest, such constant companionship and such an unfailing Friend as the true servants of Christ.

The Saviour in heaven, never slumbering and never sleeping, is always ready to help. Though we sleep Jesus wakes. Though we faint Jesus is never weary. Though we are weak Jesus is almighty. Though we die Jesus lives for evermore. Blessed indeed is this thought!

For meditation: *No situation can be faced, no circumstance arise, no problem rear its head, which the Christian has to face without Christ. Christ is always with him to help him and aid him. Oh, how foolish Christians often are not to seek his help in time of need!*

Suggested further reading: Matthew 20:20-28

We should notice in these verses Christ's command to Peter. Three times we find him saying, '*Feed* my flock': once, 'Feed my lambs' and twice, 'Feed my sheep'. Can we doubt for a moment that this thrice-repeated charge was full of deep meaning? It was meant to commission Peter once more to do the work of an apostle, notwithstanding his recent fall. But this was only a small part of the meaning. It was meant to teach Peter and the whole church the mighty lesson that usefulness to others is the grand test of love and working for Christ the great proof of really loving Christ. It is not loud talk and high profession; it is not even impetuous, spasmodic zeal and readiness to draw the sword and fight — it is steady, patient, laborious effort to do good to Christ's sheep scattered throughout this sinful world, which is the best evidence of being a true-hearted disciple. This is the real secret of Christian greatness. It is written in another place: 'Whosoever will be great among you, let him be your minister; and whosoever will be chief among you, let him be your servant: even as the Son of man came not to be ministered unto, but to minister' (Matt. 20:26-28).

Forever let the parting charge of our blessed Master abide in our consciences and come up in the practice of our daily lives. It is not for nothing, we may be sure, that we find these things recorded for our learning, just before he left the world. Let us aim at a loving, doing, useful, hard-working, unselfish, kind, unpretentious religion. Let it be our daily desire to think of others, care for others, do good to others and to lessen the sorrow and increase the joy of this sinful world. This is to realize the great principle which our Lord's command to Peter was intended to teach. So living and so labouring to order our ways, we shall find it abundantly true that 'It is more blessed to give than to receive' (Acts 20:35).

For meditation: *The desire to be useful to God should far exceed the desire to be important before men.*

Suggested further reading: Ephesians 1:3-14

Our Lord left his disciples in a remarkable manner (vv. 50-51). He left them in the very act of blessing. We cannot doubt for a moment that there was a meaning in the circumstance. It was intended to remind the disciples of all that Jesus had brought with him when he came into the world. It was intended to assure them of what he would do yet after he left the world. He came on earth to bless and not to curse, and blessing he departed. He came in love and not in anger, and in love he went away. He came not as a condemning Judge but as a compassionate Friend, and as a Friend he returned to his Father. He had been a Saviour full of blessings to his little flock while he had been with them. He would be a Saviour full of blessings to them. He would have them know this even after he was taken away.

Forever let souls lean on the gracious heart of Christ, if we know anything of true religion. We shall never find a heart more tender, more loving, more patient, more compassionate and more kind. To talk of the Virgin Mary as being more compassionate than Christ is a proof of miserable ignorance. To flee to the saints for comfort when we may flee to Christ is an act of mingled stupidity and blasphemy and a robbery of Christ's crown. Gracious was our Lord Jesus when he lived among his weak disciples, gracious in the very season of his agony upon the cross, gracious when he rose again and gathered his sheep around him, gracious in the manner of his departure from this world. It was a departure in the very act of blessing! Gracious we may be assured he is at the right hand of God. He is the same yesterday, today and for ever (Heb. 13:8), a Saviour ever ready to bless, abounding in blessings.

There is something very touching in the fact that our Lord's ascension took place close to Bethany. It was a small village bordering on the Mount of Olives. But it was the home of Mary, Martha and Lazarus.

For meditation: *God causes all his blessings to flow to us through the Lord Jesus Christ* (Eph. 1:3). *Take him away and there is no channel through which blessing can flow. He is our ladder to and from heaven* (John 1:51).

Suggested further reading: Psalm 139:1-6

The future history of Christians, both in life and death, is foreknown by Christ. The Lord tells Simon Peter, 'When thou art old, thou shalt stretch forth thy hands, and another shall gird thee, and carry thee whither thou wouldest not.' These words, without controversy, were a prediction of the manner of the apostle's death. They were fulfilled in after days, it is commonly supposed, when Peter was crucified as a martyr for Christ's sake. The time, the place, the manner, the painfulness to flesh and blood of the disciple's death were all matters foreseen by the Master.

The truth before us is eminently full of comfort to a true believer. To obtain foreknowledge of things to come would, in most cases, be a sorrowful possession. To know what was going to befall us, and yet not to be able to prevent it, would make us simply miserable. But it is an unspeakable consolation to remember that our whole future is known and forearranged by Christ. There is no such thing as luck, chance, or accident, in the journey of our life. Everything from beginning to end is foreseen — arranged by one who is too wise to err and too loving to do us harm.

Let us store up this truth in our minds and use it diligently in all the days of darkness through which we may yet have to pass. In such days we should lean back on the thought: 'Christ knows this, and knew it when he called me to be his disciple.' It is foolish to repine and murmur over the troubles of those whom we love. We should rather fall back on the thought that all is well done. It is useless to fret and be rebellious, when we ourselves have bitter cups to drink. We should rather say, 'This also is from the Lord: he foresaw it, and would have prevented it, if it had not been for my good.' Happy are those who can enter into the spirit of that old saint, who said, 'I have made a covenant with my Lord, that I will never take amiss anything that he does to me.'

For meditation: *The future that is hidden to us is an open book before a sovereign God.*

Suggested further reading: Acts 1:1-11

When our Lord left the world he went to heaven (v. 51). The full meaning of these words we cannot, of course, comprehend. It would be easy to ask questions about the exact residence of Christ's glorified body which the wisest theologian could never answer. We must not waste our time in unedifying speculations or 'intrude into things unseen' (Col. 2:18). Let it suffice us to know that our Lord Jesus is gone into the presence of God on behalf of all who believe in him as a forerunner and a High Priest (Heb. 6:20; John 14:2).

As a forerunner Jesus has gone into heaven to prepare a place for all his members. Our great Head has taken possession of a glorious inheritance on behalf of his mystical body, the church, and holds it as an elder Brother and Trustee until the day comes when his body shall be perfected.

As High Priest Jesus has gone into heaven to intercede for those who believe in him. There in the holy of holies he presents on their behalf the merits of his own sacrifice and ordains for them daily supplies of mercy and grace. The grand secret of the perseverance of the saints is Christ's appearance for them in heaven. They have an everlasting Advocate with the Father and therefore are never cast away (Heb. 9:24; 1 John 2:1).

A day will come when Jesus shall return from heaven in like manner as he went (Acts 1:11). He will not always abide within the holy of holies. He will come forth, like the Jewish high priest, to bless the people, to gather his saints together and to restore all things (Lev. 9:23; Acts 3:21). For that day let us wait and long and pray. Christ dying on the cross for sinners, Christ living in heaven to intercede, Christ coming again in glory are three great objects which ought to stand out prominently before the eyes of every true Christian.

For meditation: *Christ is in heaven. That is the Christian's destination. The Scriptures lay a present duty on the Christian to set his affections on things in heaven and not on things on earth* (Col. 3:1).

Suggested further reading: Philippians 1:20-27

A believer's death is intended to glorify God. The Holy Ghost tells us this truth in plain language. He graciously interprets the dark saying which fell from our Lord's lips about Peter's end. He tells us that Jesus spake this, 'signifying by what death he should glorify God'.

The thing before us is probably not considered as much as it ought to be. We are so apt to regard life as the only season for honouring Christ, and action as the only mode of showing our religion, that we overlook death, except as a painful termination of usefulness. Yet surely this ought not so to be. We may die to the Lord as well as live to the Lord; we may be patient sufferers as well as active workers. Like Samson, we may do more for God in our death than we ever did in our life. It is probable that the patient deaths of our martyred Reformers had more effect on the minds of Englishmen than all the sermons they preached and all the books they wrote. One thing, at all events, is certain — the blood of the English martyrs was the seed of the English church.

We may glorify God in death, by being ready for it whenever it comes. The Christian who is found like a sentinel at his post, like a servant with his loins girded and his lamp burning, with a heart packed up and ready to go, the man to whom sudden death, by the common consent of all who knew him, is sudden glory — this, this is a man whose end brings glory to God. We may glorify God in death, by patiently enduring its pains. The Christian whose spirit has complete victory over the flesh, who quietly feels the pins of his earthly tabernacle plucked up with great bodily agonies and yet never murmurs or complains, but silently enjoys inward peace — this, this again, is a man whose end brings glory to God. We may glorify God in death, by testifying to others the comfort and support that we find in the grace of Christ.

For meditation: *If God would be more glorified by your death than your life should you not be willing to die?*

Suggested further reading: 1 Peter 1:3-9

Our Lord was parted from his disciples (v. 51). Burgon remarks, 'These beautiful words denote that Jesus was rather taken away from the men he loved than that by an act of his own will left them. For his passion it is said that he was impatient (Luke 12:50); for his ascension it is not so. He did not leave his disciples, but was parted from them.'

They worshipped him (v. 52). This is the first formal act of adoration which we ever read of the disciples paying to our Lord. Their knowledge of his Messiahship and divinity was now clear and distinct. Hence came the 'joy' which the verse mentions that they felt. All things were now clear and plain to them concerning their Master. The darkness was past and the true light shone (1 John 2:8).

The veil was removed from the eyes of the disciples. The meaning of Christ's humiliation and low estate, the meaning of his mysterious agony, cross and passion, the meaning of his being Messiah and yet a sufferer, the meaning of his being crucified and yet being Son of God — all, all was at length unravelled and made plain. They saw it all. They understood it all. Their doubts were removed. Their stumbling-blocks were taken away. Now at last they possessed clear knowledge and, possessing clear knowledge, felt unmingled joy.

Let it be a settled principle with us that the little degree of joy believers possess often arises from lack of knowledge. Weak faith and inconsistent practice are doubtless two great reasons why many of God's children enjoy so little peace. But it may well be suspected that dim and indistinct views of the gospel are the true cause of the believer's discomfort. When the Lord Jesus is not clearly known and understood it must needs follow that there is little joy in the Lord.

For meditation: *Peter spoke of a fulness of joy* (1 Peter 1:8) *because he also knew a precious Jesus* (1 Peter 2:7). *This combination is a necessary one.*

Suggested further reading: 1 Corinthians 9:24-27

Whatever we may think about the condition of other people, we should think first about our own. When Peter enquired curiously and anxiously about the future of the apostle John, he received from our Lord an answer of deep meaning: 'If I will that he tarry till I come, what is that to thee? Follow thou me.' Hard to understand as some part of that sentence may be, it contains a practical lesson which cannot be mistaken. It commands every Christian to remember his own heart first and to look at home.

Of course, our blessed Lord does not wish us to neglect the souls of others, or to take no interest in their condition. Such a state of mind would be nothing less than uncharitable selfishness and would prove plainly that we had not the grace of God. The servant of Christ will have a wide, broad heart, like his Master, and will desire the present and eternal happiness of all around him. He will long and labour to lessen the sorrows and to increase the joys of everyone within his reach and, as he has opportunity, to do good to all men. But, in all his doing, the servant of Christ must never forget his own soul. Charity and true religion must both begin at home.

It is vain to deny that our Lord's solemn caution to his impetuous disciple is greatly needed in the present day. Such is the weakness of human nature that even true Christians are continually liable to run into extremes. Some are so entirely absorbed in their own inward experience and their own heart's conflict that they forget the world outside. Others are so busy about doing good to the world that they neglect to cultivate their own souls. Both are wrong and both need to see a more excellent way, but none perhaps do so much harm to religion as those who are busybodies about others' salvation and at the same time neglecters of their own. From such a snare as this may the ringing words of our Lord deliver us!

For meditation: *How often the unbelievers show a deep concern for 'those who have never heard' as an excuse by which they direct attention away from their own need!*

Suggested further reading: 1 Corinthians 15:51-58

We are told that when the disciples went forth and preached, the Lord worked with them and confirmed the Word with signs following (v. 20). We know well from the Acts of the Apostles and from the pages of church history the manner in which these words have been proved true. We know that bonds and afflictions, persecution and opposition were the first-fruits that were reaped by the labourers in Christ's harvest. But we know also that in spite of every effort of Satan the Word of truth was not preached in vain. Believers from time to time were gathered out of the world. Churches of saints were founded in city after city and country after country. The little seed of Christianity grew gradually into a great tree. Christ himself wrought with his own workmen and, in spite of every obstacle, his work went on. The good seed was never entirely thrown away. Sooner or later there were signs following.

Let us not doubt that these things were written for our encouragement on whom the latter ends of the world are come. Let us believe that no one shall ever work faithfully for Christ and find at last that his work has been altogether without profit. Let us labour on patiently each in our own position. Let us preach, teach, speak, write, warn and testify, resting assured that our labour is not in vain. We may die ourselves and see no result from our work. But the last day will assuredly prove that the Lord Jesus always works with those who work for him and that there were signs following though it was not given to the workman to see them. Let us then show the resolution to which the apostle calls us (1 Cor. 15:58). We may go on our way heavily and sow with tears; but if we sow Christ's precious seed we shall come again with joy and bring our sheaves with us (Ps. 126:6).

For meditation: *How often our despair in God's work is nothing less than faithlessness! Of course, we should look to ourselves to see if we have sin in our hearts and the Lord is therefore not hearing us (Ps. 66:18), but having searched our hearts let us hold fast to the promise and work on in the place where God has placed us.*

Suggested further reading: 2 Timothy 3:10-17

St John concludes his Gospel with these remarkable words: 'There are many other things which Jesus did, the which, if they should be written every one, I suppose the world itself could not contain the books that should be written.' To suppose that the evangelist meant the world could not hold the material volumes which would be written is evidently unreasonable and absurd. The only sensible interpretation must be a spiritual and figurative one.

As much of Christ's sayings and doings is recorded as the mind of man can take in. It would not be good for the world to have more. The human mind, like the body, can only digest a certain quantity. The world could not contain more, because it would not. As many miracles, as many parables, as many sermons, as many conversions, as many words of kindness, as many deeds of mercy, as many journeys, as many prayers, as many warnings, as many promises are recorded as the world can possibly require. If more had been recorded, they would have been only thrown away. There is enough to make every unbeliever without excuse, enough to show every enquirer the way to heaven, enough to satisfy the heart of every honest believer, enough to condemn man if he does not repent and believe, enough to glorify God. The largest vessel can only contain a certain quantity of liquid. The mind of all mankind would not appreciate more about Christ, if more had been written. There is enough and to spare. This witness is true. Let us deny it if we can.

We may well be humble when we think how ignorant we are and how little we comprehend of the treasures which this Gospel contains. But we may well be thankful when we reflect how clear and plain is the instruction which it gives us about the way of salvation. The man who reads this Gospel profitably is he who 'believes that Jesus is the Christ and, believing, has life through his name'. Do we so believe?

For meditation: *There is much about our Lord's ministry that we do not know, but all that is necessary is recorded.*

Suggested further reading: James 1:22-25

Let us close the pages of these Gospels with self-enquiry and self-examination. Let it not content us to have seen with our eyes and heard with our ears the things here written for our learning about Jesus Christ. Let us ask ourselves whether we know anything of 'Christ dwelling in our hearts by faith'. Does the Spirit witness with our spirit that Christ is ours and we are his? Can we really say that we are living the life of faith in the Son of God? Can we say that we have found by experience that Christ is precious to our own souls? (Eph. 3:17; Rom 8:16; Gal. 2:20; 1 Peter 2:7). These are solemn questions. They demand serious consideration. May we never rest till we can give them a satisfactory answer! If we have the Son we have life. If we do not have the Son we do not have life (1 John 5:12).

Let us leave the Gospels with a settled purpose of heart to seek more spiritual knowledge every year we live. Let us search the Scriptures more deeply and pray over them more heartily. Too many believers only scratch the surface of Scripture and know nothing of digging into its hidden treasures. Let the Word dwell in us more richly. Let us read our Bibles more diligently. So doing, we shall taste more of joy and peace in believing.

I now send forth this volume with an earnest prayer that the Holy Spirit may bless it and that God may be pleased to use it for his own glory and the benefit of many souls. My chief desire is to exalt Jesus Christ and make him more beautiful and glorious in the eyes of men, and to promote the increase of repentance, faith and holiness upon earth.

I have a strong conviction that we want more reverent, deep searching study of the Scriptures in the present day. We want a more clear knowledge of Christ as a living Person, a living Priest, a living Physician, a living Friend, a living Advocate at the right hand of God, and a living Saviour soon about to come.

For meditation: *Can you say from the heart, 'Even so, come, Lord Jesus'?*

Suggested further reading: John 20:30-31

I have now completed my notes on St John's Gospel. I have given my last explanation. I have gathered my last collection of the opinions of commentators. I have offered for the last time my judgement upon doubtful and disputed points. I lay down my pen with humbled, thankful and solemnized feelings. The closing words of holy Bullinger's *Commentary on the Gospels,* condensed and abridged, will perhaps not be considered an inappropriate conclusion to my *Expository Thoughts on St John.*

'Reader, I have now set before thee thy Saviour the Lord Jesus Christ, that very Son of God, who was begotten by the Father by an eternal and ineffable generation, consubstantial and coequal with the Father in all things ... but in these last times, according to prophetical oracles, was incarnate for us, suffered, died, rose again from the dead and was made King and Lord of all things... This is he who is appointed and given to us by God the Father, as the fulness of all grace and truth, as the Lamb of God who taketh away the sins of the world, as the ladder and door of heaven, as the serpent lifted up to render the poison of sin harmless, as the water which refreshes the thirsty, as the bread of life, as the light of the world, as the Redeemer of God's children, as the Shepherd and door of the sheep, as the resurrection and the life, as the corn of wheat which springs up into much fruit, as the conqueror of the prince of this world, as the way, the truth and the life, as the true vine and, finally, as the redemption, salvation, satisfaction and righteousness of all the faithful in all the world, throughout all ages. Let us therefore pray God the Father, that, being taught by his gospel, we may know him that is true and believe in him in whom alone is salvation, and that, believing, we may feel God living in us in this world, and in the world to come may enjoy his eternal and most blessed fellowship.' Amen and Amen.

For meditation: *John wrote his Gospel so that you might believe and have everlasting life. Have you?*

Suggestions for the use of these daily readings

1. As Ryle is commenting on the Word of God, the Holy Scriptures, seek God's aid in prayer to understand his Word aright. Make the psalmist's prayer your own (Ps. 119:18).

2. Remember that Ryle is commenting on God's Word. It is infallible; he is not. It must be read; his comments are aids to understanding. Resist the temptation to read his comments but not to bother to read the Bible. Where references are given, look them up.

3. God has given the Scriptures that through them our whole lives might be changed (2 Tim. 3:15-17). Read the Scriptures and the comments with the conscious aim of reading to understand and apply what is read to your life (James 1:22-25).

4. Avoid that state of mind that reads in order to quieten the conscience and which is satisfied with a superficial skimming of the surface of the truth. Read and think. There is a blessing promised to those who meditate on God's Word (Ps. 1:2-3).

5. Attempt to memorize some of the Scriptures that you read. Memorized Scripture is a useful weapon in our battles with Satan (Matt. 4:1-11) and our obedience to God (Ps. 119:11).